The Cavalries at Stones River

ALSO BY DENNIS W. BELCHER
AND FROM MCFARLAND

The Cavalry of the Army of the Cumberland (2016)

General David S. Stanley, USA: A Civil War Biography (2014)

*The 11th Missouri Volunteer Infantry
in the Civil War: A History and Roster* (2011)

*The 10th Kentucky Volunteer Infantry
in the Civil War: A History and Roster* (2009)

EDITED BY DENNIS W. BELCHER
AND FROM MCFARLAND

*"This Terrible Struggle for Life": The Civil War Letters of a
Union Regimental Surgeon* by Thomas S. Hawley, M.D. (2012)

THE CAVALRIES AT STONES RIVER

An Analytical History

Dennis W. Belcher

Foreword by Jim Lewis

McFarland & Company, Inc., Publishers
Jefferson, North Carolina

LIBRARY OF CONGRESS CATALOGUING-IN-PUBLICATION DATA

Names: Belcher, Dennis W., 1950– author.
Title: The cavalries at Stones River : an analytical history /
Dennis W. Belcher ; foreword by Jim Lewis.
Description: Jefferson, North Carolina : McFarland & Company, Inc.,
Publishers, 2017. |Includes bibliographical references and index.
Identifiers: LCCN 2017008956 | ISBN 9781476665368 (softcover : acid free paper) ∞
Subjects: xLCSH: Stones River, Battle of, Murfreesboro, Tenn., 1862–1863. |
Tennessee—History—Civil War, 1861–1865—Cavalry operations. |
United States—History—Civil War, 1861–1865—Cavalry operations.
Classification: LCC E474.77 .B45 2017 | DDC 973.7/359—dc23
LC record available at https://lccn.loc.gov/2017008956

BRITISH LIBRARY CATALOGUING DATA ARE AVAILABLE

ISBN (print) 978-1-4766-6536-8
ISBN (ebook) 978-1-4766-2851-6

© 2017 Dennis W. Belcher. All rights reserved

*No part of this book may be reproduced or transmitted in any form
or by any means, electronic or mechanical, including photocopying
or recording, or by any information storage and retrieval system,
without permission in writing from the publisher.*

Front cover: The Second United States Cavalry
at Beverly Ford (Library of Congress)

Printed in the United States of America

*McFarland & Company, Inc., Publishers
Box 611, Jefferson, North Carolina 28640
www.mcfarlandpub.com*

To all those people who work diligently to preserve our national heritage, particularly, the librarians, archivists, and all those who work with special collections. Without the dedication of these individuals, historical work would be impossible.

Table of Contents

Acknowledgments — ix
Foreword by Jim Lewis — 1
Preface — 3

PART ONE: OPENING MOVES

1. Bragg Leaves Kentucky and Two Armies Move (October 9–31, 1862) — 9
2. Two Cavalries in Middle Tennessee (November 1–30, 1862) — 35
3. A Decision to Fight (December 1–25, 1862) — 57

PART TWO: TWO CAVALRIES

4. The Cavalry of the Army of the Cumberland — 77
5. The Cavalry of the Army of Tennessee — 94

PART THREE: BATTLE OF STONES RIVER

6. The Advance on Murfreesboro—First Phase (December 26–28) — 113
7. The Advance on Murfreesboro—Second Phase (December 29–30) — 137
8. The Cavalry Battle of Stones River (December 31, Early Morning) — 153
9. The Cavalry Battle of Stones River (December 31, Late Morning) — 173
10. On the East Flank—Pegram's Cavalry (December 31) — 196
11. Stanley and Wheeler Arrive on the Battlefield (Afternoon, December 31) — 210
12. Cavalry Actions (January 1–5) — 222

Conclusion — 242
Chapter Notes — 253
Bibliography — 275
Index — 285

Acknowledgments

It is an honor to write about the cavalry actions at the Battle of Stones Rivers, and I cannot express my gratitude high enough for those historians, institutions and archivists who quietly go about their daily business of preserving our country's history. This book could not have been written without the efforts of these people.

First of all, I would offer my gratitude to Darla Brock, archivist at the Tennessee State Library and Archives. This is my third time working with Darla and I can only say that she is ever helpful, knowledgeable and efficient. She has never failed to offer her expertise in the research of the various topics in Civil War history. Likewise, Jennifer Cole, curator of Special Collection of the Filson Historical Society, has always gone out of her way to explore collections and provide excellent sources of material, which have proven to be invaluable in this Civil War research.

In addition, there are many helpful experts from various institutions who contributed to completion of this project. John Coskis, historian at the American Civil War Museum, provided much needed information regarding Southern cavalry officers. John Varner, Auburn University; Eric Honneffer, document conservator/manuscript specialist at Bowling Green State University; Lesley Martin, librarian at the Chicago History Museum Research Center; Stephanie Prochaska, archivist at the Colorado Springs Pioneers Museum; Kathy Shoemaker, reference coordinator, Research Services Manuscript, Archives, and Rare Book Library at Emory University; Peggy Dillard, special collections manager, at the Rosenberg Library in Galveston; James Capobianco, reference librarian at Houghton Library, Harvard University; Nancy Dupree, research archivist, Alabama Department of History and Archives; Tutti Jackson, Research Services Department, Ohio Historical Society; Sara Borden, librarian at the Pennsylvania Historical Society; Marlea D. Leljedal, U.S. Army Heritage and Education Center; Amy S. Wong and Simon Elliott, Library Special Collections, UCLA; Kyle Hovis, University of Tennessee Special Collections; Elizabeth Shulman and Rebecca Williams, Louis Round Wilson Special Collections Library at the University of North Carolina; Anne Causey at the Albert and Shirley Small, Special Collections Library at the University of Virginia; and finally, Melody Klaas, librarian, Missouri River Regional Library, have all been instrumental in the collection of the materials used in this book.

There a few people who deserve special attention. Jonathan Webb Deiss provided invaluable assistance with the material at the National Archives. This is inglorious duty, but the collection of this material resulted in the much-needed details about the cavalry battles. Deiss is professional, efficient, and dedicated to his tasks. In addition, Brooke Guthrie, research services coordinator at the David M. Rubenstein Rare Book & Manuscript Library, is a wonder at her position. She has been ever helpful to me and her efforts are greatly appreciated. Likewise, Jim Snider provided the much needed support in obtaining material from the collections at the Alabama Department of History and Archives. Jim is an expert with these collections and his expertise resulted in a good collection of the Southern firsthand records.

In what was one of the intriguing parts of the history of the cavalry operations at the Battle of Stones River, the details of the cavalry actions of the eastern flank led me to two important collections—the Western Reserve Historical Society and the New-York Historical Society. The information in these two collections was of major importance and I want to express my appreciation to the staff for their assistance with these materials. The efforts of Vicki Catozza, Research Center Reference Division, Western Reserve Historical Society Library Research Center and Tammy Kiter, Manuscript Department, New-York Historical Society were invaluable. I also want to thank Barbara Sontz for her efforts with the New-York Historical Society material.

I want to make particular mention of the experts of the National Park Service and express my appreciation to Jeff Patrick at Wilsons Creek National Battlefield for the use of the very complete library of Civil War material. Secondly, I cannot say how very grateful I am for the assistance of Jim Lewis at Stones River Battlefield. Jim took his valuable time to work with me at the beginning of this project and to share his understanding of the battle. He unselfishly provided input throughout the project and provided very important feedback as he read the manuscript. Jim also graciously wrote the foreword to the book and I cannot thank him enough for all his help through this endeavor.

I was very fortunate to have an excellent team of reviewers who read this manuscript before its completion—Kurt Holman, Michael Bradley, and Jim Lewis. These readers are all experts in their own right and their inputs and expertise are greatly appreciated.

Last but not least, I wish to thank George Skoch who produced the maps for this book. George is an expert in map production and his insights and skills never cease to amaze me.

Foreword by Jim Lewis

Of the three main combat branches of Civil War armies, the cavalry remains perhaps the least understood component of the great campaigns and battles of that conflict. Often obscured by the mythology surrounding the towering figures who lead the mounted arm, and clouded by the scope and pace of their operations, the story of the cavalry often ends up relegated to a postscript in examinations of Civil War combat.

I must admit that for many of the more than nineteen years that I have spent researching and writing about the Battle of Stones River and the Civil War in middle Tennessee, I fell into the trap of treating cavalry operations like a postscript to the larger story. There were many reasons for this lapse.

First, as with most of the major battles of the Civil War, the brunt of the Stones River carnage was borne by the infantry. Their successes and failures on the battlefield largely determined the ultimate outcome of the fight. Then there is the decisive role played by the artillery. Concentrations of Union guns at key points in the fight turned the tide of battle in a way that was rarely seen during the Civil War. At first glance, the actions of the mounted arm during the battle seem to pale in comparison to the other two branches.

A cursory examination of cavalry operations during the Stones River Campaign seems to confirm the long held opinions of many military historians about the mounted arm. The thesis that deciding the outcome of a battle through the sheer momentum of a charging mass of horses and men was no longer possible in the age of rifled muskets and artillery remains a powerful influence on our perceptions of cavalry's role in the fighting. Raiding, probing the enemy's lines to gather intelligence or guarding against those efforts, and flank protection make up the vast majority of the cavalry actions during the campaign seeming to confirm that the troopers in blue and gray no longer had a major role to play in the outcome.

Then there is the idea that Confederate cavalry was generally superior to its blue-clad foes. That certainly seemed to be the case in middle Tennessee. During the early years of the war, cavalry emerged as the most effective tool in the Confederate arsenal. Raids by Nathan Bedford Forrest and John Hunt Morgan strangled Union supply lines stealing momentum from campaigns that might have changed the war's trajectory in the Union's favor. Joe Wheeler's ride around the Army of the Cumberland remains the stuff of legend in the region. Through it all, Union cavalry forces seemed helpless against the cavaliers in gray and therefore were even less worthy of examination.

Dennis Belcher began to tackle the unbalanced and often dismissive treatment of cavalry in the Western Theater with his, *The Cavalry of the Army of the Cumberland*. This eye opening work traced the root causes of the initial failures of Union cavalry. It revealed the changes initiated by the likes of William Rosecrans, David Stanley, Robert Minty and others who reshaped the mounted branch and its application helping to shift the balance of power during the campaigns for the Confederate heartland.

Belcher's work also revealed that despite a lack of grandiose charges that changed the tide of battle, the evolving use of cavalry to take full advantage of its mobility had a profound impact on the successes and failures of campaigns taking place across the vast landscape of the Western Theater. Careful examination shows us that rapid and far-flung actions of mounted columns shaped the planning and execution of the campaigns throughout the war particularly the campaigns from 1863 to the end of the conflict.

In this book, Belcher sharpens his focus to examine the campaign that marks a sea change in the mounted struggle in the Western Theater. The Battle of Stones River stands as a measuring point in a shift in the mounted balance of power that will see Union cavalry equal, and even surpass at times, their gray clad adversaries. The Stones River Campaign gives us an early glimpse of a metamorphosis of organization, training, and tactics that ultimately transforms the Army of the Cumberland's cavalry into force to be reckoned with.

Belcher's exhaustive research on the cavalry operations during the Stones River Campaign has taken a major step toward helping readers of this book to appreciate the complexities and critical contributions of the mounted arm to one of the most important battles of the American Civil War. He helps us appreciate the character and motivations of the key players who grappled with each other for control of middle Tennessee with insightful descriptions that help the reader understand them as men not myths.

Belcher shows us how the early reorganization and retraining of the Union cavalry began to transform their competency and confidence. His meticulous narrative of cavalry actions from the sparring between mounted forces in the fall of 1862 through the ebb and flow of charge and counter charge as the Battle of Stones River raged allows the reader to feel as if they are seeing the action from the saddle.

Belcher's even-handed analysis will prompt the reader to reexamine long held notions about the impact of successes and failures during the campaign. Was Wheeler's December 30 raid an unequivocal success? Did the Confederate cavalry guarding the Army of Tennessee's right flank truly fail in its mission to provide accurate and timely intelligence? Belcher's answers to these and other questions effectively challenge the answers that many of us would have given before reading this book.

Most importantly, the reader will come away with a better understanding of the Battle of Stones River and its role as the harbinger of a shifting tide of war. This work coupled with Belcher's previous examination of the Army of the Cumberland's mounted arm offers us insight into the simple truth that the only way to truly appreciate the ebb and flow of the fighting in the Western Theater is through the story of the cavalry.

National Parks Service member Jim Lewis has been a park ranger, curator and de-facto historian at the Stones River National Battlefield since 1997. He has researched and presented many interpretive programs at Stones River. He is the author of Lincoln's Hard Earned Victory, *serves on the advisory board of the Tennessee Civil War Preservation Association and is a founding member of the Middle Tennessee Civil War Round Table.*

Preface

One of the most significant cavalry actions of the western theater of the Civil War began on December 26, 1862, and concluded on January 5, 1863, during the Stones River Campaign. The four brigades of Joseph Wheeler's Confederate cavalry fought daily with the three brigades of David Stanley's Federal cavalry. The most decisive of the battles occurred throughout the day of December 31, but the other actions during the campaign were very important in determining the outcome of the battle. Ultimately, the cavalry actions at the Battle of Stones River resulted in changes which defined the cavalry in the west for the remainder of the war.

As the Civil War began, the cavalry was relatively unimportant, but this changed quickly. The Federal cavalry lagged behind the Southern cavalry's development in organization and in numbers. The philosophy and the practicality of the utilization of cavalry in Civil War were vastly different from the pre-war United States Army and the actions at Stones River were important in clarifying the use of cavalry for both sides. Because the high commands of both armies understood it took one to two years to fully train a cavalry trooper, there was little focus on cavalry early in the war. At the beginning of the war many expected the conflict would be over shortly; but as the war dragged on, it was clear that mounted forces would play an important part in the Civil War.

When this work began, there were two objectives: (1) define and describe the action of the cavalry during the Stones River Campaign, and (2) to understand the important role of the Southern cavalry on the eastern flank of Bragg's army. The history of the cavalry operations during this battle has been researched in two previous works. The masterful historian, Edwin Bearss, wrote a dedicated summary of the cavalry operations at Stones River in 1959 and provided a concise summary of the cavalry during this battle. More recently, Lanny Smith authored the monumental study of the entire Battle of Stones River, which included many important details regarding the cavalry. These histories remain valuable sources today.

The greatest challenge in understanding the actions during this battle was finding creditable reports. There is confusion, the fog of war, included in many reports. The difficulty of fitting all the reports into an accurate, comprehensive history was overwhelming at times. In a single event or fight, there were oftentimes several reports giving different sequences of events. An exhaustive survey of available source material has attempted to provide a clearer picture, but there are still gaps in the exact details of events. Common in many reports were embellishments of the authors, and in many cases Union and Confederate officers wrote vastly different accounts of the same action. Often authors gave minute details of victories, while totally ignoring defeats. Claims of casualties for the enemy losses were exaggerated in many cases. In addition, the concept of "time" proved to be a major challenge but it was important to be able to frame when events occurred. There had to be some way of identifying and classifying events and "time" was a good way to do this; however, the challenge to accomplish this task was enormous.

This history of cavalry operations at the Battle of Stones River is intended to be objective and without bias as much as possible. Overall, both cavalries performed exceptionally well and at the same time, both cavalries made serious mistakes. It is important to know the records of these events most commonly come from Union cavalry sources, but as many of the Southern sources as possible are included. There are simply more Union first-hand accounts of the events of the ten-day campaign than Southern ones. In some cases, there are only Northern accounts.

The second major objective of this work was to understand the role of the Southern cavalry, specifically Brigadier General John Pegram's small brigade, stationed on the eastern flank during the battle. Historian after historian has made various references to the failure of the Confederate cavalry to provide proper reconnaissance on the morning of December 31, 1862, on the east flank. Included in the indictment of this unit are references to its observations of phantom divisions of Union infantry and references to its lackadaisically missing the withdrawal of 4,000 Union infantry. Upon examining the existing sources, it is strongly recommended that historians reconsider the role of John Pegram's cavalry during this time. Instead of assuming the Confederate cavalry failed to make proper reconnaissance, the focus should shift to understanding that this small cavalry brigade provided proper and effective service along the eastern flank during the confusion of this major battle.

While the major objectives unfolded, many other equally important points needed clarification, including: (a) explaining the repulse of the Confederate cavalry along the Union supply train on December 31; (b) understanding how the Union counterattack was accomplished on the late afternoon on December 31; (c) understanding the roles of both chiefs of cavalry, Stanley and Wheeler; (d) explaining the subsequent cavalry fights near La Vergne on January 1 and 3; and (e) understanding the roles of reconnaissance, particularly, of Wheeler's cavalry and the impact this had on Bragg's decisions.

This history is intended to be easily readable by all. Overly technical terms have been avoided as much as possible. There are references to infantry units "refusing" their right or left flank and this might require some explanation. If an infantry unit formed the end of a line of units, rather than allowing the infantry line just to end, it was common for commanders to bend the end of the line back toward itself, or "refusing" the line. This made the line less vulnerable to an attack made on the flank or rear. Also, the terms "saber" and sabre" are used interchangeably in the text. Some may argue that there are differences between these two terms, but both are used to describe the slightly curved cavalry sword carried by both Union and Confederate cavalrymen. Finally, some explanation is needed in regard to the designation of Union Tennessee cavalry regiments. At the beginning of the war, Tennessee regiments carried designations from the part of the state where they were organized, e.g., East Tennessee, Middle Tennessee, West Tennessee. Eventually these geographic designations were dropped, but at this point in the war they were still used. The 2nd East Tennessee Cavalry would be renamed the 2nd Tennessee Cavalry and the 1st Middle Tennessee Cavalry would be renamed the 5th Tennessee Cavalry. In this text, 5th Tennessee Cavalry and 2nd Tennessee Cavalry are used to designate these units.

The history of the Confederate cavalry regiments continues to be a problem even after a century and a half. Often times, multiple units were designated with the same regimental name, plus the fact that many Confederate records were destroyed during and after the war make it difficult for many people to understand which regiment participated in which action. Some of the Southern regiments have regimental histories, but far too many do not.

Finally, one bias of the work is an attempt to acknowledge that most of the participants on each side were men who were sincere, dedicated, and tried to do what was right to further their cause. Certainly, there were scoundrels aplenty in the Civil War, but most of the officers and men made their decisions based on the information they had on hand at that time. It is easy for Civil War historians to criticize, and even feel an obligation to draw conclusions about the events of the time; but the men of that time were far better than their single worst decision. In one of the most exciting and important cavalry actions of the Civil War, the men of both cavalries fully committed themselves, for glory or death, for a cause in which they believed.

"Jine the Cavalry"

If you want to have a good time, jine the cavalry!
Jine the cavalry! Jine the cavalry!
If you want to catch the Devil, if you want to have fun,
If you want to smell Hell, jine the cavalry!

PART ONE: OPENING MOVES

1. Bragg Leaves Kentucky and Two Armies Move (October 9–31, 1862)

> *O, a kingdom for four regiments of cavalry!*
> —Brigadier General A. J. Smith

One of the most significant cavalry operations in the Western Theater of the Civil War unfolded as the Army of the Cumberland began its advance on Murfreesboro, Tennessee, on December 26, 1862. The actions pitted the Union cavalry under Brigadier General David Stanley against the Confederate cavalry of Brigadier General Joseph Wheeler. The ten-day campaign was filled with desperate struggles, with successes on both sides as well as major mistakes. Ordnance officer in the Union Army of the Cumberland, Captain Gates Thruston, described the cavalry battle on the first day of the Battle of Stones River on December 31, 1862:

> The battle in the rear was a series of tumultuous cavalry fights, of charges and counter charges, at times fierce and furious, of captures and recaptures, of hand-to-hand personal combats, continuing through the day, yet the tremendous conflict of the infantry and artillery at the front almost completely overshadowed it, and has minimized its historical importance. The report of the engagements in the rear on Wednesday, made by General Stanley, our able Union cavalry commander, consists of but twenty-two lines in the official record. Those of most of his subordinate officers are almost as brief, and the Confederate reports, though more extended and satisfactory, give but a meager and disconnected history of these thrilling events.

The events which led to this cavalry battle during the Stones River Campaign fought at the end of December began when the Battle of Perryville ended.[1]

After the Battle of Perryville

On October 9, 1862, the tired and parched Army of Mississippi slowly withdrew from Perryville towards Harrodsburg after the bloody fight the day before with Major General Don Carlos Buell's Union army. At the head of the Southern column was the gaunt figure of General Braxton Bragg. Bragg, a career officer in the U.S. Army, was an organized and efficient officer, but one who had difficulty working with his superiors and subordinates alike. Bragg resigned his commission in the U.S. Army in 1856 and offered his services to the Confederacy at the beginning of the war. Although Braxton Bragg's army was bloodied, it was not defeated and Bragg withdrew to unite his army with Major

General E. Kirby Smith's Army of Kentucky, the second Confederate army which marched into Kentucky but had not participated in the Battle of Perryville. The battle at Perryville, fought the day before, was a bloody affair which resulted in over 7,000 casualties, the Union army suffering the greater losses. After Bragg withdrew from Perryville, he moved to Harrodsburg as Buell tentatively probed his flank; and a few days later after taking stock of his situation, he decided to return to Middle Tennessee by way of Cumberland Gap, and the campaign for Murfreesboro began as Bragg, who felt isolated and alone in Kentucky, slowly moved his men back to Tennessee. Bragg's march into Kentucky was part of the grand offensive of the Confederacy and becoming aware of the Confederate defeats at Iuka and Corinth, he felt he was in a vulnerable position because the "whole country in our rear was left open to the enemy's victorious forces." In addition, a large number of Federal reinforcements were moving southward from Cincinnati. Bragg wrote on October 12 in frustration that he expected the population of Kentucky to

> rise in mass to assert their independence. No people ever had so favorable an opportunity, but I am distressed to add there is little or no disposition to avail of it. Willing perhaps to accept their independence, they are neither disposed nor willing to risk their lives or their property in its achievement.

George Knox Miller, an officer in the 8th Confederate Cavalry, gave a little more balanced observation of the situation in Kentucky:

> [U]pon the whole the Kentuckians were not enthusiastic, if so at all it was those who espoused the cause of Abraham [Lincoln]. They [pro–Confederate Kentuckians] wanted some assurance that we were going to hold the state before they would compromise themselves.... But what a pity we could not hold the "dark & bloody ground"–it is inestimable value to us—so rich, so plethoric with the necessaries of life—what we now need above all things.[2]

General Braxton Bragg told his cavalry "Hold the enemy firmly" (Library of Congress).

Bragg argued that the advance into Kentucky resulted in a stronger and better supplied army as the Army of Mississippi marched to Tennessee. So, he reasoned the retrograde back to Tennessee did not signify a defeat, but rather a victorious expedition by his army. Not all of Bragg's subordinates agreed with his handling of the campaign, which resulted in the Confederate army ignobly marching back into Tennessee. After the campaign, Bragg and his wing commanders waged a war of letters about how the Perryville campaign was handled. In addition, Colonel Basil Duke, John Hunt Morgan's most effective cavalry officer, wrote that the failure in Kentucky "was the best and last chance to win the war." Bragg, West Point class of 1837, assumed command of the Army of Mississippi in June 1862 when Pierre Beauregard's illness caused him to give up command after the Union Army claimed Corinth, Mississippi, less than two months after the Battle of Shiloh. Braxton Bragg had many good qualities but he was an unpopular commander, and would remain so, as long as he commanded the Army of Mississippi, later renamed the Army of Tennessee. Subsequently,

Bragg assumed command of Confederate forces in the mid-south and finally, he led the Confederate march into Kentucky. "Bragg seemed to repel men with disarming ease," wrote historian Peter Cozzens, and as long as Bragg remained in command controversy and conflict followed him.[3]

While most historians grant the Union forces a strategic victory at the Battle of Perryville, the victory showed little dominance of the Army of the Ohio. As Bragg moved his army southward he claimed a rich booty which his Army of Mississippi needed and he also exclaimed that he saved North Alabama and Middle Tennessee for the Confederacy by drawing the Union forces northward. In addition, if Bragg could occupy central Tennessee this would allow his army to subsist from the bounty of the countryside while reclaiming Cumberland Gap as a result of the Kentucky Campaign. But not all of the booty Bragg and Smith claimed moved with the retreating Confederate armies. Much of Smith's supplies remained abandoned at supply depots set up in central Kentucky. In addition, Bragg only had a few days' rations with his retreating army and his men would be sorely tested as they marched south. George Knox Miller observed "more than 2,000 blbs [barrels] of pork destroyed in one little hour for want of wagons to transport it away. Some of our Quarter Masters succeeded in bringing away 350, or 400,000 of fine Linsey's, Jeans, Kerseys, &c., all of which will prove a blessing to our ill-clad men."[4]

On the Union side, Major General Don Carlos Buell ordered a half-hearted Union pursuit of Bragg's army which was easily handled by Bragg's two able cavalry brigade commanders, Colonel John Wharton and Colonel Joseph Wheeler, a favorite of Bragg. Wharton had just assumed brigade command of the cavalry on Bragg's Right Wing on September 25 when Bragg sent Nathan Bedford Forrest back to Tennessee to raise more cavalry and conduct operations near Nashville. Forrest, like John Hunt Morgan, another independently-minded Confederate cavalry brigade commander, demonstrated his own remarkable skill and diligently began the new assignment. In addition, Colonel John Scott's and Colonel Henry M. Ashby's small cavalry brigades accompanied Smith's Confederate Army of Kentucky. Meanwhile, Colonel John Hunt Morgan's semi-independent cavalry brigade had been given freedom to raid throughout the countryside and had just rejoined Smith's army. While the Confederate cavalry provided the rearguard duty, the Union pursuit was generally more nuisance than threat as Bragg easily slipped back into Tennessee.

While Bragg's army marched back to Tennessee, the Confederate high command was equally distressed about the situation around Nashville. Major General Earl Van Dorn's advance in northern Mississippi had just resulted in the second Confederate defeat in two weeks, this time at Corinth on October 4 which followed a tactical defeat of Sterling Price's troops at Iuka on September 19. Most recently, Van Dorn had been handily defeated by Union Major General William Rosecrans, under Ulysses S. Grant's command. Should Rosecrans march into Middle Tennessee, the entire state could be lost for the Confederacy. Forrest's role in Middle Tennessee was to prevent this from occurring until Confederate reinforcements arrived. Almost immediately after the Battle of Perryville, the Confederates focused on Middle Tennessee as a critical location for Bragg's army. On October 9, Nathan Bedford Forrest received additional cavalry, artillery and infantry for use in protecting Confederate positions around Union-held Nashville. In addition, Major General John C. Breckinridge's division which Bragg desired in the Perryville campaign, but which had been delayed, was redirected toward Murfreesboro. Breckinridge, Vice-President from 1857–1861, was popular in Kentucky and Bragg hoped his presence during the recent campaign could draw many Southern supporting citizens to rally

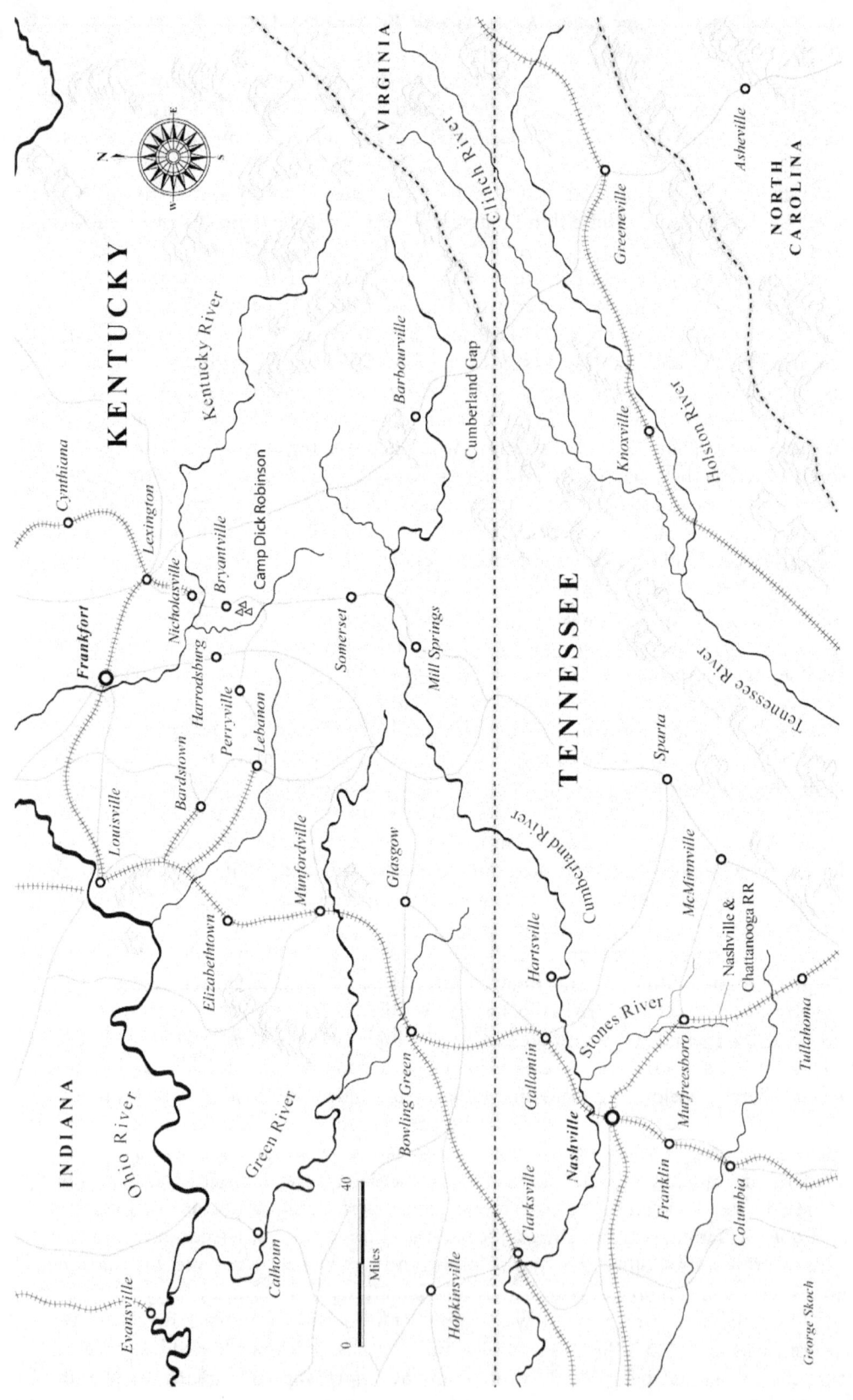

Central Kentucky and central Tennessee—October 1862.

around the Confederacy. Although Bragg understood Breckinridge's unavoidable delay, he still blamed the general from Kentucky for the lack of success in the recent campaign. The relationship between Breckinridge and Bragg would continue to deteriorate throughout the Stones River campaign.[5]

Until Breckinridge arrived, Forrest was ordered to hold Murfreesboro if possible. Bragg did not like Forrest and this was one of the reasons Bragg sent him back to Tennessee to organize the Confederate actions around Murfreesboro. John W. DuBose, Wheeler's biographer, described: "General Bragg did not appreciate Forrest; he did not like the man. Thus, about ten days after the capture of Munfordville, he ordered the cavalry leader, the ranking officer of that arm in his army, to turn his entire brigade, except four Alabama companies and his personal staff, over to Colonel Wharton ... and proceed with the four companies and his staff to Murfreesboro, there to organize a new brigade. The ostensible reason was that the enemy was moving out of Nashville in marauding expeditions."[6]

Regardless, Forrest was dedicated to the cause and Middle Tennessee remained in good hands. Tennessee-native Nathan Bedford Forrest proved to be one of the most talented Confederate cavalry officers in the war. Before the war, Forrest made a living in the Mississippi Delta and when the war began he enlisted and raised a regiment at his own expense. Forrest gained national attention when he refused to surrender his cavalry at Fort Donelson where he led his troops through Union lines rather than surrender. He had participated in the Battle of Shiloh and caused havoc to the Union army in Tennessee and Mississippi since. While Bragg fought the Battle of Perryville, Forrest returned to Tennessee and set up his headquarters at Murfreesboro.[7]

Confederate Cavalry

While Bragg had difficulty with his two infantry wing commanders and Forrest, he had better relations with his cavalry commanders. Bragg had two capable and proficient cavalry leaders with Colonel Joseph Wheeler, whom Bragg would appoint chief of cavalry on October 13, and Colonel John Wharton. Joseph Wheeler, only 26 years old, a native of Georgia and graduate of the United States Military Academy in 1859, was the type of cavalry commander Bragg wanted. In July 1862, Wheeler was given command of a cavalry brigade in Bragg's Army of Mississippi. John A. Wharton was to prove to be Wheeler's most able brigade commander. The 34-year-old Wharton, a native Tennessean, was an attorney residing in Texas prior to the war. Wharton who seemed always in the middle of a fight was severely wounded during the Battle of Shiloh and again wounded in the summer of 1862. During the Perryville Campaign, Wharton commanded the cavalry brigade attached to Leonidas Polk's right wing while Wheeler commanded the cavalry brigade attached to William Hardee's left wing.[8]

Army of Mississippi Cavalry
Col. Joseph Wheeler, Chief of Cavalry[9]

Left Wing		Right Wing	
2nd Cavalry Brig.	Col. Joseph Wheeler	**1st Cavalry Brig.**	Col. John A. Wharton
1st Alabama Cavalry	Col. William Wirt Allen	2nd Georgia Cavalry (5 co.)	Lt. Col. Arthur Hood
3rd Alabama Cavalry	Col. James Hagan	1st Kentucky Cavalry (4 co.)	Capt. Thom A. Ireland
6th Confederate Cavalry	Lieut. Col. James Pell	4th Tennessee Cavalry (5 co.)	Maj. Baxter Smith

Left Wing		Right Wing	
8th Confederate Cavalry	Col. William B. Wade	Davis's Tennessee Cava. Batt.	Maj. John R. Davis**
2nd Georgia Cavalry (5 companies)	Maj. C. A. Whaley	8th Texas Cavalry*	Lt. Col. Thomas Harrison
Smith's Georgia Cavalry Battalion	Col. John R. Hart		
1st Kentucky Cavalry (5 Companies)	Maj. John W. Caldwell		
6th Kentucky Cavalry (3 Companies)	Col. J. Warren Grigsby		
9th Tennessee Cavalry	Col. James D. Bennett		
12th Tennessee Cavalry	Lieut. Col. T. W. Adrian		
Hanley's Sect., Calvert's Ark. Battery	2nd Lieut. S. G. Hanley		

*Nicknamed—"Terry's Texas Rangers"
**Four companies

In addition to Wheeler and Wharton, John Hunt Morgan's cavalry brigade was attached to Kirby Smith's Army of Kentucky. Nicknamed, "Thunderbolt of the Confederacy," Morgan was born in Huntsville, Alabama, and was the grandson of John Wesley Hunt, an early founder of Lexington, Kentucky. Morgan attended Transylvania College for two years but was suspended in 1844 for dueling. He enlisted as a private in the U.S. Cavalry during the Mexican War. Afterwards, he became a hemp manufacturer and took over his grandfather's mercantile business in Kentucky. In 1857, Morgan raised an independent infantry company known as the Lexington Rifles and in September 1861, Morgan took his militiamen to the Confederacy. Initially, he was promoted as colonel of the 2nd Kentucky Cavalry, and Morgan gained notoriety by leading a raid deep behind Buell's lines in Kentucky in July 1862. Morgan's cavalry brigade (2nd, 7th, 8th, 9th and 11th Kentucky cavalries) moved northward as part of Smith's Army of Kentucky during the Perryville Campaign. On August 11 Morgan left Sparta, Tennessee, and rode to Gallatin, Tennessee. Arriving there on August 12, he captured a garrison of nearly 400 Union soldiers. More importantly, the Confederate cavalry destroyed the Louisville and Nashville Railroad tunnel near Gallatin effectively cutting Buell's supply line to Louisville for the 98 days it took to repair the tunnel. Next, Morgan accompanied the Confederate advance into Kentucky in the fall and was ordered, while in cooperation with Kirby Smith's Confederate column, to act independently.[10]

Kirby Smith had two additional small cavalry brigades as he marched into Kentucky: the first was the 900-man cavalry brigade under the command of Colonel John S. Scott (1st Louisiana Cavalry, 1st Georgia Cavalry, and the Buckner Guards, numbering in the aggregate 896). The headstrong Scott was a native of East Feliciana Parish, Louisiana. He began the war as a scout for Magruder's cavalry in Virginia and returned to Louisiana to help raise the 1st Louisiana Cavalry in the fall of 1861. In 1862, Scott's Louisiana cavalry operated north of the Cumberland River and participated in the Battle of Shiloh. Since that time Scott operated against the Union army in Tennessee and Alabama and had fiery interactions with his subordinate officers.[11]

The second cavalry brigade was Brigadier General Benjamin Allston's 1,200 man brigade (1st Tennessee Cavalry, 2nd Tennessee Cavalry, and Starnes' 3rd Tennessee Cavalry). Benjamin Allston was the ranking cavalry commander for Smith's cavalry but Allston was wounded during the Battle of Perryville and brigade command devolved to Colonel Henry Ashby. Both Ashby and Scott commanded relatively small cavalry commands after the Battle of Perryville.[12]

The Confederate Army Moves to Tennessee

While Bragg ingloriously marched back to Tennessee, the Union commanding general, Major General Don Carlos Buell, had troubles of his own. Buell, a career army officer, graduated from West Point in 1841. Buell commanded the Army of the Ohio in December 1861 and he successfully captured Nashville in February 1862. Buell was an industrious and efficient officer, but alienated many powerful military and political figures because of his rigid and inflexible personality. Now, in October 1862, Buell considered his pursuit of Bragg, but he delayed. Buell worried that a concentrated Confederate attack on his flank would result in disaster for his Army of the Ohio. Until he knew Bragg's intent, he was bound by caution, reasoning that the combination of Smith and Bragg roughly equaled his numbers. In addition, Buell knew Bragg would have the choice of location for a battle. Buell wrote,

> My studies have taught me that battles are only to be fought for some important object; that success must be rendered reasonably certain if possible—the more certain the better; that if the result is reasonably uncertain, battle is only to be sought when very serious disadvantage must result from a failure to fight, or when the advantages of a possible victory far outweigh the consequences of probable defeat.

Buell's lack of intensity in pursuing Bragg, in addition to his own ability to alienate important political figures, would ultimately be his undoing.[13]

Immediately after the Battle of Perryville, Joseph Wheeler was given the task to resist any pursuit which Buell ordered after Bragg's army. On October 9, Wharton's and Wheeler's cavalry screened Bragg's Confederate army which moved to Harrodsburg to unite with E. Kirby Smith Confederate army and protected the roads leading to Danville and Harrodsburg. John Scott's brigade screened the roads north at Versailles, Morgan's cavalry moved directly to Harrodsburg and Ashby's cavalry screened the right flank of the Army of Kentucky north of Harrodsburg. Bragg ordered Wheeler to hold back the enemy pursuit. Little action was taken by the Union forces to follow Bragg immediately after the battle, but on October 10, the 1st Ohio Cavalry advanced to scout the Confederate positions near Harrodsburg. Next, Colonel Edward McCook's Union cavalry brigade rode toward Danville intending to locate and hopefully cut off some portion of the Confederate forces. The location of the Confederate army was revealed when a courier from Joseph Wheeler was captured with a letter addressed to Confederate wing commander William Hardee in Harrodsburg.[14]

The first serious engagement occurred on October 11 in which Colonel William B. Wade's 8th Confederate Cavalry played an important role. Wade's cavalry had just arrived, somewhat belatedly in Wheeler's opinion from Tennessee, and was ordered to delay the Union advance toward the concentration of Bragg's army. Colonel William B. Hazen's 2,500-man Nineteenth Infantry Brigade, Army of the Ohio, led the Union advance toward Danville and camped three miles west of the town the evening before. The next morning Hazen advanced toward a Confederate battle line one mile west of Danville and Colonel Frank Wolford's 1st Kentucky Cavalry provided protection on both flanks of the Union infantry. Hazen used his infantry against the determined line of the dismounted 8th Confederate Cavalry and pushed ahead. Hazen's orders prevented him from initiating a general engagement, but he successfully dealt with Wheeler's cavalry with the 8th Confederate taking the brunt of the attack. Although successful, Hazen's appraisal of Wolford's regiment was less than complimentary as he stated: "The entire regiment seemed greatly deficient in anything approaching military drill, and it was with difficulty that my orders, given in the simplest military language, were understood."[15]

Wheeler was obliged to fall back east of Danville and then to the east side of the Dix (also referred to as Dick's) River closer to Bragg's headquarters and Confederate supply depot at Bryantsville, a small village equal distance between Lexington, Danville and Harrodsburg. During the night of October 12, Bragg sent orders to start moving back to Tennessee. The next morning, Bragg appointed Wheeler chief of cavalry and Wheeler was ordered to organize all the mounted troops and to provide rearguard action as the Confederate army withdrew. Wheeler placed his cavalry at important fords across the Dix River and the bulk of the cavalry was deployed along the two important roads of the Union pursuit. Wheeler and Wharton began a process of effectively delaying the Union advance, repeatedly causing the Union columns to move into battle line, only to mount and ride away. So pleased was Bragg with Wheeler's efforts, he sent the cavalryman a congratulatory message: "The general commanding instructs me to return you his thanks for the zeal, activity, and promptness you have manifested." Meanwhile near E. Kirby Smith's Army of Kentucky, Colonel John H. Morgan's, Colonel Henry Ashby's, and Colonel John Scott's cavalry brigades were also given duty of providing flank security and rearguard duty during the withdrawal of the two Confederate columns.[16]

Bragg was happy with his choice of chief of cavalry. Jefferson Davis described Wheeler as one of the most skillful cavalry commanders in his army. Wheeler was born on September 10, 1836, in Augusta, Georgia. He graduated from the United States Military Academy in 1859, graduating 19th in a class of 22 of which only Wheeler would distinguish himself. He was promoted second lieutenant in the 1st U.S. Dragoons upon graduation. He attended the U.S. Army cavalry school in Carlisle, Pennsylvania, before being transferred to the Mounted Rifles in New Mexico where he remained until his resignation on February 21, 1861, after Georgia voted to secede. The fires of secession drew him to the Confederate Army where he first served as first lieutenant in the Confederate artillery at Pensacola, and in September 1861, he assumed command of the 19th Alabama Infantry. He commanded the regiment during the bloody Battle of Shiloh and the subsequent siege at Corinth. In July 1862 he assumed command of a brigade of cavalry in Bragg's Army of Mississippi and aggressively raided the enemy in Mississippi and west Tennessee. Bragg continued to be impressed with Wheeler's actions during the Perryville Campaign and chose him to be his chief of cavalry because he was a "soldier of ability and competence, who scrupulously obeyed given orders, adapted quickly to fluctuating situations, and gave the fullest amount of attention and energy to his assigned duties." Also, Wheeler was educated at West Point which appealed to Bragg.[17]

While Hazen disparaged Colonel Frank L. Wolford's cavalry's action at Danville, Colonel James R. Howard, 3rd Confederate Cavalry, was more impressed as he had a running skirmish for three days and nights, from October 13 to 16, as the Union cavalry tried to maneuver to cut off the Confederate rearguard. Howard noted: "I have engaged him to the best of my ability every time. It was his purpose to cut me off. I outmanaged him, and have secured all my wagons as far as this point. In a short skirmish yesterday with about 500 of his cavalry I lost 2 men killed and 4 missing. His whole force is still after me." Howard estimated the Union cavalry on his trail to be about 5,000 men and he faced ambushes as he rode through the Kentucky countryside. In addition to the hardships involving the Union cavalry, he found in pro–Union Kentucky forage difficult to find, either because of the drought or because farmers did not welcome the cavalry in gray. Howard's account referred to Wolford's cavalry, but he fended off McCook's First Cavalry Brigade which made the Confederate rearguard duty very difficult. McCook commanded one of two cavalry brigades of the Colonel John Kennett's cavalry division of the Army of the Ohio and Lewis Zahm commanded the Second Brigade. In a confused command situation, Captain Ebenezer Gay (acting brigadier general) served as the titular chief of cavalry for Buell's troops. Gay also commanded a third cavalry brigade that was temporarily attached to Buell's army. Gay proceeded with reconnaissance efforts and effectively determined Bragg's position, but the Union infantry was cautioned not to advance in a manner which would bring on a serious engagement.[18]

As Bragg's and Smith's Confederate columns continued to march southward, John Hunt Morgan's cavalry along with Colonel Henry Ashby's Tennessee cavalry took up position as the rearguard of Smith's column, but under the overall command of Wheeler. Colonel John Scott's cavalry also screened Kirby's Confederate force. Wheeler had another heated skirmish near Lancaster on October 14 which resulted in the destruction of some of the Union artillery. Colonel Frank Wolford's 1st Kentucky was again involved in the fight and succeeded in pushing the Confederate cavalry to rear. Wolford estimated he killed or wounded thirty during the engagement. Also, Lieutenant Colonel Robert Stewart's 2nd Indiana Cavalry fought the Confederate rearguard on the Dick Robinson Road during the day. In the eastern Confederate column, Morgan and Ashby had light duty. Basil Duke recalled, "We were not pressed at all by the enemy," but Wheeler and Wharton fought off a more determined pursuit as the Confederate army moved past Crab Orchard. From this point until Bragg's column reached London (about 40–50 miles south) when the Union pursuit ended on October 22, Wharton and Wheeler formed the primary rearguard. In addition to fighting the pursuing Union troops, the cavalry ensured stragglers were not left behind. Throughout the Union pursuit, Wheeler would face primarily Union cavalry because the infantry lagged behind in the pursuit.[19]

Smith's cavalry was exhausted and Colonel John Scott had repeatedly reported that his horses were used up and he finally moved away from rearguard duty to be able to forage his horses. Scott visited with Bragg about the plight of his cavalry and gained permission to move horses to better forage in Tennessee. Bragg agreed to this but he insisted that Scott remain at Crab Orchard and determine if Wharton or Wheeler required his brigade before leaving the army. But, Scott ignored this stipulation and ordered his cavalry to Somerset. Wheeler finding Scott gone talked to Bragg and received the details of Scott's orders and then sent a party after him. Scott was arrested for disobedience of orders and removed from command. This would not be the last time in his Civil War career he ran afoul of a commanding officer. Scott's cavalry brigade was placed under direct command of Colonel John Wharton. A member of the 1st Louisiana Cavalry, Howell Carter, later wrote regarding Scott's arrest, "The particulars of which we never fully understood, though it was said that Bragg arrested him because he was contemplating an independent trip with his brigade without permission; disobedience of orders, though, I believe, was the charge."[20]

Historian Kenneth Hafendorfer declared Scott's arrest resulted from the fact that Scott refused to serve under Wheeler because he technically outranked him. Hafendorfer pointed out that Scott had refused to serve under John Adams the previous summer and N. Bedford Forrest in July. "The reason was pride, and that uncontrollable free spirit exemplified by most of the Southern cavalrymen." Ultimately, Bragg simply dropped the charges. The issue of rank was important to military men in the Civil War. Not only did rank influence Scott's actions, it most likely was important in the removal of Forrest back to Murfreesboro. If Bragg intended to name Wheeler as his head of cavalry, he could not do this while Nathan Bedford Forrest was with the army. Forrest was promoted to the rank of brigadier general the previous summer and based on his superior rank he would had to be given the position of chief of cavalry. Bragg's removal of Forrest opened the door for Wheeler's promotion.[21]

The next significant skirmish occurred on October 16, as the Union pursuit moved a few miles south of Mt. Vernon in the hilly region of the Kentucky. The 2nd Indiana Cavalry screened the advance of the Union infantry and discovered a line of Confederates supported by artillery. After the 2nd Indiana Cavalry and the Union infantry advanced, a "brisk skirmish" resulted which lasted for about thirty minutes before the Southern defenders moved away. But, the Confederate rearguard used a "fight-retreat-fight" method of slowing the Union advance as William Hazen's 9th Indiana Infantry ran into another line of dismounted Confederate cavalry supported by artillery two miles ahead. This method of fighting continued throughout the day and the felling of trees across the roads complicated the Union march. By the end of the day, the Union advance reached the Big Rockcastle Creek. Skirmishes continued more regularly on October 16–20 at Mount Vernon, Wild Cat Mountain, Big Rockcastle Creek, and Pitman's Crossroads as Bragg delayed his withdrawal to allow Smith's army to catch up. Union Brigadier General William Sooy Smith described a skirmish on October 17 near Camp Wildcat. "If [Ebenezer] Gay could have crossed over this morning into that road he might have intercepted stragglers, &c., but his horses were suffering to an extent that would not permit such movement." Acting Brigadier General Ebenezer Gay commanded Buell's cavalry during the pursuit, and the farther southeast the Union cavalry moved, the scarcer they found the forage they needed. Smith explained the efficiency of Wheeler's delaying tactics and the difficulty of the Federal cavalry in its pursuit.

> We are pressing the rebel cavalry back, skirmishing with them at every turn of the road.... They have so obstructed the road by felling timber that our progress is very slow. A cavalry force could prevent this, but our infantry cannot get ahead fast enough. They fell trees until we come up to them, then fall back rapidly and chop away again. We push them as closely as possible.[22]

The withdrawal caused the relationship between Bragg and commander of the Army of Kentucky to further deteriorate. E. Kirby Smith who commanded his own army voluntarily agreed to serve under Bragg, and he felt Bragg disproportionally favored his Army of Mississippi over the Army of Kentucky. The cooperation between the two armies was weak throughout the entire campaign and Smith had refused to concentrate his army with Bragg's in September near Louisville. During the retreat to Tennessee and while Bragg's column was approaching Mt. Vernon, Kirby Smith's army lagged some twenty to thirty miles to the rear trying to get its ordnance train over Big Hill. The intensity of skirmishing with the Confederate cavalry increased because Bragg told Wheeler the Union pursuit needed to be delayed to get the retreating infantry columns past London.

Kirby Smith was correct in his changing feelings about Bragg. Bragg had insured his army was safely retreating southward, but he had been lax in coordinating his withdrawal with Smith's Army of Kentucky. Bragg admitted to Leonidas Polk on October 16 that his withdrawal put Smith's army at risk of being cut off and surrounded. Smith's tardiness resulted because Bragg had "imposed" his trains on Smith "by which he is retarded" and allowed the Army of Mississippi to move quickly at the detriment to the other Southern column; although, Bragg kept his army between Buell and Smith for a while. As Bragg slowed to allow the Army of Kentucky to catch up, Wheeler's rearguard action became more important. The seriousness of Smith's position was stressed in his message to Bragg on October 17. "Wheeler telling me he is ordered to fall back to London. Unless the Crab Orchard roads are held for some days longer, this army and its trains will be sacrificed." Smith even contemplated abandoning his withdrawal to Tennessee in favor of another advance on Lexington, but forced marches enabled the Army of Kentucky to reach the safety of Leonidas Polk's lines which stopped to cover the flank of Smith as he hurried toward London. Carter Stevenson's division marched thirty miles and through the night to reach the main column.[23]

Smith was right to be concerned because the Union army was moving to attack the lagging Army of Kentucky, albeit too late. On October 20, Colonel John Kennett dispatched Colonel Edward McCook's cavalry brigade to ride for Big Hill but Smith had escaped by the time McCook arrived. Once McCook reached Big Hill, he found Smith's army gone.[24]

General Don Carlos Buell: "The whole cavalry force was totally inadequate for the service which the occasion demanded" (Library of Congress).

While the interactions between the two Confederate commanding generals were not good, Joseph Wheeler dodged army politics and earnestly worked for both armies. In his actions on behalf of Smith's column, he was rewarded with a message of thanks penned on Smith's behalf by Colonel John Pegram. Once the two columns united, the Confederate armies slipped back into Tennessee on October 19–24. William Hazen believed that he never caught the main body of the Confederate army, but at most, he faced a force of 1,500 to 3,000 troops whose design was to serve as rearguard and when pressed moved away from the Union pursuit.[25]

An addition to the Southern cavalry which advanced into Kentucky was the newly formed Kentucky cavalry brigade of Brigadier General Abraham Buford—3rd, 5th and 6th Kentucky cavalries. In September, Buford, newly appointed brigadier general, entered the Confederate army and brought a small three-regiment brigade of Kentucky cavalry with him. The Kentucky cavalry was new to the army and Leonidas Polk was unwilling to put any trust in this untried cavalry brigade. In addition, Polk thought that Henry Ashby's cavalry brigade was too small to resist the Federal forces pressing on the Confederate infantry. He wanted Wharton and Wheeler, two commanders he trusted, to cover his withdrawal. Polk's decision displeased Buford and it left his cavalry little to do, except to escort a wagon train down the Wilderness Road out of Kentucky.[26]

Bragg and Smith were successful in returning to Tennessee in part due to the less than aggressive pursuit ordered by Buell. Once Bragg moved past Crab Orchard, Buell concluded to stop the pursuit. He reasoned the countryside between Crab Orchard and Cumberland Gap offered no subsistence for his army. The availability of forage for the livestock was minimal. Plus Buell would be marching over the same path as Bragg and Smith and any subsistence would already have been claimed by the Southern armies. There was only one, poor route to pursue Bragg, and that was in his own footsteps down the Wilderness Road. The pursuit would go through rugged, hilly terrain along a narrow road. After marching a short distance in pursuit of Bragg the truth of the lack of forage was already felt.

> The enemy has been driven into the heart of this desert and must go on, for he cannot exist in it. For the same reason we cannot pursue in it with any hope of overtaking him, for while he is moving back on his supplies and as he goes consuming what the country affords we must bring ours forward.... For these reasons, which I do not think it necessary to elaborate, I deem it useless and inexpedient to continue the pursuit, but propose to direct the main force under my command rapidly upon Nashville ... which I have no doubt Bragg will move the main part of his army.

The decision to halt the pursuit did not sit well with those in Washington. Buell's army was battled to a standstill at Perryville and since that time Bragg and Smith simply marched back into Tennessee. Also Buell's conduct, committing only a fraction of his troops at Perryville, resulted in anger in Washington and the field. Buell's decision to stop the pursuit into East Tennessee and his focus on Nashville resulted in exasperation by his commanders in Washington, because Henry Halleck, General-in-Chief of all Union forces, wanted Buell's army in East Tennessee and not in Middle Tennessee. Henry Halleck replied to Buell's plan to move his army to Nashville:

General Henry Halleck, General-in-Chief of the Union armies, decided to replace Buell after the Battle of Perryville (Library of Congress).

> By keeping between him and Nashville can you not cover that place and at the same time compel him to fall back into the valley of Virginia or into Georgia? If we can occupy Knoxville or Chattanooga we can keep the enemy out of Tennessee and Kentucky. To fall back on Nashville is to give up East Tennessee to be plundered. Moreover, you are now much nearer to Knoxville and as near to Chattanooga as to Nashville. If you go to the latter place and then to East Tennessee, you move over two sides of an equilateral triangle, while the enemy holds the third. Again, may he not in the meantime make another raid into Kentucky?

Halleck continued in a more direct tone exclaiming that the capture of East Tennessee should be the main objective of the Union army in Kentucky and Tennessee. In response to the ability to subsist in the Nashville area instead of East Tennessee, Halleck asked if the enemy could subsist there, could not Buell's troops do likewise. Halleck concluded his message to Buell telling him that the President declared that Buell's army had to "enter East Tennessee this fall."[27]

Buell's action also precipitated political pressure being exerted on Halleck. On October 21, Indiana Governor Oliver P. Morton, upon finding Bragg and Smith had returned to Tennessee, wrote to the President:

> The butchery of our troops at Perryville was terrible, and resulted from a large portion of the enemy being precipitated upon a small portion of ours. Sufficient time was thus gained by the enemy to enable them to escape. Nothing but success, speedy and decided, will save our cause from utter destruction. In the Northwest distrust and despair are seizing upon the hearts of the people.

Meanwhile Buell wrote to Halleck of the reasons he could not advance to East Tennessee. He explained he needed 80,000 men to successfully hold that area and the resources in Middle Tennessee were greatly superior to those in East Tennessee. Buell wrote to Halleck on October 22: "I could in an hour's conversation give you my views and explain the routes and character of the country better than I can in a dispatch, and perhaps satisfactorily." Buell offered to travel to Washington to explain his decisions, but he wanted a commitment from Halleck to agree with his movements to Nashville first. While awaiting reply from Halleck and in a separate message, he informed Halleck he had halted his pursuit of Bragg.[28]

Buell simply failed to grasp the need to follow Halleck's orders. Halleck tersely replied the next day that Buell needed to march to East Tennessee "with all possible dispatch.... Neither the Government nor the country can endure these repeated delays. Both require a prompt and immediate movement toward the accomplishment of the great object in view—the holding of East Tennessee." Halleck had had enough. The same day, he ordered Major General William S. Rosecrans to proceed to Cincinnati to receive his orders. Halleck decided a change of command was needed and on October 24, Rosecrans received his orders to command the Department of the Cumberland and command of army operations which were currently under authority of Buell. When Rosecrans was given command, Buell was ordered to face a court of inquiry in November regarding the appropriateness of his actions during the Perryville Campaign.[29]

Morgan Rides for Lexington

While the two opposing armies marched southward, John Hunt Morgan initiated a raid on the rear of the Federal army. Major General Horatio Wright ordered Union troops south from Cincinnati to protect against Confederate raids, but they had not reached central Kentucky in time to prevent Morgan's actions. While Morgan initiated his raid, Wheeler and Wharton continued to protect the rear of the retreating Southern armies.[30]

When Morgan began his raid, not only did this take some attention away from the main Southern retreat, he also captured some Ohio cavalry. In position around Lexington, Major Charles Seidel, commanding the 3rd Ohio Cavalry, also had authority of some of the 4th Ohio cavalry regiment. Morgan who found he had little to do in protecting Kirby Smith's retreat and in an effort to relieve the Union pressure on the retreat, moved his cavalry brigade northward. In what was to be a model of the superiority of the Confederate cavalry and example of the faulty organization of the Union cavalry, Morgan surrounded and captured 290 men of the 3rd and 4th Ohio cavalries on October 18 with 1,800 men of the 2nd, 3rd, and 9th Kentucky CSA cavalry. The incident occurred on the estate, south of Lexington, of the late ex-senator and force behind the Compromise of 1820 and 1850, Henry Clay.[31]

Seidel reported that his troops "manfully and gallantly" fought the attacking Confederate cavalry and even fought them in hand-to-hand combat until they were overwhelmed by such disparate odds. Then, he surrendered rather than continue with the fight. Seidel had four troopers killed and another twenty-four wounded before he surrendered. Prior to the attack, Seidel guarded several roads and bridges with his cavalry regiments divided into battalions. This model of dispersing Union cavalry while facing concentrated forces of Southern cavalry at brigade strength was a disaster. Morgan's cavalry was such an overwhelming force Seidel had little hope of success. In addition to the cavalry captured at Ashland, another four companies of 4th Ohio Cavalry were captured when Morgan attacked the Union garrison at Lexington. Then the Union commanders attempted to assemble enough cavalry to catch Morgan, but Morgan easily rode through the countryside, returning to Tennessee in early November. Morgan rode through Lawrenceburg, Bardstown, Elizabethtown, Hopkinsville and finally to Gallatin.[32]

A provisional Federal cavalry brigade commanded by the aggressive Colonel Minor Millikin, 1st Ohio Cavalry, pursued John Hunt Morgan's raiders through October, but the command situation within the Union cavalry hampered Millikin's efforts. While Buell had made improvements within the cavalry, it was an arm with too many directing its efforts. Colonel John Kennett, division commander, remained very quiet through October and Ebenezer Gay, acting as chief of cavalry, also appeared to give little direction to the cavalry. The Army of the Ohio drove out pockets of Southern resistance while Morgan rode throughout the countryside in his circuitous route back to Tennessee. In frustration, Millikin wrote, "Because of the somewhat unintelligible and apparently unreasonable movements made by the forces under my command in the recent pursuit of Morgan and the fruitless result of the whole affair I suppose it proper, both in justice to myself and because some wholesome inferences may be drawn from them."

Millikin reported directly to Buell without benefit of coordination through his superior officer or the level above. As a result of confused orders, Millikin rode fifty miles to Bardstown after Morgan only to find Ebenezer Gay with cavalry already there on October 20. Then, the next day's orders from Gay kept Millikin's brigade in the area, only to be informed "incidentally" the next morning that his brigade was expected to act as an "independent one." Buell expected Millikin to be hot on the heels of Morgan while he dallied near Bardstown based on orders from Gay. "Failing to get any information or suggestions from General Gay or any one else, I started as soon as possible to Munfordville, Gay promising to go to Glasgow via Campbellsville." Millikin reached Munfordville on October 22 and then rode to Brownsville the next day when he was ordered to disband his brigade and send the regiments back to Munfordville. Millikin reported Morgan was at Bardstown on October 19, Litchfield on October 20, and Morgantown on October 24, from which he rode for Tennessee. Millikin complained about the poor coordination of the pursuit. "At no time has my force been sufficient to cope successfully with Morgan." Millikin estimated that Morgan's cavalry totaled greater than 2,000 troopers and it was accompanied with two pieces of artillery. Millikin, if successful in overtaking the Southern cavalry, would be at a numerical disadvantage. Of the 1,175 men Millikin commanded, he had only 575 troops (375 1st Ohio and 200 1st Kentucky) which had any experience in the field and another 600 troopers of the 4th Michigan Cavalry which had never been in a fight. Millikin also rode without any artillery. Millikin wrote: "In whatever way I might have met Morgan, had he had his back against the wall and shown fight, the result would have been doubtful and could not have been else than partial and unsatisfactory." In this report, Millikin summarized much of the shortcomings of the Union cavalry. In addition, as the Confederate cavalry operated behind Union lines, Brigadier General A. J. Smith moved his infantry into the area around Lexington and exclaimed, "O, a kingdom for four regiments of cavalry!"[33]

While specific regiments of cavalry accompanied Union divisions, Edward McCook's cavalry brigade, in what was the only unified cavalry action by the Army of the Ohio, was given duty of scouring the countryside for any remaining concentrations of Confederates. McCook reported he found 200–300 sick and wounded Confederates at Richmond but was convinced nothing but stragglers remained behind. McCook found that Bragg left his wounded behind in Richmond and Harrodsburg when he retreated. Carroll Henderson Clark, 16th Tennessee Infantry, was one left at Harrodsburg, and he wrote: "I was fearful that the Yanks would mistreat us Rebs in the hospital, but I was mistaken."[34]

Union Cavalry of the Army of the Ohio

The command of the Union cavalry at the Battle of Perryville was poorly organized and understood. Buell wrote: "The whole cavalry force was totally inadequate for the service which the occasion demanded." Most records show Captain Ebenezer Gay as acting brigadier general in charge of the cavalry during the battle at Perryville. Gay, West Point graduate, class of 1855, seemed to be a good choice for this position. Many West Point trained officers were promoted to the rank of brigadier general early in the Civil War. Gay served with the 2nd U.S. Dragoons at the beginning of the war and had served in various positions and campaigns including, inspector of cavalry of the Army of the Ohio during the Battle of Shiloh, the siege of Corinth, and the advance on Huntsville. In August 1862, he assisted in the organization of new cavalry regiments in Louisville and then commanded cavalry near Lexington, Kentucky. Then, Gay was named chief of cavalry for the short-lived Army of Kentucky (U.S.). The Union Army of Kentucky was abruptly named for the Union forces near Richmond, Kentucky, under the command of Major General William "Bull" Nelson. Only five days after the army was named, it was soundly defeated by E. Kirby Smith's Confederate Army of Kentucky at the Battle of Richmond on August 29–30. Afterward, Captain Charles Gilbert was promoted to the rank of major general, pending presidential approval, and placed in command of the remnants of Army of Kentucky. Gilbert remained in command of the Army of Kentucky until September 27 when it was absorbed as the III Corps of Buell's Army of the Ohio. While Gilbert commanded the Army of Kentucky, Major General Horatio Wright, commander of the Department of Ohio, told Gilbert that in regard to his cavalry: "Make Gay your chief of cavalry, and thus put him in control of that arm." This is what Gilbert did. Within ten days, Gilbert's command was absorbed into the Army of the Ohio, but in the meantime, Captain Ebenezer Gay was appointed, also provisionally, to the rank of brigadier general. Until this time, the cavalry of the Army of the Ohio was commanded by division commander, Colonel John Kennett.[35]

When Gay's command became part of the Army of the Ohio, it consisted of the 9th

Pennsylvania Cavalry (600 men); 2nd Michigan Cavalry (300 men), 6th Kentucky Cavalry (700 men), 7th Kentucky Cavalry (reported as disorganized), and finally the 11th Kentucky Cavalry (400 men). Gay's command essentially added another cavalry brigade consisting of 2,000 troops to Buell's army. Unfortunately, only two regiments had any experience in the field, and Gay wrote that only the 9th Pennsylvania and 2nd Michigan could be depended upon.[36]

Don Carlos Buell's Cavalry
Present for Duty—October 1, 1862[37]

	Officers	Men
Cavalry Division—Kennett		
First Brigade (McCook)	91	1,590
Second Brigade (Zahm)	64	1,387
Unattached Cavalry		
Negley's 8th Division	11	207
Nashville Garrison	16	722
Seventh Division	10	193
Grand Total	192	4,099

*Gay's brigade was not included in Buell's command on October 1

In Buell's report of the Battle of Perryville, he made reference to the actions of the cavalry division under the command of Colonel John Kennett and the cavalry brigades were commanded by Colonel Edward McCook, Colonel Lewis Zahm, and Captain Ebenezer Gay. The awkwardness of situation arose due to the apparent promotion of Ebenezer Gay to the rank of brigadier general which, due to his superior rank, essentially placed him in command of the division. During the pursuit of Bragg's army after the Battle of Perryville, Gay authored the cavalry report for the recent battle although his report focused primarily on his own brigade's activity. In addition, correspondence also showed James Fry, Buell's chief of staff, addressing him as chief of cavalry and Gay alternately signed his correspondence as chief of cavalry and inspector of cavalry. While Colonel Minor Millikin, 1st Ohio Cavalry, grumbled about Gay's appointment to brigade command during the battle, Colonel Kennett remained silent about losing the overall command of the cavalry. However, Gay's position was short-lived and his appointment was deemed to have been made without legal authority. By November, Gay no longer held command of the cavalry and in December, he was assigned Judge-Advocate of the Department of the Ohio. In November, Kennett again commanded the cavalry division and in the meantime, Colonel Minor Millikin who had complained about Gay's brigade command was given temporary command of his own cavalry brigade.[38]

Regardless of this confusion, the Union cavalry made only a feeble effort of pursuit after the Battle of Perryville. Several reasons have been suggested for the less than aggressive action on the part of the Union cavalry: the actions of Morgan to divert the Union attention from the withdrawal, the size of the various Confederate cavalry brigades, and deficiencies in "training, equipment, and leadership" of the Union cavalry. All of these resulted in a weak response, but perhaps, the biggest reason was the overall organization of the regiments. Buell made changes to improve the cavalry, but the overall organization still remained unsatisfactory. The various regiments and brigades still acted too independently and lacked the ability to offer a concentrated response. This organization resulted in the cavalry being subordinate to corps, division, and brigade infantry commanders who utilized the Northern horsemen to support their particular units. "Consequently the infantry step rather than the cavalry trot determined the army's pace."[39]

Organization of Cavalry of the Army of the Ohio, October 8, 1862[40]

Escort for Maj. Gen. Don Carlos Buell

Anderson Troop, Pennsylvania Cavalry   2nd Lieut. Thomas S. Maple
4th U.S. Cavalry (B, C, D, G, I, and K companies)   Lieut. Col. James Oakes

Unattached

7th Pennsylvania Cavalry, Companies A, D, F, and I   Maj. John E. Wynkoop.

Cavalry Division–Col. John Kennett

First Cavalry Brigade–Col. Edward McCook
- 2nd Indiana — Lt. Col. Robert Stewart
- 1st Kentucky — Col. Frank Wolford
- 3rd Kentucky — Col. Eli H. Murray
- 4th Kentucky — Col. Jesse Bayles

Second Cavalry Brigade–Col. Lewis Zahm
- 5th Kentucky — Major John Owsley
- 3rd Ohio — Lieut. Col. Douglas A. Murray
- 4th Ohio — Maj. John L. Pugh

[Third] Cavalry Brigade–Acting Brig. Gen. (Capt.) Ebenezer Gay
- 9th Kentucky — Lt. Col. John Boyle
- 2nd Michigan — Lt. Col. Archibald Campbell
- 9th Pennsylvania — Lt. Col. Thomas James

Unattached

3rd Ohio Cavalry   Maj. John Foster

First Army Corps
- 9th Kentucky Cavalry (detachment)
- 3rd Indiana Cavalry, Western Battalion
- 2nd Kentucky Cavalry (six companies)

Second Army Corps
- 2nd Kentucky Cavalry (4 co)
- 1st Ohio Cavalry (detachment)

Third Army Corps
- 1st Ohio (detachment)
- 7th Pennsylvania (2 battalions)
- 36th Illinois, Company B
- 4th Indiana (five companies)

Nashville Garrison
- Fry's Kentucky Scouts (Twyman's Scouts)
- 6th Kentucky Cavalry (seven companies)
- 5th Tennessee Cavalry (five companies)

Bragg Focuses on Middle Tennessee

Wheeler's cavalry performed admirable duty during the Confederate withdrawal. The overall actions of Wheeler's Confederate cavalry demonstrated an energy and effectiveness which Bragg appreciated, and George Garner, Bragg's adjutant general, wrote in a personal note: "I congratulate you, my dear fellow, upon the success with which you have conducted operations in our rear." John Pegram, Kirby Smith's chief of staff, echoed the sentiments of Bragg: "The general wishes me to express to you his appreciation of the thorough manner in which you have performed your important duties during this retreat, and to say that he will take especial pleasure in bringing your services to the notice of the Department at Richmond."[41]

While Bragg's Army of Mississippi led the march into Tennessee, the Army of Kentucky marched in a much less pleasant situation. E. Kirby Smith wrote: "This is the worst road I have ever traveled; in some places impassable, so that a new one has to be made." Smith's army marched and dragged his wagons and artillery up and down the mountains on the return to Tennessee over the same route as Bragg's army. The grueling trek resulted in men working all night and Smith's army being "very much scattered along the road." A member of the 34th Alabama Infantry, John Crittenden, wrote to his wife: "Then commenced our suffering for some thing to eat. We were allowed only one meal a day. That was two small biscuits and a plenty of meat to eat with it." As both Confederate armies returned to Tennessee, E. Kirby Smith drew a sigh of relief and dispatched his infantry to various locations to recuperate and to prepare for further action against the Union forces. Smith recorded: "My men have suffered on this march everything excepting actual starvation. There must be not less than 10,000 of them scattered through the country trying to find something upon which to live."

In regard to the cavalry, Wheeler was rightly recognized for its successful duty as rearguard and Wheeler passed his congratulations to his troops in a superb announcement on October 23:

> The autumn campaign in Kentucky is over.... Your gallantry in action, your cheerful endurance of sufferings from hunger, fatigue, and exposure render you worthy of all commendation. For nearly two months you have scarcely for a moment been without the range of the enemy's musketry. In more than twenty pitched fights, many of which lasted throughout the day, you have successfully combated largely superior numbers of the enemy's troops of all arms. Hovering continually near their lines, you have engaged in no less than one hundred skirmishes, and upon the memorable field of Perryville, alone and unsupported, you engaged and held in check during the entire action at least two infantry divisions of the opposing army. By your gallant charges on that day you completely dispersed and routed a vastly superior force of the enemy's cavalry, driving them in confusion under their artillery and infantry supports, capturing in hand-to-hand conflicts many prisoners, horses, arms, &c. Your continual contact with the enemy has taught you to repose without fear under his guns, to fight him wherever found, and to quietly make your bivouac by the light of his camp-fires. In this continual series of combats and brilliant charges many gallant officers and brave men have fallen. We mourn their loss; we commend their valor.[42]

Bragg knew where he wanted his army to concentrate—Middle Tennessee, but by October 23 Kirby Smith put his foot down after receiving the order from Bragg. Smith, a regular army officer prior to the war, was a graduate of the United States Military Academy, class of 1845. Smith commanded the District of East Tennessee after serving in the eastern campaigns early in the war. Now, he wearied of working with Bragg and he acknowledged the request in which Bragg wanted the bulk of his army in Middle Tennessee and leaving only 3,000 men to guard the Cumberland Gap. Smith responded: "The condition of my command now is such as to render any immediate operations with it impossible." Smith continued to explain that based on the recent retreat without adequate rations, clothing, blankets and due to the constant campaigning, his army was in poor condition. He had less than 6,000 men suitable for duty. As a result, Smith tried to separate his command from Bragg's. He had had enough of working with him and declared that he had his own military department responsibilities for which Richmond he held him accountable. He concluded that he had his own orders and the safety of his army was his primary concern. Smith said that his army was in such bad condition it was impossible to move it. Despite Bragg's exclamations of success during the recent campaign, he also acknowledged the recent campaign took a great toll on the Army of Mississippi, but he concluded to move his army into Middle Tennessee. He reluctantly admitted, "The Army of the Mississippi is much shattered." In the final result, Bragg's army had just marched one thousand miles and then returned to Tennessee with no positive results except "that the tarnish on Bragg's prestige was a little more tarnished," wrote historian Stanley Horn.[43]

Regardless of the position Bragg took on the recent campaign, there can be little doubt of the failure to achieve tangible results. Jefferson Davis requested a meeting with Bragg who left by train on October 24, but prior to his departure he left orders for the Army of Mississippi to proceed to Murfreesboro and take up an appropriate position against the Union forces around Nashville. During Bragg's meeting with Davis, he explained his actions during the previous campaign which were accepted by Davis as proper. Subsequently, E. Kirby Smith and Leonidas Polk met with Davis and declared the recent campaign a failure, blaming Bragg's leadership, but Davis refused to remove Bragg from command.[44]

While E. Kirby Smith, commanding the Department of East Tennessee, marched with the Army of Kentucky, Jefferson Davis appointed Major General Sam Jones to command the Department of East Tennessee without informing Smith. Smith had such success at the Battle of Richmond he was promoted to the rank of lieutenant general but the command situation in East Tennessee became confused. Smith was informed due to his superior rank he would command, but Jones would be in charge of the department. Secretary of War Randolph wrote:

General E. Kirby Smith wrote, "Bragg's movements since taking command in Ky. have been most singular and unfortunate" (Library of Congress).

> You are the second on the list of lieutenant-generals, and of course command by virtue of your rank; but until the plan of the fall campaign in Tennessee is determined General Jones will remain in the department. Such measures as you deem necessary may be immediately taken for the defense of Cumberland Gap. Show this dispatch to General Jones.

Smith reached Knoxville on October 24, only to find Bragg had left for Richmond to meet with Davis. In the meantime, Bragg had left orders for Smith to prepare to march to Murfreesboro much to the disappointment of Smith. Smith wrote his wife: "Bragg's movements since taking command in Ky. have been most singular and unfortunate." Smith privately believed Bragg had squandered opportunities and misused Smith's army during the recent campaign. Smith was invited to visit the President which he did in November. Then, Smith was ordered to join Bragg in Middle Tennessee in November, but ultimately, only Major General John Porter McCown's division from Smith's command remained in Middle Tennessee attached to Bragg's army.[45]

The Confederate Troops at Murfreesboro

General Sam Jones found himself in an awkward situation as he assumed command. Kirby Smith was unaware of the change in his department and Jones tried to make sense of Bragg's orders, who was then still in Kentucky. When Jones assumed command of the Department of East Tennessee, he cautioned Bragg against overly aggressive actions at Nashville and Murfreesboro, and he told Bragg that after the Confederate defeats at Corinth and Iuka another 6,000 Union troops had been moved to Nashville to reinforce the existing garrison of 3,000–5,000 men. Jones reminded Bragg that only two regiments of Confederate infantry remained at Knoxville and he had sent these to Murfreesboro. Jones concluded that the number of Union troops in Nashville was much larger than Bragg appeared to suppose. While Smith and Bragg were still in Kentucky, Jones acted upon Bragg's orders to bolster the Confederate presence in Murfreesboro and Nashville. He sent Dure's Battery and a battalion of cavalry to assist Forrest who had been requesting reinforcements. While directing his attention to Murfreesboro, Jones cautioned Forrest who had overall command the Confederate forces in Middle Tennessee on October 11: "If your orders from General Bragg are not positive to organize cavalry regiments, do not organize any more until the infantry are organized. The undisciplined cavalry without arms is more than useless." Isham Green Harris, Confederate governor of Tennessee, "collected some raw cavalry, or rather men on horseback, about Nashville, in whom I have no confidence," wrote Jones. The next day Jones told John C. Breckinridge that President Davis ordered him to take his Kentucky infantry to Murfreesboro.[46]

The increased activity of Confederate troops at Murfreesboro did not go unnoticed by Brigadier General James Negley who commanded Union troops in Nashville since Buell's army moved north in September. When Bragg began his retreat from Kentucky, Negley noticed the serious changes in the enemy forces he faced near Nashville. On October 13, Negley discovered Forrest commanded the Confederate forces at Murfreesboro and with whom he had had some light skirmishing. The morale of Negley's troops was high: "Our defenses are in best possible condition. Continue to improve them.... Command in good health and spirits." Two days later Negley observed the concentration of the enemy at La Vergne, just north of Murfreesboro, but he was confident in his position. The Union reconnaissance revealed three batteries of artillery, 5,000 cavalry, and 3,000 infantry in the town. Negley expected to face as many as 20,000 Confederates by the end of the week.[47]

On October 14, Sam Jones informed George Randolph, Secretary of War, of his efforts of increasing the military presence near Murfreesboro and explained his plan to hold the current Southern positions. He also optimistically contemplated moving against Negley's Nashville garrison, but the recent defeat at Corinth troubled him. If Van Dorn had been defeated as badly as he supposed, then Union troops could be moved to Nashville and a Southern offensive would not be practical. At this point, Nathan Bedford Forrest still commanded the Confederate forces at Murfreesboro and Jones wrote: "Brigadier-General Forrest is now in command at Murfreesborough, and without meaning to reflect in the slightest degree on the ability of Brigadier-General Forrest, whom I have not the pleasure of knowing, I respectfully suggest that the force which will be collected at and near Murfreesborough in a few days will be large enough to require the services of another brigadier."[48]

While Joseph Wheeler was coordinating the rearguard of Bragg's army in Kentucky, Nathan Bedford Forrest dealt with the situation at Murfreesboro and Nashville. Forrest accompanied Bragg's army into Kentucky and provided cavalry duty on the right wing until September 25, 1862, when he was ordered back to Tennessee and given control of the military operations in Middle Tennessee. Forrest was also given authority to organize four infantry regiments and two cavalry regiments. His orders directed him to patrol the various areas around Nashville and attack the enemy whenever he saw an opportunity. His attention focused on stopping the flow of supplies to Nashville. On October 16, Sam Jones ordered him not to accept any additional cavalry which was not armed. While Forrest tried to organize more cavalry, Sam Jones tried to stop him, declaring that he had more cavalry than he could possibly arm and equip. The Southerners in Tennessee felt the zeal of patriotism as they were called to arms: "[A]ll East Tennesseans must stand up as one man, proclaiming their devotion to the South and to the institutions of our fathers." Many wanted to join the cavalry instead of the infantry; however, Jones had requests for 1,900 cavalry arms and had no way of procuring them. Jones reasoned: "Cavalry without arms is of no service and very expensive. I recommend that all mounted troops for whom arms cannot be procured be dismounted and converted into infantry."[49]

Forrest, still stinging from having been sent to Tennessee while the brigade he organized remained in Kentucky, decided to side step Jones and made an appeal directly to the Secretary of War on October 20: "I am in urgent need of 5,000 stand of arms. The men only wait to receive them. If you can only send me 1,000 short arms and sabers for cavalry they will be invaluable." Randolph promptly forwarded the request to Colonel Josiah Gorgas, Confederate ordnance officer in Richmond, who flatly replied that it was impossible to furnish the cavalry arms.[50]

Jones remained uncomfortable with the independent-minded Forrest commanding the military operations at Murfreesboro although Jones appreciated the energy Forrest had shown. On October 21, Jones wrote to Forrest: "Keep the enemy hemmed in at Nashville." By October 28, Major General John C. Breckinridge assumed command of the Confederate Army of Middle Tennessee and Forrest remained in command of the cavalry in the area. Forrest's initial tasks were:

> [O]bserve the approaches to this point from Nashville, throwing his command as near the latter place as possible, striking and harassing the enemy as opportunity offers, sending also small detachments and taking such steps as he deems best to ascertain the approach of the enemy from the north to Nashville, or toward our lines from any point east or west of Nashville, or from the direction of the Tennessee River.

Sergeant Henry Clay Reynolds, 51st Alabama Partisan Rangers, echoed the objective of keeping the Federal forces hemmed in at Nashville. Reynolds wrote his wife that Confederate forces surrounded Negley's garrison and they would likely be starved until they retreated from Nashville. Meanwhile the Army of Mississippi continued its movement into Middle Tennessee and Joseph Wheeler's cavalry was assigned duty to protect the supply trains moving toward Murfreesboro.[51]

After the recent campaign, many of the regiments of the Confederate cavalry fell below 100 men and a period to transition and reorganization began in the Confederate army in Tennessee. E. Kirby Smith announced his reorganization, including the cavalry assigned to him, on October 31. While some small cavalry battalions remained dispersed throughout his army, Smith formed three substantial cavalry brigades under command of Colonel John Hunt Morgan, Colonel John Pegram and Colonel John Scott.[52]

Rosecrans Assumes Command

On October 25, 1862, the Army of the Ohio began to move south toward Tennessee across a seventy-mile front stretching from Columbia to Bowling Green, clearing Kentucky of any remaining concentrations of Confederates along the way. Buell ordered a brigade of cavalry to Bowling Green and one to Lebanon strategically placed to meet any further Confederate raids into the heart of the state. He also placed some cavalry at Munfordville as additional support. Next, he assured Negley at Nashville that Union infantry was approaching his command should he need assistance. And finally on October 31, Alexander McCook passed on intelligence that Bragg was racing toward Nashville hoping to reach there before the Union army. The two great forces were ominously converging on the countryside near Nashville.[53]

On October 24, Rosecrans received his formal orders granting him command of the Department of the Cumberland. He was ordered to travel to Buell's headquarters and formally relieve him of command. Then, Halleck assigned his strategic objectives:

> First, to drive the enemy from Kentucky and Middle Tennessee; second, to take and hold East Tennessee, cutting the line of railroad at Chattanooga, Cleveland, or Athens, so as to destroy the connection of the valley of Virginia with Georgia and the other Southern States. It is hoped that by prompt and rapid movements a considerable part of this may be accomplished before the roads become impassable from the winter rains.

Halleck acknowledged there were two ways of reaching East Tennessee. Perhaps, Halleck suggested, the most expedient was just to push Bragg's retreating army directly into East Tennessee, but Halleck also gave Rosecrans the option of securing Nashville before moving eastward. He further urged Rosecrans to move quickly and if needed, Rosecrans should support Grant, or vice versa, depending on the actions of the Confederates. Halleck concluded with a serious warning: "I need not urge upon you the necessity of giving active employment to your forces. Neither the country nor the Government will much longer put up with the inactivity of some of our armies and generals." Yet, Rosecrans would wait for two months before beginning the offensive against Bragg.[54]

Nashville was the geographic center of the state and it was a major hub of transportation in Tennessee. The city was located on the Cumberland River and was the rail center for central Tennessee. Rosecrans saw the route to East Tennessee through Chattanooga and not through the Cumberland Gap, and the railroad was the key in capturing the eastern part of Tennessee. Rosecrans knew as long as no large Union army was in east Tennessee communications, supplies and cooperation between the Confederate troops in the Mid-South and Virginia were "rapid and direct." In addition, no further movement into the Confederate territory southward was practical as long as strong Confederate forces occupied eastern Tennessee which threatened the rear of the Union army. In capturing Chattanooga, East Tennessee would be open to a well-supplied Union army which utilized the Nashville and Chattanooga Railroad; and then, the route into Georgia and East Tennessee would be within reach.[55]

Rosecrans' appointment to command came to the relief of many. The governors of Illinois and Indiana sent a joint reply to Lincoln:

> The removal of General Buell and appointment of Rosecrans came not a moment too soon. The removal of General Buell could not have been delayed an hour with safety to the army or the cause. The history of the battle of Perryville and the recent campaign in Kentucky has never been told. The action you have taken renders our visit unnecessary, although we are very desirous to confer with you in regard to the general condition of the Northwest, and hope to do so at no distant period.

Shortly afterward, Governor David Tod of Ohio added his desire to have Buell removed from command of the army; but not everyone agreed with the removal of Buell. Ex-Secretary of the Treasury James Guthrie wrote to Halleck:

> The renewed rumors of the removal of General Buell I hope are without foundation. If he should be removed a winter campaign with his army—now the best in the service—will be lost, and perhaps Nashville and all Middle Tennessee and West Tennessee in danger, without the possibility of relief to East Tennessee. His army is now again on the march south and good results must be achieved by it. He has confidence of most, if not all, of his generals and of all thinking men here.[56]

The transition of command from Buell to Rosecrans was handled poorly. Buell found out he had been superseded through the newspapers before Rosecrans reached his headquarters. Buell wrote to General George Thomas on October 29: "I judge from what appears in the papers that Rosecrans has been ordered to relieve me. Under the circumstances I am sure I do not grieve about it." Shortly thereafter, Rosecrans sent a gracious letter to Buell notifying him about the formal change of command:

> I know the bearer of unwelcome news has a "losing office," but feel assured you are too high a gentleman and too true a soldier to permit this to produce any feelings of personal unkindness between us. I, like yourself, am neither an intriguer nor newspaper soldier. I go where I am ordered; but propriety will permit me to say that I have often felt indignant at the petty attacks on you by a portion of the press during the past summer, and that you had my high respect for ability as a soldier, for your firm adherence to truth and justice in the government and discipline of your command. I beg you, by our common profession and the love we bear our suffering country, to give me all the aid you can for the performance of duties of which no one better than yourself knows the difficulties.[57]

General William S. Rosecrans appointed David Stanley, "a thorough cavalry officer," to command the Union cavalry (National Archives).

The decision to place Rosecrans in command of the Department of the Cumberland did not occur without controversy. George Thomas served as second-in-command to Don Carlos Buell in his army; and Thomas was not at all happy with Rosecrans' choice to command the Department of the Cumberland. Thomas wrote to Halleck on the date Rosecrans assumed command about his unhappiness of serving under a commander of lower rank. Thomas soon found Rosecrans' promotion to the rank of major general was antedated so that his rank superseded Thomas.' Thomas complained that Halleck had requested that he assume command of the Department of Tennessee and also of Buell's troops just the month before and now he was ordered to report to Rosecrans. He explained he had done good and loyal service for the Union and he had turned down the command so as not to impede the Union effort just as Buell prepared to follow Bragg into Tennessee. Thomas wrote:

> Feeling convinced that great injustice would be done him if not permitted to carry out his plans I requested that he might be retained in command. The order relieving him was suspended, but today I am officially informed that he is relieved by General Rosecrans, my junior. Although I do not claim for myself any superior ability, yet feeling conscious that no just cause exists for overslaughing me by placing me under my junior, I feel deeply mortified and aggrieved at the action taken in this matter.

Thomas concluded by saying an officer of superior rank would need to command the Department of the Cumberland if Thomas could be expected to stay. Halleck replied that Rosecrans' date of promotion was actually earlier than Thomas' and the decision to appoint Rosecrans resulted because Thomas refused to assume command over Buell the prior month. Thomas, thus being informed he was not serving under a junior officer, accepted command of the Center Wing of the newly named army.[58]

Rosecrans assumed command of the Department of the Cumberland on October 30 and he found his cavalry scattered and poorly organized. He knew immediately what he wanted to do improve the condition of the cavalry. On the day he assumed command, he wrote to Halleck that he had only eight regiments of cavalry to face Wheeler, Morgan and Forrest.

Would be able to do wonders under an able chief. Brigadier General Stanley, besides being an able and indefatigable soldier, is a thorough cavalry officer. He can do more good to the service by commanding a cavalry than an infantry division. I beg you for that reason to send him to me. You know the expense of cavalry, and what the rebel cavalry has done. Stanley will double our forces without expense.[59]

Summary

When the Civil War began, the United States Army had about nine hundred professionally trained officers and only a few of these were cavalry officers. Many of the top ranking officers went to the Confederacy. These officers were very important in the training of the new volunteer armies in the Civil War. Early recruitments limited the number of cavalry regiments to one for every ten infantry regiments. In the North, many high-ranking officers believed the war would be over before the one-two year training period needed for cavalry troopers to become proficient in their task. Once the fighting began, the importance of cavalry became more apparent to the Union generals and they hastened to enlist and train more cavalry regiments.[60]

In regard to organization, Union cavalry regiments consisted of twelve companies, each containing about one hundred men and officers, and at full strength totaled about one thousand two hundred men. Southern cavalry regiments consisted of ten companies of about seventy-five officers and men each. For better command and control, regiments were broken into four-company battalions under the command of majors. By the time the Union and Confederate cavalry took the field south of Nashville, it was more common to have about 300–400 men in regiments that had been active for several months. *Poinsett Tactics, Regulations and Instructions for the Field Service of the United States Cavalry in Time of War*, and *Cavalry Tactics* were all manuals from which Union cavalrymen received their training. For the cavalry of the Army of the Cumberland, David Stanley directed that *Cavalry Tactics*, written by Philip St. George Cooke, Stanley's old commanding officer, be used. While the Union cavalry would be equipped with carbine, pistol, and saber, the saber was the weapon considered to be highly effective in close combat and during charges. Sabers were often attached to the saddles of horses to be less noisy and cumbersome to use while being easily accessible. The 1840 "Old Wristbreaker" saber was replaced with the newer 1860 Light Cavalry Saber. The Southern cavalry had less standard equipment due to the difficulty in supplying regiments. The difference in cavalry tactics, particularly in regard to the saber, between Northern and Southern cavalry, would be evident during the Battle of Stones River.[61]

While the Northern cavalry was somewhat restricted at its beginning, the Southern cavalry was well respected and formed under the maxim: "[T]he best blood of the South rode in the cavalry." While difficult to make sweeping generalizations, the Southern cavalrymen were more commonly better and more experienced horsemen. Horses were part of life in the south and those in this service were accustomed to the saddle. Historians have argued that Southern horsemanship was part of the "'gentlemanly tradition'" more so than their Union counterparts because some Northerners were from urban locations and had occupations as laborers and shopkeepers. John Lee Yaryan, adjutant of the 19th Indiana Infantry, observed that the Union troopers were just not accustomed to the saddle, and that the Southern cavalry also brought the finest bred horses in the south. However, over fifty percent of the Northern cavalrymen came from the farm and even though many had experience with horses, their experience was more commonly with horses that pulled wagons and served as work animals rather than horsemanship. In the North, the government provided horses for the cavalry, even though this was a system fraught with problems. In the South, cavalrymen were generally contracted by the government to supply their own horses. While this system resulted in better horses for the Confederate cavalry early in the war, if a horse was lost, then a replacement had to be found. This became a problem as the war continued and as cavalry regiments traveled many miles from home. A cavalryman who could not replace his horse had to transfer to the infantry or artillery. As the war continued, horses became short in supply. The price of good horses skyrocketed and the common soldier could not afford to buy even a mediocre horse. As the war continued, both armies ran perilously short of mounts and dismounted cavalry regiments became more common.[62]

For the Southern cavalry, *The Trooper's Manual* was commonly used to train cavalry and in 1863, Joseph Wheeler wrote his own manual of instruction. Based on Wheeler's previous experience in the U.S. Army and first two years of service, he saw great value in cavalry operating dismounted. As a result, the Southern cavalry more commonly fought on foot. In addition, the armament of Southern cavalry in Tennessee in 1862 was not uniform, ranging from shotguns, revolvers, muskets, and carbines. Sabers, while present in the Wheeler's cavalry, were not weapons of choice. Overall, the ability of the Confederate government to supply, dress and arm cavalry would remain problematic throughout the war.[63]

By the end of October, much was defined for the Union and Confederate troops in Kentucky and Tennessee. Kentucky was preserved for the Union and would never again be so threatened as Bragg did in September and October 1862. Both armies now converged on Nashville and Murfreesboro, and these armies would again face each other at the end of the December in the Battle of Stones River. Bragg remained in command of the Southern troops and he continued to alienate many of those serving under him. E. Kirby Smith's Army of Kentucky was in a tenuous position, and part of his army would fall under the command of Bragg. In regard to the cavalry Bragg, not surprisingly, had appointed Joseph Wheeler over Forrest and Morgan as his chief of cavalry. With the addition of Forrest and Morgan to Wheeler's cavalry, the overall numbers of Confederate cavalry overwhelmed the Federal horsemen who traveled to Nashville. Buell explained what he saw as a cultural attraction of those in the South to the cavalry:

> The habits of the Southern people facilitated the formation of cavalry corps which were comparatively efficient even with instruction; and accordingly we see Stuart, and John Hunt Morgan and Forrest riding with impunity around Union armies, and destroying or harassing their communications. Late in the war that agency was reversed.

While Buell's remarks may be an over generalization, there can be little doubt of the superior numbers of Confederate cavalry around Nashville and the fact that Sam Jones repeatedly cautioned Forrest about increasing the number of additional cavalry supports the claims of popularity of this arm of the army.[64]

On the Union side of the line, Don Carlos Buell failed to draw Bragg into a decisive battle in Kentucky and did little to prevent the movement of the Army of Mississippi and Army of Kentucky back into Tennessee. Because of this, he was relieved of command and replaced with William Starke Rosecrans who was destined to fight the next major battle in Tennessee. Rosecrans saw the need to move his army to Nashville and he also saw the weakness of his cavalry. When he arrived on the scene, he had only two brigades of cavalry, which would move to Nashville. He also immediately set in motion the transfer of Brigadier General David Stanley to be his chief of cavalry. Rosecrans also began a process to re-arm and increase the number of cavalry in the Army of the Cumberland.

Finally, while it is important to understand the actions of Forrest and Morgan in months prior to the Battle of Stones River, the two primary cavalry forces which would be involved in the struggle for Murfreesboro were Wheeler's Southern cavalry and Stanley's Federal cavalry. Forrest's and Morgan's actions were of paramount importance in defining the Southern and Northern actions and philosophy about how the war was fought in Middle Tennessee even though these two commands would not be present during the Battle of Stones River.

2. Two Cavalries in Middle Tennessee (November 1–30, 1862)

Some one will have to answer for this.
—Captain George Knox Miller

November was a month of reorganizations and movement for both armies. Rosecrans assumed command of the Army of the Cumberland at Bowling Green on November 1 and marched for Nashville. Bragg, after his meeting with Jefferson Davis, consolidated his command authority and marched his Army of Mississippi for Murfreesboro. Both armies were reorganized in November after the change of command on the Federal side and after the recent campaign into Kentucky on the Confederate side. Meanwhile, Major General John C. Breckinridge arrived in Murfreesboro and took command of the Confederate troops in Special Orders No.1 from the Army of Middle Tennessee. Breckinridge would continue to refer to his forces as the Army of Middle Tennessee until the Confederate army reorganized as the Army of Tennessee later in November. Until that time, Bragg still commanded the Army of Mississippi in Tennessee.[1]

In regard to the cavalry, Bragg appealed to Richmond on November 4 for promotions for both Joseph Wheeler and John Wharton "they so justly deserve, and are so competent to fill." Three days later, Wheeler was ordered to report to Breckinridge in Murfreesboro, and arrived for duty on November 13. Also, Wheeler, still in direct command of his own brigade, assumed the responsibility for cavalry duties with Leonidas Polk's Corps while Wharton with his brigade was ordered to duty with William Hardee's Corps. Wheeler's command totaled 1,127 troopers and Wharton's brigade totaled 1,591 men present for duty. Then as the bulk of the Army of Mississippi returned to Middle Tennessee, Breckinridge was effectively removed from command of the troops in Murfreesboro when his division was attached to Polk's Corps.[2]

After his meeting with Jefferson Davis, Braxton Bragg was given command of not only his Army of Mississippi, but also command of the troops in the Department of East Tennessee in what was designated as the Confederate Department Number 2. Although both sides recognized the importance of East Tennessee, the two armies steadily converged on Nashville and Murfreesboro. E. Kirby Smith unsuccessfully tried to maintain his army in east Tennessee as Bragg pulled Smith into his newly forming army.[3]

Meanwhile on the Union side, Rosecrans assumed command of what was soon to be designated the Army of the Cumberland. By early December the Department of the

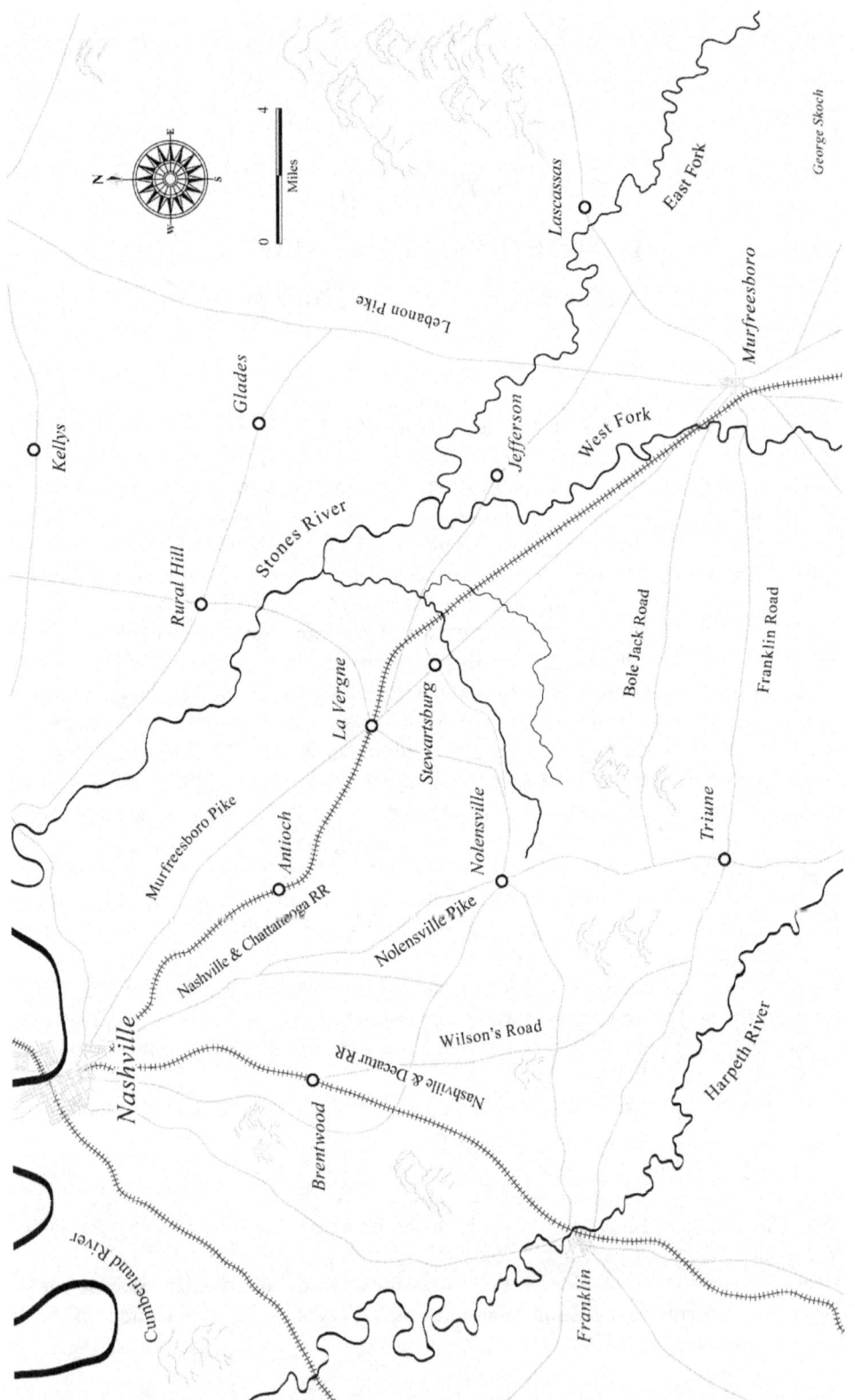

Area around Nashville and Murfreesboro—November 1862.

Cumberland was simply designated as the Army of the Cumberland, a title it would carry to the end of the war. Rosecrans initially established his headquarters at Bowling Green, Kentucky; and Brigadier General James Negley maintained command of Union troops in occupied Nashville. As Bragg's troops moved into Middle Tennessee, Rosecrans recognized the need to quickly move his troops to support Negley's garrison at Nashville. On November 3, Rosecrans sent orders to the Union cavalry to screen the advance of the Army of the Cumberland as the infantry continued forward. Rosecrans ordered John Kennett, commanding the Union cavalry division, to send a screen of five cavalry regiments from Bowling Green to Nashville, a distance of about seventy miles. The western most regiment was ordered to Springfield and the eastern most regiment would ride to the vicinity of South Tunnel, which had been destroyed by John Hunt Morgan in August. Rosecrans told Kennett to make an effort to determine Morgan's location. The orders stressed the importance of communication and called for the establishment of a courier line to headquarters. Kennett was told to cover the front and flank of the advancing Federal infantry and locate and track the Southern cavalry "with a view, if possible, of striking a blow, your further movements will depend upon circumstances." Rosecrans knew his cavalry was outnumbered but he wanted Kennett to have opportunities to strike smaller concentrations of Confederate cavalry. In the short term, Kennett needed to open communications between his cavalry, the wing commanders and headquarters. Because the Army of the Cumberland faced such large concentrations of Southern cavalry, the Federal cavalry needed to work in cooperation with the infantry advance southward. "The general commanding wishes that it should be impressed particularly upon you to have your communications thoroughly and effectually open." In short, Kennett needed to be the eyes and ears of the army, a basic principle of the cavalry during the Civil War.[4]

As the two armies moved to Middle Tennessee, the inability to arm cavalry became the major issue for both Bragg and Rosecrans. In addition, Rosecrans correctly determined he needed more cavalry and he immediately obtained permission to add cavalry regiments to his army. Most notably the 15th Pennsylvania Cavalry, also known as the Anderson Cavalry, was ordered to the Army of the Cumberland and he was given permission to raise another regiment of cavalry. Rosecrans recognized the cavalry was poorly equipped and he wrote to Henry Halleck that he needed 2,500 breech-loading or revolving rifles immediately. "Please let me know how soon I can have them. My cavalry are the eyes and feet of my army, and will be its providers." While on the Southern side, the biggest obstacle to adding cavalry was the ability to arm, clothe and equip them. There seemed to be troopers enough, but the problem was arming them.[5]

Attack on Edgefield and Nashville—November 5, 1862

As the two armies moved in the same general direction, skirmishes broke out between the opposing forces. While Rosecrans marched toward Nashville, the Southern cavalry planned a raid on the city to destroy supplies, communications and supply routes. On November 5, General James Negley, commander of the Nashville garrison, knew there was an increase in Southern troops near the city. He estimated that as many as 25,000 enemy troops, including 5,000 cavalry and forty pieces of artillery were already in the area. Negley remained unsure of Bragg's intent, and although Rosecrans had yet to arrive with the bulk of the Union army, his morale was high. Until this time, the Southern cavalry caused the greatest problem by "driving off stock and negroes" and demonstrating against Negley's lines.⁶

The nuisance of the Southern cavalry demonstrations erupted into a heated fight on November 5 when Colonel John Hunt Morgan's cavalry, recently arrived from its latest raid in Kentucky, and Brigadier General Nathan Bedford Forrest's cavalry made a coordinated attack on the Union positions at Nashville. Forrest's cavalry moved against the Union pickets on the Murfreesboro Road (south) and the Lebanon Pike (east) with an estimated 3,000 troopers. Forrest pushed the Union pickets back toward the main Union line under the protection of Federal artillery. At the same time, Morgan's cavalry, 2,500 men strong, attacked from the north intending to destroy the railroad cars, engines and bridges over the Cumberland River at Edgefield, a suburb of Nashville. Forrest planned to serve as a diversion while Morgan achieved the objective of destroying the supply and communication lines.

Forrest began his movement in the early hours of the morning and attacked at dawn. He began the fight and pushed the Federal pickets back; but when the Union artillery opened fire, he then withdrew out of range. At daylight on November 5, Morgan made his attack and ran into the 16th Illinois Infantry, nearly succeeding in capturing a company posted near a railroad station. The company barely escaped capture and joined the rest of the regiment in the entrenchments on the north side of the river. Once in the defenses, the 16th Illinois Infantry held the line until Negley sent additional infantry reinforcements and Morgan settled for burning "an old railroad building in Edgefield" on the outskirts of northeast Nashville. Negley reported Morgan lost a stand of regimental colors in the fight when the Union infantry counterattacked. Negley estimated five enemies killed and 19 wounded and the 16th Illinois recorded five wounded and six missing, probably prisoners in Morgan's hands. Of note in the action was a unit of Union mounted horsemen—Twyman's Mounted Independent Scouts, also called Fry's Kentucky Scouts. This was a unit, about company size, organized in the summer of 1862 and led by Captain Henry G. Twyman. Although the details of Twyman's action were not recorded, Colonel Robert Smith, 16th Illinois, wrote: "I cannot close my report without mentioning the excellent conduct of the mounted scouts belonging to Captain Twyman's independent command. I have rarely seen their equal for bravery and efficiency." Twyman's Scouts would be consolidated into the 3th Kentucky Cavalry (U.S.) in the summer 1863. Bragg boasted that Morgan destroyed several railcars, engines, water tanks, and bridges on Louisville & Nashville Railroad during the attack; but the *New York Times* correspondent wrote:

> For some weeks the disloyal citizens of this isolated city have predicted its capture, and have even gone so far as to name the day on which its occupation by the Confederates would take place. The rebel cavalry first attempted to fire the recently-completed railroad bridge which spans the Cumberland, but were foiled.

General Nathan Bedford Forrest battled the Union forces at Nashville on November 5, 1862 (Library of Congress).

John M. Porter, 9th Kentucky Cavalry (CSA) of Morgan's command, recalled: "The fight was quite lively for some time, but our force was inadequate to cross over. Very soon the enemy came in solid column pouring over their bridges and forced us to retire."[7]

While Morgan was fighting on the north side of town, Forrest's cavalry occupied the attention of the Union infantry and cavalry on the south and east of Nashville. At daylight, Forrest ordered the 51st Alabama Partisan Rangers and Captain W. C. Bacot's cavalry battalion to move toward the Union defenses from the direction of Lebanon. The action was accomplished at the cost one man killed during the fighting. In the meantime, Lieutenant Colonel A. A. Russell's Partisan Rangers advanced along the Murfreesboro Pike followed by Colonel Joseph B. Palmer's and Colonel Roger W. Hanson's infantry brigades accompanied by artillery. The Confederate column advanced on Nashville from Dogtown, a village just east of Nashville. The Union pickets withdrew a mile and a half and attempted to make a stand behind some rough log and dirt fortifications. The skirmishing continued heatedly as the Union pickets continued to withdraw away from the fortifications which were located on a high hill on the east of the Murfreesboro Pike. Here, Forrest placed four cannons and began shelling Jones' Hill about a mile and a half away. As Forrest unlimbered his cannon, he heard Morgan's fight on the north side of the town.[8]

The remainder of Forrest's cavalry (Colonel James Starnes's, Major Dewitt C. Douglass's battalion, Colonel George Dibrell's cavalry, Freeman's and Roberts' batteries) advanced from the west of the Murfreesboro Pike along the Nolensville, Mill Creek, and Franklin pikes. The fighting became general and continued between the Southern cavalry and Negley's troops until about 10:00 a.m. when Forrest began to withdraw. Forrest recorded a loss of three killed, ten wounded and five missing. He claimed fifteen Union soldiers killed, twenty prisoners and estimated another twenty wounded.[9]

As the fighting diminished, Negley concluded to take the offensive and marched toward Forrest's cavalry south of Nashville. Negley accompanied his infantry (69th Ohio, 78th Pennsylvania, and 14th Michigan infantries), cavalry (5th Tennessee commanded Colonel William B. Stokes and Colonel George Wynkoop's 7th Pennsylvania) and two sections of artillery along the Franklin Pike in pursuit of Forrest's cavalry. At the same time, he sent two regiments of infantry and one section of artillery on the Murfreesboro Pike. Negley's part of the advance totaled about 1,400 men and his column drove the Southern cavalry about seven miles south, primarily through the efforts of his artillery. Negley, hoping to draw Forrest into a fight, ordered Stokes' 5th Tennessee Cavalry to charge the enemy's rear and then retreat back to the Federal column. Stokes' cavalry rode forward and was so successful that he failed to notice that he chased only a small contingent of Confederate troopers to within five miles of Franklin while, unknown to Stokes, the main body of Confederate cavalry turned into a lane to the west. The Confederate cavalry's action revealed the pursued was the pursuer as Forrest moved to cut off the Stokes' and Negley's return to Nashville. Negley discovered the maneuver and ordered his infantry and remaining cavalry forward to prevent Stokes from being captured.[10]

Negley had just discovered the dangerous nature of Nathan Bedford Forrest's cavalry as the Southern cavalry maneuvered to cut off the Union column from Nashville. One of Negley's scouts found Forrest's cavalry already a mile in the rear with a battery of artillery concealed in ambush. Negley quickly gathered the 5th Tennessee Cavalry back into his column and reversed direction and marched to the position of the ambush. Negley noted "the head of the column was immediately placed to the rear" and then hurried forward to meet Forrest's cavalry. A heated fight resulted for about thirty minutes and Negley moved his men away so they were not shelled by enemy artillery. Negley felt he was outnumbered and deciding that caution was the best plan, he maneuvered around Forrest to return to Nashville. But, Forrest ordered an attack on the Union troops.[11]

The *New York Times* reported:

> Further pursuit was deemed useless, and our troops prepared to return, and had come back two miles when the pickets announced that the rebels were in considerable force on a cross road about one mile in advance. Our artillery then went forward and quickly silenced them. During this time a whirlwind of dust had arisen, and at times entirely obscured the view of each other's position. The rebel cavalry, taking advantage of this fact, made a desperate charge upon a spot where they supposed Stokes' Cavalry to be, but as Stokes had changed his position, they rode upon an ambuscade of a part of the Seventy-eighth Pennsylvania and Fourteenth Michigan infantry, who, with a well directed fire, which killed and wounded a number, soon put them to flight. Subsequently the rebels endeavored to bring their artillery to bear upon our men, but were repulsed and driven back in every instance.[12]

Report of Casualties at Nashville on December 5, 1862

	Confederate Killed	Confederate Wounded	Confederate Missing	Union Killed	Union Wounded	Union Missing
Negley's Report	Unknown	5 (Morgan) + Unknown (Forrest)	19 (Morgan) + 23 (Forrest)	0	26	19
Forrest's Report	4	13	5	45	80	40

*Morgan did not record his losses or Union losses. The losses reflect morning plus the afternoon actions.

Negley complemented his cavalry, which drew Forrest's attack into the line of the 14th Michigan and 78th Pennsylvania infantries. Negley explained that a regiment of Southern cavalry thought they were attacking Stoke's 5th Tennessee Cavalry, but instead rode directly into two regiments of infantry which unleashed a furious volley and sent the troopers running for cover. At the same time, a section of the Confederate artillery unlimbered and prepared to fire, but seeing the reversal of the momentum of the fight, also packed up and withdrew without firing a shot. Starnes's 4th Tennessee Cavalry and Dibrell's 8th Tennessee cavalry regiments supported by Freeman's and Robert's artillery carried much of the action in the fight for the Confederates. Forrest recorded the skirmish lasted for an hour before the "Abolitionists" retreated back to Nashville without an account of the repulse of the cavalry charge. This put an end to the fighting and the two forces returned to their relative positions. Because Negley marched back to Nashville, he did not claim the battlefield and he could not give an accurate estimate of losses to Forrest's cavalry. Those captured told Negley the losses were "large."

General James Negley: "[The] head of the column was immediately placed to the rear" and then hurried forward to meet Forrest (Library of Congress).

Negley reported he captured twenty-three prisoners, including two captains of artillery. According to Negley his losses were twenty-six wounded and nineteen missing.[13]

The losses reported in fights at Nashville on November 5 were vastly different. Forrest claimed his losses in the afternoon action to be one killed and three wounded and recorded that Negley had forty men killed, sixty wounded, and twenty captured. In total, Forrest estimated about 160 losses for Negley's troops during the entire day and twenty-two for his troops. On the other hand, Negley reported about forty-five casualties for his troops. In the other action during the morning, Morgan's troopers felt the attack from the north was a failure. The recent campaign, poor ammunition, improper winter clothes, and exhausted horses were cited as reasons for the poor showing. Afterward, Forrest returned to La Vergne, Morgan returned to Gallatin, and Negley marched back to Nashville.[14]

"We had quiet [sic] a little fight at Edgefield Junction near Nashville," wrote John Weatherred, 9th Tennessee Cavalry. Lieutenant A. J. Lacy, 8th Tennessee Cavalry, also wrote:

> Wee had another fight November the 5th. Our engagement lasted about 3 hours. We had 8 pieces of artillery & several Regts of cavalry. Our co got 2 fellers wounded.... Wee charged the infantry and artillery but they make the bullets whistle so that we could not get to them. They threw some bums among us. There was a bum passed in about 4 ft of my back. It blowed as it passed.[15]

Rosecrans Takes Control and Chooses David Stanley

Rosecrans assumed command of the Army of Cumberland after commanding the Army of the Mississippi which had just gone through an extensive campaign in Missouri, Tennessee and Mississippi. Rosecrans had just achieved two Union victories during the Battle of Iuka and the Battle of Corinth in September and October 1862. Although successful in both battles, he had disappointed his commanding officer, Ulysses Grant, in each engagement. In fact, Grant had concluded to relieve Rosecrans of command on the day he was ordered to supersede Buell.[16]

Ohioan, William Starke Rosecrans, was born in 1819 and graduated fifth in his class at West Point in 1842. Rosecrans was an engineer in the army until his resignation in 1854. Prior to the war Rosecrans ran a kerosene factory in Cincinnati, and he received a commission as a colonel serving as General George McClellan's aide early in the Civil War. He was soon promoted to the rank of brigadier general and distinguished himself in action at Rich Mountain, Virginia. Serving under McClellan was revealing to Rosecrans when McClellan failed to acknowledge much of the success at Rich Mountain was due to Rosecrans' efforts. As a result, Rosecrans requested a transfer to the western theater of the Civil War rather than serving under McClellan in the east.[17]

Rosecrans announced upon taking command of Buell's troops that he would reorganize his new department and knew exactly what he wanted to do about the weak cavalry component of his new command which consisted of only eight cavalry regiments. Rosecrans made a good decision when he asked for Stanley. He was a West Point graduate of the class of 1852, finishing 9th in his class, and he had nine years of service on the frontiers, first in the dragoons, and next in the U.S. Cavalry. Stanley had experience in "Bloody Kansas" as the state sought to determine if it would be a free or slave state; and since the beginning of the war, he had fought in the Wilson's Creek Campaign, commanded infantry divisions during the Siege of New Madrid and Island Number 10, the siege of Corinth, the Battle of Iuka and the Battle of Corinth. The last three engagements where under the direct command of Rosecrans who liked the way Stanley commanded his soldiers. Although Stanley had commanded infantry since the beginning of the war, the Union high command had had their eye on him to command cavalry for a long time. In January 1862 George McClellan, chief of the Union Army, wrote to Henry Halleck and asked for Stanley to serve as the chief of cavalry for Buell's Army of Ohio. McClellan gave his endorsement by adding: "[I]know him to be a first-rate officer."[18]

Although Rosecrans requested Stanley to command his cavalry, there were still a few unpleasantries which needed to be navigated. The biggest obstacle was Ulysses Grant, who didn't like Rosecrans and who was Stanley's commanding officer, and Grant seemed to be in no hurry to give Stanley up. Although Rosecrans needed him immediately, it would be three weeks before Stanley would arrive. Six days after his last message Rosecrans wrote to Halleck, "I have considerable cavalry in much confusion for want of a head. I am greatly in need of General Stanley, and request that you order him to join me at once. General Grant is pushing him south."[19]

Stanley still did not arrive at the Army of the Cumberland and on November 9 Rosecrans wrote again to Halleck, "Our great wants are arms and a chief for the cavalry. Nothing yet from Stanley." On the same day, he also appealed to Edwin Stanton, Secretary of War: "General Halleck has ordered Stanley for a chief. He has not reported. No promise of arms. What can you do for us?" Grant finally issued orders for Stanley's transfer on November 11.[20]

Brigadier General David Sloan Stanley brought years of cavalry experience to the Army of the Cumberland. After grad-

General David Stanley, Union chief of cavalry (Library of Congress).

uation at West Point, Stanley attended cavalry training at Carlisle Barracks in Pennsylvania and then accompanied Lieutenant A. W. Whipple's Topographical Engineers expedition consisting of about 20 men. The expedition began at Fort Smith, Arkansas, and then traveled west by horse and wagon; and the detachment was escorted by a group of 30 soldiers of the 7th U.S. Infantry. The engineers' task was to survey a route from Fort Smith, Arkansas, to San Diego, California. The expedition began on July 24, 1853, and reached San Bernardino on March 14, 1854. Stanley then spent years in various locations on the western frontier dealing with issues between settlers and Native Americans. While on the frontier Stanley met and served with a myriad of men who would lead troops in the Civil War. Ironically, future Confederate cavalry legend, J. E. B. Stuart, saved Stanley's life in a skirmish with Indians in Kansas. In 1857, Stanley's command went in search of a group of marauding Cheyenne Indians near Solomon Fork, Kansas. While pursuing the Indians, the quarry dispersed and as luck would have it, Lieutenant Stanley and Lieutenant Stuart rode stirrup to stirrup after one of the Indians. The chase took four miles and the horses were winded when the Indian stopped, and fired at Stuart. Stanley recorded, "I turned my horse and rode in on the Indian, firing one shot, but as I fired near my horse's ear, it scared him, and immediately jumping off my horse, tried to get a good aim at the Indian, but to my horror, my pistol stood firmly cocked and refused to fire. The Indian saw my fix in a flash and ran towards me, presenting his pistol." Stanley dropped his pistol, drew his saber and waited for the shot, but Stuart rode ahead and swung his saber at the Indian. Stuart hit his target, but at the same time the Indian's pistol went off wounding Stuart in the chest.[21]

Stanley also participated in the events surrounding slavery issues in Kansas. When the war began Stanley turned down a commission in the Confederate Army and he was commissioned a brigadier general in September 1861 and successfully led infantry divisions thus far in the war. It was during the advance on Corinth in May 1862 that Stanley first served under wing commander, William S. Rosecrans. Rosecrans grew to value Stanley's professional attitude toward the war and despite the fact Rosecrans privately censured Stanley's late arrival at the Battle of Iuka, the two men mutually supported each other. The relationship between the two men revealed a common spiritual nature. While Rosecrans was well known for his verbal tirades, he never blasphemed. Rosecrans was a devout Roman Catholic and his brother was a priest in the church, and later would become a bishop. Stanley, on the other hand, was raised in the Presbyterian Church and was also noted for his spiritual nature.

A significant event occurred during the summer of 1862 which explained much in regard to the relationship of David Stanley and his immediate commander, William Rosecrans. David Stanley was baptized into the Roman Catholic Church in Mississippi in 1862 and Rosecrans became his godfather. Rosecrans wrote his wife about the baptism,

> I had also the great joy to be God father to Genl. David S. Stanley who was baptized this morning at seven o'clock this morning previous to the Holy Sacrifice which was offered by the Rev. Father Tracy of Tuscumbia or rather of Huntsville in whose mission the region lies and who has come here to administer the sacraments to those he finds willing...

Before Stanley entered the United States Military Academy, he was a Presbyterian, but the war caused him to search the core of his personal convictions. John Ireland, chaplain of the 5th Minnesota Infantry, and after the war, Archbishop of St. Paul, Minnesota, recalled Stanley's public conversion occurred during Mass held in a public square at Iuka with a very large congregation. Before this group Stanley publicly read his profession of faith and was conditionally baptized. Word of the event swept through the army. Ireland stated, "Not many weeks later I met General Stanley, and he told me that he was most happy in realizing that he had obeyed the calling of his conscience; and that by so doing he was nearer to his God, and ready to meet Him, if death came to him in the performance of his duty on the battle field." Afterward, it was common to see Stanley kneeling on the ground with the common soldiers with his prayer book in his hand. Ireland noted, "Catholics and non–Catholics expressed their respect for him on account of his open profession."[22]

Rosecrans most certainly was influential in this decision of Stanley's conversion to Catholicism, but the presence of a remarkable Roman Catholic priest coincidentally entered Stanley's life and changed him forever. The priest was Father Jeremiah F. Trecy, a native of Ireland, and he was noted for ministering to troops on both sides during the Civil War. Trecy's involvement in the Union army began after the Battle of Shiloh when he asked to tend to the religious needs of the Southern wounded and prisoners. Permission was granted and soon the good father provided spiritual care for both sides. Trecy moved from place to place providing much needed spiritual support but he was often accused of being a spy.[23]

The Confederate Cavalry Goes to Work

The seriousness of the threat of Southern cavalry was communicated to Rosecrans from Major General Alexander McCook, commanding his Right Wing, on November 6 about the actions of Morgan and Forrest the previous day around Nashville. McCook wrote that Morgan was next seen six miles north of Nashville heading for Gallatin and that he had dispatched some of his cavalry to observe Morgan's movements and promised to relay the information to Thomas Crittenden.[24]

The Confederate cavalry seemed to be everywhere. Rosecrans revealed his evident frustration with his own cavalry when he responded to McCook through his acting Chief of Staff, Arthur Ducat,

> We have nothing from Colonel Kennett as to where he is: did he go toward Scottsville, as ordered? He has not communicated with General Crittenden, and the general does not know whether he has cavalry on his front or not. One regiment was ordered to go on General Crittenden's front. When Colonel Kennett marched it was never reported to him.

Rosecrans had clearly told Kennett the importance of communication from the cavalry.[25]

Rosecrans wrote on November 7 a chastisement of Kennett's silence in a communication to Crittenden. Rosecrans identified the intent of the Confederate cavalry to prevent the use of the railroad to Nashville, and he told Crittenden to order Kennett to strongly defend Hartsville from the enemy's cavalry. He also wanted Crittenden to use some of the cavalry assigned to his corps to serve as a screen near Lebanon. The distance was too great and Rosecrans had more to do than giving Kennett detailed orders for each action. Ducat wrote to Kennett that Rosecrans wanted him to begin communicating with the wing commanders who seemed to be unaware of the location and duties of the cavalry screening their movements. Ducat continued:

> The general commanding expects that you will exercise your own judgment in many respects, governed by the several movements ordered.... The general wishes me to state that he does not consider your dispatches satisfactory, and would like them oftener; that communication with his headquarters must at all times be kept up, wherever they are.[26]

Colonel Lewis Zahm, commanding the Second Brigade, soon grasped and accepted the need to increase communication, and on November 7 reported to Rosecrans the location of McCook's corps and information of Morgan's cavalry at Gallatin. Zahm only had 600 troopers with him and could not engage Morgan. He was unaware of the exact location of the wings of the army and sent troopers to try to find Crittenden's corps to open communications with him. Rosecrans reinforced the importance of intelligence from Zahm, and encouraged him to keep the messages going. "Inform him [Crittenden] of all you know, and keep up communications with him. If you have to communicate, will Colonel Kennett act on the principle that the cavalry are the eyes of the army? Take orders for co-operation from General Crittenden. Always keep up your communication with headquarters." While Zahm acted on Rosecrans' wishes that his cavalry work in conjunction with the entire army, it was disturbing that Zahm had to be urged to influence Kennett to serve the army through his role as commander of cavalry.[27]

Rosecrans had had enough of the cavalry operating without communication. He had gotten one of his cavalry brigades on board and he issued General Orders No. 7 announcing Captain Elmer Otis, 4th U.S. Cavalry, as chief of the courier lines. Otis organized an effective courier service utilizing troopers who had horses but no weapons. One way or another, he needed to get information from his eyes and ears of the army to his three infantry corps.[28]

Crittenden reported the efforts of his infantry to capture Morgan and on November 8 the infantry, Colonel Charles Harker's Brigade, and Zahm's cavalry reached the location where Morgan was observed only to find him gone. They managed to capture eighteen men, some horses, and equipment.

> The want of cavalry greatly embarrasses my operations. Colonel Kennett has not yet reported, so I have none to send to General Smith, as you have ordered. Without a cavalry force at Hartsville, I fear a single regiment would not be safe here, and I have no means of opening communication with General McCook.

Crittenden lamented the lack of cavalry to support his actions and the continued lack of communication from Kennett. Rosecrans responded:

> We are astonished Kennett does not move more rapidly; he has his orders such as sent you last night. Send back communication to Gallatin and find him; he is moving that way in the rear, instead of front. You must have his force, and use all that can be spared from a strong occupation of Hartsville on the front and flank of your advance across the river.... Kennett's orders are to occupy Hartsville strongly, and the balance on your front.

Ducat appealed to Alexander McCook to speed Kennett along: "Kennett is operating slowly. He should be on Crittenden's front, and also occupying Hartsville. Stir him up if you can." Lewis Zahm's brigade of cavalry made contact with Crittenden at 5 p.m., thereafter relieving some of the tension on the cavalry.[29]

Rosecrans' commander of his center wing, Major General George Thomas, arrived in Gallatin, Tennessee, on November 12 offering experience and stability to his newly forming army. Thomas's first questions went to the heart of the struggle Rosecrans faced, "Arrived here today.... Where is Crittenden and the cavalry?" Almost immediately, the weakness of the cavalry was evident. Thomas needed to know how to position the other Union troops and he needed to know the location of the Union cavalry. On November 12, Kennett with 2,000 Union cavalry arrived in Hartsville, Tennessee, and Rosecrans told Thomas that Kennett had been ordered to "keep up communications."[30]

Actions in Mid-November

As Bragg settled his army into the countryside south of Nashville, he found the communities around Nashville a far cry from the pre-war rolling hills of prosperity. As the troops approached Nashville, particularly from the north, they found fallow fields where fence posts had been pulled up to be used in campfires. Mills no longer functioned, houses were vacant, and windows were broken. In some places only a charred chimney remained as a reminder of the homestead which was once present. No children were seen and only an occasional dog made an appearance. The countryside was one of war and occupation.[31]

Bragg chose to assign Joseph Wheeler the day-to-day cavalry actions connected to the Army of Mississippi and he also utilized two independent cavalry brigades for partisan activities—Forrest and Morgan. Over the next sixty days, Bragg would use the numerical superiority of cavalry to his advantage. Forrest's, Morgan's, and Wheeler's cavalry commands had numerical and organizational superiority to the Federal cavalry in November; but although the Union cavalry was probably better armed and supplied, it struggled under Kennett's command. On November 6, Morgan's cavalry effectively put his concentration of regiments to good use and continued to harass the rail system from Louisville. The engineers working on repairing the railroad around South Tunnel, which Morgan had destroyed in the summer, complained of attacks from mounted troops. The engineers, already under pressure to reestablish rail service, sent a message to Rosecrans that work could not be completed unless he sent a force large enough to protect the construction. Kennett's cavalry sought to keep Morgan's men contained and on November 11, John Kennett's cavalry rode into Hartsville, a base for Morgan's troops, and drove out a small contingent of about 150 cavalry while capturing 20 prisoners and over 100 mules.[32]

In reply, one of the first acts of resistance to the approaching Union army by the Confederate cavalry was the disruption of the courier service which had just been established to keep communications flowing between the various Union units. The couriers rode along the front of the Union lines, often in a similar manner to Pony Express riders. On November 12, Captain G. C. Kniffin who served on Crittenden's staff reported from Stones River that twenty couriers had been captured by Confederates, effectively disrupting Union communications. One of the couriers caught by Morgan's cavalry early in November recorded his exploits in the *New York Times*. The courier threw his dispatches into a river before he was wounded, captured, searched and robbed of his money. He was taken to Morgan who threatened to hang the courier, but he prevented his execution by demanding a court martial when he showed his Confederate discharge papers. Next the courier was imprisoned while awaiting his trial, but he escaped and finally made his way back to the Union lines.[33]

Throughout November, the Confederate cavalry remained in position looking for opportunities to strike their Union opponents. On November 11 or 12, Forrest overwhelmed the 4th Ohio Cavalry and sent it fleeing. James Negley wrote:

> I regret to inform you that the picket officers report the Fourth Ohio Cavalry driven in great disorder by Forrest, with 1,200 cavalry and six pieces of artillery. Permit me to respectfully suggest extreme caution in operating against Forrest's cavalry. They are between 4,000 and 5,000 strong, are constantly moving, and are always watching for an inferior force and ready to remove from an equal one.

Negley was aware of Forrest's cavalry near La Vergne but he did not have a cavalry force large enough to engage him, and if infantry approached, the cavalry would just ride away.

Negley wrote to Rosecrans that although he desired to attack the enemy, he faced only Southern cavalry and that until the Union army had a large enough cavalry force to meet Forrest, Morgan or Wheeler any chance of success was unlikely.[34]

Of the fight with the 4th Ohio Cavalry, Forrest clashed with about two hundred and fifty Ohio troopers near the State Insane Asylum north of La Vergne and along the Nashville Pike, and after a skirmish, "they fled." Forrest could find no infantry, but observed the Union troops were trying to repair a bridge on the Lebanon Pike.[35]

Meanwhile changes were being made to reshape the defenses of Bragg's army. Joseph Wheeler's cavalry arrived in Murfreesboro on November 13 and moved to assume Forrest's position screening the Confederate troops. Breckinridge still operated under the title of commander of the Army of Middle Tennessee; and Bragg moved his headquarters to Tullahoma on November 14 and then to Murfreesboro on November 26. On November 15, Forrest, a brigadier general, ordered Wheeler, Bragg's chief of cavalry, upon his arrival to dispatch several companies of cavalry to Spencer's Springs, three miles west of Murfreesboro to be organized into a regiment and also requested Dibrell's cavalry at the same location to be armed and resupplied. Next, he recommended Wheeler move his command to Stewarts Creek because of the abundance of forage and because a good blacksmith shop was there.[36]

General Joseph Wheeler, Confederate chief of cavalry (Library of Congress).

Communication Troubles with the Union Cavalry

Meanwhile, communication and confidence continued to be a problem with the Union cavalry. On November 14, Rosecrans wrote to Thomas, "Have you any news from Kennett today? He was anxious on yesterday. Satisfied there was no cause. Find out how much of a train it will take to haul his spoils from Hartsville, and send for them. Direct your infantry at Hartsville to collect the stores discovered by Colonel Kennett." Thomas responded disparagingly of his interactions with Kennett,

> A dispatch from Colonel Kennett, just received, states that one of his scouts had just returned from Lebanon, and tells him that Morgan and Forrest are at Lebanon with 4,200 men and eight pieces of artillery. Colonel Kennett thinks it will be an unequal fight, and, therefore, would return to Hartsville. He thinks a combined movement should be agreed upon to move from this place and Lebanon on the rebels. Confess I do not understand him, and his dispatch has something of the appearance of a stampede.[37]

Within three days of Thomas's arrival in Gallatin, he summarized the cavalry situation of the Army of the Cumberland which Rosecrans had desperately tried to remedy. Thomas wrote to Rosecrans on November 15, "When will Stanley arrive? It is a great pity he is not now in command of the cavalry." Three days later, Arthur Ducat slapped Colonel Kennett verbally with an unpleasant and thinly veiled message about the way the cavalry was being handled. "Dispatch received. Had information some time before of the affair at Gallatin. It is to be regretted that our cavalry has proved too slow for Morgan. It is hoped that you will execute your orders promptly." The communications among the Union army commanders showed less than full confidence in Kennett to command the cavalry division, but Kennett was being given orders from three corps commanders and the commander of the army, often without coordination. The cavalry division commander seemed to be in an unenviable position of following one commander's orders and being taken to task by another officer. Kennett followed Rosecrans' orders to move to Lebanon on November 15, only to be told by Crittenden's chief of staff: "Before making any movement upon Lebanon you should have informed me of the orders received for that purpose, that I might have co-operated with you." Kennett was clearly struggling with communication and coordination and revealed that the organization of the cavalry was not working effectively. Kennett had too many masters and too few troops.[38]

To give Kennett credit, he was unhappy with the use of the cavalry and he welcomed Stanley's arrival. Kennett wrote: "The cavalry arm is defective. It is not numerous enough in the first place; secondly, it is not properly armed and equipped; thirdly, it requires a skillful head. When General Stanley comes it will have the later." This was a somewhat puzzling and, perhaps humble, letter, because Kennett was the head of the Union cavalry which he acknowledged needed David Stanley.[39]

On November 17, Halleck came through on his promise to furnish new and effective cavalry arms to the Army of the Cumberland. Although the type of cavalry arms was not specified in his message, the new and technically superior Colt revolving rifles were being sent to Rosecrans. Edwin Stanton promised 1,600 revolving rifles were on their way by passenger train to Louisville for use by Rosecrans. During the intervening weeks the constant struggle of communication with Kennett on one hand and the hit and run tactics of Morgan, Forrest, and Wheeler on the other was enough to distract Rosecrans. By the middle of November, Kennett's communications improved somewhat. Rosecrans had also been successful in obtaining some additional cavalry units. The 15th Pennsylvania, 1st Tennessee, and 2nd Tennessee cavalries were approved to be sent to Rosecrans. Brigadier General Joshua Sill, commanding McCook's Second Division, wrote despairingly that the two hundred men of 1st Middle (5th) Tennessee Cavalry assigned to him arrived in squads throughout the day on November 19.[40]

Bragg Renames His Army, Reorganizes the Cavalry

On November 20 Bragg reorganized and renamed his army the Army of Tennessee. The new army had three corps: Smith's, Polk's, and Hardee's. Kirby Smith's Army of the Kentucky was included in the Army of Tennessee as a corps. In addition, Wheeler's cavalry was assigned to the Army of Tennessee. Of the remaining two cavalry brigades, Bragg wrote:

Brigadier Generals Morgan's and Forrest's brigades of cavalry will, as soon as practicable after being relieved by Wharton's command, proceed to the special service assigned them by the commanding general. Much is expected by the army and its commander from the operations of these active and ever-successful leaders.... The foregoing dispositions are in anticipation of the great struggle which must soon settle the question of supremacy in Middle Tennessee. The enemy in heavy force is before us, with a determination, no doubt, to redeem the fruitful country we have wrested from him. With the remembrance of Richmond, Munfordville, and Perryville so fresh in our minds, let us make a name for the now Army of Tennessee as enviable as those enjoyed by the armies of Kentucky and the Mississippi.[41]

On November 22, Braxton Bragg reorganized the Army of Tennessee, and described his cavalry assignments:

POLK'S CORPS—Brigadier General Joseph Wheeler commanding one cavalry brigade consisting of 1,500 to 2,000 men.

HARDEE'S CORPS—Colonel John A. Wharton commanding one cavalry brigade consisting of 1,500 to 2,000 men.

INDEPENDENT CAVALRY—Brigadier General Nathan Bedford Forrest and Colonel John H. Morgan commanded a brigade of 2,500 each and these cavalry brigades would act as partisans.[42]

Colonel John Kennett, division cavalry commander, Army of the Cumberland.

The exact regiments of Confederate cavalry in Middle Tennessee are difficult to identify due to the poor records of the time. Even as Bragg reorganized his cavalry, he recognized the composition of the brigades as incomplete. Certainly many cavalry regiments were being organized from battalion-sized units. In addition, Kirby Smith's forces in East Tennessee had a significant number of cavalry units which would be included in Bragg's army. The organization remained fluid, particularly in light of Bragg's desire to reshape all the Southern troops in Tennessee; however, on November 20, Smith reported the reorganization of his cavalry. This organization was short-lived. Upon Bragg organization of the Army of Tennessee many of these regiments would be soon reassigned to different commanders.

E. Kirby Smith Reorganized Cavalry—November 1862

First Cavalry Brigade—Brig. Gen. John Pegram
Alabama Cavalry, Col. J. R. Howard
1st Tennessee Cavalry, Col. H. M. Ashby
3d Tennessee Cavalry, Col. J. W. Starnes
Tennessee Cavalry, Col. J. E. Carter
Tennessee Battery, Capt. W. R. Marshall

Second Cavalry Brigade—Col. John H. Morgan
2d Kentucky Cavalry, Col. Basil W. Duke
7th Kentucky Cavalry, Col. R. M. Gano
8th Kentucky Cavalry, Col. R. S. Cluke
11th Kentucky Cavalry, Col. D. W. Chenault
Kentucky Battalion, Lieut. Col. W. C. P. Breckinridge
Arnett's Kentucky howitzer battery

Third Cavalry Brigade—Col. J. S. Scott (at Sparta)
1st Georgia Cavalry, Col. J. J. Morrison
1st Louisiana Cavalry, Lieut. Col. J. O. Nixon
12th Tennessee Cavalry Battalion, Maj. T. W. Adrian
Louisiana Battery, Capt. William H. Holmes

Unattached
16th Georgia Battalion Partisan Rangers, Lt. Col. F. M. Nix
3d Kentucky Cavalry, Col. J. R. Butler
5th North Carolina Cavalry Battalion, Maj. A. H. Baird
7th North Carolina Cavalry Battalion, Lieut. Col. G. N. Folk
North Carolina Regiment, Col. W. H. Thomas
5th Tennessee Cavalry, Lieut. Col. G. W. McKenzie
16th Tennessee Cavalry Battalion, Maj. E. W. Rucker[43]

The number of men present for duty within the various cavalry brigades in Smith's command totaled about 6,700 troopers: Pegram 1,500, Morgan 2,000, Scott 900, and unattached about 2,300.[44]

A few days later on November 25, Colonel John Wharton's cavalry brigade arrived in Middle Tennessee and he reported his command, somewhat incompletely.

Wharton's Cavalry Brigade

3rd Confederate Regiment
2nd Georgia Regiment
4th Tennessee Regiment
Bledsoe's Tennessee battalion
8th Texas Regiment
Anderson's company of cavalry (couriers)
White's section of artillery (6-pounders)

Wharton recorded 1,586 officers and men present for duty and a total of 2,354 (aggregate) for his brigade. Also, Abraham "Abe" Buford's small and newly organized Kentucky cavalry brigade was also present for duty in Tennessee and consisted of the 3rd, 5th and 6th Kentucky regiments. Buford's brigade would also fall under Wheeler's direct command in Tennessee. Only Wheeler and Forrest did not report the composition of their respective brigades in late November. Forrest's brigade consisted of the 4th, 8th and 9th Tennessee cavalries and the 4th Alabama Cavalry.

Wheeler's Cavalry Brigade

1st Alabama Cavalry
3rd Alabama Cavalry
51st Alabama Partisan Rangers
8th Confederate Cavalry
1st Tennessee Cavalry
Douglass' Tennessee Battalion
Holman's Tennessee Battalion
Calvert's Arkansas Battery

Buford's Cavalry Brigade

3rd Kentucky Cavalry
5th Kentucky Cavalry
6th Kentucky Cavalry

On November 21, Bragg defined his expectations for Forrest and his cavalry. Forrest was given a free rein to operate west of the Nashville and Columbia road with authority to operate in western Tennessee if there was an opportunity to strike the enemy or cut communications. He was also given command of Colonel Phillip Roddey's cavalry from northern Alabama. Finally, Forrest received authority to increase his force, if he had the ability to arm the new troops; but his subsistence needed to be obtained from the area in which he operated. Bragg requested weekly updates of the activities of Forrest's cavalry and loosely defined his objectives as "fall suddenly on his rear, destroy his trains, and harass him to the extent of your ability."[45]

Bragg had most parts of his Army of Tennessee in place by November 22. Polk and

Hardee were in Middle Tennessee and Kirby Smith's corps moved toward Tullahoma. The location of the Confederate army drew its subsistence from the rich farmland and the support of the loyal population which had "once felt the yoke of Abolition despotism." While being outnumbered, Bragg assumed a defensive posture and believed an attack on Rosecrans would be imprudent because of the strong Union defenses supported by artillery. Bragg hoped the combined actions of his cavalry would force Rosecrans to fight or retreat.[46]

Meanwhile, Bragg's requests for stars for his cavalry commanders were approved. Wheeler was promoted to the rank of brigadier general effective October 30, Wharton on November 18, and John H. Morgan on December 11, 1862. Kirby Smith requested a promotion to the rank of brigadier general for John Pegram, who had recently served as his chief of staff, which was granted on November 11, 1862, and Pegram was given command of a brigade of cavalry. Forrest had been promoted to that rank the previous July and was, therefore, the highest ranking cavalry officer in Middle Tennessee. Bragg's intentions for Wheeler's cavalry was to place Wheeler's, Wharton's and Pegram's cavalry brigades covering the roads leading south and east from Nashville. With his cavalry so strategically placed, Bragg hoped to keep an eye on Rosecrans' movement and with superior numbers of cavalry to resist any foraging efforts south of Nashville by the Union army.[47]

General John Wharton, cavalry brigade commander, Army of Tennessee (Alabama Department of Archives and History).

On November 24, Bragg learned he had a new commanding officer, General Joseph Johnston, who assumed command of all the Southern forces of Western North Carolina, Tennessee, Northern Georgia, Alabama, Mississippi, and Eastern Louisiana. On the same day, Bragg reported his situation and strategy to Jefferson Davis as he concentrated his army in Middle Tennessee. In regard to cavalry, he told Davis that Morgan's and Forrest's cavalry were to cooperate independently of the Army of Tennessee. Forrest was ordered to operate south of the Cumberland River and west of Nashville with his focus on disrupting river supply and support on both the Tennessee and Cumberland Rivers. Forrest's objectives were to fight the enemy "break up railroads, burn bridges, destroy depots, capture hospitals and guards, and harass him generally. Thus we may create a diversion in favor of Pemberton, and, if successful, force the enemy to retire from Mississippi." For the remainder of his cavalry, he placed three brigades as a screen for the three infantry corps at Murfreesboro, and a fourth cavalry brigade (Buford's) remained in position near McMinnville to the east. Bragg placed his infantry all within supporting distance of each other, because Bragg felt significantly outnumbered compared to Rosecrans' army of at least 60,000 troops. If Bragg was going to be successful, then cavalry had to be a key component in his strategy. His cavalry was a large force, roughly 20 percent of the entire Confederate army in Middle Tennessee, and Bragg identified his cavalry as a way of forcing Rosecrans' hand. If communications and supplies were cut off by Forrest and Morgan,

Rosecrans would have no other choice but to advance or withdraw. As he settled into his headquarters at Murfreesboro, Bragg was more comfortable than he had been in months. Despite the criticism he had received about his retreat from Kentucky a month earlier, Bragg was "cheerful" and met with his staff in the evenings to relate his experiences in the Mexican War.[48]

Meanwhile, John H. Morgan had been on duty constantly for months and looked forward to relief when Pegram's cavalry arrived for duty. This allowed Morgan a few weeks before he started his new actions against the Louisville & Nashville Railroad which carried much of the supplies to Nashville. Morgan had perhaps caused the greatest impact to this supply line during his summer raid when he destroyed South Tunnel and stopped supplies on the railroad for one hundred days.[49]

Brigadier General John Pegram, recent chief of staff of Smith's Army of Kentucky and new to the cavalry, brought his brigade to Middle Tennessee and moved into position as Morgan withdrew to resupply and rest his command. He established his headquarters at Baird's Mill along the Confederate east flank. Pegram, a West Point graduate and ex-regular army officer, commanded four regiments in his newly reorganized brigade—1st Georgia, 1st Louisiana and the 1st and 2nd Tennessee. In one of the earliest actions of the war, Pegram had been captured during the defeat at the Battle of Rich Mountain in Virginia and later exchanged. Pegram, a Virginian, had commanded infantry and served as an engineer prior to appointment as cavalry brigade commander. Although Pegram's performance had been inconsistent, he was still a highly regarded officer for the Confederacy, commanding a brigade of cavalry for the first time in the Civil War.[50]

When Wheeler arrived in Middle Tennessee he had many duties, including, recommending officers for promotion within the cavalry ranks and this was accomplished by establishing examining boards which had the duty of "retiring those judged unqualified, incompetent, or disabled." In addition, Wheeler's cavalry had been composed of various battalions and he needed to merge battalions or increase their strength to regimental size. He set about the task of reorganizing these sub-regimental units. Bragg also erroneously felt Rosecrans' position in Nashville was tenuous at best, but he was confident in the dominance of his cavalry. Wheeler, as well as Forrest and Morgan, was charged with raiding the Federals at any opportunity. Wheeler was assigned the duty of arresting deserters and those absent without leave and returning them to their commands. And finally, if it had not been assigned enough duty, the cavalry was also given the unenviable responsibility of enforcing Bragg's General Orders 146 which prohibited the consumption of grain alcohol in the army.[51]

Colonel John Hunt Morgan, cavalry brigade commander, Army of Tennessee (Library of Congress).

Skirmishing Continues

On November 27, in one of the many skirmishes that occurred between the opposing forces, a near miss served to identify the character of one of the principle commanders of the Confederate cavalry—Wheeler. Forrest had recommended that Wheeler move to La Vergne because of good forage and excellent blacksmith facilities. The presence of increased numbers of Confederates at La Vergne drew the attention of Brigadier General Joshua W. Sill's Union infantry which conducted a reconnaissance expedition to La Vergne. The Confederate infantry was positioned about five miles to the rear at Stewarts Creek and Wheeler's 1st Alabama Cavalry and Hunley's Battalion screened the Confederate positions at La Vergne. As Sill approached, the Southern vedettes fell back as a defensive line was hastily prepared by the Confederate cavalry. The Union infantry, Colonel Edward N. Kirk's brigade, preceded by a detail of cavalry crashed into the Wheeler's line prepared just north of La Vergne. The fight intensified as the Union infantry charged a Southern battery and during the fight Wheeler was nearly killed. The first volley by Southern troopers sent the Union cavalry to the rear, but Kirk followed up with infantry and artillery support. Kirk's advance pushed the 1st Alabama and Hunley's men rearward, as they stopped, fired and rode several yards to the rear and repeated the exercise. The cavalry fighting the Union advance received orders from Wheeler to hold the line until reinforcements arrived. Wheeler arrived shortly after the fight began and encouraged his men in the fight. A Federal shell exploded and killed Wheeler's horse and his orderly. Shrapnel struck Wheeler's leg, but despite his injury, Wheeler obtained another horse and remained on the field until the skirmish ended. Wheeler's men made nine stands as they were pushed south of La Vergne but the Confederate infantry failed to reach the site of the fighting to support the cavalry. When Kirk took possession of the town, he burned the Confederate cavalry headquarters and applied "the torch to many a fine house on the road side." Upon hearing of Wheeler's wound, Bragg's adjutant general wrote of his behalf:

> The general commanding directs me to thank you for your successful engagement with the enemy today. He also desires you will express to the First Alabama Regiment (one of his old corps) his appreciation of their gallant conduct, not unexpected, which you refer to in your report. He further directs me to state that you expose yourself too recklessly in affairs of this character.

Wheeler was fearless on the field, a trait that would continue through the war. Wheeler would be wounded three times and have sixteen horses shot from under him during the war.[52]

George Knox Miller, 8th Confederate Cavalry, described the Union expedition to La Vergne in a letter on November 28 from near La Vergne:

> Yesterday the Yankees drove our pickets thro' the little village of Lavergne on the Nashville & chattanooga R. Road, and having gained possession of the town, burnt & destroyed every thing in it leaving scarcely a house standing, even tearing up & burning beds, clothing, buggies, carraiges, &c. This done they retreated back behind their fortifications in front of Nashville. Some one will have to answer for this, and what a record will be presented when man's final settlement is made with his Maker!" Private Benjamin Burke of the 8th Texas Cavalry echoed the comments of Miller. Burke, stationed near Triune, went through a series of skirmishes on the western flank of the army. Burke wrote home: "The yankess are committing many deprivations upon the citizens near Nashvill (sic) by stealing negroes, plundering & burning houses. Some of the people have great fears to our evacuating the state and leaving them to the mercy of the Yankees.[53]

The Union expedition to La Vergne could have been a bloodier fight if Bragg had followed Wheeler's earlier advice that infantry should be moved further north to support his cavalry. While the Southern cavalry effectively battled the reconnaissance expeditions and foraging parties, it was still no match for columns of infantry.[54]

Stanley Arrives

At long last, Rosecrans announced David Stanley's arrival on November 24. Stanley arrived at an army which desperately needed a chief of cavalry because communication, organization, and reliability of the cavalry were poor. Almost immediately upon the arrival of Stanley, all messages about communication and coordination with the cavalry ceased. Brigadier General John Beatty was impressed with David Stanley upon his arrival and recorded in his diary: "Major-General Stanley, the cavalryman, is of good size, gentlemanly in bearing, light complexion, brown hair."[55]

When Stanley arrived at the Army of the Cumberland, he brought with him an intimate friend who would serve with him throughout the remainder of the war, Major William Henry Sinclair. Sinclair was born near Akron, Ohio, and enlisted in the 7th Michigan Infantry and, soon thereafter, was promoted to the rank of lieutenant in Dee's 3rd Michigan Artillery. Stanley became acquainted with Sinclair during the Siege of Island Number 10 and when Stanley moved to Nashville in the fall of 1862, Sinclair came along as his adjutant general and remained in that role until the end of the war. During the Battle of Corinth, Sinclair had been sent with a message for Stanley. As he arrived, Stanley's aide was killed and he turned to Sinclair and appointed him to his staff at that moment. Stanley had no more efficient, loyal subordinate or better friend than Sinclair.[56]

Because Ebenezer Gay's cavalry brigade remained in Kentucky with the Department of the Ohio, David Stanley initially formed his cavalry into two brigades forming one division until additional regiments arrived for duty.

Cavalry—Army of the Cumberland[57]
Brigadier General David S. Stanley

Cavalry Division
Colonel John Kennett

First Brigade
Colonel Edward McCook–Colonel Robert H. G. Minty
2nd Indiana, Lieutenant Colonel Robert Stewart
3rd Kentucky, Colonel Eli H. Murray
4th Michigan, Lieutenant Colonel William H. Dickinson
7th Pennsylvania, Major John E. Wynkoop

Second Brigade
Colonel Lewis Zahm
1st Ohio, Colonel Minor Millikin
3rd Ohio, Lieutenant Colonel Douglas A. Murray
4th Ohio, Major John L. Pugh

Artillery
1st Ohio, Battery D (section), Lieutenant Nathaniel M. Newell

Unattached
4th U.S. Cavalry, Captain Elmer Otis

What was thought to be one of the more pleasant bits of news which awaited Stanley was that the 15th Pennsylvania Cavalry, also referred to as the "Anderson Cavalry," was on its way to the Army of the Cumberland. The Anderson Troop, an independent cavalry command formed in Pennsylvania, served primarily as escorts for the previous commanding generals of the Army of the Ohio. The Anderson Troop expanded by eleven companies in 1862 and officially comprised the 15th Pennsylvania Cavalry regiment. The 15th Pennsylvania would serve in the cavalry reserve brigade for the Army of the Cumberland but did not reach the army until December 24. Two Tennessee regiments were also assigned to Stanley and would arrive about the same time.

Upon his arrival, Stanley summarized his assessment of the cavalry:

> The cavalry had been sadly neglected. It was weak, undisciplined and scattered about a regiment to a division of infantry. To break up this foolish disposal of cavalry and to form brigades and eventually divisions, was my first and most difficult work. Generals commanding divisions, declared they would not give up their cavalry regiments, but I insisted that they do so and General Rosecrans sustained me.

Colonel Edward McCook—one of the "Fightin' McCooks"—cavalry brigade commander, Army of the Cumberland (Library of Congress).

Stanley's correctly assessed his new command, because the cavalry was scattered throughout the various infantry corps in old the Army of the Ohio.[58]

Both Stanley and Rosecrans wanted time for their new troops to drill, equip and train in preparation for the upcoming campaign, but by December 4, Henry Halleck informed Rosecrans the President grew increasingly impatient with the Army of Cumberland's stay in the area around Nashville. In return, Rosecrans had several issues of his own which he felt needed to be rectified before he could march, including, a supply of shoes, arms, and tents. In regard to the cavalry, he lamented the lack of horses and he felt he had about half the number the cavalrymen needed. When Stanley arrived he had 3,038 troopers present for duty and an aggregate total of 4,534 cavalrymen. The 15th Pennsylvania Cavalry, which was *en route*, as well as two regiments of Tennessee cavalry increased the number by another 2,883 men. The new total of cavalry was 7,400 and even with the new arms received from Washington, there were still 1,300 troopers without arms. Another 1,200 horses were also needed.

Summary

By the end of November, both armies had been restructured. Bragg combined his Army of Mississippi with parts of Kirby Smith's old Army of Kentucky into three corps and seven divisions. On the Union side of the field, Rosecrans had just gained command of Buell's Army of the Ohio and made changes of his own. This "turbulence" in the organization of the two armies would be important in the upcoming actions. The historic structure of divisions and brigades had yet to be established and when in the heat of the battle the mutual reliance between the various commands in the fighting was vitally important. Both armies needed time to develop the communication, trust and coordination between units and there was just not enough time for this to mature.[59]

In regard to the cavalry, this lack of maturation was similar. Within the Union cavalry, David Stanley had just arrived with too few troopers and with commanders he did not know. The Union cavalry also had a crisis in command. Stanley had never worked with any of his subordinates before and some subordinates had serious command issues. The two brigades, Zahm's and McCook/Minty's, were used to working together, but in a more disjointed manner. More men were needed by the Union cavalry and better weapons and more horses. When the three new regiments arrived for duty in December, there were serious issues, either in command or in experience. While the commanders of the Union cavalry recognized this, there was little time to remedy it.

The Confederate cavalry, while superior in numbers, also was in turbulence. The Southern cavalry was in the midst of combining the various, semi-independent battalions into regiments. It would take time for the inherent independence in these battalions to be replaced with regimental identity and integrity. In some instances the old battalions still rode with their own battle flags. Certainly, it is difficult to examine the Southern cavalry without recognizing Forrest's and Morgan's cavalry, but these two commands were given very clear orders in the new Confederate organizational structure to operate away from the Army of the Tennessee. In the meantime, Wheeler commanded four brigades, two of which were commanded by brigade commanders he had never worked with before—John Pegram and Abe Buford. While Wheeler had worked well with John Wharton, Wheeler as chief of cavalry still had titular command of his own brigade. There were several good candidates for brigade command, but Wheeler maintained this command. This decision had significant implications for the Southern cavalry actions in the upcoming months.

3. A Decision to Fight (December 1–25, 1862)

Victory is enchained to our banners.
—Brigadier General John Hunt Morgan

December began with Rosecrans dealing with several issues. One of the most immediate tasks focused on pushing the various Confederate forces south of the Cumberland River. This prevented the loss of valuable resources and it also kept his lines of communication open. Rosecrans also hastened to organize his army which he felt lacked proper discipline and which needed to be rearmed. While dealing with these issues, he also had to deal with the impatience of those in Washington.

In the first few days of December Henry Halleck exchanged communications regarding Rosecrans' failure to advance against Bragg's position south of Nashville. On December 4, Halleck told Rosecrans that the President was growing impatient about Rosecrans' delay in moving forward. Those in Washington worried that if no movement occurred soon, the winter weather would make any campaigning impossible and six months would be lost. Halleck wrote: "You give Bragg time to supply himself by plundering the very country your army should have occupied.... Twice have I been asked to designate someone else to command your army. If you remain one more week at Nashville, I cannot prevent your removal." The threat in Halleck's message was clear to Rosecrans who commanded the Army of Cumberland for about a month, but Rosecrans was not ready to move and told Halleck so. Rosecrans replied:

> In front, because of greater obstacles, enemies in greater force, and fighting with better chances of escaping pursuit, if overthrown in battle. In rear, because of insufficiency and uncertainty of supplies, both of subsistence and ammunition, and no security of any kind to fall back upon in case of disaster.... Many of our soldiers are to this day barefoot, without blankets, without tents, without good arms, and cavalry without horses. Our true objective now is the enemy's force. If the Government which ordered me here confides in my judgment, it may rely on my continuing to do what I have been trying to—that is, my whole duty. If my superiors have lost confidence in me, they had better at once put someone in my place and let the future test the propriety of the change. I have but one word to add, which is, that I need no other stimulus to make me do my duty than the knowledge of what it is. To threats of removal or the like I must be permitted to say that I am insensible.[1]

Rosecrans had just outlined the issues he wanted to correct only to be greeted with a message from Henry Halleck. Halleck, while explaining to Rosecrans his letter was not a threat, reiterated to Rosecrans that Lincoln was greatly dissatisfied with the delay of the Army of the Cumberland at Nashville. Halleck explained that European interests in the war required a rapid push of the Confederates south of the Tennessee River. In Halleck's interpretation of the President's concern, only Tennessee could be seen as a Confederate success over the past year, and this Confederate progress could be used as an argument to draw England into the war on the side of the South. Washington saw the action, or rather inaction, on the part of Rosecrans as having

> an importance beyond mere military success. The whole Cabinet are anxious, inquiring almost daily. "Why don't he move? ... Can't you make him move? ... There must be no delay.... Delay there will be more fatal to us than anywhere else." You will thus perceive that there is a pressure for you to advance much greater than you can possibly have imagined. It may be, and perhaps is, the very turning-point in our foreign relations.

Halleck reminded Rosecrans that those in Washington had little doubt that Rosecrans' predecessor, Buell, would have eventually defeated Bragg, but he was too slow in achieving this objective. Because he moved so slowly he was replaced and Rosecrans needed to consider the importance of attacking Bragg quickly.[2]

While these exchanges were made, Rosecrans continued moving his army to Nashville. McCook and Crittenden formed the front lines of the Army of the Cumberland at Nashville and Thomas's center wing continued to march southward. Rosecrans still awaited trailing infantry, ammunition and artillery. Despite being in a good position at Nashville, he had only five days' rations for his troops, and his cavalry remained a major concern. There were still too many troopers without proper arms, although Washington had sent some arms. Rosecrans wrote to Halleck that the weapons for his cavalry arrived slowly and explained the importance of fully equipping his horsemen. In addition, three cavalry regiments assigned to Federal army in Nashville remained in Louisville, 1st, 2nd and part of 5th Tennessee cavalries. Even the 15th Pennsylvania Cavalry had yet to arrive.[3]

Skirmishing Continues

As the two opposing armies settled into Middle Tennessee in December, the conflicts between the two began quickly and the Confederate cavalry made an immediate impact. From December 3 to 7 the cavalry units of the two armies struck at various locations with the most important action taking place on December 7 despite it being a snowy day. About 200 of Thomas Harrison's Texas Rangers (8th Texas Cavalry) attacked a Union forage train on the Hardin Pike near Nashville on December 3, capturing two officers in charge of the forage train but a company of the 43rd Illinois Infantry fought off the attack and saved the wagons. The next day, Colonel Robert Minty's 4th Michigan Cavalry took the offensive and began a forty-five mile reconnaissance along the Franklin Pike and ran into pickets of the enemy cavalry at Holly Tree Gap. Although Minty had about 700 men in his regiment, over half were sick with various ailments. Three hundred Michigan troopers rode nine miles down the Franklin Pike and encountered about 70 enemy pickets. Minty found some bridges had been burned but found no other obvious obstructions in the area, and a near disaster was avoided during the expedition as Minty's cavalry discovered a large group of infantry, which had quickly fallen into line. The tragedy was averted when the cavalrymen recognized the men of the 10th Michigan Infantry which prepared to fire on Minty's troopers. Also on December 4, Major Daniel W. Holman's battalion of Confederate partisan rangers, which would become part of the 11th Tennessee Confederate Cavalry early in 1863, attacked a Union outpost at Stewarts Ferry on Stones River. At 3:00 a.m., Holman's men attacked a group of ten men, one sergeant and nine others, of Powell's Mounted Scouts, an irregular company of mounted Union infantrymen.

The Union report claimed no one wounded and three captured, but the Confederate report claimed three Union men killed and the remainder wounded. Holman demanded the Union soldiers surrender but they refused and were fired upon by twenty of his men. The weakness of the Union cavalry was expressed by Brigadier General James Morgan who complained he had no cavalry to screen his men to prevent them from being attacked by mounted Confederates.[4]

Next, Wheeler's cavalry attacked another forage train at Kimbrough's Mill at Mill Creek on December 6, killing one soldier, wounding two others, and capturing about ten wagons belonging to Brigadier General Milo Smith Hascall's division. On December 6 Wheeler's cavalry attacked the forage train of Colonel Harvey M. Buckley's brigade. The affair caused great embarrassment to Buckley, who commanded a brigade of the 1st Ohio Infantry, 5th Kentucky Infantry, 97th Ohio Infantry and 93rd Ohio Infantry. Two companies of the 3rd Indiana Cavalry accompanied the expedition as Buckley's brigade marched about seven miles southeast of Nashville in search of forage. Buckley's forage train was attacked as it moved back toward Nashville and when it reached Mill Creek Wheeler's cavalry captured about ten wagons. As the infantry marched ahead it was confronted with a small force of about twenty Confederate cavalry. The forward infantry regiments deployed into battle line, the artillery unlimbered and the 3rd Indiana Cavalry, commanded by Captain Argus Vanosdol, rode ahead and dispersed the enemy cavalry. The 23-year-old, Vanosdol, a native of Switzerland County, Indiana, received the praise of the brigade commander: "[H]ere I would say that no men could have behaved better than those two companies, nor could any one have maneuvered them to better advantage than the captain in command." After dispersing the enemy cavalry, Buckley's men completed their task. Upon completion of gathering the forage, the Confederate cavalry attacked the head of the column and then made a more determined attack on the flank near the rear in an attempt to cut off that portion of the brigade. A heated skirmish resulted and the enemy captured about ten forage wagons before the Union infantry fought off the attack.[5]

General Benjamin Cheatham's infantry joined Wheeler's cavalry attack on the foraging expedition at Kimbrough's Mill on December 6 which served as a diversion for John Hunt Morgan's cavalry's expedition set for the next day. Colonel Harvey Buckley's Union brigade escorted the large forage train and a second smaller forage train was guarded by Lieutenant Colonel Milton Barnes (97th Ohio Infantry). Wheeler's cavalry attacked different parts of the smaller train while intending to separate a group of wagons from the main column. In addition, a section of Wiggins's Arkansas Artillery fired on the 97th Ohio Infantry escorting the smaller train and the 5th U.S. Artillery unlimbered and returned the fire. After firing a few rounds Wiggins limbered and moved away. In the meantime, another attack by dismounted Confederate cavalry targeted a portion of the train guarded by the 93rd Ohio, which had just reached the train while it was under attack. This attack was also repulsed and the train returned to the safety of the Union lines; but not before Wheeler had accomplished his task of diverting attention of the Union infantry to protect the foraging trains while capturing a few wagons and prisoners along the way.[6]

Little did the Union forces realize that the increased attacks masked part of a greater plan by Braxton Bragg and John Hunt Morgan to attack the Union forces at Hartsville the next day. Bragg set several units into motion on December 5 and 6 as diversions. Part of Colonel Roger Hanson's infantry brigade of Breckinridge's division (2nd and 9th Kentucky infantries and Cobb's Kentucky Artillery) marched to unite with Morgan's cavalry the next day. In the meantime, the remainder of Hanson's brigade marched as a diversion toward Nashville. Also, Benjamin Cheatham's infantry moved toward La Vergne in conjunction with Joseph Wheeler's cavalry which resulted in the attack on the forage train and served as a general demonstration along that section of the Union line. The real intent was to occupy the Union army while Morgan and Hanson marched for Hartsville.[7]

The 8th Confederate Cavalry also played its part of the diversion. Captain George K. Miller wrote in a letter on December 7 from Stewarts Creek:

> [M]y gallant boys are "in front" on picket skirmishing almost hourly with the enemy. Yesterday I was by a log fire nearly all day listening to the heavy boom of the cannon.... Yesterday morning the uninitiated were on tip-toe, expecting a general engagement which seemed all the more probable when the artillery opened about 12 o'clock. But it proved to be only an attack of our regiment and another large forging [foraging] party of Yankees who have been in the habit of coming out from 4 to 6000 strong almost daily driving in our pickets and skirmishing while their wagons were in their rear despoiling farms of grain, poultry, meal &c.

Miller proudly wrote that the Confederate cavalry stopped the Federal forces after several hours of fighting. He recorded that the Union army lost fifty-seven prisoners, twelve wagons, sixty mules, and several horses.[8]

The Action at Hartsville

"Do I understand that they have captured an entire brigade of our troops without our knowing it, or a good fight?" asked the astonished William Rosecrans on December 7. The give and take of these minor cavalry clashes developed into the serious action at Hartsville, Tennessee, as John Hunt Morgan surprised the Federal garrison there.[9]

The Thirty-ninth Brigade of the Army of the Cumberland occupied the town of Hartsville in early December. The brigade was commanded by Colonel Absalom B. Moore who had just assumed brigade command on December 2 from Colonel Joseph Scott, 19th Illinois Infantry. Moore, a La Salle County Illinois resident, had been promoted to the rank of colonel on August 27, 1862. Aware that Hartsville and Gallatin had been bases for Morgan's cavalry, Moore kept his cavalry on constant watch. Moore's total force consisted of about 2,300 men (104th Illinois Infantry, 106th Ohio Infantry, 108th Ohio Infantry, 2nd Indiana Cavalry, 11th Kentucky Cavalry and artillery), but 200 infantry and cavalry were away guarding a supply train at Gallatin. The final Union casualty count totaled approximately 2,100 men, the total of those present near the town on December 7.[10]

Hartsville was not a welcoming town to the Union troops. Colonel Edward McCook, First Cavalry Brigade commander, explained that Southern sympathizers moved within the Union held town regularly and speculated that even some of Morgan's cavalrymen examined the Union position and provided accurate intelligence regarding the best approach of the attack. McCook was correct. Prior to the attack, Morgan received intelligence from his scouts that there had been no significant changes in position or numbers of Federal troops.[11]

Lieutenant Colonel Robert Stewart's, 2nd Indiana Cavalry, diligently scouted the countryside the day before by sending troopers across the Cumberland River, and as far as Lebanon. The local citizens were questioned about Southern activity in the area and reported no movements on the parts of the local Confederates. Morgan planned well. His advance occurred after the Union cavalry had returned for the evening. Hartsville was located on the northern side of the Cumberland River. The Union camp was located on a wooded hill overlooking the Cumberland River, about midway between Hartsville and the river. A large field bordered the camp on the northwest and in addition, a ravine ran southward toward the Cumberland River.[12]

John Hunt Morgan's plan depended upon a surprise attack on the unsuspecting Union garrison. The Union army had established garrisons at Hartsville, Gallatin and Castalian Springs and prepared to begin foraging in an area which supported the Confederate army. Morgan was determined to strike back at the Union outpost at Hartsville. He left his headquarters, about eight miles south of Lebanon, at 10:00 a. m. on December 6 with 1,400 men—about 450 of his cavalry under direct command of Colonel Basil Duke; the 2nd and 9th Kentucky infantry under command of Colonel Thomas Hunt; Cobb's battery, two small howitzers, and two rifled Ellsworth cannons. Though outnumbered, morale was high. Morgan rode out of town in a "driving sleet pelting them in the face amid the shouts and waving of handerchiefs of the ladies, old men and soldiers who had gathered to see them off." Morgan rode to Lebanon and determined Moore's brigade still occupied Hartsville with about 1,300 men, somewhat underestimated. Morgan crossed his infantry and artillery at Purier's Ferry while the cavalry made a cold crossing of the Cumberland River at a nearby ford. He reached Moore's position at 5:30 a. m. on December 7, but Gano's 500 man cavalry brigade had yet to arrive. Major Robert G. Stoner's battalion of Kentucky cavalry remained on the south side of the Cumberland River with two mountain howitzers (referred to as "bull pups") protecting the Lebanon Road and Colonel James D. Bennett's 9th Tennessee Cavalry rode to Hartsville to prevent a retreat by the Federal troops. In addition, some southern troops watched the roads leading to Gallatin, Castalian Springs, Lafayette, and Carthage. Colonel John M. Harlan's and Colonel Abram Miller's Union infantry brigades were nine miles away at Castalian Springs. Morgan wanted to isolate Moore at Hartsville and placed his men to ensure he was not discovered or that Union reinforcements did not hamper his attack. Then, he launched his attack from the west and as his men found the Union pickets, they were "shot down."[13]

The Union reports explained the initial success of Morgan's attack resulted from the Confederates deceiving the Federal pickets. Moore noted the sentries were captured by Union uniform-wearing Confederates "without firing a gun." Then Morgan made a full dismounted attack on the unsuspecting Union brigade; but soon the alarms sounded and confusion reigned. Only Bennett's Confederate cavalry remained in the saddle and rushed into Hartsville and captured Company A of the 104th Illinois Infantry. Colonel Basil Duke commanded the cavalry which rode into the attack and then dismounted the 450 men of Cluke's (8th Kentucky CSA) and Chenault's (11th Kentucky CSA) cavalry regiments. The Confederate cavalry formed a battle line in a field opposite Moore's defensive line which was organizing after the surprise attack. Duke ordered the men to charge and the Federals recoiled rearward about a half a mile. At that point, Duke halted until Hanson's Confederate infantry joined in by attacking the Union left wing. Once the infantry joined the attack, the entire Union line again began to retreat. Morgan wrote; "It gave way and ceased firing, and soon after surrendered."[14]

Moore's troops attempted to withstand the attack, but were surprised, confused, and finally unable to rally, surrendered to the smaller force. Moore placed the blame for the defeat at the feet of the 106th Ohio Infantry. He wrote that battle raged from 6:45 a.m. and concluded by 8:30 a.m. He explained:

> The One hundred and fourth Illinois fought heroically, and maintained their position. The Second Indiana Cavalry and the Eleventh Kentucky Cavalry also did nobly. The One hundred and sixth Ohio acted shamefully, and left us in the midst of the fight, many of the men running for shelter in the tents of the One hundred and eighth Ohio, which were in the rear of our line of battle.

All attempts by Moore and Lieutenant Colonel Stewart, 2nd Indiana Cavalry, were unsuccessful in rallying the retreating Union troops. Moore also described the fate of those soldiers who attempted to run away. Morgan's cavalry had detached guards on the roads and "succeeded in capturing the cowards who had deserted us in the time of need."[15]

After battling the Southern force for some time, Moore observed that Duke's attack stopped and at that point he ordered his command to charge. He explained: "I gave the order to charge, feeling confident that we could cut our way through the rebel ranks." Moore thought the lull in the attack resulted because his men had battled Duke to a standstill, but Duke was just waiting for a realignment of Hanson's Confederate infantry. The charge by the Union troops proved unsuccessful. Moore described,

> Immediately upon giving the order, the stampede of the One hundred and sixth commenced, which then brought a tremendous fire upon the One hundred and eighth Ohio, they being the center, and were soon flanked on the right, and gave way in confusion. I withdrew the order to charge, and directed the One hundred and fourth to hold the rebels in check until I drew our guns, now entirely unsupported on the right, to another position.

Moore moved his cannons on top of a bluff overlooking the river and two hundred yards to the rear, and ordered the 106th and 108th Ohio infantries to form a battle line near the guns. He was to be disappointed again because the two regiments remained so disorganized that he was unable to rally them. According to Moore only the 104th Illinois still fought trying to hold off the attack of Morgan's cavalry and infantry but the last regiment was surrounded and surrendered. Moore bitterly exclaimed that one-half of his command was "captured by deserting their position without orders, I was compelled to surrender, as fighting longer would only increase the number of killed and wounded, as we were contending against a force of ten to one after forming in our new line of battle."[16]

Moore had hoped to receive reinforcements from the Union troops at Castalian Springs, but the aid came too late. One of the reinforcements, William Allen Clark, 72nd Indiana Infantry, wrote in a letter that his regiment arrived twenty minutes too late after marching over "ditches, hills & fences." Clark described the scene: "We buried 49 of our men and 14 secesh. Dont know the number of wounded. The men were all shot in the head or Breast. It was a bad sight men & horses in promiscuous confusion spred of [over] a 10 acre field." Moore expressed his appreciation for the efforts of Lieutenant Colonel Robert Stewart and Major Samuel Hill, 2nd Indiana Cavalry; and Captain Frederick Slater, 11th Kentucky Cavalry, for their efforts during the fight. He concluded his report; "I will say I love every man that fought; I hate every dog that ran. It was the first time that any of the infantry regiments engaged in the battle were under fire."[17]

Casualties at Hartsville—December 7, 1862[18]
Union Forces

Regiment	Killed		Wounded		Captured		Total
	Officers	Men	Officers	Men	Officers	Men	
104th Illinois	0	25	5	126	23	545	724
106th Ohio	2	20	3	38	16	413	492

Regiment	Killed		Wounded		Captured		Total
	Officers	Men	Officers	Men	Officers	Men	
108th Ohio	0	10	0	30	20	393	453
2nd Indiana Cav	0	0	0	0	11	346	357
11th Kentucky Cav	0	0	0	0	2	42	44
13th Indiana Battery (section)	0	1	0	2	1	22	26
Union Total	2	56	8	196	73	1,761	2,096

CONFEDERATE FORCES

Regiment	Killed		Wounded		Captured		Total
	Officers	Men	Officers	Men	Officers	Men	
Morgan's Brigade:							
Staff	0	0	1	1	0	0	2
Gano's Regiment	0	0	0	0	0	1	1
Cluke's Regiment	1	1	4	20	1	5	32
Chenault's Regt.	0	1	0	4	0	0	5
Total	1	3	6	27	1	6	44
Hanson's Brigade:							
2nd Kentucky Infty	2	6	3	51	0	6	68
9th Kentucky Infty	1	5	1	9	0	1	17
Cobb's Battery	0	3	0	7	0	0	10
Total	3	14	4	67	0	7	95
Confederate Total	4	17	10	94	1	13	139

"Danger was now imminent on every side. One could feel it in the air," exclaimed Bennett Young of Morgan's cavalry. While the fighting was taking place, Colonel John Marshall Harlan at Castilian Springs and Colonel Abram Miller's brigade at Gallatin moved to assist the Union troops at Hartsville. As Miller and Harlan approached Hartsville, they ran into the detached troops Morgan had placed to prevent reinforcements and his plan worked perfectly. Miller encountered the enemy first and requested Harlan to ride forward. Morgan, aware the Union reinforcements were marching to Hartsville, dispatched some additional cavalry to delay Harlan and Miller. Morgan believed the line of his cavalry caused the Union reinforcements to delay as they fell into line, not knowing the size of the force they faced. This gave him time to get his column of prisoners, artillery, and captured goods across to the south shore of the Cumberland River. As the reinforcements pushed ahead, they saw Morgan's cavalry crossing the river and Morgan's decision to place troops and artillery at the ford prevented Harlan and Miller from pursuing. Upon arriving at Hartsville, Harlan found fifty-five dead Union soldiers and fifteen dead Confederates.[19]

In Rosecrans' report, he chastised the actions of the 2nd Indiana Cavalry which he described as "spiritless" in its security efforts although he had no evidence for this accusation. This was an easy conclusion, but an ill-formed one. The reports by those at the battle supported the 2nd Indiana Cavalry actions at Hartsville. Major Samuel Hill filed the report for the 2nd Indiana and explained the regiment scouted the countryside the afternoon and evening before without finding any enemies. Cavalry vedettes announced the presence of the enemy preparing to attack while Morgan's men were three quarters of a mile away. The 2nd Indiana rode forward, dismounted to meet the attack, with the exception of Company G, which remained mounted. As the Union infantry formed a battle line, the cavalry mounted and secured the flank of the infantry. The Union infantry hastily formed a line, supported by artillery, and cavalry. When the infantry line was pushed rearward, the cavalry moved back to the vicinity of its camp. The Union cavalry had encamped near Hart's Ferry along the southern flank of the infantry and was assigned duty of guarding the crossing on the Cumberland River overnight. The 2nd Indiana Cavalry held its position during the fighting and even held out after the infantry surrendered for another forty minutes.[20]

The Union reports placed blame for the surrender on various persons, including Colonel Moore and the actions of the various regiments. Moore placed the principle blame on the 106th Ohio, but Lieutenant Colonel Gustavus Tafel of that regiment reported his position became untenable due to the need to face a flanking action by Morgan's cavalry after Moore surrendered the Federal battery. Carlo Piepho, 108th Ohio, wrote that "Colonel Moore having surrendered before I knew anything about it. The confusion of the battle and the inexperience of the Union infantry resulted in the surrender of the brigade."[21]

Morgan's entire force during the attack amounted to about 500 cavalry troopers, 700 infantry and a battery of artillery. Morgan reported that he

> captured three well-disciplined and well-formed regiments of infantry, with a regiment of cavalry, and took two rifled cannon—the whole encamped on their own ground and in a very strong position—taking about 1,800 prisoners, 1,800 stand of arms, a quantity of ammunition, clothing, quartermaster's stores, and 16 wagons.

Morgan proudly exclaimed:

> Three Federal regimental standards and five cavalry guidons fluttered over my brave column on their return from this expedition. With such troops, victory is enchained to our banners, and the issue of a contest with our Northern opponents, even when they are double our force, no longer doubtful!

To which, Bragg replied:

> To the other brave officers and men composing the expedition the general tenders his cordial thanks and congratulations. He is proud of them, and hails the success achieved by their valor as but the precursor of still greater victories. Each corps engaged in the action will in future bear upon its colors the name of the memorable field.

The Federal flags were presented to Jefferson Davis during his visit to Murfreesboro the following week.[22]

The effect of the victory at Hartsville boosted the morale of the common soldier in Bragg's army. William Thompson, 16th Tennessee Infantry, while encamped near Murfreesboro wrote his sister on December 11 that Morgan captured 2,000 men: "Our cavalry seemed to be playing the wild with the Yanks.... I think the invaders will never flaunt his banners through our quiet valleys & over our green mountain tops." The Confederate victory at Hartsville showed the value of Confederate cavalry acting independently and increased the expectations of the upcoming December raids of Earl Van Dorn, Forrest and Morgan. Bragg seeking a way to damage Rosecrans' army ordered Morgan: "You will assail his guards where your relative force will justify it; capture and destroy his trains; burn his bridges, depots, trestle-work, &c. In fine, harass him in every conceivable way in your power." The Confederate army needed the successes that Forrest and Morgan could achieve. This was true not only in Tennessee. Pemberton's army in Mississippi felt the pressure of Grant's Union advance toward Vicksburg and the Confederate cavalry needed to bring relief from the Federal troops. As a result, three Confederate cavalry expeditions began in December. Joseph Johnston wrote: "Two thousand cavalry will be sent to break up the Louisville and Nashville Railroad, and 4,000 will be employed in the same way in West Tennessee and Northern Mississippi." The latter included Earl Van

Dorn who would lead a large cavalry force to attack Grant's communications in Mississippi and Tennessee. As Morgan prepared for his raid, Brigadier General John Pegram's cavalry brigade (1st Georgia, 1st Louisiana, 1st Tennessee and 2nd Tennessee cavalries) moved into position to take his place in the Confederate line near Murfreesboro. On December 10, Wheeler's cavalry, four brigades strong, remained with Bragg's army with about 7,600 officers and men.[23]

In the aftermath of the affair at Hartsville, Rosecrans accepted the defeat, and initially thought the recent attacks on the forage trains and the action at Hartsville signaled a general Confederate offensive. Rumors were rampant that Kirby Smith had a large infantry force at Lebanon. He soon realized these were just opportunistic attacks, but Morgan's attack caused the Federal commanders "to see Confederates everywhere." The success at Hartsville reinforced Rosecrans' disadvantage in regard to cavalry. In a message to Halleck, Rosecrans said: "Our great difficulties will come from their numerous cavalry harassing us and cutting off our forage parties and trains. I am arming our cavalry, who are not more than one-fourth of their effective force, and much cowed from that fact and want of arms."[24]

General John Pegram, cavalry brigade commander, Army of Tennessee (Library of Congress).

Skirmishes Continue, Stanley Concentrates His Cavalry

After having success on the Union forage train on December 6, Wheeler again attacked a foraging expedition of Colonel Stanley Matthews brigade (35th Indiana, 51st Ohio, 8th Kentucky, 21st Kentucky, and Swallow's artillery) on December 9 at La Vergne. Details are sketchy about this skirmish, but the Union commanders estimated six regiments of Wheeler's cavalry, totaling 1,500 men, attacked the Union foraging party in a dismounted attack. The attack on the forge train began with skirmishing at the rear and soon the front of the train was attacked. George Swallow's 7th Indiana Artillery and a company of Union skirmishers acted quickly and prevented Wheeler's troopers from a successful attack on the front of the train. The casualties for either side were not recorded, but Matthews described the fight as a "sharp skirmish" and the Confederates recorded this as a battle and not a skirmish. Matthews lost "quite a number killed and wounded," but none of the wagons containing the forage were lost in the fight. Unofficially the Union commander recorded losses of five killed, twenty-nine wounded and five prisoners. Matthews also reported the Confederate cavalry in the fight carried Enfield muskets and navy revolvers. An informal Confederate report revealed "8 killed upon the field ... a large number of wounded." Mathews had a hard fight, and he was thrown from his horse and received a wound to his face during the skirmish.[25]

Also, on December 9, Brigadier General John Wharton's cavalry clashed with the 8th Kansas Infantry while on reconnaissance near Franklin. Wharton patrolled the area and just a few days before successfully preventing the construction of a bridge over Mill Creek, "a small and sinuous stream, with bluffy banks, and skirted with thin canebrakes, formed a good natural fosse in front." The two forces skirmished near Brentwood, Tennessee, and though both commanders reported the skirmish, there was very little similarity in the reports. Both commanders claimed having the advantage at the end of the day during this minor skirmish.[26]

After Morgan's victory at Hartsville and the other clashes with Southern cavalry, Rosecrans and Stanley insisted on more cavalry. Rosecrans requested the 7th Michigan Cavalry be sent to Nashville, but the regiment was promised to the Army of the Potomac instead. Next, Rosecrans requested more cavalry regiments from the Department of the Ohio. In response, General Horatio Wright, commanding the Department of Ohio, told Rosecrans a Tennessee cavalry regiment was awaiting transportation to Nashville, but the regiment needed weapons and horse equipment which continued to be a problem for both cavalries. Rosecrans' continuous requests for more troops and equipment resulted in a terse response from P. H. Watson, Assistant Secretary of War:

> You have recently had 4,000 sets of horse equipments, 3,600 carbines and Colt's revolving rifles, with all the necessary appurtenances, and all the swords and pistols for which you have called. Lately you have received a far larger proportion of cavalry arms than any other commander. Which of your cavalry regiments are insufficiently armed?

Rosecrans graciously responded about the situation of his cavalry:

> Three thousand and thirty-eight cavalry present; 1,496 absent; total, 4,534; 1,996 carbines; 2,554 pistols. Exclusive of Tennessee and Anderson Guard, now leaving Louisville, 1,516; Camp Dennison, 717; here, 650; total, 2,883. Total to be armed, 7,417. Carbines in hands of cavalry, 2,496; received this day, 3,600; total, 6,096; deficit, 1,321, supposing absentees return. Effective cavalry strength present December 4, 3,810, exclusive of the Tennessee and Anderson Guard, now coming down. You must remember that the first arms so kindly sent me by the Secretary of War went to cavalry in Mississippi.[27]

Reconnaissance and Skirmishes at Franklin

Since David Stanley's arrival to the Army of the Cumberland, he spent his time preparing to make changes to the Union cavalry. Stanley knew what he needed to do about the cavalry, but he was initially blocked by infantry officers who did not want to give up the cavalry which had been assigned to them. If the Union cavalry was going to be successful, it needed to act cohesively under the command of the chief of cavalry and not scattered in small units. The resolution to this impasse came when Rosecrans agreed with Stanley's plan. In addition to his regiments at Nashville, Stanley had been promised the 15th Pennsylvania, 1st Tennessee and 2nd Tennessee cavalries and he planned to form three brigades. During the month, Stanley rode with his command and assessed its ability. He concluded:

> Our cavalry had been poorly instructed and depended upon their carbines instead of the saber. I insisted on the later. I sent grindstones and had the sabers sharpened, each squadron being provided with the means for this work. This soon gave confidence to our men, and the opportunity was only lacking to show their superiority over the enemy.[28]

Stanley, an experienced cavalryman, recognized he faced large concentrations of enemy cavalry and the only way to meet this threat was to concentrate his own regiments. He wanted his cavalry to operate at brigade strength. One of the first efforts of Stanley's command began on December 11. In light of Morgan's recent raid of Hartsville, Stanley, with a considerable force, launched a large reconnaissance of his own and prepared to meet cavalry with cavalry. The intent of the mission was reconnaissance, and also the destruction of Confederate supply trains that routinely moved along the road between Brentwood and Murfreesboro.[29]

Stanley rode south out of Nashville ten miles toward Brentwood with much of the Edward McCook's First Brigade of Union cavalry (3rd Kentucky, 4th Michigan, and 7th Pennsylvania) along with the 5th Tennessee Cavalry. Once the column reached Brentwood without incident, it headed east on the Wilson Pike toward Murfreesboro. After riding two miles, the Union cavalry met enemy pickets and then the full strength of Colonel Baxter Smith's 4th Tennessee Cavalry (CSA) of General John Wharton's brigade. Stanley drove Smith's cavalry about two miles and decided to continue on his way toward Murfreesboro; but soon found Smith's regiment dismounted and prepared to make a stand. As Stanley advanced upon the outnumbered 4th Tennessee, it again retreated. Stanley bivouacked for the evening, but pickets exchanged gunfire throughout the night.[30]

The next morning came early for Edward McCook's brigade, which rode for Franklin at 4:00 a.m. and encountered enemy pickets about a mile and a half east of the town. The Federal cavalry drove them toward the town and found a concentration of Wharton's cavalry along the bank of the Harpeth River centered near a mill and a house. After the running fight on the previous day, Wharton placed 400 troopers at Franklin to meet the Union threat. The Confederate cavalry was promised infantry reinforcements but these did not reach Wharton's position in time for the fight. McCook ordered the 4th Michigan and the 7th Pennsylvania to dismount and move forward while the remainder of his brigade rode to the rear of the enemy. A stiff fight resulted but the Confederates gave way under the pressure of the McCook's brigade. Wharton lamented Smith's force at Franklin was outnumbered 5 to 1 and he was forced to withdraw until Brigadier General Patrick Cleburne's infantry could be

Colonel Baxter Smith, 4th Tennessee Cavalry—Battled Edward McCook's cavalry on December 12, 1862, at Franklin, Tennessee.

moved forward to defend the town. Stanley claimed four enemies killed, nine more wounded, and eleven prisoners; and one Union trooper mortally wounded and four horses killed. Wharton recorded he had three men killed and six wounded. Wharton also noted: "Colonel Smith lost one of his most valuable officers." Wharton dispatched the 8th Texas Cavalry to Franklin on December 11 to support Smith, but the size of Union force precluded any intervention from the Texans. Stanley initially planned to burn the grain mill which the enemy defended but decided it could result in a fire in the town. Instead, his troopers destroyed the mill equipment and confiscated four wagons of flour and ten horses. He also destroyed a wagon full of brandy and whiskey intended for the Confederate Army. Stanley gave credit for most of the fighting to the 7th Pennsylvania Cavalry and exclaimed "I am happy to be able to report that my men behaved well."[31]

This engagement did not make up for Union losses from Morgan's raid at Hartsville, but it was a first step in gaining the offensive. "It was a handsome little affair," noted historian Larry Daniel. Significant was the use of new technologically superior weapons, new troops and an experienced, professional commander. A member of the 4th Michigan proudly wrote home describing the Colt revolving rifles as "the best gun in the world." These three factors were important as the Union cavalry struggled to gain equality on the field with the Confederate cavalry. On the Confederate side, John Wharton was concerned about the vulnerable position of his cavalry at Franklin and called upon the Confederate infantry to support his position. The mill at Franklin was the only important military reason to protect Franklin and Wharton asked for permission to move his men closer to Nolensville and the main body of the army as the Union forces became more aggressive.[32]

At Murfreesboro, the atmosphere around the Confederate army remained confident. Confederate President Jefferson Davis arrived there on December 12 to discuss strategy, bolster morale, and ascertain for himself the state of Bragg's army. Davis concurred with Johnston's plan to unleash the Confederate cavalry on the rear of the Union armies pressing southward. He also felt Bragg was successful in keeping Rosecrans bottled up at Nashville, but Pemberton's troops in Mississippi caused him the most concern. Grant steadily pushed southward and threatened Pemberton in Mississippi. As a result, Carter Stevenson's division, from Kirby Smith's corps, was ordered to move from Middle Tennessee to join Pemberton's forces in Mississippi, beginning December 18; but the concerns of the citizens in northern Alabama were also on Davis's mind. Those citizens loyal to the South felt the heel of the Federal boot during the previous summer and desired more protection from the advance of the Union army into Alabama should Bragg retreat. Davis wrote: "The feeling in East Tennessee and North Alabama is far from what we desire. There is some hostility, and much want of confidence in our strength." Davis remained in Murfreesboro for a couple of days discussing the army's strategy and left on December 14.[33]

On the day Stanley began his reconnaissance to Brentwood, December 11, Nathan Bedford Forrest left Columbia, Tennessee, on his raid on Grant's communications in western Tennessee and northern Mississippi. Forrest's independence was demonstrated by his reaction to Bragg sending a lieutenant of artillery to accompany the expedition. When the officer presented his orders to Forrest, he declared that his artillery was under the command of Captain Samuel Freeman and "I don't propose to be interfered with by Bragg." Forrest was determined to act independently and the recognition of this fact probably solidified Wheeler's position and Bragg's determination to send Forrest raiding the rear of the Union armies. So, Wharton held that section of the Confederate line with his brigade upon Forrest's exit. Eleven days later, John Hunt Morgan, began his Christmas Raid into Kentucky (December 22–January 3). Morgan departed somewhat later than Forrest because he was married on December 14. Morgan married the daughter of ex-congressman, Colonel Charles Ready, Jr., of Rutherford County, Tennessee. Martha Ready was described as an ideal symbol of Southern womanhood. Morgan's promotion to the rank of brigadier general was announced just the day before and in attendance at the ceremony were the notable Confederate officers: Bragg, Hardee, Cheatham and Breckinridge, including the headquarters staff. General Leonidas Polk, Episcopal Bishop of the Diocese of Louisiana and the nephew United States President James K. Polk (1845–1849), performed the ceremony. Morgan's command rode to Kentucky on December 22, 1862, on a bright and shinning morning. A review of the troops held the evening before outlined the formality of the raid and the dangerous nature of the expedition. Confederate officers read the orders to all stating some "would find a grave before the expedition was over."[34]

For the common soldier of the Army of Tennessee, the familial bliss of Morgan's marriage caused them to think of their own homes. Alfred Tyler Fielder, 12th Tennessee Infantry, wrote in his diary:

> President Davis is at Murfreesboro and ... reviewed the troops at that place yesterday.... I thought much of home of loved ones and the comforts & pleasures of other days, but they are gone and instead of accompanying my wife to church on Sabbath.... I am on out post duty watching the movements of an inveterate foe who is seeking our destruction.[35]

With Forrest and Wheeler off on raids, the stage was set for the two cavalries that would participate in the upcoming Battle of Stones River—Stanley and Wheeler.

Preparation for the Movement on Murfreesboro

While Rosecrans prepared for the next offensive, the Union troops facing Forrest and Morgan scrambled to prevent wide-scale destruction in Kentucky and western Tennessee, but it did not cause Rosecrans to lose sight of his objective at Murfreesboro. In fact, the removal of these two formidable cavalry brigades proved an opportunity for Rosecrans. The Union commanders also realized the Confederates were concentrating at Murfreesboro, and as a result, planned to raid into the lightly held East Tennessee. General Horatio Wright, commanding the Department of Ohio, and Rosecrans discussed the raid in early December. On December 10, Wright urged Major General Gordon Granger to initiate the raid under command of Brigadier General Samuel Carter. Wright ordered the

General Horatio Wright, commander Department of the Ohio, ordered a raid into East Tennessee to assist with Rosecrans's plans at Murfreesboro (Library of Congress).

destruction of bridges, railroads and Confederate supplies by sending a raiding force of about 1,200 men. Rosecrans desired Carter's raid as a way to reduce the number of Confederate forces he faced, but in Washington, U.S. Representative Horace Maynard expressed additional reasons for the raid. The citizens of East Tennessee "have been ravaged and pillaged, and driven from their homes and imprisoned, both near home and in the far South; their wives and daughters ravished and themselves put to death, under circumstances of cruelty and ignominy." Exhorting Wright to begin Carter's raid, Rosecrans echoed Maynard's analysis. He told Wright he had evidence that East Tennessee "is clear of enemy," because the majority of the Confederate troops from that area were concentrated at Murfreesboro. He urged Wright to send an expedition as soon as possible.[36]

While Forrest and Morgan began their cavalry actions, Earl Van Dorn's cavalry, though not attached to Bragg's command, launched a successful raid on Grant's supply and medical depot at Holly Springs, Mississippi. The Union cavalry in return was not idle. Brigadier General Samuel P. Carter, detached from his career as a naval officer, began his Union cavalry and infantry raid into eastern Tennessee with the intent to support Rosecrans' position in Middle Tennessee. As Confederate reinforcements and supplies moved to Murfreesboro, Carter's expedition intended to destroy the supply depots and transportation centers in east Tennessee. Among the cavalry regiments attached to the expedition were the 2nd Michigan, 9th Pennsylvania, and 7th Ohio cavalries. Carter began his raid on December 20 and it lasted until January 5, 1863.[37]

The removal of these large cavalry forces from the area around Murfreesboro set the stage for the remaining cavalry that would participate in the actions at the Battle of Stones River. Thomas L. Connelly, author of *Autumn of Glory*, wrote of the situation of Bragg's Army at Murfreesboro: "The entire army seemed far too confident." But, rumors circulated that Rosecrans was on the verge of taking offensive action on December 13, and General John Wharton requested a meeting with Leonidas Polk at Murfreesboro to discuss the Federal movements. Wharton wrote: "Colonel [Baxter] Smith writes me from Franklin that a lady, whom he has known for years, and knows to be true, told ... that a great battle would take place in a few days on the Murfreesborough pike, between Nashville and Murfreesborough." But, nothing occurred and the situation remained unchanged when the next day Confederate cavalry attacked a foraging party of the Chicago Board of Trade Artillery capturing five men and as many horses. Negley simply wrote: "Need cavalry vedettes."[38]

Flags of Truce—The 1st Alabama and 4th Michigan

The civility of flags of truce was tested in November and December 1862. Flags of truce were a tricky endeavor during the Civil War. Not surprisingly, lack of attention during the encounters of flags of truce could result in the enemy obtaining important intelligence about the strengths and weaknesses of their opponents. As Rosecrans assumed control of the Army of the Cumberland, he outlined specific standards for the handling of the flags of truce and Bragg had guidelines of his own within the Army of Tennessee. On November 14, General Orders No. 16 outlined these details which included: the bearers of the flag of truce must remain at outposts of the army, the bearer of flag will deliver papers to an officers of equal rank, the bearer of the flag of truce would only advance to the main body of the army while blindfolded, and further conversation among parties was not be allowed.[39]

3. A Decision to Fight

While the instructions seemed to be clear, problems occurred almost immediately. The next day, W. H. Hawkins, 22nd Tennessee Volunteers and acting adjutant of a group of Confederate partisan rangers, was arrested while carrying a flag of truce. He was treated as a captured prisoner and initially sent to the prison-of-war facility at Alton, Illinois, and then transferred to Camp Chase in Ohio. The error was immediately recognized and Ulysses Grant ordered Hawkins released from Alton the next day. By the time the orders reached Alton, Hawkins had already been transferred to Ohio but subsequently Hawkins was released. The arrest caused an outage on the part of Bragg and some of his troops and resulted in a series of communications between the two opposing commanding officers. While Bragg was outraged, Rosecrans claimed ignorance of such a minor event in the army, but he did reply: "The flag must come from the senior officer commanding, and follow the most direct route."[40]

The messages between Bragg and Rosecrans continued into December. On December 15, it was the Union army's turn to be outraged as a number of the 4th Michigan Cavalry were captured by the 1st Alabama Cavalry while they attended a Confederate officer who held a flag of truce. Later the same day, Rosecrans sent a scathing letter to Bragg demanding:

> [A]nother outrage of the grossest character has been perpetrated by your troops, in the presence of your own flag, commanded by a lieutenant-colonel in your service, who but yesterday was courteously received. I cannot believe you had authorized, or will permit to go unpunished or without prompt reparation, such barbarous conduct, hardly paralleled by savages. You cannot restore life to my men who have been inhumanly murdered, but I shall leave to your own head and heart to devise such reparation as is demanded by your own honor and the honor of our common humanity.[41]

Bragg retorted in the same manner, exclaiming that the flag was sent from his lines but the Federals held the flag for hours. Because the Union troops did not appear to accept the flag, the Southern troops just assumed there was, in fact, no flag of truce and acted accordingly. Bragg replied:

> The delay of the flag was caused by the reprehensible and criminal conduct of some of your subordinates, who placed its bearer under arrest, and kept him twenty-four hours before permitting him to return. Upon being finally permitted to leave, he was again arrested, menaced, and insulted by soldiers with drawn weapons at the command of an officer who placed him under strict arrest, notwithstanding the accompanying presence of his flag. The officers most active in perpetrating this outrage gave their names as Capt George [G.] Knox and Lieutenant-Colonel Dickinson, who represented themselves as belonging to the Fourth Michigan Cavalry, a part of which command was near by. The reason assigned for his detention was that they intended making an attack on our pickets, and did not wish them notified.

Colonel Robert Minty, cavalry brigade commander, Army of the Cumberland.

Instead of apologizing to Rosecrans and correcting the situation, Bragg insisted that Rosecrans should apologize and offer reparation for the outrages of the Union troops. Bragg scoffed at the idea that any "truce" existed just because a specific flag of truce was offered by a Confederate officer. Bragg explained a flag of truce offered no immunity from attack for the remainder of the troops in the area. In an interesting twist to the argument, Bragg reasoned that the Union troops accepted the flag of truce, and therefore, it was no longer a Confederate flag, but a Union flag due to its capture. Therefore, the possession of the flag of truce "lost its sanctity by reason of your violence, and you ought to be the last one to seek a refuge beneath its folds."[42]

The Confederate and Union reports are contrary on the details prompting the attack by the 1st Alabama Cavalry. Bragg alleged Hawkins was detained inordinately long, while the Union reports recorded that Hawkins reached the Union lines at 2:00 p.m. with "several citizens and ladies, who desired to go to Nashville." While awaiting word from headquarters, the 1st Alabama attacked, capturing some of the 4th Michigan Cavalry outposts. When the Confederate cavalry withdrew, the Confederate officer went with them and returned the next morning under a new flag truce. At that point, Major General Horatio Van Cleve had him placed under arrest, but he subsequently released him. Colonel Robert Minty reported that twenty-two troopers were on duty at the time of the attack. By the next day, eight troopers returned to camp, and six more were still missing. Minty reported similar casualties on both sides—one killed and one wounded.[43]

In a more reasonable response than the bluster of his earlier reply, Bragg finally admitted that he had ordered an investigation into the matter. He found the 1st Alabama acted without the knowledge that a flag of truce had been offered and had not intended to violate the expectations of the flag of truce. These troopers, instead, had just followed their orders of the day. The 1st Alabama Cavalry had been in the saddle since the morning and found some unsuspecting vedettes. Bragg concluded, "I take pleasure in informing you that I have ordered the men to be returned to your lines, together with their equipments, arms."[44]

While so much time was being spent on how to effectively deal with flags of truce, General George Thomas seemed to have a simple solution: "I request that no more women be sent here for the purpose of passing through the lines. I consider them more insinuating and far more dangerous than men.... I do not believe in flags of truce; therefore, do not permit or receive them." Thomas was probably the most sensible regarding these exchanges and while the matter may seem trivial by today's standards, Colonel W. D. Pickett, Hardee's inspector general, and John Wharton admitted they used a flag of truce to develop General August Willich's position south of Nashville in December. After the ruse, Hardee relocated his headquarters based on the intelligence gathered during this event.[45]

Cavalry Skirmishes through December 25

The numerical advantage of the Confederate cavalry continued to be apparent to all. Forrest rode west and the Union commanders expected Morgan would soon begin his raid into Kentucky. David Stanley distributed his cavalry on the north side of the Cumberland River to monitor Morgan's activities and also sent scouts to Stones River. A demonstration in the direction of Gallatin just prior to Morgan's "Christmas Raid" was detected by the Union troops and Crittenden sent infantry to determine the extent of the threat. Stanley was called upon to furnish cavalry along the advance. He threw out a reconnaissance force toward Rural Hill to the east and formed an arc of vedettes to screen any actions by the enemy. In addition, Robert Minty's brigade provided a screen for an infantry advance the next morning toward Stewarts Ford because Wheeler was known to be in that area. As a result of the reconnaissance to the east, Minty discovered Pegram's cavalry near Rural Hill and a small fight resulted as Minty's cavalry clashed with the Confederate pickets without significant results.[46]

Meanwhile, Wheeler set up an effective picket screen in front of Bragg's army stretching from Rural Hill on the east and to Nolensville Pike on the west, including a line of scouts even farther west to Franklin. Along that arc, Wheeler worked to harass Federal movements, offer reconnaissance, and screen Bragg's movements. Contrary to earlier intelligence that Rosecrans was concentrating his army to advance on Murfreesboro, and perhaps, in a hopeful task, the Confederate cavalry was ordered to determine if Rosecrans was actually evacuating Nashville on December 20. The next day, Wharton sent a resounding negative reply: "On the contrary, the entire force is now on the Nashville side of the river." On December 21, the 4th Michigan Cavalry had another skirmish with Confederates south of Nashville. Captain Frank Mix, commanding two companies, rode on a reconnaissance and escort mission to the junction of the Franklin Pike and Wilson Creek Pike. Mix rode four miles east on the Wilson Creek Pike and encountered two regiments of Negley's infantry, and about thirty troopers of the 5th Kentucky Cavalry (U.S.), and a section of artillery in a battle with Confederate troops. David Stanley, in command of the cavalry on the expedition, ordered Mix to take his troopers and assist the 5th Kentucky Cavalry which battled a group of Confederate cavalry on the left of the pike. Mix joined the Kentuckians who were in an open wooded area firing at Wharton's Confederate cavalry behind a stone wall. Mix's Michigan cavalry had the five-shot Colt revolving carbines and because of the bulkiness of the weapon, dismounted. As Robert Burns, adjutant of the 4th Michigan Cavalry, described that with the new weapons tactics changed, "We have to dismount and play infantry." The combined Union troops still could not dislodge the Confederates behind the wall. Mix concluded to hold the enemy in place with some of his men dismounted and the remainder moved to flank the enemy position. Mix's men charged the position and received a volley, but continued the charge which caused part of the enemy troopers to rapidly retreat with Mix's troopers on their heels. When the mounted cavalry returned, the remainder of the enemy force withdrew, ending the fight.[47]

While the Union cavalry adapted to new weapons, some of the Southern cavalry were armed with shotguns. Some of the Confederate cavalry units were poorly armed, but the constant skirmishing often resulted in improved weapons for the victors. Holman's Tennessee Battalion clashed with Union troops while on a reconnaissance expedition in December. While on a scouting mission, the newly formed battalion quickly became veteranized. Major Daniel Holman found a local guide who led the Southern cavalry close to the Union position near McWhirtersville, just east of Nashville. The Southern cavalry silently crossed Stones River at 2:00 a.m. and the slipped between the Federal pickets and moved

Captain Robert Burns, adjutant 4th Michigan Cavalry—"We have to dismount and play infantry."

past a concentration of enemy infantry. No alarms were sounded as the Union soldiers silently slept in their tents. This was a bold feat of reconnaissance but the strength and position of the Union troops were observed in detail. Just before sunrise, Holman led his troops away from the Union camp and through the cold water of Stones River. Since the Southern cavalry moved past the concentration of Union troops and because it was beginning daylight, the chance of escaping unnoticed was lost. Holman ordered his troopers to surround the Union pickets and demanded their surrender. The surprised pickets refused to surrender and a fight broke out, and Holman's men responded with shotgun fire killing some pickets and sent the others looking for cover.

> Gathering up the improved arms left scattered around, and such horses as were not killed or badly wounded, the battalion re-crossed Stone's River, and moved briskly in the direction of its camps till out of reach of the enemy, who had been thoroughly aroused by the firing, as indicated by the sound of drums and bugles.[48]

Another minor skirmish occurred on December 20 near Brentwood when twenty Confederate cavalry attacked some Union vedettes. The attackers were surprised when a dozen of David Stanley's escort counterattacked and drove them away. Perhaps the most important part of the skirmish was the discovery of the type of armaments of the attackers. "One Springfield rifle and musket (cut short) was captured. The rebels wore our army overcoats; had our knapsacks in use as haversacks."[49]

The skirmishes involving cavalry, particularly John Wharton's cavalry, increased as the Stones River Campaign approached. On December 23, a group of Texas Rangers (8th Texas Cavalry) and 2nd Georgia Cavalry attacked an outpost of Phil Sheridan's troops. Wharton captured fourteen soldiers and left several others dead. The Union commanders complained that the Confederates approached the outpost dressed in Union uniforms while killing one man and capturing nine others. Wharton's cavalry and the infantry of Alexander McCook's wing again skirmished on Christmas day. An infantry brigade commanded by Colonel P. Sidney Post advanced with a 200-wagon forage train southeast from Brentwood. Wharton was also involved in a foraging detail in the same area, and the two forces skirmished throughout the day. The expedition was unpleasant on both commands. Wharton recorded:

> We have been fighting the enemy from sunrise until dark.... The country is very hilly and covered with cedar brakes, which renders it totally unfit for cavalry, and the infantry here has orders to risk nothing. I had 3 men wounded; killed 6 and wounded 14 of the enemy. They thus paid for their forage.

Meanwhile, Post complained of the impracticality of taking a 200-wagon train which extended for four miles on a foraging expedition. He explained the difficulty of protecting such a large target which was vulnerable to enemy attack without a large escort. "[I]t would not be difficult to suddenly attack so long a train and destroy some portion of it, especially while threatening it in the rear, as they did much of the way in today."[50]

Rosecrans Takes the Offensive

On December 24, Rosecrans wired Halleck and announced his plans to immediately attack Bragg. Bragg seemed content to remain on the defensive and settle into winter quarters at Murfreesboro despite the clashes with components of each army. Also, Rosecrans had finally accumulated enough rations and ammunition for a twenty day march which should take him through a reasonable campaign even if Morgan disrupted his supply line in Kentucky. Rosecrans told Halleck his army would begin its advance on Murfreesboro the next day at daylight. Rosecrans wrote: "[I]f they meet us, we shall fight to-morrow; if they wait for us, next day. If we beat them, I shall try to drive them to the wall. The detachment of Forrest to West Tennessee, and of Morgan, will materially aid us in our movement." On December 24, Rosecrans began moving his wings into position for an advance on the Confederate army at Murfreesboro. Delays prevented the advance until December 26, but initial moves revealed a strong Confederate cavalry force, Wharton's, at Franklin and Triune and the majority of Wheeler's cavalry near Stewarts Creek. The initial movements on December 24 found that the Confederate defenders withdrew rather than contest the advance. However, Negley reported: "Rebel cavalry quite numerous and impudent. There was considerable skirmishing on Wilson pike without important results."[51]

Rosecrans took stock of his cavalry and Stanley reported from his headquarters on the Lebanon Pike that he had 203 officers and 4,090 troopers ready for duty. As the advance began Stanley could only move 1,300 of his command while the remainder finished preparations for movement on December 24. The 4th Ohio Cavalry prepared to begin the march the next morning, and William Crane of that regiment recorded in his diary ominously: "It is said that Rosecrans makes a forward movement in the morning with his whole force."[52]

PART TWO: TWO CAVALRIES

4. The Cavalry of the Army of the Cumberland

Perhaps you may hear better results from the operation of the cavalry—Captain Martin Buck

As David Stanley began his march to Murfreesboro he had seven regiments of cavalry on which he could rely to fight—3rd Kentucky, 4th Michigan, 7th Pennsylvania, 1st Ohio, 3rd Ohio, 4th Ohio, 4th U.S. and one section of artillery assigned to his cavalry. In addition, he had only one company of the 2nd Indiana (the remainder captured a few weeks before at Hartsville) and a battalion of the veteran 3rd Indiana. Finally, he had three new regiments that had yet to be tested—the newly arrived 15th Pennsylvania (a regiment about to mutiny), and the Tennessee regiments—the 2nd and 5th Tennessee cavalries. While the 5th Tennessee (1st Middle Tennessee) saw action over the past month, the regiment had many carbines that did not fire.

Stanley faced quite a challenge when he arrived in November. Colonel John Kennett commanded the cavalry division as he had with the Army of the Ohio. Stanley, a professional cavalryman, found his command eager to fight but outmanned by its Confederate counterparts. The Union cavalry had faced skirmishes but had yet to be fully tested on the field of battle. The cavalry under the organization of the Army of the Ohio was dispersed throughout the army under command of specific infantry corps commanders. Colonel Edward McCook had commanded a brigade of cavalry in Thomas L. Crittenden's II Corps made up of three regiments: 2nd Indiana Cavalry, 1st Kentucky Cavalry, 7th Pennsylvania Cavalry, and Battery M of the 4th U.S. Light Artillery. Colonel Lewis Zahm also commanded a cavalry brigade of 5th Kentucky, 3rd Ohio, and 4th Ohio. The 2nd Kentucky Cavalry and 1st Ohio Cavalry served as escorts for the various commanders; and the 4th U.S. Cavalry and the "Anderson Troop" served as escorts for the commanding general. When the cavalry moved from Kentucky to Tennessee, Captain Ebenezer Gay's cavalry brigade remained in Kentucky.

Initially, Stanley reorganized the cavalry regiments into a single division:

Cavalry[1]
Brigadier General David S. Stanley

Cavalry Division
Colonel John Kennett

First Brigade
Colonel Edward McCook–Colonel Robert H. G. Minty
2nd Indiana, Company M, Captain Joseph A. S. Mitchell

3rd Kentucky, Colonel Eli H. Murray
4th Michigan, Lieutenant Colonel William H. Dickinson
7th Pennsylvania, Major John E. Wynkoop

Second Brigade
Colonel Lewis Zahm
1st Ohio, Colonel Minor Millikin
3rd Ohio, Lieutenant Colonel Douglas A. Murray
4th Ohio, Major John L. Pugh

Artillery
1st Ohio, Battery D (section), Lieutenant Nathaniel M. Newell

Unattached
4th U.S. Cavalry, Captain Elmer Otis

Stanley summarized his assessment of the cavalry when he arrived at the Army of Cumberland as neglected without consideration of the value of a fully functioning division. Many of the commanding officers were not always selected based on their ability but rather on their political influence. In addition, the cavalry was parceled out in small units for the sole benefit of individual infantry units without consideration of the use of cavalry for the entire army. This was the model used throughout the Western Theater. Grant did this and Rosecrans also accepted this model when he commanded the Army of the Mississippi. Stanley convinced Rosecrans the cavalry needed to be concentrated and needed to operate in conjunction with the movements of the entire army. Although some infantry commanders objected, Stanley was able to gain control of the cavalry under his command. Stanley's appraisal of the cavalry was accurate and Captain Martin Buck, 1st Ohio Cavalry, agreed in a letter published in the *Highland Weekly News* (Hillsboro, Ohio) where he complained about the actions of the Confederate cavalry and the inaction of the Union cavalry. He wrote: "We need a Morgan or a Forrest at the head of our cavalry. We have a Stanley, now, as our chief, so perhaps you may hear better results from the operation of the cavalry in the future." When Stanley arrived he had 3,038 troopers present for duty and an aggregate total of 4,534 cavalrymen. The 15th Pennsylvania (Anderson) Cavalry which was *en route* as well as the two regiments of Tennessee cavalry added much needed manpower to the division.[2]

Cavalry Division

The cavalry division was commanded by Colonel John Kennett, born in St. Petersburg, Russia, in 1809. He attended Harvard College and returned to Russia after completing his education. Later, he immigrated to Cincinnati where he became a United States citizen. Prior to the war, Kennett co-owned a large tobacco company in Cincinnati. He assisted in the organization of the 4th Ohio Cavalry and served as the first colonel of the regiment. Kennett was appointed commander of the cavalry division on September 5 and he commanded the Federal cavalry during the Battle of Perryville and during the movement to Nashville.[3]

THE FIRST BRIGADE

The 29-year-old Colonel Edward McCook commanded the First Brigade of cavalry under Buell and he continued in that capacity under Rosecrans. Before the war McCook was a lawyer and served in the Kansas Territory legislature. McCook, one of the "Fighting McCook's," a family of a large number Union officers, enlisted without military experience and had risen in rank through his performance in the field. In September 1862, his brigade successfully captured the 3rd Georgia Cavalry near New Haven, Kentucky; and in October McCook led the brigade in the Battle of Perryville. McCook who had recently been thrown from his horse was granted a leave of absence in mid–December and the command of the First Brigade fell to Colonel Robert Minty, 4th Michigan Cavalry. The First Brigade was made up of four regiments: 2nd Indiana, 3rd Kentucky, 4th Michigan, and 7th Pennsylvania.[4]

2nd Indiana Cavalry

The 2nd Indiana Cavalry was the first complete cavalry regiment organized in Indiana in September 1861, and John A. Bridgeland was the first colonel of the regiment. Troopers enlisting in the 2nd Indiana were promised: "Good quarters, a handsome uniform and first rate horse." In addition, those of the regiment were offered a salary of $14-$24 per month. In November 1862, the 2nd Indiana was a battle hardened regiment with service extending to the Battle of Pea Ridge and it had experience sparring with Confederate cavalry in Kentucky and Tennessee. At full strength the regiment contained 1,200 men. On December 7, 1862, John Hunt Morgan's Confederate cavalrymen captured most of the regiment in the attack at Hartsville, Tennessee, despite the notable fighting spirit by the troopers. Only Company M, commanded by Captain Joseph Mitchell, avoided this fate and was available for service in Stanley's cavalry division. Mitchell, a 26 year-old attorney from Goshen, Indiana, was a native of Pennsylvania and had no prior military experience. In mid–December, Mitchell's small command was relegated to courier duty.[5]

In December, over 150 men of the 2nd Indiana Cavalry remained in Louisville awaiting transport to Nashville; but when Morgan captured the regiment, these men remained in Kentucky and would not be transported until January.[6]

3rd Kentucky Cavalry

The 19-year-old Colonel Eli H. Murray commanded the 3rd Kentucky Cavalry. Murray, born into a prosperous family in Cloverport in Breckinridge County, Kentucky, was commissioned major when the regiment was mustered into service. Murray was educated by private tutors and then organized a company of cavalry at the beginning of the Civil War. Murray, though very young, was described as "always cool, self-possessed ... and equal to every emergency."[7]

The regiment was organized in September and October 1861 with the troopers drawn from central Kentucky. The 3rd Kentucky had active service since the fall of 1861 and was involved in a skirmish with Forrest's cavalry at Sacramento, Kentucky, the second day's battle at Shiloh, the siege of Corinth, the Battle of Perryville and the actions in northern Alabama, Tennessee and Kentucky. The regiment also participated in the capture of the 3rd Georgia Cavalry near New Haven. Murray was commissioned colonel August 13, 1862 and commanded the regiment since that time.[8]

4th Michigan Cavalry

The 4th Michigan Cavalry was mustered into service on July 29, 1862, and Colonel Robert Minty commanded the regiment. Minty had been serving as lieutenant colonel of the 3rd Michigan Cavalry. Minty, born in County Mayo, Ireland, on December 4, 1831, son of an English soldier serving in Ireland, did not consider himself an Irishman. Following in his father's footsteps, Minty enlisted as an ensign in the British Army and served five years in the West Indies, Honduras, and the west coast of Africa. Minty's service in the Union Army began when he was commissioned major of the 2nd Michigan Cavalry in 1861. Stanley had great respect for Minty and enjoyed his style of horsemanship, both officers realizing the need to wield the saber when fighting in close quarters with enemy cavalry. Minty's brigade would ultimately be nicknamed the "Sabre Brigade" because of his insistence on the use of this weapon.[9]

The 4th Michigan had traveled to Louisville, Kentucky, after its organization and clashed with Forrest's cavalry near Stanford, and later escorted the infantry to Nashville. While the 4th Michigan was a green regiment, with over 1,200 men and officers on the rolls, the influence of Minty instilled confidence and steadiness to these troopers. Lieutenant Colonel William H. Dickinson commanded the regiment after Minty assumed brigade command.

7th Pennsylvania Cavalry

The 7th Pennsylvania Cavalry was an experienced regiment which was mustered into service during the fall of 1861, and George Wynkoop was appointed as its first colonel. The regiment contained men from various counties in eastern Pennsylvania. Wynkoop, a cavalry officer for more than twenty years, provided the much needed experience to command the regiment. He had served in a three-month regiment prior to the organization of the 7th Pennsylvania Cavalry. Wynkoop's subordinate officer was Lieutenant Colonel William B. Sipes, a newspaper editor from Philadelphia. In December 1862, George Wynkoop was away from his regiment accompanying the remains of his son being transported to Pennsylvania for burial. Sipes temporarily assumed command of the regiment as it became part of the Army of the Cumberland. Sipes would permanently assume command of the regiment in April 1863 when Wynkoop resigned due to disability.[10]

The regiment under Buell's command had previously been assigned to duty primarily in central Tennessee. The duties of the 7th Pennsylvania included heavy skirmishing with Forrest's and Morgan's Confederate cavalry, including a particularly bloody affair near Gallatin, Tennessee, where the 7th Pennsylvania lost 140 men killed or wounded. In addition, Major John E. Wynkoop, whose brother, Battalion Adjutant Nicholas Wynkoop was killed in action at Gallatin, led the First Battalion during the Battle of Perryville where the regiment recorded seven casualties. Once Rosecrans gained command of the Army of the Cumberland, he told battalion commander Major William H. Jennings that the 7th Pennsylvania was the "best regiment" in the service of the United States.[11]

THE SECOND BRIGADE

Colonel Lewis Zahm commanded the Second Brigade. Zahm, born in Bavaria on August 7, 1820, came to America with his two sisters and travelled to Ohio where his brother lived. When the Civil War began, he was urged to raise a regiment of cavalry which he did after some deliberation and became the first colonel of the 3rd Ohio Cavalry which was mustered into service in September 1861. Lewis Zahm was a sincere, conscientious and capable commander; and he was described as an "indefatigable correspondent, bombarding everyone in authority" to get the support he needed for his troops.

The Second Brigade consisted of three regiments of cavalry and a section of artillery: 1st Ohio, 3rd Ohio, 4th Ohio cavalries, and 1st Ohio Artillery Battery D (Newell's section).[12]

1st Ohio Cavalry

The 1st Ohio Cavalry, with the majority of troopers being drawn from central Ohio, was one of the most experienced of Stanley's regiments. The regiment saw action in the siege of Corinth, engagements in northern Mississippi and Alabama, and participated in the Battle of Perryville. The first colonel of the regiment was O. P. Ransom, but he resigned in February 1862. Colonel Ransom, a regular army officer, was strict disciplinarian. He had been disparaged by men of the regiment who referred to him as a tyrant, but soon the training and discipline he instilled were recognized and appreciated. After Ransom's resignation, Colonel Minor Millikin assumed command. Millikin came from a prosperous family from southern Ohio, and attended Hanover College and Miami College. He graduated from the Harvard Law School and was an attorney, newspaper editor for the Hamilton *Intelligencer* and farmer before the war.[13]

Colonel Lewis Zahm, cavalry brigade commander (MOLLUS-MASS Civil War Photograph Collection).

Millikin, an outspoken and energetic officer, chafed under the command of Ransom not because of his discipline but due to his excesses. Millikin was commissioned as major when the 1st Ohio was organized as a three-year regiment. When he served as major, he wrote to his commanding officer, "Your habits, Colonel Ransom, your intemperate excesses, are of such a character as to entirely negative my faith in and respect for your other good qualities." Millikin, obviously referring to Ransom's drinking, declared he would prefer charges against his colonel if the problem continued. When Ransom resigned, Millikin was promoted to the command of the regiment. Dissatisfaction resulted in the regiment because the 30-year-old Millikin passed some older and more experienced officers. He also was promoted over the brother of the governor and another who would later be promoted to the rank of brigadier general. Millikin was assigned to the staff of General George Thomas while a board of officers determined his competence to serve as colonel of the 1st Ohio. Millikin satisfied the board, retained command of the regiment and was in the saddle when Stanley arrived.[14]

3rd Ohio Cavalry

The 3rd Ohio Cavalry recruited troopers from northern Ohio, and was also an experienced regiment. The 3rd Ohio arrived at Shiloh on the second day of the battle, participated in the siege of Corinth, served in northern Alabama, sparred with Confederate cavalry in Tennessee and Kentucky, and participated in the Battle of Perryville. When fully mustered, 1,200 men made up the regiment, which "wanted to get at it, get it done, and get home again." The first colonel of the regiment was Colonel Lewis Zahm who assumed brigade command in the fall of 1862. Next, Lieutenant Colonel Douglas A. Murray commanded the regiment. Murray, a Scotsman, was an experienced cavalryman and had been promoted from the 2nd U.S. Cavalry. Murray's experience in the regular cavalry made him the ideal choice for command of the regiment and he began training the volunteers in the skills needed to fight in the war. Sergeant Thomas Crofts recalled Murray's "very peculiar brogue, rolling his rs in a wonderful fashion."[15]

4th Ohio Cavalry

The 4th Ohio Cavalry was recruited from various locations across the state, including Hamilton, Dayton, Lebanon, South Charleston, Ironton, Lima and St. Mary's, but primarily Cincinnati. The 4th Ohio was also an experienced regiment, being mustered into service in the fall of 1861. Like other cavalry regiments in the division, it had seen action in various engagements in Kentucky, Tennessee and Alabama. Colonel John Kennett was instrumental in its organization, and when Kennett was promoted to command the cavalry division, Lieutenant Colonel Henry W. Burdsall assumed command of the regiment. Burdsall resigned the day before Stanley arrived in Nashville and Major John Pugh, a 29-year-old Madison, Indiana native, commanded the regiment through the upcoming months.[16]

In December the regiment was still 186 men short, because these troopers who had been captured at Ashland, Kentucky, by John Hunt Morgan still awaited exchange. As the Stones River Campaign began, the 4th Ohio was in command crisis. The week before the advance, officers were subpoenaed to testify in the court martial of Major Pugh for disobedience of orders and cowardice for actions taken the prior summer.[17]

Lt. Colonel Douglas Murray, 3rd Ohio Cavalry.

Newell's Section—1st Ohio, Battery D

The artillery assigned to the cavalry division was the 1st Ohio, Battery D (section) commanded by Lieutenant Nathaniel M. Newell. The main battery was captured in Munfordville, Kentucky, on September 17, 1862; but Newell's section escaped that dubious honor because it was attached to Brigadier General James S. Jackson's Tenth Division. Newell's section saw action at the Battle of Shiloh, in the siege of Corinth, northern Alabama, Tennessee and the Battle of Perryville.[18]

The battery was mustered into three-year's service in October 1861 under the command of

Colonel James Barnett, who served as Rosecrans' chief of artillery. Newell's section contained two 3-inch rifled cannon which were noted for exceptional accuracy. The artillerymen proudly claimed the cannon could hit the end of a flour barrel at any distance less than a mile.[19]

4th U.S. Cavalry

The final cavalry regiment that was attached to army headquarters was the 4th U.S. Cavalry, commanded by Captain Elmer Otis. The 32-year-old Otis, a West Point graduate in 1853, was a professional soldier and commanded an expert regiment of cavalry. He had experience on the frontier, similar to Stanley's experience, prior to the war. Otis was promoted to the rank of captain in May 1861 and had commanded the 4th U.S. Cavalry thus far in the war. This professional regiment had seen extensive service in Missouri, Fort Donelson, New Madrid, Shiloh, and Perryville.[20]

THE UNION RESERVE BRIGADE

By December 25, Stanley and Rosecrans successfully added three new regiments of cavalry—15th Pennsylvania Cavalry, 5th Tennessee (1st Middle Tennessee) Cavalry, and 2nd (2nd East) Tennessee Cavalry. A battalion of the 3rd Indiana was also loosely assigned to this brigade. At the beginning of the war, Tennessee regiments carried designations from the part of the state where they were organized, e.g., East Tennessee, Middle Tennessee, West Tennessee. Eventually these geographic designations were dropped, but at this point in the war they were still used. The 2nd East Tennessee Cavalry would be renamed the 2nd Tennessee Cavalry and the 1st Middle Tennessee Cavalry would be renamed the 5th Tennessee Cavalry.

While the 15th Pennsylvania Cavalry would not arrive until Christmas, the three new cavalry regiments, although very inexperienced, did add important numbers of men to fill the ranks of the Union cavalry. Stanley and Rosecrans concluded to add additional cavalry regiments. By December 25, the Army of the Cumberland would have ten regiments of cavalry plus the 4th U.S. Cavalry which was attached to army headquarters and Stanley formed three brigades. The First Brigade was initially commanded by Edward McCook and by mid–December, the highly regarded, Robert Minty assumed command of the brigade in McCook's absence. The capable Lewis Zahm commanded the Second Brigade and David Stanley assumed direct command of the greenest of the troops in the Reserve Brigade.[21]

Reserve Cavalry

3rd Indiana (four companies), Major Robert Klein
15th Pennsylvania, Major Adolph G. Rosengarten, Major Frank B. Ward
1st Middle (5th) Tennessee, Colonel William B. Stokes
2nd East (2nd) Tennessee, Colonel Daniel M. Ray

3rd Indiana Cavalry

The 3rd Indiana Cavalry's unique organization resulted in four companies (G–K), the West Battalion, being assigned to the Army of the Cumberland while six companies served in the Army of the Potomac. The companies assigned to the Army of the Cumberland were organized after the first six companies had been sent to fight in the east.

Major Robert Klein (center, in chair), 3rd Indiana Cavalry (Library of Congress).

These four companies performed escort, courier and provost duty until they were formed into an independent cavalry battalion commanded by Major Robert Klein who had served as captain of Company K. The battalion also saw action during the Perryville Campaign while protecting the army's supply train and served during the advance of Buell's army to Nashville. The very capable 26-year-old, German-born and ex–Prussian soldier, Klein was a resident of Switzerland County, Indiana, before the war.[22]

2nd Tennessee Cavalry (2nd East Tennessee)

The 2nd Tennessee Cavalry was organized in eastern Tennessee and began service in September 1862, and the regiment had little combat experience by November 1862. The regiment participated in the Union retreat from Cumberland Gap to Greensburg, Kentucky, and then served about a month in the Kanawha Valley before being moved to Nashville. Colonel Daniel M. Ray commanded the regiment. The 29-year-old Ray was a North Carolina native and the son of a farmer. He resided in Tennessee and taught school for three years prior to the war. Ray served in the 3rd Tennessee Infantry before the 2nd Tennessee Cavalry was organized.[23]

The 2nd Tennessee Cavalry was shuttled from place to place in November and had difficulty in making a complete organization. On November 4, the 2nd Tennessee Cavalry was in Bowling Green, Kentucky, and then it moved to Cincinnati, and then back to Louisville where it received its horses and equipment. While in Louisville an epidemic of measles, a deadly disease in the Civil War, broke out within the regiment and several members died as a result. Daniel Ray's cavalry finally arrived in Nashville on December

Company D, 2nd Tennessee Cavalry. The regiment had fewer than the required companies and was yet to be formally organized (Tennessee State Library and Archives).

24 after a whirlwind of movements over the past few months, and was hardly prepared for the fighting which would begin only two days after its arrival. The command of the regiment was also in transition. In December, Lieutenant Colonel William R. Cook was listed as the commander of the regiment in some records but during the battle Daniel Ray was officially recognized as the commander of the regiment. In fact, the regiment had less than a full complement of companies and would not be formally mustered into service until after the battle on January 26, 1863.[24]

5th Tennessee Cavalry (1st Middle Tennessee)

The 5th Tennessee Cavalry had been mustered into service as the 1st Middle Tennessee Cavalry on July 15, 1862, under the command of Colonel William B. Stokes. The 48-year-old Stokes was a farmer and had served in the house and senate in the Tennessee General

Colonel William B. Stokes, 5th Tennessee Cavalry. More than half of his Merrill carbines would not fire on December 24 (Library of Congress).

Assembly prior to the war. Previously, Stokes had served for a short time as a major in the Tennessee volunteer infantry. The 5th Tennessee Cavalry had been assigned to the Union garrison at Nashville until Stanley added the regiment to the Reserve Brigade. The regiment saw action against Forrest's cavalry on November 5 near Franklin. The 5th Tennessee, which as the war progressed would gain a reputation as regiment with discipline problems, generally performed reconnaissance but had little combat experience except in skirmishes at Nashville and Kinderhook.[25]

About 470 men of this regiment were mounted and ready for duty in mid–December. The 5th Tennessee Cavalry was a Union cavalry regiment unhappy with its armaments as the advance on Murfreesboro began. Colonel Stokes wrote to John Kennett on December 24 that his regiment was armed with Merrill carbines, and over half of the weapons that were tested would not even fire. Just two days before the action around Murfreesboro, the regiment had totally unreliable weapons.[26]

15th Pennsylvania Cavalry

The highly anticipated 15th Pennsylvania Cavalry was requested for service in the Army of the Cumberland and permission had been granted for the regiment to be transported to Nashville. This cavalry regiment was originally organized as an independent cavalry company (or troop) attached to army headquarters by Brigadier General Robert Anderson. The troop was recruited in the fall of 1861 and organized at Carlisle Barracks, Pennsylvania under command of Captain William J. Palmer. The troop moved to Louisville in December 1861 and moved with Buell's army during the Battle of Shiloh. The troop performed its assigned duty, primarily as dispatch carriers and scouts with high recommendations from the commanding general. In July 1862, permission was given to raise three more companies, but the order was changed to raise an entire regiment. The name was changed from the Anderson Troop to the Anderson Cavalry and subsequently changed to the 15th Pennsylvania Cavalry with 1,200 troopers when the regiment was assigned duty with the Army of the Cumberland.[27]

The 27-year-old William J. Palmer, a native of Delaware, was the commanding officer of the regiment. Palmer served as secretary and treasurer of the Westmoreland Coal Company before he took the post as secretary to John Edgar Thompson, president of the Pennsylvania Coal Company. Unfortunately, he was captured the day after the Battle of Antietam and would remain a prisoner of war until January 1863. The newly expanded regiment was assigned combat duty instead of courier duty, and it had just lost its commander. This combination of factors would make the 15th Pennsylvania's inclusion into the cavalry division difficult one.[28]

David S. Stanley and the Cavalry

For the first few weeks after Stanley's arrival in Tennessee, he continued training his cavalry and ensuring it was supplied with horses and arms. His cavalry scouted, guarded supply trains, screened for the infantry and struck where it could find an advantage against the Confederates. Stanley also waited impatiently for the arrival of the 15th Pennsylvania Cavalry which had been due weeks ago.

David Stanley was a professional soldier. He had a productive experience at West Point and made many important contacts and relationships which were important to his career in the army. Stanley also met a life-long friend on his way to West Point. As Stanley traveled to Cleveland on his initial trip to West Point he rode with a lovely young woman and a "little dapper, rather dandified young man." The young man happened to be Philip Sheridan, "small and red faced, long black wavy hair, bright eyes, very animated and neatly dressed in a brown broadcloth sack suit." Stanley recorded that once Sheridan reached West Point, his suit was replaced with a brown linen jacket and his locks were removed revealing a rather "insignificant" looking person. For Stanley, this new appearance meant nothing because Sheridan was a "good fellow and he and I remained friends until his death."

Sheridan also remembered his first encounter with David Stanley and recalled their friendship increased while on the steamship crossing Lake Erie. Sheridan recalled, "I found out that he had no 'Monroe shoes,' so I deemed myself just that much ahead of my companion, although my shoes might not conform exactly to regulations in Eastern style and finish." When the war began Stanley turned down a commission in the Confederate Army and later led troops during the Wilson's Creek Campaign, Siege of New Madrid and Island Number 10, Siege of Corinth, the Battle of Iuka, and the Battle of Corinth. He was commissioned a brigadier general in September 1861 and successfully led infantry divisions thus far in the war.[29]

When Stanley arrived at the Army of the Cumberland, a correspondent of the *Cincinnati Commercial Newspaper* and member of Rosecrans' staff, William D. Bickham, described him as a "man of sanguine nervous temperament, of vehement and fiery spirit, with blazing blue eyes and a lithe figure somewhat above medium stature." Stanley faced many challenges in improving the weak Union cavalry to meet his formidable adversaries. Upon his arrival, Stanley assessed the poor organization of the cavalry and gained Rosecrans' support to improve his new command. Stanley declared, "I soon had three pretty substantial brigades formed and commanded by good officers. We made several sudden marches upon the enemy's outposts, where they were collecting provisions and running mills and we ran the enemy away."[30]

If imitation is the sincerest form of flattery, then the Confederate cavalry had to be pleased with Stanley's decision to reorganize the cavalry of the Army of the Cumberland. The Confederates began organizing their cavalry in brigades early in 1862. Stanley's reorganization of the cavalry was unique to the Federal armies in the west. Stanley served under Rosecrans in Mississippi and that cavalry was organized just as it had been under Buell in the Army of the Ohio. The decision to form a fully operational cavalry division was met with almost universal approval by the cavalrymen under Stanley's command. They felt they had had hard service working for the infantry corps or division commanders and had accomplished very little. Small groups of cavalry had faced large Confederate forces and the Union troopers had no significant offensive role. The situation immediately changed with Stanley's arrival as he and Rosecrans began to develop a plan to build parity with the enemy's horsemen. The Federals needed to be able to mount a force large enough to meet the enemy on equal terms and this could not be accomplished under the old Union organization.

Next, Stanley realized he had some very experienced cavalry regiments mixed with newer regiments, and his entire command had really never participated in a battle as a significant cavalry presence. The Army of the Ohio had really participated in only two battles, Shiloh and Perryville, and in both, the cavalry played a minor offensive role. As the Army of the Cumberland faced Forrest, Wheeler and Morgan, the Union cavalry needed to learn to fight. Stanley assumed command of cavalry that had been utilized according to the policy applied to the eastern theatre. At the beginning of the war, the high command of the Union Army felt that due to the geographic obstacles, cavalry could not be efficiently used and therefore little emphasis was placed on this arm of the service. In addition, it was commonly accepted that a cavalrymen could only be fully trained after two years. Most believed the war would be over in a short period and discounted any efforts for a long-term expansion of the cavalry. This neglect was obvious as Stanley assumed command.[31]

With the increased need for cavalry, training was important. Stanley insisted on the use of the saber as a primary weapon for his troopers. This decision by Stanley has generated numerous comments from historians, some positive, most not. Stanley believed the new volunteers needed as much training as possible. Granted, the cavalry tactics were rapidly changing with the effectiveness of firearms becoming more important. This was still a time of transition for cavalry tactics and Stanley never minimized the importance of firearms for his troopers. He felt the cavalry needed to be trained to be fully capable of utilizing not only pistols, muskets, rifles and carbines, but the saber also. The cavalry in 1862 still charged and in close quarters combat the saber proved to be an effective weapon of the day. The cavalry under Stanley, and fully supported by his experienced brigade commander, Robert Minty, would need to use the saber. Discounting some views of Stanley's over reliance on the saber, Rosecrans and Stanley armed as many troopers as possible with breech loading, revolving and repeating carbines, the new technology in weaponry at the time.[32]

Next, the Union cavalry needed more men, desperately, and also better firearms and good horses. Remarkably, the Union cavalry in Tennessee had many troopers without horses and weapons this late in the war. Stanley convinced Rosecrans, who began sending messages urging Washington to send more men, weapons and horses.

Not only was Rosecrans happy to have the skills of Stanley in charge of the cavalry, so were many in the Union cavalry. W. L. Curry, 1st Ohio Cavalry, wrote,

> General D. S. Stanley, a cavalry officer of long, active service in the regular army, had just been assigned to duty as Chief of the Cavalry, Army of the Cumberland, and as he was very active and aggressive, a long felt want in that arm of the service seemed to have been supplied. He was always on the alert for duty required of his command, and he did not propose to settle down and wait for the enemy to come to him, but went after the enemy, and usually found him, as Forrest, Wheeler and Morgan were tireless riders and were making raids on the railroads almost daily.[33]

Cavalry Tactics

In December 1862, both the Union and Confederate cavalries were in a time of transition and both sides had several concerns. The leaders within the both cavalries had yet to be tried in many cases. In addition, the commanders of the division, brigades and regiments needed to be examined and changed in some cases. Stanley developed a new way of organizing the cavalry and received more technologically superior weapons, including, the five-shot Colt revolving carbine. Only a few of Union regiments had this weapon in December 1862, but most of the cavalry had breech loading carbines. Better training for the cavalry was needed in many areas, and the differences between the tactics used by Confederate and Union cavalries would become evident as the war carried into 1863. And, though there were different approaches to the roles of Union and Confederate cavalry, the duties of cavalry in the Civil War fell into six main areas: reconnaissance, screening, covering (flank security), attack, headquarters duties, and interdiction (raids). Each of these duties would be executed during the Battle of Stones River.[34]

Arguably the cavalry tactics in the United States Civil War had little similarity to the cavalry tactics used in Europe. From the outset, the cavalry in the U.S. Civil War was made up of amateurs and in most cases regiments, brigades and divisions were also commanded successfully by amateurs. In addition, war technology was changing. The fact that muskets and carbines were effective at 500 to 1,000 yards altered the effectiveness of the tactics of the time. The introduction of the Colt revolving rifle, which allowed the five or six shots being fired without reloading, increased the firepower dramatically. Many cavalry regiments, particularly early in the war, went to battle with old-fashioned weapons (shotguns, particularly for Southern cavalry) due to the inability of the quartermasters to provide more modern weapons. As the war developed, the Spencer repeating carbine would be the most effective cavalry carbine, although it remained in short supply throughout the war. Often a regiment used many different types of weapons which caused difficulty in providing and organizing the distribution of ammunition. When the breech-loading carbines or muskets were unavailable, some regiments chose to carry two or three revolvers per man, which increased firepower in close quarters fighting.[35]

In addition, it is somewhat surprising that horses remained in short supply throughout the war. In most cases, Southern troopers were required to provide their own horses, and mounting and remounting both Southern and Northern cavalry would remain a constant problem. The lack of care for horses and training for cavalrymen resulted in increased waste of mounts. Union cavalrymen often carried too much weight and offered improper feed and water rations to their horses. Horses were often used beyond their endurance and needed to be replaced. David Stanley, upon gaining command, sent an order to the cavalry division directing the proper use of horses and noted that one half of the unserviceable horses were cruelly injured by careless troopers riding at "full speed" without cause or consideration for the animals.[36]

Unidentified Union cavalryman with Colt revolver, sabre and carbine (Library of Congress).

Despite these issues, the use of cavalry was very important in the Civil War, but the role of the cavalry would evolve during the war, just as it would for the infantry. Prior to the Civil War, the United States Army had three types of mounted units—cavalry, dragoons and mounted rifles. Historian James A. Schaefer wrote: "[T]he difference among them was more in name and the color of the trim on their uniforms than in function." The distinctive duties of mounted units, which were nominally cavalry and mounted infantry, were to change dramatically in the Civil War. The shock of rapid movement combined with firepower proved to be the greatest advantage of mounted troops. Despite the introduction of new weapons, much of the cavalry actions during the Civil War were confined to raiding and reconnaissance. The mobility of cavalry still allowed for an effective offensive role but not against large numbers of infantry in line of battle without an overwhelming advantage of manpower. Cavalry versus cavalry could battle on equal terms, but cavalry against infantry only worked effectively when the infantry was disorganized, outnumbered or surprised. Both cavalries used mobility to rapidly move a fighting force to a location while the infantry followed. The ability to move rapidly while providing effective firepower allowed the cavalry to screen the movements of infantry and to serve as rearguards; but overall reconnaissance duties and mobility proved the most important assets for cavalry.[37]

The Union and Southern cavalry effectively served as the eyes and ears of their respective armies, but the method of engaging the enemy would be vastly different. The Southern cavalry often discounted the use of the saber on which the Union cavalry would rely heavily upon throughout the end of the war. The Southern cavalry often relied more on the revolver which could deliver several shots without reloading. Confederate cavalry often used 1851 Navy Colt and 1860 Army Colt revolvers, but the Le Mat revolvers (and many others) were common in various units. The Union cavalry was often more balanced in the weapons they carried and had revolvers, carbines, sabers and knives. The most common revolvers for Northern cavalrymen were Remington, Colt, and Starr revolvers. The short-barreled carbines, breech loading or muzzle loading, were easy to handle in the saddle and were generally effective at a minimum of eight hundred yards. Muzzle loading carbines and shotguns were predominant in the Southern cavalry early in the war. The Union cavalry quickly moved to breech loading carbines, and both cavalries used knives. In addition, the Southern cavalry adapted to the role of dismounted troops more quickly and more often than Union cavalry, although, the Union cavalry fought dismounted more as the war continued. With cavalry fighting dismounted, there was an increased need for "horse holders" which reduced firepower, but the accuracy of dismounted cavalrymen often offset the loss in firepower. Generally, one man of a group of four would hold the horses while the other three troopers fought on foot. The increased dismounted fighting also introduced a modified cavalry force, the mounted infantry regiments, although dragoons were common before the war. The formal introduction of mounted infantry for the Union Army was an effective innovation in the Tennessee in 1863, although some criticized this as providing inadequate cavalry and at the same time providing inadequate infantry. While cavalry regiments fought mounted and dismounted, the mounted infantry almost always fought dismounted. The proponents of this type of unit only had to point at Colonel John Wilder's Brigade as a very successful example. In addition, Joseph Wheeler's use of his cavalry resembled mounted infantry due to his reliance on dismounted attacks.[38]

In regard to organization, the Southern cavalry combined the various regiments into brigade and division strength before the Federals. An inherent attraction of cavalry for Confederate troops resulted in a larger body of cavalry by late 1862. The Confederate states recognized the importance of cavalry and accepted it before the Union army in the west. The Union cavalry lagged in organization and size of cavalry by the time of the Stones River Campaign. Historian Lawyn Edwards observed:

> To add to the militia organization, the new Confederate cavalry claimed most of the senior leadership and talent of the old U.S. Cavalry. As their home states seceded from the Union, Southerners in the army resigned their commissions and went home to help the war effort of the states and the Confederacy. Of the five pre-war mounted units, four of the full colonels commanding the regiments went South. Not only was this devastating to the U.S. units, but these officers were educated in and understood cavalry operations as it was.

Even in areas where experienced cavalry officers were present, their impact was diluted because they were distributed though the various units of volunteers where they trained the new recruits.[39]

The Mutiny of the 15th Pennsylvania

On December 24, 1862, the 15th Pennsylvania Cavalry arrived in Nashville for service in the Army of the Cumberland, specifically requested by William Rosecrans. But soon great dissatisfaction arose within the regiment, and the regiment expressed this dissatisfaction by refusing to perform its duty. This highly anticipated regiment arrived in Nashville under a veil of controversy and the events over the next week resulted in one of the largest mutinies in the Union Army during the Civil War. Although there are several accounts of the mutiny, the official version was recorded by Assistant Adjutant General, Major N. H. Davis who investigated the mutiny.

The Anderson Troop was organized in the fall of 1861, commanded by Captain William J. Palmer, to serve as an escort for Brigadier General Robert Anderson. When General Don Carlos Buell assumed command of the Army of the Ohio, he retained the Anderson Troop. This cavalry troop was made up of intelligent men of high character, and the company had proved itself highly efficient at its duties. When permission was granted to raise three additional companies, the response was overwhelming and resulted in greater than 1,000 men volunteering for service. All of the men wishing to enlist, and who met the standards set by Captain Palmer, were allowed to do so, although it was unclear if Palmer had the authority to organize a full cavalry regiment.[40]

Based on the terms of enlistment, the officers were appointed rather than elected by men of the regiment. Most of the officers were to be drawn from the old Anderson Troop and the full complement of officers had yet to be appointed as Lee's army moved northward culminating in the Battle of Antietam. The day after the battle, Captain Palmer was captured by the Confederates and made a prisoner of war. The regiment returned to Carlisle, Pennsylvania, to complete its organization and training while negotiations were made to return Palmer to the regiment. In the meantime, Rosecrans requested this new regiment of cavalry, the 15th Pennsylvania Cavalry, and permission was granted to send it to the Army of the Cumberland. The regiment arrived in Louisville on November 9, 1862, and awaited transportation to Nashville. It was while the regiment remained in Louisville that the dissatisfaction began. While the Pennsylvanians languished awaiting transportation south, the regiment drilled and trained, but Major Davis noted, "The preparations were retarded, discipline lax, and camp or garrison duties more or less neglected from insufficiency of company officers."[41]

With William Palmer in a Confederate prison, the importance of determining officers became imperative. First Lieutenant William Spencer was commissioned lieutenant colonel on October 1, 1862. Additionally two majors were appointed—Adolph G. Rosengarten and Frank B. Ward. Additional officers were appointed but only eleven other officers were commissioned for the twelve company regiment. The regiment began its movement to Nashville on December 8 and reached Bowling Green on December 15. The 15th Pennsylvania Cavalry joined the 4th Tennessee Cavalry escorting a wagon train moving toward Nashville on December 21 and finally reached Nashville on December 24.[42]

When the regiment arrived in Nashville, there were seven regimental officers, twelve officers for the companies and only two-thirds of the non-commissioned officers appointed. The regiment had a list of grievances when it arrived in Nashville and the next day during its first assignment of guarding a supply train, the Confederates attacked. The attack was successfully repulsed but one trooper, Martin Hill, of the 15th Pennsylvania was killed while attempting to chase off the raiders. Major Lewis Wolfley, 3rd Kentucky Cavalry, commanded the defense of the supply train, which was attacked and clearly recognized the regiment's unpreparedness for its duty. Wolfley explained the Confederate cavalry charged the train and nearly cut off Wolfley's 3rd Kentucky battalion. Wolfley discouragingly wrote that the 15th Pennsylvania ran away "at the first shot." Major Davis reported the evening after the first duty in Nashville the men of the regiment concluded that their officers were "inexperienced and incompetent." However, Davis determined the officers of the 15th Pennsylvania compared favorably to officers of others volunteer regiments. Nevertheless, the men decided not to do further duty and they demanded to be disbanded or discharged. The troopers decided to refuse to perform their assigned duty during meetings of the members of the regiment without consulting superior officers.[43]

Quartermaster George Fobes of the 15th Pennsylvania wrote that the mutiny resulted from Palmer's tight control of the regiment. Palmer wanted to "organize, equip, and discipline a regiment" alone. Certainly, when Palmer was captured the regiment was not organized and was "left almost alone." Another of the regiment, James Weir, felt Palmer had a more steady hand on the men and wrote that had Palmer been present, the regiment would not have "this contemptible record." Fobes noted jealousy resulted between the new enlistees and members of the old Anderson Troop. The latter felt, based on their experience, they would receive all the commissions over the new enlistees. Fobes wrote, "Witnessing the rivalry, suffering from the consequent delays and neglect, was it unreasonable that the men began at length to feel that they had been enlisted not for the good of the service, but for the purpose of the furnishing commissions to a body of men who looked upon them as their aristocratic right." Great distrust developed between the old Anderson Troop and the new 15th Pennsylvania Cavalry.[44]

Fobes explained the dissatisfaction continued in Louisville as the old Anderson Troop, which formed Company A of the regiment, received privileges not offered to the new enlistees. The lieutenant colonel of the new regiment was also constantly at odds with the two majors, who in Fobes's opinion diligently tried to get the regiment prepared for its new assignment. Fobes noted many of the problems resulted from the poor command abilities of Lieutenant Colonel Spencer. When on one occasion the 15th Pennsylvania was ordered to ride on an expedition, Fobes, serving as quartermaster, tried for a day to obtain ammunition for the regiment. Spencer only signed the requisition after

Fobes threatened to report the matter to General Stanley. Sergeant Charles M. Betts agreed with Fobes's assessment of Spencer, describing Spencer as a man thoroughly familiar with cavalry, but "lacking the ability to command and shirking the responsibility of decision." James Weir, a diarist, was more kind to Spencer. Weir recorded that Spencer was ill and traveled in an ambulance, but his absence from active duty contributed to the lack of confidence observed in the regiment.[45]

The day after the regiment's first mission at Nashville, many of the troopers stacked their arms and refused to do further duty. Major Davis recorded the dissatisfaction of the regiment which included the understanding that the new enlistees were to form a single battalion for the purpose of being a body guard for Buell. The troopers also complained they had not been properly mustered, the regiment did not have sufficient officers, they were not properly armed, they were assigned duty unsuitable for them, and that they had, in fact, been deceived into enlisting in the regular Union cavalry service. Also, the members of the regiment stated their dissatisfaction was discussed in Louisville, but they were promised their issues would be addressed once they reached the Army of the Cumberland.[46]

Davis determined no deception to entice men to enlist, but the men were told "their duties would be the same as those of the old troop, viz., scouting, secret expeditions, escorts, guards, service of a daring and dashing character, and that they would probably be kept at or about the headquarters of the commanding general, and under his orders." He also found authority was granted to raise the full regiment and that all the men were properly mustered into service with the exception of about twenty men. In addition, the men of regiment were found to have adequate officers, proper arms, equipment and mounts. However, the real rankle came when it was determined the regiment would serve as regular cavalry.[47]

The dissatisfaction within the regiment escalated according to Davis during the movement from Louisville to Nashville, when "squads of the men visited disloyal families, and reported to them their grievances, and exhibited a disposition to refuse or avoid doing a soldier's duty." When instructed by the officers to stop these practices certain individuals replied, "…they dared any general to interfere with their rights; that they had money and influence, which would secure them their rights, discharge, &c." Those at home in Pennsylvania were aware of the situation as many newspapers carried the reports of the mutiny. The *Potter Journal* (Coudersport, Pennsylvania) recorded: "Of the Anderson Troops of Philadelphia, which behaved badly previous to the battle of Murfreesboro, 391 are in the work-house, 103 in prison, and 224 in camp." The 15th Pennsylvania also received a scathing indictment from the *New York Times* which flatly stated if the troopers of the regiment were dissatisfied with its assigned duties and officers, it could be remedied by "being shot to death for cowardice and misconduct." Other soldiers in the army distanced themselves from the mutiny. In a letter written by Sergeant George Garrett, 4th Missouri Cavalry, he wanted to be sure the folks at home knew his regiment was not to be confused with those who mutinied at Stones River.[48]

These events within the 15th Pennsylvania Cavalry all occurred on the eve of the beginning of the Stones River Campaign and when David Stanley ordered the men to duty only 200–300 agreed to service while another 500 remained in Nashville under arrest. Only about a half of a battalion of this regiment would participate in the upcoming battle.

David Stanley faced many challenges within the Union cavalry on the eve of the Battle of Stones River.

5. The Cavalry of the Army of Tennessee

If they get a chance at the Yankees they will make them suffer.—Daily State Sentinel

Facing Stanley's cavalry was Joseph Wheeler with four cavalry brigades, including the one he personally commanded—Buford, Pegram, Wharton and Wheeler. While Stanley had concerns about his cavalry, Wheeler was also greeted with the fact that although he had some very experienced troopers, he also had some green troops and in some cases, he had experienced cavalrymen who had served in battalions that had recently been made part of a new regiment. Finally, Wheeler also had his own share of commanders which had never been under his command and there was much still to be proven by those in his division.

Wheeler's cavalry consisted of a mixture of partisan rangers, "Confederate" regiments, regular state regiments and independent battalions (3–5 companies). The Confederate States of America passed the Partisan Ranger Act in April 1862 to allow irregular units to operate, primarily, behind enemy lines. Henry Clark, governor of North Carolina, wrote of the controversial policy allowing partisan rangers: "[T]he idea of being in a mounted company, independent and on detached service, render that service popular and desirable, while there is but little prospect of their being of much service, unless a few with well-chosen officers and in peculiar localities." While the Confederacy intended to use to partisan rangers behind enemy lines, this policy resulted in such regiments as the 51st Alabama Partisan Rangers which served as a more typical cavalry regiment. However, many Northern sympathizers saw partisan rangers as merely guerrillas whose single purpose was to cause injury and damage to anyone supporting the Union regardless if the target was military or civilian. Wheeler's immediate challenge was to quickly convert his various cavalry units in a cohesive fighting force. These four Confederate cavalry brigades would have important duty over the next ten days.[1]

Wharton's Brigade

14th Alabama Battalion	2nd Georgia
1st Confederate	3rd Georgia
3rd Confederate	4th Tennessee
8th Confederate	Davis' Tennessee Battalion
8th Texas	Murray's Tennessee Regiment
	White's Tennessee Battery

John Austin Wharton was Wheeler's most aggressive brigade commander. He was born a short distance from Nashville on July 3, 1828, when his parents were on a shopping trip to buy furnishings for their plantation in Texas. He was the only son of William H. and Saran Ann Wharton. William Wharton was an attorney who moved to Texas in 1827, and his son, John Wharton, grew up on a plantation, Eagle Island, between the Brazos River and Oyster Creek and only twelve miles from the Gulf of Mexico. He was privately educated in the home of his uncle, and when he was fifteen he went to Columbia, South Carolina, to complete his education, which he did at the age of twenty. While at Columbia, Wharton read law under William C. Preston, a noted South Carolina attorney. Wharton's support of states' rights was solidified during his time in that state and while he was there he determined his political position as the Civil War approached. While studying law, John A. Wharton met and in 1848 married Penelope Johnson, the only daughter of the governor of South Carolina. Wharton and his bride moved to Texas where Wharton completed his legal training and became an attorney. He was active in the secession movement, and he was credited with introducing the resolution for the secession of Texas.[2]

Wharton enlisted in the 8th Texas Cavalry, nicknamed Terry's Texas Rangers, and was elected captain of a company. The regiment moved to Bowling Green, Kentucky, after its organization and Wharton fell ill to a severe case of measles. When Colonel B. F. Terry was killed in Kentucky, Wharton became colonel of the regiment. Wharton received a severe wound to his leg at the Battle of Shiloh and was again wounded in the fighting at Murfreesboro in July 1862. Wharton gained brigade command during the Perryville Campaign and proved to be a proficient cavalry commander.[3]

14th Alabama Battalion

The 14th Alabama Battalion was organized as a unit of partisan rangers in September 1862, although some records show the date as December. James Chappell Malone's 14th Alabama Battalion would be the core of the 9th Alabama Cavalry when it was organized in May 1863.[4]

Lieutenant Colonel James Chappell Malone, Jr., born May 21, 1837, in Athens, commanded the battalion in December 1862 and he was an attorney in Nashville prior to war. He completed his education at the University of Virginia and Cumberland University of Law. He enlisted in the 1st Tennessee Infantry at the beginning of the war and was elected second lieutenant. He left the infantry regiment and organized a company of cavalry, was elected major, and subsequently lieutenant colonel, of the 14th Alabama Battalion. The battalion would be consolidated with the 19th Alabama Battalion in 1863 to form a full cavalry regiment.[5]

1st Confederate Cavalry

The 1st Confederate Cavalry reflected the composition of many of the "Confederate" regiments. The Confederate States did not have regular army troops like the Union Army. Instead, regiments designated as Confederate consisted of regiments made up of troops from various states. The 1st Confederate Cavalry had Major H. C. King's western Kentucky battalion (known as King's battalion, 6th Confederate Cavalry, or Kentucky Mounted Rangers) as its core and it was supplemented with four Tennessee companies and two Alabama companies. In fact, the 1st Confederate Cavalry had connections with King's Cavalry, Lay's Cavalry, the 6th Confederate, 12th Confederate Cavalry, 16th Confederate, Claiborne's Cavalry, Memphis Mounted Rebels, and Kentucky Mounted Rangers. Various components of the regiment participated in fights at Paris, Tennessee, and Blackland, Alabama. The regiment was formally organized in April 1862 just prior to the Battle of Shiloh. The first officers were appointed by General Albert Sidney Johnston, which resulted in Colonel Thomas Claiborne of Johnston's staff being named commanding officer of the regiment. When elections were held in the fall, the men elected Henry C. King as colonel. King, born in 1821 in Burkesville, Kentucky, attended the University of Alabama and was a pre-war lawyer in Paducah and Memphis. King began the war as captain of a Kentucky company in 21st Tennessee Infantry. The company transferred with King when he formed a cavalry battalion, and became King's Battalion in 1862. The regiment's first duties were reconnaissance and security. The 1st Confederate Cavalry participated in the Perryville Campaign and served on rearguard duty as Bragg's army withdrew to Tennessee. Then the regiment was assigned "outpost and picket duty" on the Confederate left flank after returning to Middle Tennessee. In early December 1862, John T. Cox assumed command of the 1st Confederate Cavalry, which was composed of 313 troopers, but he had two companies which were detached from his command.[6]

Colonel John Threlkeld Cox was born in Washington, D.C., in 1820, son of Colonel John Cox, a merchant and mayor of Georgetown. Cox moved to Warren County, Kentucky, when he married the daughter of a United States senator from Kentucky. Prior to the war Cox was a civil engineer working with the construction of railroads. He enlisted in the Confederate Army as an engineer in 1861 and was promoted to the rank of captain in 1862. John T. Cox was described as having a fair complexion, light hair, blue eyes, and six feet tall. He was promoted to command the 1st Confederate Cavalry on December 17, 1862.[7]

3RD CONFEDERATE CAVALRY

The 3rd Confederate Cavalry was organized in the summer of 1862 and Estes's 11th Alabama Cavalry and Howard's Battalion were combined to form the regiment. Later, two companies of Georgia and one company of Tennessee troopers were added to the other Alabama companies. The combination provided enough men to form a regiment. Many of the troopers had experience in eastern Tennessee in E. Kirby Smith's command. One of the early skirmishes by the 3rd Confederate included a fight near Battle Creek, Tennessee, in August 1862. By December the regiment contained about 450 troopers present for duty. The first commander of the 3rd Confederate Cavalry was Colonel James R. Howard, and Lieutenant Colonel William N. Estes commanded the regiment in December.[8]

2ND GEORGIA CAVALRY

The 2nd Georgia Cavalry was organized in February 1862 in Albany, Georgia, and the men were drawn from Randolph, Doughtery, Clayton, Marion, Fulton, and Decatur counties. The regiment was initially positioned near Chattanooga and spent the summer skirmishing with Union forces before accompanying Bragg on the Perryville Campaign. Winburn J. Lawton was the first colonel of the regiment—a planter, railroad builder and a state legislator before the war. During the battle at Murfreesboro in July 1862, the regiment participated in Forrest's successful capture of the town from Union troops. The 9th Michigan Infantry served as provost guards in Murfreesboro for Confederate prisoners held in the courthouse, and Forrest assigned the 2nd Georgia to capture the U.S. troops in the courthouse and around the town square. Some 150 prisoners were being held in the jail, some under sentence of death. The circumstances are not clear, with each side blaming the other, but the jail was set afire and the 2nd Georgia spent some time rescuing the prisoners from the flames before going on to capture the courthouse. Lawton resigned in October 1862 and the regiment served as part of John Wharton's brigade, commanded by Lieutenant Colonel James E. Dunlop and Major Francis M. Ison, while the newly appointed colonel of regiment, physician, Charles C. Crews returned to the regiment after being exchanged. Dunlop was referred to as a "steady and efficient officer."[9]

3RD GEORGIA CAVALRY

The 3rd Georgia Cavalry was organized at Athens, Georgia, in the summer of 1862 under the command of Martin Jenkins Crawford. The troopers were from Rabun, Whitfield, and Cherokee counties in Georgia. Edward McCook's Union cavalry brigade surprised and captured the 3rd Georgia at New Haven, Kentucky, in September 1862. Colonel Crawford was court martialed and found guilty of conduct prejudicial to good order and military discipline. He was sentenced to three months suspension of rank and duties. Crawford, born in 1820, was a successful judge and U.S. congressman before the war. About 130 men escaped capture and were present for duty in December 1862 and served under the command Major Robert Thompson.[10]

4TH TENNESSEE CAVALRY (SMITH'S)

The 4th Tennessee Cavalry was not organized as a regiment until after the Perryville Campaign and then it was assigned duty near Franklin. The regiment faced several actions including Stanley's expedition to Franklin in early December. There is often confusion regarding the identity of the 4th Tennessee because there were, at least, three regiments with this name—Starnes (Stearns's) 4th Tennessee, Murray's 4th Tennessee and Smith's 4th Tennessee. Ultimately, Baxter Smith's 4th Tennessee Cavalry was "annulled" and renamed the 8th Tennessee Cavalry in 1863. The troopers from this regiment were drawn from Marshall, Sullivan, Smith, Wilson, Cannon, Rutherford, Hamilton, Fentress, Davidson, DeKalb, Sumner, Knox, and Blount counties. At least part of Smith's regiment had the nickname of the "Hell Roarers." Baxter Smith commanded the 4th Tennessee Cavalry in John Wharton's brigade during the Union advance on Murfreesboro and the battle on December 31 through January 5.[11]

Colonel Baxter Smith, born in 1832, made his home in Gallatin, Tennessee, and he was an attorney and politician before the war. He organized and commanded the regiment at the time of the Battle of Stones River. Smith was originally a captain in was what known as James Bennett's Battalion when it was first mustered into service. Upon the formation of Bennett's Battalion, Smith was elected major and this unit began its service at Bowling Green, Kentucky, and then the regiment moved to Shiloh. After that battle, Smith was ordered to Knoxville to command a battalion which would ultimately be organized into Smith's 4th Tennessee Cavalry as part of Nathan Forrest's brigade. The battalion participated in the battle at Murfreesboro in July 1862 and later in fighting around McMinnville.

The battalion also accompanied Bragg and Smith during the Perryville Campaign and upon its return the regiment was formally organized. So, though the regiment was newly organized just before the Battle of Stones River, it had many experienced troopers and an experienced colonel.[12]

Davis's Tennessee Battalion

Major John R. Davis commanded Davis's Tennessee Battalion. The battalion was made up of four companies with the majority of troopers drawn from Cannon, DeKalb, Rutherford and Wilson counties. The battalion was organized in the fall of 1862 and had initial duty at McMinnville before being attached to Wharton's brigade on December 7. The battalion would participate in the Battle of Stones River as part Wharton's cavalry. Davis's troopers would be consolidated with Baxter Smith's 4th Tennessee Cavalry on January 27, 1863.

4th (Murray's) Tennessee Cavalry Regiment

Murray's 4th Tennessee Cavalry was, yet another, cavalry regiment designated as the 4th Tennessee, as were Smith's 4th Tennessee and Starnes' 4th Tennessee. This regiment was organized in August 1862, and would be disbanded in January 1863 with the various companies being redistributed to other regiments. Initially the regiment was commanded by Colonel John P. Murray, and Willis Scott Bledsoe held the rank of major. During the Battle of Stones River, Bledsoe commanded the regiment because Murray left the regiment to take a position in the Confederate Congress. Bledsoe was an attorney in Jamestown, Tennessee, before his enlistment in the Southern cavalry and his family had prosperous business ventures in Fentress and Overton Counties. Bledsoe, who enlisted at the age of 24 in 1861, had an independent command before his cavalry was merged into Murray's cavalry.[13]

The various companies which made up this unit had extensive experience in the war including, the Battle of Mill Springs, skirmishes in Tennessee and northern Alabama, the Perryville Campaign, and a skirmish at Nolensville on December 12. Upon its organization, Murray's regiment was assigned to Forrest's Brigade and then to Wharton's brigade. There is much confusion about the organization of this regiment and how it is distinguished from Baxter Smith's 4th Tennessee. The Confederate Army attempted to organize two regiments from the troopers in Murray's cavalry and Smith's 4th Tennessee but was unable to find the men to accomplish this. As a result, Murray's cavalry was disbanded in January and four companies from this unit were included in Smith's regiment and Willis Bledsoe was elected major in Smith's regiment.[14]

8th Texas Cavalry—"Terry's Texas Rangers"

The 8th Texas Cavalry was organized in August 1861. The arms of the troopers included a shotgun or carbine, at least one, but commonly two, Colt revolvers and a Bowie knife. Unlike some other regiments, the men were not required to furnish their horses. The regiment was identified as a "picked body of men" skilled in horsemanship and weapons. This was probably the most famous regiment in Wharton's brigade and it had experience, seeing action at the Battle of Shiloh and the Battle of Perryville. When the regiment was mustered into service B. F. Terry was the colonel, Thomas S. Lubbock, lieutenant colonel, and Thomas Harrison, major. Although the 8th Texas was promised duty in Virginia, the regiment moved to Bowling Green, Kentucky, in the fall 1861 for its first active duty. Upon arrival, a measles epidemic struck the regiment resulting in many of the troopers being hospitalized. After the epidemic passed, the regiment was assigned reconnaissance duties and subsequently, Terry was killed in a skirmish near Bardstown, Kentucky, in December 1861. Upon his death Lubbock assumed command of the regiment, but he fell ill with typhoid fever and died in Nashville in early January 1862. Next, John Austin Wharton was elected colonel and John G. Walker lieutenant colonel of the regiment. Wharton was appointed to brigade command in the fall of 1862 and Colonel Thomas Harrison commanded the regiment in December 1862.[15]

Harrison, born in 1823 in Alabama, moved to Texas in 1843. He lived in Waco at the outset of the war; and Harrison was described as "of a somewhat grumpy disposition, at times irascible, and not easily understood. He got off to a rather slow start in gaining confidence of the men." Harrison won the confidence of the men when he led a cavalry charge during the Battle of Shiloh, and troopers agreed: "He was a worthy successor of Wharton."[16]

The 8th Texas was removed from Forrest's command and placed under Wheeler in the autumn of 1862, but those in the regiment generally recognized only Wharton as their commander. The regiment was actively involved with the rearguard action from Perryville. Terry's Texas Rangers settled in at Nolensville and diligently scouted around the area after returning to Tennessee after the Kentucky Campaign. Corps commander, William Hardee, enjoyed the 8th Texas screening his infantry at Eagleville and said, "I always feel safe with when the Rangers are in the front."[17]

WHITE'S ARTILLERY BATTERY

Little is known of White's Tennessee battery, which was commanded by Captain Benjamin H. White. White began the war serving as captain in Company H of Neeley's 4th Tennessee Infantry and he transferred to artillery in October 1861. Three of White's guns accompanied Forrest's cavalry as he raided into western Tennessee and the remaining section of three guns was assigned to Wharton's cavalry brigade. Sixty-three men were present for duty in this section as the actions in December began around Murfreesboro.[18]

Buford's Brigade

Abraham Buford, born on January 18, 1820, came from a prosperous family in Woodford County, Kentucky. Buford had two cousins who also became generals in the Civil War, Napoleon and John Buford. All three of the Bufords attended West Point. Abraham, "Abe," Buford initially attended Centre College in Danville, Kentucky, before attending West Point where he graduated in 1841. His initial military service was along the western frontier. Like many military men of the time, Buford participated in the Mexican War and received a promotion to the rank of captain for bravery at Buena Vista. In 1854, he resigned from the army and moved back to Versailles where he spent his time raising and training race horses. Others in his family joined the Union Army, but Abraham did not commit his services and experience to either side, preferring to remain neutral. When Bragg entered Kentucky during the Perryville Campaign, Buford decided to offer his services to the Confederacy and was appointed brigadier general on September 2, 1862, and he was given brigade command of the 3rd, 5th and 6th Kentucky cavalries. Buford was a giant of a man, reportedly weighing 320 pounds, and he had a red beard and hair. Buford was a strong advocate of states' rights, but opposed secession.[19]

3RD, 5TH AND 6TH KENTUCKY CAVALRY

Buford's Kentucky regiments were green and untried. The 3rd Kentucky Cavalry was organized in the summer of 1862 under command of Colonel J. Russell Butler, the 5th Kentucky Cavalry was organized in September 1862 under command of Colonel Dabney Howard Smith and the 6th Kentucky Cavalry was organized in the summer of 1862 under command of J. Warren Grigsby. All of Buford's three regiments were mustered into service during Bragg's Kentucky campaign. The brigade was attached to John Wharton's command when Bragg retreated to Tennessee after the Battle of Perryville and after this campaign the brigade trained and armed itself in preparation for further action with the enemy. The majority of the soldiers making up this brigade were drawn from central Kentucky.[20]

General Abraham "Abe" Buford, West Point class of 1841, advocated for states' rights but opposed secession (Alabama Department of Archives and History).

The 3rd Kentucky Cavalry suffered from some confusion about its proper title. J. Russell Butler is generally recognized as the colonel of Helm's 1st Kentucky Cavalry, second organization. Essentially, the 3rd Kentucky Cavalry was subsequently consolidated with the 1st Kentucky Cavalry and lost its identity in 1863. The Adjutant General's Report for Kentucky also documented Butler as an officer in the 1st Kentucky Cavalry.[21]

Colonel D. Howard Smith, the youngest of seven sons, was born in Scott County, Kentucky, on November 24, 1821, and received his education at Georgetown and Miami colleges before gaining his law degree from Transylvania College in Lexington. Smith practiced law and became politically active and served in the Kentucky General Assembly. Smith raised the 5th Kentucky Cavalry, with about 800 troopers, and joined Buford's brigade. The 5th Kentucky Cavalry had about 220 men present for duty for the Stones River Campaign.[22]

John Warren Grigsby was born in Rockbridge County, Virginia, on September 11, 1818. Grigsby began publishing a newspaper at the age of sixteen and when he was twenty-one he was appointed to a diplomatic mission to France where he served from 1841 to 1849. After his diplomatic experiences, he moved to New Orleans, studied law, and opened a practice there. He subsequently met and married the granddaughter of the first Kentucky governor (Isaac Shelby), and moved to Lincoln County, Kentucky, where he settled as a farmer until the beginning of the Civil War. In September 1862 he was elected colonel of the 6th Kentucky Cavalry and joined Buford's cavalry brigade.[23]

Pegram's Brigade

Brigadier General John Pegram, born in Virginia, January 24, 1832, was a handsome, almost ideal symbol of the South. He was the son of a prominent Virginia family of planters, and grew up in family at the apex of the social hierarchy in Petersburg, Virginia. His grandfather was a major general in the War of 1812 and his father was also a general in the Virginia militia and a banker. When Pegram's father died, he assumed the patriarchal role in the family. John Pegram attended West Point, class of 1854, and subsequently served in the U.S. Dragoons on the western frontier. In 1857, he became instructor of cavalry at the United States Military Academy. In 1858, he spent two years in Europe observing military tactics and strategy there. When he returned, he assumed his military duties in the U.S. Army. At the onset of the war, he resigned from the U.S. Army on May 10, 1861, and offered his services to the Confederate States of America. He was promoted to the rank of lieutenant colonel of the 20th Virginia Infantry and brigade command in Brigadier General Robert Garnett's command in Virginia. Pegram led his troops against William McClellan and William Rosecrans at the Battle of Rich Mountain where he surrendered and was subsequently imprisoned. He was later exchanged and served as chief of engineers in Bragg's army at Tupelo in July 1862. Next, he accepted a position as Kirby Smith's chief of staff before gaining command of a cavalry brigade after the Perryville Campaign upon recognition of excellent service during the Kentucky campaign.[24]

Pegram's time with the Army of Tennessee was destined to be a troubling experience for him. As happens with many changes of command, Pegram replaced Colonel Henry Ashby who had been serving as brigade commander and he also commanded Colonel John Scott who commanded a brigade in the Perryville Campaign. On November 12, Sergeant Tucker St. Joseph Randolph, a Virginian serving in the Army of Tennessee, wrote to his father:

> Genl. John Pegram is to be assigned to Col. Ashby Brigade which throws him back to his Regt and me back to the Company, which I am very sorry for, as my position in it is very disagreeable, in fact I don't wish to go back even if I were Captain as it is composed of a class of men I don't admire, and if I can get any other position, I will gladly accept it.

Randolph was dissatisfied with his lot in Tennessee and desired to return to Virginia. He continued:

> [T]here is such great dissatisfaction in this department, we have or aught to have enough of Cavalry officers to command our Cavalry, without assigning Infantry Colonels as Pegram was, I have not found out anything to do yet but hope to be able to find something before long. I am like a "bandy ball" knocked first one side then another, if I do get a good permanent position I will stick to it like "grim death to a dead nigger" as the boys say.

Perhaps in this fragment of the letter might be found some of attitudes of some Virginians toward westerners and those who were promoted.[25]

Perhaps even more interesting is the letter written by Randolph after Pegram assumed command: "Genl Pegram has taken command of the Brigade. I think the command will like him though they were very much prejudiced against him."[26]

1st Louisiana Cavalry

The 1st Louisiana Cavalry Regiment was well supported financially, militarily, and politically when it was organized in Baton Rouge in September 1861, and then re-mustered a month later. Over 900 troopers made up the regiment, and once mustered the regiment moved to Bowling Green, Kentucky, and remained in that vicinity until February 1862 when the Confederate forces moved south to counter the Union threat to the Confederate positions along the Mississippi River. The 1st Louisiana Cavalry participated in the defenses at Fort Donelson and once it fell, the regiment moved to Nashville.[27]

Next, the regiment participated in the Battle of Shiloh as part of Forrest's cavalry command. Subsequently, it withdrew to Corinth and then moved to northern Alabama to resist the Union actions there. On May 1, the 1st Louisiana Cavalry drove a group 18th Ohio Infantry out of Athens, Alabama, only to have the Union infantry return the next day in force. The resulting action by the Colonel John Turchin's Union infantry brigade was referred to the "Rape of Athens." John Scott was a controversial commander of the regiment and his actions at Athens caused much upheaval within the officer ranks of the regiment. After driving the Union troops out Athens, Scott burned the Limestone Bridge between Decatur and Huntsville, captured a supply train, and claimed thirty-four Union casualties in this successful cavalry action. While Turchin was marching on Athens, the Union cavalry arrived and set out in pursuit of the 1st Louisiana and caught the regiment crossing the Elk River. After successfully repulsing two charges the 1st Louisiana made its escape. However, the actions of Scott at the Elk River crossing caused his officers to rebel. Many believed Scott's orders were reckless which endangered the men and allowed the Union cavalry to successfully capture the ferry. As result of what was deemed to be Scott's incompetence, nine captains marched to P. T. Beauregard's headquarters in Corinth and preferred charges against Scott. But, Beauregard, displeased with the captains' actions of leaving their commands and riding to his headquarters, ordered the arrests of all the captains, except two, who were not with the regiment at that time, for abandoning their posts in the face of the enemy. Ultimately no charges were made against these officers and they returned to duty, but there was little doubt the command situation within this regiment was stressed.[28]

The 1st Louisiana Cavalry joined in Bragg's and Smith's Kentucky Campaign where John Scott was rewarded with command of a cavalry brigade, but he was arrested for disobedience of orders during the retreat to Tennessee. (He would subsequently be charged with disobedience of orders in March 1863 and court martialed.) After returning to Tennessee, the regiment was posted at Sparta, a staunchly, pro–Southern town in eastern Tennessee. In mid–December, Scott was ordered to Murfreesboro and the 1st Louisiana remained on the right flank of the army through December.[29]

The fiery John Sims Scott was a planter from East Feliciana Parish, Louisiana. Scott began the war serving in Magruder's cavalry in Virginia and then returned to Louisiana to raise a cavalry regiment from his home state. Despite his aggressive nature in the Confederate cavalry, Scott was known in Louisiana as "genial companion and intelligent gentleman, distinguished especially as a good judge of horse flesh, a bold rider and a brilliant shot." Scott's reputation within the army was one of concerns about his command ability and his quarrelsome nature toward other officers. He was physically described:

> In person Mr. Scott is about five feet nine inches high, with a rather florid and full face—regular, and when in repose, almost feminine; dark gray eyes, brown wavy hair, broad shoulders, full chest, and a body, from neck to ankle, far from lean and angular, yet not soft and rounded to a degree of obesity.

Scott would remain a controversial member of the Confederate cavalry, receiving the highest praise, but his relations with others in the Confederate army resulted in volatiles exchanges.[30]

During the Battle of Stones River, the 1st Louisiana was commanded by Lieutenant Colonel James O. Nixon, who moved from his home in Cedarville, New Jersey as a teenager, to open a branch of the family clothing business in New Orleans. In 1854, he became the editor of the pro-slavery newspaper, the *New Orleans Crescent*. At the time of the Battle of Stones River, Nixon was stout man with a gray-streaked beard. Lieutenant Colonel Nixon's brother remained in the New Jersey and served as a U.S. Representative.[31]

Colonel John S. Scott, 1st Louisiana Cavalry.

1ST TENNESSEE CAVALRY (CARTER'S)

Carter's 1st Tennessee Cavalry was organized in November 1862 and the 3rd Tennessee Battalion (Brazelton's) served as the nucleus of the new regiment. Brazelton's Battalion was organized in 1861 as a one-year regiment under the command of Lieutenant Colonel William Brazelton, Jr. It was planned that the regiment be redesignated as the 1st Tennessee Cavalry as early as March 1862, but the order was never implemented. Instead in May 1862, the regiment was reorganized as the 14th Tennessee Battalion under the command of Lieutenant Colonel James E. Carter, who was described as a "brave and knightly Southron, cool, clear-headed and fearless." Four additional companies were added to the battalion in November 1862 when the regiment was officially renamed the 1st Tennessee Cavalry. The troopers of this regiment were primarily from Rhea, Bradley, McMinn, Roane, Bledsoe, Union, Knox, Jefferson, and Claiborne counties. The original companies saw action primarily in eastern Tennessee and Kentucky, operating at Cumberland Gap and Big Creek Gap. Finally, two additional companies would be added but not until 1863. When the regiment was organized, it was attached to Pegram's cavalry brigade. On December 29, the regiment was detached to Wheeler's brigade and it participated in Wheeler's raid on the Union supply line.[32]

2ND TENNESSEE CAVALRY

When Tennessee seceded from the Union, Governor Isham Harris formed the Provisional Army of Tennessee and from this organization, two cavalry battalions were organized which would become the 2nd Tennessee Cavalry (CSA). Lieutenant Colonel Benjamin M. Branner's Fourth Tennessee Cavalry Battalion and Lieutenant Colonel

George R. McClellan's the Fifth Tennessee Cavalry Battalion were composed of men drawn from eastern Tennessee. The battalions participated in the early actions in Kentucky during the war, including the Mill Springs campaign.[33]

A trip to his uncle's home in east Tennessee resulted in Henry Marshall Ashby's decision to join the Confederate Army. Ashby assisted in the organization of a company of cavalry from Knox County, Tennessee, and was elected captain. Ashby, a native Virginian, attended William and Mary College in 1853–1854. Henry Ashby's cousin, Turner Ashby, commanded cavalry in Virginia in Stonewall Jackson's corps. Ashby came from a politically divided part of the state, and for the Tennessee cavalry drawn from the mountains, great political and philosophical divisions existed. Although Tennessee seceded from the Union, many counties in the east were decidedly pro–Union. Those Confederates from eastern Tennessee felt they were already outnumbered and animosity ran high among neighbors.[34]

In April 1862, Captain Henry Marshall Ashby, commanding portions of Branner's and McClellan's battalions, encountered a group of Union sympathizing East Tennessee men marching for Kentucky through Woodson's Gap. During the fight that resulted when Ashby attacked the body of men, Ashby succeeded in killing about thirty men, wounding the same number, and capturing four hundred twenty-three prisoners. For this type of energy and initiative, Ashby became a favorite of E. Kirby Smith who commanded the Department of East Tennessee in the spring of 1862.[35]

The two battalions combined to form the 1st Tennessee Cavalry in May 1862, but subsequently became the 2nd Tennessee Cavalry; and Ashby was given command of the regiment, primarily because of his actions at Woodson's Gap. The regiment operated in East Tennessee before moving northward when Smith and Bragg began the Kentucky Campaign. When the campaign ended, the 2nd Tennessee Cavalry was assigned duty of protecting the approaches into Tennessee from the north, and by the end of October the 2nd Tennessee was assigned to General John Pegram's cavalry brigade.[36]

Colonel Henry M. Ashby of the 2nd Tennessee Cavalry (Library of Congress).

1st Georgia Cavalry

The 1st Georgia Cavalry was organized in the fall of 1861 at Rome, Georgia, at which time more than a thousand officers and men were mustered into service. The troopers came primarily from Meriwether, Floyd, and Lumpkin counties. Its first service was at Chattanooga and then Knoxville. The regiment served with the Department of East Tennessee until the end of 1862 and then joined the Army of Tennessee. The 1st Georgia Cavalry was also known as Morrison's Cavalry and was commanded by Colonel James J. Morrison. The regiment served under command of General Nathan Bedford Forrest and General Joseph Wheeler. The 1st Georgia had notable service under the command of Forrest in the Union defeat at Murfreesboro in June 1862 where it attacked artillery "with great efficiency ... made a gallant charge almost to the mouths of the cannon." Next, the 1st Georgia participated in the overwhelming Confederate victory at the Battle of Big Hill, near Richmond, Kentucky, during the Perryville Campaign.[37]

Colonel James J. Morrison was a planter before the war and was veteran of the Mexican War. He initially enlisted at the rank of lieutenant colonel of the 21st Georgia Infantry. He resigned in March 1862 and became the lieutenant colonel of the 1st Georgia Cavalry. Morrison commanded the regiment through extensive cavalry operations and received recognition for the exceptional performance of his regiment. Lieutenant Colonel Armistead Harper, who would command the regiment at Stones River due to Morrison's absence, also received accolades for his command of portions of the regiment since it had been mustered into service.[38]

Wheeler's Brigade

1st Alabama	McCann Tennessee (detachment)
3rd Alabama	Douglass' Tennessee Battalion
51st Alabama Partisans	Holman's Tennessee Battalion
8th Confederate	2nd Kentucky Battalion
Wiggin's Arkansas Battery[39]	

1st Alabama Cavalry Regiment

The 1st Alabama Cavalry was organized in November 1861 in Montgomery, Alabama, although some of the companies were already active in the war. For example, the Montgomery Mounted Rifles, which would be mustered in as Company K, had been organized since February 1860. Upon organizing the regiment, the *Daily State Sentinel* of Selma declared: "[T]ruly fine looking men, well equipped in every particular. We will guarantee if they get a chance at the Yankees they will make them suffer." The 1st Alabama Cavalry once organized became an experienced regiment of cavalry seeing action in the Battle of Shiloh, Boonville, Blackland, Perryville, and in the skirmishes around Nashville in November and December 1862. Troopers were drawn from various counties in Alabama, including, Autauga, Montgomery, Morgan, Tallapoosa, Calhoun, Pike, Dale, Coffee, Monroe and Butler. At Shiloh, the regiment received praise for its action of covering the flank of the Confederate infantry. In May 1862, Joseph Wheeler again commended the regiment's performance at Bridge Creek. "The conduct of the officers and men in this affair was commendable, subjected as they were to a heavy fire of both artillery and infantry, from a foe secreted by a density of undergrowth. They advanced steadily, not using their arms until they were ordered, when they fired with good effect." During the Perryville Campaign, the 1st and 3rd Alabama Cavalries, as part of Wheeler's brigade, were identified as performing exceptional service. Wheeler, pleased with the addition of the 1st Alabama Cavalry to his brigade, perceived it to be well disciplined with good officers.[40]

James H. Clanton, an attorney from Montgomery, was instrumental in the formation of the regiment and was named colonel in December 1861. (Clanton was initially the captain of the Montgomery Mounted Rifles and William Wirt Allen served as his lieutenant.) Clanton resigned in 1862 after a disagreement with Braxton Bragg and command fell to William Wirt Allen. Allen, a New York native, was born in 1835 and his family subsequently moved to Alabama where he received his childhood education. Next, he attended and graduated from Princeton University in 1854 and returned to Montgomery and became a planter. Allen "laid down the peaceful vocation" of planting and enlisted in the Confederate Army in 1861 and served with Braxton Bragg's command in Pensacola. Allen was "tall, stout, making a stalwart figure. He is cordial in manner, and of ardent public spirit. As a soldier he was cool amid danger, and faithful and tireless in the discharge of his duty."[41]

3RD ALABAMA CAVALRY

The 3rd Alabama Cavalry was organized in June and July 1862 in Tupelo and like other Confederate regiments, the unit was a consolidation of other companies and battalions that had actively participated in the war. Three companies of the 3rd Alabama Cavalry were originally organized as Woods's Regiment, part of Wirt Adams' Mississippi cavalry, and the bulk of the remainder of the regiment came from the 1st Alabama Cavalry Battalion. The 3rd Alabama Cavalry was organized and the officers were appointed and elected on July 1, 1862. The troopers of this regiment were drawn primarily from Monroe, Choctaw, Wilcox, Mobile, Perry, Dallas, Calhoun, and Autauga counties.[42]

The various companies were previously organized as Ruffin Rangers, Percy Walker Rangers, Robbins' Rangers or Wilcox Rangers, Jackson County or Alabama Mounted Rifles, Mobile Humphries Dragoons, Curry or Murphy's Independent Company, Floyd Bush Rangers, Prattville Dragoons, Lenoir County or Mathews Rangers Cavalry, and Crocheron Light Dragoons. The Mobile Humphries Dragoons, Percy Walker Rangers and Ruffin Dragoons were part of Adams' Mississippi Cavalry; all three companies were mustered into service in September 1861 and served during the Battle of Shiloh. The Wilcox Rangers, Curry Dragoons, Prattville Dragoons and the Mathew Rangers were all previously designated in the 1st Alabama Battalion, and all four companies also saw action at the Battle of Shiloh. These four companies were all mustered into service in 1861. The Floyd Bush Rangers were included in the 3rd Alabama Cavalry in September 1862, and some of the troopers from that company were part of the 2nd Alabama for the past year. The regiment was well armed with some companies entering service with Colt revolvers and Sharps carbines.[43]

The 3rd Alabama often served with the 1st Alabama and was part of Wheeler's brigade in the recent Perryville Campaign; and the regiment was complemented on its performance during the campaign by Wheeler. Barton Ulmer wrote in a letter to his mother in November: "The 3rd Alabama I believe has won a name for itself. General Wheeler calls it the 'honest Third' and the 'brave Third.'" He reported General Bragg declared the 3rd Alabama was the only regiment "that a shell could burst in its center, and it would not give way."[44]

James Hagan commanded the 3rd Alabama Cavalry. Hagan, born in Ireland, came to America with his parents and grew up in Pennsylvania, where his father was a farmer. Later, Hagan became a businessman in his uncle's firm in Mobile, Alabama, before the Mexican War. Hagan served

Colonel James Hagan, 3rd Alabama Cavalry (Library of Congress).

in the Texas Rangers in the Mexican War and was commissioned captain in the 3rd Dragoons during the conflict. At the outset of the war with Mexico, Hagan joined the Texas Rangers and participated in the storming of Monterey. After the war, Hagan returned to Alabama and took up agriculture as a vocation. He remained a planter until the beginning of the Civil War when he was commissioned a captain, and shortly thereafter, major. When the 3rd Alabama was organized Hagan was appointed colonel of the regiment. John W. DuBose, Wheeler's biographer, described Hagan: "Hagan was an imposing figure, a notable horseman, trained for service in the Mexican War. He had become an Irish citizen of Mobile, and in no little degree distinguished as the successful suitor for the hand of the famous belle of Alabama, Miss Bettie Oliver."[45]

51ST ALABAMA PARTISAN RANGERS

The 51st Alabama Partisan Rangers was organized at Oxford, Alabama, in August 1862 when Colonel John Tyler Morgan returned from a year's service in Virginia. Its members were from the counties of Calhoun, Pike, Talladega, Dallas, Saint Clair, Tuscaloosa, Perry, Mobile, and Montgomery. While this regiment was designed to be partisan rangers, it acted more like a regular Confederate cavalry regiment. Upon its organization, it was placed in Nathan Forrest's brigade in Middle Tennessee and participated in a fight at La Vergne. A few weeks later, the regiment was assigned to Joseph Wheeler's brigade and it remained near La Vergne until the Stones River campaign where it saw its first significant fighting. The men of the regiment became veterans quickly and participated in eleven skirmishes from November 27 to December 29, 1862.[46]

John Tyler Morgan commanded the 51st Alabama Partisan Rangers. Morgan, a native of Athens, Tennessee, was born in 1824, a son of a merchant. His family moved to Calhoun County, Alabama, when he was nine years old. He prepared for a career as an attorney by studying law at a private school in Tuskegee under the guidance of the Honorable William P. Chilton. He began practicing law in 1845 and in 1855 he moved to Dallas County, Alabama, where he settled in the community of Cahaba. Morgan participated in the Alabama state constitutional convention that decided upon Alabama's secession from the Union. In April 1861, he enlisted for twelve months and was elected as major in the 5th Alabama Infantry. He spent his time with the 5th Alabama in Virginia and returned to his home state with authority to raise a mounted regiment. He successfully raised, and personally helped to equip, the 51st Alabama Partisan Rangers in the fall of 1862.[47]

MCCANN'S CAVALRY BATTALION

McCann's Cavalry Battalion was organized during the summer of 1862 under the command of Major J. R. "Dick" McCann. McCann had a fair complexion and he was five feet eight inches in height

Colonel John Tyler Morgan of the 51st Alabama Partisan Rangers (Alabama Department of Archives and History).

and weighted about 140 pounds. He was described as being "polished and humorous in conversation." He was born in Virginia, the son of Irish parents. He declared that he opposed the dissolution of the Union but when Tennessee voted to secede, he followed his state. McCann was highly effective in his duties and would be labeled a notorious guerrilla by the Union Army in 1863.[48]

The battalion was first organized with five companies from Davidson and Williamson counties, and the battalion joined in Morgan's Kentucky raid in the summer of 1862. McCann's Battalion returned to Tennessee after the Perryville Campaign and joined Wheeler's brigade.[49]

Douglass's and Holman's Tennessee Partisan Rangers

Douglass's Partisan Rangers was organized in October 1862 under the command of Major DeWitt C. Douglass, who had previously been a captain in the 7th Tennessee Infantry. There is little historical detail regarding this battalion. The battalion was probably initially armed with shotguns, as was, Holman's. Douglass's battalion saw action in the November 5 skirmish with Negley and Forrest south of Nashville and the battalion served under Wheeler's command during the actions at the Battle of Stones River.[50]

Holman's Battalion was organized in June 1862 under the command of Major Daniel W. Holman, born in 1832 in Mulberry, Tennessee. He attended Union College and was an attorney in Lincoln County, Tennessee, prior to the war. Holman began the war in the 1st Tennessee Infantry in the Army of Virginia and was appointed to the rank of major in the Holman's Partisan Rangers in October 1862 when the battalion was organized. The battalion had little opportunity for action prior to actions at Murfreesboro in December, but the troopers trained for two months and assisted in "enforcing the conscript law and arresting deserters from the army." Holman's Battalion joined Wheeler's command about December 1, 1862, at La Vergne.[51]

The initial armament of these units was poor. "When the battalion first went into service it was badly armed and equipped. Double-barrel shot-guns—the most of them of inferior quality—for the most part constituted the armament. There were a few smoothbore muskets, and scarcely a long-range gun in the command." Douglass's and Holman's Tennessee Partisan Rangers operated as separate units as part of Wheeler's brigade in December 1862. These two units would be consolidated, along with two additional companies, in February 1863 to form the 11th Tennessee Cavalry.[52]

8th Confederate Cavalry (Wade's)

The 8th Confederate Cavalry (Wade's) was one of two regiments with that name, and the second was Dearing's 8th Confederate Cavalry. Wade's 8th Confederate was originally designated the 2nd Mississippi and Alabama Cavalry and the regiment was organized after the Battle of Shiloh by uniting three battalions, Brewer's, Bell's and Baskerville's under Brigadier General James R. Chalmers command. In all, there were six Alabama and four Mississippi companies in the regiment. Brewer's and Baskerville's battalions participated in the Battle of Shiloh.[53]

The companies comprising the regiment at the time of its organization were primarily from the Alabama Counties of Talladega, Chambers, Pickens, Randolph, Tallapoosa and Chickasaw; and Lowndes County, Mississippi.[54]

Richard H. Brewer was given command of the new regiment, and Lieutenant Colonel Charles Baskerville and Major Solon Bell made up the new upper command of the 8th Confederate Cavalry. Brewer, West Point graduate, class 1858, served in the 1st Dragoons in California and Nevada before resigning to join the Confederate Army. Almost immediately after the organization of the regiment, Brewer resigned and transferred to the war in Virginia. Then, Baskerville assumed command of the regiment. Due to a disagreement with Brigadier General James Chalmers on the field at Blackland, Mississippi, Baskerville resigned. That action resulted in William B. Wade serving as colonel of the regiment.[55]

Wade was not a member of the regiment and Braxton Bragg, by virtue of his position, appointed Wade, a Mississippian, to command.

> Colonel Wade was a remarkable soldier; combining the great skill in handling a brigade of cavalry in desperate, aggressive action; in careful disposition while covering a retreat, and yet personally taking the lead in acts calling for desperate intrepidity. Unfortunately, much of his capacity as a commander was negatived by an irascible and, at times, uncontrolled temper that led to insubordination and serious friction between him and those in authority over him. He was a veteran of the Mexican war, led a company of accomplished riders, expert with pistol, and was at home in a charge with sabres.

Wade, born in Virginia in 1823, was the son of a prosperous planter who moved to Lowndes County, Mississippi. Wade joined the 1st Mississippi Regiment and served as a lieutenant in the Mexican War. After the war, he took up planting and served in the U.S. Congress for one term in 1854. When the war began, Wade organized a company, "Lowndes Southrons," later designated the 10th Mississippi Infantry which served in Pensacola and also in the Battle of Shiloh.[56]

George Knox Miller wrote: "Our regiment has again changed name—some one having re-baptized it 8th Confederate, making the name, I suppose, from the nature of the organization." During the spring and summer of 1862, the regiment was involved with fights at Blackland and Boonville, Mississippi, and was constantly in motion scouting and harassing the enemy's positions. Chalmers gave up brigade command due to his deteriorating health and Joseph Wheeler assumed command of the brigade in July 1862.[57]

The 8th Confederate remained in Aberdeen, Mississippi, as Bragg moved into Kentucky to complete the organization of the regiment. As soon as the organization was complete the regiment joined Wheeler's brigade in Kentucky, but it did not arrive until October 10 much to Wheeler's displeasure. The 8th Confederate missed the fighting at Perryville and George Knox Miller recorded that Wheeler

> was not quite satisfied with Colonel Wade's excuse of not joining him earlier. This was perhaps the inception of that lack of cordiality between the two officers that eventuated in insubordination on the part of Col. Wade and materially affected the discipline of a portion of the regiment during its last year of heroic service.

Colonel William B. Wade, 8th Confederate Cavalry (*Confederate Veteran*).

Wheeler wasted no time in putting the regiment to work and the day after its arrival, the 8th Confederate

Cavalry performed the primary rearguard action as the Union infantry began its pursuit of Bragg's army near Danville.[58]

Wiggins' Artillery Battery

Captain Jannedens H. Wiggins commanded one of the artillery batteries assigned to the Confederate cavalry during the Stones River Campaign. The battery was also known as the Clark County Artillery or the 2nd Arkansas Light Artillery and had been organized in May 1861 in Arkadelphia, Arkansas. Wiggins commanded the battery since May 1862. The battery began its service in garrison duty but when Wiggins gained command of the battery, it became a horse artillery unit. Wiggins' Artillery generally operated as two three-gun sections.[59]

Joseph Wheeler and the Cavalry

Joseph Wheeler was born in Augusta, Georgia, on September 10, 1836, the youngest son of Joseph and Julia Wheeler. His parents were native New Englanders who had moved to Georgia after the War of 1812. The senior Joseph Wheeler had been a merchant, banker and landowner but had lost most of the family's wealth in the Panic of 1837. Afterwards, the younger Wheeler went to Connecticut to complete his education while living with two of his aunts. At seventeen, he graduated and received an appointment to West Point on June 8, 1854, most likely through the influence of the Wheeler family and other extended family. But, Wheeler's experience at West Point was not a success. His biographer wrote that Wheeler had "a rather dismal record at the Academy, one that started poorly, and then went downhill." Wheeler performed poorly in just about all areas of study, but he was not disruptive and recorded no large numbers of demerits. Neither was Wheeler one to excel in sports. He received the nickname "Point" because of his small stature and because he had "neither length, breadth, nor thickness." Wheeler was an introvert, but was recognized as gentlemanly and quiet. He graduated 19th in a class of 22 in 1859. Yet he was the only one in his class to achieve recognition for military success.[60]

Upon graduation, Wheeler was initially appointed lieutenant in the 1st U.S. Dragoons, but after the completion of his training for mounted duty at Carlisle Barracks he was assigned to the Mounted Riflemen at Fort Craig in the New Mexico Territory. On the way to his new posting in 1860, he was assigned to duty as escort to a wagon carrying a surgeon and the pregnant wife of an army officer. When the woman went into labor, Wheeler, the doctor and the teamster remained behind the column to deliver the child. Immediately after giving birth, an Indian war party attacked the small group. Wheeler charged the party, firing a musket which was immediately discarded, and attacked with his Colt revolver, supported by the teamster. He successfully drove off the attacking Indians. Because of his aggressive action, he lost the nickname "Point" which was replaced by "Fightin' Joe," a name which remained with him for the remainder of his life.[61]

Wheeler had a relatively quiet life in his short stay at Fort Craig. The fires of rebellion burned in the east and Wheeler was faced with a decision. Although he had connections to the South, he also had connections in the North. Wheeler's home state of Georgia followed the other Southern states of South Carolina, Mississippi, Florida and Alabama and voted for secession on January 19, 1861. Wheeler's brother, William, immediately began organizing an artillery battery and interceded with authorities in Georgia for a commission for Joseph. On February 27, Wheeler offered his resignation to the United States Army and traveled to Georgia to take up arms against his country as a lieutenant in an artillery battery in the Confederacy. He was initially assigned to Pensacola where the Southern troops were commanded by Braxton Bragg. Based on Wheeler's confidence and performance, he received command of the 19th Alabama Infantry in Mobile in September 1861.[62]

Wheeler was a dedicated and diligent commander of the new regiment and worked tirelessly to make the 19th Alabama a premier fighting unit. In February 1862, Wheeler's regiment joined Albert Sidney Johnston's army at Jackson, Tennessee. Upon Bragg's arrival at Jackson, Wheeler was appointed acting brigade commander of Alabama infantry. In late March, Wheeler returned to command the 19th Alabama. During the Battle of Shiloh, the months of training paid off for the 19th Alabama which maintained its integrity and cohesion throughout the battle. In July, Wheeler assumed command of a cavalry brigade and began to organize his troopers, who were scattered across a large geographic area without much organization. His 1,000 man brigade consisted of Colonel William "Red" Jackson's 1st Mississippi, Colonel R. A. Pinson's 2nd Arkansas, Colonel James Hagan's 3rd Alabama, and Lieutenant Colonel William B. Wade's 8th Confederate Cavalry. Based on his experience, Wheeler concluded to utilize his cavalry primarily as mounted infantry. One of his initial efforts was a raid through Union-held outposts at Grand Junction, Bolivar and Middleburg, destroying supplies and communications along his path.[63]

Next, Wheeler, 5'5" in height and weighing a mere 120 pounds, was ordered to east Tennessee in August in preparation for Bragg's Kentucky Campaign and ultimately Wheeler's and Wharton's brigades performed duty during the Battle of Perryville and then returned to Middle Tennessee. Wheeler's promotion to chief of cavalry was based on Bragg's assessment of his ability to train and lead cavalry. Colonel Baxter Smith wrote of Wheeler: "[A] thorough solider and gentle as a woman, and as courteous as a cavalier, of the olden time, he possessed the finest courage." Bragg saw in Wheeler a commander who could adapt to rapidly changing situations, one who was serious and dedicated, and a commander that followed orders. Certainly, Wheeler's West Point education was appreciated by Bragg, and with Bragg's tendency to alienate others, he needed a commander loyal to him. He believed Wheeler was such a commander. One of Wheeler's biographers wrote: "He never displayed the audacity and flash of Forrest and Stuart, but in performing the true functions of cavalry attached to the flanks of an army he was unsurpassed." Wheeler was well-liked by his troopers and he often shared camps and food with them. Sir Arthur Fremantle, a British military observer, traveled with the Confederate army in 1863 and described Wheeler as a "little man" but a very "zealous officer."[64]

Summary

While the Confederate cavalry outnumbered the Union cavalry in Middle Tennessee, there was a great deal of independence, unruliness and even distrust within some of the regiments. Some commanders felt some of the east Tennessee troops, in particular, could not be trusted to remain loyal to the South. Colonel J. Stoddard Johnston, a member of Bragg's staff, wrote: "East Tennesseans were 'wild cavalry'—the inefficiencies of which there was constant complaint almost daily." E. Kirby Smith wrote in March 1862: "The people are against us, and ready to rise whenever an enemy's column makes its appearance. The very troops raised here cannot always be depended upon." Smith was unfair in his assessment of the troopers drawn from the mountains, but his comment reflected the appraisal, unfair or not, of some of the high command of the Confederacy. His remarks probably more accurately reflected his frustration with the strong Union sentiment in parts of the South.[65]

While Wheeler dealt with the lack of cohesiveness of his cavalry, he also dealt with his primary issue—an inability to adequately arm and supply his troopers. He had a hodge-podge of armaments, uniforms, and equipment for his men. Some of his regiments were armed primarily with revolvers and had only a small numbers of carbines or muskets, while others were primarily armed with carbines and others with muskets only. Many troopers carried shotguns only, and the Confederate cavalry distained the use of the saber. These various abilities to fight at short-range and long-range impacted the Southern cavalry command decisions. The cost of cavalry was an expensive effort for both sides, but particularly so for Southern troopers who were expected to furnish their own horses. Horses commonly cost more than $100 which was ten times the monthly wages of a Southern trooper.[66]

One additional factor which affected the Southern cavalry was the "raiding strategy" described by historian Christopher Dwyer. As Union forces penetrated deeper in the South, the paradigm of using Confederate cavalry to attack extended enemy communications and supply lines supplemented the traditional role of cavalry. The commanding generals of the western Confederate armies all accepted this strategy. The praise and recognition heaped upon Forrest and Morgan in Tennessee demonstrated the importance of these tactics to all Confederate cavalrymen, including their commanding officers. Joseph Wheeler while attached to the Army of Tennessee watched as both Morgan and Forrest set off on raiding expeditions in mid–December amid the cheers of the citizens and the soldiers. Although Wheeler served in the more traditional role where decisions held dramatic results, he too understood that glory awaited those who successfully raided Union communication lines. This strategy held important implications for the upcoming battle near Murfreesboro.[67]

Another important concern in December was the fact that the overall command structure of the Southern cavalry had yet to be demonstrated. Some regimental commanders were new, as was the overall structure of some regiments; and two brigade commanders were still untried. Only Wheeler and Wharton worked together over the past three and a half months. John Pegram, although the most formally trained cavalry officer in Wheeler's command, had just gained command of cavalry for the first time in the war and Abe Buford commanded a relatively inexperienced, small Kentucky cavalry brigade. Finally, Wheeler, like David Stanley, still commanded the second largest cavalry brigade in his division. Wheeler chose not to act solely as chief of cavalry, but he chose to retain direct command of a brigade operating in the field. While Stanley chose to do the same thing, he still had a cavalry division commander, Kennett, who had direct command of the three Union cavalry brigades. So, while similar, the chiefs of cavalry had different command structures.

Finally, Wheeler was also untried. He had never commanded a division in a major battle. The upcoming Battle of Stones River would be his first battle as chief of cavalry and it is important to realize that Wheeler was still a very young officer. Despite the issues facing the Southern cavalry, the numbers were in Wheeler's favor.

PART THREE: BATTLE OF STONES RIVER

6. The Advance on Murfreesboro— First Phase (December 26–28)

> *With the blessing of God, General,*
> *I will whip my friend Hardee tomorrow!*
> —Major General Alexander McCook

On December 26, Rosecrans' army of 43,000 seized the initiative to attack Bragg's army of 37,000. Murfreesboro, generally considered the geographic center of Tennessee, is located about thirty miles southeast of Nashville. The Nashville and Chattanooga Railroad ran through Murfreesboro and provided an important transportation link between Nashville and points east. The town lay in a large, fertile plain that extended from Nashville to the Cumberland Mountains. The nature of the plain and rolling hills made the area an important center of agriculture. The west fork of Stones River, a tributary of the Cumberland River, ran just west and north of the town and provided little difficulty for infantry seeking to cross. At the fords, the water was very shallow, and only heavy rainfall made the stream an obstacle. The area north and west of Murfreesboro was scattered with cultivated fields, limestone outcrops, cedar breaks, and woods in the slightly rolling, almost flat, terrain.[1]

David Stanley's orders to advance sent the three Union cavalry brigades across the front of Rosecrans' army. Lewis Zahm's brigade screened the advance along the right flank while Minty's brigade advanced along the Murfreesboro Pike on the left flank. The Reserve Brigade planned to advance in the center along the Nolensville Pike. The detached 4th U.S. Cavalry remained with army headquarters which advanced along the Murfreesboro Pike. While the Union army's objective was Bragg's army concentrated at Murfreesboro, Rosecrans was concerned about the Confederates at Franklin. The Union army marched in a southeasterly direction which potentially left the rear open to a Confederate attack, particularly from the southwest. Rosecrans estimated 700 Southern troops remained in Franklin and he wanted his cavalry to deal with them. Lewis Zahm's Ohio cavalrymen were ordered to "dash" the enemy and drive them out of Franklin. Afterwards, Zahm planned to move toward Nolensville.[2]

In addition, Rosecrans needed to be sure communications flowed efficiently to and from his headquarters initially located near Concord Church at La Vergne. Stanley needed to keep the communications open with Alexander McCook's Wing, which moved in the center along the Nolensville Pike, and Zahm was directed to report to Thomas who moved from his position on the Franklin Pike to the Wilson Pike southward, on the Union right flank. Minty also cooperated with Crittenden regarding his movements. Some of the Reserve

Brigade was assigned courier duty while endeavoring to keep communications open. Elmer Otis, 4th U.S., had overall command of the courier line and Stanley ordered his cavalry to coordinate actions with the regular army officer as the advance began.[3]

The skies on December 26 were dark and ominous as the Union army began its advance over the rolling hills interspersed with wooded thickets, streams, farms and rocky bluffs. The day was to prove dismal as incessant rain fell "in torrents during the entire morning." The weather had been relatively dry and the rain began as the march began. The soldiers tried to drink their morning coffee only to have the rain drops splash the coffee from their cups onto their faces. Rosecrans determined Polk's and Kirby Smith's (now only a single division) forces held the line at Murfreesboro, and Hardee's troops were concentrated between Triune and Eagleville, on the Shelbyville and Nolensville Pike with an advance guard at Nolensville. His strategy was to press Hardee. Alexander McCook's corps moved in the center of Rosecrans' army with three divisions, Thomas advanced on his right (west) with Negley's and Rousseau's divisions. Crittenden's three divisions moved directly toward Murfreesboro on the left flank. McCook planned to attack Hardee at Triune and if Bragg moved to support Hardee then Thomas would join the Union attack. If McCook successfully defeated Hardee, or if Hardee retreated, and Bragg held his line north of Murfreesboro then Crittenden would attack, supported by Thomas and then McCook would, while holding Hardee in place, swing the remainder of his wing into Polk's rear. If Hardee moved to join Bragg and Polk at Murfreesboro, then Rosecrans would concentrate his army to oppose Bragg's entire force.[4]

Rosecrans held Stanley in high regard, but the cavalry situation worried him. The superiority of Confederate cavalry in Middle Tennessee since the bulk of Union army arrived caused Rosecrans much concern. Rosecrans acknowledged the disparity between the two cavalry forces which "gave the enemy control of the entire country around us. It was obvious from the beginning that we should be confronted by Bragg's army, recruited by an inexorable conscription, and aided by clans of mounted men, formed into a guerrilla-like cavalry, to avoid the hardships of conscription and infantry service." The two Union generals would do the best they could with the cavalry they had on hand—an effective force of 3,200.[5]

All of the Union wings were vulnerable to attack, but perhaps, the most important wing according to Rosecrans' plan was McCook. McCook received a telegram from Rosecrans at 4:30 a.m. on December 26 ordering him to begin moving and Jefferson C. Davis's and Phil Sheridan's divisions began their advances an hour and a half later. Davis marched for Prim's Blacksmith Shop over a rough country road and then directly marched for Nolensville while Sheridan marched on a more direct route to Nolensville followed by Brigadier General Richard W. Johnson's division which served as the reserve of the right wing. David Stanley's Reserve Cavalry Brigade planned to lead the advance, but by the time Stanley's cavalry began its march the roads were blocked with McCook's infantry and trains. As Davis's division marched toward Nolensville, it encountered Wharton's cavalry. The bulk of Hardee's infantry held a line near Eagleville, about fifteen miles south, and Patrick Cleburne's infantry division was the target of McCook's advance southward. Cleburne, the Irish-born general from Arkansas, had three brigades located near College Grove on December 26 and his fourth brigade under command of Brigadier General S. A. M. Wood was four miles north near Triune on the Nashville and Shelbyville Turnpike. While on the eastern flank, Polk corps along with three brigades of Breckinridge's infantry of Hardee's corps remained at Murfreesboro. The Confederate cavalry stretched across the front of Bragg's army. John Wharton held the Confederate left flank, Wheeler's brigade in the center at Stewarts Creek along the Murfreesboro Pike, and Pegram's brigade remained on the right flank and covered any approaches from Lebanon. Finally, Abraham Buford's brigade was on the extreme right at McMinnville about forty miles to the east.[6]

Action at Nolensville

The Union infantry ran into Wharton's Confederate cavalry after marching two miles and the Southern cavalrymen resisted McCook's advance throughout the day. About a mile north of Nolensville was a line of hills and along the ridge Wharton concentrated his cavalry, supported by White's Tennessee Artillery. Nolensville, a small village in a fertile agricultural community, was the home of the 20th Tennessee Infantry. John Wharton had established his headquarters on the Page Plantation, between Nolensville and Triune, and the evening before Wharton enjoyed a delightful Christmas evening with eggnog and a group of friends. Today, he faced the Union army. As the Union column advanced, it moved directly for the center of Wharton's cavalry. Jefferson C. Davis fortunately had Company B, 36th Illinois Cavalry, as his escort and had to rely on this unit for his reconnaissance. In fact, there was no 36th Illinois Cavalry regiment. The 36th Illinois Cavalry was a mounted company of the 36th Illinois infantry, which served as dragoons or mounted infantry. It was a unique role for an infantry company in the Army of the Cumberland, but the company provided valuable service during the day. Davis ordered his escort to screen and push the enemy pickets. The Illinois mounted company did this duty so well that Davis's division, which led McCook's advance on Nolensville, moved unimpeded until it reached the line of enemy a mile north of Nolensville. As the Union infantry approached Nolensville, Colonel William Carlin's brigade successfully thwarted a flank attack by the Southern cavalry. After pushing past the defensive line, Davis's division again marched ahead and ran into another line of Wharton's Confederate cavalry at Knob Gap, just south of Nolensville. Wharton chose his position well and Knob Gap, an excellent defensive position, also allowed White's artillery to fire "long range" as the Union infantry advanced. William Carlin declared: "The ridge itself, with the knobs, forms as fine a military position to hold an attack as I ever saw in open territory." Davis deployed his division to meet the resistance before him. Colonel P. Sidney Post's brigade formed on the left of the road, Colonel William Carlin's infantry brigade on the right of the road and Colonel William Woodruff's brigade formed on Carlin's right. The 2nd Minnesota Battery and 5th Wisconsin Battery unlimbered and began to fire on the Confederate cavalry. As the Union line attacked, Wharton's troopers gave way leaving one of White's guns on the field. So far, the skirmishing at Nolensville, with the exception of the 36th Illinois Cavalry, was confined to Wharton's cavalry resisting the advance of Union infantry.[7]

One of the Confederate regiments in front of McCook's advance on December 26 was the 8th Texas Cavalry. The vedettes observed the columns of blue coated soldiers marching in their direction and the regiment quickly assembled to delay the advance. Once the Union skirmishers saw the Texans, the artillery began shelling the defenders. James Blackburn of the 8th Texas was in the saddle as the shells started to fall:

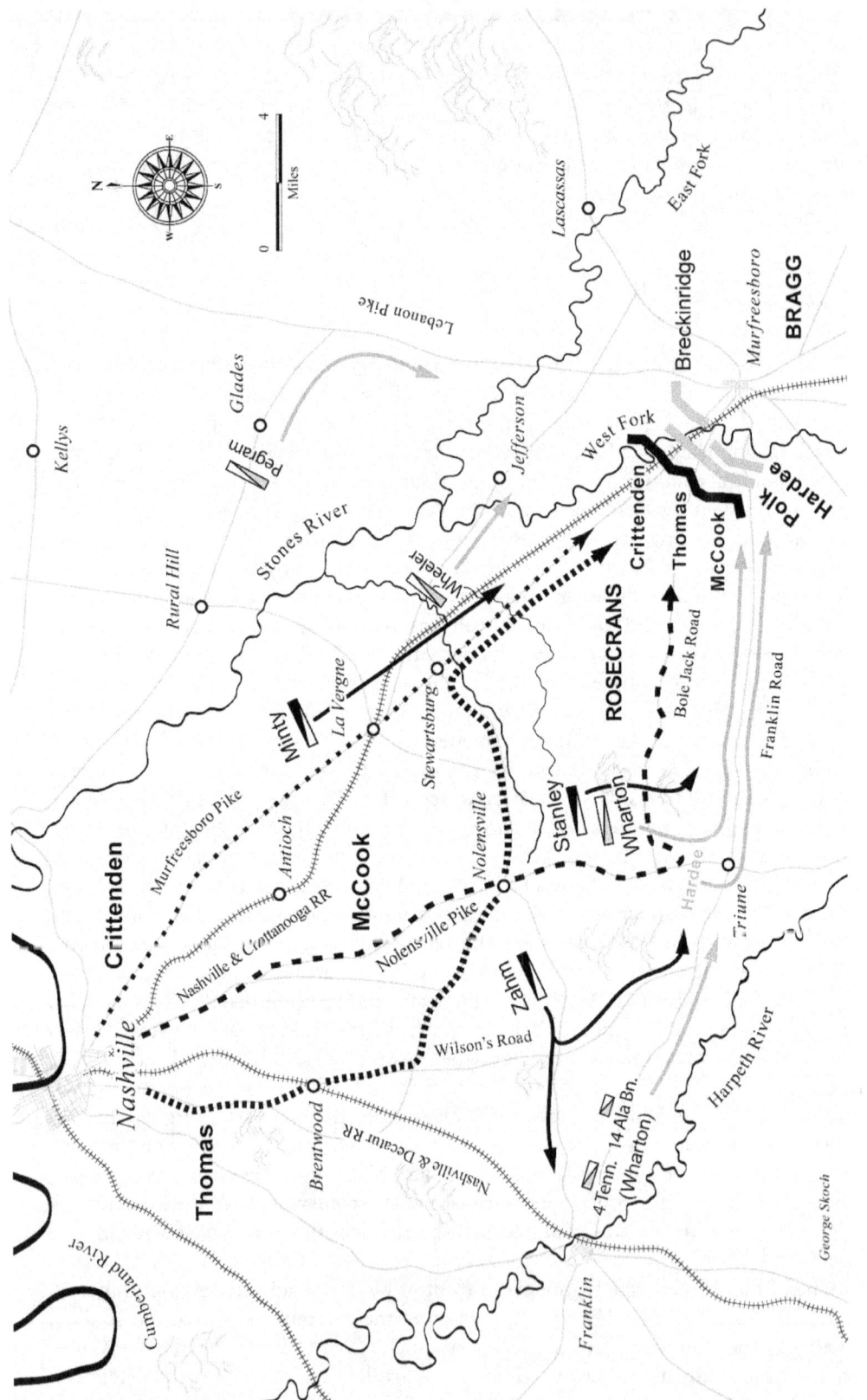

The march on Murfreesboro—December 26–30, 1862.

One shell burst in rear of my company doing slight damage, another one entered the body of a horse near my horse's head, bursting inside the horse and knocked my horse to his knees and covering him and me with blood and flesh from the other horse. Strange to say the trooper riding this torn up horse escaped without the slightest injury.

The next shell struck a cedar tree and cut it in half. The Southern cavalry moved off to the left away from the artillery only to discover Union soldiers attempting to attack the west flank and the Texans moved to face this new threat, Carlin's infantry, when the seriousness of the situation became evident. As the Harrison's Texas cavalry opened fire on those along the left flank, an explosion of gunfire revealed another Union regiment firing from the front. There were just too many Yankees and Harrison withdrew his men to a safer spot.[8]

The Union advance did not come as a complete surprise to the Confederates. Only two days before John Wharton wrote: "The enemy are threatening to visit us tomorrow." E. Kirby Smith wrote to Joseph Johnston on the day of Rosecrans' advance: "Rosecrans is enterprising; his force is, I think, underestimated, and I would look for offensive operations rather than the abandonment of Middle Tennessee." Rosecrans' initial movements had alerted the Southern cavalry to the possibility the Federal army might be moving. Wheeler prepared to resist any movement southward with his four brigades. Wheeler who had been in Murfreesboro moved to the front at La Vergne the evening before and upon observing the full extent of the movement during the day was convinced that the Union activity signaled a general advance.[9]

While Stanley's Reserve Brigade did not precede McCook's advance, the brigade provided assistance to Sheridan's division when it ran into Southern cavalry at Bole Jack Pass and pushed the defenders aside allowing Sheridan to advance to Nolensville. Stanley's troopers charged ahead and drove the defenders two miles which resulted in two hand-to-hand skirmishes along the way. Stanley sought to keep the morale of his troopers high and remarked: "They went into the fight like they liked it; and were unwilling to stop." One encounter included a Confederate trooper and Major Adolph Rosengarten, 15th Pennsylvania Cavalry, and they made the fighting personal. The combatants rode toward each other but the rain had moistened the gunpowder so that neither weapon fired. Instead, the major and the Southern trooper continued the contest with their fists. Rosengarten won the contest by knocking his assailant off his horse, but not before receiving a "stinger" of a punch to his eye. In the end, the Confederate cavalryman was taken prisoner.[10]

Wharton's role during the day was simply to delay McCook's advance and he effectively accomplished all that could be expected. McCook's corps was much too strong for Wharton and Wood to handle, but their efforts gave Hardee time to determine how he intended to meet the threat. The resistance of Wharton's troopers was effective enough to result in seventy-five casualties to Davis's division and also allowed the Confederate infantry south of Nolensville time to prepare to meet the Union advance. The day ended for McCook as he gained his objective, Nolensville, although his troops were exhausted from marching through the rain and mud during the day, and he was joined by Stanley and Rosecrans that evening. When Stanley arrived at McCook's headquarters, he rode with the 15th Pennsylvania Cavalry, 5th and 2nd Tennessee Regiments, once the congestion of troops on the roads allowed his cavalry to move ahead. McCook explained his actions during the day and verbally received his orders from Rosecrans to move directly south seven miles to Triune seeking to engage Hardee's corps.[11]

Cavalry Skirmish at Franklin

While the center of the Union column marched toward Hardee's corps at Nolensville, Lewis Zahm's Ohio cavalry brigade rode on the right of George Thomas' infantry corps moving along the Franklin Pike. Zahm was more successful than Stanley in getting his cavalry into position and away the congestion along the Franklin Pike. Zahm had orders to coordinate his actions during the day with those of George Thomas, but Thomas was delayed by the movement of his troops and those of McCook's. As Zahm sought Thomas, he was directed to the head of the infantry column about two miles beyond Brentwood on the Wilson Creek Pike only to learn that Thomas had returned to the rear of the column. The diligent colonel from Ohio then proceeded to ride another six miles to the rear only to find Thomas had ridden across country to the vicinity of Nolensville. Zahm realized he could chase Thomas throughout the day, but his orders directed him to neutralize the Confederate threat at Franklin.[12]

Zahm then proceeded down the Franklin Pike at the head of 950 troopers of the 1st, 3rd, and 4th Ohio cavalries. About two and a half miles from Franklin, Zahm ran into the first pickets of Wharton's cavalry, and pushed them to the rear. The approach of the Ohio troopers surprised the Southern cavalry which hastily prepared a more determined defense about a half a mile from Franklin where a "sharp skirmish ensued." Zahm successfully pushed ahead and the Southern cavalry retreated again into Franklin where they planned to make a stand. Zahm used six companies of cavalry as dismounted skirmishers supported by mounted cavalry and began flanking Wharton's troopers on both sides. Then the flanking Union cavalry attacked across the Harpeth River causing the Confederates to retreat. A running fight continued for another two miles and the Ohio cavalry pursued close on the heels of the Southern horsemen. Due to the lateness of the day, the pursuit ended and Zahm concluded his success: "The enemy was taken by surprise; could not get their forces together before we were upon them; therefore made it rather an easy task to drive them, as they were in several directions, formed several lines, but as we advanced and fired they invariably fled." William Crane, 4th Ohio, recorded in his diary: "[T]he 1st O[hio], being in advance had a sharp fight lasting about twenty minutes. The enemy was driven back by the column then charged, routing him from his camp and driving him in every direction."

The Union cavalry captured ten prisoners, one of which was a lieutenant of Bragg's escort. Zahm also claimed several horses, mules, weapons and the destruction of the Southern cavalry camp which had been abandoned. The information from the prisoners led Zahm to conclude that he faced 900 men of Colonel Baxter Smith's regiment plus the 14th Alabama Battalion commanded by Lieutenant Colonel J. C. Malone. The actual number of Southern cavalry was probably much less than this number. Zahm, while commanding the Ohio cavalry brigade, was the first colonel of the 3rd Ohio cavalry, and he naturally took pride in his own regiment. He concluded his report on the action at Franklin: "My command behaved nobly, both officers and men. The Third [Ohio] Cavalry had the advance, and did the principal part of the fighting; there was no flinch to them." Colonel Baxter Smith, commanding the Confederate forces at Franklin, recalled in his memoirs that he was "unceremoniously" driven from the town.[13]

While Zahm was occupied in Franklin, his scouts discovered a large concentration of Hardee's infantry nine east along the Franklin Road which led from Franklin to Murfreesboro. Zahm returned to Thomas' corps at 9:00 p.m. hoping to find Thomas and give him the report of his actions during the day, but again, he was unable to find Thomas. Instead, he found Major General Lovell Rousseau whose division formed the extreme right flank of the Federal army. Rousseau confirmed a large infantry force to be at Triune and the two officers decided to use about half of Zahm's cavalry brigade to reconnoiter the infantry in the front and right of the infantry advance toward Triune. The remainder of Zahm's cavalry would return to Franklin the next day to ensure Baxter Smith's and J. C. Malone's cavalry would not harass the flank and rear of the Union army.

The congestion and rain proved to be a challenge to all. George Thomas did not progress as far as he had hoped due to the conditions of the roads but planned to advance the next morning without delay. He had successfully moved Negley's division near Nolensville while Rousseau's division remained on the right flank of the Union army; however, Thomas advanced throughout the day without interference from the enemy. Thomas' wing which started moving on the right flank prepared to shift so that his divisions would move to the center between McCook and Crittenden. At the end of the first day of the Federal advance, Stanley's reserve brigade moved into place to lead the Union movement toward Triune the next morning with Richard Johnson's infantry division following behind.[14]

Fighting Along Murfressboro Pike

On the left (east) flank, Thomas L. Crittenden began his march toward La Vergne on the morning of December 26. Three regiments of cavalry in Minty's cavalry brigade succeeded in reaching the front of Crittenden's wing and screened the Union advance. Colonel John Kennett, cavalry division commander, rode with Minty's brigade and assumed overall command of the cavalry operations on the Union left flank. There was reason to suspect this would be the most difficult movement of the day. Crittenden's wing moved directly toward the concentration of Bragg's army at Murfreesboro by the most direct route and Wheeler's cavalry was based at Stewarts Creek, a few miles south of La Vergne. Although Kennett had direct command of Minty's brigade, he had little to do. Minty's actions were governed by Major General John Palmer but the orders were transferred to Minty via Kennett.

Minty threw his scouts several miles in advance of Crittenden's main body. The

General Thomas Crittenden, commander of the Union left wing (Library of Congress).

advanced guard rode about a half mile in front of the cavalry regiment and a quarter mile behind them followed a company of cavalry. Minty also used "flankers" which consisted of about 100 to 150 troopers. As expected, Minty found the enemy pickets in front of his advance about ten miles south of Nashville but his troopers drove them to the rear. Among those screening the Confederate infantry was trooper, W. M. Webster, a member of the 51st Alabama Partisan Rangers, a regiment that would have extensive duty over the next few days. The vedettes of the Confederate cavalry had the cold and unpleasant duty in the dark and long nights in December of protecting the forward positions. Webster lamented his duty in preparation of the Union advance: "[W]e did shiver with cold while on picket duty ... while the infantry were back a few miles taking their ease with nothing to molest them." But as the Union cavalry preceded Crittenden's advance, the 51st Alabama sounded the alarm, and the Confederate infantry and cavalry prepared to resist the Federal march. Minty continued his advance intending to reach La Vergne by the end of the day. Minty positioned the 3rd Kentucky Cavalry on the left of the Murfreesboro Pike, the 7th Pennsylvania on the right and the 4th Michigan in the center on the pike. As Crittenden's column continued to drive forward the sounds of the fighting at Nolensville could be heard by Union troops. The closer to La Vergne the Union column advanced, the greater the resistance from the Wheeler's cavalry and when Minty neared La Vergne he faced 1,000 cavalry supported by a four gun battery, Wiggins' Arkansas Artillery.[15]

Crittenden's trailing infantry moved forward to face the bulk of Wheeler's cavalry, supported by Brigadier General George Maney's brigade of Tennessee infantry which held a position north of Stewarts Creek. As Crittenden began his march he moved through some of the country which proved troublesome for both armies, large agricultural fields, now fallow in December, but filled with tall weeds and between the fields were stones and woods "often interspersed with almost impenetrable cedar thickets." As the day developed, General Leonidas Polk concluded that Crittenden was moving in force and he also heard the noise of battle along McCook's advance to the west. Polk ordered Maney and Wheeler to delay the Union advance while Bragg determined what reaction he would make. Wheeler's scouts reported the extent of the Union movement approaching his position and he decided to throw his full command in an attempt to delay Crittenden. Wheeler also alerted Bragg to the Union movements and he sent orders to Pegram and Wharton to prepare for a general Union advance.[16]

About two miles north of La Vergne, Wheeler made a determined stand and a section of Wiggins' Artillery began to shell the advancing cavalry. Minty ordered his cavalry off the road and adjutant Robert Burns of the 4th Michigan Cavalry described Wiggins' initial fire: "[T]he enemy fired a ball which would have raked our whole column and killed many. It went skimming along the road just where the men had been standing and within a few feet of us." Burns, riding with Minty, observed a near miss as another cannonball passed within eight feet of the two officers. Minty moved his cavalry behind a slight rise and Newell's section of two 3-inch Rodmans of 1st Ohio Artillery unlimbered to counter-fire Wiggins's guns. Two companies of the 4th Michigan moved to support the artillery behind a fence. Meanwhile, Wiggins's Arkansas artillery sent the rest of Minty's cavalry looking for cover. Newell returned the favor when he began firing. His first target was a body of cavalry and Confederate artillery, which dispersed after four rounds from Newell's guns. The Union column advanced another mile only to run into the Confederate artillery and cavalry again. Newell recorded: "I fired 60 rounds, losing, during the action,

1 man killed ... and 1 horse disabled. I then moved into a field on the right of the pike and opened fire. The enemy retired from their position to the left and rear." The exchange of artillery lasted about thirty minutes when General John Palmer sent one of his batteries forward to assist Newell, and the defenders withdrew.[17]

Next, Brigadier General Charles Cruft sent the 1st Kentucky and 31st Indiana infantries forward to deal with the Confederate defenders. Minty moved his cavalry to support Cruft's left flank. Then, Colonel Walter Whitaker ordered two infantry regiments forward and drove Wheeler's cavalry back to La Vergne. Lieutenant Colonel J. D. Webb, 51st Alabama Partisan Rangers, was called to move his regiment into the fight north of La Vergne. Webb dismounted his men and formed a battle line on the west side of the Murfreesboro Pike. As the Union infantry moved ahead, Wheeler ordered Webb to fall back under the support of the Confederate artillery. Webb withdrew, resting his right flank on the pike, and remained in line until 10:00 p.m. and then returned to Stewarts Creek. Crittenden noted the intensity of the skirmishing: "In all these skirmishes the enemy fought with such determination as to induce the belief that there must have been a large force in the neighborhood. Our troops are in excellent condition, and manifest the finest military spirit and enthusiasm." Crittenden established his headquarters one and a half miles north of La Vergne that evening.[18]

Captain George Knox Miller, 8th Confederate Cavalry of Wheeler's Brigade, wrote in a letter of his actions during the day. Around noon the advance of the Union infantry was confirmed by the Southern cavalry and for Miller's regiment, the sounds of cannons booming in the distance signaled the serious threat of the enemy. As Crittenden moved forward, Wheeler sent his brigade to La Vergne to slow them. The 8th Confederate Cavalry had been five miles south and reached the town about 3:00 p.m. The movement of Union troops was a fairly common occurrence. The Southern cavalry had clashed with Union foraging expeditions for the past two months and this signaled nothing out of the ordinary. Upon arriving in the town and observing the size of the force, the alarm bells sounded for the Confederates. Crittenden's entire corps was clearly not on a foraging expedition.[19]

When the 8th Confederate Cavalry arrived, it moved to the east side of the Nashville Pike to support the 3rd Alabama Cavalry which was being "pressed vigorously" by the Union troops. Miller's regiment moved a mile forward and then dismounted to add its guns to those of the 3rd Alabama. The troopers of the 8th Confederate found the enemy well concealed in grove of cedar trees about a 150 yards away and then opened fire on them. Then the orders were given to charge them. The Southern cavalry ran ahead over two fences and at thirty yards away from the enemy they were surprised to find the Union soldiers in an excellent defensive position. Miller wrote, "Here we had as hot a little brush as one would want on a Dec. day. The Yanks were better posted than we and as it was growing dark had the light in their favor, besides their clothes were so near the color of the cedars behind which they were posted that it was almost impossible to see them; for nearly an hour we fought them, each man to his tree"[20]

Here a heated skirmish resulted as the Union soldiers refused to budge and the Confederate cavalry did likewise. The soldiers in blue had the advantage of better cover and some of the Confederates remained exposed. Miller found cover behind the trunk of a tree and aimed at a Union soldier when he felt a Minié ball hit the leg of his pants, tearing the yellow cords and barely avoiding a serious injury. As he fired, the return fire was so rapid and accurate that the balls knocked bark into his eyes several times. Those troopers facing Crittenden's soldiers had no doubt what was happening. "It took no ghost to us that Rosencranz had begun his long expected advance from Nashville, and what confirmed it, we could distinctly hear heavy cannonading all day to our left on the Nolensville pike, showing that he was advancing with a heavy column on each road." Miller's men withdrew after determining the size of the Union force.[21]

Later, the curious adjutant of the 4th Michigan Cavalry, Robert Burns, rode ahead at about 5:00 p.m. to see the positions of the two armies. As he rode, he heard a gunshot but he had heard gunfire all day and thought nothing of it until

> a ball whistled about a foot from my ear. I did not think much of it supposing it to be one of the enemy balls flying around sent on no particular message. In a moment I heard another and a ball came so close to my head I could almost feel it. I then concluded that I had been shot at and had no business so far in front.[22]

End of Day One

So, by the end of the first day of the advance toward Murfreesboro, Wheeler had fallen back about three miles and Crittenden's corps moved just north of La Vergne; and McCook pushed beyond Nolensville. The cavalry components of both armies had performed well during the first day. Naturally, the scope of Rosecrans' advance surprised Bragg and Wheeler, but Wharton's and Wheeler's cavalry responded in a professional and efficient manner. A stiff resistance by the Southern cavalry had accomplished its objective—the prevention of a rapid penetration of the Confederate line and gave time for the infantry to prepare a defense. Bragg was still unsure of Rosecrans' intent. If Rosecrans wanted to develop the Confederate position, this could be just a bluff and Rosecrans could easily return to Nashville during the night. However, the extent of the advance had gained the attention of the Southern commanders and the next day would be critical in determining Rosecrans' plan.

On the Union side of the line, the day proceeded pretty much as expected and the objectives were gained. Crittenden met the greatest resistance as expected and had moved to La Vergne, a ruin of a town with only a handful of structures still intact. "[B]lackened chimneys standing lone and desolate above gray beds of ashes—significant monuments of the folly and crime of rebellion—told the fate of the rest." Minty's cavalry effectively screened the advance and the Union infantry moved ahead to push Wheeler back. The infantry appreciated the work by Minty's cavalry that moved the enemy away from the front and cleaning out sharpshooters along the flanks. The next day would be important for Minty and Crittenden. As Crittenden moved south, the bridge over Stewarts Creek, if it could be captured intact, would allow his march toward Murfreesboro to go faster. Crossing a bridge in a wet, cold December day was much quicker and more convenient for the troops than crossing a stream on foot. Crittenden wrote to Rosecrans early the next morning that he expected the bridge to be burnt by the time he arrived.[23]

Thomas Wood, commanding the Left Wing First Division, described the terrain Crittenden faced:

> The country occupied by these bodies of hostile troops affords ground peculiarly favorable for a small force to retard the advance of a larger one. Large cultivated fields occur at intervals on either side of the turnpike road, but the country between the cultivated tracts is densely wooded, and much of the woodland interspersed with thick groves of cedar. The face of the country is undulating, presenting a succession of swells and subsidences.[24]

At the end of the day, Minty performed good duty and Lewis Zahm's brigade had accomplished its objectives during his expedition to Franklin, despite his inability to locate Thomas. The Ohio cavalry brigade had sent the Southern troopers scampering away from Franklin. Zahm prepared to work with Thomas' corps the next day in a reconnaissance mission toward Triune while sending half of his brigade back to Franklin. Finally, Stanley's reserve cavalry had been tardy in reaching the front of McCook's advance. However, the 36th Illinois mounted infantry performed the necessary screen for Jefferson Davis's division and it is unlikely Stanley could have provided greater service to Davis. Stanley's reserve brigade was still trying to gain confidence and had light, but productive, duty in the advance of Sheridan's division.

The rain continued to fall into the night. Rosecrans, after his ride to McCook's headquarters at Nolensville on the evening of December 26, verbally directed McCook to continue his advance the next day to Triune and attack Hardee's infantry. This was the key to Rosecrans' plan and Hardee's response would determine Rosecrans' next action. Thomas' two divisions also moved ahead. Rousseau still held the Union right flank, south of Brentwood at Owen's Store and Negley's division pushed ahead toward Nolensville in support of McCook. On the Union left flank, Crittenden settled into his headquarters just north of La Vergne while he planned to march on Stewarts Creek the next day. As Rosecrans left McCook's headquarters, McCook said, "Good night, General ... with the blessing of God, General, I will whip my friend Hardee tomorrow!"[25]

While the Union high command was making plans, so were the Confederates. Colonel W. D. Pickett, Hardee's inspector general, and Colonel Thomas Harrison, 8th Texas Cavalry, made a night reconnaissance. Because Harrison was familiar with the countryside, the two rode in relative silence through the soggy fields without alerting the enemy pickets. They came over a ridge and looked into a valley. They saw the entire valley filled with Union infantry and this dispelled any question to them of seriousness of the Federal advance. They returned and sent a message to Hardee describing what they had seen.[26]

At Confederate headquarters, Bragg met with his commanders

General Alexander McCook, commander of the Union right wing (National Archives).

and decided to pull Hardee closer to Murfreesboro. He asked Wheeler how long he could delay Rosecrans' advance and Wheeler responded two to four days, depending on the source. William Hardee thought Wheeler was too confident, "They will run right over you!" But Wheeler's plan brought good news to Bragg. It gave him time to determine the Union actions the following day and also time to prepare to concentrate his army to face a determined advance, if it really was one. So, Wheeler's cavalry moved to absorb the blows while punishing the Union soldiers who slowly moved south. William Hardee, like Rosecrans, had ridden to the front to determine the opposing force he faced. In light of the large Union force, Pat Cleburne's infantry, facing McCook south of Nolensville, was ordered to prepare to move to Murfreesboro. Although Cleburne would not receive his orders to move until early the next morning, S. A. M. Wood's infantry and John Wharton's cavalry were ordered to delay the Union advance at Triune. In the meantime, Wheeler prepared to slow Crittenden's advance north of Murfreesboro.

General William Hardee, commander of the Confederate corps that met McCook's advance (Library of Congress).

While Rosecrans' intent was still totally unclear, Bragg prepared to concentrate his army at Murfreesboro. The Union actions on Saturday would reveal the seriousness of Rosecrans' intent. Isaac Barton Ulmer, 3rd Confederate Cavalry, wrote a letter during the evening: "Firing has been very severe on both the Murfreesboro and Nolensville Pikes all day. The Yankees may have commenced their forward movement. Tomorrow I suppose will decide."[27]

December 27—Saturday

One of the soldiers of the Union army wrote of the day before: "It had rained, rained all night and all the next day. I did not have a dry foot for ten days," and the cold rain on Friday resulted in a dense fog on the morning of December 27. McCook initially ordered his infantry to march to attack the enemy at Triune, but the fog changed his plans.[28]

Meanwhile, Cleburne's division, McCook's target, hastily began a march of its own toward Murfreesboro under orders from Hardee who was convinced after his late night reconnaissance that a general Federal advance was taking place and early on December 27, Hardee ordered Cleburne's three brigades to Murfreesboro. S. A. M. Wood and John Wharton remained at Triune with orders to resist the Union advance. Cleburne's three brigades marched "over a miserable road and through a cold, drenching rain." He arrived at Murfreesboro that evening and camped a mile from town. As Cleburne marched eastward, S. A. M. Wood's (16th Alabama, 33rd Alabama, and 45th Mississippi infantry) brigade of 950 men supported by Darden's artillery and John Wharton's cavalry fell into position about a mile and a half north of Triune. Wood, an experienced officer from Alabama, began his Civil War service as captain in the Florence Guards. Wood's infantry moved into position at 4:00 a.m. along the hills just north of the town and Lieutenant Colonel Richard Charlton's 45th Mississippi Infantry held the forward position on the Nolensville Pike. John Wharton's cavalry brigade, that faced McCook's column the day before, also held its position north of town. The 45th Mississippi's and the cavalry's task was to skirmish and fall back, delaying McCook's advance.[29]

At 9:00 a.m., McCook's column found Charlton's Mississippi infantry and the Union cavalry sent the Southern soldiers seeking safety. Confederate soldier, F. M. Martin, described his skirmishing with 3rd Indiana Cavalry which led the Union advance:

> Our regiment (Forty-Fifth Mississippi now) engaged the advance cavalry force. In the melee I ran with the command, and forgetting my blankets, I ran back to get them; but finding them wet and too heavy to carry, I dropped them. All of a sudden bullets came hissing around my head. I thought I would be killed anyway, so I wheeled around and deliberately fired on my pursuers. There were three cavalrymen all in a bunch, so I fired and started on my run again. I saw some cavalry to my right, and I thought I would get them to take me up behind them, but decided to go on. I overtook my command just in time to stop them from firing into Wharton's Texas Cavalry, so I saved our own men. We halted in a skirt of woods out of a drenching rain, when suddenly the Yankee cavalry commenced firing on us. Our company had just got some shirts from Summit. The ladies of Summit had made them out of ... Brussels carpet, which made them look like British soldiers. These shirts were scattered over the field, and as I had not gotten one in the draw I picked one up as I was running.[30]

Despite the fog, Charlton observed McCook's column approaching and ordered Darden's artillery (four Napoleon cannons) to open fire. McCook continued to advance and Darden's artillerymen sent a hundred rounds into the rows of blue soldiers. Both Battery E, 1st Ohio Artillery, commanded by Captain Warren P. Edgarton, and Peter Simonson's 5th Indiana Artillery unlimbered and began to return fire. Simonson's artillery sent some of Wharton's cavalry seeking safety. As McCook continued his advance the 45th Mississippi infantry opened fire, but Union troops continued forward forcing Darden to limber his guns and head for the rear. As the 45th Mississippi and Darden's artillery made their initial stand, they were immediately threatened by Stanley's Reserve Cavalry Brigade. Major Joseph Collins, 29th Indiana Infantry, sent his skirmishers ahead to take over the ground vacated by Wood's infantry which had been "just wrested from the enemy by our cavalry." The Union cavalry which removed the Confederate defenders was the 3rd Indiana Cavalry commanded by Robert Klein. Klein proudly acknowledged David Stanley's compliment that morning: "Third knew how to take these rebels." Stanley also ordered Klein to move forward to Triune and Klein intended to do just that. As the Union cavalry moved ahead it detected "the enemy in considerable force drawn up in line of battle." Klein galloped forward and his forward company received the full volley of the defenders. Klein deployed his battalion on the Nolensville Pike and either side. Due to the soggy condition, the flanking companies were slower on the advance. Once the remaining companies arrived, the defenders retreated and moved to the protection of the Southern artillery. Klein again charged ahead and drove the defenders from a hill and back to Triune. McCook expected a fight with Hardee's Corps at Triune and the dense fog caused him to stop his advance. McCook described the fog as so dense, it "prevented us from seeing 150 yards in any direction.... The fog at this time being so thick that friend could not be distinguished from foe, and our cavalry having been fired upon by our infantry skirmishers, on the flanks, the enemy being conversant with the ground, my troops strangers to it, and from prisoners captured having learned that Hardee's corps had been in line of battle since the night before." McCook knew he faced infantry, cavalry and artillery but he prudently decided to wait until he could see what he faced. In the meantime,

Wharton ordered Charlton to withdraw 300 yards to the rear to stone wall to a line held by the 16th Alabama Infantry near the Franklin Road and again resist McCook's advance. Darden's artillery also unlimbered and was joined by a section of White's artillery as the Confederate defense intensified. During the withdrawal, Wood's engineers destroyed the bridge over Nelson's Creek.[31]

At 1:00 p.m., the fog lifted to such a degree that McCook decided to advance. Wood now waited for the Union infantry behind the stone wall supported by Wharton's cavalry on the flanks. Stanley's Reserve Cavalry Brigade and part of Zahm's cavalry preceded the Union advance and appeared on both flanks of Wood's infantry while McCook's infantry marched ahead. Seeing the Union cavalry riding forward, the Union soldiers watched large bodies of Wharton's cavalry move into position to resist the Union cavalry. As the opposing forces were drawing into a battle line, Edgarton's six-gun Union battery unlimbered on a hill near Triune outside the range of Wood's artillery and began to fire. This caused Wood to move his artillery to the rear. Not only was the Confederate artillery a target, so was Wharton's cavalry. Lieutenant Albert Ransom, 1st Ohio artillery, recorded; "When we first came in sight of Triune, the road was filled with rebel cavalry, and one section, unlimbering in the road, made them its especial mark. The town was soon made untenable." The 29th Indiana Infantry moved forward to assist in silencing the Confederate artillery. The Indianans found the guns supported by a dismounted cavalry whose "leaden compliments attracted our attention," commented Major Joseph Collins. As Collins's infantry continued forward, it was surprised by when a regiment of Southern cavalry appeared on the left of his infantry moving "leisurely to the front." Collins ordered his men to fire into the 1st Confederate Cavalry and troopers reeled in their saddles. Collins charged forward knocking four or five troopers out of their saddles and capturing two men. After rapidly ordering his men to fire, Collins feared the cavalry was the 5th Tennessee Cavalry (U.S.), part of Stanley's command, but he had made the correct order.[32]

While Stanley and McCook pushed directly south in the early afternoon, Union cavalry continued to threatened Wood and Wharton from the west. The cavalry was again commanded by Major Robert Klein who had had success during the morning by pushing the Confederate skirmishers before the infantry advance. Klein had been ordered by Stanley to take his battalion with one company of the 15th Pennsylvania Cavalry to attack the Confederate left (west) flank. The cavalry moved out under the shouts of the infantry: "[G]o for 'em boys, give 'em thunder." If the flank could be turned, then this could give the Union infantry more room to maneuver. The Union cavalry had the task of attacking the Confederate defenders behind the stone wall with the only visible targets being the heads of the enemy, a difficult shot for troopers on horseback. Wood and Wharton held a strong position behind a rock wall and supported by artillery. Despite the difficulty of the task, Klein felt his men were making good progress against the defenders. Then the Southern artillery focused on Klein's troopers. Klein observed two guns on his left about 500 yards away and two guns in front which opened fire and sent the Union cavalry back to the cover of some woods. Klein recorded the retreat was "done promptly, but in good order," but S. A. M. Wood recorded: "Many saddles were emptied and the whole thrown into confusion." Klein recorded three men killed and three wounded during the day. In addition, Major Adolph Rosengarten, 15th Pennsylvania, who seemed to have a knack of being in the center of all the action, narrowly escaped capture. Just as a hard rain and hail began falling and realizing that this was a battle which could not be won, Wharton and Wood concluded to retire under the cover of their artillery. The weather continued to deteriorate and Wood observed the might of the Union infantry approaching his position "extending a mile in length." Wood credited the success of the withdrawal to his artillery "but, above all, the disposition of cavalry made by Brigadier-General Wharton." Wood moved his division to within three miles of the Eagleville Pike where he camped for the night. Wood recorded six casualties in the resistance of McCook's columns.[33]

The sheer size of McCook's corps won the day, but Private Benjamin Burke, 8th Texas Cavalry, proudly wrote his description of the day: "Although they had force enough to drive us, we contended [contested] every inch of ground with them as fare as they followed us." The chaplain of the 8th Texas Cavalry also noted the strategy utilized by the Federal cavalry. He described that the blue-coated cavalry would charge ahead and then withdraw under the support of infantry and artillery. He felt that Wharton and his cavalry had performed its duty well during the day.[34]

George Thomas's wing still trailed McCook's wing. Rousseau reached Nolensville during the evening after an arduous march during the day, Negley moved to the right of Crittenden at Stewartsborough and Moses Walker's brigade reached the Nolensville Pike, having moved from Brentwood. As Thomas advanced, Lewis Zahm worked on the flank and rear of Thomas's column. Zahm proceeded during the day according to the plan developed in cooperation with Rousseau the evening before. The 1st Ohio, 3rd Ohio and 4th Ohio cavalries rode down the Wilson Creek Pike to the proximity of Triune on a reconnaissance mission, perhaps fruitlessly, because the bulk of McCook's wing and Stanley's reserve brigade were also near Triune. Had Bragg or Wheeler planned a flank attack on McCook or Thomas, Zahm's presence would have detected it. Near Triune, the Ohio cavalry approached the Confederate line and received a barrage of about fifty artillery rounds. William Crane recorded that the 4th Ohio Cavalry halted and the 1st Ohio and the 3rd Ohio regiments moved a mile further in advance and were shelled by Confederate artillery. The 1st Ohio and 3rd Ohio were "driven back.... Sharp skirmishing then occurred & artillery firing was kept up about an hour, the rebels being attacked about the same time by Gen. [Richard] Johnson's Brig. which came upon them from another side." Zahm claimed six prisoners for his efforts during the day. Meanwhile, a battalion of the 3rd Ohio Cavalry returned to Franklin, the site of Zahm's successful charge the day before with much less success. Baxter Smith's 4th Tennessee (Confederate) Cavalry and the 14th Alabama Battalion were prepared when the Union cavalry returned and "quite a skirmish ensued." Certainly, Zahm's single battalion was a much smaller force than the

General George Thomas, commander of the Union center (Library of Congress).

one used the previous day and Smith was prepared for the Union cavalry's return. Zahm reported the enemy had returned in force and repaid the Ohio cavalry for their actions the day before. The skirmish lasted for two hours but the "enemy was too strong to drive" and the 3rd Ohio returned to camp. The repulse of the Federal cavalry increased the morale Smith's 4th Tennessee (CSA) regiment. In addition, the fact that Bragg was not retreating was greeted with support from the members of the Confederate Cavalry. "We were buoyant with the hope he would send Genl. Rosecranz howling back to Nashville."[35]

Capture of Stewarts Creek Bridges

Meanwhile, Robert Minty's cavalry brigade again worked to assist Thomas Crittenden's movements. Crittenden's wing pushed forward during the day and the Union general felt he was vulnerable should Bragg decide to counterattack rather than just waiting for Rosecrans' movements. In particular, Crittenden needed support on his right flank. As McCook and Thomas began their movements during the day, Crittenden remained idle, but his objective was getting his wing over Stewarts Creek which promised to be a cold, wet process. Brigadier General Thomas Wood described Stewarts Creek as a "narrow and deep stream, flowing between high and precipitous banks." With the bridges destroyed the forward progress by Crittenden's troops would either be delayed while the bridges were rebuilt or the crossing would be made via fords in the cold December water. While Crittenden waited he planned how to make his crossing. He sent a brigade to the east on the Jefferson Pike to attempt to capture a bridge over Stewarts Creek because his scouts reported a relatively small number of cavalry defending the bridge. Negley's division of Thomas' wing was still moving from the west to cover Crittenden's right flank, but McCook was still fifteen miles away. At 7:30 a.m. as Crittenden waited, cannon fire was heard from the west. McCook was moving.[36]

Minty ordered the 7th Pennsylvania Cavalry under command of Major John Wynkoop to screen General Palmer's division which was on the left of Crittenden's wing. A battalion of the 4th Michigan Cavalry (about 90 men), commanded by Captain Frank Mix, cooperated in the movement of William B. Hazen's infantry brigade along the Jefferson Pike as it moved toward Stewarts Creek. The 3rd Kentucky Cavalry and the one company of the 2nd Indiana Cavalry covered the other flank of Crittenden's wing which began moving at 11:00 a.m. While Mix's men moved to the east in hopes of securing the bridge over Stewarts Creek on the Jefferson Pike, Thomas Wood's infantry marched ahead with the same objective along the Murfreesboro Pike. Wood determined the terrain in front of his division to be unsuitable for cavalry and dispatched the cavalry to the rear and advanced with his infantry. Milo Hascall's infantry brigade took the lead, flanked by Wagner's and Harker's brigades on either side of the road. Hascall's infantry led the attack and pushed the defenders out of La Vergne, Wood's first objective, and then moved to secure a crossing over Stewarts Creek, Wood's second objective. In a steady, drenching rain, Wood's division rushed ahead with such vigor that the defenders "could not materially retard the advance." Wheeler's cavalry saw that Wood's division could not be stopped and attempted to set fire to the bridge; but the 3rd Kentucky Infantry rushed forward securing the bridge and threw the flaming material into the stream. While the 3rd Kentucky secured the bridge, Wheeler's cavalry tried to capitalize on the unsupported movement of the infantry. The Southern cavalry struck the left flank of the leading brigade but the attack backfired on the cavalry. The 51st Alabama Partisan Rangers tried to cut their way through to the bridge, but the Alabamans made a desperate but ill-planned attack. Hascall's infantry confronted the Southern cavalry and demanded their surrender. When Lieutenant Colonel James D. Webb's men refused, the Union infantry "pressed upon them, drove them into the fence corners, and captured 24 of them, including Lieut. J[oseph] J. Seawell. They called themselves 'Alabama Partisan Rangers.' With them were captured 12 horses and saddles and 12 guns." The remainder of the Alabama cavalry saw those in front surrendering to the 100th Illinois infantry and "wheeled to the left behind a house and escaped." The 100th Illinois Infantry rushed ahead and cut off a portion of Southern cavalry claiming a total of 75 prisoners, but importantly Wheeler failed to destroy the bridge over the creek.[37]

The second Stewarts Creek bridge was about four miles east of the Murfreesboro Pike on the Jefferson Pike and Captain Frank Mix rode at the head of a battalion of the 4th Michigan Cavalry consisting of Companies B, E, H, and L. About two and a half miles from the bridge, Mix ran into enemy pickets and the Union cavalry began chasing them toward the bridge. Mix noted: "At every rod their number increased, so that when we came to the bridge we were chasing about 200 of them." The 51st Alabama Partisan Cavalry, Lieutenant Colonel J. D. Webb commanding, had just participated in the failed defense of the Stewarts Creek bridge on Murfreesboro Pike, which was claimed by Hascall's infantry, when its rear was attacked by the hard charging 4th Michigan riding at top speed. The remainder of 51st Alabama which just avoided a disaster at the hands of Wood's infantry rode to the east when it clashed with the 4th Michigan Cavalry. The 4th Michigan, on an expedition of its own, had been ordered by Hazen "to put spurs to his troop, and not slack rein until the bridge was crossed" as it screened the advance of a brigade of infantry to the Stewart Creek bridge on the Jefferson Pike and it was doing just that. Despite Hazen's attempt to take credit for the success of Mix's action, the 4th Michigan Cavalry serendipitously clashed with Webb's 51st Alabama Partisan Rangers and drove the pickets toward Stewarts Creek. What started as a rear guard action, resulted in a full retreat as the rearguard unnerved the main body of the 51st Alabama Partisan Cavalry. The Southern cavalry pickets scrambled across the bridge and they were so crowded some were shoved off the side of the bridge and were taken prisoner. Mix's troopers followed close on the heels of the retreating cavalry. After claiming the bridge which was still intact, Mix sent riders to hurry the infantry forward. Mix's men began to prepare defenses while they waited for the infantry to rush forward. In the meantime, the Confederates rallied through the efforts of Captain M. L. Kirkpatrick, Captain Lee W. Battle, and Lieutenant William M. Fitt, and turned and attacked Mix. Mix wrote: "[S]trong force, but our boys nobly stood their ground and repulsed them." To make matters worse for Mix, he found another hundred Confederate cavalry in his rear cutting him off from the infantry. "I then attempted to draw part of my command (Company L) back of the bridge, but I no sooner started them back than they came down on us like bees, yelling as if they had us sure." Next, Mix ordered Lieutenant Julius Carter to position Company B on each side of the road where they could observe the Confederate movements. Company L hurried back to the newly forming Union position being chased by Southern cavalry, but Mix ordered them to turn about after reaching his line and they faced their pursuers. The Michigan cavalrymen turned around "which they did handsomely, not a man flinching or wavering in the least. They immediately opened a fire upon the enemy, which soon made them leave for the woods."[38]

Musket fire exploded in the rear of Mix's cavalry and he dispatched Captain Benjamin Pritchard's company to assist with the fighting. Expecting his small group of cavalry to be attacked from all sides, Mix moved Company B on the bridge itself and not a moment too soon as Confederates rushed ahead trying to drive the Michigan cavalry away "[O]ur boys were too much for them, and again drove them back under cover of the woods." Finally, a charge by the troopers of Company H secured the bridge for Hazen's infantry which were hastening forward with artillery support.[39]

Mix continued,

> The officers and men of these four companies are deserving of great praise. With 50 men we charged and drove for 2½ miles 200 of the [Fifty-]First Alabama Cavalry, and held the bridge for one-half hour against the whole regiment. The prisoners we took admit that their regiment was all there, and another regiment in Wheeler's brigade was 2 miles in the rear, on Stone's River.

In a letter written on January 9, Mix was more reflective about the fight and explained taking and holding the bridge resulted in an intense skirmish. "It was the hottest place I ever got into in my life," explained Mix when the Confederates counterattacked his position.[40]

Mix's battalion held on to the bridge for thirty minutes as Hazen's infantry and artillery hastened forward and secured the prize. Mix had one man wounded and three men taken prisoner during the fight. In return the 4th Michigan captured nine men of the 51st Alabama Partisan Rangers and killed one officer and one trooper. The plucky Michigan cavalry had gained a crossing over Stewarts Creek and demonstrated the morning belonged to the bold. Lieutenant Colonel James Webb, 51st Alabama, explained "being heavily pressed by greatly superior numbers, and opened upon by their artillery with grape, canister, and shell vigorously," he had no choice but to withdraw. As Hazen's infantry moved to claim possession of the bridge the fight was over. The regiment had had a difficult morning. It was somewhat ironic that Confederate infantryman James R. Riggs declared in a letter he wrote to his sister on December 26, 1862, that he wanted to join the 51st Alabama Partisan Rangers because "they have quite an easy time." After the day's actions, many of the troopers of the regiment may have desired to change places with him.[41]

Crittenden's success of capturing two intact bridges over Stewarts Creek boded well for his advance the next day. Facing primarily cavalry during the day, his infantry had achieved its objective although Crittenden was still several miles away from McCook who had determined that Hardee had moved his corps but where, was still an uncertainty—Shelbyville or Murfreesboro. Conflicting reports suggested movement south while others suggested Bragg intended to fight along Stewarts Creek but McCook believed the Confederate army was concentrating at Murfreesboro.[42]

George Knox Miller's 8th Confederate Cavalry remained on duty during the day as part of Wheeler's brigade; and in an effort to give his men some much needed rest Wheeler rotated his regiments which faced the Union advance. After getting rations for the day,

Captain Frank Mix, 4th Michigan Cavalry—"It was the hottest place I ever got into in my life."

Miller's regiment moved to a field and watched Crittenden's corps advance. Miller's men fired and then slowly fell back but at one point his company was surprised when the company on his right fell back faster. Miller found himself temporarily in the rear of the Union infantry and cavalry which moved past him without knowing of his presence. He was so close he saw a regiment of cavalry on white horses and heard the commands clearly. Miller was able to withdraw without being seen beyond Stewarts Creek which he described: "Stewarts Creek is a driving stream with very steep banks, and our intention was to cross it at the bridge on the pike, but as we neared that point we found that our artillery had already crossed over & Gen. Wheeler had destroyed the bridge and the enemy's cannon were then raking the pike." Miller's company found a narrow path leading to the rear out of sight of the Union troops and made it back to the newly forming Confederate lines just as Minty's cavalry captured the path. The 8th Confederate Cavalry remained on picket just south of Stewarts Creek and prepared to withdraw closer to Murfreesboro where Bragg was concentrating his forces.[43]

The "fight-withdraw-fight" method of delaying Crittenden's corps was difficult for the Southern cavalry and the weather offered no relief. Miller described:

A cold drenching rain had been falling all day, and there was another cheerless night before us. My Squadron formed the second relief and was to stand 4 hours, from 11 p.m. to 3 a.m. I was lying on a wet blanket nearly freezing. I was called to go on duty and immediately roused up my wet & sleepy boys. The enemy's picket line was on the opposite side of creek and so near to our own that we could hear them in low conversation, and while I was passing along the bank going from one of my posts to the other, one of their pickets fired at me not more than 50 yds. distant & came very near taking my head off. I told him he had but little to do & moved on.[44]

During the evening of December 27 the rain finally stopped and the weather turned cold, and Crittenden remained along Stewarts Creek. At 6:00 p.m., James Negley's division moved to the right of Crittenden's wing after a long day of marching in the cold rain and on muddy roads. The remainder of Thomas's wing remained near Nolensville during evening, but Thomas planned to march to join Crittenden the next day, taking up position as the center wing of Rosecrans' army. Lewis Zahm in cooperation with Thomas maintained a close eye on the Confederate cavalry at Franklin and patrolled the Wilson Pike.[45]

On the Southern side of Stones River, the Union advance proved to be real and Bragg began to pull his army together at Murfreesboro. Bragg issued the following orders:

1st. The line of battle will be in front of Murfreesborough; half of the army, left wing, in front of Stone's River; right wing in rear of river.
2d. Polk's corps will form left wing; Hardee's corps, right wing.
3d. Withers' division will form first line in Polk's corps; Cheatham's, the second line. Breckinridge's division forms first line Hardee's corps; Cleburne's division, second line Hardee's corps.
4th. McCown's division to form reserve, opposite center, on high ground, in rear of Cheatham's present quarters.
5th. Jackson's brigade reserve, to the right flank, to report to Lieutenant-General Hardee.
6th. Two lines to be formed from 800 to 1,000 yards apart, according to ground.
7th. Chiefs of artillery to pay special attention to posting of batteries, and supervise their work, seeing they do not causelessly waste their ammunition.
8th. Cavalry to fall back gradually before enemy, reporting by couriers every hour. When near our lines, Wheeler will move to the right and Wharton to the left, to cover and protect our flanks and report movements of enemy; Pegram to fall to the rear, and report to commanding general as a reserve.
9th. Tonight, if the enemy has gained his position in our front ready for action, Wheeler and Wharton, with their whole commands, will make a night march to the right and left, turn the enemy's flank, gain his rear, and vigorously assail his trains and rear guard, blocking the roads and impeding his movements every way, holding themselves ready to assail his retreating forces.

> 10th. All quartermasters, commissaries, and ordnance officers will remain at their proper posts, discharging their appropriate duties. Supplies and baggage should be ready, packed for a move forward or backward as the results of the day may require, and the trains should be in position, out of danger, teamsters all present, and quartermasters in charge.
>
> 11th. Should we be compelled to retire, Polk's corps will move on Shelbyville and Hardee's on Manchester pike; trains in front; cavalry in rear.[46]

The decision had been made and the fight would take place at Murfreesboro.

December 28—Sunday

The gloom of the previous days was gone on December 28: "Weather beautiful all day & the night bright." The morning of December 28 found Crittenden's wing firmly in control of the crossings on Stewarts Creek. In addition to the good bridge captured at Jefferson the day before, fords, although poor ones, and two other bridges nearby were available for use by the Federal infantry, if needed. Importantly, William Hazen found there were no enemy troops south of his position along the Jefferson Pike. Alexander McCook also awoke and found the enemy in front of his wing, gone. Even Wharton's tenacious cavalry could not to be found. He wrote: "No enemy visible. Cavalry vedettes all gone." Despite the removal of the enemy, McCook still faced poor conditions with which to march. McCook also faced the destruction of the bridge over Nelson's Creek which left "very ugly bluff banks to the river; the river rising…." David Stanley had his cavalry up early and screening the front of McCook's infantry. McCook concluded, through the efforts of August Willich's infantry and Robert Klein's 3rd Indiana Cavalry, Hardee's route of retreat was not south, but east to Murfreesboro.[47]

Rosecrans accomplished what he desired during the first two days of his advance. He wanted to know if Bragg would retreat southward, or concentrate his army and contest Rosecrans. It was the latter, and Bragg appeared to choose Murfreesboro as the location to fight. Scouts determined that other Southern units were ordered up to Murfreesboro. Rosecrans concluded: "Everything indicates a determination to fight us." McCook was ordered to turn east, pushing all resistance aside and converge on Murfreesboro, sixteen miles away, starting early on December 28, despite Rosecrans' inclination not to move his army on the Sabbath. The wings were still too disconnected to suit McCook and he decided to march on Sunday, via the Bole Jack Road and close up on Thomas's right flank. McCook knew his march threated Bragg's flank and expected stiff resistance during the day.[48]

Stanley's cavalry was ordered to protect McCook's right flank, but he also sent a screen of cavalry in front of the advance. In a surprising message, McCook reported that Stanley's Reserve Brigade had "not a round of ammunition, and General Stanley reports that there is none in Nashville for these arms." Despite this situation, Stanley needed to have his cavalry in advance of McCook's infantry primarily protecting the Bole Jack Road and on the right flank of the march.[49]

As Stanley's cavalry kept pace with McCook's movement, members of the 15th Pennsylvania Cavalry encountered two ladies in the house near Triune. As the troopers searched the Pett's house, one of ladies pulled a pocket pistol and threatened the officer of the search party. No one was found in the house and as the cavalry prepared to ride away, she exclaimed, "'Mark my words … you cowardly Yankees will go flying back to Nashville tomorrow quicker than you came—though I hope to heaven'—here she raised her clenched fist—'that not one of you will live to reach there.'" Many in central Tennessee were unhappy to see the Union army marching in the countryside.⁵⁰

On the left flank of Rosecrans' army the only notable cavalry action during the day occurred when the 7th Pennsylvania moved over the Stewarts Creek Bridge on the Jefferson Pike to relieve the 4th Michigan which dutifully protected the approach to the bridge from the south. Otherwise, Lewis Zahm's Ohio cavalry brigade rode from its position on the Wilson Pike and took up position at Triune and prepared to screen McCook's flank. Zahm's Cavalry was joined by the 5th and 2nd Tennessee cavalries of Stanley's Reserve Brigade. Stanley's brigade performed the only active duty during the day. Major Robert Klein's cavalry rode in advance of Willich's brigade toward Shelbyville and found no evidence of Hardee moving south. Willich, a native Prussian, wrote to McCook: "The enemy is no more here; all gone to Murfreesborough." This information which defined the intent of Bragg to concentrate at Murfreesboro was transferred to McCook by Willich. Klein's cavalry scooped up sixteen enemy stragglers during the march.⁵¹

General Leonidas Polk, the "Fighting Bishop," commanded a corps of Confederate infantry at Murfreesboro (Library of Congress).

Only the 2nd Tennessee Cavalry reported skirmishing on December 28 and if the report was correct, the unlucky 51st Alabama Partisan Rangers had another unpleasant encounter with the Union cavalry. Lieutenant William Hall, adjutant of the 2nd Tennessee Cavalry, reported his regiment clashed with the 51st Alabama Partisan Rangers near Triune which resulted in an "obstinate engagement." The 2nd Tennessee attacked the Alabamans and sent them riding for Shelbyville. The Tennessee cavalry captured a lieutenant and five troopers and reported a loss of four horses killed in the skirmish.⁵²

Meanwhile, Thomas continued his march toward Murfreesboro on Sunday. Rousseau marched for Stewarts Creek joining Negley's division, and Moses Walker's brigade was assigned duty at Nolensville covering the extreme right flank of the army. Thomas lamented that the road was in poor condition and his march might be delayed, but Rosecrans was having none of that. The enemy intended to fight and Rosecrans was ready to fight. At noon on December 28, Lieutenant Colonel Julius Garesché wrote to hurry Thomas forward. Garesché emphasized that Bragg showed "a stubborn determination on the part of the enemy to fight this side of Murfreesborough ... close in upon them as rapidly as possible ... you must lose no time." Garesché, a West Point graduate, class of 1841, was Rosecrans' very efficient chief of staff.[53]

Bragg did not exhibit any reluctance of moving his troops on Sunday as his troops were ordered to move to their assigned positions. At 9:00 p.m. on December 27, Bragg sent orders directing Wheeler, Wharton and Pegram to "fall back before the enemy tomorrow. The move of the enemy is evidently on this place." He ordered Hardee's corps to fall into position on the right of Murfreesboro with his left on the Nashville Pike. Breckinridge's division formed the first battle line and Cleburne's division fell 800–1,000 yards behind him. Leonidas Polk's corps formed on the left of Hardee with John Withers's division in the forward position and Benjamin Cheatham occupied the second battle line. McCown's division served as the reserve. The cavalry continued to cooperate with the movement of their relative infantry corps. During the day, Wharton sent a reconnaissance expedition to Franklin and Columbia to determine the route of Rosecrans' march. Bragg ordered all the troops to be in position to meet the Federals at 9:00 a.m. the next morning. At 10:00 a.m., Bragg had time to prepare and confidently wrote: "Enemy stationary, 10 miles in our front. My troops all ready and confident."[54]

Scouts from Baxter Smith's 4th Tennessee Cavalry formed the reconnaissance to Triune and Franklin. The movement of August Willich and Robert Klein's 3rd Indiana was observed as it marched south and then returned to join McCook's wing. John Wharton concluded any concern that Rosecrans was attempting a flanking movement of Bragg at Murfreesboro proved unlikely. Willich and Klein marched over six miles to determine Hardee did not retreat south toward Shelbyville. Wharton found McCook tracking Hardee, not trying to flank him. Wharton decided to make his headquarters on the Wilkinson Pike, a dirt road running in a western direction from the Nashville Pike just north of Murfreesboro, and he extended his cavalry to connect with Wheeler's brigade on his right. With Bragg's decision to fight at Murfreesboro, Wharton wrote to Polk: "This is my proper position as your cavalry officer," but all illusion of Bragg's intent was lost. Wharton concluded: "My falling back on this place convinces them that General Bragg will fight here."[55]

The civility of not practicing war on the Sabbath was also part of Bragg's army. Captain George K. Miller, 8th Confederate Cavalry, wrote: "Gen. Bragg has by a general order dispensed, as much as possible, with all military duties such as drills, drawing and issuing commissaries on the sabbath day.... The soldier should at least be reminded when the Sabbath comes." As the Confederate cavalry moved back to the main Confederate lines, the life of a cavalryman was contemplated by some. The 8th Confederate Cavalry, like many of the other Confederate regiments had no complete uniforms. Equipping the Southern cavalry was still a work in progress. Miller described his uniform:

> My company has, really, no complete uniform, nor ever has had since it was an old volunteer.... You may say its uniform at present is plain gray jeans frock coats, with a single row of brass buttons, pants of same color, high boots and black felt hats. Some few of them are dressed a little different from this, but the above is the standard.

In addition to being without standardized uniforms, the Confederate cavalry routinely slept outdoors and ate as a regiment in camp. Miller believed an officer's position was with his men and he spent his time with his company. He explained: "[I]t ensures discipline and gives them confidence in those who are, for the most part arbitrarily, called their superiors."[56]

Bragg selected his position for battle. He reasoned that because Murfreesboro was the junction so many of the roads in the area, he had no choice but to defend this position. This way he could control the movements of the Union army. In regard to the actions of Wharton and Wheeler, Bragg had nothing but praise. He recognized the cavalry supported by infantry had given him what he needed most—time to pull his army together.

> To the skillful manner in which the cavalry, thus ably supported, was handled, and to the exceeding gallantry of its officers and men, must be attributed the four days' time consumed by the enemy in reaching the battlefield, a distance of only 20 miles from his encampments, over fine macadamized roads.[57]

Captain George Miller whose 8th Confederate Cavalry battled the Union advance observed that the bridge over Stewarts Creek being re-built and in working order the next morning. When the sun came out the next morning [28 December], Miller described it: "[A]s genial as on a spring day, and taking advantage of a house near the creek I stood and viewed the Yankee horde as it filled the open woods and fields in front of us." As the day progressed, the Southern cavalry and the Union sharpshooters took shots at one another. Miller described a fairly common practice in the Civil War when peace unexpectedly broke out between some of the opposing soldiers. After exchanging shots with a Yankee soldier for some three hours,

> John bartered him to stop shooting and exchange [news]papers with him. After considerable parleying it was agreed to on both sides, and in a few minutes an armistice was agreed upon and all ceased firing. John got a paper & went down to the creek, the Yankee did likewise while their whole army came out & looked on. Papers were exchanged & compliments passed. I went down and exchanged papers with several of the Yankees, or rather Federal Kentuckians. They asked many questions about friends & acquaintances in our army and we parted at Sundown.[58]

Summary

Edward Longacre, Wheeler's biographer, summarized the Confederate cavalry's efforts in delaying Rosecrans' march through December 28, and he acknowledged that historians generally give high accolades, including Bragg himself, to Wheeler but also acknowledged historian Edwin Bearss' alternate point of view. Bearss gives more credit to the poor weather conditions, which included fog and a quagmire of mud, as the reason for the successful slowing of the Union advance. Regardless, there can be little doubt Wheeler brought a fighting spirit to the Confederate forces at Murfreesboro and he was successful in his ability to slow the Union movement. Wharton and Wheeler's brigades calmly, doggedly, and in a disciplined manner resisted the Federal advance and prevented a quick strike to any vulnerable Confederate positions. All the while, Bragg pulled his infantry and artillery into place; and in the end, Wheeler's cavalry successfully delayed the Union advance.

From the Union side, the cavalry also performed well. Zahm and Stanley protected the flanks of McCook's corps while effectively dealing with Wharton's resistance. The 4th Michigan Cavalry had claimed an intact bridge over Stewarts Creek and screened Crittenden's advance. The efficient Robert Klein's 3rd Indiana made notable successes, as did the Ohio cavalry brigade in its efforts to deal with Baxter Smith's 4th Tennessee Cavalry and Malone's 14th Alabama Battalion. Even the recalcitrant 15th Pennsylvania Cavalry was rising to meet the call of duty. No serious mistakes occurred on either side to this point and the two armies slowly moved to meet on the ground chosen by Braxton Bragg, along Stones River just north of Murfreesboro.

7. The Advance on Murfreesboro— Second Phase (December 29–30)

We will now take the enemy in hand & and by the grace of God give him his due.—General Braxton Bragg

December 29–Monday

Crittenden's wing started its advance at 10:00 a.m. expecting to find stiff resistance at the Stewarts Creek crossing after a series of enemy troop movements and signals observed during the night. Instead, Crittenden found only Wheeler's cavalry resisting the movement. Palmer's, Wood's and Van Cleve's divisions pushed ahead and had little problem moving the Southern cavalry out of the way. Brigadier General John Palmer resorted to his artillery to fire a few shells at the cavalry defenders and then marched forward. The Union infantry advanced against Wheeler's cavalry which, even though clearly outnumbered, stubbornly resisted the lines of blue soldiers. James Negley's division joined the right flank of Crittenden's wing about 3:00 p.m., finally linking Crittenden with Thomas' division. At 4:00 p.m. Crittenden's march was over. Three-quarters of a mile north of Murfreesboro, Crittenden observed Bragg's infantry in plain view and he had no option but to stop. General Thomas Wood observed the Confederates troops "displayed in battle array, were plainly to be seen in our front." Some initial reports from the Federal infantry erroneously reported the Confederate troops were retreating. This miscommunication resulted in Colonel Charles Harker's infantry brigade advancing across Stones River where he held his position until 10:00 p.m. before re-crossing to the north bank of the river after Bragg firmly held his position. Harker's crossing threatened a key Confederate artillery position at Wayne's Hill until he returned to main Union lines.[1]

Wheeler's intent was not to stop the Union advance toward Murfreesboro but to slow it so the Confederate infantry and artillery could prepare for the upcoming battle. Wheeler's troopers were doing their job well. George Knox Miller wrote:

> Another cold night on picket and Monday 29th dawned upon us. The sun was an hour high but all was yet quiet and we began to think the day might pass as Sunday had. Soon, however, we saw a column moving down to the ford at which we had crossed. A company was sent down to oppose the crossing. The enemy opened with artillery upon it. Our regiment was covered by a house, and when Col. Wade gave the order to fall back across an open field they turned their guns on us. In this firing a shell struck a horse and burst inside of him, tearing the animal up but injuring the rider not at all. The enemy crossed the creek in full force and we slowly fell back toward Murfreesboro. General Bragg's order to the cavalry was not to fight back the advance too steadily but to let them come on.[2]

Crittenden's troops formed a double battle line and then refused his vulnerable left flank. Part of Thomas's wing had joined Crittenden, and Thomas ordered Rousseau's division to Jefferson to bolster the left flank. In the meantime, Minty's cavalry screened the flanks to prevent a surprise attack from Bragg. Minty's cavalry was in the saddle throughout the day providing protection along the flank. As Crittenden's wing connected with Thomas's division, the 7th Pennsylvania Cavalry, commanded by Major John Wynkoop, remained on duty along the left flank and Eli Murray's 3rd Kentucky Cavalry rode on the right. Part of the 4th Michigan rode in the rear of the infantry and the rest of the regiment went on a scouting expedition seven miles to the east of the armies to make sure there was no effort to flank Crittenden's wing. Captain Joseph Mitchell, commanding the only company of the 2nd Indiana Cavalry with the army was ordered to courier duty between Nashville and Crittenden's wing. Robert Minty simply reported, "Light skirmishing with the enemy all day.... Bivouacked for the night immediately in rear of our line of battle."[3]

McCook's wing remained separated; but it marched down the Wilkinson Pike and at the end of the day it would be only three miles away from Murfreesboro. About an hour after Crittenden began his movement that morning, gunfire was heard to the west. Stanley's Reserve Brigade and Lewis Zahm's First Cavalry Brigade were already involved in more action than Minty would have during the entire day. Stanley's and Zahm's cavalry clashed with Wharton's cavalry whose headquarters was directly in the path of McCook's march to Murfreesboro.[4]

Stanley's and Zahm's brigades successfully screened McCook's advance as Rosecrans moved his various wings into a solid line outside of Murfreesboro. Certainly the resistance was intensifying along McCook's flank as he approached from the west. More concerning was the repeated message McCook sent to headquarters that Stanley's cavalry had no ammunition. Garesché snapped that there was plenty of ammunition in Nashville for all types of weapons and in reply to the fact that Stanley had no ammunition: "It is his fault if he is out, and he must provide without delay; if he can do no better, he must go back." The mystery of the missing ammunition might be explained by Major Lewis Wolfley, 3rd Kentucky Cavalry, of the First Cavalry Brigade which accompanied Crittenden's march. Wolfley was in charge of 150 cavalry supply wagons and only 100 wagons were designated for his brigade. As the advance began Wolfley was approached by an officer of Zahm's 2nd Cavalry Brigade inquiring about his supply train which appeared to have been sent along with Minty's train by mistake. In addition, two of the wagons assigned to the 2nd Brigade were lost during the cavalry raid in which the 15th Pennsylvania saw its first duty on Christmas day. Most likely, the remainder of Zahm's supply train was still *en route* to his brigade at the time McCook sent his message. Meanwhile, McCook's wing plodded throughout the day on the muddy roads progressing eastward. By noon, he was still nine miles from Murfreesboro and six miles from Stewartsborough, and he optimistically noted no gunfire from Crittenden's wing.[5]

Shortly after 4:00 p.m., McCook's wing reached its objective, Wilkinson's Crossroads, about three miles from Murfreesboro. McCook, after much marching finally joined the rest of the Army of the Cumberland drawing up in front of the Confederate army, reported that he had marched over a "miserable road today." The arriving Union troops faced a line of Confederates on the west side of Murfreesboro extending in an arc from the Franklin Pike to the Murfreesboro Pike, and then extending east to the Lebanon Pike. Upon his arrival, McCook wrote to Rosecrans: "I neglected to inform you that I have failed to find Negley, Thomas, or Rousseau. I heard Negley was coming up right bank of Stewart's Creek. He is not here. I will persevere, and try and find him by morning." McCook and

Negley still had not connected despite urgings from army headquarters for them to do so and McCook sent some of Zahm's cavalry in an attempt to find him, but this was unsuccessful. He would wait until the next morning to connect his left flank with Thomas' wing which continued to advance through the day and took up position in the center of the Army of the Cumberland after an uneventful, but equally plodding day.[6]

Action on McCook's Flank and the Charge of the 15th Pennsylvania

The cavalry protecting the flanks of McCook's wing had a busier day but Zahm's and Stanley's troopers performed their duty well and at the end of the day Stanley informed McCook: "Our cavalry are about 2 miles beyond this. Zahm is abreast with us; he has been fighting some. The burning going on seems to be the Nashville pike bridge over Stone's River. The prisoners and negroes say the rebs are in line of battle from the Franklin to the Nashville pike." As McCook reported his position to Crittenden he noted: "My cavalry, I hear, have just made an unfortunate dash on some rebel infantry, on the right of Wilkinson pike." McCook described a cavalry attack made by the 15th Pennsylvania Cavalry during the day.[7]

For Stanley's cavalry, the Reserve Brigade continued forward in front of McCook's advance and rode on the Bole Jack Road while Lewis Zahm paralleled this movement on the Franklin Pike. The cavalry brigades initially advanced along these routes and then moved forward to Wilkinson's Crossroad by the end of the day. Stanley's cavalry would have three skirmishes during the day. Zahm cavalry's moved forward in three columns parallel to each other and first skirmish occurred when the 3rd Ohio advanced to Wilkinson's Crossroad. The 4th Ohio moved on the right flank on the Franklin Road, the 3rd Ohio held the center and the 1st Ohio moved on the left flank. Each regiment rode about a mile and a half apart, and skirmishers connected each of the regiments. The 2nd Tennessee Cavalry, which joined Zahm's cavalry the previous night, accompanied the infantry advance and did not participate in the screening actions of the Ohio cavalry regiments. So, Zahm's advance presented a solid front about three miles wide. After riding about five miles on the morning of December 29, the 3rd Ohio Cavalry clashed with pickets of Wharton's cavalry and pushed them to the rear. Lieutenant Colonel Douglas Murray, reported "when attacked by the enemy's pickets in force, which we drove, skirmishing, they frequently making a stand, which we each time broke, and still drove them about 5 miles." John Wharton set up a defense to meet Zahm's formation, and shortly thereafter, the 1st Ohio and 4th Ohio also ran into Wharton's pickets. Captain William Crane recorded in his journal: "[H]ad several encounters with them, driving them before us. The skirmishes on the left of the column, towards Nashville & M. Pike were also busy & their carbines were constantly echoing through the woods." After pushing Wharton's pickets about a mile, Zahm found Wharton's main body of cavalry in line prepared to resist any further advance. A general skirmish resulted along the front which lasted about three hours. Zahm recorded how the skirmish ebbed and flowed:

> [S]ome time the right wing, then the left, then the center, receiving several charges, which were repulsed, driving the enemy some 2 miles, when the brigade concentrated, repelling a heavy charge from the enemy, driving him back under his guns, which were only a short distance from us. We then retired some 2 miles and went into camp. Some few casualties occurred this day. The officers and men

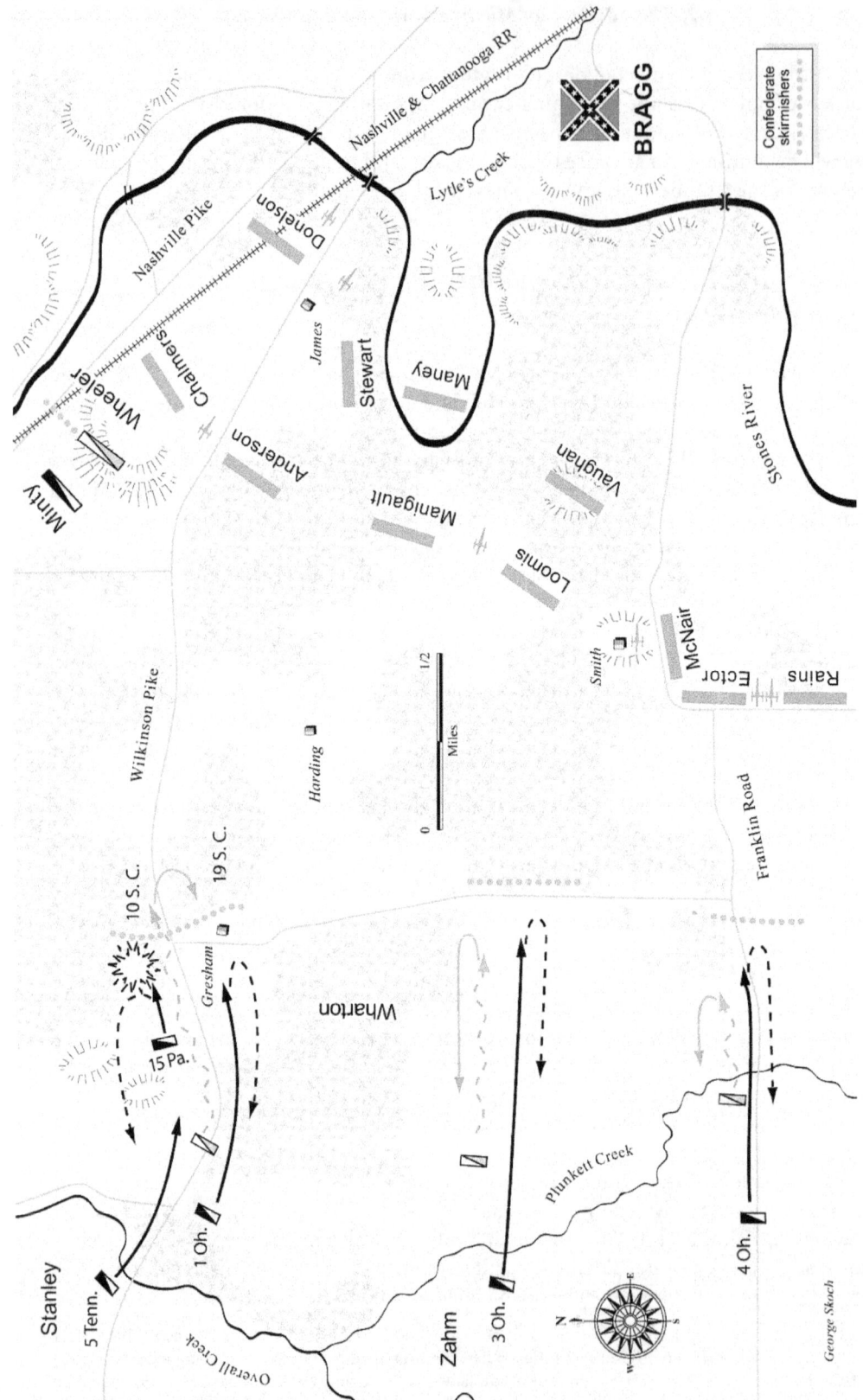

The Union cavalry actions on December 29, 1862, along the western flank of Bragg's army.

7. The Advance on Murfreesboro—Second Phase   141

behaved admirably during the whole day. The Fourth had proceeded until the enemy threw shells into them pretty rapidly, when they retired.

A wall of infantry skirmishers protecting the front of Bragg's army lay behind Wharton's cavalry screen. Wharton's entire brigade, including the 8th Texas Cavalry, faced Zahm's cavalry and trooper Ephraim Dodd recorded in his diary: "Met the Yankees and skirmished with them all day, falling back gradually. Their cavalry charged us once but paid dear for it. A number of prisoners were taken. We fell back to our infantry this evening."[8]

When Major John Pugh's 4th Ohio Cavalry found the enemy pickets, it drove them rearward skirmishing with small squads of Confederate cavalry which Pugh thought were on reconnaissance missions of their own. The troopers of 4th Ohio carried Sharps .52 caliber carbines, .44 caliber Colt revolvers, and sabers. About three or four miles from Murfreesboro, Pugh discovered a line of enemy in a wooded area supported by a section of artillery. As Pugh moved to investigate, the artillery opened up with grape shot. Pugh noticed a large group of Confederate cavalry swinging around toward his rear attempting to cut him off. The situation became serious quickly and Pugh directed his cavalry to face Wharton's troopers. He also found another smaller group of cavalry along the other flank. He ordered a company to immediately charge the smaller group of enemy cavalry, and then sent the rest of his regiment in a charge on the enemy attempting to flank his position. A severe fight resulted which resulted in two of Pugh's troopers being killed, seven more wounded and nine captured. In return, Pugh claimed seven prisoners as he made his escape.[9]

In his journal, William Crane recorded additional details of the actions of the 4th Ohio Cavalry:

William Crane, 4th Ohio Cavalry—"We met the charge with showers of bullets."

[A]bout 2½ miles from Murfreesboro & had a spirited engagement with Secesh cavalry who finally opened a battery & forced our boys back. The column was then countermarched & several cos. moved out into the woods on the right flank where another fight occurred in which we lost several men in killed & prisoners & a few were wounded. We took a number of prisoners—rebel casualties not ascertained. Being now reinforced with the 3rd [Ohio], another advance was made. Took position in a field to the left & in a short time saw the enemy advancing in considerable force, with cavalry & infantry. For half an hour our skirmishers held them in check but finally their cav. dashed forward on a charge & our flankers fell back. We met the charge with showers of bullets, our regiment alone sustaining the brunt of the fighting as the 3rd O[hio] had broken position, some distance off. Being thus unexpectedly repulsed, the enemy attempted a flank movement and galloped off to our right, yelling and hooping like so many Indians. But, in the road, they encountered one of our companies (G) which had been sent to the rear and was just moving up. Supposing another of our columns, the rebel horsemen made a rapid wheel about and galloped back. This fortunate incident saved us the day for they were triple our numbers. We now charged upon their left flank with a yell as demoniac as their own & their entire force made a most precipitate retreat. We then moved over toward the pike into close proximity to McCook's line, meeting the 1st O[hio] again. The whole brigade was employed on picket duty during the night which was very dark & rainy. Several prisoners taken today.[10]

The third cavalry skirmish of the day involved the 15th Pennsylvania Cavalry. Stanley's Reserve Brigade rode parallel and north of Zahm's cavalry and the action of this brigade resulted in an ill-fated charge of the 15th Pennsylvania which moved along the Bole Jack Road until it reached Wilkinson's Crossroads. About three hundred men of the regiment committed to perform their duties while the remainder of the regiment remained in Nashville under arrest. Those wishing to fight referred to themselves as the "Noble Three Hundred" or the "Gallant Three Hundred." Stanley hoped to inspire a fighting spirit in the troublesome and mutinous Pennsylvanians and had made progress under the leadership of two battalion commanders—Adolph Rosengarten and Frank Ward. Had these two sincere and effective commanders been given command of the regiment much of the problems which occurred might have been prevented. A line of Confederate cavalry held its position on the west side of Overall Creek and the Union cavalry decided to push ahead. The 15th Pennsylvania, supported by the 5th Tennessee Cavalry, charged the defenders on the west side of Overall Creek and as it advanced the Confederates gave way under the pressure of the Union cavalry. The 272 troopers of the 15th Pennsylvania who obeyed their orders had a running fight which covered a few miles. The fighting spirit heightened and the fight continued, but experience was needed as the Pennsylvanians approached the Confederate lines. The skirmish continued to within a half mile of the Confederate line manned by the 10th and 19th South Carolina infantry regiments. The attack of the 15th Pennsylvania Cavalry almost accomplished all it hoped, but South Carolina infantry stood firmly in line. A member of the 10th South Carolina Infantry recorded as the 15th Pennsylvania "thundered down the line," capturing Lieutenant Carrol White and a group of skirmishers, but "detecting indecision in the faces" of the troopers of the inexperienced 15th Pennsylvania, White ordered his soldiers still in line to "[c]ommence firing; don't mind us." White and the other skirmishers then dropped to the ground and a volley from the Southern infantry emptied the saddles of the 15th Pennsylvania. The Union troopers rode into a line of infantry and received a full volley from the South Carolina infantry. The two majors immediately became casualties. Rosengarten was killed during the exchange and Ward was mortally wounded, and died on January 11, as the 15th Pennsylvania was repulsed. In the attack eleven troopers were killed, twenty-five wounded, and nine missing. Trooper C. Lewis Diehl was among the wounded during the fight when he was shot in the face as he dismounted to assist one of his fellow soldiers. One of the troopers of the 15th Pennsylvania, Joseph Eckman, explained the South Carolinians were protected behind a wall and the regiment found itself riding parallel to the wall. Eckman wrote "We paid dearly for it." David Stanley explained the 15th Pennsylvania had shown great courage in the charge but he remarked discouragingly: "With the loss of these two most gallant officers the spirit of the Anderson Troop, which gave such fine promise, seems to have died out, and I have not been able to get any duty out of them since." Major Frank Ward would die of his wounds, but the efforts of Sergeant Major Washington Airey were described in the records of Charles Betts. Betts wrote, "Major Ward who had fallen mortally wounded was helped to the rear by Sgt. Maj. Airey after the regiment had retired but he [Ward] continued trying another charge while bleeding from several wounds."[11]

For the remainder of Stanley's reserve brigade, the day was uneventful. The 2nd Tennessee Cavalry accompanied the advance of the infantry and in the afternoon came in full view of the Confederate army. The regiment connected with Eli Murray's 3rd Kentucky Cavalry of Minty's brigade forming a complete screen of cavalry extending to the

Franklin Pike. At the end of the day, Stanley realigned his cavalry and sent the 2nd Tennessee to extreme right flank. There was no longer any need for the cavalry to screen the front of the infantry as the two armies faced each other over the fields north of Murfreesboro.[12]

Meanwhile Bragg waited and watched the dispositions of the various Union forces on December 29 and concluded to draw Rosecrans into a fight on his chosen ground. Bragg continued to pull his infantry closer to Murfreesboro and he ordered his cavalry to slacken its resistance, allowing Rosecrans to develop his line. Bragg's only real questions were where Rosecrans would place his strength and when he would attack. The next day would answer these questions.

December 30—Tuesday

December 30 would be an important day for both armies as the infantry lines faced each other. Rosecrans had finally moved his army into position before Murfreesboro but Bragg had had two days to prepare to meet his opponent and he was becoming impatient with Rosecrans. It was to prove to be a long day for the two cavalries. The soldiers awoke that morning shivering because it was so cold and because they had slept on the rain-soaked ground. Again, the cavalry moved out early. An orderly of the 4th U.S. Cavalry was greeted with death as he attended to the needs of the commanding general when a sharpshooter claimed his life. Afterward, the band of the 4th U.S. began playing

Top: Major Adolph Rosengarten, 15th Pennsylvania Cavalry, killed in action—"We paid dearly for it" (Civil War Photograph Collection, USAHEC). *Bottom:* Major Frank B. Ward, 15th Pennsylvania Cavalry, mortally wounded in a clash with South Carolina infantry (Civil War Photograph Collection USAHEC).

the "Star Spangled Banner" in response to the act. The rest of the Union cavalry worked to protect the flanks of Rosecrans' army and light skirmishing occurred throughout the day. Zahm's brigade bivouacked near McCook's headquarters during the evening at a small Methodist brick meetinghouse, Asbury Church, and awoke early to again push toward Murfreesboro. Zahm personally commanded the 2nd Tennessee, 1st and 3rd Ohio and he ordered his regiments forward along the Franklin Road, quickly encountering more enemy pickets. The 4th Ohio Cavalry rode on a reconnaissance expedition southward on the Salem Turnpike where it met Wharton's cavalry and a "brisk skirmish ensued." Soon, heavy concentrations of cavalry and artillery advanced to meet Zahm's probes and after an hour's fighting, he made no further progress.[13]

While the 4th Ohio skirmished on the Salem Turnpike, Zahm discovered another "heavy force of the enemy was encamped some little distance south of the Franklin road, and east of where my column halted." The main body of Wharton's Confederate cavalry formed a defensive line in a stand of timber and an approach was not practical for the Union cavalry. Zahm withdrew to the area where he encamped the night before in a large open field and fell into battle line as the Southern cavalry followed him. The Union skirmishers made the first contact with the approaching Southern horsemen who fell into battle line and attempted to flank Zahm's cavalry. Zahm recorded: "I forestalled him every time. With the exception of severe skirmishing, nothing transpired. The enemy retired…." A potentially heated cavalry battle was avoided and the cavalries disengaged.[14]

To fully develop the battle line for Rosecrans' army, McCook's wing pushed forward during the day and moved closer to Bragg's army at Murfreesboro, but the Southern resistance stiffened as McCook advanced toward Hardee's main line of infantry. In the late afternoon, Stanley arrived at Zahm's position with Colonel Philemon Baldwin's infantry brigade from Brigadier General Richard Johnson's division and with Zahm's cooperation marched directly forward. As the combined Union line advanced, the Southern defenders fell into a battle line and prepared to resist the attack. Again a heated skirmish lasted for about thirty minutes but Stanley and Johnson decided to withdraw. Baldwin's brigade and Zahm's cavalry ran into a "very large cavalry force … drawn up in line of battle. We advanced to a fence and commenced firing at them; but, the range being so great and our loads having been long wetted, our shots did no apparent execution." Stanley told Zahm not to continue the skirmish because Rosecrans did not intend to initiate a full attack. As the Union line withdrew the Southern cavalry advanced, but did not take any further action except for a weak demonstration. No further action took place. The tension in Union ranks was palpable as Zahm camped about a mile and a half away from the Confederate line and the troopers slept on their arms during the night.[15]

Private Benjamin Burke, 8th Texas Cavalry, recorded the late day action with Zahm, Stanley and Johnson:

> We had several encounters with them that day principly with their cavalry as they were in the advance though their infantry was close behind them we succeeded in tolling them into our infantry lines and late in the eavening of 30th Dec. they run afoul of our infantry and had a right tight fight for about two hours. The canonadeing (sic) was very heavy on both sides though this little fight was merely an introduction to the great battle.

Wharton ended his day forming a line perpendicular to Hardee's infantry south of the Franklin Pike.[16]

Wheeler's Raid

The Confederate commanding general greatly appreciated the actions of Wheeler's and Wharton's cavalry. The cavalry had given Bragg the time he needed to prepare his defenses. On December 29, Wheeler marched his cavalry behind the lines of the infantry for the first time in the campaign. "They came in columns of four. Well ordered, rough men." Bragg expressed this appreciation to Wheeler: "Your command had already done more than their duty most nobly." Bragg exclaimed in the presence of Hardee and Polk his appreciation for Wheeler's effort and stated: "We will now take the enemy in hand & and by the grace of God give him his due." While Rosecrans' attention had been focused on Bragg's concentrating army to his front, General Joseph Wheeler decided it might be opportune to utilize his superior numbers of cavalry to attack the Union rear. Bragg and Wheeler decided to distract Rosecrans by creating problems with his communications while a full infantry attack was planned

Major Daniel W. Holman's Tennessee Battalion arrived just in time to join Wheeler's Raid (Tennessee State Library and Archives).

for the Union right flank on morning of December 31. Observing a lack of concentration of Union troops on the Jefferson Pike, Wheeler's brigade and the 1st Tennessee Cavalry from Pegram's brigade began riding for the rear of the Union army on Monday night. Wheeler's cavalry moved forward past the Confederate infantry on the Confederate right and at midnight began the raid. George Knox Miller, 8th Confederate Cavalry, also added his account of the raid: "Promptly at midnight we were aroused from our stolen slumbers and in a few minutes had saddled and mounted and were following General Wheeler up the Lebanon pike at full gallop. The rain was falling and the darkness so dense that a man could not see the comrade riding at his side. Two miles further on, we left the Lebanon pike and took the one leading to the little village of Jefferson, which was directly in the rear of the Yankee army. Daylight found us near that village, where we halted and fed our horses." At daylight Wheeler's large cavalry force reached Jefferson and soon thereafter found an infantry baggage train. An account from Holman's Tennessee Battalion also reported attacking the Union train at Jefferson shortly after sunrise and after a fight of about an hour captured the train with "many prisoners, wagons, mules." As Bragg drew in infantry divisions, so Wheeler had called in his cavalry. Holman's Tennessee Battalion had been on detached duty and was ordered to Murfreesboro. Holman's cavalry returned to Murfreesboro on the night of the raid, reaching there just in time to join the expedition with the remainder of the cavalry under Wheeler's command. Taking the Lebanon Pike, Wheeler reached the rear of Rosecrans' army before daylight.[17]

Wheeler's Cavalry Brigade During the Raid on Union Rear December 30, 1862

1st Alabama	1st Tennessee (from Pegram's brigade)
3rd Alabama	Douglass' Tennessee Battalion
51st Alabama Partisan Rangers	Holman's Tennessee Battalion
8th Confederate	2nd Kentucky Battalion
McCann Tennessee (detachment)	Wiggin's Arkansas Battery

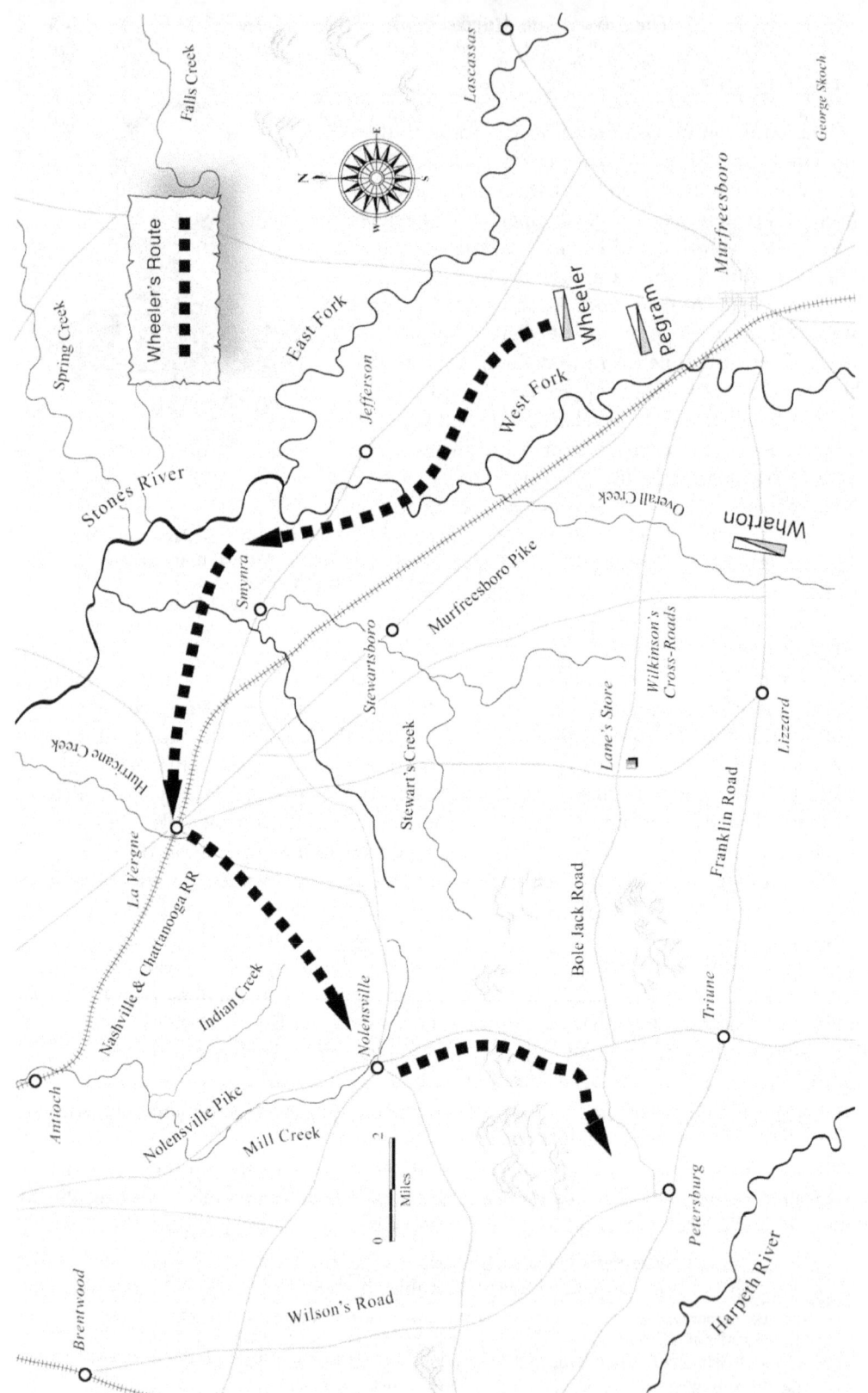

The route of Wheeler's December 30 raid.

Colonel John Starkweather reported the Union account of the attack on the 28th Brigade's supply train of sixty-four wagons heading for Jefferson consisting of "camp equipage, stores, officers' baggage, knapsacks." The train was sent without protection except for a small number of guards and therefore it made an ideal target for the Confederate cavalry. Ten wagons also carried rations for the Starkweather's infantry. Just as the train reached Jefferson, Wheeler's cavalry attacked the center and rear of wagon train and Colonel William Wirt Allen led a separate attack on the Union infantry guarding the wagons by riding down the both sides of the train. Starkweather hastily threw his brigade in line and prepared to meet the attackers. During the heated engagement, the train was quickly ordered to gallop ahead and to be parked and defended by the infantry. The 21st Wisconsin Infantry divided and moved to the front and rear of the train, and the 24th Illinois Infantry was sent to protect the bridge over Stewarts Creek from being burned. Then Starkweather hurried the 79th Pennsylvania, supported by two sections of artillery, to meet the Southern attack. Even a company of the 2nd Kentucky Cavalry, which was detached from the cavalry division, pitched into the fight.[18]

The heated engagement along the wagon train lasted for about two hours with give and take on both sides of the field. Wheeler's intention was not to capture Starkweather's brigade but to disrupt communications in the rear of Rosecrans' army. After this particularly heated fight, he withdrew and moved further to the rear of Rosecrans' army in search of more targets. Starkweather just survived a serious situation but his troops battled for their lives. Starkweather concluded, "[D]eeming my rear unsafe, I ordered the command to retire, and went into camp on the north side of Stone's River, near Jefferson."[19]

Captain John Henry Otto, 21st Wisconsin Infantry, was just beginning his meal when the shouts "Fall In! Fall In!" echoed. When Otto's company was positioned, it fell in line behind a fence and then saw the headquarters wagon being whipped, dashing ahead, and another wagon frantically following it. Behind the wagons Confederate cavalrymen rode in hot pursuit. The regiment rushed ahead and saw a line of wagons on fire. Then a quarter mile further on, the regiment saw the Southern cavalrymen in the woods and loosed a volley into their ranks. The cavalry returned the fire. Then a Federal battery began shelling Wheeler's men who disengaged. Otto wrote that over eighty Southerners were killed, but he lamented, "It was a bad pi[e]ce of business for us." Otto blamed the loss of the wagons on a captain who allowed those guarding the wagons to fall asleep, resulting in the surprise attack.[20]

Starkweather reported his casualties as:

Officers and Men	Killed	Wounded	Missing	Prisoners	Total
79th Pennsylvania	–	1	1	5	7
21st Wisconsin	1	3	37	–	41
1st Wisconsin	–	4	13	3	20
1st Kentucky Battery	–	–	1	1	2
24th Illinois	–	–	52	–	52
	1	8	104	9	122

Starkweather estimated Wheeler's strength to be in excess of 3,000 men and his brigade strength was about 1,700. In reality, the two forces were pretty evenly matched. Starkweather recorded eighty-three enemies killed and an unknown number wounded. Unfortunately, Starkweather reported most of the Union casualties were "convalescents, who were with the train when attacked." In addition, twenty wagons were lost in battle which were plundered and then burnt.[21]

Next, Wheeler turned his attention to La Vergne where he had greater success, and on his way he discovered a small party of Union foragers "stealing and gathering stock" and Wheeler scooped up the group and the forage train. At noon, he reached La Vergne and found large trains parked in a field, but he also found many soldiers guarding the trains. With surprise and boldness on his side, Wheeler attacked in three columns and quickly surrounded the soldiers who showed "but slight resistance.... We immediately paroled the prisoners, amounting to about 700, and destroyed immense trains and stores, amounting to many hundred thousands of dollars." John Witherspoon DuBose, 3rd Alabama Cavalry, observed: "[E]verywhere there was the ringing of captured mules, the shouts of the victors & the moaning of the wounded foe with long lines of white top smoking wagons." George Knox Miller's account also supported Wheeler's:

> We dashed in, four or five regiments, at full speed, fired a few shots and we had possession of an army train of over three hundred wagons, richly laden with quartermasters and commissary stores. The officers went quickly to work patrolling prisoners, while the men set fire to the train. It was a scene that would have rejoiced all rebeldom to behold! Mules stampeded, Yankees running for dear life a multitude of appliances brought out to subdue us. We tarried only one hour at LaVergne and then turning in a westward direction had gone only a mile or two when we heard the Yankees in revenge shelling the innocent village of LaVergne, thinking no doubt they were scattering death in the rebel ranks.

And trooper John N. Smith, 1st Alabama Cavalry, wrote in a letter: "We burnt up two hundred wagons, cut out the mules from the wagons and turned them loose seven hundred mules and taken four hundred prisoners. Colonel [John T.] Morgan taken the prisoners out in the cedars and paroled them."[22]

Colonel John Starkweather battled Wheeler during the cavalry raid on December 30 (Library of Congress).

The echoes of Wheeler's action reverberated throughout the Union army on December 30. The first indication things were amiss arrived via a message from Rosecrans to Thomas about 11:00 a.m.: "Firing heard in the direction of Jefferson. Have sent to ask Rousseau if brigade there has been withdrawn, and to order it back if it has left." Colonel John Starkweather's brigade had been posted along the Jefferson Pike and Wheeler's cavalry rode past the infantry during the raid, but the attack was aided by the movement of a brigade of Confederate infantry which occupied Rousseau's attention. As Wheeler moved to Stewarts Creek, Colonel Joseph Burke, 10th Ohio Infantry, whose regiment served as provost in charge was guarding the headquarters train, reported the capture of Federal baggage train shortly before noon.[23]

Wheeler's success was complete and then he rode northward to Rock Spring and found another large supply train, which he promptly sacked, capturing a large amount of supplies and arms, and about 300 prisoners. Any of the Southern cavalry, which had been poorly equipped, was now fully supplied thanks to the United States government. Finally, Wheeler began moving southward to complete his sixty-mile ride around the entire Army of the Cumberland. George Knox Miller, 8th Confederate Cavalry, wrote in a letter:

> A liberal application of the spur for two hours, and down we swooped like a tornado upon quiet, little Nolensville. It was scarcely more than LaVergne repeated. We found scattered squads of Yankees, here and there, and 150 wagons, mostly loaded with ammunitions and medicines. Also several fine ambulances, which we took along. The rest of the spoils of war were consigned to the flames, and the Yankees sent on their way rejoicing, with paroles in their pockets. You could not have made them happier, by presenting them a western homestead.

Miller ended his day west of Nolensville after a very fruitful expedition.[24]

Wheeler's raid on the rear of Rosecrans' army resulted in actions by the Federals to bolster the defenses at Jefferson and La Vergne. During the raid the action was described "like the breaking of millions of sticks, and the cannons boomed like a trip hammer sounds over a stubborn piece of heated iron. Then followed the woo-oo-ooing of the solid shot, the w-h-i-z-z-i-n-g howl of a steel, as with a shuck tied to it." More importantly Starkweather and more Union cavalry remained in the rear to protect against further raids while Bragg intended to attack the Federal army early the next morning at Stones River. The advantage of the utilization and numbers of Confederate cavalry was instrumental in achieving a significant success. After leaving Starkweather, Wheeler pushed on to La Vergne and attacked another supply train shortly after noon. The Southern cavalry swept down on a train of over 300 wagons with an estimated value of a million dollars and it was set aflame. Colonel Moses Walker's infantry hastened to site of the attack and only just managed to make contact with Wheeler's rear guard. Next, the column rode two hours to Rock Spring, just northwest of Stewartsboro and attacked a third train which he burned. Then, he found another train as he advanced to Nolensville after a three hours ride, again capturing and burning the train. It is unknown the full extent of Wheeler's destruction on the Union supply train, but one estimate was a million dollars' worth of property destroyed, 500 wagons burned or captured, 600 prisoners, and a large number of mules.[25]

Final Preparations

In response to the Confederate raid, Robert Minty accompanied the 4th Michigan Cavalry and a battalion of the 7th Pennsylvania Cavalry rearward along the Nashville Pike to prevent further ravages of Wheeler's cavalry which had just caused havoc on the Union supply trains. When Minty arrived he found about one hundred Confederate raiders, in what he described as Union uniforms. The 7th Pennsylvania pursued this group, which retreated, but Wheeler's main force had long since moved westward in his raid around the rear of Rosecrans' army. Minty dismounted and decided to spend the night with Colonel Moses Walker, 31st Brigade, about two and a half miles south of La Vergne. Companies B and D of the 3rd Kentucky Cavalry operated on courier duty during the day in the rear of the army but were also in the vicinity of Minty's cavalry at Stewarts Creek. These two companies would remain with Minty during the following day.[26]

As McCook's corps advanced on Murfreesboro, David Stanley recorded in his memoirs that he brought information which could have changed the battle. At 2 p.m. on December 30, Stanley sent a local citizen who had knowledge of the Confederate concentration of forces to McCook who subsequently sent the citizen to Rosecrans. The civilian stated,

> I was up to the enemy's line of battle twice yesterday and once this morning, to get some stock, taken from me. The enemy's troops are posted in the following manner: The right of Cheatham's division rests on the Wilkinson pike; Withers is on Cheatham's left, with his left resting on the Franklin road; Hardee's corps is entirely beyond that road, and his left extending toward the Salem pike.

McCook recorded,

> This made me anxious for my right. All my division commanders were immediately informed of this fact, and two brigades of the reserve division, commanded, respectively, by Generals Willich and Kirk, two of the best and most experienced brigadiers in the army, were ordered to the right of my line, to protect the right flank and guard against surprise there.

At 6 p.m., Rosecrans sent an order to McCook to work in conjunction with Stanley to try to deceive the enemy. McCook and Stanley made very large campfires, some outside the Union lines, to make the enemy think there were more soldiers on the Union right.[27]

Rosecrans met with his generals on the evening of December 30 and laid out a plan to initiate the battle the next morning against Bragg. "McCook was to occupy the most advantageous position, refusing his right as much as practicable and necessary to secure it, to receive the attack of the enemy; or, if that did not come, to attack himself." Thomas' corps and Palmer's division of Crittenden's wing were ordered to begin skirmishing and occupy the center of Bragg's army. Crittenden was ordered to move Van Cleve's division, followed by Wood's, across the river and attack Breckinridge's division. Once the two Union divisions dislodged Breckinridge then batteries would be placed in the heights on the Union left which

> would see the enemy's works in reverse, would dislodge them, and enable Palmer's division to press them back, and drive them westward across the river or through the woods, while Thomas, sustaining the movement on the center, would advance on the right of Palmer, crushing their right, and Crittenden's corps, advancing, would take Murfreesborough, and then, moving westward on the Franklin road, get in their flank and rear and drive them into the country toward Salem, with the prospect of cutting off their retreat and probably destroying their army.[28]

In the evening, Stanley wanted to determine the veracity of citizen's description of the Confederate position. He recorded, "[I] rode, with only an escort, beyond our extreme right and so I reported to McCook and Rosecrans. One division of two brigades, sent this evening to support Johnson's right would have averted disaster. McCook seemed utterly indifferent," noted Stanley.[29]

For many, the day was over and weary soldiers began to sleep. As the soldiers went to sleep, two parallel battle lines faced each other over a three mile long line running roughly northeast to southwest. The east flank extended past Stones River to the Lebanon Pike and the western line extended south of the Franklin Pike. Willich's brigade of McCook's corps was refused and positioned roughly perpendicular to the main battle line. McCook's troops occupied a wooded, slight ridge with open ground in front. About four hundred yards away lay Hardee's troops positioned in a wooded area behind rough breastworks. The center was located along the Nashville Pike and Breckinridge's large division covered the Confederate eastern flank. While the Union army settled in for the night, the report that General Joseph Wheeler had caused havoc to Union supply trains by moving along the rear of the Union army resulted in more action on the part of Rosecrans. Even though Robert Minty had been dispatched earlier in the day to protect the

Union rear, Rosecrans wanted more action from his cavalry to prevent further attacks. But for the majority of the Union army, the soldiers settled into a tense, fretful night. James Knight, 11th Michigan Infantry, unaware of what tomorrow would bring, wrote, "We slept soundly that night."[30]

When Stanley returned to his bed after meeting with McCook, an orderly roused him with a message from Colonel Garesché, Rosecrans' chief of staff, about the attack of Confederate cavalry on the supply trains in the Union rear. Rosecrans ordered Stanley to see to the protection of the trains. At 11 p.m. on the December 30, Stanley prepared to ride to La Vergne with the 5th Tennessee and the 15th Pennsylvania cavalries. Stanley rode toward the Union supply trains arriving at Stewarts Creek at 5 a.m. where he met Minty and his cavalry. He found three infantry regiments, safe and sound. Father O'Higgins, chaplain of the 10th Ohio Infantry, was also present and the officers had of a pot of tea and some Irish whiskey. Stanley visited with the colonel and the chaplain until his scouts returned reporting the trains were safe. No Confederate cavalry was found lurking in the countryside.[31]

Rosecrans' battle plans called for little action on the part of his cavalry and there was little he could do to the Confederate cavalry at this point. Wheeler was in the rear and perhaps the offensive action he planned the next day would alleviate this problem. If the attack was successful, certainly Wheeler would be needed to defend the retreating Confederate army. Also, he had Stanley and Minty now in the rear and despite the disparity in numbers, these two able commanders, supported by infantry, would take care of Wheeler. It was a reasonable plan, if the situation remained static for another eight hours. Rosecrans concluded the night reasoning:

> It was explained to them that this combination, insuring us a vast superiority on our left, required for its success that General McCook should be able to hold his position for three hours; that, if necessary to recede at all, he should recede, as he had advanced on the preceding day, slowly and steadily, refusing his right, thereby rendering our success certain.[32]

On the Confederate side of the field, Bragg's army also prepared for the battle, but not all in the Confederate army were pleased with Bragg's selection of position for the battle. William Hardee acknowledged that the open terrain allowed for the advantageous use of artillery, but wrote the field "offered no peculiar advantage for defence." Bragg felt his 37,000 men faced up 60,000 Union soldiers and certainly a strong defensive position was needed. Key to Bragg's decision to fight at this location was the fact that Murfreesboro was his supply center and that part of Middle Tennessee provided the food and support for his army. By defending Murfreesboro, the Confederate army also controlled most of the roads in the area which converged on the town. The Southern defense was developed along Stones River, which presented little if any difficulty in crossing. Breckinridge's division was placed in an advantageous position to provide artillery support to Polk's flank, and Breckinridge had placed a concentration of Confederate artillery at Wayne's Hill, a few hundred yards in advance of Breckinridge's assigned position. Breckinridge had one brigade entrenched there and the remainder of his division was a half mile to the rear. But, the decision had been made and the ground chosen. They would fight were they were.[33]

Throughout the day Bragg observed Rosecrans' troop placement and was confident about Wheeler's attack on Union communications. Bragg who became impatient with the inaction from Rosecrans also concluded to attack the next morning although he felt he was outnumbered and he felt much of the success of the battle would hinge on which army attacked first. While the Union commanders focused the brunt of the attack on the eastern end of the line, Bragg had correctly identified the weakest part of the Union line to be McCook's wing. Rosecrans was also concerned about McCook and the success of the Rosecrans' plan called for McCook to hold or slowly withdraw under a determined Confederate attack. In return, Bragg planned to capitalize on this weakness by making his attack on McCook an "unequal contest." It appeared to the Southern general that McCook's line was attempting to extend past the Confederate left flank. Because of this, McCown's division was moved to that location. The resistance Stanley and Johnson received on December 30 was an attempt by Bragg to stop any further movement on his flank. In addition to McCown, Cleburne's division was moved from the second line to the left also. On the same morning the Union attack was planned, Bragg planned to attack McCook's flank with Hardee's Corps, led by McCown's division and followed by Cleburne's division. Bragg planned:

> These dispositions completed, Lieutenant-General Hardee was ordered to assail the enemy at daylight on Wednesday, the 31st, the attack to be taken up by Lieutenant-General Polk's command in succession to the right flank, the move to be made by a constant wheel to the right, on Polk's right flank as a pivot, the object being to force the enemy back on Stone's River, and, if practicable, by the aid of the cavalry, cut him off from his base of operations and supplies by the Nashville pike. The lines were now bivouacked at a distance in places of not more than 500 yards, the camp-fires of the two being within distinct view. Wharton's cavalry brigade had been held on our left to watch and check the movements of the enemy in that direction, and to prevent his cavalry from gaining the railroad in our rear, the preservation of which was of vital importance. In this he was aided by Brig. Gen. A. Buford, who had a small command of about 600 new cavalry.

Wharton also received his direct orders on December 30, "Being drawn up on the extreme left, I was ordered to reach the enemy's rear as soon as possible, and to do them all the damage I could."[34]

In what would be debated after the battle were orders by Rosecrans to Stanley and McCook to build the large campfires outside the Union lines on the western flank as a ruse to make the Confederates believe the Union forces were greater than they were. Bragg had chosen to extend his attacking force past the western flank of McCook's corps and this raised the question of whether the Southern infantry extended even further west due to these campfires. This movement could have exacerbated the effect of McCown's attack the next morning. The Southern reports of the battle do not comment on this point and Ephraim Otis, adjutant to General Horatio Van Cleve, commented: "[I] have always doubted whether Bragg was misled or deceived by this subterfuge; and not unlikely he considered it rather a confession of weakness on our right, and formed his own plans accordingly." In his memoirs, General Richard Johnson agreed that the fires demonstrated a weakness rather than strength to Bragg. McCook's Inspector General wrote that the exact location of Hardee's troops was unknown except for a strong force in the woods ahead. On the Confederate side of the field, the soldiers of the 10th South Carolina Infantry quietly moved into place watching these fires. The Southern soldiers believed the fires were camps of Union soldiers who were overly confident in their strength who "prepared their suppers and passed the camp joke."[35]

The night was filled with tension. Henry Cist, author of the *Army of the Cumberland*, wrote: "Every soldier on that field knew when the sun went down on the 30th that on the following day he would be engaged in a struggle unto death, and the air was full of tokens that one of the most desperate of battles was to be fought."[36]

8. The Cavalry Battle of Stones River (December 31, Early Morning)

It was a glorious sight, as with their sabres drawn and their horses at their fastest speed.—Colonel J. B. Dodge

The tension remained high on both armies as sunrise approached on December 31. Rosecrans sent a message overnight to his army:

> Soldiers! the eyes of the whole nation are upon you. The very fate of the nation may be said to hang on the issues of this day's battle. Be true, then, to yourselves; true to your own manly character and soldierly reputation; true to the love of your dear ones at home, whose prayers ascend this day to God for your success. Be cool. I need not ask you to be brave. Keep ranks. Do not throw away your fire. Fire slowly, deliberately. Above all, fire low, and always be sure of your aim. Close readily in upon the enemy, and when you get within charging distance, rush upon him with the bayonet. Do this, and victory will certainly be yours.

No better advice was to be offered for the soldiers on both sides of the field.[1]

The day before, Bragg met with his corps commanders. Bragg mistakenly assumed that Rosecrans intended to attack with McCook's wing and Leonidas Polk suggested the plan that would be implemented by the Army of Tennessee—with Cleburne and McCown in position and overlapping McCook's wing, the attack would be made on the western flank. Hardee would strike the vulnerable end of McCook's line of infantry and then wheel to the right and while pushing forward, Wharton's cavalry would swing to the rear of the Union army and Polk would attack the center of Rosecrans' line. While the plan seemed simple enough in concept, the broken terrain interspersed with cedar thickets, woods and rocks concerned the Southern officers. After the meeting, William Hardee met with his subordinate officers and positioned his infantry throughout the night for the attack planned for early December 31. Under the cover of darkness, Hardee placed McCown's division facing Jefferson C. Davis's and Richard Johnson's Union divisions, about five hundred yards away. Then Pat Cleburne's division moved into position behind McCown.[2]

2:00–6:22 a.m.

While the Confederate infantry quietly moved into position, Rosecrans prepared his own troops for his attack scheduled for 8:00 o'clock the next morning. Rosecrans felt confident that Crittenden's attack on the Confederate eastern flank would yield good results. The previous evening Rosecrans met with McCook to ensure he understood the necessity of holding his position for three hours during the initial attack the next morning and gave him authority to adjust his lines if he felt he needed to. As Rosecrans' army settled in for the night, those on the western flank heard the noise of moving troops and artillery into the early morning hours. Brigadier General Joshua Sill rode to his commander's tent at 2:00 a.m., Phil Sheridan, and explained he heard troops moving along the Union right flank. Sheridan rode to investigate and confirmed the sounds and both generals rode to McCook's tent with the news. McCook "dismissed their concerns on the grounds that Crittenden's early morning attack would put a swift end to any Confederate designs against the Union right."[3]

As dawn approached, Confederate corps commander William Hardee prepared for the attack. Some the Southern infantry were given a drink of whiskey to bolster them in the early hours on the late December morning. Just before 6:00 a.m. General John P. McCown and General Patrick Cleburne reported to Hardee's headquarters for their final orders. They had moved their commands into place in preparation for the morning's attack and then rode to a small house where they found Hardee and Bragg, who remained mounted on his horse. The Union line was about 500–800 yards ahead of the newly arranged Southern line and the final order was given to begin the attack at 6:00 a.m. The two generals rode back to their commands and the long lines of gray infantry slowly began to march forward. John A. Wharton began his cavalry movement along the west flank of the Southern infantry at the same time.[4]

The Battle of Stones River had begun.

6:22–9:00 a.m.

While the Army of the Cumberland also prepared to attack, Bragg won the race and Hardee's infantry moved swiftly and effectively. Brigadier General August Willich, First Brigade of Richard Johnson's division, held the far right of the Union infantry line. Willich positioned his infantry along the east-west Franklin Road with Gresham Lane running perpendicular through his command and Willich, being the end of McCook's line, properly refused his flank but the events of the morning might suggest not far enough. Next in line, and to the east, was Brigadier General Edward Kirk's Second Brigade, and Colonel Philemon Baldwin's Third Brigade held its position as the reserve, about a half a mile to the rear on the edge of a wooded area and facing south across a large cornfield, behind Johnson's other two brigades. Baldwin's brigade was placed as a reserve and also protected McCook's flank which was vulnerable to an attack from the west. To the east of Johnson's division was Jefferson C. Davis's division—P. Sidney Post's First Brigade, William Carlin's Second Brigade and William Woodruff's Third Brigade, from west to east. These two divisions, Johnson's and Davis's, were positioned to receive the full force of Bragg's attack that morning. Phil Sheridan's division held the next position in line to the east of Davis.[5]

The noise the Union sentries heard in the early morning hours came from Major General John P. McCown's division of 4,400 infantrymen followed by Pat Cleburne's division five hundred yards to the rear. McCown and Cleburne moved their divisions forward in the early morning light and marched with the full might of their infantry first on Willich's and Kirk's brigades and then planned to pivot to the right after gaining the flank and rear of McCook's corps. McCown led the attack with James Rains,' Mathew D. Ector's, and Evander McNair's brigades from west to east. Cleburne followed with the Lucius E. Polk's, St. John R. Liddell's, and Bushrod Johnson's brigades.[6]

8. The Cavalry Battle of Stones River (Early Morning)

At 6:22 a.m., the Confederate lines emerged from the fogs and the trees, and quietly made a steady advance on McCook's brigades. At 200 yards distance, the Union artillery opened up on McCown's advancing Confederates and then McCown ordered his men to double-quick, march and slammed into Willich's troops as they hastily prepared for the attack. The attack struck McCook's extreme western flank and the Confederates surprised the Union infantry many of whom had begun their breakfast. The Southern cavalry was concealed in a large wooded area in preparation for the attack and as the infantry surged forward, Wharton's cavalry brigade, Wheeler's largest cavalry brigade, swept along the western flank of Hardee's infantry.[7]

Cavalry Units and Positions

On the evening of December 30, John Wharton's cavalry formed along the left flank of McCown's division about one half to three quarters miles south of the Franklin Road. Early on December 31, Wharton moved his cavalry into position on the left flank of McCown's division keeping contact with the infantry by stretching

General Richard Johnson's division was on the western flank during the morning attack—"The attack was sudden & fierce & our infantry could not withstand its impetus" (Library of Congress).

McCown's Escort cavalry company to the east and prepared for the day. Wharton decided to divide his cavalry into three combat teams or wings to have better control of their actions. Colonel Thomas Harrison, the Texas Ranger, and Colonel John T. Cox, the Kentucky engineer, were given command of the two wings which would carry most of the Southern fighting. The remaining wing served as a reserve and support for White's Tennessee Battery. Wharton's cavalry would serve in different roles during the morning—assisting with the infantry attack, shuttling prisoners to the rear, fighting Union cavalry, and all the while realizing the ultimate objective to gain the Federal rear to sever the communications and supply route.

Wharton's Cavalry Wings[8]

Colonel Thomas Harrison	Colonel John T. Cox	Reserve & Artillery Support
8th Texas, Col. Thomas Harrison	1st Confederate, Col. John T. Cox	3rd Confederate, Lieut. Col. William N. Estes
2nd Georgia, Lieut. Col. J. E. Dunlop	14th Ala. Batt., Lt. Col. J. C. Malone	2nd Tennessee, Col. H. M. Ashby
3rd GA, Maj. R. DeWitt C. Thompson	Davis's Tenn Batt., Maj. J. R. Davis	4th Tennessee, Col. Baxter Smith
	Murray's (TN), Maj. W. S. Bledsoe	Escort Company, Capt. Paul F. Anderson
		McCown's Escort Company, Capt. L. T. Hardy
		White's (Tennessee) Battery, Capt. B. F. White

Three other Confederate cavalry brigades were active on the morning of December 31. John Pegram's two-regiment brigade, which served as a reserve, operated on the flank of Breckinridge's division on the eastern side of the Confederate army. Pegram's command was so small his duty was primarily reconnaissance on the Lebanon Pike and along Stones River. In addition, Abe Buford's cavalry brigade rode hard from its position near Rover, Tennessee, and would not arrive on the scene until about noon. Joseph Wheeler's cavalry brigade moved from its camp just west of Nolensville after its successful raid the day before. Wheeler would not reach the battlefield until noon.[9]

The morning began calmly for the Union cavalry, even though a battle was expected later in the day. As daylight approached, Colonel Lewis Zahm had his brigade up and moving early on a cold December morning, and had the misfortune of being on the right flank of the Army of the Cumberland. The men began their breakfasts and prepared for the day. Zahm bivouacked his brigade, three Ohio cavalry regiments (1st, 3rd, and 4th) plus the 2nd Tennessee Cavalry, the previous evening along McCook's infantry line about a mile and a half from Hardee's headquarters. By 6:00 a.m. he had sent two squadrons on reconnaissance riding through the morning fog and soon heard heavy firing and cannonading to his left and front. "The roar of the cannon and the rattle of the musket were terrific," noted Sergeant Thomas Crofts, 3rd Ohio Cavalry. Then, Zahm observed General Richard Johnson's 2nd Division of McCook's wing in full retreat being chased by Major General J. P. McCown's Confederates. Bragg's infantry crushed the Union right, which was flowing to the rear.[10]

The positioning of the Union cavalry included Zahm's brigade posted on the right flank of McCook's infantry, Klein's 3rd Indiana was on the extreme right flank at Wilkinson's Crossroad, Stanley and Minty at Stewarts Creek, and the remainder served as a reserve in the center of Rosecrans' army. Overall, the Federal cavalry units present for duty on the morning of December 31 were generally dispersed around the army. Only Zahm's brigade on the west flank and Minty's units at La Vergne could be considered to operating at or near brigade strength.

Union Cavalry Division at Daybreak at Stones River
Brigadier General David Stanley—La Vergne
Colonel John Kennett—Near Rosecrans' Headquarters

First Brigade
3rd Kentucky, Colonel Eli H. Murray	Near Rosecrans Headquarters—straggler duty on Dec. 30
	8 companies
7th Pennsylvania, Major John E. Wynkoop	8 companies

Second Brigade–Colonel Lewis Zahm
1st Ohio, Colonel Minor Millikin	South of Wilkinson Pike—west of Overall Creek
3rd Ohio, Lieutenant Colonel Douglas A. Murray	South of Wilkinson Pike—east of Overall Creek
4th Ohio, Major John L. Pugh	South of Wilkinson Pike—east of Overall Creek
2nd East (2nd) Tennessee, Col. Daniel M. Ray	No records

Unattached
4th U.S. Cavalry, Captain Elmer Otis	Attached to Rosecrans' headquarters (six companies)
3rd Indiana Cavalry (West Battalion—4 com)	Assigned duty beyond Wilkinson's Crossroads
Newell's artillery	At Stewarts Creek in the rear

[The remainder of the First Brigade (one battalion of 7th Pennsylvania, 4th Michigan, 2 companies of 3rd Kentucky) and Reserve Brigade (5th Tennessee, 15th Pennsylvania) began the day at Stewarts Creek.]

One of the greatest losses to the Union cavalry during the day's fighting was the placement of Newell's Ohio artillery at Stewarts Creek. The presence of Newell's section would have greatly assisted in the Union cavalry defense in the morning as Wharton's cavalry participated in the attack, but these guns were placed at Stewarts Creek on December 30 and remained there until January 1.[11]

The battle along the western flank would be fought by the cavalries on terrain conducive for cavalry operations and well known by both commanders. For the past two days, the respective cavalries operated in the area where much of the fighting would take place. The ground was remarkably flat and due to the agriculture in the area much of the area was covered with fallow corn and cotton fields. On the morning of December 31, Wharton's cavalry moved in concert with the infantry and before them lay a large fallow cornfield, perhaps 300–400 acres in size. The cornfield was notched with a wooded area on the northeast where Baldwin's reserve brigade was located and the remainder of the field extended through some light woods to Wilkinson Pike, a dirt road running roughly east and west, and about a mile north. Along the Franklin Pike and to the west of the corn field was Puckett's Branch, a small stream running northward, connecting with Overall Creek about three quarters of a mile south of Wilkinson Pike. Overall Creek was not a large creek, but the banks were lined with trees and dropped steeply about ten feet to the actual creek and it proved a moderate obstacle to movements across the stream. Despite the problems, and sometimes the advantages of the cedar thickets which marked much of the fighting for the infantry, the cavalry had relatively good terrain to utilize on the western flank during the day. Finally, Gresham Lane, a small dirt road, ran north and south and connected Wilkinson Pike and Franklin Pike. The lane ran directly through August Willich's western most Federal brigade.

The Initial Attack Along the Franklin Pike

While the amount of Union cavalry was not insignificant, only Zahm's 2nd Tennessee and three Ohio regiments could be called a cavalry brigade on the morning of December 31. Captain William Crane, 4th Ohio Cavalry, offered an insight into the distribution of the Union cavalry that remained with Army of the Cumberland before Bragg at Murfreesboro. Much of the Union cavalry was with Stanley far in the rear at Stewarts Creek after Wheeler's raid the day before. Crane wrote in his journal that at daylight Zahm moved his cavalry into a large field south of the Wilkinson Pike. He also described how some of the Union batteries were captured while the horses were being watered.

"On our part the attack was a complete surprise, the enemy having obtained position inside our lines by falling & capturing the pickets in the thick fog mist that prevailed. The attack was sudden & fierce & our infantry could not withstand its impetus. Regiment after regiment gave way, some making no stand at all, others fighting with desperation until they were cut to pieces, the men being mowed down by ranks.... The right flank had been turned (the rebel left overlapping it by two divisions).... The slaughter was most fearful & the men could not be rallied. On came the victorious hordes of a tremendous force of Infantry & Cavalry appeared on our cavalry's front & right. We retired & formed again as they came up. Fought them for a while & again changed position. Now they appear on our other flank & Zahm sends to Stanley for succor. Meanwhile, hundreds of volleys are exchanged and, for a while, we check their progress. Men are falling on every side & horses fast go down."[12]

When the fighting began, Colonel Zahm rode forward toward the sound of the battle into a large field with his escort, put his field glasses to his eyes and scanned the scene before him. Then, he ordered his cavalry to prepare to meet the attack and then moved his line forward toward the unfolding battle. To his front was Wharton's cavalry which moved along with the Confederate infantry as the Union right was propelled rearward. Hardee instructed Wharton the evening before and explained what he wanted from Wharton—"to reach the enemy's rear as soon as possible, and to do them all the damage I could," recorded Wharton. He intended to do just that but the collapse of McCook's infantry was so sudden and so complete, he was surprised and had to hurry his horsemen forward.[13]

"Onward swept that outer wing. The horses seemed to catch the spirit, and they dashed forward with fresh speed," wrote the chaplain of the 8th Texas Cavalry. The decisions made by Bragg and Wheeler capitalized on the strength of the Southern horsemen. Wheeler's foray in the Union rear now yielded its fruit. Much of the Union cavalry, including the Federal chief of cavalry, was ten miles to the rear at Stewarts Creek protecting the Union supply line and what remained was scattered on the various flanks of the Army of the Cumberland. Wheeler, the Confederate chief of cavalry, was also not on the field, but he was still away from the fighting after the raid the day before. Lewis Zahm's brigade would have the hardest duty of the morning for the Union cavalry as John Wharton's cavalry advanced along the western flank of the armies. Because Stanley showed such an ability to lead with a steady hand, the orders sending Stanley with a large portion of cavalry to the rear was lamented by those along the Union right flank. Nevertheless, Zahm had several tasks—attempt to rally the retreating troops, engage the enemy, and keep the Confederate cavalry from gaining the Union rear.[14]

At least some of the Southern cavalry was dismounted for a while and moved ahead as skirmishers assisting the infantry fights. James Blackburn, Harrison's 8th Texas Cavalry, explained that the men of the regiment were placed in line ten feet apart and moved through a very weedy field. The advance of the dismounted cavalry was hidden because the weeds were five to six feet tall. On the other side of the field were the Federal troops. Blackburn wrote: "Our skirmishers were armed with rifles or muskets for the occasion. I was told to keep the men to their places so there would be no weak spot and no bunching of our men on the line, to keep them firing continually." Blackburn remained mounted, but he was the only member of his company on horseback. While the 8th Texas acted in cooperation with the advancing infantry, the 2nd Georgia and 3rd Confederate cavalries formed a battle line and faced the line of Zahm's Union cavalry. The action of the Southern cavalry along the right flank provided significant duty whether in the fights with infantry, artillery or cavalry.[15]

Because the two opposing infantry lines faced teach other near the Franklin Pike the evening before, there had been no need for Zahm's cavalry at the front. Instead, his task was to protect McCook's flank and rear from either an infantry or cavalry attack. Zahm diligently had his troopers in the saddle with two squadrons near the front and flanks of the Union infantry. Like the rest of

General August Willich's brigade was attacked first on December 31 (Library of Congress).

Rosecrans' army, Zahm was surprised with an explosion of "heavy firing" both from muskets and artillery. Various reports recorded the firing began between 6:22–7:00 a.m. and Zahm soon observed blue-coated infantrymen running for the rear followed by Confederates surging ahead in three columns. In addition, Zahm observed Wharton's 2,000 cavalrymen approaching on his right flank and he correctly surmised the intent of the Confederate cavalry to circle into the rear of McCook's infantry.[16]

Captain Valentine Cupp, 1st Ohio Cavalry, provided a detailed account of the arrangement of Zahm's cavalry along the Union right flank on the morning of December 31. Zahm's cavalry, along with the 3rd Indiana Cavalry, formed an arc, which extended across the Union right flank. McCook's corps dangled in the air and to prevent a surprise flank attack greater than the one McCown and Cleburne had just executed, the Union cavalry extended from Philemon Baldwin's reserve brigade's position to Wilkinson's Crossroad. In the arc was the 3rd Ohio Cavalry in position in a wooded area on the east and next, the 4th Ohio Cavalry extended to Overall Creek. On the west side of the creek was the 1st Ohio Cavalry, and finally the 3rd Indiana Battalion was near Wilkinson's Crossroad. Cupp made no mention of the location of the 2nd Tennessee and there are no surviving records from the regiment regarding its exact location. The regiment might have been positioned connecting the 1st Ohio with the 3rd Indiana on the western side of Overall Creek or it could be held in a reserve position behind the other regiments. The Union commanders knew the Confederate cavalry, in particular, Wheeler, was already operating in their rear and they wanted no surprises.[17]

Captain Cupp commanded two companies on the scouting mission which left camp at 6:00 a.m. Cupp rode with Companies F and K south along the west side of Puckett Creek and after about a mile he heard the explosion of cannon and muskets to his east. Cupp moved to the sound of the gunfire to investigate and rode into a field only to find Johnson's infantry retreating northward. Cupp rode to the infantrymen and found out about the Confederate attack and then a rider from Zahm arrived with a message for them to hurry back to the brigade. But Cupp found he was already flanked on his left by Confederate infantry and cavalry.

> I at once moved my command at full speed to the rear, past the enemies left (three columns infantry) crossing the creek within one hundred and fifty yards, and under a heavy fire. Here I had one man and three horses wounded. I was then at least three fourths of a mile from my regiment, and the rebel cavalry coming at full speed and within range of my left. After reaching my camp we had occupied the night before, I found I could not cross without running into their lines. The infantry that were in our front and left were already retreating in the utmost disorder.[18]

Sergeant Isaac Skillman, 3rd Ohio Cavalry, recorded the attack in his diary. Upon hearing the gunfire and cannonading as McCown and Cleburne attacked Johnson's division, he observed a line of gray-clad soldiers rapidly moving forward and "at the same time a full division of rebel cavalry to our front and right working toward our rear." Skillman's diary reads as if he was writing during the attack itself. Skillman continued, "It seems that Bragg has massed his force on his left to crush our right and get possession of the Nashville pike which would prevent our retreat."[19]

Meanwhile, John Wharton made decisions of his own. Once Harrison's Texas Rangers were relieved from their position by advancing infantry, they mounted and joined in Wharton's move along the flank. What started as a trot from Wharton's cavalry, increased to a gallop as McCook's wing crumbled under the Southern attack. Wharton ordered his cavalry ahead toward Wilkinson's Turnpike while keeping contact with the infantry as it

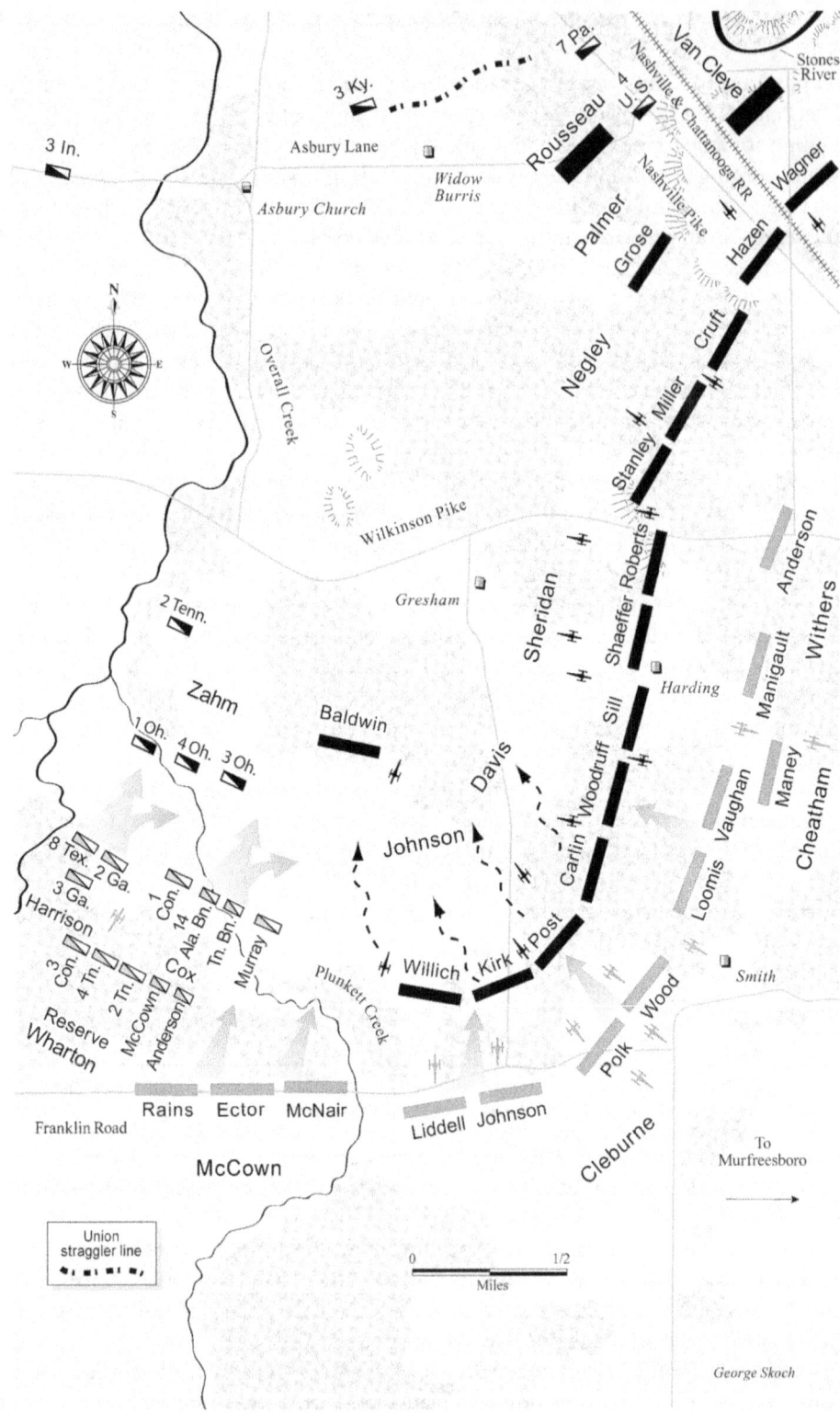

Wharton's cavalry sweeps along the western flank (6:22–7:30 a.m. December 31, 1862). There are no existing records of the order or position of individual Confederate cavalry units during this attack, or of the position of the 2nd Tennessee Cavalry (U.S.).

wheeled right. Wharton faced the enemy and next, he ordered John Cox's wing of cavalry to charge the disorganized Union troops. White's Tennessee artillery unlimbered and began to shell the retreating soldiers. In addition to supporting Hardee's infantry, Wharton faced Zahm's cavalry, which was also falling into a battle line. As Wharton pushed forward Zahm prepared for battle, first fending off the Confederate cavalry with his skirmishers and then repulsing a cavalry charge.[20]

Colonel Baxter Smith, 4th Tennessee Cavalry (CSA), recalled: "The early and sudden movement was made with such impetuosity that it was irresistible." The Confederate cavalry was ordered to attack "anything in sight." Valentine Cupp's squadron barely made it to Zahm lines and Zahm held his position along the Union right flank. Zahm recorded his situation, "[T]he enemy pressing hard on me; kept him at bay with my skirmishers. I retired in this wise for a mile, when I formed a line of battle with the First and Third [Ohio Cavalry]." Wharton, on the other side, had his two cavalry teams, Cox and Harrison, moving northward while assisting with the capture of prisoners, trains and cannons. Captain Gates Thruston, in charge of McCook's ammunition train, observed the impact of the Southern cavalry on the retreating soldiers of the Johnson's division: "Soon Wharton's Confederate cavalry appeared upon the scene and charged upon our broken regiments' stragglers and trains and all hope of resistance upon our extreme right was lost." Then the Union cavalry made its first stand south of Wilkinson's Pike. Zahm held a line on the east side of Puckett Creek in a cornfield, protecting McCook's flank and at the same time blocked a route to the rear of Rosecrans' army. Zahm moved back with the retreating infantry and continued to keep Wharton's cavalry at a distance with his skirmishers. Sergeant E. P. Burlingame, 1st Ohio Cavalry, recorded in his journal:

> Hastily forming we proceeded to join the regiment, and hardly had we done so when the rebels opened on us with artillery; one of the first shots killing our major, David A. B. Moore. Acting under orders, we fell back to a new position. The enemy, mistaking the movement for a retreat, set up a cheer and charged. Upon our again facing them, however, they came to a sudden halt, and we engaged them with our carbines. Colonel Miliken was cool and brave. "Give it to them, boys," said he, "and if they get too close take your sabres to them."

South of Wilkinson Pike, Wharton made his first charge on Zahm's brigade but the Ohioans held their position and Wharton was repulsed.[21]

Fire from Benjamin White's Tennessee artillery sent Zahm again moving to the rear. Sergeant Isaac Skillman, 3rd Ohio, wrote in his diary that the first charge of Wharton's cavalry was repulsed and driven to the rear when White's artillery came into play with an immediate impact. "The enemy's artillery had come up and were shelling us ... shell bursting in the air and one of the pieces struck and killed Major Moore.... It was getting too hot so we retreated a short distance near the Wilson [Wilkinson] pike."[22]

When the Union infantry collapsed along the right flank, instead of moving to the Nashville Pike, many retreated northward in the direction of Overall Creek, a little to the west. The ferocity of the morning's attack was a surprise even though the movements of Southern troops were heard overnight. Captain Warren Edgarton, 1st Ohio Artillery, dispatched his men to take the horses away from the guns for water before the battle started and could not move his guns to safety. Even the brigade commander, August Willich, was away from the front conferring with Richard Johnson when the attack came. As the infantry lines buckled under Hardee's attack, the men streamed rearward and some sought cover and increased hope of safety along Overall Creek. The result of this was two-fold. It led the retreating infantry in the area where both cavalries were operating and it caused some of Hardee's infantry to move away the Union center. This gave the Union cavalry the opportunity to offer some assistance and also allowed Rosecrans precious seconds to assemble a defense. Ector's and Rain's brigades followed the retreating Union soldiers toward Overall Creek instead of following the plan of sweeping into the rear of McCook's corps. Ector was so far west that he and Wharton pursued the same group of retreating Union soldiers, but the impact of Wharton's cavalry on the retreating Union troops was enormous. Alpheus S. Bloomfield, a private in the 1st Ohio Artillery, explained that the artillerymen tried to hold their position against the attacking infantry only to observe Southern cavalry already behind them.[23]

While some of McCown's troops moved too far to the west, Pat Cleburne's troops successfully wheeled right and struck the vulnerable right flank of the McCook's infantry still in line. Cleburne was so successful in his maneuver that the soldiers on the outer edge of the wheel had to run to stay in contact with the line on their right. Hardee realizing this potentially exposed his flank sent S. A. M. Wood's reserve brigade forward to ensure a Union counterattack would not halt Cleburne's success. While Wood's brigade moved forward, Hardee committed reserves he would need later in the battle.

Both Willich's and Kirk's brigades were propelled rearward. Willich who had been away from his brigade rode quickly back to his men and met the success of the Confederate attack when he rode into a line of Ector's Texas Dismounted Cavalry. The soldiers demanded Willich's surrender, but he tried to wheel and ride away. His horse became entangled in the undergrowth and the horse was shot and Willich was promptly captured. Meanwhile, Ector's, Rains' and McNair's infantry continued in their assault past Willich's line and slammed into Kirk's brigade. Kirk's men bravely resisted the attack and the Southern infantry continued its relentless advance. Kirk, encouraging his men to hold the line, was almost immediately shot as the battle rolled past his lines. Lieutenant R. J. Heath, 34th Illinois, of Kirk's brigade observed the effectiveness of having Confederate cavalry on the flank of retreating Union soldiers: "At about the same time a large force of cavalry attacked the 39th Indiana [Willich's brigade] on the flank line and drove them back toward us. The Regiment and the Battery were routed, and we, on the picket line, attempted to get to what was left of the 34th."[24]

W. R. Friend, 8th Texas Cavalry, described the actions of the regiment during the first part of the morning:

> The enemy was routed and retreating, some apparently for dear life. There could be seen squads, companies, and fragments of regiments in measurably good order, doggedly falling back, and while doing so, wheeling and firing on the advancing Confederates, who soon became a mixed mass of cavalry and infantry. The Terry Rangers on horse and Ector's infantry on foot were whooping, and screaming and yelling, hungry and dirty. The game was noble and the pursuit was that the veriest coward on earth could not have skulked to the rear.

A bugle sounded and the troopers of the 8th Texas were recalled and formed, charged and captured two artillery pieces. Throughout the morning, Union soldiers were to dread seeing the 8th Texas riding with their regimental flag flowing in the wind bearing the words: "We Conquer or Die."[25]

The Battle Comes to Baldwin's and Post's Brigades

At 7:30 a.m. St. John Liddell's and Evander McNair's Confederate infantry brigades reached Philemon Baldwin's Union reserve brigade which had been positioned in the rear of Richard Johnson's other troops. At the same time, Bushrod Johnson's brigade converged on P. Sidney Post's troops, the next brigade still in McCook's original line established the evening before. Captain Wilbur Goodspeed, 1st Ohio Artillery, sent two guns to a knoll to his left to help delay the attacking Confederates and after he sent his guns to the west, a hatless sergeant came running forward to report that Wharton's cavalry had already claimed the hill and his guns. After a thirty minute bloody fight, both Union brigades collapsed adding to the confused mass of blue-coated soldiers running for safety. As the Union positions gave way, Mathew Askew, 1st Ohio Infantry, watched the Confederate infantry move to attack Baldwin's brigade in conjunction with Wharton. The 1st Ohio Infantry, Baldwin's brigade, received an attack of infantry and "a large amount" of cavalry joined in the attack. The cavalry and infantry moved along the flanks of the 1st Ohio which gave way when the regiments on their flanks moved to the rear. The actions of Southern cavalry focused not only on the Union cavalry, but on the infantry as well. Askew observed Confederate infantry "marching up 4 regements deep in front of us and the Texes Raingers on our flank, bad for all the roring of musketry and artilery it beat all. I bellive it was about 8 oclock in the morning, the calvery run over me. I was knocked down and taken prisnar." The Union infantry suffered severely from the movement of Wharton's cavalry on the flank and rear. Alexis Cope, 15th Ohio, wrote that he was enjoying a hot cup of coffee when "blowing our coffee cool enough to drink, suddenly came the sharp zt, zt of bullets." The bullets startled the men into action and they observed the enemy advancing along their flank and even reaching their rear. Then the soldiers broke for the rear to evade capture. They ran a short distance and came upon a fence. Next, they scrambled across a small stream and any semblance of order was gone by this point. "Our compact, close, efficient organizations had apparently gone all to pieces and one could see only a disorganized crowd moving to the rear, apparently under no command whatever. The enemy's cavalry appeared on our flank, and some one called out 'fix bayonets' and every man fixed his bayonet to be ready for a cavalry charge."[26]

After McCown's success with Willich's and Kirk's brigades, Philemon Baldwin's reserve Third Brigade folded under the Southern attack along the extreme right flank. Baldwin's brigade had some advance warning and he prepared his men for the attack. Without the support of Willich and Kirk on his east, he became the western most Union brigade in line and found he was an island among a forming sea of gray. Baldwin concluded the futility of making a determined stand and then ordered his men to move toward the Nashville Pike. In addition, to the east P. Sidney Post's brigade of Jefferson's Davis Division was the next target of the Confederate attack. Baldwin's, and subsequently Post's, withdrawal opened the rear of the Union army, except for the small groups of Johnson's division still trying to reorganize

General Evander McNair's Arkansas brigade swept the Union lines before them (Library of Congress).

while retreating northward. The battle for the Union rear between the Union and Confederate cavalry began in earnest.[27]

Next, Hardee directed his infantry toward Jefferson C. Davis's division, in particular, P. Sidney Post's brigade which was in the third position from the western flank of McCook's wing. Upon the collapse of Willich, Kirk, and Baldwin, the next brigade to the east was Colonel P. Sidney Post's brigade of Indiana and Illinois infantry in Davis's First Division which began the morning facing the southeast. Post's soldiers heard the battle begin before they saw any enemies, and his right flank extended into a "dense and almost impenetrable thicket of cedars" as it connected with Kirk's infantry. For a half an hour the battle raged on their right as Post waited in line as the Confederate infantry moved toward his line and he heard the cheers of the enemy which signaled the direction of the impending attack. Post's heart sunk because he knew they had defeated Johnson's brigades and they "were already in our rear." Post moved his brigade into a perpendicular line to his previous position as he heard the Confederates approaching. Pinney's 5th Wisconsin Battery was placed in a cornfield to support Post's shifting line. The 74th and 75th Illinois infantries moved behind a fence to face the timber, while 59th Illinois held the left of the line. The 22nd Indiana Infantry moved into position to support the battery and the 6th Indiana was placed 400 yards in the rear as a reserve.[28]

Captain William Henry Harder, 23rd Tennessee Infantry, in Bushrod Johnson's brigade recorded the attack and pursuit.

> There was no halt. Yet our center moved steadily under the terrible fire from two batteries and the infantry in front. The 23rd found herself under scarcely any fire as the near approach to the low ridge covered it front. I charged my company first to the right and poured a steady, and incessant fire on the stone fence … and the nearest battery, which was silenced, our fire covered the right flank of the Federal center sweeping the whole line…. We … advanced rapidly to find the federal[s] that faced us in full retreat, scarcely firing a shot at us.

John Routt, 44th Tennessee Infantry, described the battle: "[M]en engaged in deadly conflict and heard sharp cracking of small arms and the dreadful booming of cannon and the loud bursting of shells and the rattling of fragments as they went tearing and whizzing through the air and timber."[29]

Then, the lines of gray rushed Post's position and Pinney's 5th Wisconsin Artillery exploded in a barrage with solid shot and shifted to canister as the Confederates got nearer. The infantry and artillery fired into the attacking line which wavered, rallied and again advanced. The battled raged for thirty minutes when Post saw the enemy in his rear and realized he could not hold the position without being captured. The 5th Wisconsin Artillery had paid a terrible price for its efforts so far. Captain Pinney was mortally wounded and eighteen of the battery horses were shot and one gun had to be abandoned as Post ordered the battery to withdraw. Post's infantry and artillery fell back as the Confederate line overwhelmed his brigade, capturing large numbers of prisoners.[30]

The Cavalry Battle Intensifies

The rout of the Union infantry was observed by the cavalry on the west flank, and Lieutenant Colonel Douglas Murray commanding the 3rd Ohio Cavalry saw a large body Confederate cavalry all across his front, left and right trying also to sweep past his men. Once Baldwin's brigade gave way, only the Federal cavalry held the western flank. The 3rd Ohio remained in line and prepared to meet the attack. Colonel Murray wrote:

> The brigade of infantry to our left gave way, retreating in confusion through our lines, letting the whole force of the enemy's artillery, cavalry, and infantry fall upon us, which compelled us gradually to retire toward the main body of our army. The regiment covering the entire rear of the brigade, supporting one infantry regiment on our right, drove back, with heavy loss, a large force of cavalry which charged upon us, under cover of a piece of artillery, firing well-directed shells, which passed over us.

With Baldwin's infantry in retreat, Wharton was able to focus his attention on Zahm's cavalry, the last Union force protecting to the Federal rear.[31]

Among the various obstacles for retreating soldiers were stones, woods, dense cedar brakes, and fences. The fences became a place to find some cover for the retreating troops, but in some cases the fences became such an impediment that it corralled those retreating into a choke point which made killing and capturing easier for the pursuing Southern troops. For the cavalry which often had troopers tear down fences before a battle, fences were potentially the most dangerous part of the battlefield. Isaac Skillman, 3rd Ohio Cavalry, rode to the 1st Ohio Cavalry after the death of Major Moore with orders to fall back and reform. Skillman delivered the message from Lewis Zahm to Colonel Minor Millikin and as he returned to the brigade commander, he rode down the Wilkinson Pike to find a passage through a fence. He observed that the Confederate infantry had just reached Wilkinson Pike but he found he was mistaken. Instead of Confederate infantry, he found Confederate cavalry ahead, and then he rode for his life.

> As I turned to the left through the gap in the fence, they yelled for me to halt. My horse was on the dead run and I didn't have time to halt. They fired at me but I didn't even get a scratch. My poor horse was not quite as lucky, he got a bullet through the top part of his neck just ahead of where the horse collar would come, quite a bad wound.[32]

While William Hardee's attack achieved dramatic success, Leonidas Polk had not been idle but he had the misfortune of attacking Rosecrans' strength without the advantage of a vulnerable flank. He pushed ahead and ran into Phil Sheridan's division which held its place and stubbornly resisted the attacking Confederate infantry. Meanwhile, both Thomas' and Crittenden's corps were still intact and yet to be fully engaged, despite the fact that McCook's wing was folding like a pocket knife toward the Nashville Pike. Rosecrans hastily began forming a new defense with the remnants of his army. For the rest of the day the infantries of the two armies would batter each other, but much of the cavalry actions concentrated on the right and rear of the Union army.

The Fight Along Wilkinson Pike (9:00 a.m.–10:00 a.m.)

While Zahm was fighting Wharton's cavalry, the 3rd Kentucky and 7th Pennsylvania cavalries were in the rear of the army stretched in a line across the Nashville Pike. Eli Murray's 3rd Kentucky Cavalry and Major John Wynkoop's 7th Pennsylvania Cavalry had been detailed to straggler duty the day before. They formed a line in the rear of Rosecrans' army with orders to push soldiers forward to their respective units. Neither expected much action during the day as the infantry planned to carry the major effort of the battle. At least, a company of the 3rd Kentucky began the day posted near the front and in the center of the Union army behind a battery of Parrott guns that were "blazing away." Trooper H. L. Ambrose described that the morning's work had begun very calmly because the extent of the collapse of the right flank was not initially known. After hearing the firing on the Union right flank, he saw Confederate soldiers standing on top of the rifle pits across Stones River and yelling and waving their hats. Ambrose's captain ordered him to eat what breakfast he could and to feed his horse. It had the makings of a long day, but soon an enemy battery located the Union battery the 3rd Kentucky supported. The position became a "hot place" and the troopers tried to calm their horses "amidst the bursting shells, whistling solid-shot and falling treetops." Then, the first signs of the collapse on the right flank began to be noticed. The loud thumps of cannons and the explosions of musket fire alerted all along the line and then a few men were noticed racing to the rear. Then many men were observed running and finally "squads and whole companies.... The stampede increased." Officers begged and cursed the retreating men to stand and fight as the flood of men moved to the rear.[33]

Meanwhile, Zahm moved his cavalry in pace with the retiring infantry and he maintained a line keeping Wharton's troopers from gaining the rear of McCook's infantry which would have made the morning even more disastrous than it already was for the Union troops. About 9:00 a.m., Zahm positioned the 1st and 3rd Ohio cavalries facing Wharton's troopers and moved the 4th Ohio and 2nd Tennessee regiments as the reserve. Zahm's cavalry formed a line from the retreating Union infantry to Overall Creek. Then Wharton charged, but the Ohioans held their position and repulsed the second attack of the morning. What Wharton's troopers couldn't do, his artillery could. White's Battery of Tennessee (CSA) artillery followed the advance and shelled the Union cavalry at every opportunity. The Confederate artillery again opened on Zahm's Ohio cavalry with precision. Realizing his precarious position, Zahm retreated out of the range of the artillery and formed a new line as Wharton charged but was repulsed again by the Union cavalry. Zahm recorded during this attack his troopers "made many of the rebels bite the dust." But the Confederate artillery again found Zahm's range and he retired again. During one of the cavalry fights, the adjutant of the 1st Ohio Cavalry was severely wounded while attempting to capture a flag of a Southern cavalry regiment. Zahm made another stand along the Wilkinson Pike and received some support from Willich's brigade which had rallied; and again Wharton charged and, again, he was repulsed.[34]

In one of the cavalry charges, the differences in the cavalry tactics became evident. James Blackburn, 8th Texas Cavalry, recalled:

> On another occasion the Colonel, while standing in front of his line ready to make or receive a charge as it might happen, was looking through his field glass at a body of cavalry some distance off. Suddenly he exclaimed, "Now boys, we will have some fun. There is a regiment out there preparing to charge us, armed with sabres. Let them come up nearly close enough to strike and then feed them on buckshot." So they came up with great noise and pretense, hoping to demoralize and scatter their opponents and then have a race in which they could use their sabres effectively. But as the Texans stood their ground the Yankees ran up to within a few steps and halted suddenly, giving our boys the chance they were wishing for. One volley from the shotguns into their ranks scattered these sabre men into useless fragments of a force.[35]

During the initial attack General Willich became one of the first casualties when his horse was shot under him and he was taken prisoner. Brigade command devolved to Colonel William H. Wallace, but Colonel William Gibson, 49th Ohio Infantry, assumed command of the brigade because Wallace could not be found. After the attack began, Gibson attempted to organize a defense but the center of Hardee's attack struck his brigade. Gibson observed to the right of the position of his re-forming troops, the arrival of "an immense force of cavalry." Gibson's brigade was assailed in the front and left with infantry and Wharton's cavalry menaced the right. He had no choice but to retreat. Gibson rallied his command and tried to make a stand several times, but he could not withstand the Southern assault. Finally, with his command in shatters he arrived at the Wilkinson Turnpike, a short distance from his ammunition train, and made one last stand and counter attacked to keep the enemy at bay, but to no avail, losing a cannon in the process. Wharton's cavalry attacked and captured the remnant of his brigade. Gibson's sword was demanded. Gibson's wrote in his after action report: "[A]ll of us being in the enemy's power." But help was on the way as a wave of blue charged ahead amid the sound of hoof beats sending Wharton's cavalry to the rear. "[I]n the confusion of the moment most of us fought our way out and escaped," exclaimed Gibson. Zahm's Union 3rd Ohio Cavalry counterattack successfully stymied Colonel John Cox's 1st Confederate Cavalry and part of the 8th Texas Cavalry which had captured some cannons and men of Gibson's First Brigade. Gibson's men made their escape and continued running for the rear.[36]

Upon General Edward Kirk's wounding, Colonel J. B. Dodge, 30th Indiana, assumed command of Kirk's brigade, and he, like Gibson, struggled to organize a defense against the Confederate cavalry and infantry and observed the Union cavalry charge after he crossed Wilkinson's Pike: "In a moment the enemy came in sight, his solid columns moving in splendid style. We waited until they came to the fence along the pike, and then gave them three or four volleys which they returned with interest." Dodge's infantry hurried northward in the same general direction as Gibson's brigade. Dodge knew his command was in trouble when he sent six men to the rear for ammunition and was informed that all six were captured by the enemy already in the rear. While Dodge successfully formed a line to halt the advancing Confederate infantry, it was Wharton's cavalry which turned the tide. As Dodge's men were firing, they "received a galling fire from a force of rebel cavalry that were on our right and rear, and again we were forced back, keeping just in the edge of the woods so as to have what protection we could from the large force of rebel cavalry that was on our flank, and between us and Overalls creek." Dodge fought again to get a substantial defensive line formed and he moved into a strip of woods. He wisely utilized the timber to reduce the advantage when Wharton's troopers again drew up in line to make a mounted charge. Dodge described,

> They were in some fields, on a strip of slightly elevated ground, that was covered with grass, and had room and ground suitable to move on as they wanted to, and accordingly formed a heavy line and came towards us. When I first saw them coming they were moving in a close compact line, extending as far as I could see in our rear and some little distance in our front, charging at a sweeping trot. It looked gloomy; but I formed my line promptly, facing them, and we stood there awaiting their onset with fixed bayonets. They were now within seventy-five yards, when they sounded the charge. At about fifty yards distance my line gave them a well directed volley.... In a moment a division of our cavalry came sweeping up on a full charge on the rebel flank and rear. It was a glorious sight, as with their sabres drawn and their horses at their fastest speed, they came down on the foe. They used no weapons but their sabres, and in a moment the enemy were wavering and struggling to change their front; but it was no use, they were literally ridden down and cut to pieces. They could not stand it and gave way in confusion, our cavalry showering blows upon them until they took refuge behind their infantry columns. By this time the enemies' infantry was crowding us again, and we moved on out.[37]

Zahm's cavalry freed Gibson, Dodge and their men but they were not out of the woods as the infantry hurried to the rear only to be pursued by the Southern cavalry and infantry again, and the colors of the 39th Indiana Infantry was captured. Over 700 men of Willich's/Gibson's brigade were captured at Stones River but the remainder made it back to the main Union line. "A complete panic prevailed. Teams, ambulances, horsemen, footmen, and attaches of the army, black and white, mounted on horses and mules, were rushing to the rear in the wildest confusion." Gibson tried to stop the panic as his soldiers continued to flow northward and it wasn't until he moved to the Nashville Pike and to the west of Overall Creek that he started to gain control of his men when he encountered Colonel Moses Walker infantry brigade moving toward the battle. Walker's infantry formed a strong line across the Nashville Pike and the panic subsided; and the panicked men started reforming into regiments. Lyman Ayer, 2nd Minnesota Artillery of Jefferson C. Davis's division, watched as the troops of the Federal Right Wing retreated in panic and became separated from their command. At that point in the war, there were no outwardly visible designations or badges for soldiers to identify their brigades or divisions which added to the confusion. A mob of soldiers milling around had no way to readily identify their brigade or regiment.[38]

Then, Cox's cavalry again struck the retreating Union infantry, encircled a mass of retreating infantry and captured sixty soldiers of the 75th Illinois Infantry regiment. In addition, a battalion of Texas Rangers (8th Texas Cavalry) commanded by Captain S. P. Christian, Company K, charged a battery and captured four guns and all the equipment. Wharton's troopers also scooped up an abandoned gun left on the field as the Union infantry and artillery retreated. In all, Wharton's cavalry captured six guns south and along the Wilkinson Pike, four guns of the 5th Wisconsin Artillery and two guns of Battery A, 1st Ohio Artillery. In this first phase of Wharton's attack, he collected about 1,500 prisoners and five or six artillery pieces and sent them to the rear. Private Benjamin Burke, 8th Texas Cavalry, described that while Cox and Harrison were attacking the Union forces at various intervals during the morning, the reserve wing of Wharton's cavalry shuttled prisoners to the rear. One of the prisoners captured was Corporal Morris Cope, 15th Ohio, who assisted a wounded comrade to a log cabin. He recalled,

> I carried Fenton back until we came to an old log-house filled with corn shucks. I put him inside near a window and covered him up with my overcoat and started out, when I saw ... not less than twenty revolvers pointing at me and several gentlemen very emphatically invited me to surrender. I notified them that I would do so at once. It was the Texas Rangers who captured us. They were a bully set of fellows and treated us very nicely. We had seen, as we were going into the cabin, a long line of blue-coated cavalry on our flank, and thought they were our own men.[39]

In the confusion and fighting during the morning, a brash private of the 2nd Georgia Cavalry was unhorsed while charging a group of Union infantry. James Fambro, a native of Monroe County, Georgia, was aggressively following his orders when a ball from an infantryman's musket killed his horse. Fambro, undaunted, continued on foot until he was able to capture a Federal horse, and he continued on his task of gathering up prisoners. For his actions, he was subsequently promoted to the rank of captain.[40]

Wharton pushed Zahm north of Wilkinson Pike and the Union cavalry passed into a strip of woods and moved out of sight. As the Confederate cavalry moved forward in pursuit, Lieutenant Colonel John Pugh's 4th Ohio Cavalry struck back and held the Confederate cavalry temporarily. Once the Union cavalry moved into the woods, the pursuers lost sight and followed them across a cornfield and toward the woods. Just at that moment the 4th Ohio burst forward and attacked. The Ohioans held their pursuers at bay while delivering a volley in the column, but reinforcements arrived and Pugh's cavalry again hastened northward through the woods. Pugh reported that he was successful in holding a line for a little while but was again flanked.[41]

During the various fights, Sergeant Thomas Osborn, 4th Ohio Cavalry, was a victim of the confusion on the field. As he was riding in rearguard action between Wharton's troopers and his own, he watched the enemies move in pursuit. Just at that moment, he horse fell into one of the sink holes in the area and both the horse and rider became entangled. The horse first fell on Osborn, but finally righted itself and leapt out of the hole. Osborn was in a precarious situation, the cavalry fight was going on outside the hole, but the enemy was now closer to him than his own troops. So close were Wharton's troopers, Osborn could hear the officers giving commands. Osborn recalled, "Their shot and shell was playing over and around me, and the panorama of my life passed before me. I thought my time had come." Osborn contemplated his next move, when he was startled by a noise in the hole. He discovered an enemy soldier in the hole with him, but fortunately for Osborn, the soldier

> proved worse scared than I, as he kept crawling for the bottom, not having seen me. At this juncture, I took courage, secured my pistol, which I had hidden, and boldly demanded his surrender. The position was ludicrous in the extreme. I disarmed him.... I ventured to raise my head above ground, and to my great joy, a few hundred yards in my front was a company of our troops with colors flying. Never did the Stars and Stripes look more beautiful. I took my "Johnny" and swapped him for a horse, and soon after joined my own command, happy to think I was alive, and greatly excited over my strange experience. It is but fair to say that had "Johnny" called upon me at this juncture, to surrender, I would have done so, and doubtless have pled for my life as earnestly as he did for his.[42]

The Confederate cavalry continued to push north and Cox's wing moved to the right and Harrison's wing rode on the left. While Wharton focused on capturing retreating soldiers and increasing the pressure on Zahm's cavalry, another battalion of Union cavalry joined in the fight. Major Robert Klein's 3rd Indiana Cavalry joined in the fight after riding from Wilkinson's Crossroad where he was posted on the extreme west flank of the Union army. If Klein cooperated with Zahm officially, it is unknown because Zahm made no mention of the 3rd Indiana in his after action report; but Klein described fighting, skirmishing and falling back through the morning. The cohesion of his small command was broken at this time by the retreat of an unidentified cavalry regiment, but presumably the 2nd Tennessee Cavalry. Klein wrote:

> When our forces first gave way before the overwhelming numbers of the enemy, the efficiency of my battalion was destroyed in being divided by one of our own cavalry regiments running through our ranks and scattering the men. This movement, had it been in the opposite direction, would have been a most gallant charge, and, doubtless, from its determination, an efficient one.[43]

Meanwhile, Vincent Dunn, a member of the 3rd Kentucky Cavalry, and some of the regiment had been assigned courier duty. As the battle progressed Dunn and Major Aaron Shacklett rode to investigate the sounds of battle. The two rode over a slight rise and near a battery of artillery firing on the enemy. The two cavalrymen were shocked by the sight they observed. They were "amazed at the retreat of our men. It put me in mind of a large flock of black birds rising out of a cornfield when our men retreated back." Lewis Wolfley, 3rd Kentucky, also described the morning for his battalion which had previously been assigned to courier duty. At the sound of the battle Wolfley moved to the right and observed:

> [H]ere they came over fences & ditches as hard as they could tear. Wagons, ambulances, cannons and infantry almost by Regt. Officers and men trying to out do each other. While in their rear and almost on them was the rebel cavalry with one or two pieces of artillery. This was our first notice of our Right having giving [given] way. Our orders were to stop all stragglers. This we at first tried to do but finding it impossible we next turned to the Rebels. Who by this time were right on us.[44]

The remaining Union cavalry regiment on the field was part of the 7th Pennsylvania Cavalry. One battalion of the regiment was in the rear with Stanley and Minty. For the remainder of the regiment, which began the day on straggler duty, they were hastily

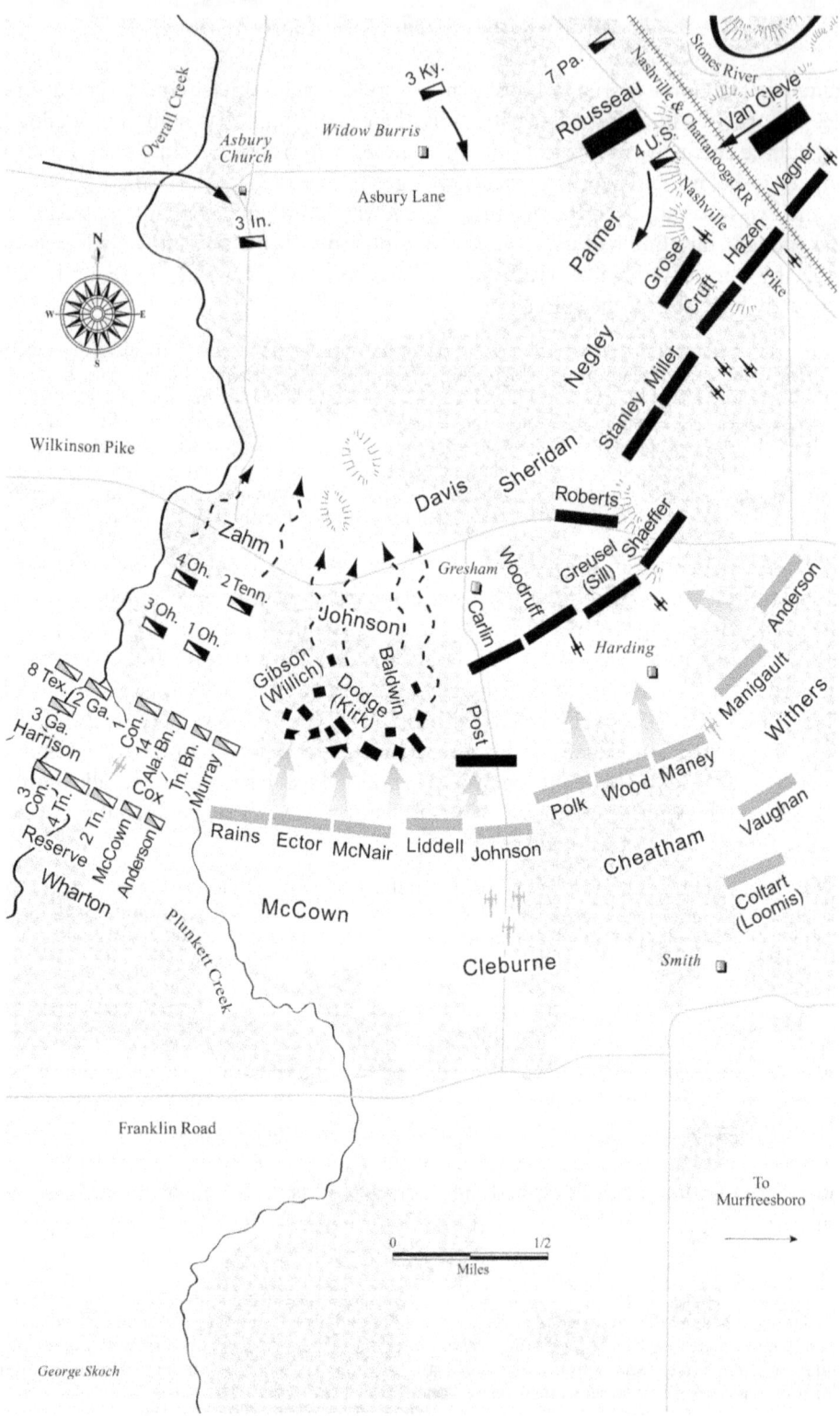

The cavalry battle moves south of the Wilkinson Pike (8:00–9:00 a.m. December 31, 1862). There are no existing records of the order or position of individual Confederate cavalry units during this attack.

assigned to rallying the troops and performing courier duty, carrying messages from one part of the battlefield to another.[45]

Not only did Zahm have to deal with Wharton's men, but the Southern infantry continued its relentless pursuit of the retreating Union infantry. The Confederate infantry's success left Zahm in a position of holding the enemy's cavalry but being nearly cut off by the advance of the Southern infantry. Zahm moved his troopers through a wooded area and passed "by a line of rebel infantry [McNair's], marching parallel with my column, not over 200 yards from us, so that we were nearly surrounded." While the Confederate infantry advanced so closely to Zahm, Wharton's cavalry continued on its assigned task of reaching the rear of the Union army. At 9:00 a.m., Zahm held the position near the Wilkinson's Turnpike and faced 2,000 Southern horsemen compared to about 1,000 of his own. He observed: "They had cavalry enough to spare to strike, or to take position, when ever required."[46]

Summary

The Southern infantry and cavalry clearly won the early morning. Wharton's contributions were remarkable and significant. The presence of two thousand enemy cavalry on the flank of the routed Union infantry was unnerving and helped prevent the Federal soldiers from rallying and establishing some sort of a defense. The efforts against Zahm's cavalry were also significant as Wharton forced Zahm to retreat; although Zahm successfully repulsed several cavalry charges. Wharton wisely brought White's Tennessee Artillery which generally forced Zahm to continue his retreat. The concentration of cavalry and clear objectives resulted in effective use of Southern cavalry during the morning, but Wharton needed some additional support, either from cavalry or infantry. He was operating successfully, but on his own.

The biggest error on the Confederate side during the early part of the attack was the absence to Wheeler, the chief of cavalry. While the actions on the west flank were proceeding well, the small Confederate presence on the eastern side of the battlefield would be problematic, one which needed a chief of cavalry. Certainly, one has to question if Wheeler was, in fact, acting as chief of cavalry, or was Wheeler acting as a cavalry brigade commander in this action. While Wheeler successfully destroyed supplies intended for the Union army, the result did not weaken Rosecrans' ability to fight at Stones River. In addition, if Wheeler could have coordinated his return to Murfreesboro with Wharton's action on the morning of December 31, the results could have been even greater in favor of Bragg's attack. But, it is important to remember this was Wheeler's first battle as chief of cavalry and he was still learning his new role.

For the Union cavalry during the morning's fighting, it was clearly roughly handled. While many commanders embellished their reports during the Civil War, Lewis Zahm provided a refreshingly straight forward account. His four regiments of cavalry were pushed back during the morning, but he had held a steady line and thus far thwarted Wharton's real objective, Rosecrans' rear. Zahm had prevented this, while assisting the retreating Union infantry, and successfully repulsing Wharton's cavalry charges.

As with Wheeler, David Stanley, the Union chief of cavalry, was not on the battlefield where he was desperately needed. He had been ordered to the rear to prevent further destruction by Wheeler, and so, in this regard Wheeler successfully pulled a third of the

Union cavalry to the rear. The Union cavalry was already outmanned and this exacerbated the situation which the Confederates took full advantage. Although, John Kennett commanded the full Union cavalry division and was present on the battlefield, there was no evidence of his efforts to coordinate a cavalry defense with his remaining regiments on the field, at this point—3rd Kentucky, 3rd Indiana, 7th Pennsylvania, and the detached 4th U.S. About three hours had passed and Zahm's cavalry stood alone on the Union right flank. The decision to send David Stanley to the rear of the Union army was a poor one.

9. The Cavalry Battle of Stones River (December 31, Late Morning)

*Commending their souls to God,
they charged home.*—Captain W. L. Curry

Between 9:00 and 10:00 a.m., the cavalry battle on the western flank moved north of Wilkinson Pike. Just north of the pike and east of Overall Creek was another cornfield bordered by light woods on three sides. On the north side of the cornfield, the route of the Northern retreat passed through a strip of woods about 300–400 yards wide. North of these woods was a vast set of fallow agricultural fields stretching to the Nashville Pike, which ran diagonally from the northwest to the southeast. On the east side of the Nashville Pike was a slightly elevated strip of ground on which the Nashville & Chattanooga Railroad track was built. Roughly parallel to the Wilkinson Pike and about a mile north was a dirt road, Asbury Lane, connecting Asbury Church and Widow Burris's house and extending east to the Nashville Pike. The concentration of Federal supply and ordnance wagons was located along the Nashville Pike and the cavalry battle moved in the direction of the wagons.

The Wagon Trains

The lifeblood of the troops on the field was the supply and ammunition wagons. These were large, lumbering wagons that carried camp equipment, foods, supplies, tools, ammunition and clothing. The wagons held the ever-important supplies for regiments, artillery batteries, brigades and corps; and there were many in use by the Army of the Cumberland. The invaluable and often contrary components of the wagons trains were the army mules. The backbone of the wagon trains was the mule, described by veteran teamsters as: "He cannot be trusted even when appearing honest and affectionate." These animals were "tough and hardy" and invaluable during the war. Wheeler spent the previous day destroying four supply trains destined to support those in the desperate battle taking place, but there were still many wagons on the field. Bragg certainly wanted to defeat Rosecrans, and he seemed well on his way of doing that by mid-morning; but if he couldn't defeat him, then he would settle for sending him back to Nashville and even back into Kentucky. The cavalry battle on the right and rear of Rosecrans' army clarified and focused on Wharton's intent to destroy or capture the bounty of Federal supplies in

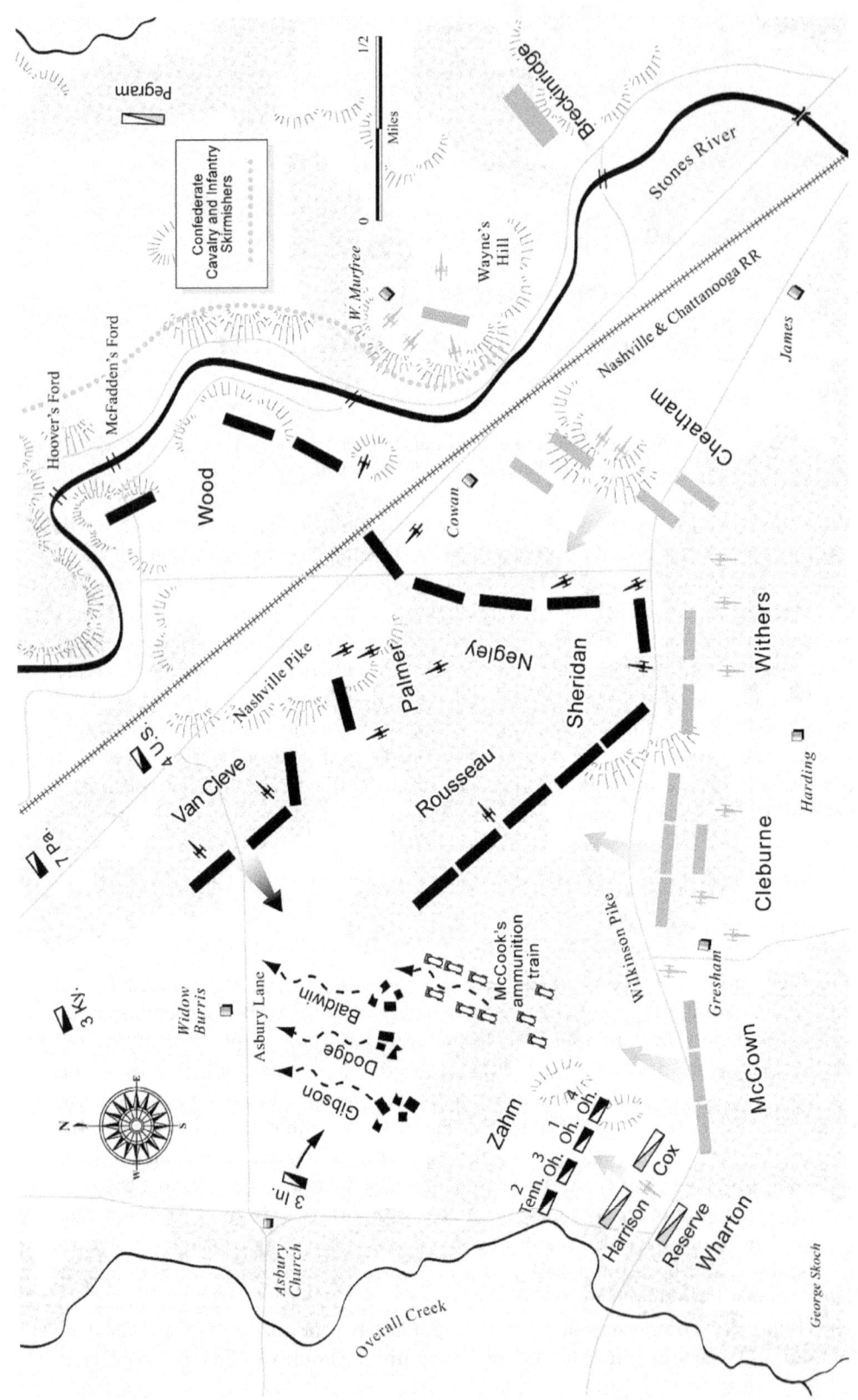

Cavalry actions along Wilkinson Pike (9:00–10:00 a.m. December 31, 1862). There are no existing records of the order or position of individual Confederate cavalry units during this attack.

wagon trains parked on the Nashville Pike. Without ammunition or rations, Rosecrans would have to return to Nashville. As the Union infantry continued its retreat on the western flank, Wharton saw the opportunity to cause more havoc, and he was determined to destroy the supply trains in the rear of Rosecrans' army. And there were a lot of wagons from which to choose.[1]

After the Battle of Perryville, ammunition trains were ordered closer to the fighting units. At Perryville, there was the loss of critical time and firepower because the ammunition wagons were too far to the rear. As a result, on December 31 the wagon trains were about six hundred yards behind the reserves, which were about six hundred yards behind the main infantry line. Because the Union troops retreated so quickly, the ammunition wagons about two-thirds of a mile in the rear were at risk of being captured within the first hour of the attack. In addition to ammunition trains, the various supply wagons, caissons, ambulances, and wagons containing regimental books and personal effects were all on the battlefield at a distance from the front presumed to be "safe." As the battle began, many of the teamsters were calm because both sides expected a battle during the day and the noise was not unexpected. As the battle developed, the entire army became involved and what started out as calm routines for the teamsters evolved into a scramble. Lieutenant Alfred Pirtle, 10th Ohio Infantry, was in charge of an ammunition train in Thomas's wing and he had moved Thomas's ammunition train about two-thirds of a mile behind the main infantry line along the Nashville Pike, and soon men began clamoring for ammunition which Pirtle distributed. Next, his wagons were ordered to move because it occupied an excellent spot for artillery. Soon afterward, he found he was being shelled by Confederate artillery and he attempted to move again, but his wagons became stalled

Union ammunition wagon train—the invaluable and often contrary components of the wagon trains were the army mules (Library of Congress).

The lifeblood of the troops on the field was the supply and ammunition wagons (National Archives).

along the railroad track. The teamsters desperately wanted to move the wagons because troops were falling in around the area of his wagons. If the Confederate artillery hit a wagon, it might explode killing everyone around the wagons. Next, the quartermaster fell under Confederate musket fire and finally he was able to move further to the rear. This train was located in the center of army and had a challenging morning; but outside the reforming Union lines, the morning became a nightmare for the teamsters with their wagon trains.[2]

Many of the supply trains were drawn closer to the original front line on the evening on December 30. For example, the wagon train of the 11th Michigan Infantry moved to the west of the Nashville Pike to provide the men with their rations and meals. As the battle began, the supply trains made a wild dash to the rear. James King, 11th Michigan, who was with one of Negley's trains, hastily moved the brigade's train about two miles where the regimental quartermaster thought the wagons would be safe. But none of the Union commanders considered the scope of the collapse of the Union right flank. To aid in the confusion, those who moved the trains tried to return to their regiments while the trains were left unattended "safely" in the rear. The concentration of supply wagons which were moved to safety became the targets of Wharton's cavalry which moved along the western edge of the battle. As King left the wagons, he observed the fighting was like a "crop fire which killed many of our brave boys. All day the battle raged."[3]

The confusion of the day was also described by G. C. Kniffin of Crittenden's staff:

> Wharton in command of ten regiments of cavalry and a battery of artillery, moved over towards the Nashville pike and turned his attention to the immense supply train of the army. A portion of this

train, six miles long when stretched out upon the road, was moving across the country from the Wilkinson to the Nashville pike. The scene was one of the most indescribable confusion. Urged by impending calamity the canvas-covered wagons flew across the fields with the velocity of four-mule power, each driver plying whip and spur; sutler wagons, bounding over rocks, distributed their precious contents along the way.[4]

Among the wagons trains that were at risk of being captured by the attacking Confederates was the baggage train of the 15th Pennsylvania Cavalry. Five wagons of the regiment moved eastward after the unsuccessful charge which claimed Adolph Rosengarten's life and mortally wounded Frank Ward on December 29. When the 15th Pennsylvania was sent to the rear the evening before, the wagons continued eastward and joined one of the infantry supply trains near Gresham's farm just south of the Wilkinson Pike. John Williams, 15th Pennsylvania, described that the morning was bitterly cold and he and his fellow teamsters were up early. They planned to continue to the Nashville Pike when they heard the explosion of gunfire and cannons as the Confederate attack began. Williams told his fellow teamsters the sounds were "more than a skirmish." Williams pulled his watch and noted in his journal the time was 7:10 a.m. Recognizing the need to hurry toward the main body of the Union army, Williams hurried the teams forward along the pike. As Williams's wagon emerged from a cedar grove, he was met with the full display of the battle unfolding on the western flank of the armies. Soon Williams saw the result of Johnson's rout from the seat of his wagon. Streaming across the road ahead of him was a mob of soldiers, many with no weapons at all. The retreating soldiers ran head long across the road into the cedar groves beyond. Williams observed some of retreating infantry move northward "straight into the arms of Wheeler's Rebel cavalry." He whipped

The Federal supply train extended for miles—photograph depicts an example of a supply train in Virginia (Library of Congress).

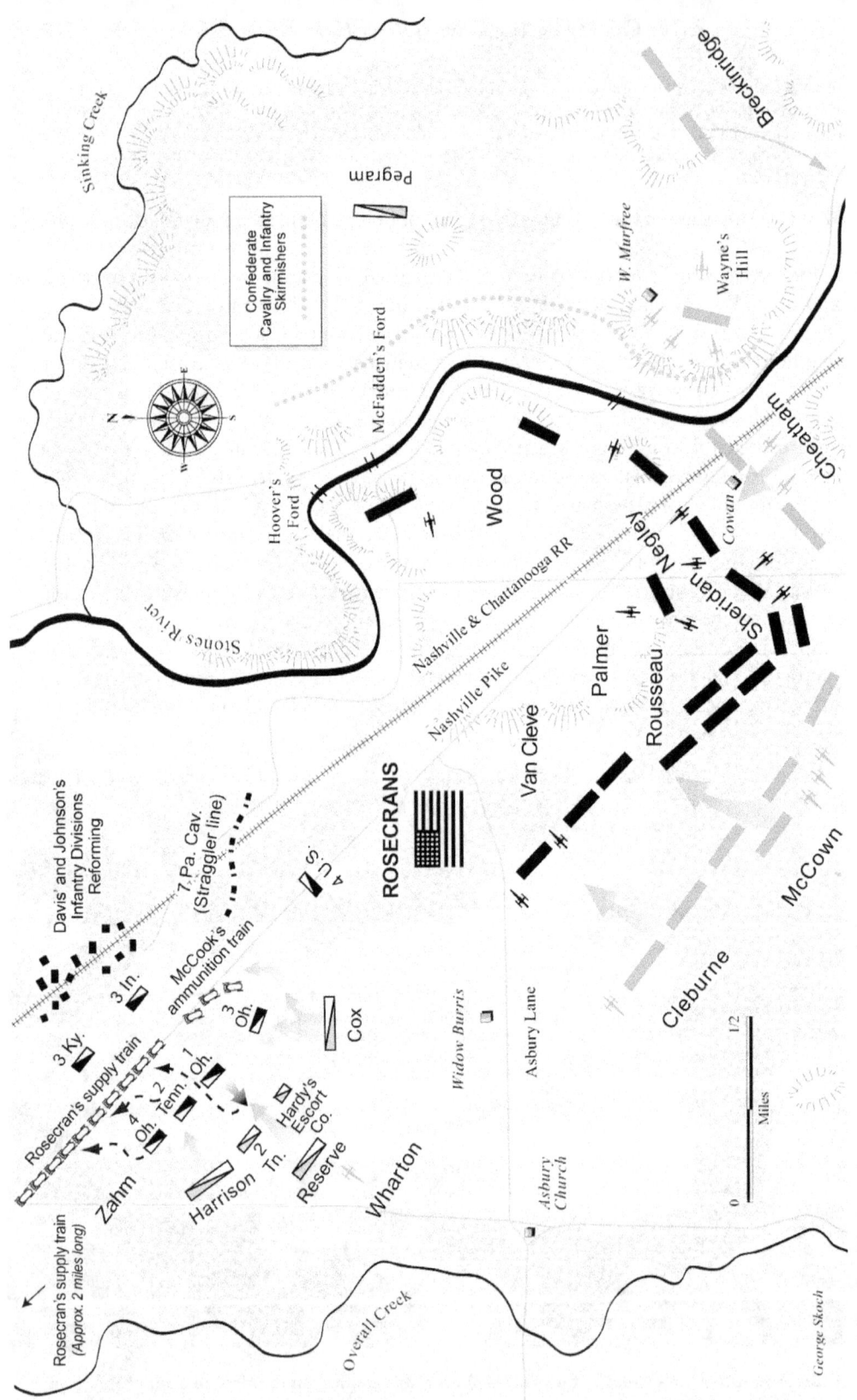

Wharton's cavalry defeats Zahm's brigade defending the ammunition and supply trains (10:00–11:00 a.m. December 31, 1862).

the teams forward and came upon a brigadier general calmly giving orders while sitting on a black horse—Phil Sheridan. But the battle raged and drew closer and Williams concluded to continue his route by another road. Luckily for Williams his small train reached the Nashville Pike and he moved to safety near the position of the 7th Pennsylvania Cavalry.[5]

Several regimental wagon trains hurried to the safety of the center of the army including the train of the 7th Pennsylvania Cavalry. Sergeant Gerould Gibson recorded in his diary: "We had to skeddale with the teams." Gibson drove his wagons five miles to the rear during the day. William H. Colony, a teamster in the 7th Pennsylvania Cavalry, found the wagon trains to be a very dangerous place to be. Three times, during day of the battle he missed being seriously injured or captured. As the wagon train moved to the rear it moved past a four gun battery and Colony rode further to the rear and then turned to assist the battery. By the time he reached the battery it had already been captured and the horses shot.[6]

Captain Gates Thruston's large and vitally important ammunition train for McCook's corps became one of the first objectives of Wharton's cavalry as it moved across the Wilkinson Pike. Thruston began the morning with sixty-six or sixty-seven "heavily-laden" ammunition wagons drawn by either four horses or four mules in the field directly behind Richard Johnson's division. He had been assigned only seventy-five men and two orderlies for the ammunition train. Thruston was aware of his precarious situation as the right collapsed and he had barely saved the ammunition train from an early attempt of the Confederate cavalry to capture his train. "I was proud of this new command, but these ordnance treasures carried with them grave responsibilities. I hastened back to my train, located near corps headquarters. Danger already threatened, and it was soon prepared for movement." With Alexander McCook and his headquarters staff at the front trying to rally his command there was no one to give Thruston orders about the ammunition train. Thruston took the matter into his own hands and decided to start his long wagon train toward the center of the army near the Nashville Pike. As Thruston started to move, a detachment of Wharton's discovered the slow moving train and attacked. The gray-clad cavalry tried to stampede the horses and mules while shooting at the teamsters, but this was not a concentrated attack and the train guards picked up their muskets and fired away. Some Federal cavalry and some stragglers from various infantry units joined in the defense of the wagon train. Thruston's teamsters were joined by a Captain Henry Pease, Inspector General of Jefferson C. Davis's division, who assisted in the defense of the wagons and Thruston was successful in driving off the attackers. The near miss after the Confederate attack caused Thruston to attempt to find safety by heading across country. The wagons continued to roll along and for the moment the Confederate cavalry looked for other targets.

Captain Gates Thruston commanded McCook's important ammunition wagon train throughout the morning (Tennessee State Library and Archives).

It was a toilsome struggle to guide and push our unwieldy trains through byways, ravines, and fences, and to cut our way through cedar thickets. We soon reached a series of open fields, where new dangers confronted us, but we managed to move on and on until we found ourselves in the midst of a veritable battlefield, stormy with conflicts and tumult.

McCook's ammunition train was blocked by the battle raging to the east along Wilkinson Pike as the two infantries surged forward. Thruston had no choice but to try to move his wagons northward across country to reach the safety of the Union lines.[7]

For most of those wagon trains that successfully reached the Nashville Pike in the center of the army, they were soon in the way of advancing troops. T. F. Dornblaser, 7th Pennsylvania Cavalry, observed as Rousseau's division moved to the Union right flank to stem the tide and marched toward the Nashville Pike which was full of wagons. When Rousseau saw the situation, he yelled, "Clear this field: on this ground the battle must he fought!" The teamsters who had a reputation for their independence immediately began moving their wagons. "They mounted the saddle-mule, cracked the whip, and off they went up the pike, four wagons abreast, on a full charge." The trains moved northward along the Nashville Pike and moved to the apparent safety in the rear of the army.[8]

Distressing is the consideration of the contents of the wagons trains as the day progressed. Certainly, these wagons, heading for the rear and some for Nashville, did not just carry ammunition or supplies, which would be needed on the battlefield. More realistically, many of these wagons carried the bodies of the wounded and perhaps the dead from the day's battle to the hospitals and morgues in the rear.[9]

The Battle Moves North of Wilkinson Pike

At 10:00 a.m., Zahm's cavalry was pushed north of the Wilkinson Turnpike and away from the infantry. The new phase of the battle for the two cavalries, North and South, focused on the Union wagon trains which offered booty for the Southerners and provided the ammunition and food the Northerners needed to keep fighting. The wagon trains were critical for the Union army's ability to stay on the battlefield. As Zahm withdrew his cavalry from the collapsing right flank, his cavalry rode through a strip of woods and he found himself in the flat, open ground of large agricultural fields. A few hundred yards ahead was a dirt road running east and west- Asbury Lane. To the west was the sight of his bivouac two evenings before along Overall Creek and near Asbury Church. To the east was the temporary hospital of Widow Burris' house and beyond that was the Nashville Pike where Rosecrans' infantry was making a determined defense. Further north along the Nashville Pike was the large wagon train of the Federal army which had been placed at a location presumed to be a safe distance from the fighting. Over the fields, Thruston's teamsters continued onward and whipped their teams while they hurried away from Colonel John T. Cox's three-regiment wing close on his heels. As Zahm moved into the open ground, Thruston rode to him and explained the importance of his ammunition train. The withdrawal was over for Zahm and his cavalry, and he had found the place to stand and fight. Zahm's position near the ammunition train was about three quarters of a mile north from where the major infantry action was occurring at the time. Zahm had the task of trying to protect two wagon trains, McCook's ammunition wagons hurrying to the rear and Rosecrans' large army supply train.[10]

Meanwhile, the Confederate cavalry was filled with exultation from the victory of the morning. Baxter Smith, 4th Tennessee Cavalry (CSA), recorded: "Charge after charge we made carrying everything before us." As the Southern attack continued, Union hospitals were overrun and the personnel captured. Dr. F. G. Hickman, a surgeon in Johnson's Division watched as the Southern troops flowed forward. He received the badly wounded General Kirk. Hickman exclaimed that General Kirk would not let them remove him from the ambulance: "'Boys, get out of here as soon as possible, or you will be captured.'" Then, the ambulance proceeded rearward. Hickman ordered his ambulance hitched and for his staff to move to the rear, but "they were too late, for the Confederate cavalry soon overtook them." Further to the rear, Thruston observed Wharton's cavalry "sweeping everything before him."[11]

Zahm's Defense of the Wagon Trains

While on the Southern side of the field, Wharton's cavalry doggedly followed Zahm's troopers through the same patch of woods three hundred yards wide and as he emerged, he saw the large wagons trains to the north and also saw the Federal cavalry turning into line to face the his command. Wharton also observed some of the Federal cavalry escorting Thruston's large ammunition train attempting to reach the Nashville Pike. Wharton, observing the advance of the Confederate infantry across Wilkinson Pike, concluded: "I determined to move across the country, give the cavalry battle, and to attempt to capture the train." Wharton's brigade reached the rear of the Union army and fell into line about three quarters of a mile from the Nashville Pike. Wharton saw his prize, but he also saw Zahm's cavalry in line in front the trains—four regiments of Union cavalry. In addition, some Union additional cavalry had moved in proximity of the train in the rear of the forward Union cavalry line, probably the 3rd Indiana Cavalry and the 3rd Kentucky Cavalry. Colonel Baxter Smith exclaimed as he beheld the Union supply trains extending northward on the Nashville Pike: "[O]ne of the prettiest sights I had ever seen." Actually Smith and Wharton probably saw two trains–Rosecrans' large army supply train which extended about two miles and McCook's sixty-six wagon ammunition train dashing for the main Union line. Wharton responded by forming his larger cavalry force in an arc parallel to the Nashville Pike (two-thirds of a circle) with Ashby's 2nd Tennessee (borrowed from Pegram's brigade) and Hardy's Escort Company in the center. Harrison's command (8th Texas, 2nd and 3rd Georgia regiments) formed on the left. Cox's cavalry team which was still in action on the right of Wharton's command in pursuit of McCook's ammunition train was recalled to join in the fight with the line of Union cavalry. In the meantime the remainder of Wharton's cavalry completed the arc and in support, White's artillery unlimbered and faced the defenders in blue. Wharton wrote, "The battery opened with considerable effect."[12]

Quartermaster Thruston described the scene as Zahm moved to face Wharton:

> There was a succession of conflicts over a wide field, with varying fortunes. The whole area in rear between our right and left was a scene of strife and confusion that beggars description. Stragglers from the front, teamsters, couriers, negro servants, hospital attendants, ambulances, added to the turmoil. Wounded and riderless horses and cattle, wild with fright, rushed frantically over the field. While in the open ground, moving our ammunition train rapidly to the left, it was discovered by the enemy.

Thruston was a conscientious officer and he rode to every cavalry officer he could find explaining the importance of the ammunition train to the battle. He reached Zahm who also realized the importance of the train and began to form a battle line with his four regiments. As the ammunition train lumbered eastward, John Pugh moved the 4th Ohio Cavalry between Wharton's men and the train. Next the 2nd Tennessee fell in line, followed by the 1st Ohio, and lastly the 3rd Ohio. Zahm initially reformed his four regiments in a line along a dirt road, running east from Asbury Church to Widow Burris's house and Thruston's ammunition train raced northeasterly toward the Nashville Pike past Widow Burris' house. He placed the 4th Ohio near Asbury Church and to the east, the 2nd Tennessee fell into line. The 3rd Ohio moved to the eastern end of the line around Widow Burris's house. The 1st Ohio fell into line between the 2nd Tennessee and 3rd Ohio and prepared to meet a charge from Wharton's cavalry. As Wharton's cavalry advanced across the field, Zahm slowly moved his line of cavalry back toward the Nashville Pike.[13]

Wharton prepared to charge the Union line with Ashby and Hardy, and he ordered White's artillery to cease firing to prevent injury to the Southern troopers. Then the Southern troopers charged and they were met by a countercharge by the 1st Ohio Cavalry commanded by Colonel Minor Millikin. In what could only be described as a suicidal charge, Millikin led his troopers directly into the center of Wharton's line and at the heart of Ashby's and Hardy's attack. The 1st Ohio successfully disrupted the attack, winning the fight against Ashby and Hardy; but Wharton ordered an attack by Harrison's 8th Texas, 2nd and 3rd Georgia regiments to relieve Ashby's and Hardy's predicament with the Ohioans. There were just too many Southern cavalry for a single Union regiment to defeat. Zahm recorded:

> The First had been ordered to proceed farther on into another lot, to form and to receive a charge from another line of the enemy's cavalry. The Third moved to the left, in the vicinity of a white house. About the time the First was formed, the enemy charged upon the Fourth, which, being on the retreat, owing to the shells coming pretty freely, moved off at a pretty lively gait. The Third moved farther to the left, and, somewhat sheltered by the house and barns, the First charged upon the enemy; did not succeed in driving them back.[14]

Captain Valentine Cupp of the 1st Ohio Cavalry recalled the charge into the midst of the Confederate cavalry which resulted in Colonel Minor Millikin's death, the serious wounding of his adjutant, Lieutenant William Scott, and the death of Lieutenant Timothy Condit. Millikin was described as "a rare character, intense, impatient and dramatic" and he lived up to this description during the battle. Cupp noted Millikin reasoned to permit Wharton's cavalry to proceed any further into the Union flank would have been "ruinous." The 1st Ohio's charge fulfilled Colonel Minor Millikin's stated desire to lead his regiment in a full blown saber charge. Millikin, a highly regarded cavalry officer who had led the Provisional Brigade of cavalry after the Perryville Campaign, had been frustrated leading the Union cavalry and he lamented that in no instance were the resources at his disposal sufficient to meet his Southern cavalry adversaries. Millikin's brigade was disbanded after the campaign, and he now faced Wharton's cavalry brigade. The 1st Ohio Cavalry, like the rest of Zahm's brigade, had been roughly pushed to the rear throughout the morning and now the sun was high in the sky. He was in no better position now than he was as the day began. Throughout the morning he had lost men, first Major David Moore in the first artillery barrage, his adjutant W. H. Scott had been severely wounded in one of the cavalry attacks, and another officer, Lieutenant Sam Fordyce was wounded as well as several of his enlisted men. Millikin watched as Wharton's grand show of strength unfolded before him. Millikin reasoned: "He must act at once, or his regiment would be stampeded and driven from the field, as they were being pushed and crushed ... then

Colonel Millikin ... gave the command 'Charge!' which was repeated to right and left along the line.... Commending their souls to God, they charged home." The 1st Ohio's charge cut through the Confederate cavalry and when Wharton ordered all of his cavalry to join in the attack, Private John Bowers shot Millikin in the neck during the fight and he died. There were too many of the Wharton's troopers and the charge had little hope of success. The charging Union cavalry regiment had good initial results but was overwhelmed by the Southern cavalry. One of the 1st Ohio Cavalry appealed to Millikin to surrender and explained that Millikin responded with a "heavy swinging of the saber. With a cut to the rear, one assailant was cloven down, and with a stroke to the front another." Then Millikin was shot. As the Confederate cavalry closed around the 1st Ohio, the regiment lost thirty-one killed and wounded in this charge, including five officers; and many of the remainder taken prisoners.[15]

Colonel Minor Millikin, 1st Ohio Cavalry.

Along with Millikin, Timothy Condit, the regiment's adjutant, was also killed. Condit was born in Cleveland, Ohio in 1837 and at the age of fifteen he began working at a newspaper. Later, he earned a living as a printer. Condit worked his way through Marietta College and was the Valedictorian of the class of 1860. Ironically, Condit entered the Congregational Church in 1856 and had entered theological studies in 1861. He struggled with the direction of his life and the theology student decided to join the Union Army for the cause of "freedom and good government." He was promoted to the rank of second lieutenant in May 1862 and led a squadron during the charge at Murfreesboro. It was reported by a member of the regiment: "When the Lieutenant was killed they were all around us, we could not see any way out. The Lieutenant said the only way was to charge and then retreat. He rode forward to lead and was killed."[16]

After the unsuccessful charge of the 1st Ohio, the regiment attempted to retire but was attacked again and surrounded by their pursuers. The 8th Texas, 2nd Georgia and 3rd Confederate cavalries arrived as the 1st Ohio charged the 2nd Tennessee (CSA). "The Ohio men had gained the day, and the Georgians fleeing for their lives. Then the Rangers moved in. With the wildest yells, they charged. It was the same story as that as nearly all such impetuous surges: the Ohioans gave way and fled to the rear." The Southern cavalry chased those not captured. In this charge, some of the Rangers concluded the success was as much from superior weapons as fighting ability. The Texans used revolvers while the Union troopers used carbines and sabers. "Where are your sabers?" they would ask. "How far can you kill with a saber?" was the reply.[17]

At least one Confederate cavalryman attributed the initial success of Millikin's charge against Ashby's Tennessee cavalry to the fact the Southern troopers were armed with only long muskets. It is also important to note that it is generally accepted that Millikin attacked Ashby's 2nd Tennessee and Hardy's Escort company, although numerous reports include descriptions of the counterattack also relieving the pressure on Georgia cavalry. Whether this is confusion in the individual accounts or a gap in records remains unclear. Millikin's troopers rapidly reached their target and the Southern troopers had no time to reload.

By that time, the 1st Ohio cavalry was among them with sabers flashing. Fortunately for Wharton he had plenty of reserves and Millikin's lone regiment made the charge. The remainder of Wharton's cavalry handily took care of the attack.[18]

White's artillery which had been so effective during the morning continued to have a significant impact on the Union cavalry. Zahm wrote: "They prepared to charge upon us; likewise commenced throwing shells, at which the Second East Tennessee broke and ran like sheep. The Fourth [Ohio], after receiving several shells, which killed some of their men and horses, likewise retired from their line, as it became untenable." John Pugh would write about the actions of the 4th Ohio which initially shielded Thruston's wagon train. The regiment retreated due to the shells of White's Battery falling among the troopers and he observed that the panic resulted in the regiment retreating in disorder.[19]

White's was not the only artillery which found Zahm's cavalry. Captain William Harder, 23rd Tennessee Infantry, observed as his regiment continued to attack the Union line formed along the Nashville Pike that off to his left "appeared a cloud of cavalry," Zahm's, which protected the Union right flank. His attention was soon directed to the forming Union infantry line supported by artillery. Harder, part of Brigadier General Bushrod Johnson's brigade, recorded the Southern artillery unlimbered and directed its fire northward into the lines of Union cavalry. Brigadier General St. John R. Liddell, who had been informed that his son was killed earlier in the day, ordered his artillery to join in the barrage near Zahm's cavalry and the ammunition train, "I ordered the battery to fire upon that part of the train to the right of the cavalry, which caused the train to break in confusion." Gates Thruston noted he received some "hot shots" fired from Confederate artillery on the main battlefield just as his train had finally and successfully reached the Nashville Pike. Liddell's and Johnson's infantry brigade battled northward throughout the morning and finally reached the dirt road running east and west in front of Widow Burris's house. Charles Harker's brigade of Union infantry had moved into position on the high ground directly behind her house. While moving into position, the Southern artillery began firing shells into the Union cavalry and the supply trains.[20]

Then, Wharton's entire brigade swept down on Zahm's three waiting Ohio and Tennessee regiments. Wharton wrote:

> Availing myself of the confusion caused by the rout of the enemy's advanced cavalry, the entire brigade was ordered to charge the enemy's whole cavalry force, drawn up in line half a mile in rear of their main line of battle, protecting their wagon train. The order was responded to in the most chivalrous manner, and 2,000 horsemen were hurled on the foe. The ground was exceedingly favorable for cavalry operations, and after a short hand-to-hand conflict, in which the revolver was used with deadly effect, the enemy fled from the field in the wildest confusion and dismay, and were pursued to Overall's Creek, a distance of 2 miles. After they had crossed Overall's Creek, the enemy reformed out of range of our guns.

Corps commander William Hardee would exclaim: "The field was favorable, the charge irresistible, the conflict short." With the collapse of Zahm's brigade, what seemed like the end of a successful day was within reach for Wharton. He claimed several hundred wagons of the supply train with his troopers. He turned the wagons around and started them for Murfreesboro.[21]

Zahm had clashed with Wharton throughout the morning and finally his troopers facing Wharton's cavalry, White's artillery, and artillery fire from the main Confederate line, fled; except for two battalions of the 3rd Ohio Cavalry. Louis Zahm recorded that the remainder of the 1st Ohio and 4th Ohio cavalries "retired pretty fast" and the enemy cavalry rode hard in pursuit. The 2nd Tennessee was given the dubious honor of being in the lead of the Union cavalry retreating from the field. Zahm who had commanded a commendable defense throughout the morning was frustrated and disgusted. Zahm joined the three regiments which retreated and he still needed to rally the men. But, rallying the troops proved difficult as Zahm described, "I was with the three regiments that skedaddled, and among the last to leave the field." Zahm endeavored to rally his command, but the final attack by Wharton so unnerved the Union cavalry he could not pull his men into a cohesive fighting unit. Zahm accompanied the panicked troopers to the west side of Overall Creek and finally succeeded in reforming his command. As Zahm's brigade moved off, two battalions of the 3rd Ohio remained on the field and still successfully shielded Thruston's frantic teamsters from Southern cavalry.[22]

While Zahm disparaged the performance of the 2nd Tennessee Cavalry (U.S.), it is important to recall the regiment had yet to be formally organized and rode with an incomplete complement of troopers. The regiment had been moved from hither to yon for two months and had only been in Nashville since December 25. The 1st Ohio Cavalry had several men captured and was disorganized after its unsuccessful charge. The 4th Ohio Cavalry retreated after receiving fire from White's Tennessee Battery. However, Zahm's cavalry was not finished and reformed in the rear with the assistance of James Parkhurst's 9th Michigan Infantry near Wade's Hill and would engage Abraham Buford's Kentucky cavalry later that afternoon.[23]

W. R. Friend, 8th Texas, described the preparation of the attack on Zahm's cavalry.

> The division had advanced from a woods in which it had been formed into open fields in sight of the pike, on which, to my eye, seemed a flying mass of wagons as compact as the space would permit. About one hundred yards this side of them was a blue line of cavalry, looking as if, on full rations, they breathed nothing but hatred and defiance.

Friend explained that much of Wharton's brigade was armed primarily with Enfield rifles and they were really nothing more than mounted infantry. The exception was the 8th Texas Cavalry which carried three revolvers and a breech loading carbine. Friend also described the Union cavalry as "poorest horsemen I ever saw."[24]

Captain William Crane described the capture of the Union train as Millikin of the 1st Ohio Cavalry was killed. Crane believed the action which broke the Union ranks was the Southern artillery. Crane wrote: "[A]nd shot & shell rain around us on every side. No cavalry could stand firm before such a storm. We had not a single cannon to reply with & lines began to waver. The enemy sees it & yelling like hell hounds make a charge." While most of the 4th Ohio Cavalry retreated a battalion rallied and turned to face their pursuers, identified by Crane and also Captain Henry B. Teeter, to be a group of the 8th Texas Cavalry. The 8th Texas seemed to be intent on attacking the retreating 2nd Tennessee when the battalion of the 4th Ohio surprised them. Captain Peter Mathews rallied the Ohio troopers and contemplated what action to take. The excitement of unfolding events caused Crane to exclaim,

> "Mathews, let's go for them!" He hesitated a moment, said they were too many for us, then gave the command & we made the charge—fifty against five hundred! Greek met Greek & there was a fierce tug of war. The Rangers were evidently deceived as to our numbers. They turn & flee.... The rear of their fleeing column also suffers severely. But the rebel hordes were pressing into the field against us unchecked by the infantry.... With a single battery, or the support of a regt. of infantry, the cavalry might then have saved the day, but the infantry were rushing in every direction, throwing down their arms & each man looking out for himself.[25]

Wharton Captures the Supply Train and the Federals Counter Attack

So far, Wharton had had everything much his own way. He had successfully captured prisoners, both cavalry and infantry, and collected artillery pieces, and he had successfully sent the Union cavalry fleeing from the field and before him was a magnificent prize, the Army of the Cumberland's supply train only lightly protected. Then, Wharton descended on the supply train. The prize was there for the taking. But the day was not over for the Union cavalry as Wharton tried to escape with his booty. Wharton was to be undone by the remnants of the Union cavalry, but also by the lack of discipline and organization of his own troops. The 3rd Indiana Cavalry (West Battalion), part of the 3rd Kentucky Cavalry, the 4th U.S. and the 3rd Ohio Cavalry were still active on the field. In the meantime, David Stanley was moving the 4th Michigan, 15th Pennsylvania and 7th Pennsylvania to the fight. But, Wheeler's cavalry which had just ridden a circle around the Union army and Abe Buford's Kentucky (CSA) cavalry brigade were also riding hard toward the fight.

W. R. Friend, 8th Texas, described the attack on Rosecrans main supply train being made in columns of companies.

> [I]t was child's play to outride the wagons, and shoot down drivers and lead mules and destroy or carry off the train … regiment after regiment becoming mingled in a confused mass, and when the opportunity presented a gratification of the insatiate lust for plunder, the bane of the army, the Rangers dashed along, shooting and banging without restraint.

Friend explained he thought many of the teamsters were German and were killed because they could not understand English and failed to comply with the orders to halt. Along with train, Wharton's cavalry scooped several hundred stragglers. Sergeant Major John Dollinger, 1st Ohio Cavalry, described the carnage in the wagon train did not result from men who misunderstood the language:

> The poor negro teamsters were shot in their tracks like dogs; the mules were killed while yet hitched to the wagons, and the finest artillery horses I ever saw shared a like fate, while all along the pike to Overalls Creek the stiff and blue coated forms of our comrades were stretched, still in death.[26]

Along the supply and ammunition trains, the results of the cavalry battle were disheartening for Quartermaster Gates Thruston. After defeating Millikin's 1st Ohio Cavalry charge and with the artillery shells falling among the Zahm's cavalry, regiment after regiment began to retreat. Then, Wharton sent his entire command racing forward, unstoppable. Thruston wrote "Alas, when the crisis came…. There was no staying the Confederates. They outnumbered and outflanked us, and to tell the melancholy truth, our defending cavalry retired in confusion to the rear and left the ammunition train to its fate—high and dry in a cornfield."[27]

Thruston still had James W. Paramore's two battalions of the 3rd Ohio Cavalry screening McCook's ammunition train from John Cox's Southern cavalry, and Paramore stood his ground. Of Zahm's cavalry, the 3rd Ohio held its ground. Major James W. Paramore, 3rd Ohio Cavalry, held two battalions of the regiment in line after retreating as far as the ammunition train after the collapse of the Union right. The 32-year-old James Wallace Paramore, born in Mansfield, Ohio, commanding a battalion of the 3rd Ohio, had been a lawyer before the war; and he now faced the challenge of his life. He noted, "We had been forced back as far as General McCook's ammunition train, and were drawn up in front of it for its protection, the furious charge of the enemy's cavalry, Cox's, preceded by a shower of shells, caused a pretty general stampede of our cavalry, led off by the Second Tennessee on our right, and followed by the Fourth and First Ohio, and the First Battalion of the Third Ohio Cavalry.'" The 3rd Ohio provided the last hope to preserve ammunition for one third of the Union infantry. Paramore ordered his battalion to hold its position although it was receiving a "galling fire," but his troopers suffered the attack without budging. Paramore escorted McCook's ammunition train to the apparent safety along the Nashville Pike just as the Southern cavalry converged on the entire supply train.[28]

With Rosecrans' main wagon train in his hands, Wharton decided to carry off his booty, but Colonel Baxter Smith recalled this mistake. He wrote the mistake was not burning the wagon train which could have been done quickly and efficiently by a small number of troopers. He stoically declared: "Instead of burning it as we could have done we tried to bring it off. We had ventured too far, for we were immediately in the rear of Genl. Rosecrans' line of battle. We could not hold the prize and had to give up most of the wagons."[29]

The 4th U.S. Cavalry Turns the Tide

Then a solid rank of blue cavalry emerged from a lightly wooded area on the east flank of Wharton's cavalry. The best regiment in the Union cavalry was the 4th U.S. Cavalry which had yet to join the fight. This regiment was detached from Stanley's cavalry division and placed under direct command of Rosecrans' headquarters. Earlier in the day, the sound of the battle reached Rosecrans and groups of Rosecrans' staff began to discuss the cause of the musket firing and cannonading along McCook's wing. Julius Garesché sent Otis's 4th U.S. to discover what was unfolding. And Otis made a quick reconnaissance and he sent a lieutenant back with the news the right was being propelled rearward with the enemy advancing on the heels of the retreating troops. Otis initially detailed his command along the Union right flank with the duty to rally the retreating infantry. The 4th U.S. Cavalry rallied some of troops, which were not too disorganized, including two regiments which still had their colonels with them.[30]

Next, the 4th U.S. Cavalry rode to assist in dealing with Wharton's cavalry. From his position, Captain Elmer Otis rode to the right and after moving about one half mile he found the Southern troopers in possession of the train. Newspaperman William Bickham described that Garesche had ordered Otis to take his regiment and "look after" the enemy cavalry on the right flank. Otis marched his men through a lightly wooded area and

Captain Elmer Otis, 4th U.S. Cavalry—"'Charge!' Now they gallop—away they fly! It is an avalanche."

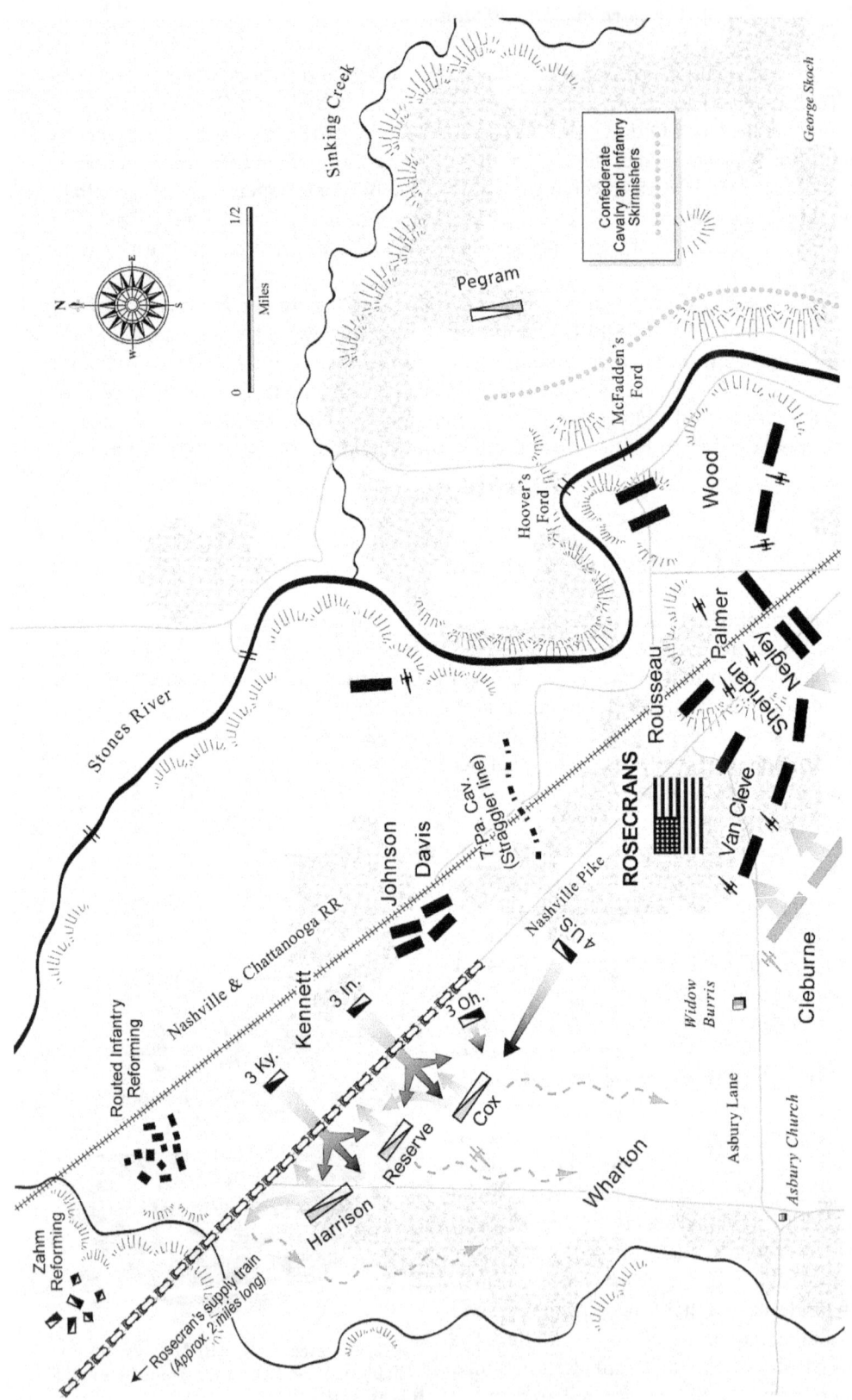

The Union cavalry counterattack initiated by the 4th U.S. Cavalry, and followed with attacks by the 3rd Kentucky, 3rd Ohio, and 3rd Indiana cavalries (11:00 a.m. December 31, 1862).

9. The Cavalry Battle of Stones River (Late Morning)

discovering a cloud of mounted gray-backs in the distance, he quickly directed his command to charge, pistol in hand. But said Otis, "Don't you fire a shot until you take each your man by the scalp. Forward—trot!" Away they go gallantly, the ground trembling beneath them. There is a heavy column of gray before them, but no cheek blanches. Each rider gathers his reins firmly. Their eyes flash lightning. The trot bears them swiftly; Otis rises in his saddle and thunders, "Charge!" Now they gallop—away they fly! It is an avalanche. The rebels vainly strive to disperse it by shot and shell. A storm of grape is scattered among those wild riders, but in vain. Their shock falls upon the enemy with terrific momentum. "Horse, rider, and all, in one red burial blent," go down together. Our gallant [Captain Eli] Long and some of his fellows went down in the tumult, but the glory of the charge made the noble fellows forget their pain. It was a thunderbolt, which drove the enemy from center to flank.[31]

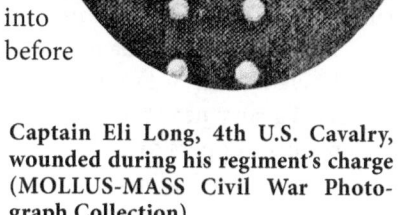

Captain Eli Long, 4th U.S. Cavalry, wounded during his regiment's charge (MOLLUS-MASS Civil War Photograph Collection).

Otis's charge was also described by a trooper of the regiment, "Our Commander gave the word, "Front, into line, charge!" And such a charge! I have been in several before upon the Indians, but the splendor of this eclipsed them all. Our column, small in number, consisting of but a few companies, closed up, and in good order we advanced. When we neared them they broke. On we came, yelling like so many savages, and scattering them like chaff. Two-thirds of our men were fresh recruits, but nobly and well did they march with the regulars…. Owing to the sudden belching forth of a masked battery, they were enabled to retake their wounded."[32]

Reports from various sources recorded the result of Otis's charge on Wharton's cavalry. The *New York Times* reported that Otis captured sixty-seven Southern cavalry and released another 300 Union soldiers which were held as captives. Otis reported capturing about 200 Confederate cavalry in his two attacks during the day. The charge of the 4th U.S. and the disorganization of the Confederate cavalry which occurred after it gained possession of the wagon train turned the tide in favor of Federal cavalry. Trooper Friend, 8th Texas, lamented the lack of planning and organization once the Southern cavalry gained possession of the wagon train. Friend could only watch the solid line of Union cavalry descend on those trying to escape with wagon train, now unprepared for such an attack. Captain Christian of the 8th Texas tried to organize a defense but could not assemble more than thirty men as the 4th U.S. charged. Historian Edwin Bearss wrote that the Federal attack was so aggressive that the Confederates thought they were being attacked by Zahm's full brigade in addition to the 4th U.S. Cavalry. The lack of control of the Southern cavalry and lack of a formal plan to deal with the Union train was Wharton's undoing. Friend declared: "It is plain that this result could have been avoided by retaining two regiments in order; in fact, one regiment would have sufficed to capture all the train, for it was without a guard." After Wharton's cavalry gained possession of the wagon train, it lost its organization and composition. The Southern cavalrymen were no longer cavalry, they were teamsters. The 4th U.S. Cavalry led the first of a series of counterattacks, followed by Paramore's 3rd Ohio, Klein's 3rd Indiana, and the 3rd Kentucky supported by a brigade of infantry just emerging from the trees near the Nashville Pike.[33]

Next, James Paramore's 3rd Ohio Cavalry escorted McCook's ammunition train to safety and then turned its attention to the Wharton's cavalry closing in on the large army supply train. The 3rd Ohio and 3rd Indiana cavalries were able to charge the Confederate cavalry. The 3rd Ohio wheeled around and charged on the Confederates that had been trailing them: "With terrible effect (scattering their columns in worse confusion, if possible, than they had just routed the balance of our brigade)." Paramore recorded the charge effectively dispatched the Confederate cavalry, killing an unrecorded number and claiming 10–12 prisoners. Paramore's charge released several prisoners which were in Confederate hands. "The enemy, seeing our determination and bold resistance, turned and left us…"[34]

Robert Klein's 3rd Indiana Cavalry battalion had participated in the morning's battle as it fought and retreated, over and over. Klein had a steady hand on his men despite the chaos which reigned after one of the routed cavalry regiments stampeded through Indiana troopers. He reformed his battalion along the Nashville Pike and joined in the Union counterattack. The Indiana cavalry set their spurs to their mounts and charged the captured wagon train shooting and slashing the Confederate troopers along the way. In Klein's first charge, he captured eleven prisoners, recaptured ambulances, and released a Federal surgeon who had been captured while dispersing the small groups of Southern cavalry.[35]

Now the 3rd Indiana and 3rd Ohio joined in another attack on the Wharton's confused cavalry. The 3rd Ohio and the 3rd Indiana cavalries encountered a group of Confederate cavalry near the Union hospital intending to capture a supply train. Paramore ordered his troopers to attack although Klein estimated he faced twice his numbers. The battle was severe and several were lost on both sides. A squadron of Paramore's cavalry engaged another group of Southern cavalry further along the pike in an effective counterattack led by Colonel John Kennett. Paramore proudly wrote in his after action report, "Then be it spoken to their praise that the Second and Third Battalions of the Third Ohio Cavalry did not run nor break their lines during that day's severe fighting."[36]

Kennett's Counter Attack with the 3rd Kentucky Cavalry

In addition to the charge made by the 4th U.S. Cavalry, Wharton's advance on the Union right flank was also stopped when Colonel James B. Fyffe's infantry brigade emerged from the woods on the Nashville Pike. Colonel Fyffe's brigade quickly moved through a stretch of woods and emerged to find a long line of wagons parked on the Nashville Pike. Past the wagon train was a large open field and then to his dismay, he observed the Confederate cavalry slowly moving the wagons to the rear. To make matter worse, he saw the Confederate cavalry held a group of the 1st Ohio Cavalry as prisoners.[37]

Fyffe's infantry brigade startled the Southern cavalry guarding the 1st Ohio prisoners, and with the emergence of the Federal infantry the Ohioans began attacking their guards, succeeding in capturing one guard and killing another. Fyffe quickly assessed the situation and ordered Captain George Swallow's 7th Indiana Artillery into action and Swallow hurried his men to unlimber their guns in some rough terrain. Fyffe's artillery quickly came into play. Swallow "soon had his pieces in position, and opened fire on the rebel lines, which began dispersing, and were charged by three of our cavalry, which had passed down the road to the right of the train, doing excellent service." M. B. Butler, a soldier in the 44th Indiana Infantry observed, "[T]he Parrott guns poured canister through their battalion leaving horses and riders scattered over the field." Fyffe watched the 4th U.S., 3rd Kentucky and 3rd Ohio cavalries countercharge, and confident about

9. The Cavalry Battle of Stones River (Late Morning)   191

The Battle of Stones River (Library of Congress).

the situation along the Union cavalry's front, turned his attention to the infantry battle which was still unfolding. Fyffe ordered Swallow to move his artillery onto higher ground with a better command of the field of battle and open up on the Confederate infantry.[38]

Shortly after the charge of the 4th U.S., cavalry division commander, Colonel John Kennett, arrived on the field. John Kennett's service to the Army of the Cumberland had been inconsistent; and there is no record that Kennett had tried to assist Zahm in his morning battles with Wharton. During the battle on December 31, Rosecrans ordered Kennett, in Stanley's absence, to attempt to rally the collapsed right wing and organize the cavalry in an effective screen. The 4th U.S., 3rd Kentucky, and 7th Pennsylvania cavalries had this duty during the morning. Next Kennett focused his attentions on the Union supply trains. As Kennett rode with Colonel Eli Murray's 3rd Kentucky Cavalry, they observed the Union wagon train being moved away by the Confederate cavalry. Colonel James Paramore observing the arrival of Kennett on the field dispatched two companies to aid in the attack. Kennett's absence from the morning's cavalry fight remains puzzling and his first notable presence on the field occurred at 11:00 a.m. He noted, "We found a complete stampede—infantry, cavalry, and artillery rushing to the rear, and the rebel cavalry charging upon our retiring forces on the Murfreesborough pike."[39]

Eli Murray's 3rd Kentucky Cavalry (U.S.) was positioned near the rear and center of the army as the battle began in earnest and as the cavalry action moved northward, he ordered his troopers "To horse!" Murray hurried his men forward as Wharton's men captured the supply train. Murray's cavalry emerged from a cedar thicket into a 100 acre cotton field and observed a mass of yelling Confederate cavalry. Trooper Ambrose observed the field was covered with bodies from the earlier fighting. Murray recorded that riding ahead he found the entire supply train captured by Confederate cavalry. He ordered his cavalry to attack and they quickly charged into the fray. "We came upon the enemy in all directions. Here were engagements hand-to-hand, but dashing onward my men were doing in earnest the work before them."[40]

Kennett commanded the attack by the 3rd Kentucky and part of the 3rd Ohio cavalries which joined in the attack of the disorganized Confederate cavalry in possession of the wagon train,

> Colonel [Eli] Murray, with great intrepidity, engaged the enemy toward the skirts of the woods, and drove them in three charges. His men behaved like old veterans. Between his command and the field the space was filled with rushing rebel cavalry, charging upon our retreating cavalry and infantry, holding many of our soldiers as prisoners.

This newly forming group of Union cavalry fell into line behind a fence and began making orderly volleys into the disorganized Confederate cavalry still trying to move the wagons to the rear. Next Paramore's battalions the 3rd Ohio attacked another group of Southern troopers and sent them reeling to the rear. Murray, 3rd Kentucky Cavalry (U.S.), ordered his men to make another charge and his successes mounted.

> The open field gave us the place for charging. The enemy were marching about 250 of our men to their rear as prisoners. These we recaptured ... saved the baggage and ammunition of a great part of our army; recaptured a portion of the Fifth Wisconsin Battery and a section of, I think, the First Ohio Battery, and, at least calculation, 800 of our men.

Colonel Eli Murray, 3rd Kentucky Cavalry—"We charged into this mass, recaptured the prisoners, several pieces of artillery and the wagons" (MOLLUS-MASS Civil War Photograph Collection).

Kennett who joined his cavalry in the fight was nearly killed by Confederate troopers. Private James Farrish and Corporal Wilson Jaggers, Kennett's orderlies, shot two Southern troopers converging on Kennett and captured a third who had a pistol leveled in Kennett's face.[41]

After clearing the train of Wharton's cavalry, Murray ordered his 3rd Kentucky to charge ahead. Murray found the Hord House, a hospital of General John Palmer's division, occupied by Wharton's cavalry and he decided to clear the enemy away. Murray ordered a detachment of cavalry to charge, and sent the occupiers seeking safety. The cavalry battle surged around the Hord House, a temporary hospital. Thomas and Mildred Amelia Hord lived in the house and they had a son in the Confederate Army, but they were ardent Unionists. In addition, Amelia Hord was pregnant and despite her condition she helped move the wounded into her house and assisted with their care. Thomas Hord related that "the house was unexpectedly and suddenly taken for a hospital and the wounded brought in so rapidly that there was not time or means of removing the carpets or furniture."[42]

Afterwards, Murray paused to assess the situation on the field and so successful was the Union counterattack that many of the 3rd Kentucky's troopers were busy taking prisoners to the rear. Murray was not satisfied and ordered his troopers to take the prisoners to the nearest infantry unit and then hurry back to the train. He knew the day had yet to be won. No sooner did his men return when they faced an attack by the Confederate cavalry which attempted to rally and retake the train. Murray's troopers formed a line near the hospital just as they were attacked, but the Kentucky cavalry charged ahead and repulsed the enemy. Major Lewis Wolfey, 3rd Kentucky, recorded that he moved his men about a quarter mile and "met this hurricane of confusion…. We charged into this mass, recaptured the prisoners, several pieces of artillery and the wagons & in fact, whipped their whole brigade, took more than 100 prisoners & killed & wounded a great many." Wolfey's later letter modified his estimate to 70 prisoners and 25–30 killed and wounded."[43]

When the supply train was attacked, only the regular quartermaster guard was present with the train which stretched for two miles. Trooper Ambrose, 3rd Kentucky, observed the advantage fell to the Union cavalry which was still in formation while the Confederate cavalry, claiming the train, was disorganized in various smaller groups. Ambrose estimated Wharton had 2,000 cavalry while the counterattacking Federal force was about 400, but the Southern cavalry were busy driving the train and others were firing upon the teams and their drivers. Then, Murray ordered "Charge!" and the 3rd Kentucky rode ahead. The guards still around the train added their firepower to fight. The fighting was hand-to-hand and Murray kept the enemy between his regiment and the White's artillery. J. A. Holman, 8th Texas Cavalry, recalled he was assigned a squad of twelve troopers to move some Union cannons to the rear when they were attacked and captured by Eli Murray's Kentuckians. While the 3rd Kentucky attacked, Ambrose noticed another line of Confederate cavalry form on the crest of a small hill and he observed the gleam of brass as White's artillery was moved into position. After the counter attack of the Federal cavalry, Wharton's troopers withdrew and re-formed around the White's artillery which began shelling the 3rd Kentucky which moved back to the supply train. Then, Ambrose observed the arrival of the 4th U.S. Cavalry which was the "grandest picture" of professional horsemanship as the regulars charged toward a group of Wharton's men which had re-formed sending them to the rear. Ambrose noted that once the 4th U.S. and 3rd Kentucky pushed Wharton away from the supply train, Kennett arrived with the remainder of the cavalry and formed a line in front of the supply train. (It is worthy to note that Ambrose's sequence of events varies from some of the other reports.) After Otis's, Murray's, Klein's, and Paramore's attacks, Kennett's troopers had effectively reclaimed and cleared the Southern cavalry from the train. During these fights, Kennett declared he was successful in saving the entire supply train while recapturing one piece of artillery and releasing a large number of prisoners.[44]

The author of the history of the 8th Texas Cavalry, C. C. Jeffries described:

> At length, while deep within the Federal line, they discovered a large wagon train, and Wharton decided to attempt its capture. It was a hazardous undertaking, but Wharton thought that such a prize would justify the risk. The actual taking of the train proved no great task: they drove off the guard, captured the wagons—three hundred in number—together with a battery, and started back with them. But the rest of brigade failed to come to their assistance, and since the enemy cavalry was now coming up in force, they had to relinquish their prize. They did succeed, however, in bringing off the captured battery. The rest of the day they were engaged in their old task of guarding the flank of the army.

As the Confederate attack ground to a halt, the 8th Texas cavalry would conclude the day when they were fired upon by their own troops.[45]

During the charge of the 4th U.S. Cavalry, it also came to the aid to a portion of the 1st Ohio Cavalry who had been captured after Millikin's charge. When the regulars attacked, many of Millikin's regiment were freed and returned to the fight. G. C. Kniffin, Crittenden's staff officer, wrote that the 4th U.S. dashed "forward with the velocity of a locomotive, the battalions" and went to work. Then, Elmer Otis focused on the Confederate artillery causing so much trouble. Otis observed the battery of Southern artillery only lightly supported and rode to gain support for a charge on the artillery, but the other organized cavalry units declined to participate due to duty of protecting the wagon trains. Although Otis declined to identify the commander he spoke to, but it was presumably Robert Klein. He replied "that he was placed there to protect a train, and would not charge with me." Klein had been ordered to protect the wagon train and he felt his duty was with the train. By the time Otis returned to his command, he had been ordered to other duty also.[46]

It was John Wharton's time to be in a precarious situation and his cavalry was driven from the slow-moving, cumbersome wagon train and the remaining Union cavalry regiments supported by what infantry regiments which could be assembled took the fight to the Southern cavalrymen. He found himself in a tense situation as the 4th U.S. and 3rd Kentucky discovered his lightly support section of artillery. In addition, Swallow's Union battery was shelling his cavalry. Wharton had to be dismayed by the events unfolding in front of him. The sweet taste of the morning's actions was turning bitter. He had committed his entire force without thoughts of holding a reserve or providing for security. Then he noticed the 4th U.S. Cavalry reforming and facing in the direction of the White's battery which also had a day unmarred by the opposition. Wharton recorded:

> Knowing that it would be impossible to withdraw my men from the pursuit, and having no disposition to do so, I immediately returned in person with two of my staff ... and found the battery with no support save Colonel Smith and 20 of his men, the balance, with too much zeal, having engaged in the pursuit of the fleeing enemy. My arrival was most opportune. About 300 of the enemy's cavalry, not over 400 yards distant, were bearing down upon the battery with a speed that evinced a determination to take it at all hazards. A few men, with Colonel Smith, were promptly formed, and the battery unlimbered and ordered to fire upon the approaching enemy. Several shells were exploded in their ranks and they retired in confusion.

Wharton was lucky as the day ended for him. If Otis had found support from one of the other Union regiments, he was poised to ride for Wharton and his artillery. Likewise the 3rd Kentucky Cavalry also noticed the unprotected battery but it did not attack. Wharton recorded his tally for a very productive day for his men despite the repulse along the supply train.

> The command that had captured the wagons, thinking that they had driven the entire force of the enemy's cavalry across Overall's Creek, and apprehending danger alone from that quarter, were prepared to meet it only from that direction. Besides, many were scattered along the entire length of the wagon train, directing its movements and guarding the numerous prisoners taken. In this condition they were attacked by the same party of cavalry from the direction of Murfreesborough that I had repulsed with the artillery, the enemy's cavalry that we had driven across Overall's Creek being in condition likewise to attack them in the rear. Owing to this and to my being detained to defend the battery, we were able only to bring off a portion of the wagons, 5 or 6 pieces of artillery, about 400 prisoners, 327 beef cattle, and a goodly number of mules cut from the wagons.

By 1 p.m. Wharton was "fought out" after a productive, but ultimately frustrating, day operating on Hardee's left flank.[47]

Gates Thruston was also lucky and he summarized the countercharge by the Union cavalry which saved his train:

Happily this appalling state of affairs did not last long. Some of our cavalry rallied, other Union detachments came to the rescue. Wharton had soon to look to his own flanks, and was kept too busy to carry off our train. The conflict fortunately shifted.... Everybody—even officers and stragglers—helped, and nearly every wagon was finally recovered.

Thruston lost "but a few wagons" as he whipped his teams through hills, rocks, cedars, dirt roads, and Confederates to successfully save the train.[48]

The morning cavalry actions were finished by noon and most likely by 11:00 am. One of the teamsters of the 15th Pennsylvania recorded seeing David Stanley arrive with the cavalry from La Vergne after 11:00 am. Meanwhile on the Union left flank, Major John Wynkoop commanded the remainder of the 7th Pennsylvania near Murfreesboro while Minty rode with Stanley from Stewarts Creek. During the morning Wynkoop's command screened the left flank of the army and served as couriers. The 7th Pennsylvania performed a yeoman's task of rallying the retreating troops. Once the Union right collapsed, he pulled his troopers together and began the duty of stopping the panic stricken solders running to the rear, but Wynkoop was unable to stop the stampede of men running away. In exasperation, Wynkoop asked for orders from Rosecrans who directed him to proceed to the rear and try his best to pull the troops together into fighting units. The 7th Pennsylvania rallied the troops until about 2 p.m., when the regiment was ordered back to the front by Kennett.[49]

William Henry Harder, 23rd Tennessee Infantry (CSA), summed up the day in his diary: "Our left had achieved a great success but the center was thwarted, and the right had its trial to make yet. Rosecrans had ceased to advance and Bragg had failed to drive him back." Trooper William "Joe" Short, 2nd Georgia Cavalry, wrote to his wife: "From daybreak to dark the fight raged. The rattle of musketry, the roaring of cannon, the bursting of bombs, and crashing of wagons, timbers, burning of houses, &c. All conspired to make it an awful but grand scene." Trooper Dunbar Affleck, 8th Texas, also acknowledged the heavy fighting of the day. He wrote that this was the most losses the regiment had experienced yet in the war, with fifteen or twenty men killed and many others wounded.[50]

Sometime later Rosecrans found his ammunition and supply trains were safe and he asked Quartermaster Thruston how he was able to accomplish the deed. Thruston replied, "Well, General," I replied, "we did some sharp fighting, but a great deal more running." Colonel W. D. Pickett of Hardee's staff would write after the war: "First win the battle, and the enemy's wagon trains fall into your hands." Pickett was critical of the decision of sending Wheeler on raid around the Union rear when he was needed on the battlefield. Pickett acknowledged the good results of Wheeler's raid, but he pointed out that hurling Wheeler's cavalry onto the western flank at the critical moment in addition to Wharton's brigade might have yielded "great results." The battle had almost been won during the day, but the Federal line held and likewise, the wagon trains had *almost* fallen into Wharton's hands.[51]

10. On the East Flank—
Pegram's Cavalry (December 31)

A pretty strong infantry force of the enemy ... has just crossed over.—Brigadier General John Pegram

While the intense fighting was taking place on the western flank and in the center of both armies, Major General John C. Breckinridge's large Confederate infantry division remained unengaged on the eastern flank. As the battle began, the relationship between Breckinridge and Bragg was dismal at best. Bragg commanded the Army of Tennessee and Breckinridge was arguably the most powerful Kentuckian in the Confederate Army. Breckinridge was the ex–Vice President of the United States and made an unsuccessful bid for the presidency in 1860; and like many commanders in the Army of Tennessee, he did not like Bragg. Historian Peter Cozzens noted the relationship between Breckinridge and Bragg had "deepened to a state of near mutiny." Bragg appeared to have the same disregard for Breckinridge and his division. Historian William C. Davis wrote a few days earlier that Bragg was "sick of the Kentuckians' grumbling and troublemaking. He would put a stop to it." This resulted in Bragg's ordering the execution of a Kentucky private for desertion over the objections of Breckinridge. The poor relationship which existed before would deepen on December 31, two days later and in the months after the battle.[1]

The bulk of the Confederate cavalry, Wheeler's, Buford's and Wharton's brigades, was engaged or still on its way to western flank while John Pegram's reserve cavalry consisting of only two Confederate regiments, 1st Louisiana and 1st Georgia, remained on duty protecting the right flank of Bragg's army. Pegram's cavalry, a mere 480 men, held the position on the Confederate right flank along the Lebanon Pike. To complicate things for Pegram, both of his regiments were commanded by the lieutenant colonels. This was frustrating duty for the remaining regiments of Pegram's brigade. Two of his regiments, 1st Tennessee and 2nd Tennessee, had been appropriated by Wheeler and Wharton for their various actions on December 30–31. In fact, Pegram was relegated to important but inglorious duty; however, his actions during the morning of December 31 were perhaps the most important and controversial of the entire campaign. It is unfortunate that Pegram filed no report of his actions during the battle. Nor were reports made by the 1st Louisiana Cavalry and the 1st Georgia Cavalry; but John Pegram's reputation would suffer as much as any Confederate commander after the Battle of Stones River despite being away from the significant fighting during the day. Some would actually blame Pegram for the loss of the battle. As the day began, Pegram's cavalry stretched across the Confederate eastern flank with reconnaissance responsibilities and with the assignment of protecting the Confederate right flank.[2]

The records of the events on the Confederate eastern flank on December 31, and the later events on January 2, are sketchy, but it is critical to understand the sources of the existing records. Both Bragg and Breckinridge made counter claims about the events during these two days, and ultimately in March 1863, Breckinridge asked for a court of inquiry to examine the allegations made by Bragg in his battle report. The two main sources of information regarding the events of December 31 come from Bragg's records at the Western Reserve Historical Society and Breckinridge's records held at the New-York Historical Society. These records are an accumulation of those reports, letters and orders which supported the claims being made by officers, generally staff officers for the two generals. In regard to the cavalry, there were no reports and historians have since relied heavily upon these two repositories without comment from the cavalry officers involved. What may be most important is what is not included in these collections, rather than what is included.[3]

Breckinridge Prepares Defenses on the Confederate Eastern Flank

John C. Breckinridge's large division of greater than 6,000 men held the Confederate right flank on the east side of Stones River. His command consisted of five brigades under the command of Brigadier General Daniel Adams, Colonel J. B. Palmer, Brigadier General William Preston, Brigadier General Roger W. Hanson, and Brigadier General John K. Jackson. Breckinridge's command, stretched from Stones River to the Lebanon Pike, held the eastern most part of Bragg's line and the general from Kentucky worried about a flank attack. The Confederate generals knew there was a considerable Union force in Gallatin but they were unaware how these troops fit into Rosecrans' plans for Murfreesboro. Both Bragg and Breckinridge feared Rosecrans, at any time, would swing infantry from the north down the Lebanon Pike. Indeed, Breckinridge was Rosecrans' intended target on the morning of December 31, but the day before Breckinridge placed an extensive screen of infantry skirmishers in front of his division to guard against that very threat. He even issued Special Orders No. 60 which ordered his skirmishers to "report promptly to these head quarters any movements of the enemy." He wanted to be sure he was not surprised and his over vigilance, ironically, still did not prevent confusion from reigning on December 31.[4]

Breckinridge was right to be concerned about an attack on eastern flank of the Army of Tennessee, and this concern began two days earlier when Colonel Charles Harker somewhat serendipitously marched his brigade across Stones River on the evening of December 29. Breckinridge's

General John C. Breckinridge's large division held the Confederate eastern flank (Library of Congress).

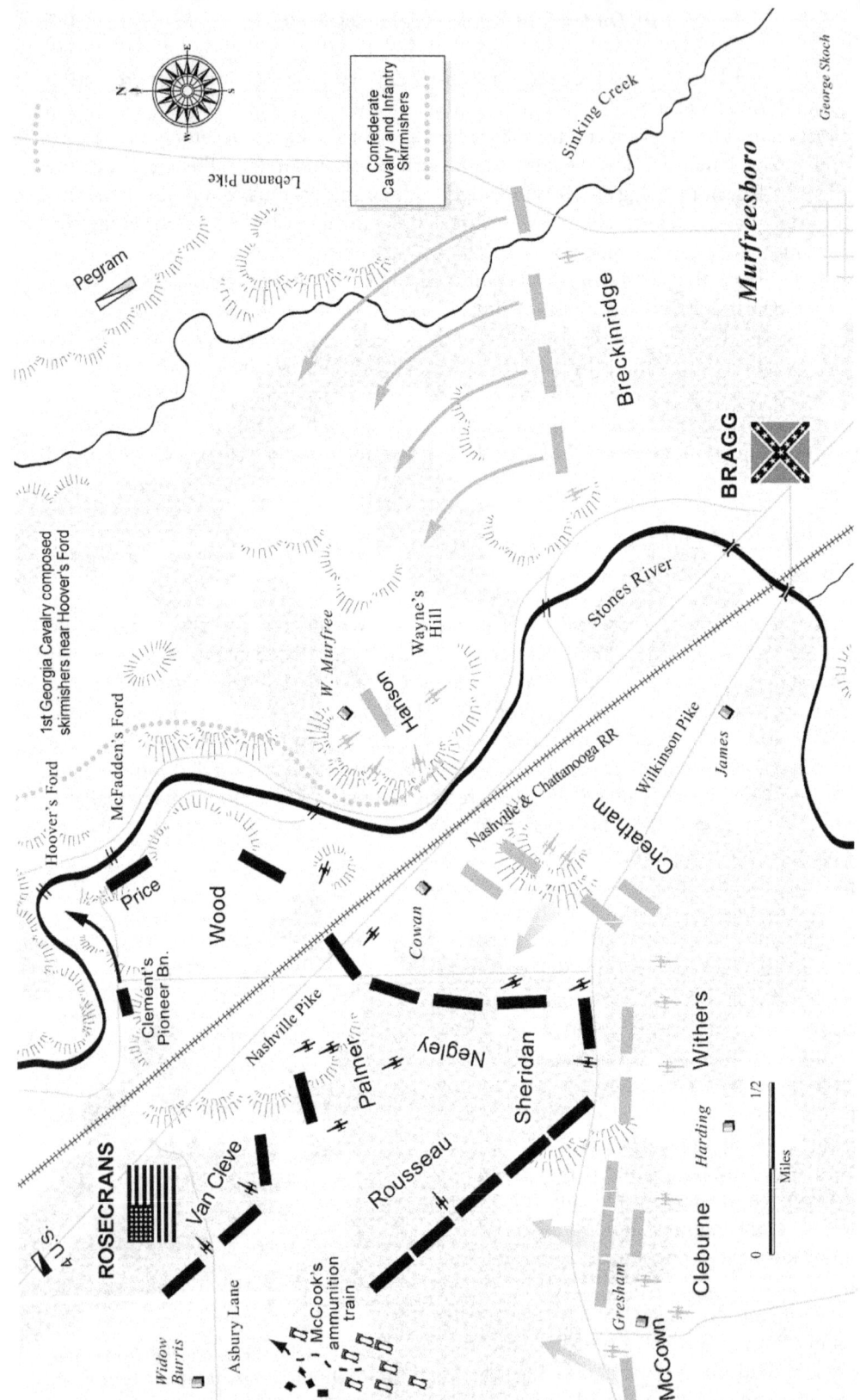

Pegram's cavalry on the east flank during the Battle of Stones River (10:00–11:30 a.m. December 31, 1862).

troops fought Harker's infantry for possession of Wayne's Hill, where Cobb's Kentucky Battery was placed, before Harker moved back to the west side of Stones River. Afterwards, Brigadier General Roger Hanson and Breckinridge agreed about the vital tactical importance of artillery placed on this elevated position which overlooked the plain where the heart of the Army of the Cumberland was located. By December 31, Hanson's brigade was entrenched, fortified and supported a concentration of artillery on Wayne's Hill—Cobb's, Lumsden's, Washington's, and Semple's guns. The remaining four brigades of Breckinridge's division fell into a rather thin line about one half mile to the rear and stretched from the Stones River to the Lebanon Pike. Pegram's two-regiment cavalry brigade operated a mile or so north of Breckinridge's main line along the Lebanon Pike.[5]

On December 31, Bragg successfully began his attack first, but Rosecrans' orders were still in place. So, at 7:00 a.m., the tenacious, bespectacled Brigadier General Horatio Van Cleve marched his 3,800 soldiers of the Third Division of Thomas Crittenden's corps across Stones River near McFadden's Ford intending to carry out his orders to attack Breckinridge at eight o'clock. However, after McCook's wing was attacked, it was apparent to Rosecrans that his planned attack on the east was no longer feasible and to save his army he needed to support his right flank with units intended for the attack. Van Cleve was ordered to re-cross Stones River to support the collapsing western flank of the Federal army. In perhaps, a convoluted set of events, John C. Breckinridge's division on the Confederate right flank remained in place anticipating an attack from a large Union force which began with Van Cleve's early morning movements. Van Cleve's initial crossing was reported to Breckinridge by Pegram's cavalry. As the morning progressed on western side of the battlefield, the Confederate momentum finally ground to a halt when the Southern infantry encountered Phil Sheridan's division in large wooded area called the Cedars.

Because of the desperate infantry battle being fought for the Union salient at Round Forest which William B. Hazen, and later Milo Hascall, stubbornly refused to yield, Bragg decided additional Confederate troops were critical to reinforce the attack on the Union line to tip the battle in his favor. Breckinridge's troops could potentially have made the difference, but he was convinced he was about to be attacked and refused to move. He believed he was threatened by a heavy force of Union infantry.[6]

The confusion, which would paralyze Breckinridge's division, centered on misunderstandings, bad intelligence, and bad communications. The arguments continued for months after the battle, particularly as Breckinridge and Bragg defended the decisions they made during the day.

Bragg Orders Breckinridge to Send Reinforcements

According to Breckinridge's orders the night before, Major J. J. Cox's, 2nd Georgia Battalion

Colonel William B. Hazen's infantry tenaciously held its ground against the Confederate attack (Library of Congress).

Sharpshooters, provided skirmishers and security in front of the left part of Breckinridge's line and Major John E. Austin, 4th Louisiana Battalion (sharpshooters), covered the right side of the front of Breckinridge's line. Breckinridge ordered these two officers to "cooperate in all these movements and report promptly to these headquarters any movement of the enemy." There are no records of Pegram's orders for the day, but presumably he was ordered to scout the extended front of Breckinridge's division including the area near Stones River to the Lebanon Pike. In Bragg's report, he stated Pegram's position as being on the Lebanon Pike.[7]

Around ten o'clock Bragg sent a member of his staff, Colonel J. Stoddard Johnston, with orders which called for Breckinridge to send a brigade to support the main Confederate attack and then shortly after he asked for a second brigade. Earlier that day, Breckinridge reported Pegram's cavalry observed a large force of Union soldiers crossing the fords of Stones River and advancing toward Breckinridge's line. At that point, both Pegram and Breckinridge correctly identified Van Cleve's division moving toward the Southern right flank. Pegram's cavalry was in position and actively firing on the Union Pioneer Brigade, a construction unit made up of carpenters and masons, which began working on improving the fords across Stones River at daybreak. Sometime around 8:30 to 9:00 a.m., Van Cleve moved his division to support the Union fighting along the Nashville Pike. Many historians have concluded that when the Union troops were removed, the withdrawal was apparently unobserved, and more likely unreported, by the Confederate cavalry on the right flank. As a result, Breckinridge continued to believe he was about to be attacked by a significant infantry force which some have assumed to be Van Cleve's division. Upon receiving orders from Bragg requesting reinforcements, Breckinridge declined because he believed he faced this imminent attack. Bragg recorded: "His [Breckinridge] reply to the first call represented the enemy crossing Stone's River in heavy force in his immediate front, and on receiving the second order he informed me they had already crossed in heavy force and were advancing on him in two lines." Bragg then ordered Breckinridge not to delay, but to attack the Union troops in front of his division, which, in fact, were no longer there. But Breckinridge denied that he received an order to attack. Instead, he recalled that Colonel J. Stoddard Johnston, Bragg's staff officer, "suggested" that Breckinridge should move against the enemy. Bragg explained he ordered Breckinridge to attack, but Breckinridge heard "suggested." Breckinridge would later write that he subsequently became aware Johnston interpreted this as an order, but he discounted the misinterpretation because he moved his division forward to attack at once, regardless of the semantics. Breckinridge, believing he was about to be attacked, reasoned Bragg intended Breckinridge's movement to serve as a diversion that would assist with the battle raging on the western flank, and Breckinridge moved his division toward the direction he expected the Union infantry to attack. Although Breckinridge wrote that he would rather fight the advancing Union troops on the "ground which I occupied," he began his attack and moved his entire division forward one half mile, except for Hanson's brigade which remained entrenched around the Confederate artillery on Wayne's Hill.[8]

Much of the criticism for the Southern cavalry comes from a single surviving record from John Pegram sent to Bragg at 10:00 a.m. The message sent to Bragg stated:

> General—Col. Harper [Armistead R. Harper, 1st Georgia Cavalry] sends word that his pickets near Hoover's ford over the West Fork of Stones River have retired a short distance before a pretty strong infantry force of the enemy which has just crossed over. I shall at once go in that direction, & I will report from time to time.

Many conclusions have been drawn from this single message; however, the absence of the prior messages and subsequent messages makes this important but incomplete. Breckinridge's aides, in their reports of the battle, were unanimous in the fact that cavalry reports had been received throughout the morning. This message did not indicate that Pegram still thought Van Cleve was on the east side of the river, which many have concluded. This message actually demonstrated the exact opposite of that, and suggests that Pegram had already reported Van Cleve's withdrawal. However, Bragg, and presumably Breckinridge, would use this single message to justify their subsequent orders. Harper's pickets were forced back from the east bank of Stones River by Morton's Pioneer Brigade supported by infantry around 8:00 a.m. Captain Robert Clements, Morton's brigade, described that "Major Stewart crossed with the balance of his men, and drove the enemy from the ground, and commenced work." Subsequently, the Pioneer Brigade withdrew to support the battle on the east side of the river. Colonel Samuel Price's infantry brigade remained in position at the ford with orders from Van Cleve to continue to "overlook and command the ford" and Milo Hascall's brigade was also in that general vicinity and was the last brigade to join in the fight to bolster the Union right flank due to the congestion of troops. To delay in sending this message, based on the intelligence he received from his cavalry, would have been negligent on Pegram's part. Pegram, who was not at the ford himself, promised to investigate at once and give an update to Breckinridge and Bragg. No further message has been preserved.⁹

Lieutenant Colonel James O. Nixon commanded the 1st Louisiana Cavalry on December 31.

Confusion Over the Threats to Breckinridge's Position

In regard to Pegram's action, the messages he sent before and afterward are more important, but there are no records of them. The message which was preserved should be considered in context. The message was used by Bragg to justify his actions in a long running argument with Breckinridge. Pegram included in the message a promise to provide subsequent updates, and presumably, he had already sent messages before this time. Importantly, several historians have referred to the fact that the Confederate cavalry failed to record that Van Cleve had re-crossed Stones Rivers. Upon examination, it is clear that the cavalry did not miss this movement, because if the 1st Georgia Cavalry reported being pushed back from it position near Hoover's Ford, it is unlikely it could have held that position if 4,000 Union infantry were still on the east side of the river. And, Pegram made the point that infantry "just crossed over" Stones River which indicated a new force just crossed the river. So, Pegram and most likely Bragg and Breckinridge knew Van Cleve had moved back to the east side of the river earlier. The new movement needed to be reported and developed. This was the prudent action for the cavalry—report the movement and then determine what was going on. In the Civil War, this took time to accomplish and communicate. Pegram promised to ride to the point of the Federal movement, and in the meantime Lieutenant Colonel Harper could have provided clarification of his own. Finally, the message does clearly say the cavalry was withdrawn only a short distance, which indicated that a serious forward movement had not taken place at that time.

Also, General Lovell Rousseau substantiated the claim that the Confederate cavalry was very active on the eastern flank during the morning of December 31. The 2nd Kentucky Cavalry (U.S.) reported directly to Rousseau's division and not to Stanley. In Rousseau's report he observed:

> On the morning of the 31st, six companies of the Second Kentucky Cavalry, Maj. Thomas P. Nicholas commanding, were ordered down to watch and defend the fords on Stone's River, to our left and rear. The cavalry of the enemy several times, in force, attempted to cross these fords, but Nicholas very gallantly repulsed them, with loss, and they did not cross the river.

The cavalry working in the area of Rousseau division could only have been Pegram's two regiments. Had four thousand Union infantry been in place on the east side of Stones River, the Confederates could not have acted as described in this report.[10]

Theodore O'Hara, a lifelong friend of Breckinridge and member of his staff, wrote his report of the actions on the Confederate left flank on December 31 and recorded that the cavalry provided "frequent reports" about the enemy in front of Breckinridge's line. Colonel John Buckner of Breckinridge's staff substantiated the frequent communications with the cavalry throughout the morning. Next, O'Hara recalled that a message was received from Bragg stating that Breckinridge faced a Union infantry line to his front at 10:00 a.m. This report from Bragg seemed to convince Breckinridge that the threat he faced was real, but Bragg would claim that it was Breckinridge that reported he faced two heavy lines of infantry advancing on his position. While the details of Pegram's exact message are often overlooked, it is somewhat ironic both Breckinridge and Bragg blamed each other for the intelligence declaring the presence of the enemy to the front. The 10:00 a.m. message from Pegram was apparently interpreted by each of the generals to indicate Breckinridge faced a significant threat; and both generals reinforced the threat to each other.[11]

When Pegram's and Breckinridge's messages reached Bragg, Bragg simply responded by telling Breckinridge to attack the enemy that was before him, and Breckinridge did exactly that. Bragg made the correct order based the information from Pegram and Breckinridge. Breckinridge put his division in motion and began marching ahead perhaps a mile (for the most eastern brigades) when Breckinridge received another set of orders asking from for reinforcements for the battle at Round Forest. This strongly suggested that Bragg became aware there was no large force crossing at Hoover's Ford and this

General Horatio Van Cleve's division's movements were a source of controversy for the Confederate generals.

prompted the message (although there is no substantiation of this in any of the records). Bragg wanted two brigades to move across Stones River to assist Hardee's attack, and Breckinridge promptly ordered Jackson's and Adams' brigades to comply with these orders. With the removal of these brigades, Breckinridge stopped his forward advance, and then he sent officers of his own staff and several of his escort to find out the position and strength of the enemy in front of his division. Breckinridge never recorded the outcome of this reconnaissance, but the issue was no longer important. Next, Breckinridge received yet another set of orders from Colonel Johnston and Colonel George Grenfell of Bragg's staff to bring all of his command, except for the artillery and Hanson's brigade to assist in the battle. This can only mean that Bragg now knew Breckinridge faced no imminent attack from Hoover's Ford.[12]

Major William Clare, the third of Bragg's staff officers to ride Breckinridge, recalled that Bragg sent a reply in regard to Breckinridge's delay that unless Breckinridge was sure the enemy was threatening him to send reinforcements. Breckinridge's reply was "he could be certain of nothing, or something similar, but that he had taken steps to ascertain the correctness or falsity of the report." Clare noted that he observed Grenfell and Johnston moving back and forth from Bragg's headquarters.[13]

In summary, at this point, the situation regarding the Union infantry movement near Hoover's Ford had been clarified. Upon receiving the intelligence from the 1st Georgia Cavalry, Breckinridge was prudently concerned about an attack on his position. No one knew what was unfolding—the cavalry, Bragg or Breckinridge. It simply took time to develop this. Upon receiving Bragg's message substantiating the claim of infantry to his front, this convinced Breckinridge that he should prepare for an attack and he moved forward. Finally, it was determined there was no threat, and upon determining this fact, Bragg ordered reinforcements. Instead of blaming the Confederate cavalry for missing a significant troop movement or for seeing something that wasn't there, it is a more reasonable and accurate to give credit to an enemy, whether Federal infantry or the Pioneer Brigade, which forced the Confederate cavalry away from sharpshooting across the river near Hoover's Ford. This movement simply caused a delay in the movement of Breckinridge's division until the full extent of the Union advance at the fords on Stones River was determined.

Another Rumor About Federal Infantry on the Eastern Flank

It took an hour or so for Bragg, Breckinridge and Pegram to clarify that a significant infantry advance across Stones River was not occurring. Once the situation was clear, Bragg's original request for troops to support the Confederate attack at Round Forest was reinstated. Bragg ordered Breckinridge to send reinforcements at 11:30 a.m.; but now Bragg heard another rumor of his own, probably from Breckinridge himself. Bragg wrote in his battle report that he received information, from an unidentified source, that a large force of Union infantry was advancing along the Lebanon Road five miles away. Could this be the flank attack that both Breckinridge and Bragg feared? Then, Bragg ordered Pegram to develop this movement, cover the flank and prevent the attack of a large force of Union infantry, which, again, was not there. Believing a potentially damaging flank movement by Rosecrans was imminent, Bragg countermanded Breckinridge's attack order and request for reinforcements for Round Forest. Again, confusion reigned while Pegram's cavalry determined the phantom infantry on the Lebanon Pike was not real. There is no evidence or intimation that this rumor originated from Pegram's cavalry.

Bragg recorded in his after action report:

> About this same time a report reached me that a heavy force of the enemy's infantry was advancing on the Lebanon road, about 5 miles in Breckinridge's front. Brigadier-General Pegram, who had been sent to that road to cover the flank of the infantry with his cavalry brigade (save two regiments detached with Wheeler and Wharton), was ordered forward immediately to develop any such movement. The orders for the two brigades from Breckinridge were countermanded, while dispositions were made, at his request, to re-enforce him. Before they could be carried out, the movements ordered disclosed the facts that no force had crossed Stone's River; that the only enemy in our immediate front there was a small body of sharpshooters, and that there was no advance on the Lebanon road. These unfortunate misapprehensions on that part of the field (which, with proper precaution, could not have existed) withheld from active operations three fine brigades until the enemy had succeeded in checking our progress, had re-established his lines, and had collected many of his broken battalions.

Bragg would write an addendum to Breckinridge's battle report in which he would point the finger for the poor intelligence regarding the Union force moving by the Lebanon Pike directly at Breckinridge. Bragg wrote, that in Breckinridge's reply regarding the orders to attack the infantry thought to be in front of Breckinridge's division, that Breckinridge expressed his concern about exposing his right flank. Bragg explained that he received a message from Breckinridge stating: "I am obeying your order"; but expressing the opinion that the move would expose him "to a heavy force of the enemy advancing from Black's (on the Lebanon road)." Although Breckinridge might have argued that he never directly stated an attacking enemy force was on the Lebanon Pike, but merely stated *if* an attack came from that direction, his flank would be vulnerable. Bragg implied his message declared he was exposed to a heavy force moving on the Lebanon Pike. He supported his conclusion by his staff officer, Major William Clare, who subsequently wrote that it was Breckinridge that told him that his right flank was being threatened. Captain H. B. Clay of Pegram's staff clarified the part the cavalry played in this situation. Clay reported this rumor was carried by Colonel George St. Leger Grenfell of Bragg's staff who arrived at Pegram's cavalry brigade headquarters with orders to determine if the enemy was attacking by way of Black's Crossroads on the Lebanon Pike. Pegram was not at headquarters because he was probably in the Hoover's Ford vicinity developing the enemy activity in that area. Clay was surprised by this request but promptly carried out the reconnaissance; and reported no enemy was found there. The threat of an enemy column appears to have been a misunderstanding carried to Bragg in response to Breckinridge's concern about a potential threat to his right flank. It is unclear if Bragg read Breckinridge's reply as a declaration of the presence of an enemy erroneously, or if Breckinridge seriously believed there was a threat of the attack along the Lebanon Pike. But, clearly this rumor did not originate with Pegram or his staff.[14]

Theodore O'Hara substantiated Breckinridge's account of the report of the phantom Federal force on the Lebanon Pike. He wrote that as Breckinridge was moving his division forward and while using Hanson's brigade as a pivot, swinging to the west, he received a message from Bragg. O'Hara wrote: "[Y]ou received another message from the Commanding General that the enemy was advancing on the Lebanon road and ordering you to fall back to your original position." Some historians have attributed the message about a "heavy force" of Union infantry on the Lebanon Pike as being reported by Pegram, but there is no indication in Bragg's report who made that claim and Pegram's staff officer denied this. Colonel David Urquhart, Bragg Staff's, in his description of the battle made no accusation of dilatory duty on the part of Pegram or the cavalry. He simply recorded that by the time Breckinridge moved his brigades to support the Confederate attack in the afternoon Rosecrans had already strengthened his positions.[15]

Major James Wilson of Breckinridge's staff wrote a report regarding the events of December and made no mention of the confusion about an infantry threat at Stones River or the Lebanon Pike. Finally, Colonel John Buckner filed the most critical report of Breckinridge's three staff officers. Buckner also recalled that the cavalry made frequent reports and reported that the enemy was on the east side of the river. Buckner also recalled that Bragg sent a message that the enemy was on the east side of the river, reinforcing the cavalry reports. In the subsequent discussions of these events, Breckinridge's staff stated the rumor came from Bragg, Bragg in return said the rumor came from Breckinridge and Pegram's staff declared that they had no knowledge of the movement until Colonel Grenfell of Bragg's staff arrived ordering them to determine if the enemy was moving south along the Lebanon Pike. The real situation on the eastern side of the Army of Tennessee was finally determined after one o'clock and Breckinridge sent his troops to support the main Confederate attack.[16]

Pegram's brigade not only covered Hoover's Ford which required attention, but also made several reconnaissance expeditions on the Lebanon Pike. Pegram's cavalry had one additional action. It also joined an infantry combat mission during the morning which targeted Hoover's Ford, and this certainly did not indicate a belief that Van Cleve's division lay in wait unseen ahead. While the cavalry on the eastern flank of the Confederate army has been maligned, it appears to have been anything but lax in its duties on December 31. Bragg finally concluded,

> Having now settled the question that no movement was being made against our right, and none even to be apprehended, Breckinridge was ordered to leave two brigades to support the battery ... on his side of Stone's River, and with the balance of the force to cross to the left.... The three brigades of Jackson, Preston, and Adams were successively reported for this work. How gallantly they moved to their task, and how much they suffered in the determined effort to accomplish it, will best appear from reports of subordinate commanders and the statement of losses, herewith.

Breckinridge appears to have taken the brunt of Bragg's criticism for the action, or inaction, on the eastern flank during the morning and early afternoon.[17]

Breckinridge wrote in his battle report that the intelligence which observed "the enemy, having crossed at the fords below, were moving on my position in line of battle. This proved to be incorrect, and it is to be regretted that sufficient care was not taken by the authors of the reports to discriminate rumor from fact." Breckinridge stated the report came from the cavalry, presumably Lieutenant Colonel Harper, 1st Georgia Cavalry. He therefore pointed his finger at the cavalry but never blamed Pegram for the erroneous report which caused all the confusion and lost opportunities. However, Breckinridge did not state when he received this message and subsequent messages. If Breckinridge was referring to the reconnaissance observing Van Cleve's initial crossing, the intelligence was correct. Breckinridge did not refer to the fact that the ten o'clock message from Pegram stated the enemy had "just crossed over." Because of the lack of Pegram's report of the battle, which remains a mystery, it is unclear what he perceived about the day's activity. Pegram's cavalry correctly identified Van Cleve's division movement across Stones River as it prepared for the early morning attack. Did Pegram report the re-crossing of Van Cleve? This is unknown, but there is strong evidence that this was reported and the threat reported by Harper at 10:00, and reinforced by Bragg, caused Breckinridge to anticipate an attack. If this was the case, then there is no blame to be assigned. Only the report of the movement of a Union force across Stones River delayed the movement of Breckinridge's division to reinforce the attack at Round Forest. The lack of preservation of subsequent messages and the counter claims by Breckinridge and Bragg make it impossible to determine the accountability of any of the parties. Again, it is also important to know what was preserved outside of the official records of this event was used to add to support to the arguments between Bragg and Breckinridge after the battle.[18]

Despite the effort of finding fault or blame, it is still hard to believe that responsible cavalry officers, not only Pegram, but all very capable regimental cavalry officers of the two regiments on the field, missed so badly. Not only was Pegram a West Point trained professional officer, he served on the staff of Smith's Army of Kentucky and knew the importance of accurate communication and intelligence. Both the 1st Louisiana and 1st Georgia cavalries were experienced regiments with exemplary officers. Certainly subsequent messages were sent to give the proper description of the situation. The frequent messages received throughout the morning from the cavalry did not begin and stop at ten o'clock. In addition, the infantry had men gathering information also. This is particularly true in light of reports from the battle, such as those of Joseph Palmer who was aware of the Union cavalry moving on the east flank of the battle and Palmer detected the presence of the supply train a mile and a half away. Palmer dispatched a group of infantry commanded by Captain D. H. S. Spence to attack the Union wagon train during the morning in the very location Van Cleve's infantry was spotted early in the day. Certainly, responsible infantry commanders, expecting an advance of enemy infantry would have thrown forward skirmishers of their own who would have reported seeing no troops in front of them at some time between 7:00 a.m. and noon.[19]

Breckinridge's orders also assigned the duty of reconnaissance to infantry officers, not only to Pegram's cavalry, and not only was Captain Spence's infantry combat team operating freely in front of Breckinridge's command when he was still contemplating the possibility of an attack. Another infantry commander, Colonel Robert Trabue, had skirmishers and scouts moving with impunity. Hanson's, and subsequently Trabue's, command held the forward position of Breckinridge's division and recorded: "All this while the brigade covered more than a mile of front with skirmishers and pickets, using for that purpose from six to ten companies daily. These advanced to within 100 yards of the enemy in many places, and were hourly engaged."[20]

What appears more likely is that Bragg interpreted Harper's message to support Breckinridge's claim that Union infantry was in front of his division, and Breckinridge prudently decided to get a clear understanding of the situation. Bragg's report supported Breckinridge's earlier intelligence about Van Cleve's division threatening to attack. Perhaps, credit should be given to Morton's Pioneer Brigade and the supporting Federal infantry which pushed the 1st Georgia Cavalry from Stone Rivers as a feint on the Confederate positions on the east side of Stones. In the Civil War, that took some time to determine the exact situation. Finally, the rumor regarding the phantom Union infantry force on the Lebanon Pike appears to have been a simple misunderstanding.

On January 1, General Breckinridge sent more definite instructions for his skirmishers. He ordered his skirmishers from the brigades in the rear and supporting Hanson's forward position on Wayne's Hill to move "boldly" forward. He wanted to push the skirmishers even across the river if no opposition was found and he ordered his men to locate the enemy artillery positions. The admonishment was clearly directed to prevent the confusion from the day before.[21]

Finally, in regard to the potential success of moving Breckinridge's brigade, had he not been delayed, it is unlikely this would have changed the outcome of the battle given the command situation which existed. Many historians have analyzed the stalled Confederate attack at Round Forest and there are various opinions if additional reinforcements from Breckinridge's division would have carried the day. Even when Breckinridge's men arrived, some question if they were utilized properly and whether Polk's decision to add reinforcements in a piecemeal fashion throughout the day doomed the attack to failure. However, if Breckinridge's division was added in a swift, well-coordinated attack, the pressure on the Union line could have made the situation critical, but this type of attack was never made. Leonidas Polk's, biographer, simply explained there was too few cavalry on the Confederate right flank that morning to provide proper intelligence about the presence of Union troops in the front and the possibility of a Union infantry marching from the north down the Lebanon Pike. He and others theorized that if Morgan's cavalry had been retained with Bragg's army, much of the problems on the Confederate right flank would have been averted.[22]

General Roger Hanson commanded the Confederate position on Wayne's Hill—"All this while the brigade covered more than a mile of front with skirmishers and pickets" (Library of Congress).

Pegram's Afternoon Action

Around two o'clock in the afternoon, Pegram's small brigade found an opportunity for offensive action in cooperation with Colonel Joseph Palmer's infantry, 18th Tennessee Infantry. Palmer dispatched Captain D. H. C. Spence earlier in the day to investigate the opportunity of attacking a wagon train observed in front of Breckinridge's command. Pegram's troopers had heard constant musket fire and cannonading as the Federal troops advanced for the last five days and observed the fighting on December 31 without much involvement. Captain Henry B. Clay, commanding a squadron of 1st Louisiana Cavalry, got into the fight by engaging two mountain howitzers and attacking across Stones River.[23]

The Southern cavalry discovered a hospital, a large numbers of stragglers, and a large wagon train just north of the main battle. The wagon train gained the attention of

Pegram who sent a member of his staff to confirm if the rumors were true. Upon finding the wagon train, Pegram's cavalry attacked across Stones River, captured five to eighteen wagons (depending on which account was correct) and 170 prisoners. The cavalry and infantry supported by mountain howitzers fired on the defenders. Pegram, personally, led the charge against the Union position. A member of Pegram's escort, David Anderson Deaderick recorded:

> We charged up a lane, Gen. [Pegram] in front, our company following, & the other Co. behind us. The line which we charged was composed of the wagon guard about 300 in all. When they saw us coming they threw down their arms & ran and by the time we got to them they were scattered all over a 10 acre field.... They were very much frightened, held up their hands, hat or handkerchiefs, and made every demonstration to let us know they had surrendered.... We did not shoot any of them, as they seemed to expect. By this time the enemy had got a battery in a position that commanded us & threw the shell in very thick.[24]

The 58th Indiana Infantry was the target of Pegram's attack. The regiment moved from the left flank to the center to support the McCook's collapsing troops and as the battle unfolded in front to them on the Nashville Pike, the soldiers heard a "defiant 'rebel yell'" in their rear. Pegram's small cavalry force attacked a weakly defended wagon train, the hospital at Collins' House and charged on the retreating soldiers still moving to the rear. The regimental supplies and some of the soldiers of the 58th Indiana, including the surgeon and hospital steward, were captured and the remainder of the regiment felt pressed in on all sides—Pegram in the rear and the Confederate infantry in the front.[25]

The 3rd Wisconsin Artillery joined in the fight against Pegram's cavalry. Lieutenant Cortland Livingston, commanding the battery, reported:

> I saw a great stampede among the ambulances, wagons, and stragglers opposite, and was told some rebel cavalry were charging on them. I was fearful of making a mistake and firing on our own cavalry. We could not see the enemy until he got among the wagons and was taking them off. We then opened upon them and disabled 2 wagons, which blocked the lane and obliged them to leave without their booty. I think they got off with only 5 wagons. They left 1 man killed, and carried off their wounded.[26]

Colonel Samuel Price, Van Cleve's Third Brigade commander, reported Pegram's afternoon action. Price recorded that Pegram attacked at two o'clock with 300 or 400 cavalry, almost all of Pegram's available troopers. As the Confederate cavalry attacked, Price ordered his artillery to fire on them which killed three and wounded others; but not before Pegram alarmed Price's men on the east flank and escaped with some wagons and prisoners.[27]

Summary

In regard to the Confederate cavalry on the eastern flank, Pegram's small brigade has been criticized severely for many years; but it important to see these actions in a new perspective. Believing that experienced cavalryman serving as pickets during one of the largest battles of the Civil War missed the movement of an entire division of 3,800 Union infantry and, even more incredulous, of imagining the movement of a Union division marching down the Lebanon Pike is much too simplistic and one dimensional. The records that exist are contradictory, incomplete, and hand-picked to support actions taken by Bragg and Breckinridge.[28]

It must be concluded that there is not enough evidence or information to assign blame to anyone on the eastern flank for the confusion during the day, but certainly Wheeler's decision to act as a brigade commander and to diminish Pegram's cavalry to such a

Captain James St. Clair Morton commanded the Pioneer Brigade—the brigade's movement most likely confused the Confederate generals.

small force was a poor one. The communication problems on the Confederate right flank (east) between the cavalry and Breckinridge would not end on December 31, but would continue on January 2 when the problem would also include John Wharton, as well as Pegram. These problems demonstrated the importance Joseph Wheeler acting as chief of cavalry. If the problem on the east flank rested with Pegram, a chief of cavalry, acting in that capacity and on the field, should have been able to identify and rectify the problem. While Wheeler might not have been able to rectify the problem on December 31 when presumably the first indication of trouble presented itself, he might have prevented the continuation of the problem on January 2.

For those involved in the actions in the field, the information that exists does not show John Pegram or the Confederate cavalry to be the principle cause of the problems on December 31. The existing evidence relieves the cavalry from any of the rumors about an enemy infantry column marching down the Lebanon Pike. In none of the reports is there any intimation the rumor originated with the cavalry. In regard to confusion about enemy infantry crossing Stones River, certainly there can be blame assigned for incomplete or unclear intelligence reports; but this is unknown. Could the cavalry have failed to report Van Cleve's withdrawal or misrepresenting the Union army's crossing of Stones River at 10:00 a.m.? The answer is yes; however, this is unlikely. If the cavalry made frequent reports about Van Cleve during the morning, it is unlikely the reports ceased at 8:30 a.m., except for the report at 10:00 a.m. Cavalry reports were routinely sent at twenty to thirty minute intervals. To conclude, there is no indication these reports stopped at 8:30, and it is unlikely the 1st Georgia Cavalry moved in closer proximity to Stones River without reporting this. When the new movement began at 10:00 a.m., this regiment properly reported it. What did the cavalry reports say through 8:30 to 10:00 and afterward? And why were these not preserved by Breckinridge and Bragg?

While giving the cavalry the benefit of professionally doing its assigned duty, it is more likely Pegram's cavalry reported Van Cleve's crossing at 7:00 a.m. and re-crossing at 8:30. Some additional force apparently pushed the cavalry pickets, who were firing into the Union troops throughout the morning, away from Hoover's Ford. As a result, Breckinridge still believed he faced a double line of infantry crossing at Stones River. Even if he had received information about Van Cleve's withdrawal, this second message about the enemy moving on his front, substantiated by Bragg himself, caused Breckinridge to believe he was about to be attacked. Rather than dilatory duty on anyone's part, the event just unfolded as it did. There is just not enough information to conclude otherwise, and the years of assigned blame to John Pegram and/or his cavalry must be reconsidered in the light that cavalry competently accomplished it duty.

11. Stanley and Wheeler Arrive on the Battlefield (Afternoon, December 31)

The man who does not follow me is a damned coward!
—Brigadier General David S. Stanley

At Stewarts Creek at 9:30 a.m., David Stanley received a message from Colonel Julius Garesché, "The enemy have attacked McCook's corps in great force, and the Corps is falling back in a good deal of disorder. Fasten to the right and do your best to restore order." David Stanley's reserve cavalry and portions of Minty's First Brigade mounted and rode to assist Zahm's and Kennett's troops ten miles away. Stanley and Minty rode hard to the collapsing wing of the army with the 5th Tennessee and a portion of the 15th Pennsylvania Cavalry and with the First Brigade in tow (two companies of 3rd Kentucky, 4th Michigan and Jennings Battalion, 7th Pennsylvania), the combined cavalry moved to the right to support McCook's damaged flank. Minty left 130 men of the 4th Michigan to provide cover for the Battery D, 1st Ohio Battery (Newell's section) which remained at Stewarts Creek; and as they hastened to Overall Creek, Stanley's cavalry came under friendly fire, ironically ordered by John Kennett. After a half dozen shells were fired into the approaching Union cavalry, Minty ordered a flag of truce sent to the Union lines to convince them the approaching cavalry was Federal cavalry and not Confederates which had been so predominant in the area during the morning. But the return of Minty's cavalry was delayed initially due poor intelligence. The cavalry moved about two miles when word was received that a large body of Confederate cavalry was approaching. Expecting that Wheeler had returned for more pillaging, at least, some of the troopers stopped and sought shelter in block houses until the threat was proven to be wrong. Then the cavalry rode back toward the battlefield.[1]

As Stanley reached the right wing of the army he met many stragglers–"first a few dozen, then a hundred and finally not less than five thousand." He left a troop of cavalry to rally the men of Johnson's and Davis's shattered divisions and return them to their lines. He later learned that his troopers assisted with the return of over two thousand soldiers to their regiments. On the return ride, Minty's column observed the Union hospitals, really houses and other buildings impressed into service, but designated with a red flag on the chimneys. Upon arrival to the battlefield, Stanley consulted with Rosecrans and then he joined Minty's fresh cavalry before assessing the situation in the field.[2]

By the middle of the day, both armies slowed their attacks. Rosecrans girded his infantry divisions into a new line of defense and Bragg realized the advantage he demonstrated during the morning had ground to a halt. He sought fresh troops to throw into the fight in an attempt to dislodge the stubborn Union resistance, which had prompted his orders to Breckinridge. On the Union side of the field, Rousseau's troops reinforced Sheridan's division and Negley's division moved into position to support Palmer's division. Rosecrans maneuvered his artillery on high ground along the railroad to protect the newly formed defensive line. Meanwhile, Bragg moved to capitalize on the Union effort to bolster the western flank with an attack on Crittenden's line as he scrambled to find fresh troops to add to the fight. While the armies repositioned, Minty crossed his cavalry over Overall Creek near McGregor's house, a few hundred yards north of Asbury Church, when he was mistakenly fired upon by Union artillery. One trooper of the 15th Pennsylvania was severely wounded by the friendly fire. Once over Overall Creek and about three-quarters miles southwest of the Nashville Pike, the 4th Michigan dismounted and formed a line of skirmishers and drove some Confederate cavalry from a wooded area to their front. Minty formed his command into a semicircle. The 4th Michigan was supported by a portion of the dismounted 5th Tennessee which moved to the edge of the woods and which looked east over the field toward Widow Burris's house. To the west and rear of the 4th Michigan, Captain William Jennings's battalion of the 7th Pennsylvania and two companies of the 3rd Kentucky Cavalry joined in the preparation for battle in the woods near Asbury Church. The 15th Pennsylvania Cavalry moved immediately behind the 4th Michigan. The entire Union cavalry defense comprised 950 men. Minty's arrangement of his cavalry was aligned in this manner in response to the action of Abraham Buford's Kentucky (CSA) cavalry brigade's movements on the west side of Overall Creek and Wheeler's cavalry south of Asbury Lane.

Buford's Advance on the West Side of Overall Creek

Buford's small cavalry brigade of 631 men began the day about twenty miles south of Murfreesboro, protecting the flank of Bragg's army. At midnight, Buford received his orders to move to Murfreesboro and he had his troopers in the saddle and riding northward about the time of the first gunfire of the battle. The three-regiment brigade arrived around noon and participated in joint actions with Wheeler's brigade for the remainder of the day. To streamline his command, Buford combined his 5th and 6th Kentucky regiments into a single regiment, so his brigade functioned as two regiments. Buford's cavalry moved to the extreme western flank of the battle and he initially moved northward on the west side of Overall Creek. He soon encountered a group of Union troops, infantry, cavalry and artillery, positioned on a hill near the Miller house along the Nashville Pike. Buford encountered Zahm's reforming cavalry brigade along with the 9th Michigan Infantry. Buford's cavalry advanced on the Federal line with the 5th/6th Kentucky Cavalry on the left and the 3rd Kentucky Cavalry on the right. The Federal artillery opened up on the advancing Kentucky skirmishers and Buford, being recalled by Wheeler, withdrew his men. He captured a few stray Union soldiers on this movement up Overall Creek, but moved to rejoin Wheeler's brigade. Buford referred to his actions as a mere skirmish which resulted in one man killed and three wounded; but he was able to find a lightly protected wagon train and thirty stray Union soldiers who quickly became prisoners.[3]

During his movement up Overall Creek, Buford encountered Lieutenant Colonel

John Parkhurst's 9th Michigan Infantry, which had served as provost guard which performed straggler duty the day before. This regiment began the morning about two miles north of the main Union line. The regiment was in high spirits because Parkhurst had just been cleared by a court of inquiry for his actions at Murfreesboro the previous summer. Parkhurst spent most of the day halting retreating troops and because he was unsure of the extent of the McCook's defeat, he drew his line of infantry into a strong defensive position on the west side of Overall Creek as he continued to re-form the disorganized troops flowing to the rear. As Parkhurst handled this duty, he was informed that Moses Walker's reserve Union infantry brigade was marching from the rear toward his regiment. Captain Josiah Church who commanded the 1st Michigan Artillery, Battery D, placed his guns on the left and center of hill where Parkhurst positioned his regiment and dug in awaiting a full attack. Seeing the confusion before him, Parkhurst thought it might be reasonable to send his train back to Nashville. Once his train started its movement to the rear, Buford's cavalry appeared and attacked it; but the 1st Michigan Battery sent a few shells into the attacking cavalry as Walker's infantry joined in the firing. Buford was compelled to break off his attack. Zahm's cavalry, which had finally reorganized, rode in pursuit of Buford, but Parkhurst, in his report, described the pursuit as half-hearted. However, Charles Bennett, 9th Michigan Infantry, explained that Parkhurst wrote a more favorable description of Zahm's actions, not included in the *Official Records*:

> At this juncture the rebel cavalry following our routed army made a charge upon my advanced lines, which was handsomely repulsed by the cavalry I had organized from the troops which but a few minutes previously had given way in despair and were fleeing for dear life. After the repulse of the rebel cavalry our cavalry pursued the enemy till he reached the woods to the right of the pike.

Zahm's cavalry had had enough fighting for the day but his troopers still provided defensive actions in the afternoon.[4]

Henry Cooley, 9th Michigan Infantry, recorded in his diary that Buford's troopers drew up in battle line about one half mile from his regiment which had moved across the Nashville Pike to face the threat and to protect the bridge over Overall Creek. Everyone expected Buford to charge at any moment, but Buford chose to draw away from the infantry, pursued by Zahm's reformed cavalry. Colonel Moses Walker's infantry brigade, recently arrived from La Vergne, fell into line next to Parkhurst and Buford wisely chose to withdraw.[5]

Wheeler Moves to Attack Minty

Around four o'clock, Minty's cavalry saw the approaching troopers of General Wheeler's cavalry, which had moved, onto the battlefield after its circuitous ride around Rosecrans' army. Minty knew the fighting was not over for the day and rode among his men encouraging them to maintain the line.[6]

When Minty and Stanley arrived, Wharton's brigade was "fought out," but Wheeler's and Buford's brigades were still present and effective on the field. Now, the Confederate cavalry approached Minty's position: "[T]he Rebels appeared in small numbers and commence desultory skirmish fire which lasted perhaps an hour; then their whole force appeared in line opposite us," explained N. W. Sample, 15th Pennsylvania. Wheeler's entire command, some mounted and others dismounted, advanced forward supported by two guns of Southern artillery. Wheeler's combined force including Buford probably totaled around 1,800 men. Minty, who commanded the newly arrived contingent of Union cavalry while Stanley and his staff visited Rosecrans, described,

> They drove back the Fourth Michigan to the line of the First [Middle] Tennessee skirmishers, and then attacked the Seventh Pennsylvania with great fury, but met with determined resistance. I went forward to the dismounted skirmishers and endeavored to move them to the right, to strengthen the Seventh Pennsylvania, but the moment the right of the line showed itself from behind the fence where they were posted, the whole of the enemy's fire was directed on it, turning it completely around.

The unreliable 15th Pennsylvania Cavalry continued to be so, rapidly riding to the rear. This left the 7th Pennsylvania Cavalry dismounted and without any support and in a very vulnerable position. Trooper John C. McLain of the 4th Michigan explained that half his regiment was dismounted and a flanking movement caused his regiment to give way. The Union cavalry fell back and reformed, unseen and outside the range of the Southern artillery. Lancaster Thomas, 15th Pennsylvania, explained the Confederate troopers advanced through the woods and pressed Minty's cavalry back. Thomas concluded the Southern troopers had had so much success during the day they planned to "ride us down and capture us so out of the woods, they came cheering."[7]

Eugene Bronson, 4th Michigan Cavalry, described in a letter written after the battle that the Confederate cavalry had two artillery pieces shelling the Union cavalry position, but he explained the value of multiple shot Colt revolving rifle. "[O]ur guns shoot five times and the rebs are afraid of them. They would not come out of the woods to meet us on an open field." Bronson explained the other Federal cavalry regiments "ran away" and only the 7th Pennsylvania held its position in support of the Michigan cavalry. Trooper Francis Weigley, 7th Pennsylvania, wrote of his experience during this fight: "[A]bout two hundred and fifty of us were dismounted to fight on foot ... then we met our enemy and then we commenced firing and in about five minutes we had to fall back but in that time I shot ten balls and every ball found a man."[8]

As the Union skirmishers fell back before Wheeler's initial attack, a precipitous withdrawal by the 5th Tennessee Cavalry also resulted. The 5th Tennessee boldly entered the fight despite their unreliable Merrill carbines, only to be pushed back. Minty observed: "[A]n officer of that regiment called to his men fire and run. This caused a partial pause, his men fired in any and every direction and came back across the large cotton field north of Widow Burris's house." Minty's cavalry withdrew and reformed in a line strong enough to stop Wheeler's advance; and David Stanley arrived on the field with his staff. Eugene Bronson, 4th Michigan, explained that Minty ordered his troops to fall back and form a dismounted line behind a fence. Once the Union troops assembled behind the fence the Confederate cavalry opened up on them. Bronson wrote, "The bullets fell like hails around us, one knocked a sliver off a rail about 2 inches from my head.... We were ordered back to our horses and when they saw us leave they shouted and poured the lead into us, a perfect storm."[9]

Wheeler's cavalry brigade had just ridden around the rear of Rosecrans' army and spent the night just west of Nolensville. Wheeler's cavalry reached Wilkinson Pike at 2:00 p.m. and he had little time to rest before he received a message from Bragg to hasten forward to the battle and take position on the west flank of the Confederate army. Bragg wanted Wheeler on the same duty as Wharton, probing the enemy's rear while destroying "trains, ammunition and camps" and capturing prisoners. Buford's cavalry pushed across Overall Creek from the west, attacking the flank of the 7th Pennsylvania and Wheeler pushed northward on the east side of the creek. As Buford's brigade joined in the fight

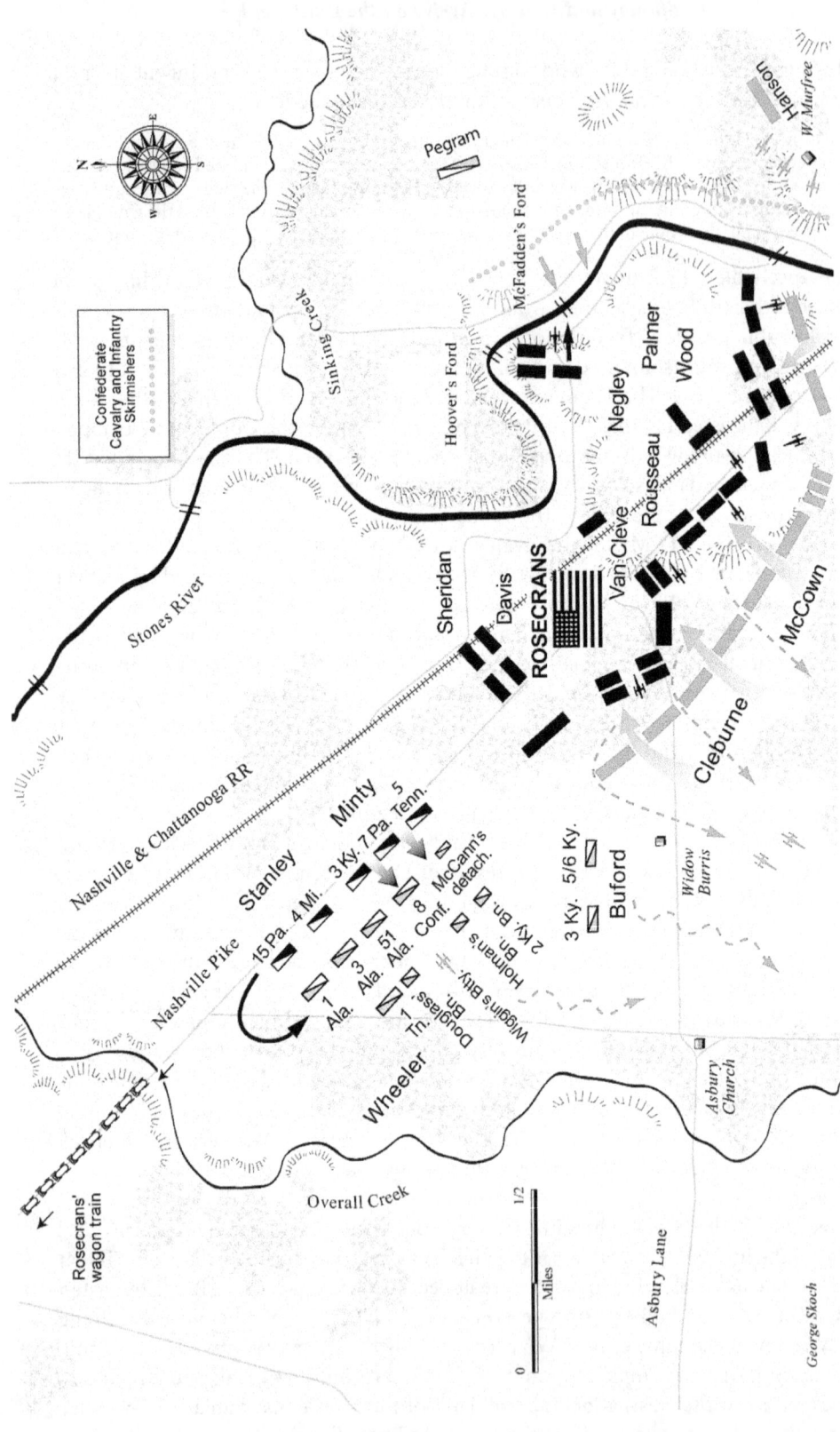

Stanley's and Minty's repulse of Wheeler and Buford (4:00 p.m. December 31, 1862). There are no existing records of the order or position of individual Confederate or Union cavalry units during this attack. Wheeler had about 1,100 men compared to 950 for Stanley and Minty. Stanley attacked the flank of Wheeler while Minty attacked the center.

he found Minty's men on the east side of Overall Creek in the woods. Buford ordered Colonel J. Warren Grigsby's 5th and 6th Consolidated Kentucky Cavalry to lead the attack across the creek while Butler's 3rd Kentucky regiment remained in reserve and the attack was successful. Buford wrote that he "charged the enemy, and drove him back with severe loss upon the lines of his heavy infantry." During this engagement he recorded casualties of eight men, including Major James Chenoweth and Captain William Campbell. He also claimed 10–15 prisoners.[10]

Minty and Stanley Charge the Southern Cavalry

While the situation looked bleak for Stanley's men, the Union cavalry was not to be pushed aside so easily and Stanley met with Minty on the field. At four o'clock, Minty observed Wheeler's cavalry, in force, moving to the right collecting more Union infantry as prisoners. Shadowing the Rebel cavalry, Minty moved at a distance of about six hundred yards. Stanley saw the gray coated enemy moving across the large fallow fields collecting prisoners and he was concerned that the enemy's infantry had moved further north. He soon discovered these were part of Wheeler's dismounted cavalry. The Union cavalry skirmishers held the Southern cavalry at a distance for about half an hour through the volleys fired by the 4th Michigan and 7th Pennsylvania. Stanley pulled all his cavalry together, mounted and moved to face Wheeler. The Federal cavalry formed a battle line in a semicircle about 800 yards long. Together, Minty and Stanley led a coordinated charge, which would end the day for the cavalry.[11]

Teamster John Williams of the 15th Pennsylvania was the wagon master that moved his regimental baggage train near the 7th Pennsylvania cavalry earlier in the day. At this point, Williams, who left his wagons at Stewarts Creek, returned to the regiment in preparation for further action. Williams rode past the area of the Wharton's and Zahm's earlier fight and observed Union corpses devoid of their overcoats, hats and shoes. When he arrived, Stanley was standing with a group of officers in front of a line of dark blue cavalry.

> Almost immediately after, a few mounted figures appeared and halted on the ridge—it was the enemy. More followed; then a long column filed up over the hill, and down the slope a short distance, where they wheeled very prettily into line. A second column soon followed and performed the same manoeuver. Their skirmishers advanced boldly to the base of the hill, and commenced firing at ours. There was artillery, too, we noticed, posted in a clump of trees on the rebel left.

Frank Mix, 7th Pennsylvania, also recalled the grandeur of the two cavalry lines. "They came out with their colors flying formed in line of battle and then we pitched in." By all accounts the emergence of the Southern cavalry onto the field was one of the grandest sights of the war. Lancaster Thomas, 15th Pennsylvania, remarked: "[They] formed a splendid line of battle (which looked as though they were forming dress parade) and in another moment be ready to devour the yankees in front of them."[12]

Wheeler's cavalry faced Stanley, and Buford's small brigade swung to the east toward Widow Burris' house behind Wheeler's men. Without Buford, Wheeler's cavalry outnumbered Minty by only a couple of hundred men. Minty recorded,

> The rebel cavalry had followed us up sharply into the open ground, and now menaced us with three strong lines, two directly in front of my position and one opposite our left flank, with its right thrown well forward, and a strong body of skirmishers in the woods to our right, and threatening that flank.

The adjutant of the 15th Pennsylvania observed, "General Stanley was everywhere, and in a moment he saw the best that could be done was to order a charge. Let's charge them boys! Let's charge them!"[13]

At this point in the day, Stanley was fearless and he decided to put the fighting spirit into his horsemen despite the odds. He knew he had to inspire whatever part of the 15th Pennsylvania Cavalry that would fight. As he divided the assignment of the cavalry, he said to Minty, "You look after those fellows in the front and I will take care of this force," pointing at a group of Wheeler's cavalry on the western flank. Stanley prepared to lead the 4th Michigan. He stopped, considered and Minty recalled Stanley told the men of the 4th Michigan, "'Wait here and I will bring you assistance." He rode over to the reluctant troopers of the 15th Pennsylvania Cavalry. He told the men to prepare to charge the Confederates,

> I then witnessed one of the most heroic scenes of the war. Stanley, standing in his stirrups, his soldierly figure erect, his saber raised straight above his head, in a voice distinctly heard above the noise of battle exclaimed, "The man who does not follow me is a damned coward!" and wheeling his horse dashed back to the two companies of the of the 4th Michigan. The 15th followed and the 4th, and with a raging cheer this little band of heroes, led by the gallant Stanley, charged home into the center of Wharton's [Wheeler's] Brigade and drove it from the field.

Then, Minty moved to face the main body of the Confederate cavalry and Stanley initially moved his command in line with Minty's troopers. Then, he executed a "great right wheel" movement and ordered his men to draw their sabers. He ordered the charge and while Minty's command held the attention of the main Confederate line, Stanley's command slammed into the left flank of Wheeler's cavalry. The attack was successful and the Confederate troopers hustled away. While Stanley was leading his troopers, Minty charged with his regiments which made two charges. Minty recorded the capture of one stand of colors and he noted, "The enemy was again broken and driven from the field."[14]

James Weir, 15th Pennsylvania, recorded in his diary that in the charge the color bearer of the 3rd Tennessee Battalion, which had been reorganized into Carter's 1st Tennessee Cavalry, was hit and dropped the colors. J. C. Reiff, adjutant of the 15th Pennsylvania described the capture of the flag:

> The name of one was Sergeant Henry C. Butcher, of Company B; the other Private L. B. Holt, of Company L. They saw the enemy's flag and coveted it as a prize, but to attempt its capture was to expose themselves to our own as well as the enemy's fire. After deliberating a moment, the prize was too tempting and they rode up, shot the standard bearer, who had advanced some distance in front of his command, and brought the flag into our lines—the two men riding one wounded horse, the other being killed. It was an heroic and audacious act.

The captured flag, from the 3rd Tennessee Cavalry Battalion, carried the motto "Death Before Subjugation." Stanley and Minty fought Wheeler's entire brigade which included the 1st Alabama Cavalry and during the fight Colonel William Wirt Allen's hand was severely, and permanently, wounded.[15]

Captain Frank Mix, 7th Pennsylvania Cavalry, participated in the charge and he wrote to his brother a few days later: "[O]f all the cavalry fighting I ever saw[,] that knocked the spots off from them all.... I do not believe there has been such a cavalry fight during the war." When the charge was over, Sergeant Eugene Bronson, 4th Michigan, recorded, "The number of horses that was killed almost covered the ground." Mix's horse was killed under him during the fight as was Stanley's. Josiah Lewis's horse was killed during the charge, and Lewis barely escaped death. He wrote in a letter of the action during the 4th

Michigan's attack, "My horses head was shot off with a cannon ball and he fell crossways of the cotton rows and fell between them and under him. So, I pulled by boot off trying to get from under him."[16]

The presence of Stanley and Minty leading the charge was very important for the success of the Union cavalry and Trooper John Williams recorded that Stanley riding at the front of the 15th Pennsylvania made a tremendous impact on the men. Williams wrote:

> It was a graceful and fatherly kindness in General to take personal command of our little battalion, for we were almost orphaned of officers. The Colonel had been a prisoner in Richmond since the battle of Antietam; the Lieut.-Colonel was an invalid in Nashville, where he started with us, but was compelled to return, the two majors, were we had learned to confide in and admire, were dead.[17]

As Minty led his section of the charge, he rode out in front of his troops, drew his saber and shouted, "Come on." Then, he turned to his men and yelled, "Shout!" One of the troopers wrote: "[T]he shout we set up drowned the din of battle and we drove them from the field but many a good mare bit the dust there." Next, Minty observed Buford's cavalry brigade which was still south of the lane running by Widow Burris's house, and two opened fences separated these two cavalries. Buford also saw Minty's cavalry riding for him. Buford had just moved his cavalry from the west side of Overall Creek, crossing near the Washington house. Minty moved his cavalry toward Buford at a hard gallop or "lope," as he referred to it. Minty was just about to order a charge when Buford's troopers turned and "made for the cover of the trees." Minty's command held the field north of Widow Burris's house through the night. Both Buford and Wheeler moved back to the Wilkinson Pike and joined Wharton's cavalry there.[18]

Despite Stanley's and Minty's final actions, the Confederates cavalry felt they had won the day. Private Benjamin Burke, 8th Texas Cavalry, recorded, "[T]he day closed after our boys drove them about two or three miles on our left, leaving a great many dead on the field ... the open corn fields was almost blue with dead Yankees." Wheeler wrote little of his actions during this campaign. Of the actions of December 31, he recorded that he arrived at Murfreesboro after sleeping five hours. He had his troopers in the saddle at 2:00 a.m. and moved to the battle "On arriving the line was engaged. We pressed on and attacked enemy on the Murfreesborough and Nashville pike, just north of Overall's Creek. After a brisk engagement we moved across the creek and made an attack on the enemy at that point, driving him for 2 miles and successfully engaging him until dark, when we fell back to the left of our line, where we remained during the night." He made no comments about the final cavalry action of the day.[19]

Colonel J. D. Webb was also wounded along with several others of his 51st Alabama Partisan Rangers in the afternoon action. He was wounded when a shell exploded and a fragment struck his forehead. In addition, eleven troopers of that regiment were wounded in the engagement. The regiment, which had been in numerous fights, had truly become veterans after its actions over the past few days. During this charge the difference in cavalry tactics between the Union and Southern cavalry was again highlighted. While the troopers of the 8th Texas Cavalry expounded the value of revolvers, the Federal troopers saw the value of sabers. N. W. Sample, 15th Pennsylvania, described:

> In this charge, however, we were very successful, the enemy being without sabres and having only single fire guns, which after they delivered one discharge could not be reloaded in time to prevent us from being up on them, so they retreated in not very good order. We got prisoners and their battle-flags.[20]

The Union Cavalry Determines Rosecrans' Decision to Stay and Fight

After the day's battle Rosecrans met with his commanders on the evening of December 31. He asked the question, "Shall we fight it out here, or withdraw to an advantageous position covering our depots at Nashville?" Crittenden declined to offer an opinion but agreed to obey any orders of Rosecrans, and Thomas gave a similar answer. It was McCook who said, "I therefore advise that we retire on Nashville and await reinforcements." The officers looked toward Stanley who said he agreed with McCook's recommendation. Rosecrans thanked the officers for their opinions and inspected the ground he held with Stanley for two hours.[21]

Rosecrans, Stanley, and others rode along the defenses of the army and they spied fires along the west flank of the Union army and to the rear. This caused Rosecrans to conclude to stay and fight, because if the Confederates were that close to cutting off his route of retreat back to Nashville, he had no choice. Ironically, what Rosecrans, McCook and Stanley observed were the campfires of the Union cavalry, in violation of Rosecrans' order, along Overall Creek. Rosecrans exclaimed to McCook, "They have got entirely in our rear, and are forming a line of battle by torchlight." Unknown to Rosecrans, these were not the fires of the enemy, but his own men, the cavalry. At 1 a.m., Stanley asked him, "'General, what are you going to do.' He immediately answered, 'By God's help, I am going to beat the enemy right here.' No more was said and we immediately went to bed."[22]

Rosecrans returned to headquarters and told the commanding generals, "Well, gentlemen, we shall not retreat, but fight it out here and to the front. Go at once to your posts and hold your commands ready to receive any attack from the enemy." Rosecrans concluded to establish a defensive position and not resume his advance until the arrival of ammunition and supplies from Nashville.[23]

Lieutenant Colonel James D. Webb, 51st Alabama Partisan Rangers, wounded when a shell fragment struck his forehead (Alabama Department of Archives and History).

Summary of the Fighting on December 31

At the end of a difficult day, the Union cavalry had stabilized the extended right flank of the army. Rosecrans' and Stanley's policy of rearming the cavalry contributed to its efficiency during the battle. The Confederate cavalry had many troopers armed only with shotguns, while others had revolvers only, and still others had only long muskets. The 4th Michigan, 5th Tennessee, and 7th Pennsylvania cavalries held the Union line and the remainder of the Union cavalry settled in for the night north of Asbury Church. While Wharton's cavalry had gotten some booty from the Union supply train, it was minimal. General John Wharton recorded he was only able to capture five or six guns, 400 prisoners, some mules and 327 cattle. The actions of Wheeler's brigade on the battlefield during the day were also minimal. On the other hand, Wharton's cavalry played a paramount role along west flank of the Union army and swept all before it, infantry and cavalry for most of the morning. Perhaps Wheeler had been concerned that Stanley's and Minty's afternoon actions were an attempt to turn the Confederate left flank, but he soon determined the Union cavalry was making no further efforts to drive forward. Confident there no further risk to the flank, Wheeler retired his cavalry for the day, exhausted after the entire expedition around Rosecrans' army and the day's battle. Edward Longacre, Wheeler's biography, gave the victory to Stanley and Minty because the charge by the Union cavalry surprised and caught Wheeler's men in "mid-movement." Joseph Vale, 7th Pennsylvania, supported Longacre's conclusion and explained the while Wheeler was moving to face Minty's larger force, Stanley's charge struck the Confederate line in the flank.[24]

While the day was difficult for the Union cavalry, it was no picnic for Confederate cavalry. An analysis of the 2nd Tennessee Cavalry (CSA) at Stones River concluded: "At Stones River, the regiment faltered when it charged Federal cavalry, and had to be reinforced. In both instances, a lack of effective weapons may have contributed to the regiment's inability to successfully execute offensive tasks." William Tarver, 1st Alabama Cavalry, recalled "I received a slight wound at Murfreesboro. and the Yankees killed two horses under me, and I had many narrow escapes." Perhaps, the most visible casualty was Colonel William Wirt Allen's hand injury:

> At a critical stage of this battle one of the most brilliant charges of the war was made by Wheeler's First brigade, and conspicuous at the head of his regiment was the handsome and intrepid Allen, his sabre flashing high in the air. Suddenly his right hand was shattered and at the same moment his horse was killed. Mounting behind his bugler, he refused to be taken from the field until he was carried to the head of his column, and, holding his bloody hand aloft, several of his fingers dangling, he called upon his boys "to avenge this."

Allen's wound caused permanent damage and he was unable to use his hand afterward. In addition, Lieutenant Colonel James Webb received a wound to his head during the day's battle.[25]

John Pegram's Confederate cavalry brigade remained in place on the east side of the Army of Tennessee during the fight on December 31 and would not see action again until January 2. The poor communications on the Confederate right flank resulted in the criticism of Pegram's actions during the day and this was significant, although poorly understood. The communication problems between the cavalry and infantry command would continue into January 2.[26]

On the Confederate side of the battlefield, Colonel Baxter Smith explained the Southern forces were celebrating because the action was "victorious and exultant." Wheeler had just destroyed several wagon trains while circling Rosecrans' army and Wharton had an exceptional day. Baxter Smith accompanied Wharton to Murfreesboro to Bragg's headquarters. He described Polk as "buoyant and in the finest spirits." Bragg, on the other hand, was not happy and Smith felt Bragg had received "depressing" news even though the Confederates had carried the day.[27]

The human results of the day's battle were described by a member of Thomas Crittenden's staff, G. C. Kniffin, who rode by the wounded along Overall Creek where much of the cavalry action had taken place. He described the situation:

> All through the night the ambulances passed to and fro on the road to the hospitals, where further torture awaited the wounded, unless the angel of death kindly relieved them of the ministrations of the surgeons. A space twenty yards in front of the White House, near Overall's Creek, was covered with the mangled forms of men awaiting their turn upon the operating tables. Inside were groups of surgeons with sleeves rolled up to the elbows, their brawny arms red with blood, one handling the saw, another the knife, another the probe, while others bound up the bleeding stumps and turned the patient, henceforth the Nation's ward, over to nurses, who bore them tenderly away. In a corner lay a ghastly heap of arms and legs and hands and feet, useless forevermore. The busy fingers which had indited the last fond message to the anxious wife or mother would never caress them more. Does this horrible recital grate upon the ear? It is as much a part of the history of a battle as is the furious charge and repulse from which it resulted.

W. L. Curry, 1st Ohio Cavalry, recorded that the wounded cavalrymen who were captured were taken to a large storeroom with a dirt floor covered with straw. There were no cots and only a few blankets for the two hundred men crammed into the room to get them out of the cold night air. There was a single fireplace in the room, which held a large fire. The surgeon of the 1st Ohio, Dr. Randolph Wirth, and his hospital steward worked throughout the night, caring for the wounded and amputating limbs. Wirth had no chloroform and only a small amount of morphine as he worked on the wounded men. When Wirth appealed to their Southern captors for chloroform, he was told none was available. Wirth and his steward remained with the men until the Union army captured the town and freed the wounded.[28]

Confederate artillery officer, James E. Magee, recorded in his diary: "The groans of the poor wounded was heartrending. I could not repress a few falling tears.... Many, many were chilled to death.... Alas! Alas! The horror of war."[29]

At the end of the day's fighting, Lucy Virginia French, a civilian, wrote of the tension of those not in the battle and the great happiness of the Southern fighting forces:

> God be praised the Tidings were glad tidings of great joy! ...They had whipped the enemy—loss heavy on both sides.... And when I went to bed—as I lay there so comfortable & cosy I could not go sleep for thinking of the many poor fellows who were then lying on the battle-field—some cold in death—others shivering with cold & writhing with pain. The cold dear moon looked down upon them, for it was a brilliant, frosty night—but who was there with a warm kind glance to cheer their last agonized hours? And who when they lay stiff and stark would bend over them with a tear, & linger by a moment to look upon the clay-cold lips & kiss him for his mother? The surgeons are busy tonight—the little city of Murfreesboro is full of the wounded. God help them.[30]

For the cavalrymen in the saddle, they were in for a long cold night after the fighting during the day. T. F. Dornblaser, 7th Pennsylvania, recalled:

> We sat on our horses weary and hungry. With heavy eyelids and distended pupils, we strained the optic nerve to penetrate the thickening fog—to catch the outline of the victor of yesterday and the antagonist of tomorrow. We shall never forget how hard it was to keep wide awake. The eyelids would drop in spite of all we could do. By beating the skull with the fist, and pinching the ears, we managed to keep sufficiently wakeful to halt the "Grand Rounds."[31]

The bloody first day of the Battle of Stones River was over for the cavalry of both sides. The Confederate cavalry had won the day, despite some nagging problems: Wharton's failure to control his troopers with the Union's large supply train and repulse; Wheeler's inability to deal with Stanley and Minty; and finally the poor communications on the Confederate right flank. The Union cavalry had issues of its own, Zahm's brigade was driven off the field, the lack of coordination of the cavalry regiments deprived the Union cavalry an ability to fend off Wharton's attack, and Wheeler's success at the rear of the Union army. If Kennett could have combined all his regiments to form a solid defense north of Wilkinson Pike, there is little doubt Wharton could have been contained. In war, the defensive position generally trumped an offensive one even with unequal numbers of men. Zahm alone had a thousand men, was driven from the field but combined with the 3rd Kentucky, 4th U.S., 3rd Indiana and 7th Pennsylvania cavalries, this would have been a more equal fight. Even throwing regiments in piecemeal, the Union cavalry supported by infantry eventually stopped the attack. Finally, the presence of White's Tennessee Battery with Wharton's brigade was an important factor in the Southern cavalry's success during the fighting. Historian, Thomas Connelly, would conclude: "All Wharton needed to hold the pike was support." He had none and was repulsed.[32]

In summary, the Confederate army had won the day. Could there be little doubt Rosecrans would withdraw back toward Nashville? But Rosecrans had faced situations like this before, at Iuka and Corinth, where he was roughly handled on the first day of the battle and won the battles. He realized his army remained undefeated. Being on the defensive gave an army great advantages, and Rosecrans had a good position for his artillery. Perhaps, this was why Bragg was in such a foul mood when Wharton and Baxter Smith reached headquarters full of victory. Bragg was a smart, though unlikeable, general. He realized he had squandered an opportunity during the day and he faced an unbeaten foe as the new year began. Despite his gloomy countenance, Bragg believed Rosecrans would retreat.[33]

12. Cavalry Actions (January 1–5)

I there saw enough of war.—
Captain Robert Burns

A New Year

While the Union and Confederate cavalries clashed, it was the infantry regiments that suffered the carnage of the hard fought battle on December 31. Bragg had hoped Rosecrans would withdraw after the previous day's battle, but at daybreak the Union line remained unchanged. On January 1, the two opposing armies stared across the fields and streams at each other; but the Confederate cavalry was not idle. Bragg ordered Wheeler to make a reconnaissance of the enemy's position and to stop any flow of supplies by again attacking the rear of Rosecrans' army. More importantly, Bragg needed to know if Rosecrans intended to withdraw or if he received reinforcements. This meant another long day for Wheeler, Wharton and Buford, and also for the Union cavalry of Zahm's Second Brigade and part of the Union Reserve Brigade. Wheeler moved his brigade, along with Buford's and Wharton's, to La Vergne and planned to operate on the rear of the Union army.[1]

Nathaniel W. Sample, 15th Pennsylvania Cavalry, slept in battle line after the final action along the Nashville Pike the day before. It was dark when Sample laid down on his blanket and when he awoke he found his head was touching the dead body of a Confederate cavalryman. Sample merely commented, "He was frozen stiff." Several of the regiment had the same experience. Trooper Wilmon Blackmar also commented, "The dead lay all around us, covered with frost." The regiment soon found a breakfast of corn on the cob and horse steaks. They mounted and resumed their duty north along the road to Nashville. The Confederate soldiers found the same sleeping arrangements as the 15th Pennsylvania. John Crittenden, 34th Alabama Infantry, wrote his wife: "We camped that night upon the battle field surrounded with the dead and wounded. It was a terrible thing to lay and listen to the calls of the wounded for help."[2]

Many of the wagon trains which were so vulnerable the previous day had been moved further to the rear and the process began of sending convoys of wagons carrying the wounded to Nashville, then returning loaded with fresh supplies. The Nashville Pike was the best and most direct route for resupplies to reach the Union army. While Rosecrans and Bragg faced each other along Stones River on January 1, Rosecrans' supply line soon became a target for the Confederate cavalry. Wheeler had previously raided Rosecrans' supply trains on December 30, and the Union army had lost valuable supplies during the first day of the battle. For the soldiers to be able to fight, they needed rations and ammunition, and the trains needed to pass between Murfreesboro and Nashville for Rosecrans to remain on the field. Many of the Confederate generals expected Rosecrans to withdraw after the previous day's battle. Baxter Smith, 4th Tennessee Cavalry, agreed with the expectation of an imminent withdrawal of the Federal army still in such confusion.[3]

The Confederate Cavalry Attack North of Murfreesboro

The Union cavalry was assigned duty to cover the movement of two wagon trains from the battlefield at Murfreesboro to Nashville on the morning of January 1. The larger of the two trains proceeded first to Nashville under the guard of Lewis Zahm with the largest body of cavalry. Zahm reasoned if the Confederate cavalry was in the rear, it probably prepared to ambush the first in the convoy of wagons. A second wagon train of about thirty wagons followed the first train and it was guarded by the 2nd Tennessee Cavalry and the 22nd Indiana Infantry. "Long before daylight the first of the year, Wheeler & his bold followers were on the way around the wearied & broken army," wrote historian John Dubose. Wheeler took most of the Confederate cavalry (three brigades) north to the rear of the Union army and, at noon, discovered the wagon trains along the Nashville Pike. "Quick as thought, Wheeler formed his men by fours, taking position at the head of the column. The bugler at his side, he spoke in quick, low tones, 'Sound the Charge!'" Wheeler and Buford rode together to attack the larger train and Wharton's brigade descended on the smaller train. Seeing the large number of enemy cavalry, the 2nd Tennessee (U.S.) rode for their lives, the teamsters panicked, and ninety-five of the infantrymen surrendered to the cavalry in gray. With the 2nd Tennessee Cavalry retreating in face of the larger force, and after burning 30 wagons, Wheeler sought more booty.[4]

For Lewis Zahm's Second Cavalry Brigade, January 1 began early after the difficult time his troopers had experienced the previous day, but his horses were fresher than the other Union regiments. Zahm's brigade was saddled and moving at 3:00 a.m., being ordered to escort ambulances and empty ammunition wagons to Nashville and then to escort badly needed supplies to replenish those used, destroyed or captured on the previous day. When Zahm's cavalry reached Stewarts Creek, it was delayed by the movement of an infantry division's supply train moving along the same road for about an hour. His patrols reported the movement of Confederate cavalry converging on his position from the west and Zahm hastened the wagon train he guarded to move at a "brisk walk." The supply train successfully reached La Vergne and Zahm allowed the train to continue on a northern route; and he placed his cavalry in battle line on the "flats" at La Vergne facing Wheeler's two brigades which were riding in his direction. Zahm's flankers first encountered Wheeler's advance guard and sent a volley into them. Then, Zahm sent riders to the wagon train telling the teamsters to head north at a trot.[5]

Wharton's attack on the smaller wagon train totally unnerved all present. Colonel Joseph Burke and his 10th Ohio Infantry, acting as the provost guard and positioned at Stewarts Creek, observed the chaos that reigned as the survivors of the attack ran for a safe position. Colonel Joseph Burke and the 10th Ohio Infantry protected the bridge which had been won during Crittenden's advance a few days before. At one o'clock, Burke saw the remnants of the Southern cavalry's attack rush northward along the Nashville Pike. "[A] squadron of affrighted negroes came charging at full gallop from Murfreesborough toward Stewarts Creek, and with such impetuosity and recklessness that over 100 passed the bridge before I could check the progress of the main cavalcade." When Burke ordered his men to stop the panic, many of the panicked men ran past the provost guard and continued northward. Included in the rush were riderless horses, cavalry, and infantry which "came streaming down the road and pouring through the woods on their way toward the bridge." Despite his best efforts to curb the panic, the men were so terrified no attempt of stopping them worked and they continued toward safety. Burke also had added support of four companies of the 4th Michigan Cavalry under command of Lieutenant Colonel William H. Dickinson, and Lieutenant Nathaniel Newell's section of 1st Ohio Artillery was already in place at Stewarts Creek. Burke's soldiers detected the presence of the Wheeler's cavalry that morning but he was in a secure position, supported by cavalry and artillery. Wheeler concluded to look for easier prey and by-passed Burke and the Stewarts Creek bridge. Baxter Smith's Tennessee cavalry participated in the raid and he described the scene: "It looked like war indeed to see that long line of wagons on fire and to hear and see the frequent explosion of shells."[6]

There were many wagons several miles in the rear of Rosecrans' army and many stragglers still wandered along the Nashville Pike. James King, 11th Michigan Infantry, explained that the quartermaster sent the regiment's supply wagon another mile to rear and away from the fighting near Murfreesboro. After completing this task, the teamsters of the regiment were pressed into escorting the convoys of wagons moving northward to Nashville. As he moved north, Wheeler's cavalry attacked. King wrote: "[A] body of Rebel cavalry had attacked in the rear and were burning wagons and supplies. We started and were near La Vergne when the train was attacked in front and a number of the wagons burned."[7]

The train of the 7th Pennsylvania Cavalry was also part of the wagons destroyed by Southern cavalry on January 1. The 7th Pennsylvania's train had moved five miles to the rear during the previous day's battle and was parked just south of La Vergne when it was attacked. The train, consisting of twenty-three wagons, were all captured and burned. All of the company books were burned during the raid. Gerould Otis Gibson, a teamster, recorded the train was attacked by a large body of cavalry with three artillery pieces. To compound the problem for Gibson's wagon train was the disorganization along Nashville Pike "jammed full of stragglers ... they could not be brought to a stand or nearly all the train could have been saved, but run like sheep." Despite the attempt to reform the regiments after the previous day's battle, many of the soldiers still wandered unnerved and aimlessly in the rear of the army.[8]

While Wharton burned the first wagon train guarded by the 2nd Tennessee, Wheeler rode toward Zahm's column protecting another larger wagon train. Along the way, he dispatched Wharton's brigade to deal with the 1st Michigan Engineers and Mechanics' small outpost at La Vergne; but Wharton was to find a regiment which would obstinately defend its position. Meanwhile, Zahm, with only the 3rd Ohio Cavalry, 4th Ohio Cavalry, and 15th Pennsylvania Cavalry, faced Wheeler's and Buford's brigades. Zahm discovered he was being attacked when he found the 2nd Tennessee Cavalry riding hard north, toward him and toward the rear. Zahm threw a company of cavalry across the road to stem the retreat. Zahm proceeded to stop the Confederate pursuit, only to see the 2nd Tennessee again race to the rear "like sheep." While the 2nd Tennessee showed no willingness to fight, the 15th Pennsylvania Cavalry which had duty as rearguard showed even less. When the Confederates attacked, the 15th Pennsylvania ran off in every direction to avoid the fight. Zahm's remaining cavalry repulsed the Confederate attacks twice at the rear of the train at the cost of only 2 or 3 wagons and he saved some cannons which were almost captured. While Wheeler attacked the rear, Zahm was held in check and the wagon train proceeded northward until the Union cavalry was one half mile from the rear wagon. He noted, "The Anderson Troop, I am sorry to say, were of very little benefit to me, as the majority of them ran as soon as we were attacked." Trooper James Weir of the 15th Pennsylvania merely recorded in his diary that the regiment worked with the 3rd Ohio Cavalry and when Wheeler attacked "we repulsed them."[9]

Zahm observed Wheeler moving into line and prepared his cavalry to receive another charge from Wheeler and Buford. Skirmishers from both sides exchanged fire. Expecting a full charge from Wheeler's larger force, Zahm was surprised to see the Southern troopers re-form in columns of four and move northward intent on destroying the supply train. Wheeler took his troopers around a hill and toward the train, now about a half mile ahead. Zahm sent his flankers ahead to attempt to prevent the attack and a courier reported to Zahm that Wheeler had not reached the head of the train. Zahm's column rode hard to reach the train. After riding for two miles, Wheeler's cavalry attacked Zahm's rear and the Federals successfully repulsed the attack, and the Southern cavalry again attacked only to be repulsed. Then, Zahm sent a charge of his own into the pursuers and chased them for over a mile. During the skirmishing, the Union cavalry recorded killing nine of Wheeler's troopers, wounding eleven and capturing two. In return, Zahm reported only minor wounds to his men and exclaimed that none of the wagons fell into the hands of the enemy, although four or five wagons were damaged and left behind. The damage to the wagons resulted from the "stampede" of the 2nd Tennessee riding through Zahm's column after they had been attacked by Wharton. Zahm arrived in Nashville at nine o'clock p.m. after a long day in the saddle.[10]

Sergeant Isaac Skillman, 3rd Ohio Cavalry, described the fight which began half way between Nashville and Murfreesboro, near La Vergne, in his diary,

> We met Wheeler. He tried to get to the train but we fought his men off each time. We kept the mule teams on the run. Two miles further on, they charged us in the rear. The Anderson Troop was our rear guard, or supposed to be. At the first charge of the rebs, the Troops came rushing through ... each one trying to be the first one to Nashville. Perhaps they are running yet.... The Third Ohio checked the attacking rebs after the Anderson fighters got out of the way. Had a quite a hard little fight but repulsed them.

History was not kind to the 15th Pennsylvania Cavalry's actions during the day and one record remains of the action of the 15th Pennsylvania Cavalry. Lancaster Thomas recorded in a letter that the teamsters began the rout, by cutting the teams from the wagons and trying to escape; and finally he felt much too exposed to the gun fire and simply rode into the woods to avoid the attack.[11]

Not all of the 15th Pennsylvania Cavalry joined in the stampede of the regiment. One member of the regiment described the fate of a squad of six men assigned to protect the wagon train. When the Southern cavalry swept down on the train near La Vergne, panic ensued. Someone yelled for the cavalry to abandon the wagons which resulted in a panic among the teamsters who whipped their teams. A few of the 15th Pennsylvania Cavalry tried to stop the panic and hold a line against the raiders. Suddenly, the Confederate cavalry surrounded the troopers demanding, "Do you surrender?" Seeing the futility of his situation, Trooper Ball Colton and others said yes. As he was hurried away as a prisoner, Colton observed trooper Orlando Weikel lying "with his head over the edge of the bridge just gasping." Zahm's counter attack sent the Southern cavalry riding for the trees but not before they successfully burned part of the train and captured several prisoners.[12]

Many of the wagons which moved northward carried the wounded and the bodies of the dead after the previous day's battle. A teamster of the 15th Pennsylvania Cavalry described the gruesome situation as those on wagons attempted to avoid capture:

> We had left the road ... cutting across fields, and all the time at a jog trot. The tailboard of our wagon got loose and the body of Major Rosengarten commenced sliding down from a pile of bodies. There was nothing to do but stop our wagon, crawl in over the bodies and lift the major's body back to its place, then start off again.

The problem kept recurring and the wagon plodded along, but it stopped so many times it became separated from the other wagons. The teamsters were not attacked, and they concluded the Confederates thought since they were all alone they must be a decoy. Eventually, the wagon made it safely to Nashville.[13]

Wharton Attacks the 1st Michigan Engineers

Colonel William P. Innes commanded three hundred and ninety-one men of the 1st Michigan Engineers and Mechanics on the morning of January 1. The 1st Michigan Engineers had had a rocky few months recently with the Union Army and the bureaucracy of the government had prevented the men of the regiment from being paid. Like the 15th Pennsylvania Cavalry, about 100 men mutinied and refused to perform their duty on November 8 until they were paid. Two days later about one quarter of the regiment joined the mutiny, but on December 1 the issue was resolved. However, those who mutinied were arrested and sentenced to thirty days of hard labor. For the remainder of the regiment the daily duties continued and Innes moved toward La Vergne after building a bridge over Mill Creek on December 30. When he arrived, Innes found confusion and destruction in the aftermath of Wheeler's raid on the supply train that day. He settled his regiment about three-quarters of a mile south of the town on a hill and he set up his headquarters in a cabin. After seeing the destruction of the Southern cavalry, he placed his wagons in a semicircle and built a defensive position behind cedar logs on December 30 and 31. While the men were engineers and mechanics, they were also armed. Most of the men carried 1842 vintage muskets, although about twenty-five percent of the men had newer Enfield and Springfield muskets. About one third of the men were veterans, having seen action during the Perryville Campaign.[14]

On the morning after the first day's battle, Union supply wagons, ambulances, and ammunition wagons rolled between Murfreesboro and

Colonel William P. Innes, 1st Michigan Engineers—"We don't surrender much."

Nashville, and Innes's men formed a line across the Nashville Pike and tried to stop as many stragglers as possible from going to Nashville. From Innes's position east of the Nashville Pike and south of La Vergne on January 1, he observed Lewis Zahm's cavalry escorting ambulances and empty supply and ammunition wagons northward. Still to the south, the 2nd Tennessee Cavalry and the soldiers from the 22nd Indiana Infantry escorted thirty wagons. Wharton's cavalry swept down on the 2nd Tennessee and sent the troopers riding for their lives. Innes became aware of the presence of the Confederate cavalry when he heard the explosion of gunfire as Wharton attacked the smaller wagon train. Next, Innes heard more gunfire north when Wheeler attacked Zahm's wagon train. In addition, Innes had his own small mounted patrol which reported back to him that Wharton's troopers were destroying the wagon train. This gave Innes time to pull his command together and to further prepare the defenses. It didn't take long and as Innes feared, a Confederate cavalry patrol discovered his position, but his men, securely behind their walls, unleashed a volley into the patrol. The patrol quickly rode away, but reported to Wharton the presence of an isolated regiment on a hill south of La Vergne. Wharton then decided to capture them, but he was to be surprised by the tenacity of the defenders.[15]

At two o'clock, Wharton's cavalry arrived and surrounded the engineers. Having such a large force and effectively surrounding Innes, he sent a flag truce and a demanded that Innes surrender. The Federal colonel refused and according to newspaperman William Bickham, Innes's reply was "Tell General Wheeler I'll see him d—d first." Then Wharton gave the command to attack the encampment with his cavalry supported with artillery, but Innes's regiment held its position through several attacks. According to Innes, Wharton made seven attacks; but in Wharton's report he stated that he attacked four times simultaneously from three different sides with Cox's 1st Confederate, Malone's 14th Alabama Battalion, and Baxter Smith's 4th Tennessee cavalries. The attacks, mounted and dismounted, were described by one the defenders as the Confederate attack surged forward "discharging their pieces and wheeling to the left when they found our defenses so good they could not gallop their horses over them." Then, the Southern cavalry settled into an afternoon of attacks on the small outpost.[16]

Wharton tried all he could to dislodge the stubborn Union regiment, including, sending a group of Southern cavalry in the guise of Union soldiers in an attempt to breach the Union defense. Innes's men remained out of sight in their defenses until the Confederates attacked and then they appeared and unleashed furious volleys into the attackers. At five o'clock Wharton sent another demand for surrender under a flag of truce and alternate versions of the event are recorded. One records Captain Marcus Grant, representing Innes, under the flag of truce, who replied: "We don't surrender much." Another version of the events attributes the reply to Innes. But this defiant reply would become famous and provide the identity of the regiment for the remainder of the war. The principles returned to their respective lines and the battle continued. Soon, the sun began setting and Wharton sent a final flag of truce asking permission to remove his wounded and dead. Innes stoutly replied, "No." Instead he said he would handle that chore once Wharton departed.[17]

Baxter Smith, part of Wharton's brigade, described the attacks on the 1st Michigan Engineers: "We made repeated efforts to dislodge a Federal force that was fortified near La Vergne, but without success. We destroyed wagons and captured prisoners within 100 yards of them," but could not defeat them. Wharton broke off his attacks and recorded, "My loss in Murray's, Smith's, and Cox's regiments and Malone's battalion in officers and men was very considerable." James Blackburn, 8th Texas, recounted the wounding of Colonel Harrison, who was thought to be invincible by those in his regiment.

> On the second day of this battle, Billy Savers, his Adjutant, sat on his horse beside him under a heavy fire. Colonel Harrison leaned over to Savers and whispered, "I am wounded, but don't say anything about it on account of the men." Billy wanted him off the field, but he refused to go. It proved to be a flesh wound in the hip, not very serious, and he stayed with and commanded the regiment throughout the battle.[18]

In the battle, the 1st Michigan Engineers lost two men killed, nine wounded and five missing. Innes remained in possession of Wharton's casualties of six killed, six wounded and seven prisoners. Innes noted that the prisoners reported Wharton's losses to be between forty and fifty. The casualties were not insignificant. Innes demonstrated the value of having good engineers construct defenses and he demonstrated the 1st Michigan Engineers were not to be taken lightly. At the end of the day, the soldiers of the regiment surrounded their colonel, picked him up and carried him on their shoulders while marching around their camp shouting, "'We don't surrender much.'"[19]

In a less than flattering event, the 4th Michigan Cavalry failed to relieve the pressure on Innes's position. The regiment had been assisting Joseph Burke's 10th Ohio Infantry defend the Stewarts Creek bridge. Burke became aware of Innes's situation and he sent four companies of the 4th Michigan Cavalry supported by a section of artillery to break the siege. For two hours Burke heard the battle rage and the muskets and cannons were clearly heard. Burke assumed all was going as planned until a civilian arrived at his headquarters with a dispatch from Innes asking for reinforcements. Burke wrote, "[T]he astonishing information that the troops I sent up under Lieutenant-Colonel Dickinson were on their way back to me without having fired a shot, and the rebels were burning the trains."[20]

Concluding Events on Janaury 1

Meanwhile along Zahm's path, the retreat of the two Federal cavalry regiments stampeded some of the supply wagons and resulted in a few breakdowns of wagons, otherwise the wagons successfully moved north. Despite the poor performance of the 2nd Tennessee and 15th Pennsylvania Cavalry, Zahm coordinated his remaining regiments with the 4th Michigan Cavalry and some infantry and finally drove Wheeler away. Lieutenant Colonel Joe Burke, in charge of provost duties, made a point in his report to mention Lieutenant James Gilbert, 2nd Tennessee Cavalry, as a member of the cavalry who was connected with "the disgraceful panic," but Burke also noted that Lieutenant Joseph Rendelbrook, 4th U.S. Cavalry, and the non-commissioned officers and men of his command, and also Lieutenant Thomas Maple, 15th Pennsylvania Cavalry, for their exemplary service during this engagement. But overall, the Southern cavalry had another successful raid the Union supply trains, but less so than before. John Wharton claimed possession of about 100 wagons, 150 prisoners, 300 mules, and 1 piece of artillery during his part of the raid. Wheeler, on the other hand, came away with little.[21]

While Zahm escorted supply trains, Minty's First Cavalry Brigade stayed at the front with the Army of the Cumberland and skirmished with enemy cavalry pickets. Robert Burns, adjutant of the 4th Michigan, recorded the cavalry was positioned in battle line along the right flank of the army. Burns recorded in his letter, "I had not been there 15 minutes when the enemy opened on us with artillery. The shells burst in all directions about us, and but two or three men were wounded. I could distinctly see the shells flying over us." Minty maintained this duty on January 1, 2, and 3. Part of Stanley's Reserve Brigade also remained with the army on January 1 and had little to report, except some skirmishing.[22]

The day had been too much for the remainder of the 15th Pennsylvania Cavalry. Even of those who had fought on December 31 and January 1, many returned to Nashville and joined their fellow soldiers in refusing to do their duty on January 3. Many of those who fought during the first few days of the Battle of Stones River joined the mutineers in an attempt to force a resolution of the complaints of the regiment.[23]

While the cavalry actions were taking place in the rear, Rosecrans continued to develop his defenses while he awaited the attack from Bragg. The 15th Ohio Infantry which had suffered during the attack the day before was put to work in deluding Bragg about the condition of the Federal Army.

> We were shortly called into line and the brigade, Colonel Gibson in command, moved back along the pike. We moved out behind a ridge which hid our movement from the enemy and then marched back in plain view of his skirmishers and cavalry. We did this a number of times, for the purpose, it was said, of giving the rebels the impression that we were receiving reinforcements. We were a nervous lot, although we made a bluff of seeming as brave as ever.[24]

Despite Wheeler's successes on January 1, the Union army and cavalry were adapting to prevent further destruction of communications and supply lines. Zahm's Ohio cavalry was successful in its efforts as were the 1st Michigan Engineers, but the 15th Pennsylvania, 2nd Tennessee and some of 4th Michigan Cavalry had less than stellar performances. On the Confederate side of the field, Wharton suffered a decided setback and had the casualties to prove it. In the end, Wheeler reported that his cavalry had again carried the day and Bragg was ecstatic and he reflected this in his communications to Richmond:

> The enemy has yielded his strong position and is failing back. We occupy whole field and shall follow him. General Wheeler with his cavalry made a complete circuit of their army on the 30th and 31st; captured and destroyed 300 wagons loaded with baggage and commissary stores; paroled 700 prisoners. He is again behind them and captured an ordnance train today. We secured several thousand stand small-arms. The body of General Sill was left on the field and three others are reported killed. God has granted us a happy New Year.

But, Bragg's elation was premature. Rosecrans was still firmly in place north of Stones River and his infantry and cavalry remained undefeated. Wheeler's biographer, Edward Longacre, reflected on Wheeler's repulse during the day and his report.

> Wheeler's repulse ended his efforts to wreak havoc on Rosecrans' communications. It also gave the lie to Wheeler's boast that he had 'captured and destroyed a large number of wagons and stores.' No more than a dozen vehicles, which had broken down and become defenseless, had fallen into his clutches this day.

The Union infantry and cavalry were adapting to deal with Wheeler's raids in rear.[25]

At the end of the first day of January, Wheeler returned with good news for the commanding general of the Army of Tennessee. It appeared that Rosecrans was ready to withdraw, but Wheeler's claims of success and description of the rear of the Federal army gave Bragg the wrong impression. Bragg wrote; "No doubt this induced the enemy to send large escorts of artillery, infantry, and cavalry with later trains, and thus the impression was made on our ablest cavalry commanders that a retrograde movement was going on." This faulty intelligence from Wheeler helped Bragg form the decision to firmly hold

January 2—Wharton and Pegram in Breckinridge's Attack

Wheeler's cavalry returned to the friendly confines of the Confederate line after dark on January 1 and the following morning they were given an opportunity to rest and resupply; but Bragg wanted further evidence that Rosecrans planned to stay and fight or retreat to Nashville. Wheeler's and Buford's brigades were ordered again to strike the Union rear on January 3 and at the same time, definitely determine Rosecrans' intentions. John Wharton's brigade which had been heavily involved in fighting over the past few days joined Pegram's brigade on the right flank of the Army of Tennessee. In addition, Wharton was given command of all the cavalry in this section of the battlefield, even though Pegram outranked him by a week or so. While the Confederate cavalry was attacking wagon trains near La Vergne the day before, Rosecrans ordered Colonel Samuel Beatty, in command of Van Cleve's division supported by Colonel William Grose's brigade of John Palmer's division, to move to the east side of Stones River. This Federal line of infantry threw up hastily prepared defenses and faced Breckinridge's division. During the night, Grose's brigade returned to the west side of the river, but returned early the next morning to support Beatty accompanied by the 3rd Wisconsin Artillery. This movement presented a significant problem for Bragg. The placement of artillery on the east side of the river made the Confederate infantry around Round Forest vulnerable to shelling from Beatty's position. Bragg could not allow the Union troops to remain in position on the east side of Stones River and at the same time if Bragg could capture and hold the high ground at this location he could continue to shell Rosecrans' army utilizing the concentration of artillery on Wayne's Hill. At two o'clock on January 2, Bragg summoned Breckinridge and then ordered him to lead an attack on Beatty's troops. Breckinridge's attack which began at 4:00 p.m. was initially successful and his large division of more than 5,000 men sent the Union troops retreating back across Stones River. Rosecrans moved reinforcements to support the retreating Union infantry and then turned to his artillery to stop the Confederate attack. As Breckinridge's Confederates advanced, a "murderous fire" of fifty-seven Union cannons decimated them resulting in the loss of more than 1,800 Confederate soldiers, killed or wounded, in an hour's time.[27]

Many watched in awe as the Confederate attack ground to a halt. On the Union side, Lewis Wolfley, 3rd Kentucky Cavalry (U.S.), observed the battle on January 2 and understood the implications. "I have never heard anything equal it since I have been in the service. In fact, all the time it was going on as though it was the turning point. I know things were looking bad for us and if we drive this time we were lost."[28]

In the assessments of the fighting on January 2, Breckinridge and Bragg both wrote that Wharton and Pegram had been ordered to cooperate in the attack, but both reports revealed that the Confederate cavalry played no part in the fighting except in covering the retreat of Breckinridge's division. A cursory view of these reports reflect poorly on Pegram, who was still stinging from allegations of poor intelligence on December 31, and on Wharton, Wheeler's ablest brigade commander. The details of the events involving the cavalry during this attack show the state of poor communications and the poor relationships between Bragg and Breckinridge rather than a negative performance by the cavalry, but the Confederate cavalry would again suffer a blow to its reputation.

The same problem of communication between the cavalry, Bragg, and Breckinridge which existed on December 31 still existed on January 2. While historians have repeatedly criticized Pegram for his lack of up-to-date intelligence on December 31, the same problem appears to have included Wharton, on January 2. The communication issues demand a better explanation than two cavalry brigade commanders not performing their duty during a major battle. And the communication problem during this action also lies with Bragg's inability to communicate with his cavalry and his infantry commanders. Breckinridge clearly stated in his report of the attack: "Pegram and Wharton, who, with some cavalry and a battery, were beyond the point where my right would rest when the new line of battle should be formed, were directed, as the general informed me, to protect my right and co-operate in the attack." But Bragg simply wrote: "The cavalry force was left entirely out of the action." Breckinridge's report puts the responsibility of ordering Wharton and Pegram to support the attack on Bragg while Bragg, in return, blamed Breckinridge for not utilizing all the resources allotted for his attack.[29]

Breckinridge made no further comment on the cavalry's inaction, but the author of the history of the Orphan Brigade simply recorded:

> The main body of cavalry which had been ordered to join in the attack failed to come up in time; but the order to Gen. Breckinridge was of such a nature that he did not deem himself allowed that discretionary power which would justify delay; and he made his dispositions at once. The infantry, two batteries of the artillery, and the cavalry present, were put under arms, and the order to march was given.

In other words to some in the infantry, it appeared that the cavalry saw the futility of the attack and chose not to sacrifice themselves. This was not the case. Simply, the cavalry had no clear orders to join in the fight.[30]

Unfortunately, John Pegram's records of the actions of his brigade are not recorded and only John A. Wharton's record exists regarding the cavalry actions in support of Breckinridge's attack. Wharton's report reflected negatively on Pegram's ability to direct the action of his artillery.

> When Breckinridge's division attacked the enemy's left on Friday afternoon, having received no intimation that such an attack was contemplated, I accompanied Pegram's battery to the front.... Capt. Paul [F.] Anderson not being able to induce General Pegram to open with his battery (he being fearful of firing into our own troops), I took charge of the battery, placing it upon a commanding hill, and opened fire upon a heavy column of the enemy advancing from their extreme left to turn Breckinridge's right. The fire was so effective (the range not being over 500 yards) as to shoot down their standard and throw them into confusion. The fire was continued until my horse was shot. I was thrown in his struggles, and when I succeeded in getting another horse the battery had been run off without any occasion whatever.

After this Breckinridge's division began to retreat and then Wharton ordered his brigade to support the withdrawal. Wharton's cavalry moved forward a short distance on the foot to cover any pursuit from the Union infantry, which did not come. Wharton was assigned overall command over Pegram by Bragg, ostensibly because of his greater experience commanding cavalry. Since Wharton had overall command of the cavalry, it fell to him to direct the actions of Pegram during Breckinridge's attack. In addition, Bragg reassured Pegram that Wharton would be present and also participating in the attack. Clearly, Wharton was not in position and Pegram remained without orders from Bragg (other than to prepare for the battle), Breckinridge or Wharton.[31]

What Wharton did not include in his critical report of Pegram's artillery skill was an attempt by Pegram's staff to induce a more vigorous action on part on the battery just

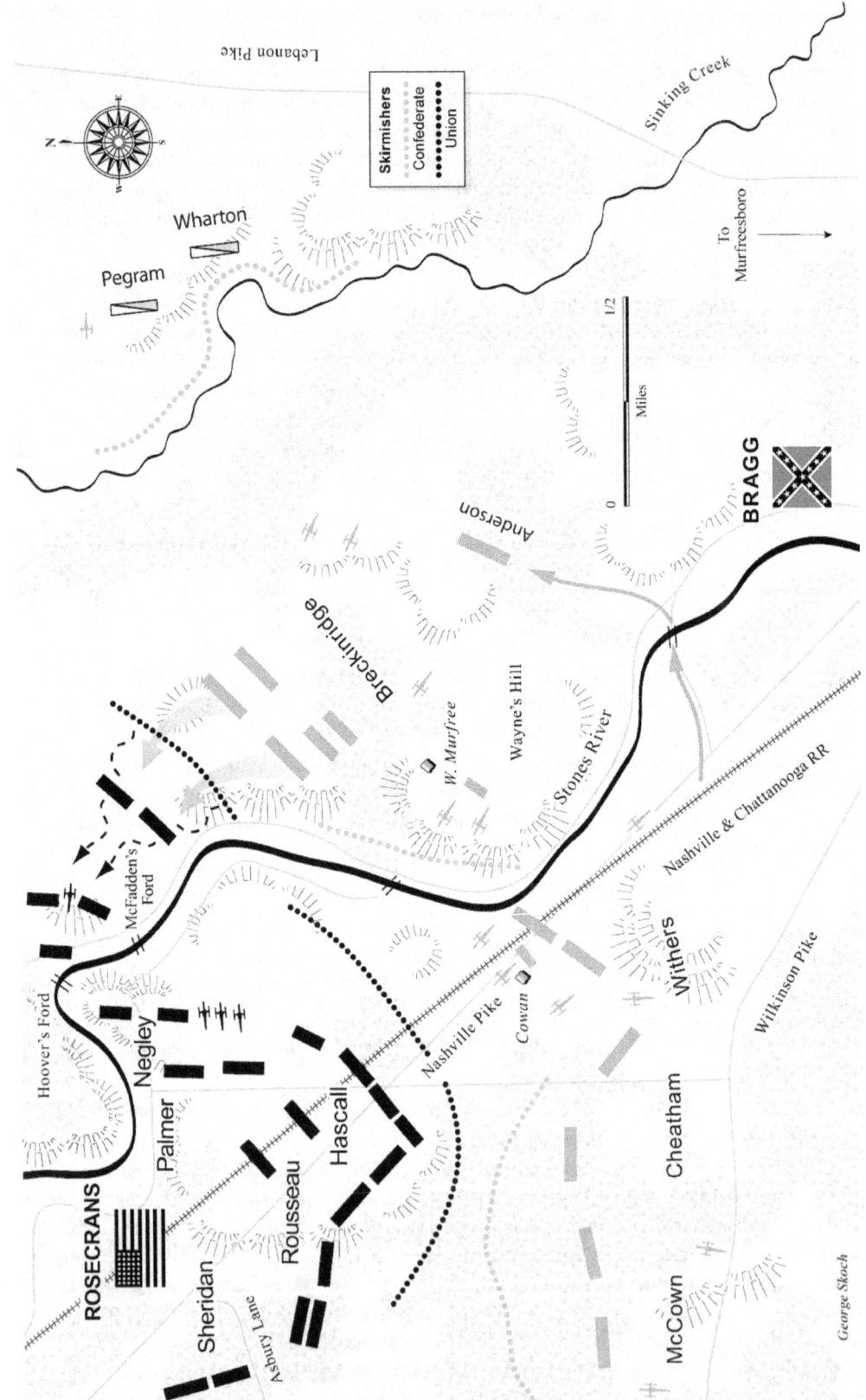

Wharton's and Pegram's brigades hold their position during Breckinridge's charge (4:00 p.m. January 2, 1863).

moments before. The grandeur of Breckinridge's attack seemed to awe the members of Huwald's Battery which was attached to Pegram's cavalry brigade. Captain Henry B. Clay of Pegram's staff recalled:

> So wonderful was the sight that for some moments I did not notice that our gunners seemed to be moving to and from guns and limber chests as if they were on parade. Riding to them, I ordered them to move faster, as they at once did so. Resuming my position near General Pegram, I lost all sense of danger in the tremendous scene until a horse reared high near and I discovered that Gen. John A. Wharton in some way and from somewhere had come to us. Some of his escort were "taking to the timber," behind nearby trees, and it occurred to me that when Texans took to the trees it must be a hot place.

According to Clay's report, Wharton's presence surprised everyone and where Wharton was during the afternoon is unknown. While Wharton reported a member of his staff had tried to initiate firing, Clay, of Pegram's staff, also encouraged the gunners to fire. To give a full description of Huwald's performance, when Wharton was unhorsed, the battery under Wharton's direct command at that point, and to the exasperation of Wharton "the battery had been run off without any occasion whatever." Taken as a whole, Wharton appeared to fare no better with the recalcitrant artillery than Pegram, but Wharton still decided to be hyper critical of Pegram. Also, it was ironic that Wharton attempted to make his second display of the masterful firing of his artillery over Confederate infantry only to be cautioned not to do it. Brigadier General William Preston wrote that when his Third Brigade of Breckinridge's infantry withdrew, he met with Wharton and declared: "Wharton with his battery and the cavalry, with which he was covering our right. He was about opening fire with the battery, when I advised him not to do so, as he might fire on some of our men."[32]

Both Wharton and Pegram suffered under the pen of Colonel J. Stoddard Johnston who served as a member of Bragg's staff during the fighting. Johnston wrote that Wharton and Pegram with artillery extended past the right flank and were ordered to protect the right and participate in the attack. Because Breckinridge's Kentucky artillery had little infantry support and fearing an enemy attack from the right, two staff officers were sent to Wharton and Pegram requesting details about their actions and reconnaissance on the right. Breckinridge received no indication from either Wharton or Pegram of what lay on the right flank and he wrote, "[B]ut received no intelligence up to the moment of the assault."[33]

To cloud the story of the Confederate cavalry's actions on the January 2, a report by Captain Henry B. Clay of Pegram's staff suggested that the 1st Louisiana and 1st Georgia cavalry, in fact, participated somewhat in Breckinridge's attack. Clay reached Pegram's headquarters and the cavalry "loitered about, until just before three o'clock, the 1st Georgia and 1st Louisiana were dismounted and formed in skirmish formation. The short time seemed long as with strained nerves—to me at least—we listened for the signal gun." Clay wrote that as Breckinridge's division began the attack, he was ordered to "move our line forward faster, and at the command we took up our yell." Clay's statements indicated that there was some expectation of the cavalry and actual cooperation in the attack; but Pegram was under orders from Wharton and still awaiting more instructions from Breckinridge. In addition, Pegram was told that Wharton would be there also and Wharton's location was unknown until he surprised everyone by his appearance near Huwald's guns.[34]

A member of Van Cleve's division observed Confederate cavalry on January 2 as they prepared for an attack from Breckinridge's infantry. M. B. Butler, 44th Indiana

Infantry in Fyffe's brigade, participated in the Union defense on the east side of Stones River which received the full attack of Breckinridge's division:

> Ours was but a single brigade line, no support visible to us. A river that we could neither jump nor climb its precipitous banks, running around us on the right and rear, with only a narrow ford, a heavy body of the enemy's cavalry on our left, in an open field in plain sight and Breckinridge with his rebel hosts in front … our own guns planted above the ford, turned their muzzles toward the cavalry and the grape and canister came pouring through the trees immediately over my head. I moved more behind the building and there a volley from the rebel cavalry struck like hail, against the house, and I started for the river, jumped down its precipitous bank and into the ice cold water.

Butler's recollection supports the claims of H. B. Clay, but no other records indicate any participation of the Southern cavalry during this attack other than covering the retreat of the Confederate infantry. Reinforcements of Union infantry moved into line and with the Federal artillery stopped the Confederate attack with heavy losses.[35]

The reason for the lack of participation by Wharton and Pegram was clear. They were waiting for orders from Breckinridge or Bragg; but Bragg's preemptory orders to attack consumed Breckinridge's thoughts. Breckinridge was summoned to meet with Bragg in the early afternoon and he found that Bragg was committed to attack the Union position on the east side of Stones River even though he had not discussed this with Breckinridge or Breckinridge's commanding officer, Hardee. During the meeting, Bragg told Breckinridge that his division had relatively small losses on December 31 and therefore, he was best prepared to make the attack. Breckinridge argued that his personal reconnaissance revealed the Federal position was heavily supported by artillery and the attack would not be successful. In response, Bragg simply told Breckinridge he had his orders and they were expected to be carried out. Bragg ordered him to form his division in two lines and Bragg told him that Pegram and Wharton "were instructed to protect the general's flank and cooperate in the attack." Pegram received the vague message, but Wharton would record he had no knowledge of the attack at all. Both cavalry officers awaited their instructions defining their role in the attack which never came.[36]

Breckinridge returned to his headquarters and informed his brigade commanders who all opposed the order. Even one brigade commander reportedly considered going to army headquarters and shooting Bragg. At 3:30 p.m. Breckinridge busily prepared for the attack, and his new brigade commander, Brigadier General Gideon Pillow, rode up to Breckinridge and asked him about the support along the right flank. Breckinridge told Pillow that Bragg had ordered the cavalry to cooperate in the attack and Pillow asked him if there had been an attempt to communicate with Wharton or Pegram. Breckinridge responded negatively and Pillow said that it "would not only be proper but important to communicate" with the two cavalry officers. By the time staff officers were sent to find Wharton and Pegram, it was too late for the cavalry to join in the attack, except in assisting with the withdrawal.[37]

The actions of the January 2 would be fought on paper for many months after the disastrous attack. While Breckinridge felt Bragg had ordered the cavalry to join in the attack, Bragg criticized Breckinridge for failing to include Pegram and Wharton in the attack. George Brent, Bragg's adjutant general sent a message to John Pegram at 1:00 p.m.: "The general is about moving to take by force a position between Hower's house and the right of our line, on this side of the river. General Wharton will be there. You will arrange and dispose your command in the vicinity of Hower's, so as to cooperate with this movement." The message was unclear and vague. It was not possible to move to Hower's house because the Union infantry already occupied that location. Also, the message clearly stated that Wharton would be present for the attack and Pegram simply marked the message "received." Breckinridge's biographer referred to this order as vague and one which was interpreted as "to be ready to cooperate with Breckinridge's attack." Wharton and his cavalry held the position between Pegram and Breckinridge, and Bragg's headquarters was less than one half mile from Breckinridge's headquarters. And if Wharton was not notified at the same time as Pegram, it is difficult to imagine not finding Wharton or a member of his staff during the three hour interlude. The recurring problems in communication were evident because Wharton claimed he had no indication his cavalry was expected to join in the attack. While Bragg criticized Breckinridge's use of cavalry, Breckinridge did not respond to the comments about this utilization of the cavalry, but, in so many words, just referred to the poor decision to criticize him and his command which had just lost over 1,800 men, or about one third of his force, based on Bragg's preemptory orders to attack such an unassailable position. Despite the reassurance that Wharton would join in the attack, Wharton reported; "Upon Friday I was ordered by General Bragg to the right. When Breckinridge's division attacked the enemy's left on Friday afternoon, having received no intimation that such an attack was contemplated." It simply seemed that Bragg sent messages to the cavalry commanders, and which, at least, Pegram received preparing them for the attack, but no further orders were sent by Bragg or Breckinridge, each expecting the other to direct the cavalry. Wharton, instead of joining the attack, was directing artillery fire and when he discovered he was expected to participate in the attack he only had time to order his men to assist in the Confederate retreat. Baxter Smith recorded in his memoirs that the cavalry was ordered to assist in the attack, but the orders were received too late to participate except with the retreat. And the chaplain of the 8th Texas Cavalry, R. F. Bunting, would later write that Wharton was under no orders to participate in the attack.[38]

The assignment of blame for Breckinridge's failed attack raged for months. The interaction between Gideon Pillow and Breckinridge remains noteworthy in regard to the role of the cavalry. During the attack, Pillow was not with his brigade and Breckinridge reportedly found him hiding behind a large tree. Breckinridge then ordered him to join his men. When Pillow was asked by Bragg to write his observations about the attack on January 2, he placed the blame on Breckinridge for the misuse of the cavalry. He wrote:

General Gideon Pillow—It "would not only be proper but important to communicate" with the cavalry (Tennessee State Library and Archives).

> At this point in the conversation, General Bragg asked, "Why did not General Breckinridge protect you from the flanking force by the large body of cavalry I had placed under his orders?" I replied I did not know he had any cavalry under his orders. General Bragg then said that he had a large force of cavalry placed under his orders for the

express purpose of providing for such a contingency. I remarked to him that I saw a large body of cavalry on the heights to my right and below the ford when Negley crossed the river, but that it did not make any attempt to arrest the advance of the flanking force, and I felt certain it could not have received orders to do so. The above is the substance of that conversation on the part of those operating. General Bragg gave me the first intelligence that I received of this body of cavalry being under the orders of General Breckinridge. I expressed astonishment that it was not used for the protection of my right flank and rear. I also expressed myself as clear that the position of the line of battle was a most important error of judgment in the operations of the day.

However, some historians have speculated that Breckinridge's allegations of cowardice tainted Pillow's view of the events of the day and resulted in the negative description of Breckinridge's command of the cavalry.[39]

In an unrelated event, Captain H. B. Clay of Pegram's staff explained the difficulty and importance of reporting enemy troop movements. Intelligence of the enemy's movement was an important part of the cavalry's duty, but in the heat of battle this duty was difficult. On January 2, Clay suffered much remorse in regard to the actions of Breckinridge's attack. Clay's cavalry scouted the east flank and tried to determine the movement of trains, artillery and troops movements. After the war, he wrote that his command observed a movement which led him to believe the Federals were withdrawing. Clay made a report to John Pegram who sent him directly to Bragg. After delivering the information, Bragg replied, "I have ordered General Breckinridge to assault that position this afternoon." Years after the battle, Clay believed Bragg made his decision ordering Breckinridge to attack based on this intelligence.[40]

Both Pegram and Wharton were able officers and ones who did not intentionally disobey orders. These two cavalry units remained on the flank uninformed about their expected involvement in the disastrous attack on January 2. The animosity between Breckinridge and Bragg carried through 1863 and was publicly covered in the newspapers.[41]

Skirmish at Cox's Hill and Bragg's Decision to Withdraw— January 3

On January 2, Lewis Zahm found time to gather his troopers and forage the horses after several days of activity. The remainder of Stanley's cavalry maintained its position and scouted the flanks of the army. During the evening, the soldiers on both sides suffered through a miserable night as more rain began to fall. On January 3, it continued raining throughout the morning and most of the day. During the day, some of the Union cavalry regiments went on reconnaissance missions, and Zahm again guarded hospital, supply wagons and ammunition trains supplying Rosecrans' army. Not surprisingly, Zahm found himself again fighting the Confederate cavalry. Much to his relief, he had the 1st Ohio, 4th Ohio and 3rd Tennessee cavalry regiments to perform this duty with much better results. The cavalry formed the escort around a hospital supply and ammunition train, and accompanied by two and half regiments of infantry, the train began to move at 11 a.m. After marching for eight miles, Wheeler's cavalry attacked and was repulsed, and then attempted a second attack later. Fourteen hours later the train arrived safely and Zahm recorded he had killed 15 Confederate troopers, wounded an unknown number and captured twelve prisoners. This was a much better day for Zahm.[42]

The major skirmish during this escort duty took place at 2:00 o'clock. Wheeler discovered the large supply and ordnance train at Cox's Hill (also referred to as Blood's Hill or Insane Asylum Hill) early in the afternoon. He claimed: "[S]ucceeded in driving off the cavalry guards and in breaking down and upsetting a large number of wagons. The enemy's infantry being in such force (quite treble our numbers), we were prevented from destroying the train, but succeeded in preventing its making any further progress that day." Wheeler's report was incorrect and by all other accounts, the wagon proceeded to Murfreesboro without delay. Wheeler claimed he broke off the fight due to the receipt of orders from Bragg ordering him back to the main Confederate lines. Abe Buford's Kentucky cavalry brigade trailed Wheeler. Buford's brigade fell into line about eight miles south of Nashville on the Murfreesboro Pike in the rear of Wheeler's brigade and prepared to join in the fight. Buford moved his brigade into a cornfield along the left of Wheeler's troopers along the pike. Buford dismounted his men, threw out skirmishers and he moved toward the enemy. However, Wheeler began pulling his men back into a wooded area and Buford received orders to return to Murfreesboro before really engaging the Union soldiers. Wheeler broke off the fight at four o'clock, withdrew about sunset and rode back to Bragg's lines through the night in a cold rain.[43]

The Union reports described a repulse of Wheeler's cavalry. Sergeant Isaac Skillman, 3rd Ohio Cavalry, again described some of the cavalry action near Cox's Hill.

> We found our old friend Gen. Wheeler with his whole brigade waiting for us. I suppose he thought we had something to eat. He seemed determined this time to see what we had in the wagons. So we had quite a fight in preventing him from capturing the train, but we saved the whole train complete.[44]

Meanwhile at Murfreesboro, it rained throughout the day on January 3 as the two armies remained in their positions. Much to chagrin of many in the Southern cavalry, Bragg decided to move his army southward. Baxter Smith moved his Tennessee cavalry across Stones River and occupied the trenches just vacated by the infantry.

> We who were citizens of Middle Tenn. felt a sudden realization of the truth that the high hopes that we had so fondly cherished of driving the invaders from our homes and that within a few days, were suddenly darkened. No funeral cortege ever presented a more solemn aspect.[45]

As Zahm's cavalry escorted the supply trains to and from Nashville, additional troopers were added to the numbers of the regiments. Some of the troopers remained in Nashville as the advance on Murfreesboro began and some of those who retreated in fear also returned. William Crane, 4th Ohio, wrote that 120 cavalrymen returned. "These 120 were the troopers who been left behind at N[ashville] & the skedaddlers of Wednesday." On January 4, Zahm scouted toward Murfreesboro and found Bragg had withdrawn. After receiving reports from Wheeler's reconnaissance that Rosecrans was not withdrawing, but was, in fact, moving forward what appeared to be reinforcements, Bragg withdrew southward from Murfreesboro. Rosecrans marched into Murfreesboro claiming the victory on January 5. George W. Dillion, 18th Tennessee Infantry, was astonished at the order to withdraw:

> It seemed hard indeed and also surprised us for all indications during the battle seemed at lead us to a glorious victory and then to leave our homes and friends and all that is near and dear to us upon this earth ... exposed to an invading foe with cold hearts and proud, hauty, subjugation desires, desires to plunder peaceable citizens.... It went hard for us to retreat.

The 1st Tennessee Cavalry (CSA) burned the bridge over Stones Rivers by pouring turpentine on the structure and setting it on fire. For the Union cavalry "Boots & Saddles" sounded and Zahm's brigade rode cautiously for Murfreesboro supported by Colonel John Miller's infantry brigade of Negley's division accompanied by Loomis's artillery.

Loomis fired a few shells into what was thought to be the position of Confederate guns but received "no response." The town had been evacuated.⁴⁶

Zahm's brigade "then returned & went into camp near the scene of our defeat last Wednesday. All was quiet now, but that ensanguined battle, where the strife had raged for three days so fiercely," William Crane philosophically concluded. Robert Burns described the result of the battle:

> I saw a good many butternuts lying there. Some of the trees were literally covered with bullet holes from the ground to 25 feet high. Not a tree for a mile but what was marked. I saw one tree two feet in diameter with a hole about the size of your fist directly through the center of it through which you could see. Others were cut in two by cannon balls. I there saw enough of war.

Vincent Dunn, 3rd Kentucky Cavalry (U.S.), wrote to his father that after riding over the battlefield. "It made my veins raise in anguish to see the dead bodies of our army laying over the battle ground stripped of their clothing."⁴⁷

By the end of Sunday, the tension which was so palpable for the past week was gone. The 4th U.S. Cavalry unsaddled their mounts for the first time since Wednesday morning when the battle began. Othniel Gooding, 4th Michigan, also wrote, "[W]e did not unsaddle our horsses for six days and nights and ware on them a goodeal of the time." Sergeant Ganum Vineyard in the Confederate Tennessee cavalry also reported the constant movement during the battle: "I never left the horse in the battle." Vineyard would write in a letter that he had lived for three days on parched corn and he expected his horse to die as a result of the exertions over the past week. Some of the soldiers lamented the only food they had to eat during the battle was scavenged from the haversacks of the dead on the field.⁴⁸

Based on the decision to withdraw from Murfreesboro, allegations of poor intelligence from the Southern cavalry were laid at the feet of Joseph Wheeler in regard to Bragg's orders to abandon Murfreesboro. Wheeler's biographer, Edward Longacre, suggested that Wheeler at this point in the war had not clearly learned the nuances and skills of intelligence gathering and reporting. Bragg publicly placed the responsibility of the Southern withdrawal on Wheeler's reconnaissance, and he wrote in his battle report:

> [On January 3] Before noon, reports from Brigadier-General Wheeler satisfied me the enemy, instead of retiring, was receiving re-enforcements. Common prudence and the safety of my army, upon which even the safety of our cause depended, left no doubt on my mind as to the necessity of my withdrawal from so unequal a contest. My orders were accordingly given about noon for the movement of the trains, and for the necessary preparation of the troops.

Wheeler erroneously interpreted the movement of Union troops as a signal of reinforcements moving to the aid of Rosecrans troops in Murfreesboro. In fact, a single infantry brigade marched from Nashville to Rosecrans' army and Wheeler failed to properly interpret and communicate this to Bragg. This report would be used by Bragg to move southward to Tullahoma. While Wheeler would take some blame for Bragg's decision, Wheeler's report was likely used as an excuse. Generals Benjamin Cheatham and Jones Withers sent a letter to Bragg on the evening of January 2 urging the retreat of the army and stated there were only three divisions which could be relied upon in the Army of Tennessee. In addition, Bragg had other commanders who objected to the allegations of reinforcements. General St. John Liddell disagreed with Wheeler's report and exclaimed, "It can't be so, for I have just come from the extreme left, I could have clearly seen the reinforcements approach, and I have seen none. Where is Rosecrans to get them from?" Bragg's response suggested concern that some in his army had lost the will to continue the fight, and certainly, Bragg had the option of further investigation of the reported Union reinforcements. Instead, he simply decided to withdraw.[49]

Bragg had other reasons for his withdrawal. In addition to Wheeler's intelligence, Bragg captured McCook's headquarters papers during the battle of December 31 and as his staff looked over the figures, they found McCook had eighteen thousand men, far more than he thought. Bragg concluded he faced more enemy than he could defeat, and coupled with low morale after the previous day's battle and Wheeler's information, he reasoned to defend Murfreesboro was impractical.[50]

On January 3, Bragg sent orders to his commanders to prepare to move south. He ordered those sick or wounded who could travel to begin marching toward Tullahoma, Manchester and Shelbyville. Those who could not march were left in Murfreesboro. The decision to leave the wounded was a difficult one for Bragg and he wept over the necessity of moving without them. Over two thousand wounded and sick were left behind because there were not enough wagons to carry them and the necessities of war. Bragg's army marched with three days rations and the Confederate wagons were filled with supplies and ammunition. The Confederate cavalry was again on duty providing rearguard security for the Army of Tennessee.[51]

Lucy Virginia French, who had written so optimistically of the battle on December 31 wrote her thoughts again on January 4:

> Mollie & I sat here in the greatest suspense ... we asked breathlessly. Go South immediately, he replied! Go South immediately ... were the ominous words. Our army was then retreating! ... Many citizens returned from Murfreesboro today—indeed the road has been full of horsemen & wagons all afternoon. Gov. Harris, Andrew Ewing, Judge Humphreys & many others have come in. They report our victory decided—the Yankees re-inforced, & our men having got off all prisoners & things captured—were retreating in good order to Wartrace & Shelbyville. They say this—but they will retreat to Chattanooga, as sure as you live—and we will be left here at the mercy of those savages, the Yankees. What is to become of us God only knows.[52]

Rosecrans Claims Murfreesboro—January 5

On the morning of January 5, Stanley's cavalry pursued Bragg's army. The 4th Ohio Cavalry was the first unit into Murfreesboro and rode past the courthouse as the clock struck 9 o'clock. Many Confederate tents remained, as did the sick, wounded and dead. "[E]very public building & many private dwellings being used as hospitals," recorded William Crane. Most of the local citizens remained hidden behind closed doors in fear of the retribution of the Union army. Only Confederate medical personnel, marked with hospital insignias, moved freely throughout the town. Minty's cavalry advanced through Murfreesboro and down the Manchester Pike southward and within a mile encountered Confederate pickets. David Stanley took command of the advance and drove ahead, riding with the 4th U.S. Cavalry. As the advance continued, the Union cavalry crossed a creek another mile forward and came under attack from Confederate artillery. The advance which included the 1st Tennessee, 3rd Kentucky, 7th Pennsylvania, 4th Michigan, 4th U.S. and 2nd Tennessee cavalries pushed onward. Six miles south of Murfreesboro, a stiff skirmish resulted with most of the fighting being successfully done by the 4th U.S., 5th Tennessee and 7th Pennsylvania. Afterward the Union cavalry withdrew and camped just south of Murfreesboro.[53]

In what was described as "delightful" weather, Zahm's brigade advanced down a parallel road, the Shelbyville Pike, and likewise skirmishing resulted through the morning. An estimated 500 Southern cavalry resisted the pursuit and at noon Zahm halted and returned to Murfreesboro. As the Southern cavalry again provided the effective rear guard action, Bragg slowly marched to Tullahoma abandoning Murfreesboro and giving Rosecrans the victory.[54]

The 1st Louisiana Cavalry provided rearguard action during the Confederate withdrawal.

> On the 4th the Federals quietly took possession of Murfreesboro. On the 5th they moved forward and not very far from town overtook our command. We drove back their advance, and being somewhat protected behind a fence succeeded in repulsing their second charge, but when the third came and in such tremendous force we had to leave our fence corners with considerable alacrity.[55]

Trooper Edward Amsden, 3rd Ohio Cavalry, summed up the situation from the Union perspective in a letter to his cousin on January 5, "General Rosecrans is a stubborn Dutchman and says he don't know when he is whipped." Amsden continued in his letter the good news from Kentucky, John H. Morgan was sent packing back to Tennessee and Basil Duke, a highly regarded part of Morgan's command, was wounded in the process. Trooper James Wiswell, 4th U.S. Cavalry, wrote to his father of his pride of the fighting of the men of the Army of the Cumberland, "I used to brag on the eastern 'Yankees' but these Western Volunteers with Rosecrans to lead them can whip the world." Of the Battle of Stones River, William Rosecrans wrote to his wife "*Non nobis, Domine, non nobis, sed nomini tuo da gloriam*" (Not unto us, O Lord, not unto us, but to thy name give the glory.) He rode across the battlefield at 3:00 a.m. with only an aide and an orderly after Breckinridge's attack on January 2 and while he believed that victory was his, the sound of the wounded soldiers crushed his heart. He told his wife there was little for him to do but offer a little whiskey and water and urge them to pray.[56]

Bragg's commanding officer, Joseph Johnston, upon hearing of the withdrawal from Murfreesboro immediately sought the Confederate cavalry as a possible remedy. "Ask General Bragg if his cavalry cannot operate upon the enemy's rear, to compel him to fall back. We must abandon no ground that it is possible to hold." The confidence of the high command of the Southern army in the cavalry was apparent, but the problem was much larger than the Southern horsemen could handle.[57]

Despite the viciousness of the battle which showed no clear superiority of one side over the other, except in the power of the Union artillery, the Army of the Cumberland was deemed victorious and for a while William Rosecrans was seen as hero in the eyes by many in the North. On the heels of Fredericksburg and Grant's prolonged attempt to reach Vicksburg, Rosecrans brought victory when it was needed. On the Confederate side, the withdrawal from Murfreesboro was lamented by many civilians, military men, and politicians. Charles George, 5th Georgia Infantry, summed much of the feelings of the Confederate army; "Why we left Murfreesboro, I dont know the Yanks left two hours before we did, but Gen Bragg didnt believe it I suppose so or he would have pursued them if he had not had been too badly frightened he was the only one the Yanks whipped." Bragg's withdrawal also exploded into a crisis of command and discontent for the Army of Tennessee. Bragg was severely criticized in newspapers and many felt Bragg had lost the confidence of his army. Among the charges made about Bragg was the loss of confidence by his officers and the decision to withdraw against the advice of his commanders. In response, Bragg sent letters to his corps commanders asking them to confirm that they agreed with the decision to withdraw, but the letter was distributed beyond corps commanders and reached division commanders who added their opinions. The opinions extended past the question about the decision to withdraw, but also included comments about a loss of confidence in the commanding general. Bragg would remain in command over the displeasure of his subordinates. William Hardee's biographer, Nathaniel Hughes, Jr., wrote: "Bragg did not feel that the 'confidence of my army' had been impaired; but everyone else did." The aftermath of the Battle of Stones River continued the discontent with Bragg which began in earnest after the Battle of Perryville and would continue until December 1863.[58]

Conclusion

We must have cavalry and cavalry arms.
—Major General William S. Rosecrans

Summary of the Cavalry's Role at the Battle of Stones River

Both cavalry divisions, Union and Confederate, provided commendable service at the Battle of Stones River and both commands lost valuable men during the conflict. The discrete cavalry actions at the Battle of Stones River include:

1. The advance on Murfreesboro from December 26 to December 30;
2. Wheeler's raid on the rear of the Army of the Cumberland on December 30;
3. The cavalry battle along the west flank on the morning of December 31;
4. The afternoon cavalry battle on the west flank on December 31;
5. The cavalry actions, reconnaissance and security, in conjunction with Breckinridge's division on December 31;
6. The cavalry action, and reconnaissance, of the Union rear on January 1;
7. Wharton's and Pegram's actions in conjunction with Breckinridge's January 2 attack;
8. Skirmish at Cox's Hill and Wheeler's reconnaissance on January 3.

The advance on Murfreesboro requires little additional comment. Both the Union and Confederate cavalries performed their duties well. Much has been made of Wheeler's boast that he could delay the Union advance for two to four days and the impact the weather had in achieving Wheeler's success. Most importantly, the Confederate cavalry, supported by infantry, performed remarkable duty in preventing a rapid penetration of the Southern defenses during Rosecrans' march to Murfreesboro. Both Wheeler and Wharton had their men organized and on duty throughout the five day Union advance. This provided Bragg with the time he needed to meet this threat. Likewise, Stanley's cavalry also achieved its objectives and operated in an effective and efficient manner, overall, during the advance.

In regard to Wheeler's raid on December 30, this is a more complicated event to consider. Certainly, Wheeler dramatically demonstrated the ability of his cavalry to ride circles around Rosecrans' army and he effectively destroyed over a million dollars of supplies while increasing the morale of his troops. The "raiding strategy" accepted by the

Confederate cavalry was demonstrated in this action and was an important part of the Confederate military psyche. The obvious renown Forrest and Morgan achieved during their daring raids was recognized by the Confederate high command and became a critical part of the military strategy in Tennessee in December 1862. The Confederate government felt these raids contributed important successes so desperately needed as Union armies marched into the Confederacy.

The other intended, or unintended, result of Wheeler's raid drew David Stanley, the Union chief of cavalry, and Robert Minty, Stanley's most effective brigade commander, away the battlefield on the morning of December 31. As a result, about a third of the Union cavalry remained in the rear when the battle began. This was important in regard to Wharton's actions on the first day of the battle. On the morning on December 31, John Wharton achieved a remarkable success and this was the high point for the Confederate cavalry during the battle. Wharton's cavalry provided incalculable benefit by preventing the Union infantry from reorganizing in addition to capturing prisoners, cannons, and other equipment. Perhaps, Wharton's wisest choice was the inclusion of White's Tennessee Battery with his command. It is unclear if Wharton's cavalry alone could have driven Zahm's Union cavalry to the rear, but the effect of the Southern artillery was significant in the actions during the day. There can be little fault found in Wharton's actions until he gained possession of the Army of the Cumberland's large supply train. Then, Wharton's lack of supervision resulted in his repulse. At that point in the day, the Union army was in such disarray Wharton could have had greater success in burning the train rather than trying to carry it away. His greatest mistake was the lack of security and as a result he no longer had a cavalry command, but a mob of men carrying away the spoils. He had had such complete success, but he failed to consider a counter attack, which began with the 4th U.S. Cavalry's charge into the Southern flank. Three other Union cavalry regiments attacked and effectively sent Wharton to the rear. Historian Thomas Connelly wrote that all John Wharton needed to complete his success of attacking the Union supply train was support. The "what ifs" have been asked by many about the cavalry actions at Stones River. If Wheeler was with Wharton in a command presence, would he have urged a few regiments to serve as security, or would he have suggested burning the train rather than move it away? Even, more importantly, if Wheeler's two thousand men were present and operating in conjunction with Wharton, it is not hard to imagine the extent of the damage which could have occurred.

Wheeler did not operate as chief of cavalry during the Battle of Stones River which was detrimental to the overall performance of the Southern cavalry. He was acting as brigade commander, and he allowed each of his other brigade commanders to operate independently. Even if Wheeler's raid took place, but under the command of Colonel William Wirt Allen a worthy brigade commander, Wheeler's command presence would have aided Wharton on the west flank and Pegram on the east flank. Instead, he was away from the battlefield on the morning of the first day of the battle along with about a third of the Confederate cavalry. In Wheeler's defense, it is important to realize that this was his first battle as chief of cavalry and he had much to learn. He just needed the time and experience to develop into a premier chief of cavalry.

On the Union side of the field on the morning of December 31, the cavalry regiments were dispersed except for Lewis Zahm's brigade that did most of the fighting. Overall, Zahm's brigade performed well considering the force it faced. It conducted an organized, fighting withdrawal and assisted in freeing some infantry along the way. Just as Wharton needed support for his success, so did Zahm. John Kennett, commanding the cavalry division, in Stanley's absence failed to organize the cavalry defense in the area of Wharton's cavalry attack. If Kennett could have pulled the 7th Pennsylvania, 3rd Kentucky, 4th U.S. Cavalry, and 3rd Indiana Cavalry into a unified defense, the morning most likely would have yielded much different results for Zahm's cavalry. This was not accomplished and a single organized regiment, the 4th U.S. Cavalry, charged Wharton's disorganized command and this action began a series of individual charges from the Union cavalry which effectively stopped the Confederate advance along the right flank. If David Stanley had remained on the field, it is possible he could have accomplished a more unified defense, as he demonstrated throughout his Civil War career. He had such an ability to ride to the sound of the guns, gain Rosecrans' support of his decisions, and gain support from other commanders, that his loss during the morning's action was significant.

The actions on the afternoon of December 31 between Wheeler's and Buford's brigades and Stanley and Minty's commands are also an interesting consideration. Wharton's command had withdrawn to Wilkinson's Pike at this point when Wheeler moved onto the field. There is great pride from the Union cavalry standpoint in regard to this action, but almost no mention of the action recorded by the Confederate cavalry. Because Stanley's cavalry gained the upper hand, this might have caused the Confederates to try to forget this fight, and the disparity of the Union success over a larger Confederate force remains somewhat puzzling. Stanley wisely ordered the charge as Buford's brigade moved toward the Nashville Pike and dealt with Wheeler's troops alone—a more equal fight. The events were recorded in various Union accounts and, at least, two Confederate cavalry colonels were wounded during the battle which adds credence to the descriptions by the Union authors. Therefore, the only conclusion to be drawn is that Stanley shrewdly and successfully executed a flank attack while Minty charged the front of Wheeler's command. Stanley and Minty attacked Wheeler's brigade before Buford's brigade could join the Confederate attack. Also, significant in this action was likely the fact that Wheeler's cavalry was not adequately armed and as a result could not successfully deal with a full blown saber charge. This charge forcefully repulsed Wheeler's attempt to push further along the western flank. This successful action added a boost to the Union cavalry which had been roughly handled during the day.

Meanwhile, the actions of John Pegram's reserve cavalry brigade of 480 troopers on the right flank during the day on December 31 continue to be controversial. The dismal relationship between Breckinridge and Bragg would continue to deteriorate even further after the Battle of Stones River, and the events of December 31 were the first of two clashes the commanders would have during the battle. Historians have blamed the Southern cavalry for poor intelligence during the day. Some even had suggested the report of a phantom Union force marching down the Lebanon Pike might have resulted due to Pegram's negligence. Pegram was not the source of the rumor about Union infantry advancing down Lebanon Pike and quickly silenced that concern. He did correctly and promptly observe Van Cleve's division move into line at seven o'clock. The only question was whether he was accountable for not reporting Van Cleve's movements back across the river at 8:30 a.m.; but the only surviving record of his messages strongly suggested Van Cleve's movements were observed and reported by the Southern cavalry. Upon examination of the single message, which many have used to criticize the efforts of Pegram's cavalry, it appears to demonstrate that Pegram reported the withdrawal of Van Cleve's division. The surviving message actually stated that the 1st Georgia Cavalry withdrew a short distance when a strong force crossed over Stones River. A serious reconsideration of Pegram's performance is demanded upon the examination of the existing materials, one in which the Southern cavalry accurately performed its duty.

On January 1, both cavalries had mixed results. Wheeler's cavalry was able to destroy a thirty-wagon train protected by the 2nd Tennessee and also burned some wagons guarded by the 15th Pennsylvania Cavalry. Both of these are notable successes, but both of the Union regiments were not prepared for the Battle of Stones River for various reasons. The less than acceptable actions by these regiments were a result of trying to throw new and unprepared troops against a foe with superior numbers and experience. The results were not surprising. The remainder of Zahm's command successfully fought off Wheeler with good results as the Union cavalry adapted to counter the actions of their adversaries. For Wheeler's command, reconnaissance was probably far more important than burning some empty wagons or wagons filled with the dead or wounded. In this role, Wheeler was not successful. The Union stragglers, still in a state of confusion, filled the roads and led Wheeler to conclude that Rosecrans' army could not stand. This was Wheeler's first experience as chief of cavalry in a major battle and the message he brought back to Bragg erroneously convinced Bragg that Rosecrans was preparing to withdraw.

On January 2, again confusion and disagreements resulted on the Confederate right flank. The disastrous attack by John C. Breckinridge ended any hopes of victory for Bragg at Murfreesboro. Poor communications between division and army headquarters resulted in no clear orders to the cavalry assigned to the attack and John Wharton's and John Pegram's cavalry brigades did not participate in the attack. But realistically, their participation would probably not have affected the outcome. On January 3, Wheeler and Buford returned to the rear of the Army of the Cumberland raiding the supply line and determining Rosecrans' real intent—fight or withdraw. Again, Wheeler brought back the wrong message. Wheeler told Bragg than instead of withdrawing, Rosecrans was gaining reinforcements. As result Wheeler was criticized for bringing the wrong intelligence to Bragg, but Bragg probably used Wheeler as an excuse, having decided on his own to withdraw. In the skirmish at Cox's Hill, the Union army showed a complete evolution of tactics to deal with Wheeler's cavalry. The combination of infantry, artillery and cavalry effectively repulsed Wheeler who was not successful in his attempts to capture the supply trains.

Finally, Bragg belatedly realized that he had other cavalry units which could be of great value during the battle, namely Forrest and Morgan, and before the battle he sent riders to urge John Hunt Morgan's 3,000 troopers to pitch into the fight. There are several reports that Bragg intended Morgan to hurry back to Murfreesboro to aid in disrupting the communications and supply lines of Rosecrans near Nashville. Colonel Basil Duke confirmed this comment, but he suggested the raids by Morgan and Forrest could actually have aided Bragg during the battle. "General Bragg had sent officers (who never reached him until it was too late) to Morgan with instructions to him to hasten back, and attack the enemy in the rear.... These expeditions drew off and kept employed a large a large number of troops whose presence in the great battle would have vastly aided Rosecrans." In a letter written to Morgan by his new wife, she told her husband that those in Murfreesboro asked over the week long battle; "When will Morgan be here?" Likewise, Forrest was operating in western Tennessee in a raid of his own.[1]

Union Cavalry Conclusions

The Union cavalry recorded 357 casualties and losses of 77 horses. In addition to the losses recorded, Colonel Minor Millikin, Major David Moore, and 2nd Lieutenant Timothy Condit, all of the 1st Ohio Cavalry were killed. Major Frank B. Ward (died January 11) and Major A. O. Rosengarten, 15th Pennsylvania, were killed in the campaign. Although, not listed in Stanley's official report, the cavalry would soon receive resignations from Colonel John Kennett (February 1863) due to ill health and Colonel Lewis Zahm (January 1863) who had been wounded during the battle. In addition, Captain John Wortham, 1st Middle (5th) Tennessee Cavalry; Captain Eli Long, 4th U.S. Cavalry; Lieutenant William H. Scott, 1st Ohio; and Lieutenant Thomas V. Mitchell, 4th Michigan Cavalry, were all wounded during the battle.[2]

Perhaps one of the most interesting casualties during the Battle of Stones was that of Private Frank Martin, 2nd Tennessee Cavalry. The 18-year-old Martin had enlisted about six months prior to the battle and while being examined for a shoulder wound, was found to be a woman. Martin was, of course, discharged, but she later enlisted, while again hiding her gender, in the 8th Michigan Infantry.[3]

Casualities for the Union Cavalry
(During the advance from Nashville on the 26th December, including the Battle of Stones River[4])

	Killed		Wounded		Missing		Total
	Officers	Men	Officers	Men	Officers	Men	
First Brigade—Robert Minty							
2nd Indiana (Co. M)	–	1	–	–	1	13	15
3rd Kentucky	–	1	1	7	–	1	16
4th Michigan	–	1	1	6	–	12	26
7th Pennsylvania	–	2	–	9	–	50	61
Total First Brigade	–	5	2	22	1	76	106
Second Brigade—Lewis Zahm							
1st Ohio	3	2	1	10	1	14	31
3d Ohio	–	6	–	15	–	13	34
4th Ohio	–	7	–	18	–	31	56
Total Second Brigade	3	15	1	43	1	58	121
Artillery							
1st Ohio Light, Battery D	–	1	–	–	–	–	1
Total First Cavalry Division	3	21	3	65	2	134	228
Reserve Cavalry							
3rd Indiana (West Battalion)	–	–	–	–	–	–	–
15th Pennsylvania	1	8	1	8	–	53	71
1st Middle (5th) Tennessee	–	–	1	5	1	8	15
2d Tennessee	1	2	–	10	–	5	18
Total Reserve Cavalry	2	10	2	23	1	66	104
Unattached							
4th United States	–	3	1	9	–	12	25
Total Cavalry	5	34	6	97	3	212	357

Certainly, accounts vary regarding the number of men present for duty, but Rosecrans recorded 3,200 Union cavalry troopers participated in the battle. The refusal of most of the 15th Pennsylvania Cavalry to participate in the battle accounts for some of the reduction for Union troopers. Although the casualty list for the cavalry appears relatively light compared to certain infantry regiments, the toll was severe. For example, the 3rd Ohio Cavalry reported 538 men present for duty on December 22, 1862, but on January 19, only 263 men were available for duty. The same trend occurred in the 4th Ohio, which reported 533 men and officers present for duty on December 25, but only 351 on January 12.[5]

The important and successful actions of the Union cavalry were: successful screening of the infantry during the advance on Murfreesboro, Zahm's defense on the Union right flank during the morning of December 31, the counterattack during the same conflict led by the 4th U.S. Cavalry, Stanley and Minty's repulse of Wheeler during the afternoon, the adaptation to the Confederate raiding strategy and successful protection of the wagon trains on January 1 and January 3. For the less than successful events for Stanley's division, the list includes: mutiny of the 15th Pennsylvania Cavalry, the unpreparedness of the 2nd Tennessee Cavalry, the failure of the Union cavalry to relieve the 1st Michigan Engineers, the failure of John Kennett to organize a coordinated cavalry defense on the morning of December 31, and David Stanley's absence on the field during the first part of the battle. While Lewis Zahm's cavalry brigade was driven from the field on the morning of December 31, it is difficult to rate his actions as anything other than commendable. He held a superior foe, supported by artillery, for four hours as the Union lines crumbled around his command and protected the Union supply trains until other cavalry regiments joined in the battle. Zahm's defense, while he was finally defeated, remains one of the most important Union cavalry's actions at Stones River.

On January 6 the battle was over and the Union cavalry of the Army of the Cumberland marked a new beginning. Stanley really had eight dependable, complete regiments during the battle: Minty's First Brigade, Zahm's Second Brigade and the 4th U.S. Regulars, although this regiment was not attached to the Union cavalry division. The 15th Pennsylvania and the 2nd Tennessee Regiments were just too unprepared for reliable service at Murfreesboro. Stanley had only a month to work with his cavalry; however, Reginald Stuart, in his analysis of the Union cavalry at Stones River, noted that despite the early retreats during the Battle of Stones, the cavalry demonstrated increased aggressiveness and energy under "Stanley's guiding hand in combination with Rosecrans' lavish attention" which produced positive results.[6]

Certain changes in command were necessary after the actions at Stones River. Major Frank Mix, 4th Michigan Cavalry, did not shy away from his thoughts about the commander of that regiment, Lieutenant Colonel William Dickinson, after Minty assumed command of the brigade. Mix wrote to his brother,

> That d___ coward of a Dickenson has spoiled all I done for the Regt. and more too. It is like this. Minty is in command of the Brigade and Dickenson was left in command of the Regt. Two of our Majors have gone home and the other one on standby staff, so I was sent in one direction with six companies and Dickenson another.... On the other hand, Dickenson was attacked and was scared to death. Showed the white feather and his ass too. Lost our wagons, came near losing his men. And I will not attempt to tell you all, only has brought a pile of disgrace on himself and the Regt and he had some of the best officers under him we have in the Regt. And if he does not leave the Regt. you will soon see your humble servant and a number of others at home in quick time. I never will march a rod under his command if I am cashiered for it.[7]

Lieutenant Colonel Dickinson resigned six weeks later due to ill health. The author of the 1st Michigan Engineer's history also commented on Dickinson and speculated that in light of the controversy of Dickinson's command decisions at Stewarts Creek that "his departure was not entirely voluntary."[8]

In addition, a change in command occurred in the 4th Ohio Cavalry, commanded by Major John Pugh, but Pugh was not to command the regiment for long. On November 20, the officers of the regiment signed a petition demanding Pugh to "resign immediately and unconditionally." The demand was based on charges of cowardice, for deserting his company, "took to the mountains at Battle Creek" Tennessee and disobedience of orders for taking a route contrary to orders. Pugh resigned on February 25, 1863. Oliver P. Robie, who would be promoted to the rank of lieutenant colonel in February 1863, replaced Pugh. The 29-year-old, Robie, was captured at Lexington, Kentucky, in October 1862 by John Hunt Morgan's raiders and subsequently paroled. Now, the three men who were responsible for the organization of the 4th Ohio Cavalry were all gone. Subsequently, Colonel Eli Long, recently of the 4th U.S. Cavalry, assumed command and improved the command of this worthy regiment. Long was destined to become an exemplary cavalry brigade commander during the war.[9]

In addition, John Kennett resigned in January citing ill health as the reason. Kennett, as commander of the cavalry division, appeared to have little impact on his command since the Battle of Perryville. He certainly struggled under Rosecrans' command and, presumably, Stanley. Stanley makes almost no reference to Kennett in any of his memoirs or records. Captain William Crane, 4th Ohio and Kennett's own regiment, wrote of Kennett departure on January 24: "Col. Kennett has resigned & his resignation was today accepted.... Considerable rejoicing seemed to be manifested among officers & men who are left in camp." The next day Crane wrote: "Kennett went into town last evening & this morning started homeward. Besides his staff, Adj. Johnson & Maj. Pugh, none of the officers thought sufficient of him to go in & say "good bye." Kennett's nicknames were "Black Jack" and "Major General Jack," and his staff returned to their respective regiments where they would "again be introduced to the mysteries of *work*—something they have long been unused to," exclaimed Crane.[10]

There were moments of absolute embarrassment for the Union cavalry at Stones River, but there were also moments of ultimate heroism and glory. It was a start and having David Stanley in the saddle leading this command had been invaluable. Others noted the efforts of the cavalry, too. Alexander McCook wrote of the actions of Stanley and the cavalry after the battle was over. "To Brig. Gen. D. S. Stanley, chief of cavalry, my thanks are particularly due. He commanded my advance from Nolensville and directed the cavalry on my right flank. A report of the valuable services of our cavalry will be furnished by General Stanley. I commend him to my superiors and my country." Rosecrans also lauded the role of the cavalry

> Brig. Gen. D. S. Stanley, already distinguished in four successful battles ... at this time in command of our ten regiments of cavalry, fought the enemy's forty regiments of cavalry, and held them at bay, or beat them wherever he could meet them. He ought to be made a major-general for his service, and also for the good of the service.

Stanley would be greeted with a promotion to the rank of major general in March 1863.[11]

The 15th Pennsylvania Cavalry would be reorganized after the Battle of Stones River and despite the events during the battle, provided excellent service for the remainder of the war. When Colonel William Palmer regained command of the 15th Pennsylvania, he described the situation in a letter in March 1863,

> I pity the poor fellows who mutinied so many of them were led into it without reflection and in that careless accidental way by which it is so easy to stray from the right path into the wrong. These men take it very much to heart, now that the proper soldierly feeling has been restored, and seem abashed and down hearted. It is a good sign however and promises good fruits and is much better than the bold, defiant, reckless air of audacity which characterized them when I first came out.

The 15th Pennsylvania Cavalry was removed from the cavalry division and attached to Rosecrans' headquarters after the Battle of Stones River and the 4th U.S. Cavalry formally joined the cavalry division.[12]

Stanley mentioned in his report those individuals in his opinion who deserved recognition for their actions during the battle. He identified:

Major Robert Klein	3rd Indiana Cavalry	For Action on December 27
Major Frank Ward	Anderson Cavalry	Great Bravery
Major Adolph Rosengarten	Anderson Cavalry	Great Bravery
Colonel Robert Minty	4th Michigan Cavalry	Command in Several Actions
Captain Eli Otis	4th U.S. Cavalry	Important and Distinguished Service
Colonel Eli Murray	3rd Kentucky Cavalry	Important and Distinguished Service
Major John Wynkoop	7th Pennsylvania Cavalry	A Model to Faithful Soldiers
Colonel Lewis Zahm	Second Brigade	Personal Example
Colonel John Kennett	Divisional Command	Rendered Good Service[13]

Of the Battle of Stones River, Stanley wrote, "The battle of Stones River was no great victory but retreating to some extent demoralized, the rebel army, and coming about the time of Burnside's miserable failures in the east, our victory helped to sustain the courage of the country." Much was learned by Stanley and Rosecrans in regard to the Union cavalry at the Battle of Stones River and the first lesson learned was the need to have parity in arms, experience, and numbers to meet the Confederate cavalry. Finally, the reorganization of the cavalry of the Army of Cumberland was of great importance in the Battle of Stones River and subsequently for the Union cavalry. Only by concentrating the full force of cavalry, although still outnumbered, could Stanley have made the progress he did. It is not difficult to imagine the havoc Wheeler's cavalry could have made had the Union cavalry regiments remained dispersed throughout the various infantry corps working directly under the command of divisional or infantry brigade commanders. Stanley receives credit for this improved organization despite complaints of the infantry commanders. This organization was the first step in gaining parity with Wheeler, Forrest, and Morgan who, until this point, had literally ridden circles around the Union army.[14]

Confederate Cavalry

Joseph Wheeler began the campaign for Stones River with 4,237 men present and ready for duty. This amounted to about thirty percent more cavalry than the Union forces. Wheeler recorded 450 casualties during the campaign, and about the same percent loss as reported by the Union cavalry around 11–12 percent. Rosecrans' after action report claimed 257 Confederate cavalry troopers and officers captured during the battle, about fifty more than Wheeler reported.[15]

	Killed	Wounded	Missing
Wheeler's Brigade	22	61	84
Wharton's Brigade	20	131	113
Pegram's Brigade*	–	–	–
Buford's Brigade	2	11	6
Total	44	203	203

*Pegram did not report any losses.

Among the Confederate officers wounded during the battles over the ten-day campaign included: Colonel William Wirt Allen, 1st Alabama Cavalry; Lieutenant Colonel James D. Webb, 51st Alabama Rangers; Colonel Thomas Harrison, 8th Texas Cavalry;

Major James Quilbert Chenoweth, 3rd Kentucky; Major C. J. Prentice, 1st Alabama; Captain William Campbell, 3rd Kentucky Cavalry; Captain R. J. C. Gailbreath, Murray's Regiment; Lieutenant William Ellis, 8th Texas; Lieutenant W. H. Sharp, 8th Texas; Lieutenant and Adjutant N. D. Rothrock, 3rd Confederate; Lieutenants E. S. Burford and William E. Wailes of Bragg's staff. In addition, John Wharton's inspector general was mortally wounded and subsequently died after the battle.[16]

Wheeler also identified Colonel William W. Allen, Captain V. M. Elmore, and Lieutenant Edward S. Ledyard, of the 1st Alabama Cavalry; Major C. J. Prentice and Captain Richard McCann, commanding cavalry detachments; and Lieutenants E. S. Burford and William E. Wailes, (the last two being on Wheeler's staff) for gallantry.[17]

The important and successful actions of the Confederate cavalry are more easily assessed by examining the four cavalry brigades separately. First, Abraham Buford's brigade was ordered somewhat belatedly to join in the battle and thereafter, it was assigned primarily as support of Wheeler's brigade. While Buford made the deepest penetration into the Union western flank on December 31, overall Buford's troopers saw light action. After the Battle of Stones River, Abraham Buford transferred to the war in Mississippi and he would command an infantry brigade during the Vicksburg Campaign. Buford had only been in the war a few short months; and by January 1863 he had had two clashes with other officers, first E. Kirby Smith and then after the Battle of Stones River with his subordinate, Colonel R. J. Butler of the 3rd Kentucky Cavalry. Bragg sent Buford, who had a "contentious personality," to Mississippi presumably to remove Buford from the charges and counter charges made by Butler. Wheeler's other two brigade commanders, John Pegram and John Wharton, continued to command cavalry. It is of particular interest that both Buford and Pegram, both United State Military Academy graduates, struggled in the cavalry of the Army of Tennessee.[18]

While Wharton demonstrated a remarkable ability to command cavalry at Stones River, he also had a somewhat contentious personality that would result in his ambitious desire for promotion and subsequent death at the hands of one of his subordinate officers in 1865. Wharton's spirit was evident during the December 31 cavalry actions in the battle on the west flank. Wharton clearly had the edge on the Union cavalry, a two to one numerical advantage, plus a dedicated section of artillery which offered a significant advantage over his Federal counterparts. Perhaps the greatest contribution made by Wharton's cavalry during the day's fighting was the ability to quickly move to the rear of the routed Federal infantry. The Federal infantry facing the enemy in the front and the cavalry in the rear resulted in panic and the inability to reorganize or set up a good defensive position. Had Wharton had some additional support, from cavalry or infantry, there is little doubt he would have carried the day. The fighting on December 31 was the high point for Wharton, and the Confederate cavalry at Stones River. The next day he claimed a lightly defended small wagon train, only to be severely repulsed by a single Union regiment, the 1st Michigan Engineers. Finally, on January 2, a lack of communications on the east flank resulted in Wharton's brigades being unprepared to assist Breckinridge's attack, as intended.

John Pegram, while he remained with the cavalry in Tennessee, would have a difficult time. It is unclear why this occurred. Pegram's first infantry command was captured at the Battle of Rich Mountain earlier in the war and allegations of vacillation haunted Pegram. However, Pegram was one of the most experienced and well trained cavalry officers of the Southern cavalry. He was West Point educated, served as a cavalry training officer, and had experience on the western frontier. Compared to the volunteers who commanded the various regiments, Pegram was well suited for his role. It is also important to note that Pegram was socially and culturally a Virginia gentleman and perhaps some found this difficult to accept. Pegram was also an accomplished artist. In the rough and tumble atmosphere of the Confederate cavalry, he might have alienated some in the cavalry. It is past time to reevaluate his performance at Stones River. The conclusions drawn about poor reconnaissance on the east flank on the morning of December 31 are perhaps true. There are certainly enough historians who have drawn this conclusion; however, Pegram needs to be given the benefit of the doubt. And there are doubts, a plenty. The single surviving piece of evidence pointing at reconnaissance from the cavalry originated with the 1st Georgia Cavalry which Pegram promptly reported the movement of a Federal force moving across to the east of Stones River and properly forwarded this information to the Confederate division and army command. What messages Pegram sent before and after have not been preserved. The actions of the Confederate cavalry on the eastern flank deserve a more positive reconsideration.

The final brigade was Wheeler's own brigade. Wheeler's and Wharton's brigade provided excellent service while contesting Rosecrans' advance on Murfreesboro. Afterward, Wheeler's largest contribution came from the raid on December 30 which resulted in a large amount of damage to Rosecrans' supply trains. Both of these actions provided positive results. However, the raid on December 30 is more complex. The net result of this raid was the destruction of property, but it caused little overall impact on the battle. It can be argued that Wheeler's brigade might have been more useful in support of Wharton during the Battle of Stones River. Finally, Wheeler's brigade was repulsed on the afternoon of December 31, and had little success with the wagon trains on January 1 and 3.

One of greatest criticisms of the Southern cavalry at the Battle of Stones River rests with Joseph Wheeler acting as chief of cavalry. The allure of the "raiding strategy" which permeated the Southern cavalry worked against the Army of Tennessee at the Battle of Stones River. Not only did Bragg have two valuable commands away from this army at a critical time, the emphasis on this strategy kept Wheeler away from the main battle. There can be no doubt that Wheeler's raid on December 30 caused a significant loss to Union resources, but it did not affect the Army of the Cumberland's ability to fight and win the battle. Subsequent raids on January 1 and January 3 can only be described as failures in regard to impact and to reconnaissance. Bragg's acceptance of this role for his cavalry removed much of its positive use on the battlefield itself. Only Wharton's brigade had success on the morning of December 31 of the four cavalry brigades under Wheeler's command.[19]

The process that Joseph Wheeler began in November of organizing his various units, often battalions, into regiments yielded positive results during this battle and for future actions. The independent minded cavalry commanders needed to operate more as regiments assigned to the Army of Tennessee rather than partisans or raiders. In regard to Confederate cavalry itself, it is hard to imagine a more dedicated and committed group of troopers in history. These were brave men who fought and died for their homes, family, and their beliefs. Discipline was needed to enhance the already obvious skills of horsemanship and a willingness to aggressively engage the enemy. After the battle, Wheeler needed to find a way to instill discipline, arm and equip his men to match his Federal adversaries.

Tactics between the Southern and Federal cavalry remained vastly different in 1862 and 1863. Wheeler would author his own manual for the training of Southern cavalry which would be published early in 1863; and in the field, he would emphasize dismounted cavalry and cavalry with a reliance on revolvers. He would also arm his cavalry with carbines whenever possible. The Union cavalry on the other hand still remained in the saddle more often, although they did fight dismounted. In obvious contrast to Wheeler, the Union cavalry relied heavily on the saber and would throughout the war. There are numerous accounts and various comments from Union cavalrymen which stated: "They won't stand the sabres"; but this is in direct contrast to the distain for the saber the 8th Texas troopers demonstrated in the recent battle. The disagreements of the relative value of sabers compared to pistols continued for years after the war. In the early 1900s the argument still raged. Colonel E. S. Godfrey, 9th U.S. Cavalry, reported to the War Department in 1905 the results of exercises to determine the effectiveness of these weapons. Godfrey explained with troopers in the saddle firing a revolver that only one in five shots hit a target and that firing revolvers in close combat was equally dangerous not only for the enemy but for friends alike. Godfrey concluded, "The role of the pistol and the role of the saber are different; one cannot displace the other. The cavalry that is without the saber will be unable to take advantage of all the opportunities of a war."[20]

After the Battle of Stones River, Forrest and Morgan returned to Middle Tennessee and joined Wheeler's and Wharton's cavalry. Earl Van Dorn's cavalry also would join Bragg's army in March 1863, but Abraham Buford's stay in Tennessee was short-lived. In January, his brigade was distributed to other commands and Buford was sent to service in Mississippi where he was assigned to an infantry brigade. John Pegram was assigned duty in the Department of East Tennessee and commanded a large cavalry brigade of four regiments, two battalions and a battery of artillery. Pegram would command a cavalry division under Forrest's command at the Battle of Chickamauga before transferring to Army of Northern Virginia. He was a highly regarded general when he reached Virginia and would be killed in action in Virginia in 1865.[21]

Final Remarks

Overall, both cavalries performed very well at Stones River, but the long term effect of the battle sounded an ominous tone for the dominance of the Confederate cavalry. The Confederacy quickly and willingly accepted the cavalry as an integral part of their military strategy early in the war, and moved to offer a superior organization of their cavalry regiments. Because the cavalry of Army of Tennessee was so formidable in Middle Tennessee and at the Battle of Stones River, it became a primary objective of Rosecrans and Stanley to add more cavalry that was well armed, and prepared to fight. By June 1863, Rosecrans had two cavalry divisions under Stanley's command with twenty regiments and in May 1864, that number would swell to four divisions and thirty-eight regiments. The cavalry actions south of Nashville in 1862 and 1863 gave the Union Army the clear objective of meeting the Confederate cavalry on equal terms and this began in earnest as a result of the Battle of Stones River.

Chapter Notes

Chapter 1

1. Gates P. Thruston, "Personal Recollections of the Battle in the Rear at Stone's River, Tennessee, with Two Maps," In *Sketches of War History 1861–1865, Papers Prepared for the Commandery of the State of Ohio, Military Order of the Loyal Legion of the United States*, Volume IV, Theodore F. Allen, Edward S. McKee, and J. Gordon Taylor, eds. (Cincinnati: Monfort & Co., 1908), 219–220.

2. George Knox Miller, *An Uncompromising Secessionist: The Civil War of George Knox Miller, Eighth (Wade's) Confederate Cavalry*, Edited by Richard M. McMurry (Tuscaloosa: University of Alabama Press, 2007), 93; Braxton Bragg, *The War of the Rebellion. A Compilation of the Official Records of the Union and Confederate Armies*, Series 1, Volume 16, Part 1, 1088, 1093. [Hereafter referred to as *Official Records*.]

3. Peter Cozzens, *No Better Place to Die: The Battle of Stones River* (Urbana and Chicago: University of Illinois Press, 1991), 3; Basil W. Duke, *History of Morgan's Cavalry* (Cincinnati: Miami Printing and Publishing Co., 1867), 270; Braxton Bragg, *Official Records*, Series 1, Volume 16, Part 1, 1093, 1095–1107; Leonidas Polk, *Official Records*, Series 1, Volume 16, Part 1, 1096–1107; William Hardee, *Official Records*, Series 1, Volume 16, Part 1, 1095–1107.

4. Braxton Bragg, *Official Records*, Series 1, Volume 16, Part 1, 1087, 1094; George Knox Miller, *An Uncompromising Secessionist*, 93.

5. Charles Stringfellow, *Official Records*, Series 1, Volume 16, Part 2, 929; Sam Jones, *Official Records*, Series 1, Volume 16, Part 2, 934; Peter Cozzens, *No Better Place to Die: The Battle of Stones River*, 32–33.

6. John W. DuBose, *General Joseph Wheeler and the Army of Tennessee* (New York: The Neale Publishing Co., 1912), 91.

7. Clement A. Evans, editor, *Confederate Military History*, Volume I (Atlanta: Confederate Publishing, 1899), 699–702.

8. Edward Longacre, *A Soldier to the Last: Maj. Gen. Joseph Wheeler in Blue and Gray* (Washington, D.C.: Potomac Books, Inc., 2007), 7–11, 55–60; J. P. Dyer, "The Civil War Career of General Joseph Wheeler," *The Georgia Historical Quarterly*, Vol. 19 No. 1 (Mar. 1935), 17–46; William Wharton Groce, "Major General John A. Wharton," *Southwestern Historical Quarterly*, Vol. 19, No. 3 (Jan., 1916), 271–278; C. C. Jeffries, *Terry's Rangers* (New York: Vantage Press, 1961), 17–29.

9. Robert S. Cameron, *Staff Ride Handbook for the Battle of Perryville, 8 October, 1862* (Fort Leavenworth, KS: Combat Studies Institute Press, n.d.), 205–206.

10. Robert S. Cameron, *Staff Ride Handbook for the Battle of Perryville, 8 October, 1862*, 215; Basil Duke, *Morgan's Cavalry* (New York: The Neale Publishing Co., 1909), 14–17.

11. Joseph Wheeler, "Bragg's Invasion of Kentucky," in *Battles and Leaders of the Civil War*, Volume III (New York: The Century Company, 1888), 4; John S. Scott, *Official Records*, Series 1, Volume 16, Part 1, 938–939.

12. Kenneth Hafendorfer, *They Died by Twos and Tens: The Confederate Cavalry in the Kentucky Campaign of 1862* (Louisville, KY: KH Press, 1995), 739, 742.

13. Don Carlos Buell, *Official Records*, Series 1, Volume 16, Part 1, 51.

14. Braxton Bragg, *Official Records*, Series 1, Volume 16, Part 2, 930; George Brent, *Official Records*, Series 1, Volume 16, Part 2, 935, 941; Joseph Wheeler, *Official Records*, Series 1, Volume 16, Part 1, 898; Kenneth Hafendorfer, *They Died by Twos and Tens*, 753.

15. William Hazen, *Official Records*, Series 1, Volume 16, Part 1, 1137; Cyrus Thomas, Diary, 1862, October 13, 1862, entry, United States Civil War, Thomas, Cyrus, b. ca. 1832, Papers, Archives and Regional History Collections, Western Michigan University; collection A-563; James B. Frye, *Official Records*, Series 1, Volume 16, Part 2, 600; John W. Dubose, "8th Confederate Cavalry," SG024922, Folder 14, Alabama Department of History and Archives, Montgomery.

16. George Thomas, *Official Records*, Series 1, Volume 16, Part 2, 600; George Brent, *Official Records*, Series 1, Volume 16, Part 2, 935, 941.

17. Edward Longacre, *A Soldier to the Last*, 11, 61; John W. DuBose, *General Joseph Wheeler and the Army of Tennessee*, 113; J. L. M. Curry, *Legal Justification of the South in Secession* (Atlanta: Confederate Publishing, 1899), 705.

18. Ebenezer Gay, *Official Records*, Series 1, Volume 16, Part 2, 605; James R. Howard, *Official Records*, Series 1, Volume 16, Part 1, 1143–1144; Eastham Tarrant, *The Wild Riders of the First Kentucky Cavalry* (Louisville: Press of R. H. Caruthers, 1894), 123.

19. Joseph Wheeler, *Official Records*, Series 1, Volume 16, Part 1, 898–899; Basil Duke, *Morgan's Cavalry*, 195; Edward McCook, *Official Records*, Series 1, Volume 16, Part 2, 618; Carroll Henderson Clark, "Memoir," Confederate Collection, Box 12, Folder 9, page 28, Tennessee State Library and Archives, Nashville, TN; Eugene Bronson, Letter—November 3, 1862, Eugene Bronson Collection, Kalamazoo College, Kalamazoo, Michigan.

20. Howell Carter, *A Cavalryman's Reminiscences of the Civil War* (New Orleans: American Printing Co., n.d.), 50; Joseph Wheeler, *Official Records*, Series 1, Volume 16, Part 1, 898–899; Thomas Lawrence Connelly, *Army of the Heartland: The Army of Tennessee, 1861–1862*

(Baton Rouge: Louisiana State University Press, 1967), 277.

21. Kenneth Hafendorfer, *They Died by Twos and Tens*, 792.

22. Anonymous, *Official Records*, Series 1, Volume 16, Part 1, 1136; George Brent, *Official Records*, Series 1, Volume 16, Part 2, 948; Joseph Wheeler, *Official Records*, Series 1, Volume 16, Part 1, 898–899; William Sooy Smith, *Official Records*, Series 1, Volume 16, Part 1, 1140; George Wm. Brent, *Official Records*, Series 1, Volume 16, Part 2, 949.

23. Kirby Smith, *Official Records*, Series 1, Volume 16, Part 2, 958; Braxton Bragg, *Official Records*, Series 1, Volume 16, Part 2, 952.

24. John Kennett, *Official Records*, Series 1, Volume 16, Part 2, 633.

25. William Hazen, *Official Records*, Series 1, Volume 16, Part 1, 1138–1139; John Pegram, Letter, October 20, 1862, Joseph Wheeler Papers, MSAm1649.24-717-1, Pegram, John, 1832–1865 to Joseph Wheeler; [n.p.] 20 Oct 1862, Harvard University, Houghton Library, Cambridge, MA.

26. Leonidas Polk, *Official Records*, Series 1, Volume 16, Part 2, 963.

27. Henry Halleck, *Official Records*, Series 1, Volume 16, Part 2, 623, 626–627; Don Carlos Buell, *Official Records*, Series 1, Volume 16, Part 2, 619.

28. O. P. Morton, *Official Records*, Series 1, Volume 16, Part 2, 634; Don Carlos Buell, *Official Records*, Series 1, Volume 16, Part 2, 637.

29. Henry Halleck, *Official Records*, Series 1, Volume 16, Part 2, 638; John Lillyett, Letter April 14, 1863, Don Carlos Buell Papers, 1818–1898, Correspondence, Letters Received, Mss A B928, 15, Filson Historical Society, Louisville, KY.

30. Horatio Wright, *Official Records*, Series 1, Volume 16, Part 2, 626; Jeremiah T. Boyle, *Official Records*, Series 1, Volume 16, Part 2, 625.

31. Horatio Wright, *Official Records*, Series 1, Volume 16, Part 2, 626; Jeremiah T. Boyle, *Official Records*, Series 1, Volume 16, Part 2, 625; Leonidas Polk, *Official Records*, Series 1, Volume 16, Part 2, 963; Charles Seidel, *Official Records*, Series 1, Volume 16, Part 1, 1147–1148.

32. Charles Seidel, *Official Records*, Series 1, Volume 16, Part 1, 1148; James B. Fry, *Official Records*, Series 1, Volume 16, Part 2, 629; Basil Duke, "Morgan's Cavalry During the Bragg Invasion," In *Battles and Leaders of the Civil War*, Volume III (New York: The Century Company, 1888), 28; George Kryder, Letter October 22, 1862, George Kryder Papers—MS 163, Bowling Green State University, Special Collections, Bowling Green, Ohio; George Walsh, *Those Damn Horse Soldiers* (New York: Thom Doherty Associates, 2006), 69–70.

33. Minor Millikin, *Official Records*, Series 1, Volume 16, Part 2, 648–649; A. J. Smith, *Official Records*, Series 1, Volume 16, Part 2, 633.

34. Edward McCook, *Official Records*, Series 1, Volume 16, Part 2, 1142; Carroll Henderson Clark, "Memoir," 28.

35. George Cullum, *Biographical Register of the Officers and Graduates of the U.S. Military Academy, 1841–1867*, Vol. II (New York: D. Van Nostrand, 1868), 396; Horatio Wright, *Official Records*, Series 1, Volume 16, Part 2, 523; Horatio Wright, *Official Records*, Series 1, Volume 16, Part 2, 908–909; William Polk, *Leonidas Polk—Bishop and General*, Volume 2 (New York: Longmans, Green & Co., 1915), 179.

36. Ebenezer Gay, *Official Records*, Series 1, Volume 16, Part 2, 552.

37. Don Carlos Buell, *Official Records*, Series 1, Volume 16, Part 2, 563–564.

38. Don Carlos Buell, *Official Records*, Series 1, Volume 16, Part 1, 1031: Joseph Clement, *Official Records*, Series 1, Volume 16, Part 1, 693; Napoleon J. T. Dana, *Official Records*, Series 1, Volume 16, Part 1, 662; Ebenezer Gay, *Official Records*, Series 1, Volume 16, Part 2, 606; James B. Fry, *Official Records*, Series 1, Volume 16, Part 2, 628.

39. Robert Cameron, *Staff Ride Handbook*, 232.

40. Don Carlos Buell, *Official Records*, Series 1, Volume 16, Part 2, 591–596.

41. George Garner, *Official Records*, Series 1, Volume 16, Part 2, 965; John Pegram, *Official Records*, Series 1, Volume 16, Part 2, 971.

42. Kirby Smith, *Official Records*, Series 1, Volume 16, Part 2, 967, 975; Joseph Wheeler, *Official Records*, Series 1, Volume 16, Part 2, 976–977; John Crittenden, Letter to Wife, October 25, 1862, Crittenden, John Crittenden letters (1862–1865), Record Group 765, Auburn University, Auburn, Alabama.

43. Kirby Smith, *Official Records*, Series 1, Volume 16, Part 2, 975; Braxton Bragg, *Official Records*, Series 1, Volume 16, Part 2, 974; Stanley Horn, *The Army of Tennessee* (Norman: University of Oklahoma Press, 1952), 189.

44. Braxton Bragg, *Official Records*, Series 1, Volume 16, Part 2, 976; George Wm. Brent, *Official Records*, Series 1, Volume 16, Part 2, 976; Robert Cameron, *Staff Ride Handbook*, 101.

45. G. W. Randolph, *Official Records*, Series 1, Volume 16, Part 2, 979; Joseph Howard Parks, *General Edmund Kirby Smith, C.S.A.* (Baton Rouge: Louisiana State University Press, 1992), 243–250.

46. Sam Jones, *Official Records*, Series 1, Volume 16, Part 2, 934, 938–939; S. Cooper, *Official Records*, Series 1, Volume 16, Part 2, 935.

47. James Negley, *Official Records*, Series 1, Volume 16, Part 2, 613, 619; Alfred P. James, "General James Scott Negley," *Western Pennsylvania Historical Magazine*, Volume 14, Number 2 (April 1931), 77.

48. Sam Jones, *Official Records*, Series 1, Volume 16, Part 2, 945.

49. Jonathan Otey, *Official Records*, Series 1, Volume 16, Part 2, 876–877; Sam Jones, *Official Records*, Series 1, Volume 16, Part 2, 953, 956, 969.

50. Nathan Bedford Forrest, *Official Records*, Series 1, Volume 16, Part 2, 970–971; J. Georgas, *Official Records*, Series 1, Volume 16, Part 2, 971; John Allan Wyeth, *Life of General Nathan Bedford Forrest* (New York and London: Harper & Brothers Publishers, 1899), 104.

51. Sam Jones, *Official Records*, Series 1, Volume 16, Part 2, 973; John A. Buckner, *Official Records*, Series 1, Volume 16, Part 2, 981–982; George G. Garner, *Official Records*, Series 1, Volume 16, Part 2, 983; H C. Reynolds, letter, October 4, 1862, Henry Clay Reynolds Papers, 1838–1920, LPR61, Alabama Department of Archives and History, Montgomery.

52. E Kirby Smith, *Official Records*, Series 1, Volume 16, Part 2, 984–985.

53. James B. Fry, *Official Records*, Series 1, Volume 16, Part 2, 643; Don Carlos Buell, *Official Records*, Series 1, Volume 16, Part 2, 641, 644–647.

54. Henry Halleck, *Official Records*, Series 1, Volume 16, Part 2, 640–641; L. Thomas, *Official Records*, Series 1, Volume 16, Part 2, 642.

55. Ephraim Otis, "The Murfreesboro Campaign," In *Campaigns in Kentucky and Tennessee including the Battle*

of Chickamauga, 1862–1864, *Papers of the Military Historical Society of Massachusetts* Vol. VII (Boston: Military Historical Society of Massachusetts, 1908), 296–297; Basil Duke, *Morgan's Cavalry* (New York: The Neale Publishing Co., 1909), 193–194.

56. James Guthrie, *Official Records*, Series 1, Volume 16, Part 2, 647; Richard Yates and O. P. Morton, *Official Records*, Series 1, Volume 16, Part 2, 642; David Tod, *Official Records*, Series 1, Volume 16, Part 2, 652.

57. Don Carlos Buell, *Official Records*, Series 1, Volume 16, Part 2, 652; William Rosecrans, *Official Records*, Series 1, Volume 16, Part 2, 653.

58. George Thomas, *Official Records*, Series 1, Volume 16, Part 2, 657; Henry Halleck, *Official Records*, Series 1, Volume 16, Part 2, 663.

59. William Rosecrans, *Official Records*, Series 1, Volume 16, Part 2, 655.

60. William A. Ganoe, *The History of the United States Army* (New York: D. Appleton & Co. Publishers, 1924), 250; T. F. Rodenbough, *From Everglade to Canon with the Second Dragoons* (New York: D. Van Nostrand, 1875), 232–37.

61. Grady McWhiney and Perry Jamieson, *Attack and Die: Civil War Military Tactics and the Southern Heritage* (Tuscaloosa: University of Alabama Press, 1982), 63–68; Stephen Starr, "Cold Steel: The Saber and the Union Cavalry, *Civil War History*, Volume 18, Number 2, 1965, 110–111; United States War Department, *Cavalry Tactics*, Volumes 1–3 (Philadelphia: J. B. Lippincott, & Co. 1862), 1–13; Kenner Garrard and Lewis Edward Nolan. *Nolan's System for Training Cavalry Horses* (New York: D. Van Nostrand, 1862), 3–8; Harris, Moses. "Some Thoughts on Equipment," *Journal of the United States Cavalry Association*, Vol. 4 (1891), 166–167; W. H. Sinclair, Orders, December 16, 1862, Letters and Orders, First Cavalry Division, Record Group 393, Part 2, Number 2468, National Archives.

62. Lloyd Lewis, *Sherman: Fighting Prophet* (Lincoln: University of Nebraska Press, 1960), 337; Charles W. Ramsdell, "General Robert E. Lee's Horse Supply, 1862–1865," *The American Historical Review*, 35 (July 1930), 758; Chelsea A. Medlock, "Delayed Obsolescence: The Horse in European and American Warfare from the Crimean War to the Second World War," Master's Thesis, Oklahoma State University, 2009, 17–27; John Lee Yaryan, "Stone River," In *War Papers Read before the Indiana Commandery MOLLUS* (Indianapolis: MOLLUS, 1898), 161; James Arthur Schaefer, "The Tactical and Strategic Evolution of Cavalry During the American Civil War," Ph.D. Dissertation, The University of Toledo, 1982, 28.

63. J. Lucius Davis, *The Trooper's Manual* (Richmond: A. Morris Publisher, 1861), 1–306.

64. Don Carlos Buell, "East Tennessee and the Campaign of Perryville" In *Battles and Leaders of the Civil War*, Volume III (New York: The Century Company, 1888), 51.

Chapter 2

1. John C. Breckinridge, *Official Records*, Series 1, Volume 16, Part 2, 1003.

2. Braxton Bragg, *Official Records*, Series 1, Volume 20, Part 2, 385–388; George Brent, *Official Records*, Series 1, Volume 20, Part 2, 393; John C. Breckinridge, *Official Records*, Series 1, Volume 20, Part 2, 402.

3. Peter Cozzens, *No Better Place to Die: The Battle of Stones River* (Urbana and Chicago: University of Illinois Press, 1991), 31.

4. Arthur C. Ducat, *Official Records*, Series 1, Volume 20, Part 2, 7–8.

5. William Rosecrans, *Official Records*, Series 1, Volume 20, Part 2, 9.

6. James Negley, *Official Records*, Series 1, Volume 20, Part 1, 3.

7. James Negley, *Official Records*, Series 1, Volume 20, Part 1, 4; Robert Smith, *Official Records*, Series 1, Volume 20, Part 1, 5; Thomas Speed, *Union Regiments of Kentucky*, Volume I (Louisville: The Courier Journal Job Printing, Co., 1897), 140; Braxton Bragg, *Official Records*, Series 1, Volume 20, Part 1, 6; John M. Porter, "Memoirs," Confederate Collection, Box 14, Folder 11; p. 70, Tennessee State Library and Archives, Nashville; *New York Times*, "Our Nashville Correspondence—The Attack Upon the City by Morgan Gen. Negley Repulses, the Rebels," November 15, 1862.

8. Nathan B. Forrest, *Official Records*, Series 1, Volume 20, Part 1, 6.

9. *Ibid.*

10. James Negley, *Official Records*, Series 1, Volume 20, Part 1, 4.

11. *Ibid.*

12. *New York Times*, "Our Nashville Correspondence; The Attack Upon the City by Morgan Gen. Negley Repulses, the Rebels," November 15, 1862.

13. James Negley, *Official Records*, Series 1, Volume 20, Part 1, 4–5; Nathan B. Forrest, *Official Records*, Series 1, Volume 20, Part 1, 6–7.

14. Nathan B. Forrest, *Official Records*, Series 1, Volume 20, Part 1, 7; Dee Alexander Brown, *Morgan's Raiders* (New York: Smithmark Publishers, 1959), 138.

15. John Weatherred, "The Wartime Diary of John Weatherred," private collection of Jack Masters, Gallatin, TN. November 9, 1862; James Lacy, Andrew Jackson Lacy, November 9, 1862, letter, Confederate Collection, Box C28, Folder 17, Tennessee State Library and Archives, Nashville.

16. Ulysses Grant, *Personal Memoirs of U.S. Grant, Volume I* (New York: Charles L. Webster & Co., 1894), 349.

17. Dennis W. Belcher, *General David S. Stanley, USA: A Civil War Biography* (Jefferson, NC: McFarland, 2014), 59.

18. William McClellan, *Official Records*, Series 1, Volume 7, 931; Dennis W. Belcher, *General David S. Stanley*, 19–91.

19. William Rosecrans, *Official Records*, Series 1, Volume 20, Part 2, 27.

20. William Rosecrans, *Official Records*, Series 1, Volume 20, Part 2, 31; Ulysses Grant, Special Order No. 15, Union Generals Records—David S. Stanley, Record Group 94, Entry 159, Box 28, National Archives, Washington, D.C. November 11, 1862; *Official Register of the Officers and Cadets of the U.S. Military Academy* (West Point, NY: U.S. Military Academy, June 1852), 7.

21. David Stanley, *An American General—The Memoirs of David Sloan Stanley*, Samuel W. Fordyce IV, ed. (Santa Barbara, CA: The Narrative Press, 2004), 98; Eli Long, Diary, July 29, 1857, United States Army Heritage and Education Center, Eli Long Papers—1855–1892, Carlisle, Pennsylvania; David S. Stanley, "David Stanley Diary, United States 2nd Dragoons of a March from Fort Smith, Arkansas, to San Diego, California, made in 1853," Crimmins (Martin Lalor) Papers, Briscoe Center for American History, University of Texas at Austin, Austin.

22. William S. Rosecrans, Letter—Undated, William

S. Rosecrans Papers, Box 59, Folder 54, University of California—Los Angeles; Thomas M. Vincent, "David Sloane Stanley," *The Thirty-fourth Annual Reunion of the Association Graduates of the United States Military Academy at West Point, New York* (Saginaw, MI: Seeman and Peters Printers and Binders, 1903), 62.

23. David Power Conyngham Papers (CON), "Soldiers of the Cross," University of Notre Dame Archives (UNDA), Notre Dame, IN., 26–29.

24. Alexander McCook, *Official Records*, Series 1, Volume 20, Part 2, 15.

25. Arthur Ducat, *Official Records*, Series 1, Volume 20, Part 2, 15.

26. Arthur Ducat, *Official Records*, Series 1, Volume 20, Part 2, 19, 21.

27. Arthur Ducat, *Official Records*, Series 1, Volume 20, Part 2, 23.

28. Arthur Ducat, *Official Records*, Series 1, Volume 20, Part 2, 23.

29. Thomas Crittenden, *Official Records*, Series 1, Volume 20, Part 2, 28; Arthur C. Ducat, *Official Records*, Series 1, Volume 20, Part 2, 28–29; John Large, Letter—November 13, 1862, John W. Large Papers. 1862–1863. [VFM 455], Ohio Historical Society, Columbus, Ohio.

30. George Thomas, *Official Records*, Series 1, Volume 20, Part 2, 29.

31. William D. Bickham, *Rosecrans' Campaign with the Fourteenth Army Corps, of the Army of the Cumberland* (Cincinnati: Moore, Wilstach, Keys & Co., 1863), 50.

32. J. B. Anderson, *Official Records*, Series 1, Volume 20, Part 2, 14; Thomas Crittenden, *Official Records*, Series 1, Volume 20, Part 2, 38.

33. G. C. Kniffin, *Official Records*, Series 1, Volume 20, Part 1, 9; *New York Times*, "A Federal Courier's Tale," November 24, 1862.

34. James Negley, *Official Records*, Series 1, Volume 20, Part 2, 41.

35. Joseph Wheeler, "The Battle of Murfreesboro," Joseph Wheeler Papers, Chicago Historical Society, Chicago.

36. John C. Breckinridge, *Official Records*, Series 1, Volume 20, Part 2, 402; David Urquhart, "Bragg's Advance and Retreat," In *Battles and Leaders of the Civil War*, Volume III (New York: The Century Company, 1888), 603; M. J. M. Mason, *Official Records*, Series 1, Volume 20, Part 2, 404.

37. William Rosecrans, *Official Records*, Series 1, Volume 20, Part 2, 45; George Thomas, *Official Records*, Series 1, Volume 20, Part 2, 45–46.

38. Lyne Starling, *Official Records*, Series 1, Volume 20, Part 2, 55; George Thomas, *Official Records*, Series 1, Volume 20, Part 2, 56; Arthur C. Ducat, *Official Records*, Series 1, Volume 20, Part 2, 66.

39. Nancy Pape-Findley, *The Invincibles: The Story of Fourth Ohio Veteran Volunteer Cavalry* (Tecumseh, Michigan; Blood Road Publishing: 2002), 112.

40. James G. Spears, *Official Records*, Series 1, Volume 20, Part 2, 60; Ulysses Grant, "Special Order No. 15"; Joshua Sill, *Official Records*, Series 1, Volume 20, Part 1, 12.

41. Braxton Bragg, *Official Records*, Series 1, Volume 20, Part 2, 411–412; Edwin Bearss, "Rebels Concentrate at Stones River," Research Project Number 5, 1960, Stones River National Park, Technical Information Center, Murfreesboro, TN, 148–150.

42. Braxton Bragg, *Official Records*, Series 1, Volume 20, Part 2, 420.

43. E. Kirby Smith, *Official Records*, Series 1, Volume 20, Part 2, 414.

44. E. Kirby Smith, *Official Records*, Series 1, Volume 20, Part 2, 413–415.

45. George Brent, *Official Records*, Series 1, Volume 20, Part 2, 415.

46. Braxton Bragg, *Official Records*, Series 1, Volume 20, Part 2, 416–418.

47. Edwin Bearss, "The Battle of Hartsville and Morgan's Second Kentucky Raid," Research Project #4—Stones River, Stones River National Park, Technical Information Center, Murfreesboro, TN, 1960.

48. Braxton Bragg, *Official Records*, Series 1, Volume 20, Part 2, 422; Jonathan Withers, *Official Records*, Series 1, Volume 20, Part 2, 424; David Urquhart, "Bragg's Advance and Retreat," 604.

49. G. St. Leger Grenfell, *Official Records*, Series 1, Volume 20, Part 2, 428.

50. George Brent, *Official Records*, Series 1, Volume 20, Part 2, 434; Terry L. Jones, *Historical Dictionary of the Civil War*, Volume 1 (Lantham, MD: Scarecrow Press, 2011), 232–233, 1091.

51. Edward Longacre, *Soldier to the Last*, 70.

52. George W. Brent, *Official Records*, Series 1, Volume 20, Part 1, 19; Longacre, *Soldier to the Last*, 71; A Staff Officer, *Synopsis of the Military Career of Gen. Joseph Wheeler* (New York: n. p., 1865), 8; "Mrs. L. Kirkpatrick's Scrapbook," 1st Alabama Cavalry's File, Alabama Department of History and Archives, Montgomery; Edward Kirk, *Official Records*, Series 1, Volume 20, Part 1, 13; Joshua Sill, *Official Records*, Series 1, Volume 20, Part 1, 12.

53. George Knox Miller, *An Uncompromising Secessionist The Civil War of George Knox Miller, Eighth (Wade's) Confederate Cavalry*, Edited by Richard M. McMurry (Tuscaloosa: University of Alabama Press, 2007), 99; Benjamin Burke, *A Terry's Ranger Write Home: Letters of Pvt. Benjamin F. Burke*, Jessie Burke Head, ed., November 30, 1862 letter, compiled 1965, Missouri History Museum, St. Louis.

54. Joseph Wheeler, "The Battle of Murfreesboro"; John Crittenden, Letter to Wife, November 27, 1862, Crittenden, John letters (1862–1865), Record Group 765, Auburn University, Auburn, Alabama.

55. J. P. Garesché, *Official Records*, Series 1, Volume 20, Part 2, 94; John Beatty, *The Citizen Soldier: The Memoirs of a Civil War Volunteer* (Lincoln and London: Bison Books University of Nebraska Press, 1998), 235.

56. Society of the Army of the Cumberland, *Twenty-seventh Reunion* (Cincinnati Ohio: The Robert Clark Company, 1898), 149–150.

57. William Rosecrans, *Official Records*, Series 1, Volume 20, Part 1, 182.

58. David Stanley, *An American General*, 150.

59. David P. Goebel, "Organizational Turbulence and Army Performance: A Comparison of the Confederate Army of Northern Virginia and the Army of Tennessee," Master's Thesis, U.S. Army Command and General Staff College Fort Leavenworth, Kansas, 1993, 45.

Chapter 3

1. William S. Rosecrans, *Official Records*, Series 1, Volume 20, Part 2, 118; Henry Halleck, *Official Records*, Series 1, Volume 20, Part 2, 117–118.

2. Henry Halleck, *Official Records*, Series 1, Volume 20, Part 2, 123–124; William Rosecrans, *Official Records*, Series 1, Volume 20, Part 2, 118.

3. William Rosecrans, *Official Records*, Series 1, Volume 20, Part 2, 115–116; Horatio Wright, *Official Records*, Series 1, Volume 20, Part 2, 120.

4. D. W. Holman, *Official Records*, Series 1, Volume 20, Part 1, 30–31; James D. Morgan, *Official Records*, Series 1, Volume 20, Part 1, 30; Robert Minty, *Official Records*, Series 1, Volume 20, Part 1, 29; George W. Roberts, *Official Records*, Series 1, Volume 20, Part 1, 28–29; Robert Burns, Letter book, November 23, 1862, M642, Minnesota Historical Society; Thomas Thompson, Diary, December 7, 1962, entry, Mss A T477, Thompson, Thomas B. 1862-1906, Diary, Filson Historical Society, Louisville, KY.

5. Charles Anderson, *Official Records*, Series 1, Volume 20, Part 1, 35–36; "Capt. Argus D. Vanosdol," *Biographical and Historical Souvenir for the Counties of Clark, Crawford, Harrison, Floyd, Jefferson, Jennings, Scott and Washington, Indiana* (Chicago: John M. Gresham & Co., 1889), 298–299; H. M. Buckley, *Official Records*, Series 1, Volume 20, Part 1, 34–35.

6. Edwin Bearss, "The Battle of Hartsville and Morgan's Second Kentucky Raid," Research Project #4—Stones River National Park, Technical Information Center, Murfreesboro, TN, 1960; Nimrod Long, Letter to wife, December 7, 1862, Nimrod William Ezekial Long papers, 1860–1865, Alabama Department of Archives and History, Montgomery.

7. Braxton Bragg, *Official Records*, Series 1, Volume 20, Part 1, 63.

8. George Knox Miller, *An Uncompromising Secessionist: The Civil War of George Knox Miller, Eighth (Wade's) Confederate Cavalry*, Edited by Richard M. McMurry (Tuscaloosa: University of Alabama Press, 2007), 100.

9. William Rosecrans, *Official Records*, Series 1, Volume 20, Part 1, 41.

10. Absalom Moore, *Official Records*, Series 1, Volume 20, Part 1, 52–53; William Rosecrans, *Official Records*, Series 1, Volume 20, Part 1, 45.

11. Edward McCook, *Official Records*, Series 1, Volume 20, Part 1, 51; Edwin Bearss, "The Battle of Hartsville and Morgan's Second Kentucky Raid."

12. Edwin Bearss, "The Battle of Hartsville and Morgan's Second Kentucky Raid."

13. George B. Guild, "Memoirs," Confederate Collection, Box C27, Folder 8, 1915, 47, Tennessee State Library and Archives, Nashville; John H. Morgan, *Official Records*, Series 1, Volume 20, Part 1, 66; Edwin Bearss, "The Battle of Hartsville and Morgan's Second Kentucky Raid."

14. John H. Morgan, *Ibid.*; Thomas Franklin Berry, *Four Years with Morgan and Forrest* (Oklahoma City: Harlow-Ratliff Company, 1914), 188–190.

15. Absalom Moore, *Official Records*, Series 1, Volume 20, Part 1, 54.

16. *Ibid.*

17. William Allen Clark, "Please Send Stamps: The Civil War Letters of William Allen Clark," Part IV, Edited by Margaret Black Taturn, *Indiana Magazine Of History*, XCI (March, 1995), 103; Absalom Moore, *Official Records*, Series 1, Volume 20, Part 1, 54–55.

18. William Rosecrans, *Official Records*, Series 1, Volume 20, Part 1, 45; Braxton Bragg, *Official Records*, Series 1, Volume 20, Part 1, 65.

19. Bennett Young, *Confederate Wizards of the Saddle* (Boston: Chapple Publishing Co., 1914), 240; John M. Harlan, *Official Records*, Series 1, Volume 20, Part 1, 47–49; John H. Morgan, *Official Records*, Series 1, Volume 20, Part 1, 67–68.

20. Samuel Hill, *Official Records*, Series 1, Volume 20, Part 1, 51–52; William Rosecrans, *Official Records*, Series 1, Volume 20, Part 1, 44.

21. Gustavus Tafel, *Official Records*, Series 1, Volume 20, Part 1, 57–58; Carlo Piepho, *Official Records*, Series 1, Volume 20, Part 1, 59–60.

22. John H. Morgan, *Official Records*, Series 1, Volume 20, Part 1, 66–68; George Garner, *Official Records*, Series 1, Volume 20, Part 1, 64.

23. William Thompson, Letter, December 11, 1862, [warr002], Civil War Collection, Tennessee State Library and Archives, Nashville; George Brent, *Official Records*, Series 1, Volume 20, Part 1, 63–64; Joseph Johnston, *Official Records*, Series 1, Volume 20, Part 2, 441; Braxton Bragg, *Official Records*, Series 1, Volume 20, Part 2, 446; Edward Longacre, *Mounted Raids of the Civil War* (Lincoln, Nebraska and London: University of Nebraska Press, 1975), 64–65; Michael R. Bradley, *The Raiding Winter* (Gretna, LA: Pelican Publishing, 2013), 17.

24. William Rosecrans, *Official Records*, Series 1, Volume 20, Part 1, 41, 44; Edwin Bearss, "The Battle of Hartsville and Morgan's Second Kentucky Raid"; Erastus Newton Bates, Letter, December 16, 1862, Erastus Newton Bates Papers, University of Georgia, Hargett Rare Book & Manuscript Library, Athens.

25. Thomas Crittenden, *Official Records*, Series 1, Volume 20, Part 1, 73; M. C. Woodworth, *Official Records*, Series 1, Volume 20, Part 1, 73–74; *Supplement to the Official Records*, Volume 3, 620–623.

26. John A. Martin, *Official Records*, Series 1, Volume 20, Part 1, 74–75; John A. Wharton, *Official Records*, Series 1, Volume 20, Part 1, 75; William D. Bickham, *Rosecrans' Campaign with the Fourteenth Army Corps, of the Army of the Cumberland* (Cincinnati: Moore, Wilstach, Keys & Co., 1863), 73.

27. Horatio Wright, *Official Records*, Series 1, Volume 20, Part 2, 135; P. H. Watson, *Official Records*, Series 1, Volume 20, Part 2, 135; William Rosecrans, *Official Records*, Series 1, Volume 20, Part 2, 135.

28. David Stanley, *An American General—The Memoirs of David Sloan Stanley*, Samuel W. Fordyce IV, ed. (Santa Barbara, California: The Narrative Press, 2004), 150; Stephen Z. Starr, "Cold Steel: The Sabre and Union Cavalry," In *Battles Lost and Won: Essays from Civil War History*, John T. Hubbell, ed. (Westport, Conn.: Greenwood Press, 1975), 116.

29. David Stanley, *Official Records*, Series 1, Volume 20, Part 1, 76.

30. *Ibid.*

31. David Stanley, Edward McCook, John Wharton, *Official Records*, Series 1, Volume 20, Part 1, 76–77; Ephraim Dodd, *Diary of Ephraim Shelby Dodd* (Austin: Press of E. L. Steck, 1914), 4; Elisha Peterson, Letter to parents, December 15, 1862, Elisha Peterson Papers, Section A, Box 104, David M. Rubenstein Rare Book & Manuscript Library, Duke University.

32. John A. Wharton, *Official Records*, Series 1, Volume 20, Part 1, 75; Larry Daniel, *Days of Glory, The Army of the Cumberland 1861-1865* (Baton Rouge: Louisiana State University Press, 2006), 196; Othniel Gooding, Letter, December 12, 1862, Othniel Gooding Letters (c.00275), Michigan State University Archives & Historical Collections, Michigan State University, East Lansing.

33. Jefferson Davis, *Official Records*, Series 1, Volume 20, Part 2, 449–450; Jefferson Davis, *Papers of Jefferson Davis*, Volume 8, "Letter to Varina Howell Davis," December 15, 1862, ed., Linda Lasswell Crist, Mary Seaton

Dix, and Kenneth H. Williams (Baton Rouge and London: Louisiana State University Press, 1995), 548; Alexander McCook, *Official Records*, Series 1, Volume 20, Part 2, 175.

34. John M. Porter, Memoir, Microfilm 824, Confederate Collection, Box 14, Folder 11, 73, Tennessee Library and Archives, Nashville; John Watson Morton, *The Artillery of Nathan Bedford Forrest's Cavalry* (Nashville, Tennessee and Dallas, TX: Publishing House of the M. E. Church, 1909), 45–46; W. W. Ward, *For the Sake of My Country: The Diary of Col. W. W. Ward, 9th Tennessee Cavalry, Morgan's Brigade, C.S.A.*, R. B. Rosenburg, editor (Murfreesboro: Southern Heritage Press, 1992), 10.

35. Alfred Tyler Fielder, "Diaries of Alfred Tyler Fielder," Microfilm 1003, Sunday December 14, 1862, entry, Microfilm 1003, Tennessee State Library and Archives, Nashville.

36. Horatio Wright, *Official Records*, Series 1, Volume 20, Part 2, 153–154; Horace Maynard, *Official Records*, Series 1, Volume 20, Part 2, 168–169; William Rosecrans, *Official Records*, Series 1, Volume 20, Part 2, 186.

37. William Rosecrans, *Official Records*, Series 1, Volume 20, Part 2, 114; Thomas Jordan and J. P. Pryor, *The Campaigns Lieut.-Gen. N. B. Forrest, and of Forrest's Cavalry* (New Orleans, Memphis, and New York: Blelock & Co., 1868), 193–194.

38. James Negley, *Official Records*, Series 1, Volume 20, Part 2, 176; John Wharton, *Official Records*, Series 1, Volume 20, Part 1, 448; Thomas L. Connelly, *Autumn of Glory: The Army of Tennessee 1862–1865* (Baton Rouge: Louisiana State University Press, 1971), 42.

39. J. P. Garesché, *Official Records*, Series 1, Volume 20, Part 2, 50.

40. Braxton Bragg, *Official Records*, Series 1, Volume 20, Part 2, 108; William Rosecrans, *Official Records*, Series 1, Volume 20, Part 2, 109; Henry Clay Greer, Compiled Service Record Colonel, November 20, 1862, 20th Tennessee Cavalry, Series M268; W. Hoffman, *Official Records*, Series 2, Volume 4, Part 1, 761; U.S. Grant, *Papers of Ulysses S. Grant: September 1–December 8, 1862*, John Y. Simon, ed. (Carbondale: Southern Illinois University Press, 1977), 229; Mamie Yeary, *Reminiscences of the Boys in Gray* (Dallas, TX: Smith and Lamar Publishing House, 1912), 319.

41. Thomas Crittenden, *Official Records*, Series 1, Volume 20, Part 1, 80; William Rosecrans, *Official Records*, Series 1, Volume 20, Part 1, 84; Braxton Bragg, *Official Records*, Series 1, Volume 20, Part 1, 84–85.

42. Braxton Bragg, *Official Records*, Series 1, Volume 20, Part 1, 84–85.

43. Horatio Van Cleve, *Official Records*, Series 1, Volume 20, Part 1, 282; Robert Minty, *Official Records*, Series 1, Volume 20, Part 1, 83; Bragg, *ibid.*

44. Braxton Bragg, *Official Records*, Series 1, Volume 20, Part 2, 187.

45. George Thomas, *Official Records*, Series 1, Volume 20, Part 2, 194; W. D. Pickett, "A Reminiscence of Murfreesboro," *Nashville American*, November 10, 1907.

46. Julius Garesché, *Official Records*, Series 1, Volume 20, Part 2, 204; J. M. Palmer, *Official Records*, Series 1, Volume 20, Part 2, 211; Lyne Starling, *Official Records*, Series 1, Volume 20, Part 2, 204–205.

47. Frank Mix, *Official Records*, Series 1, Volume 20, Part 1, 131–132; W. E. Hill, *Official Records*, Series 1, Volume 20, Part 2, 455; John Wharton, *Official Records*, Series 1, Volume 20, Part 2, 458; Robert Burns, Letter book, December 18, 1862, M642, Minnesota Historical Society, St. Paul.

48. John Berrien Lindsley, *The Military Annals of Tennessee, Confederate* (Nashville: J. M. Lindsley & Co., Publishers, 1886), 715.

49. James Negley, *Official Records*, Series 1, Volume 20, Part 2, 205.

50. John Wharton, *Official Records*, Series 1, Volume 20, Part 1, 159, 164; P. Sidney Post, *Official Records*, Series 1, Volume 20, Part 1, 164; Alexander McCook, *Official Records*, Series 1, Volume 20, Part 2, 158.

51. William Rosecrans, *Official Records*, Series 1, Volume 20, Part 2, 219–222; James Negley, *Official Records*, Series 1, Volume 20, Part 2, 224–225; H. W. Graber, *The Life Record of H. W. Graber, A Terry Texas Ranger, 1861–1865* (n. p.: H.W. Garber Publisher, 1916), 186–187.

52. David Stanley, *Official Records*, Series 1, Volume 20, Part 2, 227; George Thomas, *Official Records*, Series 1, Volume 20, Part 2, 227; William E. Crane, "William E. Crane's Daily Journal of Life in the Field during the War of the Rebellion," December 24, 1863, entry, Mss. 980, Cincinnati Historical Society, Cincinnati Museum Center; Daniel Prickitt, 3rd Ohio Cavalry, Diary, December 25, 1862, entry, ed. Edwin Stoltz, Bowling Green State University.

Chapter 4

1. William Rosecrans, *Official Records*, Series 1, Volume 20, Part 1, 182.

2. David Stanley, *An American General—The Memoirs of David Sloan Stanley*, Samuel W. Fordyce IV, ed. (Santa Barbara, CA: The Narrative Press, 2004), 150; Martin Buck, "From Capt. Buck's Co.," *Highland Weekly News*, December 25, 1862, 3; W. R. Carter, *History of the First Regiment of Tennessee Volunteer Cavalry* (Knoxville: Gaut-Ogden Co., Printers and Binders, 1902) 59; James Arthur Schaefer, "The Tactical and Strategic Evolution of Cavalry During the American Civil War," Ph. D. Dissertation, The University of Toledo, 1982, 132–133.

3. Lucien Wulsin, *The Fourth Regiment Ohio Veteran Volunteer Cavalry* (Cincinnati: Fourth Ohio Volunteer Cavalry Association, 1912), 8.

4. *National Cyclopedia of American Biography*, Volume VI (New York: James T. White Co., 1896), 448.

5. George Hazzard, *Hazzard's History of Henry County, Indiana, 1822–1906*, Volume 1 (New Castle, IN: George Hazzard Publisher, 1906), 187; *The Daily Wabash Express*, "Cavalry," Terra Haute, Indiana, November 16, 1861, 3.

6. Joseph Frederick Shelly, "Shelly Papers," Sophie S. Gemant and Fanny J. Anderson, editors, *Indiana Magazine of History*, Volume 44 (1948), Issue 2, 181–198.

7. Edward Tullidge, editor, "Governor Murray and Family," *Tullidge Quarterly Magazine*, Volume 1, Number 3 (1881), 496–501; David Evans, *Sherman's Horsemen* (Bloomington: Indiana University Press, 1996), 445.

8. Third Kentucky Cavalry, Officer Register, November 23, 1862, Record Group 94, Box 1366, Third Kentucky Cavalry Papers, National Archives, Washington, D.C.

9. William Henry Powell, editor, *Officers of the Army and Navy (volunteer) Who Served in the Civil War* (Philadelphia: L. R. Hamersly, 1893), 313.

10. William Sipes, *History and Roster of the 7th Pennsylvania Veteran Volunteers* (Pottsville: Miners' Journal Print, 1905), 1–3; Chester Bailey, *The Mansfield Men in the Seventh Pennsylvania Cavalry, Eighth Regiment*

(Mansfield, PA: Published by Author, 1986), 1–6; Gerould Otis Gibson, Diary—November 19, 1862, Pennsylvania Regimental Files, Stones River National Park, Technical Information Center, Murfreesboro, TN; T. F. Dornblaser, *My Life Story for Young and Old* (USA: Privately printed, 1930), 55.

11. George C. Wynkoop, Biography, MS-076: George C. Wynkoop Papers, Gettysburg College, Musselman Library, Special Collections & College Archives, Gettysburg; Francis W Reed, Letter December 19, 1862, Civil War Times Illustrated Collection, United States Army Heritage Education Center [hereafter referred to as USAHEC].

12. Stephen Z. Starr. "The Third Ohio Volunteer Cavalry: A View from the Inside." *Ohio History*, Volume 85 (Autumn 1976) Number 4, Ohio Historical Society, Columbus, Ohio (306–318), 310.

13. W. L. Curry, *Four Years in the Saddle: History of First Regiment Ohio Volunteer Cavalry* (Columbus: Champlin Printing Co., 1898), 20; Stephen D. Cone, *Biographical and Historical Sketches and a Narrative of Hamilton and Its Residents* (Hamilton, OH: Republican Publishing Co., 1896), 105.

14. W. L. Curry, *Four Years in the Saddle*, 28–29; Whitelaw Reid, *Ohio in the War: Her Statesmen, Generals and Soldiers* (Columbus: Eclectic Publishing Co., 1893), 993; Alexander C. McClurg, "An American Soldier, Minor Millikin," In *Military Essays and Recollections: Papers Read Before the Commandery of the State of Illinois* (Chicago: A. C. McClurg & Co., 1894), 363–364.

15. Thomas Crofts, *History of the Service of the Third Ohio Veteran Volunteer Cavalry* (Toledo: Stoneman Press, 1910), 12–13, 239.

16. W. L. Curry, *Four Years in the Saddle*, 9–12; Absolom H. Mattox, *A History of the Cincinnati Society of Army and Navy Officers* (Cincinnati: Peter G. Thomson, 1880), 187; William E. Crane, "Bugle Blast," *Ohio Commandery of the Military Order of the Loyal Legion of the United States* (Cincinnati: Peter G. Thompson, 1884), 7–8; Nancy Pape-Findley, *The Invincibles: The Story of Fourth Ohio Veteran Volunteer Cavalry* (Tecumseh, Michigan; Blood Road Publishing: 2002), 30.

17. William E. Crane, "William E. Crane's Daily Journal of Life in the Field during the War of the Rebellion," December 16–19, 1863, entry, Mss. 980, Cincinnati Historical Society, Cincinnati Museum Center.

18. *A Military Record of Battery D, First Ohio Veteran Volunteers, Light Artillery* (Oil City, PA: The Derrick Publishing Co., 1908), 39, 57.

19. *A Military Record of Battery D*, 9, 58.

20. John Fitch, "Captain Elmer Otis," *Annals of the Army of the Cumberland* (Philadelphia: J. B. Lippincott & Co., 1864), 215–218.

21. R. H. G. Minty, "The Saber Brigade," *National Tribune*, August 11, 1892.

22. *The Vevay Reveille*, "Necrology Col. Robert Klein," Volume 85, number 13, Thursday 27 March 1902, page 5, columns 3 and 4; W. N. Pickerill, *History of the Third Indiana Cavalry* (Indianapolis: Aetna Printing Co., 1906), 40–46; Frederick H. Dyer, *A Compendium of the War of the Rebellion* (Des Moines: The Dyer Publishing Co., 1908), 1105–1106.

23. L. Wallace Duncan and Charles F. Scott, editors, *History of Allen and Woodson Counties, Kansas: Embellished with Portraits of Well-Known People of These Counties, With Biographies of Our Representative Citizens, Cuts of Public Buildings and a Map of Each County* (Iola, KS: Iola Registers, Printers and Binders, 1901), 880–894.

24. John Andes and Will McTeer, *Loyal Mountain Troopers: The Second and Third Tennessee Volunteer Cavalry in the Civil War* (Maryville, TN: Blount County Genealogical and Historical Society, 1992), 38, 41–42; Second Tennessee Regimental Papers, Letter, January 29, 1863, Record Group 94, Box 4661, Second Tennessee Cavalry Papers, National Archives, Washington, D.C.

25. James Alex Baggett, *Homegrown Yankees: Tennessee's Union Cavalry in the Civil War* (Baton Rouge: Louisiana State University, 2009), 30, 46–47.

26. Fifth Tennessee Cavalry Papers, Letters, December 14, 24, 1862, Record Group 94, Box 4667, Fifth Tennessee Cavalry Regiment, National Archives, Washington, D.C.

27. Samuel P. Bates, *History of the Pennsylvania Volunteers, 1861–65* (Harrisburg: B. Singerly, State Printer, 1870), 902–903.

28. Walter Hines Page and Arthur Wilson Page, editors, "Gen. William J. Palmer, Builder of the West," In *The World's Work: A History of Our Time*, Volume 15 (New York: Doubleday, Page, & Co., 1908), 9899.

29. David Stanley, *An American General*, 49–50; Philip Sheridan, *Personal Memoirs of Philip H. Sheridan, General United States Army*, Volume 1 (New York: D. Appleton & Co., 1902), 8–9.

30. William D. Bickham, *Rosecrans' Campaign with the Fourteenth Army Corps, of the Army of the Cumberland* (Cincinnati: Moore, Wilstach, Keys & Co., 1863), 81; David Stanley, *An American General*, 150.

31. John Londa, "The Role of Union Cavalry during the Chickamauga Campaign," Master's Thesis, Command and General Staff College, Fort Leavenworth, Kansas, 1991, 28.

32. David Stanley, *An American General*, 150.

33. W. L. Curry, *Four Years in the Saddle: History of First Regiment Ohio Volunteer Cavalry*, 82.

34. Laurence D. Schiller, "Of Sabers and Carbines: The Emergence of the Federal Dragoon," *The Papers of the Blue & Gay Education Society*, Monograph Number 11, August 1, 2001, 9.

35. Lawyn C. Edwards, "Confederate Cavalry At Chickamauga: What Went Wrong," Master's Thesis, U.S. Army Command and General Staff College, Fort Leavenworth, Kansas, 1990, 10–18, 31–32; Jonathan J. Boniface, *The Cavalry Horse and His Pack* (Kansas City: Hudson-Kimberly Publishing Co., 1908), 24.

36. William Sinclair, General Order No. 3, December 2, 1862, Letters and Orders, First Cavalry Division, Record Group 393, Part 2, Number 2468, National Archives; Chelsea A. Medlock, "Delayed Obsolescence: The Horse in European and American Warfare from the Crimean War to the Second World War," Master's Thesis, University of Kansas Lawrence, KS., 2007, 18–19.

37. James Arthur Schaefer, "The Tactical and Strategic Evolution of Cavalry During The American Civil War," Ph. D. Dissertation, The University of Toledo, 1982, 20–24.

38. Ibid.; Berkley Lewis, *Notes on Cavalry Weapons of the Civil War, 1861–1865* (Washington, D.C.: American Ordnance Association, 1961), 5–30.

39. Berkley Lewis, *Notes on Cavalry Weapons of the Civil War* 33–34; Willard Glazier, *Three Years in the Federal Cavalry* (New York: R.H. Ferguson, 1870), 22; Lawyn C. Edwards, "Confederate Cavalry At Chickamauga: What Went Wrong," 33.

40. N. H. Davis, *Official Records*, Series 1, Volume 20, Part 2, 346.

41. Ibid.; Paul Hersch, Letter—October 12, 1862,

Hersh, Paul Papers (Civil War Misc. Collection), Sergeant's Transcribed Letters, Oct. 12, 1862–May 25, 1865, USAHEC, Carlisle, PA.

42. James Weir Diary, William Palmer Papers, Colorado Springs Pioneers Museum.

43. James Weir, *Ibid.*; Lewis Wolfley, Letter, January 23, 1863, Mss. Murfreesboro (Tenn.), Battle of, 1862–1863 C. Wolfley family, Letters, 1860–1865, Filson Historical Society, Louisville; H. C. Fry, "The Death of Martin L. Hill," In *History of the Fifteenth Pennsylvania Volunteer Cavalry* (Philadelphia: n. p., 1906), 77–79.

44. George Fobes, "An Account of the Mutiny in the Anderson Cavalry, at Nashville, Tenn., December 1862," In *Leaves of a Trooper's Dairy*, by John Williams (Philadelphia: Published by Author, 1869), 78–103; James Weir Diary, William Palmer Papers, Colorado Springs Pioneers Museum.

45. *Ibid.*; C. M. Betts, Journal—December 7, 1862, entry, Charles Malone Betts papers (#1889), Historical Society of Pennsylvania, Philadelphia.

46. N. H. Davis, *Official Records*, Series 1, Volume 20, Part 2, 346: William E. Carraway, "The Mutiny of the 15th Pennsylvania Volunteer Cavalry," *The Denver Westerners Monthly Roundup*, Volume XVII, No. 11 (November, 1961), 5–17.

47. William E. Carraway, "The Mutiny of the 15th Pennsylvania Volunteer Cavalry," 5–17; N. H. Davis, *Official Records*, Series 1, Volume 20, Part 2, 347–348.

48. *Ibid.*; *Potter Journal*, "News Items," (Coudersport, PA), 2, column 2, January 28, 1863; *New York Times*, January 9, 1863; T. Harry Williams, "Voters in Blue: The Citizen Soldiers of the Civil War," *The Mississippi Valley Historical Review*, Vol. 31, No. 2 (Sep., 1944), 187–204; George Garrett, Letter February 22, 1863, Stones River National Park, Technical Information Center, Murfreesboro, TN.

Chapter 5

1. Henry T. Clark, *Official Records*, Series 4, Vol 2, 31; Barton Myers, *Rebels Against the Confederacy* (New York: Cambridge University Press, 2014), 131; Thomas Speed, *The Union Cause in Kentucky: 1860–1865* (New York: G. P. Putnam's Sons, 1907), 249–250.

2. William Wharton Groce, "Major General John A. Wharton," *The Southwestern Historical Quarterly*, Vol. 19, No. 3 (Jan., 1916), 271–278; C. C. Jeffries, *Terry's Rangers* (New York: Vantage Press, 1961), 17–29.

3. William Wharton Groce, "Major General John A. Wharton," *ibid.*

4. Joseph H. Crute, *Units of the Confederate States Army* (Midlothian, Midlothian, AL: Derwent Books, 1987), 13–14.

5. Bruce S. Allardice, *Confederate Colonels: A Biographical Register* (Columbia: University of Missouri Press, 2008), 250.

6. Bruce Allardice and Lawrence Lee Hewitt, *Kentuckians in Gray: Confederate Generals and Field Officers of the Bluegrass State* (Lexington: University of Kentucky Press, 2008), 298; Claud Estes, *List of Officers, Regiments and Battalions in the Confederate States Army* (Macon, GA: J. W. Burke Co., 1912), 13; Joseph H. Crute, *Units of the Confederate States Army*, 65; 1st Confederate Cavalry File, SG024915, Folder 1, Alabama Department of History and Archives, Montgomery.

7. Bruce S. Allardice, *More Generals in Gray* (Baton Rouge: Louisiana State University Press, 1995), 65; United States Record and Pension Office, "Compiled Service Records of Volunteer Union Soldiers Who Served in Organizations from the State of Tennessee," Washington, D.C.: National Archives, 1962.

8. Joseph H. Crute, *Units of the Confederate States Army*, 67; John W. Dubose, "3rd Confederate Cavalry," SG024915, Folder 3, Alabama Department of History and Archives, Montgomery.

9. Joseph H. Crute, *Units of the Confederate States Army*, 82; Michael Bradley, *They Rode with Forrest* (Gretna: Pelican Publishing, 2012), 41–42; Bruce Allardice, *More Generals in Gray*, 66–67; *National Cyclopedia of American Biography*, Volume II (New York: James T. White Company, 1892), 244; Lanny Smith, *The Stone's River Campaign: 26 December 1862–5 January 1863, Army of Tennessee* (n.p.: Lanny Smith, 2010), 634; Lucian Lamar Knight, *A Standard History Of Georgia and Georgians*, Volume IV (Chicago and New York: The Lewis Publishing Co., 1917), 2281–2282; John Randolph Poole, *Cracker Cavaliers: The 2nd Georgia Cavalry Under Wheeler and Forrest* (Macon, GA: Mercer University Press, 2000), 53; Frank Battle, "Colonel Baxter Smith's Orders," In *Gray Riders: Stories from the Confederate Cavalry*, Lee Jacobs, compiler (Shippensburg, PA: Burd Street Press, 1999), 136–138.

10. Joseph H. Crute, *Units of the Confederate States Army*, 83; George Garner, *Official Records*, Series 1, Volume 16, Part 1, 1017–1018; Julius Lafayette Dowda, Diary, AC 70-069, MF 159; Drawer 283, Box 24, Georgia Department of Archives and History, Atlanta.

11. Joseph H. Crute, *Units of the Confederate States Army*, 283; Baxter Smith, "8th Tennessee Cavalry Regiment, Confederate, History of Regiment and Biographical information," Box 107, Folder 10, undated, USAHEC, 10; Military Units, Hand written sketch of the 4th Tennessee Cavalry, Box 17, folder 13, Confederate Collection, Civil War Collection 1861–1865, Tennessee State Library and Archives, Nashville.

12. George B. Guild, "Memoirs," Confederate Collection, Box C27, Folder 8, 1915, 180–181, Tennessee State Library and Archives, Nashville.

13. Joseph H. Crute, *Units of the Confederate States Army*, 317; Aaron Aster, *Civil War along Tennessee's Cumberland Plateau* (Charleston: History Press, 2015), 77–79.

14. *Tennesseans in the Civil War*, Vol 1. (Nashville: Civil War Centennial Commission of Tennessee, 1964), 59–61.

15. C. C. Jeffries, *Terry's Rangers* (New York: Vantage Press, 1961), 17–29.

16. C. C. Jeffries, *Terry's Rangers*, 59.

17. C. C. Jeffries, *Terry's Rangers*, 60–62.

18. *Ibid.*; *Tennesseans in the Civil War*, Vol 1. 156–157.

19. Ezra J. Warner, *Generals in Gray: Lives of the Confederate Commanders* (Baton Rouge: Louisiana State University Press, 1959), 39; Myron J. Smith, Jr., *Civil War Biographies from the Western Waters: Confederate and Union Naval Officials, Steamboat Pilots and Others* (Jefferson, NC: McFarland, 2015), 39; Bruce S. Allardice and Lawrence Lee Hewitt, eds., *Kentuckians in Gray*, 50–51; A. C. Quisenberry, "The Confederate Campaign in Kentucky: The Battle of Perryville," *The Register of the Kentucky Historical Society*, Volume 17 (January 1919) (30–38), 36.

20. Joseph H. Crute, *Units of the Confederate States Army*, 130–133; J. Tandy Ellis, *Report of the Adjutant General of the State of Kentucky: Confederate Kentucky Volunteers* (Hartford, KY: McDowell Publications, 1979), 486–540, 594–596, 634–686.

21. E. Polk Johnson, "The First Kentucky Cavalry," *Confederate Veteran*, Volume 21, 479; J. Tandy Ellis, *Ibid.*
22. D. Howard Smith, "Biography," D. Howard Smith Papers, 1821–1889, 85M03, Library Special Collections and Archives, Kentucky Historical Society, Frankfort; D. Howard Smith, *Life, Army Record, and Public Services of D. Howard Smith* (Louisville: Bradley and Gilbert Company, 1890), 2–25.
23. Bruce Allardice, *More Generals in Gray*, 108.
24. Ezra J. Warner, *Generals in Gray: Lives of the Confederate Commanders*. Baton Rouge: Louisiana State University Press, 1959), 231–232; Evans, Clement A., ed. *Confederate Military History: A Library of Confederate States History*. Vol. 3 (Atlanta: Confederate Publishing, 1899), 19–22; Peter Carmichael, *Lee's Young Artillerist: William R.J. Pegram* (Charlottesville: University of Virginia Press, 1995), 12–13, 32; The *Daily Dispatch* (Richmond), "Col. John Pegram," July 24, 1861; Walter Griggs, Jr., *Hidden History of Richmond* (Charleston, S.C.: Arcadia Publishing Co., 2012), 62–63; David Powell, *The Chickamauga Campaign: A Mad Irregular Battle* (El Dorado Hills, CA: Savas Beatie, 2014), 61–62.
25. Tucker Randolph, "Letter—November 12, 1862," Sgt. Tucker St. Joseph Randolph, Co. F, 21st Virginia Infantry and staff of Gen. John Pegram, 38 letters, May 1861–May 1864, American Civil War Museum, Richmond, VA.
26. Tucker Randolph, "Letter—December 8, 1862."
27. Arthur W. Bergeron, Jr. *Guide to Louisiana Confederate Military Units, 1861–1865* (Baton Rouge: Louisiana State University Press, 1989), 39–41; Stephen B. Oates, *Confederate Cavalry West of the River* (Austin: University of Texas Press, 1961), 26.
28. O. M. Mitchell, *Official Records*, Series 1, Volume 10, Part 1, 878–879; John Scott, *Official Records*, Series 1, Volume 10, Part 1, 878–879; Howell Carter, *A Cavalryman's Reminiscences of the Civil War* (Port Hudson, LA: Old South Books, 1979), 26–30.
29. John Pegram, *Official Records*, Series 1, Volume 23, Part 1, 171–174; Howell Carter, *A Cavalryman's Reminiscences of the Civil War*, 65–70.
30. Howell Carter, *A Cavalryman's Reminiscences of the Civil War*, 13–15; David Powell, *Failure in the Saddle* (New York and California: Savas Beatie, 2010), xxxv.
31. Rudi Keller, "Nixon Unwilling to Restore Confederate Battle Flag Despite Civil War Family Ties to Both Sides," *Columbia Daily Tribune*, May 13, 2014.
32. *Tennesseans in the Civil War*, Volume 1 (Nashville: Civil War Centennial Commission, 1964), 49–51; Walter Clarke, editor, *Histories of the Several Regiments and Battalions From North Carolina in the Great War, 1861–1865*, Volume III (Goldsboro, NC: Nash Brothers, Book and Job Printers, 1901), 745.
33. Stirling D. Popejoy, "The Second Tennessee Cavalry In The American Civil War," Master's Thesis, 2014, U.S. Army Command and General Staff College, Fort Leavenworth, KS, 19–21.
34. Stirling D. Popejoy, "The Second Tennessee Cavalry in the American Civil War," 32–33, 36–37; James P. Coffin, "Col. Henry M. Ashby," *Confederate Veteran*, Volume 14, 121.
35. Stirling D. Popejoy, "The Second Tennessee Cavalry In The American Civil War," 32; E. Kirby Smith, *Official Records*, Series 1, Volume 10, Part 1, 650; "The Lookout Rangers Colonel Henry Marshall Ashby and the 2nd Tennessee Cavalry," *The Silver Gray*, Volume 17, Number 11 (November 2012), 204.
36. Stirling D. Popejoy, "The Second Tennessee Cavalry in the American Civil War," 42–44; *Tennesseans in the Civil War*, Volume 1 (Nashville: Civil War Centennial Commission, 1964), 52.
37. N. B. Forrest, *Official Records*, Series 1, Volume 16, Part 1, p. 811; Stewart Sifakis, *Compendium of the Confederate Armies; Compendium of the Confederate States Army for South Carolina and Georgia* (New York: Facts on File, 1995), 147–149; Charles E. Jones, *Georgia in the Civil War 1861–1865* (Augusta: n. p., 1909), 41.
38. Robert Krick, *Lee's Colonels: A Biographical Register of the Field Officers of the Army of Northern Virginia* (Dayton, OH: Morningside Bookshop, 1992), 271; Terry L. Jones, *Campbell Brown's Civil War: With Ewell and the Army of Northern Virginia* (Baton Rouge: Louisiana State University Press, 2001), 59; Michael Bradley, *They Rode with Forrest* (Gretna, LA: Pelican Publishing, 2012), 39–40; J. W. Tench, "Detailed Account of the Operations of Col. Morrison's 1st Ga. Cav.," *Rome Tri-Weekly Courier*, November 20, 1862, 1.
39. Lanny Smith, *The Stone's River Campaign*, 632–633.
40. Ron Field, *The Confederate Army 1861–1865: Florida, Alabama & Georgia* (New York, Oxford: Osprey Publishing, 2005), 45; Edward Longacre, *A Soldier to the Last: Maj. Gen. Joseph Wheeler in Blue and Gray* (Washington, D.C.: Potomac Books, Inc., 2007), 4; Joseph H. Crute, *Units of the Confederate States Army* (Midlothian, VA: Derwent Books, 1987), 1; *Daily State Sentinel*, February 16, 1862; 1st Alabama Regimental File, SG024910, Folder 1, Alabama Department of History and Archives.
41. *American Civil War: The Definitive Encyclopedia and Document Collection*, edited by Spencer C. Tucker (Santa Barbara: ABC-Clio LLC, 2013), 34; T. A. De Land and A. Davis Smith, *Northern Alabama Historical and Biographical Illustrated* (Birmingham: Donohue and Henneberry Printers, 1888), 621; Willis Brewer, *Alabama, Her History, Resources, War Record, and Public Men* (Montgomery: Barrett & Brown, Steam Printers and Book Binders, 1872), 469; William B. Jones, "The Late Maj. Gen. William Wirt Allen," *Confederate Veteran*, Volume 2, Number 11, November 1894, 324.
42. Joseph H. Crute, *Units of the Confederate States Army*, 4.
43. James, Hagan, "3rd Alabama Cavalry," SG024911, folder 2, Alabama Department of History and Archives; Michael M. Bailey, *From Pensacola to Bentonville: The War History of the Pruttville Dragoons*, 3rd Alabama Regimental File, SG024911, folder 8, Alabama Department of History and Archives; 3rd Alabama Regimental File, Correspondence, SG024911, Folder 9, Alabama Department of History and Archives.
44. Corporal Barton Ulmer, November 7, 1862 letter, Perryville Battlefield State Historic Site, Ulmer Letters, Perryville.
45. James Hagan And Family Papers Mss. 1485 1833–1901, LSU Libraries Special Collections, Louisiana and Lower Mississippi Valley Collections, Special Collections, Hill Memorial Library, Louisiana State University Libraries, Baton Rouge; Willis Brewer, *Alabama, Her History, Resources, War Record, and Public Men*, 430; R. R. Gaines "Reminiscences of the 3rd Alabama Cavalry," SG024911, Folder 3, Alabama Department of History and Archives; John W. DuBose, *General Joseph Wheeler and the Army of Tennessee* (New York: The Neale Publishing Co., 1912), 99.
46. John W. DuBose, *General Joseph Wheeler and the Army of Tennessee*, 1–32; Fifty-First Alabama Partisan

Rangers, Regimental File, Alabama Historical and Archives Division, SG024914, Folder 3, Montgomery Alabama; William H. Hardie, *Brothers In Arms: The Hardie Family In The Civil War* (Mobile, Mobile, AL: Thornhill Foundation, 1994, 1998), n. p.; Wilbur F. Mims, *War History of the Prattville Dragoons* (Prattville, Prattville, AL: n.p., n.d.), 3–7; Rex Miller, *Wheeler's Favorites: A Regimental History of the 51st Alabama Cavalry Regiment* (Depew, NY: Patrex Press, 1991), 3.

47. Willis Brewer, *Alabama, Her History, Resources, War Record, and Public Men*, 225.

48. *Franklin Sentinel*, "Capture Of Dick McCann: The Celebrated Guerrilla Chief, Fifteen of His Men," August 22, 1863.

49. *Tennesseans in the Civil War*, Vol 1. (Nashville: Civil War Centennial Commission of Tennessee, 1964), 44.

50. *Tennesseans in the Civil War*, 41.

51. Bruce S. Allardice, *Confederate Colonels: A Biographical Register* (Columbia: University of Missouri Press, 2008), 200–201; John Berrien Lindsley, editor, *The Military Annals of Tennessee*. Confederate (Nashville: J. M. Lindsley & Co., Publishers, 1886), 714–715.

52. John Berrien Lindsley, *The Military Annals Of Tennessee*, 716.

53. Dunbar Rowland, *The Official and Statistical Register of the State of Mississippi* (Nashville: Brandon Printing Company, 1908), 800; 8th Confederate Cavalry, Director's Correspondence, SG024922, Folder 15, Alabama Department of History and Archives.

54. George Knox Miller, "Eighth Confederate Cavalry 1861–1865," Original deposited in Alabama, Department of Archives and History, Montgomery, Alabama.

55. George Knox Miller, "Eighth Confederate Cavalry 1861–1865"; George W. Cullum, *Biographical Register of Officers and Graduates of the U.S. Military Academy*, Volume II (New York: D. Van Nostrand, 1879), 472.

56. George Knox Miller, "Eighth Confederate Cavalry 1861–1865"; *Journal of the Congress of the Confederate States of America, 1861–1865* Vol. III (Washington: Government Printing Office, 1904), 184; John W. DuBose, "8th Confederate Cavalry," SG024922, Folder14, Alabama Department of History and Archives, Montgomery; Bruce S. Allardice, *More Generals in Gray* (Baton Rouge: Louisiana State University Press, 1995), 227–228.

57. George Knox Miller, *An Uncompromising Secessionist: The Civil War of George Knox Miller, Eight (Wade's) Confederate Cavalry*, Edited by Richard McMurry (Tuscaloosa: The University of Alabama Press, 2007), 93–94; John W. DuBose, *General Joseph Wheeler and the Army of Tennessee*, 99.

58. *Ibid*.

59. Michael R. Bradley, *The Raiding Winter* (Gretna, LA: Pelican Publishing, 2013), 176.

60. Edward Longacre, *A Soldier to the Last: Maj. Gen. Joseph Wheeler in Blue and Gray* (Washington, D.C.: Potomac Books, Inc., 2007), 7–11; J. P. Dyer, "The Civil War Career of General Joseph Wheeler," *The Georgia Historical Quarterly*, Vol. 19 No. 1 (Mar. 1935), 17–46; Lawyn C. Edwards, "Confederate Cavalry At Chickamauga: What Went Wrong," Master's Thesis, U.S. Army Command and General Staff College, Fort Leavenworth, Kansas, 1990, 49.

61. Edward Longacre, *Soldier to the Last*, 14–15; J. P. Dyer, *Ibid*.

62. Edward Longacre, Soldier to the Last, 16–17.

63. J. P. Dyer, "The Civil War Career of General Joseph Wheeler," 17–46.

64. Edward Longacre, *A Soldier to the Last*, 55–60; Baxter Smith, "8th Tennessee Cavalry Regiment, Confederate, History of Regiment and Biographical information," Box 107, Folder 10, undated, USAHEC; J. P. Dyer, "The Civil War Career of General Joseph Wheeler," *The Georgia Historical Quarterly*, Vol. 19 No. 1 (Mar. 1935), 17–46; John Randolph Poole, *Cracker Cavaliers: The 2nd Georgia Cavalry Under Wheeler and Forrest* (Macon, GA: Mercer University Press, 2000), 54; Arthur Fremantle, *Three Months in the Southern States, 1864* (New York: John Bradburn Co., 1864) 158; William Brooksher and David Snider, "The War Child Rides: Joe Wheeler at Stones River," *Civil War Times Illustrated* 14: (1976): 4–10.

65. W. Todd Groce, *Mountain Rebels: East Tennessee Confederates and the Civil War, 1860–1870* (Knoxville, University of Tennessee Press, 1999) p. 36–37, 84, 104; E. Kirby Smith, *Official Records*, Series 1, Volume 10, Part 2, 321; J. Stoddard Johnson, "Sketches of Operations of General John C. Breckinridge," *Southern Historical Society Papers* 7 (1879): 319; Bruce S. Allardice, Lawrence Lee Hewitt, editors, *Kentuckians in Gray: Confederate Generals and Field Officers of the Bluegrass State* (Lexington: University Press of Kentucky, 2008), 49–51.

66. Paddy Griffith, *Battle Tactics of the Civil War* (New Haven, CT.: Yale University Press, 2001), 180–183.

67. Dwyer, Christopher S. "Raiding Strategy: As Applied by the Western Confederate Cavalry in the American Civil War." *The Journal of Military History*, 63 (April 1999): 263–281, 266–272.

Chapter 6

1. William Hardee Papers, Hardee Family Papers, "Report of the Battle of Murfreesboro," (1862–1962), LPR121, 17, Alabama Department of History and Archives, Montgomery.

2. Julius P. Garesché, *Official Records*, Series 1, Volume 20, Part 2, 241.

3. *Ibid*.

4. William Rosecrans, *Official Records*, Series 1, Volume 20, Part 1, 184, 189–190; C. Goddard, *Official Records*, Series 1, Volume 20, Part 2, 242; Jefferson C. Davis, *Official Records*, Series 1, Volume 20, Part 1, 262.

5. William Rosecrans, *Official Records*, Series 1, Volume 20, Part 1, 189, 201; B. F. Nourse, Diary, December 26, 1862, B. F. Nourse Diary (1862–1878), David M. Rubenstein Rare Book & Manuscript Library, Duke University.

6. Patrick Cleburne, *Official Records*, Series 1, Volume 20, Part 1, 843; Braxton Bragg, *Official Records*, Series 1, Volume 20, Part 1, 663.

7. Alexander McCook, *Official Records*, Series 1, Volume 20, Part 1, 253; Jefferson C. Davis, *Official Records*, Series 1, Volume 20, Part 1, 262–263; Henry H. Eby, *Observations of an Illinois Boy in Battle, Camp and Prisons—1861 to 1865* (Mendota, IL: Published by the Author, 1910), 66; William Carlin, "A Noted Kentuckian: On to Stones River," *National Tribune*, 1, col. 6, March 19, 1885; W. N. Mercer Otey, "Organizing a Signal Corps, *Confederate Veteran*, Vol. 7, 549–550; L. G. Bennett And William. M. Haigh, *History of the Thirty-Sixth Regiment Illinois Volunteers, During the War of the Rebellion* (Aurora, IL.; Knickerbocker & Hodder, Printers And Binders, 1876), 750–757; Vickie Wendel, "Ordinary Heroes: The Second Minnesota Battery of Light Artillery," *Minnesota History Quarterly*, Volume 59, Number 4 (Winter 2004–2005) (141–153), 143.

8. J. K. P. Blackburn, *Reminiscences of the Terry Rangers* (n. p.: University of Texas, 1919), 35–36.

9. E. Kirby Smith, *Official Records*, Series 1, Volume 20, Part 2, 462; John Wharton, *Official Records*, Series 1, Volume 20, Part 2, 461; Joseph Wheeler, Stones River Report, Joseph Wheeler Family Papers, 1809-1943, LPR50, Alabama Department of History and Archives, Montgomery.

10. William Denison Bickham, *Rosecrans Campaign with the Fourteenth Army Corps or the Army of the Cumberland: a Narrative of Personal Observations, With an Appendix, Consisting of Official Reports of the Battle of Stone River* (Cincinnati: Moore, Wilstach, Keys & Co., 1863), 152–153; John McElroy, "Important Position of Kentucky and Tennessee," *National Tribune*, June 7, 1907, page 1.

11. Alexander McCook, *Official Records*, Series 1, Volume 20, Part 1, 253; William Carlin, "A Noted Kentuckian: On to Stones River," *National Tribune*, 1, col. 6, March 19, 1885.

12. Lewis Zahm, *Official Records*, Series 1, Volume 20, Part 1, 633.

13. Lewis Zahm, *Official Records*, Series 1, Volume 20, Part 1, 633; William E. Crane, "William E. Crane's Daily Journal of Life in the Field during the War of the Rebellion," December 26, 1862, entry, Mss. 980, Cincinnati Historical Society, Cincinnati Museum Center; Baxter Smith, "8th Tennessee Cavalry Regiment, Confederate, History of Regiment and Biographical information," Box 107, Folder 10, undated, USAHEC; Isaac Skillman, Diary—December 26, 1862, MMS1083, Bowling Green State University, Bowling Green Ohio.

14. George Thomas, *Official Records*, Series 1, Volume 20, Part 2, 242.

15. "Six Brothers Confederate Survivors," *Confederate Veteran*, Vol. 10, 114; Robert Minty, *Official Records*, Series 1, Volume 20, Part 1, 623; Robert Burns, January 11, 1863. Letter, Robert Burns Letter Book, 1862-1865 Burns, Robert Papers, 1832-1891, Minnesota Historical Society, St. Paul.

16. Leonidas Polk, *Official Records*, Series 1, Volume 20, Part 1, 685–686; Joseph Wheeler, *Official Records*, Series 1, Volume 20, Part 1, 958; Edward Longacre, *A Soldier to the Last: Maj. Gen. Joseph Wheeler in Blue and Gray* (Washington, D.C.: Potomac Books, Inc., 2007), 73; Robert Burns, Letter, January 11, 1863; John Fitch, "Battle of Stone River," In *Annals of the Army of the Cumberland* (Philadelphia: J. B, Lippincott & Co., 1863), 385.

17. Robert Minty, *Official Records*, Series 1, Volume 20, Part 1, 623; Nathaniel Newell, *Official Records*, Series 1, Volume 20, Part 1, 622; J. H. Wiggins, *Official Records*, Series 1, Volume 20, Part 1, 965.

18. Thomas Crittenden, *Official Records*, Series 1, Volume 20, Part 1, 446; J. D. Webb, *Official Records*, Series 1, Volume 20, Part 1, 962.

19. George Knox Miller, *An Uncompromising Secessionist: The Civil War of George Knox Miller, Eighth (Wade's) Confederate Cavalry*, Edited by Richard M. McMurry (Tuscaloosa: University of Alabama Press, 2007), 113.

20. George Knox Miller, *An Uncompromising Secessionist*, 113–114.

21. *Ibid.*, John Berrien Lindsley, editor, *The Military Annals Of Tennessee*. Confederate (Nashville: J. M. Lindsley & Co., Publishers, 1886), 714–715.

22. Robert Burns, Letter January 11, 1863.

23. Thomas Crittenden, *Official Records*, Series 1, Volume 20, Part 2, 243–44; Ebenezer Hannaford, "In the Ranks at Stone River," *Harper's Magazine*, 27 (1863), 810.

24. Thomas Wood, *Official Records*, Series 1, Volume 20, Part 1, 457.

25. Alexander McCook, *Official Records*, Series 1, Volume 20, Part 1, 253; William D. Bickham, *Rosecrans Campaigns*, 162.

26. W. D. Pickett, "Reminiscences of Murfreesboro," *Nashville American*, November 10, 1907.

27. Patrick Cleburne, *Official Records*, Series 1, Volume 20, Part 1, 843; Longacre, *As Soldier to the Last*, 73; Robert D. Jackson, letter January, n. d., 1863, Robert D. Jackson family papers, 1857-1914: LPR290, Alabama Department of History and Archives; John W. DuBose, *General Joseph Wheeler and the Army of Tennessee* (New York: The Neale Publishing Co., 1912), 120; Isaac Ulmer, Letter, December 26, 1862, Isaac Barton Ulmer Papers, #1834, Southern Historical Collection, The Wilson Library, University of North Carolina at Chapel Hill.

28. Robert Burns, Letter January 11, 1863.

29. Patrick Cleburne, *Official Records*, Series 1, Volume 20, Part 1, 843; William Henry Harder, Diary 1861-1865, December 27, 1862, Microfilm 574, Tennessee State Library and Archives; S. A. M. Wood, *Official Records*, Series 1, Volume 20, Part 1, 896.

30. Mamie Yeary, *Reminiscences of the Boys in Gray, 1861-1865* (Dallas: Smith and Lamar Publishers, Dallas, 1912), 464–465.

31. Alexander McCook, *Official Records*, Series 1, Volume 20, Part 1, 253; Peter Simonson, *Official Records*, Series 1, Volume 20, Part 1, 299; Richard Johnson, *Official Records*, Series 1, Volume 20, Part 1, 297; R. Charlton, *Official Records*, Series 1, Volume 20, Part 1, 906; Robert Klein, *Official Records*, Series 1, Volume 20, Part 1, 646; Joseph Collins, *Official Records*, Series 1, Volume 20, Part 1, 328.

32. Albert Ransom, *Official Records*, Series 1, Volume 20, Part 1, 302; Joseph Collins, *Official Records*, Series 1, Volume 20, Part 1, 328–329.

33. S. A. M. Wood, *Official Records*, Series 1, Volume 20, Part 1, 896–897; Robert Klein, *Official Records*, Series 1, Volume 20, Part 1, 646–647; James Weir Diary, William Palmer Papers, Colorado Springs Pioneers Museum; John Williams, *Leaves of a Trooper's Diary* (Philadelphia: Published by Author, 1869), 37.

34. Benjamin Burke, *A Terry's Ranger Write Home: Letters of Pvt. Benjamin F. Burke*, Jessie Burke Head, ed., compiled 1965, January 16, 1863 letter, Missouri History Museum, St. Louis; Thomas W. Cutrer, *Our Trust is in the God of Battles: The Civil War Letters of Robert Franklin Bunting, Chaplain, Terry's Texas Rangers* (Knoxville: University of Tennessee Press, 2006), 109.

35. Lewis Zahm, *Official Records*, Series 1, Volume 20, Part 1, 635; William Crane, Diary, December 27, 1862; Baxter Smith, "8th Tennessee Cavalry Regiment, Confederate, History of Regiment and Biographical information," Box 107, Folder 10, undated, USAHEC; Lucien Wulsin, *The Fourth Regiment Ohio Veteran Volunteer Cavalry*, 34.

36. Thomas Crittenden, *Official Records*, Series 1, Volume 20, Part 2, 243–244; Thomas Wood, *Official Records*, Series 1, Volume 20, Part 1, 458.

37. Robert Minty, *Official Records*, Series 1, Volume 20, Part 1, 623; Thomas Wood, *Official Records*, Series 1, Volume 20, Part 1, 458–459; Milo Hascall, *Official Records*, Series 1, Volume 20, Part 1, 466.

38. Milo Hascall, *Official Records*, Series 1, Volume 20, Part 1, 466; Frederick A. Bartleson, *Official Records*,

Series 1, Volume 20, Part 1, 482; William Hazen, *Official Records*, Series 1, Volume 20, Part 1, 543; Frank Mix, *Official Records*, Series 1, Volume 20, Part 1, 629–639.

39. Frank Mix, *Ibid.*

40. *Ibid.*; Frank Mix, Letter from Frank Mix, January 9, 1863, Elisha Mix Papers, 1818–1898, Bentley Historical Library, University of Michigan, Ann Arbor.

41. James Webb, *Official Records*, Series 1, Volume 20, Part 1, 962–963; Frank Mix, *Official Records*, Series 1, Volume 20, Part 1, 630; Elisha Mix papers, letter, January 9, 1863; James R. Riggs, Letter—December 26, 1862, James R. Riggs Civil War letters, Box Number SPR710, Folder Number 4, Alabama Department of History and Archives, Montgomery.

42. Julius P. Garesché, *Official Records*, Series 1, Volume 20, Part 2, 245; Alexander McCook, *Official Records*, Series 1, Volume 20, Part 2, 248.

43. George Knox Miller, *An Uncompromising Secessionist*, 114–115. [Federal records dispute Miller's claim that the Stewarts Creek bridge was destroyed by Wheeler's men.]

44. *Ibid.*

45. James Negley, *Official Records*, Series 1, Volume 20, Part 2, 246; George Thomas, *Official Records*, Series 1, Volume 20, Part 2, 248.

46. Braxton Bragg, *Official Records*, Series 1, Volume 20, Part 1, 672–673.

47. William Hazen, *Official Records*, Series 1, Volume 20, Part 2, 253, Lyne Starling, *Official Records*, Series 1, Volume 20, Part 2, 253; Alexander McCook, *Official Records*, Series 1, Volume 20, Part 2, 254; William Crane, Diary, December 28, 1862; John Daeuble Journal, John Daeuble Papers (1839–1864), Mss. A D123 1, Filson Historical Society, Louisville.

48. Julius Garesché, *Official Records*, Series 1, Volume 20, Part 2, 255; Alexander McCook, *Official Records*, Series 1, Volume 20, Part 2, 257.

49. Alexander McCook, *Official Records*, Series 1, Volume 20, Part 2, 256.

50. John Williams, *Leaves of a Trooper's Diary*, 43.

51. Robert Klein, *Official Records*, Series 1, Volume 20, Part 1, 647; Alexander McCook, *Official Records*, Series 1, Volume 20, Part 2, 254.

52. William S. Hall, *Official Records*, Series 1, Volume 20, Part 1, 648.

53. Julius P. Garesché, *Official Records*, Series 1, Volume 20, Part 2, 257–258.

54. George Brent, *Official Records*, Series 1, Volume 20, Part 2, 464; Braxton Bragg, *Official Records*, Series 1, Volume 20, Part 2, 467.

55. John Wharton, *Official Records*, Series 1, Volume 20, Part 2, 467.

56. George Knox Miller, *An Uncompromising Secessionist*, 103–110; William D. Bickham, *Rosecrans' Campaign with the Fourteenth Army Corps*, 44.

57. Braxton Bragg, *Official Records*, Series 1, Volume 20, Part 1, 663; Samuel Seay, "A Private at Stone River," *Southern Bivouac* (1887), 156–160.

58. George Knox Miller, *An Uncompromising Secessionist*, 115–116.

Chapter 7

1. Charles Harker, *Official Records*, Series 1, Volume 20, Part 1, 501; Thomas Crittenden, *Official Records*, Series 1, Volume 20, Part 2, 261–263; Lyne Starling, *Official Records*, Series 1, Volume 20, Part 1, 262; John Palmer, *Official Records*, Series 1, Volume 20, Part 2, 262; Thomas Wood, *Official Records*, Series 1, Volume 20, Part 1, 459.

2. George Knox Miller, "Eighth Confederate Cavalry, 1861–1865," Alabama Department of Archives and History, Montgomery, Alabama.

3. Robert Minty, *Official Records*, Series 1, Volume 20, Part 1, 623; Joseph Mitchell, *Official Records*, Series 1, Volume 20, Part 1, 626; Robert Burns Letter Book, January 11, 1863, M642, Minnesota Historical Society, St. Paul; Julius P. Garesché, *Official Records*, Series 1, Volume 20, Part 2, 263–264.

4. Julius P. Garesché, *Official Records*, Series 1, Volume 20, Part 2, 265.

5. Julius P. Garesché, *Official Records*, Series 1, Volume 20, Part 2, 266–267; Alexander McCook, *Official Records*, Series 1, Volume 20, Part 2, 266; Lewis Wolfley, Letter, January 23, 1863, Wolfey Family Papers, Mss. CW, Filson History Society.

6. Alexander McCook, *Official Records*, Series 1, Volume 20, Part 2, 267, 269.

7. Alexander McCook, *Official Records*, Series 1, Volume 20, Part 2, 269; David Stanley, *Official Records*, Series 1, Volume 20, Part 2, 268.

8. Lewis Zahm, Official Records, Series 1, Volume 20, Part 1, 635; William E. Crane, "William E. Crane's Daily Journal of Life in the Field during the War of the Rebellion," December 29, 1862, entry, Mss. 980, Cincinnati Historical Society, Cincinnati Museum Center; Douglas Murray, *Official Records*, Series 1, Volume 20, Part 1, 641; Ephraim Dodd, *Diary of Ephraim Shelby Dodd* (Austin: Press of E. L. Steck, 1914), 5.

9. John Pugh, *Official Records*, Series 1, Volume 20, Part 2, 644; Fourth Ohio Cavalry, Letter August 7, 1862, Record Group 94, Box 3518, Fourth Ohio Cavalry Papers, National Archives, Washington, D.C.

10. William E. Crane, Daily Journal, December 29, 1862.

11. David Stanley, *Official Records*, Series 1, Volume 20, Part 1, 618–619; S. Emanuel, "Promoted on the Field for Gallantry," *Confederate Veteran*, Volume 13, 17; James Weir Diary, William Palmer Papers, Colorado Springs Pioneers Museum; Eleanor Diehl Papers (1899–1918), Mss. C/D, Filson Historical Society, Louisville, Kentucky; John Williams, *Leaves of a Trooper's Diary* (Philadelphia: Published by Author, 1869), 46; *Lancaster Daily Evening Express*, "Local Intelligence," January 16, 1863; J. C. Reiff, "Fifteenth Pennsylvania (Anderson) Cavalry at Stone River," In *History of the Fifteenth Pennsylvania Volunteer Cavalry*, Charles Kirk, ed. (Philadelphia, PA: Society of the Fifteenth Pennsylvania Cavalry, 1906), 84–87; C. M. Betts, Notation, Charles Malone Betts papers (#1889), Historical Society of Pennsylvania, Philadelphia.

12. William Hall, *Official Records*, Series 1, Volume 20, Part 1, 648.

13. William D. Bickham, *Rosecrans' Campaign with the Fourteenth Army Corps, of the Army of the Cumberland* (Cincinnati: Moore, Wilstach, Keys & Co., 1863), 182; Ebenezer Swift, *Official Records*, Series 1, Volume 20, Part 1, 219.

14. Lewis Zahm, *Official Records*, Series 1, Volume 20, Part 1, 636.

15. Lewis Zahm, *Official Records*, Series 1, Volume 20, Part 1, 636; William Rosecrans, *Official Records*, Series 1, Volume 20, Part 1, 191; Charles Anderson, *Official Records*, Series 1, Volume 20, Part 1, 345.

16. Benjamin Burke, "A Terry's Ranger Write Home: Letters of Pvt. Benjamin F. Burke," Jessie Burke Head,

ed., compiled 1965, January 16, 1863 letter, Missouri History Museum, St. Louis.

17. Joseph Wheeler, *Official Records*, Series 1, Volume 20, Part 1, 958–959; Edward Longacre, *A Soldier to the Last*, 75, 78; James Hagan, "3rd Alabama Cavalry," SG024911, Alabama Department of History and Archives, Montgomery; John Witherspoon Dubose, "3rd Alabama Cavalry," unpublished manuscript, SG024911, Alabama Department of History and Archives; Montgomery; John Berrien Lindsley, *The Military Annals of Tennessee. Confederate* (Nashville: J. M. Lindsley & Co., Publishers, 1886), 715–716; George Knox Miller, "Eighth Confederate Cavalry, 1861–1865," Alabama Department of Archives and History, Montgomery, Alabama.

18. John Starkweather, *Official Records*, Series 1, Volume 20, Part 1, 391–392; John P. Dyer, *From Shiloh to San Juan: The Life of "Fightin' Joe Wheeler"* (Baton Rouge: Louisiana State University, 1989), 66–68.

19. Ibid.

20. John Henry Otto, *Memoirs of a Durch Mudsill*, David Gould and James B. Kennedy, editors (Kent and London: Kent State University Press, 2004), 79–80.

21. John Starkweather, *Official Records*, Series 1, Volume 20, Part 1, 391–392.

22. Joseph Wheeler, *Official Records*, Series 1, Volume 20, Part 1, 958–959; DuBose, "3rd Alabama Cavalry," Ibid.; J.B. Lindsley, *The Military Annals Of Tennessee*, 715–716; George Knox Miller, "Eighth Confederate Cavalry, 1861–1865"; John N. Smith, Letter, January 10, 1863, The Confederate Civil War Letters of John N. Smith, Technical Information Center, Stones River National Battlefield, Murfreesboro, TN; Newton Cannon, *The Reminiscences of Newton Cannon: First Sergeant, CSA*, Campbell Brown, editor (Franklin, TN: Carter House Association, 1963), 23.

23. Julius P. Garesché, *Official Records*, Series 1, Volume 20, Part 2, 277; G. C. Kniffin, "Army of the Cumberland and Battle of Stone River: Preliminary Movements," *National Tribune*, 3, column 4, January 7, 1882.

24. Joseph Wheeler, *Official Records*, Series 1, Volume 20, Part 1, 958–959; George Knox Miller, "Eighth Confederate Cavalry, 1861–1865," Alabama Department of Archives and History, Montgomery, Alabama.

25. Edward Longacre, *A Soldier to the Last*, 77; G. C. Kniffin, "Army of the Cumberland and the Battle of Stone River: The Preliminary Movements"; Bromfield L. Ridley, *Battle Sketches of the Army of Tennessee* (Mexico, MO: Mexico Printing & Publishing Co., 1906), 150.

26. John Wynkoop, *Official Records*, Series 1, Volume 20, Part 1, 631; Robert Minty, *Official Records*, Series 1, Volume 20, Part 1, 624.

27. Alexander McCook, *Official Records*, Series 1, Volume 20, Part 1, 256.

28. William Rosecrans, *Official Records*, Series 1, Volume 20, Part 1, 192.

29. David Stanley, *An American General—The Memoirs of David Sloan Stanley*, Samuel W. Fordyce IV, ed. (Santa Barbara, California: The Narrative Press, 2004), 152.

30. Edwin C. Bearss, Cavalry Operations—Battle of Stones River, Unpublished, Stones River National Park, Technical Information Center, Murfreesboro, TN, 1959, 59; James Knight, Letter January 3, 1863, Federal Collection Box F 25, Folder 8, Tennessee State Library and Archives, Nashville.

31. David Stanley, *An American General*, 153.

32. William Rosecrans, *Official Records*, Series 1, Volume 20, Part 1, 192; Henry M. Kendall, *The Battle of Stones River* (District of Columbia: Military Order of the Loyal Legion United States, 1903), 9.

33. William Hardee Papers, Hardee family papers, "Report of the Battle of Murfreesboro," [1862–1962] LPR121, 17, Alabama Department of History and Archives; Peter Cozzens, *No Better Place to Die: The Battle of Stones River* (Urbana and Chicago: University of Illinois Press, 1991), 60; Grady McWhiney, *Braxton Bragg and the Confederate Defeat*, Volume I (New York and London: Columbia University Press, 1969), 347–348.

34. John Wharton, *Official Records*, Series 1, Volume 20, Part 1, 966; Braxton Bragg, *Official Records*, Series 1, Volume 20, Part 1, 663–664; George Brent, Diary, December 30, 1862, Braxton Bragg Papers, Ms 2000, Series II, Box 4, Folder 22, Western Reserve Historical Society, Cleveland, Ohio,.

35. Ephraim Otis, "The Murfreesboro Campaign," In *Campaigns in Kentucky and Tennessee including the Battle of Chickamauga, 1862–1864*, Papers of the Military Historical Society of Massachusetts Vol. VII (Boston: Military Historical Society of Massachusetts, 1908), 304; Dennis W. Belcher, *General David S. Stanley, USA: A Civil War Biography* (Jefferson, NC: McFarland, 2014), 111; Horace Cecil Fisher, *The Personal Experiences of Colonel Horace Newton Fisher in the Civil War; a Staff Officer's Story* (Boston: Thomas Todd Company, 1960), 53; Richard Johnson, *A Soldier's Reminiscences in Peace and War* (Philadelphia: J. P. Lippincott & Co., 1886), 211; C. I. Walker, *Rolls and Historical Sketch of the 10th Regiment So. Ca. Volunteers* (Charleston, SC: Walker, Evans and Cogswell Printers, 1881), 93.

36. Henry M. Cist, *The Army of the Cumberland, Campaigns of the Civil War*, Volume VII (New York: Charles Scribner's Sons, 1909), 105.

Chapter 8

1. J. P. Garesché, *Official Records*, Series 1, Volume 20, Part 1, 183; Ira S. Owens, *Greene County Soldiers in the Late War. Being A History of the Seventy-Fourth O. V. I* (Dayton, OH: Christian Publishing, 1884), 29.

2. Peter Cozzens, *No Better Place to Die: The Battle of Stones River* (Urbana and Chicago: University of Illinois Press, 1991), 75–76.

3. Peter Cozzens, *No Better Place to Die*, 79–80.

4. John W. DuBose, *General Joseph Wheeler and the Army of Tennessee* (New York: The Neale Publishing Co., 1912), 129; Nathaniel Cheairs Hughes, Jr., *General William J. Hardee: Old Reliable* (Baton Rouge: Louisiana State University, 1965), 141.

5. Peter Cozzens, *No Better Place to Die*, 81–83; Richard Johnson, "Losing a Division at Stones River," In *Battles and Leaders of the Civil War*, Volume 5 edited by Peter Cozzens (Urbana and Chicago: University of Illinois Press, 2002), 296.

6. Ibid.

7. *New York Daily Tribune*, "From General Rosecrans's Army: A Terrible Battle at Murfreesboro," January 3, 1863, 1; L. B. Williams, *A Revised History of the 33rd Alabama Volunteer Infantry Regiment: In Cleburne's Elite Division, Army of Tennessee, 1862–1865* (Auburn, AL: Auburn University Printing Service, 1998), 31; Thomas W. Cutrer, *Our Trust Is in the God of Battles: The Civil War Letters of Robert Franklin Bunting, Chaplain, Terry's Texas Rangers* (Knoxville: University of Tennessee Press, 2006), 112.

8. John Wharton, *Official Records*, Series 1, Volume 20, Part 1, 966.

9. Nelson Gremillion, *Company G, 1st Regiment Louisiana Cavalry CSA: A Narrative* (Lafayette, LA: W.N. Gremillion, Sr., in cooperation with Center for Louisiana Studies, University of Southwestern Louisiana, 1986), 27.

10. Thomas Crofts, *History of the Service of the Third Ohio Veteran Volunteer Cavalry* (Toledo: Stoneman Press, 1910), 60.

11. *A Military Record of Battery D, First Ohio Veteran Volunteers, Light Artillery* (Oil City, PA: The Derrick Publishing Co., 1908), 60–61; Valentine Cupp, "Letter from the 1st O. Cavalry," *Lancaster (Ohio) Gazette*, January 29, 1863, 2; Lewis Zahm, *Official Records*, Series 1, Volume 20, Part 1, 636; Robert Minty, *Official Records*, Series 1, Volume 20, Part 1, 624; Eli Murray, *Official Records*, Series 1, Volume 20, Part 1, 627; John Wynkoop, *Official Records*, Series 1, Volume 20, Part 1, 631; Robert Klein, *Official Records*, Series 1, Volume 20, Part 1, 647.

12. William E. Crane, "William E. Crane's Daily Journal of Life in the Field during the War of the Rebellion," December 31, 1862, entry, Mss. 980, Cincinnati Historical Society, Cincinnati Museum Center.

13. John Wharton, *Official Records*, Series 1, Volume 20, Part 1, 966; William Hardee, Battle of Stones River Report, Hardee Family Papers, 1862–1962, LPR 121, Alabama Department of History and Archives, Montgomery; John S. Dollinger, "Recollections of the Battle at Stone's River, Tenn., In *W. L. Curry, Four Years in the Saddle: History of First Regiment Ohio Volunteer Cavalry* (Columbus: Champlin Printing Co., 1898), 302.

14. Lewis Zahm, *Official Records*, Series 1, Volume 20, Part 1, 637; G. C. Kniffin, "The Third Day at Stone's River," In *War Papers*, Paper Number 69, Military Order of the Loyal Legion of the United States, Commandery Of The District of Columbia, 1907, 5; Gilbert Kniffin, "The Battle of Stone's River," In *Battles and Leaders of the Civil War*, Volume 3 (New York: The Century Company, 1888), 621; Thomas W. Cutrer, *Our Trust is in the God of Battles*, 113.

15. J. K. P. Blackburn, *Reminiscences of the Terry Rangers* (n.p.: University of Texas, 1919), 37; John Randolph Poole, *Cracker Cavaliers: The 2nd Georgia Cavalry Under Wheeler and Forrest* (Macon, GA: Mercer University Press, 2000), 60.

16. Lewis Zahm, *Official Records*, Series 1, Volume 20, Part 1, 636.

17. Valentine Cupp, "Letter from the 1st O. Cavalry," *Lancaster (Ohio) Gazette*, January 29, 1863, 2.

18. Ibid.

19. Isaac Skillman, Diary—December 31, MMS 1083, Bowling Green State University, Bowling Green Ohio.

20. Lewis Zahm, *Official Records*, Series 1, Volume 20, Part 1, 636–637; John Wharton, *Official Records*, Series 1, Volume 20, Part 1, 966; George Guild, *A Brief Narrative of the Fourth Tennessee Cavalry Regiment* (n.p.: Nashville, 1913), 13; J. K. P. Blackburn, *Reminiscences of the Terry Rangers*, 38.

21. Baxter Smith, "8th Tennessee Cavalry Regiment, Confederate, History of Regiment and Biographical information," Box 107, Folder 10, undated, USAHEC, 19; William D. Bickham, *Rosecrans' Campaign with the Fourteenth Army Corps, of the Army of the Cumberland* (Cincinnati: Moore, Wilstach, Keys & Co., 1863), 209, 232–233; Lewis Zahm, *Official Records*, Series 1, Volume 20, Part 1, 637; Lanny Smith, *The Stone's River Campaign, 26 December 1862–5 January 1863: Army of Tennessee* (n.p.: Lanny Smith, 2010), 442; E. P. Burlingame, "Company L, First Ohio Volunteer Cavalry," In *History of Washington County Ohio with Illustrations and Biographical Sketches* (Cleveland: W.W. Williams Publishers, 1881), 188; Gates P. Thruston, "Personal Recollections of the Battle in the Rear at Stone's River, Tennessee, with Two Maps," In *Sketches of War History 1861–1865, Papers Prepared for the Commandery of the State of Ohio, Military Order of the Loyal Legion of the United States*, Volume IV, Theodore F. Allen, Edward S. McKee, and J. Gordon Taylor, eds. (Cincinnati: Monfort & Co., 1908), 223.

22. Issac Skillman, Diary—December 31, MMS 1083, Bowling Green State University, Bowling Green, Ohio.

23. Peter Cozzens, *No Better Place to Die*, 82–83,88–90; Lanny Smith, *The Stone's River Campaign*, 439; M. D. Ector, *Official Records*, Series 1, Volume 20, Part 1, 927; A. S. Bloomfield, Letter—January 16, 1863, Battery A, 1st Ohio (Artillery), Johnson's division, Stones River National Park, Technical Information Center, Murfreesboro, TN; Wilson J. Vance, *Stone's River: The Turning-Point of the Civil War* (New York: The Neale Publishing Co., 1914), 45.

24. Wilson J. Vance, *Stone's River: The Turning-Point of the Civil War* 45–46; Cozzens, *No Better Place to Die*, 85–87; Larry Daniel, *The Battle of Stones River* (Baton Rouge: Louisiana State University Press, 2012), 81; Edwin W. Payne, *History of the Thirty-Fourth Regiment of Illinois Volunteer Infantry* (Clinton, IA: Allen Printing Company, 1902), 347.

25. W. R. Friend, "Rout of Rosecrans," In *New Annals of the Civil War*, edited by Peter Cozzens and Robert Girardi (Mechanicsburg, PA: Stackpole Books, 2004), 211: C. C. Jeffries, *Terry's Rangers* (New York: Vantage Press, 1961), 62.

26. Peter Cozzens, *No Better Place to Die*, 92–100; Mathew Askew, Letter—January 21, 1863, Askew Family Correspondence, MMS 1380, Bowling Green State University, Bowling Green, Ohio; Alexis Cope, *The Fifteenth Ohio Volunteers and Its Campaigns, 1861–1865* (Columbus, OH: Published by Author, 1916), 234–237; Alexander Stevenson, *Battle of Stones River near Murfreesboro, Tennessee* (Boston: J. R. Osgood & Co., 1884), 39; Joab Stafford, *Official Records*, Series 1, Volume 20, Part 1, 343.

27. Philemon Baldwin, *Official Records*, Series 1, Volume 20, Part 1, 337; Edwin W. Payne, *History of the Thirty-Fourth Regiment of Illinois Infantry, September 7, 1861—July 12, 1865* (Clinton, IA: Allen Printing Company, 1902), 46; Unknown, Letter, January 18, 1863, Philemon Baldwin Papers, Technical Information Center, Stones River National Battle Field, Murfreesboro, TN.

28. P. Sidney Post, *Official Records*, Series 1, Volume 20, Part 1, 269–70; Alfred Tyler Fielder Diaries, December 31, 1862, entry, Ac #341, Box 1, Tennessee State Library and Archives, Nashville.

29. William Henry Harder, Diary 1861–1865, December 31, 1862, Microfilm 574, Tennessee State Library and Archives, Nashville 46–56; John M. Routt, Microfilm 824, Confederate Collection, Reel 4 (Box 11, Folder 15), Tennessee State Library and Archives, Nashville.

30. P. Sidney Post, *Official Records*, Series 1, Volume 20, Part 1, 29: 269–70; Charles B. Humphrey, *Official Records*, Series 1, Volume 20, Part 1, 267.

31. Douglas Murray, *Official Records*, Series 1, Volume 20, Part 1, 641–642; Dan Fleming, "Major David A. B. Moore: A True American Soldier," *Newark Advocate*, August 7, 2011.

32. Isaac Skillman, Diary—December 31, MMS 1083, Bowling Green State University, Bowling Green Ohio.

33. H. L. Ambrose, "Kentucky Troopers, Saved Rosecrans's Ammunition Train at Stone River," *National Tribune*, January 20, 1887, 8; Joseph Vale, *Minty and the Cavalry: A History of Cavalry Campaigns in the Western Armies* (Harrisburg, PA: Edwin K. Myers Printer and Binder, 1886), 113.

34. William E. Crane, "William E. Crane's Daily Journal of Life in the Field during the War of the Rebellion," December 31, 1862, entry, Mss. 980, Cincinnati Historical Society, Cincinnati Museum Center; Lewis Zahm, *Official Records*, Series 1, Volume 20, Part 1, 636; W. L. Curry, *Four Years in the Saddle: History of First Regiment Ohio Volunteer Cavalry* (Columbus: Champlin Printing Co., 1898), 83.

35. J. K. P. Blackburn, *Reminiscences of the Terry Rangers*, 38-39.

36. William Gibson, *Official Records*, Series 1, Volume 20, Part 1, 304; H. B. Teeter, *Official Records*, Series 1, Volume 20, Part 1, 645; Ezra T. Stringer, Letter, January 9, 1863, Ezra T. Stringer Correspondence, MS.2780, Folder 1, University of Tennessee Libraries, Special Collections, Knoxville.

37. J. B. Dodge, "What I Saw at Stone River," *Northern Indianian*, Thursday Mar. 11, 1875, front page. [In Dodge's report it appears that this action occurred near Wilkinson Pike, but it is unclear is Dodge is referring to the cavalry action of the 4th U.S. Cavalry which occurred later in the morning or of Zahm's cavalry near Wilkinson Pike. Because of further details in his description, this account appears to have occurred in the same vicinity of Gibson's similar events and most likely involves the action along Wilkinson Pike.]

38. William Gibson, *Official Records*, Series 1, Volume 20, Part 1, 306; Lyman Ayer, Letter—April 23, 1863, Civil War Collection, Box F 25, Folder 6. Lyman Ayer Letters, 1863, Tennessee State Library and Archives, Nashville; J. B. Dodge, "What I Saw at Stone River."

39. John Wharton, *Official Records*, Series 1, Volume 20, Part 1, 966; William Hardee Papers, Hardee family papers, "Report of the Battle of Murfreesboro," [1862-1962] LPR121, Alabama Department of History and Archives, 17-20; Benjamin Burke, *A Terry's Ranger Write Home: Letters of Pvt. Benjamin F. Burke*, Jessie Burke Head, ed., compiled 1965, January 16, 1863, letter, Missouri History Museum, St. Louis; St. John Liddell, *Liddell's Record*, Nathaniel Hughes, Jr., ed. (Baton Rouge: Louisiana State University Press,1997),110; Alexis Cope, *The Fifteenth Ohio Volunteers and Its Campaigns, 1861-1865* (Columbus, OH: Published by Author, 1916), 250; Lanny Smith, *The Stone's River Campaign*, 443.

40. F. M Ison, Letter, May 20, 1863, Letter from Lt. Col. accounting the actions of Private James F. Fambro, Technical Information Center, Stones River National Battle Field, Murfreesboro, TN.

41. H. B. Teeter, *Official Records*, Series 1, Volume 20, Part 1, 645; William E. Crane, "William E. Crane's Daily Journal of Life in the Field during the War of the Rebellion," December 31, 1862.

42. Thomas Osborn, "Osborn, Thomas H.," In *The History of the Cincinnati Society of Army and Navy Officers* (Cincinnati: Peter G. Thomson, Publisher, 1880), 185-186.

43. Robert Klein, *Official Records*, Series 1, Volume 20, Part 1, 647; Lanny Smith, *The Stone's River Campaign*, 443.

44. Vincent Dunn, Letter, January 19, 1863, Dunn Family Papers, 1854-1977, Mss./A/D923, Filson Historical Society, Louisville, Kentucky; Lewis Wolfley, Letter, January 23, 1863, Mss. Murfreesboro (Tenn.), Battle of, 1862-1863 C. Wolfley Family, Letters, 1860-1865, Filson Historical Society, Louisville.

45. T. F. Dornblaser, *Sabre Strokes of the Pennsylvania Dragoons in the War of 1861-1865* (Philadelphia: Lutheran Publication Society, 1884), 99.

46. Lewis Zahm, *Official Records*, Series 1, Volume 20, Part 1, 637.

Chapter 9

1. John D. Billings, *Hardtack and Coffee, or, The Unwritten Story of Army Life* (Boston: George M. Smith & Co., 1887), 279-294, 352-359.

2. Alfred Pirtle, "Stone River Sketches," In *Sketches of War History*, edited by Theodore Allen, Edward McKee and Gordon Taylor (Cincinnati: Monfort & Co., 1908), 95-100.

3. James Knight, Letter January 3, 1863, Federal Collection Box F 25, Folder 8, Tennessee State Library and Archives.

4. G. C. Kniffin, "Stone River—The Second Day," *National Tribune*, January 21, 1882, 1. column 1.

5. John Williams, *Leaves of a Trooper's Dairy* (Philadelphia: Published by Author, 1869), 150-155.

6. Gerould Otis Gibson, Diary—December 31, 1862, Pennsylvania Regimental Files, Stones River National Park, Technical Information Center, Murfreesboro, TN; Chester Bailey, *Mansfield Men in the Seventh Pennsylvania Cavalry, Eightieth Regiment* (Mansfield, PA: Chester Bailey Publisher, 1986), 35.

7. Gate Thruston, "Personal Recollections of the Battle in the Rear at Stone's River, Tennessee, with Two Maps," In *Sketches of War History 1861-1865, Papers Prepared for the Commandery of the State of Ohio, Military Order of the Loyal Legion of the United States*, Volume IV, Theodore F. Allen, Edward S. McKee, and J. Gordon Taylor, eds. (Cincinnati: Monfort & Co., 1908), 225.

8. T. F. Dornblaser, *Sabre Strokes of the Pennsylvania Dragoons* (Philadelphia: Lutheran Publication Society, 1884), 100.

9. J. Ferrell Colton and Antoinette Smith, editors, *Column South with the Fifteenth Pennsylvania Cavalry* (Flagstaff: J. P. Colton & Co., 1960), 44.

10. Lewis Zahm, *Official Records*, Series 1, Volume 20, Part 1, 637.

11. F. G. Hickman "Events in the Battle of Murfreesboro," *Confederate Veteran*, Vol. 3, 162; Baxter Smith, "8th Tennessee Cavalry Regiment, Confederate, History of Regiment and Biographical information," Box 107, Folder 10, undated, USAHEC, 19; Gate Thruston, "Personal Recollections of the Battle in the Rear at Stone's River," 227.

12. John Wharton, *Official Records*, Series 1, Volume 20, Part 1, 966-967; Baxter Smith, "8th Tennessee Cavalry Regiment, Confederate, History of Regiment and Biographical information," Box 107, Folder 10, undated, USAHEC, 19; Lanny Smith, *The Stone's River Campaign: 26 December 1862-5 January 1863, Army of Tennessee* (n.p.: Lanny Smith, 2010), 445.

13. Gate Thruston, "Personal Recollections of the Battle in the Rear at Stone's River," 227.

14. Lewis Zahm, *Official Records*, Series 1, Volume 20, Part 1, 636-637.

15. W. L. Curry, *Four Years in the Saddle: History of First Regiment Ohio Volunteer Cavalry* (Columbus: Champlin Printing Co., 1898), 83–84; *The Catalogue and History of Sigma Chi* (Chicago: Published by the Fraternity, 1890), 4; *Perrysburg Journal* (Perrysburg, Ohio), "The First Ohio Cavalry at Murfreesboro," January 21, 1863, 2; John Wharton, *Official Records*, Series 1, Volume 20, Part 1, 968.

16. R. R. Dawes, "Lieutenant Timothy L. Condit," In *Marietta College in the War of Succession: 1861–1865* (Cincinnati: Peter Thomson, 1878), 31–33.

17. C. C. Jeffries, *Terry's Rangers* (New York: Vantage Press, 1961), 64–65; John Randolph Poole, *Cracker Cavaliers: The 2nd Georgia Cavalry Under Wheeler and Forrest* (Macon, GA: Mercer University Press, 2000), 60–61; Benjamin Franklin Batchelor and George Batchelor, *Batchelor-Turner Letters, 1861–1864:Written by two of Terry's Texas Rangers*, H. J. H. Rugeley, editor (Austin: The Streck Company, 1961), 41.

18. Benjamin Batchelor, *Batchelor-Turner Letters*, 42.

19. Lewis Zahm, *Official Records*, Series 1, Volume 20, Part 1, 636–637; John Pugh, *Official Records*, Series 1, Volume 20, Part 1, 644–645.

20. William Henry Harder, Diary 1861–1865. December 31, 1862, Microfilm 574, 46–56, Tennessee State Library and Archives; St. John Liddell, *Official Records*, Series 1, Volume 20, Part 1, 858; St. John Liddell, *Liddell's Record*, Nathaniel Hughes, Jr., ed. (Baton Rouge" Louisiana State University Press, 1997), 115; Gates Thruston, "Personal Recollections at the Battle of Stones River," 229; Michael R. King, "Brigadier General St. John R. Liddell's Division at Chickamauga: The Study of a Division's Performance in Battle," Master's Thesis, U.S. Army Command and General Staff College, Ft. Leavenworth, Kansas, 1997, 42.

21. John Wharton, *Official Records*, Series 1, Volume 20, Part 1, 967–968; William Hardee Papers, Hardee family papers, "Report of the Battle of Murfreesboro," [1862–1962] LPR121, Alabama Department of History and Archives, 17–20.

22. Lewis Zahm, *Official Records*, Series 1, Volume 20, Part 1, 637.

23. James Alex Baggett, *Homegrown Yankees: Tennessee's Union Cavalry in the Civil War* (Baton Rouge: Louisiana State University Press, 2009), 58.

24. W. R. Friend, "Rout of Rosecrans," In *New Annals of the Civil War*, edited by Peter Cozzens and Robert Girardi (Mechanicsburg, PA: Stackpole Books, 2004), 212; Lewis Zahm, *Official Records*, Series 1, Volume 20, Part 1, 637.

25. William E. Crane, "William E. Crane's Daily Journal of Life in the Field During the War of the Rebellion," December 31, 1863, entry, Mss. 980, Cincinnati Historical Society, Cincinnati Museum Center.

26. W. R. Friend, "Rout of Rosecrans," 213–214; John S. Dollinger, "Recollections of the Battle at Stone's River, Tenn., In *W. L. Curry, Four Years in the Saddle: History of First Regiment Ohio Volunteer Cavalry* (Columbus: Champlin Printing Co., 1898), 304.

27. Gates Thruston, "Personal Recollections at the Battle of Stones River," 228.

28. J. W. Paramore, *Official Records*, Series 1, Volume 20, Part 1, 643.

29. Baxter Smith, "8th Tennessee Cavalry Regiment, Confederate, History of Regiment and Biographical information," Box 107, Folder 10, undated, USAHEC, 19.

30. Elmer Otis, *Official Records*, Series 1, Volume 20, Part 1, 649–650; William D. Bickham, *Rosecrans' Campaign with the Fourteenth Army Corps, of the Army of the Cumberland* (Cincinnati: Moore, Wilstach, Keys & Co., 1863), 209, 232–233.

31. William D. Bickham, *Ibid.*; Eli Long, Diary and Papers 1855–1892, Civil War Collection, USAHEC.

32. "The Story of a Cavalry Soldier," *Lancaster Daily Evening Express*, January 28, 1863.

33. *New York Times*, "The Murfreesboro Battle," January 4, 1863; Elmer Otis, *Official Records*, Series 1, Volume 20, Part 1, 649–650; W. R. Friend, "Rout of Rosecrans," In *New Annals of the Civil War*, edited by Peter Cozzens and Robert Girardi (Mechanicsburg, PA: Stackpole Books, 2004), 214; Edwin C. Bearss, "Cavalry Operations in the Stones River Campaign," *The Battle of Stones River*, Volume 4, Timothy Johnson, editor (Nashville: Tennessee Historical Society, 2012), 37.

34. J. W. Paramore, *Official Records*, Series 1, Volume 20, Part 1, 643.

35. Robert Klein, *Official Records*, Series 1, Volume 20, Part 1, 647.

36. J. W. Paramore, *Official Records*, Series 1, Volume 20, Part 1, 643.

37. James P. Fyffe, *Official Records*, Series 1, Volume 20, Part 1, 596.

38. *Ibid.*; M. B. Butler, *My Story of the Civil War and Underground Railroad* (Huntington, IN: United Brethren Publishing Establishment, 1914), 265.

39. Edwin Bearss, "Cavalry Operations—Battle of Stones River," 37; John Kennett, *Official Records*, Series 1, Volume 20, Part 1, 621.

40. E. H. Murray, *Official Records*, Series 1, Volume 20, Part 1, 627–628; H. L. Ambrose, "Kentucky Troopers, Saved Rosecrans's Ammunition Train at Stone River," *National Tribune*, January 20, 1887, 8.

41. John Kennett, *Official Records*, Series 1, Volume 20, Part 1, 621; E. H. Murray, *Official Records*, Series 1, Volume 20, Part 1, 627–628; John Kennett, "History of the First Cavalry Division from November 1, 1862, to January 1, 1863," In *G.A.R. War Papers* (Cincinnati, OH: Fred C. Jones Post, 1891), 348; Thomas Speed, "Cavalry Operations in the West Under Rosecrans and Sherman," In *Battles and Leaders of the Civil War*, Volume IV (New York: Century Company, 1888), 413.

42. Sean Styles, *Stones River National Battlefield: Historical Resource Study* (Atlanta: National Parks Service, 2004), 49–50.

43. Eli Murray, *Official Records*, Series 1, Volume 20, Part 1, 627–628; H. L. Ambrose, "Kentucky Troopers"; Lewis Wolfley, Letter, January 23, 1863, Mss. Murfreesboro (Tenn.), Battle of, 1862–1863 C. Wolfley family, Letters, 1860–1865, Filson Historical Society, Louisville.

44. J. A. Holman, "Letters from Veterans," In *Confederate Veteran*, Volume 2, 227; H. L. Ambrose, "Kentucky Troopers."

45. C. C. Jeffries, *Terry's Rangers* (New York: Vantage Press, 1961), 65; L. B. Giles, *Terry's Texas Rangers* (n.p.: L. B. Giles Publisher, 1911), 51.

46. W. L. Curry, *Four Years in the Saddle*, 85; Elmer Otis, *Official Records*, Series 1, Volume 20, Part 1, 648–650; G. C. Kniffin, "Stone River—The Second Day," *National Tribune*, January 21, 1882, 1. column 1; *New York Times*, "The Murfreesboro Battle," January 4, 1863.

47. John Wharton, *Official Records*, Series 1, Volume 20, Part 1, 967–968; W. B. Corbitt, December 31 entry, Subseries 1.1 Civil War-era documents, 1860–1865, Box 2, Folder 37—Corbitt, W.B.; 64-page diary (carbon typescript) from September 13, 1862–October 31, 1864, Manuscript, Archives, and Rare Book Library, Emory Uni-

versity, Atlanta; Edwin C. Bearss, "Cavalry Operations in the Stones River Campaign," 39.
48. Gates Thruston, "Personal Recollections of the Battle at Stone's River," 228–229.
49. John Wynkoop, *Official Records*, Series 1, Volume 20, Part 1, 631–632.
50. William Henry Harder, Diary 1861–1865, December 31, 1862, Microfilm 574, 46–56, Tennessee State Library and Archives; William Short, Letter to wife, January 23, 1863, William Joseph and Nancy Wallis Short Family Papers, MS 3863, University of Georgia, Athens; Bryan S. Bush, *Terry's Texas Rangers: History of the Eighth Texas Cavalry* (Paducah, KY: Turner Publishing, 2002), 71.
51. Gates Thruston, "Personal Recollections of the Battle at Stone's River," 231; W. D. Pickett, "Reminiscences of Murfreesboro," *Confederate Veteran*, Vol 16, 451.

Chapter 10

1. Peter Cozzens, *No Better Place to Die: The Battle of Stones River* (Urbana and Chicago: University of Illinois Press, 1991), 162; John W. Green, *Johnny Green of the Orphan Brigade: The Journal of a Confederate Soldier* (Lexington: University of Kentucky Press, 1956), 59–60; William C. Davis, *The Orphan Brigade: Kentucky Confederates Who Couldn't Go Home* (Garden City, NY: Doubleday & Co., 1980), 148.
2. George Brent, *Official Records*, Series 1, Volume 20, Part 1, 675; Lawrence Lee Hewitt and Arthur Bergeron, *Confederate Generals in the Western Theater*, Volume 3 (Knoxville: University of Tennessee Press, 2011), 160; Walter Griggs, *General John Pegram, CSA* (Lynchburg, VA: H. E. Howard, Inc., 1993), 60–62; Lanny Smith, *The Stone's River Campaign: 26 December 1862-5 January 1863, Army of Tennessee* (n.p.: Lanny Smith, 2010), 633; Michael Bower Cavender, *The First Georgia Cavalry in the Civil War: A History and Roster* (Jefferson, NC: McFarland, 2016), 48.
3. John C. Breckinridge, *Official Records*, Series 1, Volume 20, Part 1, 791; Braxton Bragg Papers, William Palmer collection, Western Reserve Historical Society; Breckinridge Papers, New-York Historical Society.
4. Theodore O'Hara, "Special Orders No. 60, Theodore O'Hara Papers, MS 11914, University of Virginia, Charlottesville, VA.; Larry Daniel, *Days of Glory, The Army of the Cumberland 1861-1865* (Baton Rouge: Louisiana State University Press, 2006), 217.
5. Peter Cozzens, *No Better Place to Die*, 66–72; Theodore O'Hara, O'Hara to Breckinridge, January 16, 1862, Breckinridge Papers, New-York Historical Society.
6. Peter Cozzens, *No Better Place to Die*, 156–159; Lanny Smith, *The Stone's River Campaign: 26 December 1862-5 January 1863, Army of Tennessee* (n.p.: Lanny Smith, 2010), 328; Daniel Wait Howe, Diary, December 31, 1862, Daniel Wait Howe Papers, 1824–1930, Collection #M 0148 Box 1, Folder 15, Indiana Historical Society, Indianapolis; J. J. Womack, *A Civil War Diary of Captain J. J. Womack, Company E 16th Tennessee Volunteers* (McMinnville, TN: Womack, 1961), 78.
7. Theodore O'Hara, Special Orders No. 60, Theodore O'Hara Collection; Ed Porter Thompson, *History of the Orphan Brigade* (Louisville: Louis N. Thompson, 1898), 170, 174.
8. John C. Breckinridge, *Official Records*, Series 1, Volume 20, Part 1, 782–783; Braxton Bragg, *Official Records*, Series 1, Volume 20, Part 1, 665–666; Horatio Van Cleve, *Official Records*, Series 1, Volume 20, Part 1, 574; Robert J. Dalessandro, "Major General William S. Rosecrans and the Transformation of the Staff of the Army of the Cumberland: A Case Study," Strategy Research Project, U S Army War College, Carlisle Barracks, Pennsylvania, 2002, 14.
9. John Pegram, "10:00 a.m. message, December 31, 1862," Braxton Bragg Papers, William Palmer Collection, Western Reserve Historical Society, Cleveland, Ohio; Breckinridge Papers, New-York Historical Society; Peter Cozzens, *No Better Place to Die*, 130; Robert Clements, *Official Records*, Series 1, Volume 20, Part 1, 249; Samuel Price, *Official Records*, Series 1, Volume 20, Part 1, 607.
10. Lovell Rousseau, *Official Records*, Series 1, Volume 20, Part 1, 379.
11. Theodore O'Hara, O'Hara to Breckinridge, January 16, 1863, Breckinridge Papers, New-York Historical Society; J. Stoddard Johnston, "Sketch of Theodore O'Hara," *The Register of the Kentucky State Historical Society*, Volume 11, Number 33 (September 1913): 65–72.
12. Braxton Bragg, *Official Records*, Series 1, Volume 20, Part 1, 665–666; John C. Breckinridge, *Official Records*, Series 1, Volume 20, Part 1, 782–783; Thomas Connelly, *Autumn of Glory: The Army of Tennessee 1862-1865* (Baton Rouge: Louisiana State University Press, 1971), 59; John Buckner, Letter to Breckinridge, May 20, 1863, Breckinridge Papers, New-York Historical Society.
13. William Clare, Letter, June 2, 1863, Braxton Bragg Papers, William Palmer Collection, Western Reserve Historical Society.
14. Braxton Bragg, *Official Records*, Series 1, Volume 20, Part 1, 665–666; John C. Breckinridge, *Official Records*, Series 1, Volume 20, Part 1, 782–783; H. B. Clay, "On the Right at Murfreesboro," *Confederate Veteran*, Volume 21 (Nashville: S. A. Cunningham Publisher, 1913), 588.
15. David Urquhart, "Bragg's Advance and Retreat," In *Battles and Leaders of the Civil War*, Volume III (New York: The Century Company, 1888), 608–609; J. Stoddard Johnston, Diary, J. Stoddard Johnston Papers, MssA72-16, Filson Historical Society, Louisville, KY.; Theodore O'Hara, O'Hara to Breckinridge, January 16, 1863.
16. James Wilson, Letter to Breckinridge, January 20, 1863, Breckinridge Papers, New-York Historical Society.
17. Braxton Bragg, *Official Records*, Series 1, Volume 20, Part 1, 665–667.
18. Braxton Bragg, *Official Records*, Series 1, Volume 20, Part 1, 665–666; John C. Breckinridge, *Official Records*, Series 1, Volume 20, Part 1, 782–783; Henry V. Freeman, "Some Battle Recollections of Stone's River," In *Military Essays and Recollections*, Volume III (Chicago: The Dial Press, 1899), 232.
19. Joseph Palmer, *Official Records*, Series 1, Volume 20, Part 1, 804.
20. Robert Trabue, *Official Records*, Series 1, Volume 20, Part 1, 826; John Pegram, "10:00 a.m. message, December 31, 1862," Braxton Bragg Papers, William Palmer collection, Western Reserve Historical Society; Robert Clements, *Official Records*, Series 1, Volume 20, Part 1, 249; Samuel Price, *Official Records*, Series 1, Volume 20, Part 1, 607.
21. John C. Breckinridge, Orders to General Palmer,

January 1, 1863, Breckinridge papers, Chicago Historical Society, Chicago, Illinois.

22. William Polk, *Leonidas Polk—Bishop and General*, Volume 2 (New York: Longmans, Green & Co., 1915), 193; Howard Swiggett, *The Rebel Raider: The Life of John Hunt Morgan* (Garden City, NY: Garden City Publishing, 1937), 97; Thomas Connelly, *Autumn of Glory*, 56; Grady McWhiney, *Braxton Bragg and the Confederate Defeat*, 364-365.

23. H. B. Clay, "On the Right at Murfreesboro," *Confederate Veteran*, Volume 21 (Nashville: S. A. Cunningham Publisher, 1913), 588; Braxton Bragg, *Official Records*, Series 1, Volume 20, Part 1, 667; Samuel Price, *Official Records*, Series 1, Volume 20, Part 1, 607.

24. David Anderson Deaderick, "Inslee Deaderick Memoir," Stones River National Park, Technical Information Center, Murfreesboro, TN; Joseph Palmer, *Official Records*, Series 1, Volume 20, Part 1, 804.

25. John J. Hight, *History of the Fifty-Eighth Regiment Indiana Volunteer Infantry* (Princeton: Press of the Clarion, 1895), 145.

26. Cortland Livingston, *Official Records*, Series 1, Volume 20, Part 1, 582.

27. Samuel W. Price, *Official Records*, Series 1, Volume 20, Part 1, 608.

28. Theodore O'Hara, Letter, January 16, 1863; John Buckner, Letter, May 20, 1863; Wilson Letter, January 20, 1863, Breckinridge Papers, New-York Historical Society; John C. Breckinridge, Official Records, Series 1, Volume 20, Part 1, 782-783; June 2, 1863, Braxton Bragg Papers, William Palmer collection, Western Reserve Historical Society.

Chapter 11

1. David Stanley, *An American General—The Memoirs of David Sloan Stanley, Samuel W. Fordyce IV, ed. (Santa Barbara, California: The Narrative Press, 2004)*, 152; Robert Burns, Letter Book, January 14, 1863, M642, Minnesota Historical Society, St. Paul; J. B. Dodge, "What I Saw at Stone River," *Northern Indianian*, Thursday March 11, 1875 front page; John Kennett, "History of the First Cavalry Division From November 1, 1862, to January 1, 1863," In *G.A.R. War Papers* (Cincinnati, OH: Fred C. Jones Post, 1891), 348-349; Lancaster Thomas, Letter—January 4, 1863, Civil War Collection, USAHEC, Carlisle, Pennsylvania.

2. David Stanley, *An American General*, 153; Lancaster Thomas, *Ibid*.

3. Abraham Buford, *Official Records*, Series 1, Volume 20, Part 1, 970.

4. John G. Parkhurst, *Official Records*, Series 1, Volume 20, Part 1, 653: Lewis Zahm, *Official Records*, Series 1, Volume 20, Part 1, 637; Charles W. Bennett, *Historical Sketches of the Ninth Michigan Infantry* (Coldwater, MI: Daily Courier Print, 1913), 27-29.

5. Henry G. Cooley, Diary, December 31, 1862, entry, Technical Information Center, Stones River National Battlefield, Murfreesboro, TN.

6. F. W. Weatherbee, *The 5th (1st Middle) Tennessee Cavalry Regiment, USA* (Carrollton, MS: Pioneer Publishing Co., 1992), 8; Robert Minty, *Official Records*, Series 1, Volume 20, Part 1, 624; J. C. Reiff, "Fifteenth Pennsylvania (Anderson) Cavalry at Stone River," In *History of the Fifteenth Pennsylvania Volunteer Cavalry*, Charles Kirk, ed. (Philadelphia, PA: Society of the Fifteenth Pennsylvania Cavalry, 1906), 93; Robert Minty, Letter to Backus—November 11, 1906, Robert Minty Papers, Civil War Collection, USAHEC, Carlisle, Pennsylvania.

7. Robert Minty, *Official Records*, Series 1, Volume 20, Part 1, 624; John C. McLain, Diary—December 31, 1862, John McLain Diary and Papers (c.00111), Michigan State University Archives & Historical Collections, Michigan State University, East Lansing; N. W. Sample, "Autobiographical Sketch of N. W. Sample," 15th Pennsylvania Regimental Files, Stones River, 10; Lancaster Thomas, Letter—January 4, 1863, Civil War Collection, USAHEC, Carlisle, Pennsylvania.

8. Eugene Bronson, Letter—January 22, 1863, Eugene Bronson Collection, Kalamazoo College, Kalamazoo, Michigan; Francis Weigley, Letter to his brother Jacob, January 4, 1863, Francis Weigley Papers, Private Collection.

9. Eugene Bronson, January 22, 1863 letter; Robert Minty, Letter to Backus—November 11, 1906, Robert Minty Papers, Civil War Collection, USAHEC, Carlisle, Pennsylvania.

10. John Witherspoon Dubose, "3rd Alabama Cavalry," unpublished manuscript, SG024911, Alabama Department of History and Archives, Montgomery; Abraham Buford, *Official Records*, Series 1, Volume 20, Part 1, 970-971.

11. David Stanley, *An American General*, 153; David Stanley, *Official Records*, Series 1, Volume 20, Part 1, 618; J. C. Reiff, "The Fifteen Pennsylvania Cavalry at Stones Rivers," In *History of the Fifteenth Pennsylvania Volunteer Cavalry*, Charles Kirk, ed. (Philadelphia, PA: Society of the Fifteenth Pennsylvania Cavalry, 1906), 93.

12. John Williams, *Leaves of a Trooper's Diary* (Philadelphia: Published by Author, 1869), 56; Frank Mix, Letter January 9, 1863, Elisha Mix Papers, Bentley Historical Library; J. D. Webb, *Official Records*, Series 1, Volume 20, Part 1, 964; Lancaster Thomas, Letter—January 4, 1863, Civil War Collection, USAHEC, Carlisle, Pennsylvania.

13. J. C. Reiff, "The Fifteen Pennsylvania Cavalry at Stones Rivers," 93; Robert Minty, *Official Records*, Series 1, Volume 20, Part 1, 624.

14. Robert Minty, "The Saber Brigade," *National Tribune*, August 11, 1892; Eugene Bronson, Letter—January 22, 1863, Eugene Bronson Collection, Kalamazoo College, Kalamazoo, Michigan; David Stanley, January 9, 1863, Report, Stanley, Wright, West Papers, USAHEC, Carlisle, Pennsylvania; William D. Bickham, *Rosecrans' Campaign with the Fourteenth Army Corps, of the Army of the Cumberland* (Cincinnati: Moore, Wilstach, Keys & Co., 1863), 246; Robert Minty, Letter to Backus—November 11, 1906, Robert Minty Papers, Civil War Collection, USAHEC, Carlisle, Pennsylvania; Robert Minty, *Official Records*, Series 1, Volume 20, Part 1, 624-625; Joseph Vale, *Minty and the Cavalry: A History of Cavalry Campaigns in the Western Armies* (Harrisburg, PA: Edwin K. Myers, Printer and Binder, 1886), 115.

15. James Weir Diary, William Palmer Papers, Colorado Springs Pioneers Museum; W. C. Dodson, *Campaigns of Wheeler and His Cavalry, 1862-1865* (Atlanta: Hudgins Publishing Co., 1899), 53; J. C. Reiff, "The Fifteenth Pennsylvania at Stones River," 94.

16. Robert Minty, "The Saber Brigade," *National Tribune*, August 11, 1892; Eugene Bronson, Letter—January 22, 1863, Eugene Bronson Collection, Kalamazoo College, Kalamazoo, Michigan; Frank Mix, Letter from Frank Mix, January 9, 1863, Elisha Mix Papers, 1818-1898, Bentley Historical Library, University of Michigan,

Ann Arbor; Josiah Lewis, Undated letter, Technical Information Center, Stones River National Battlefield, Murfreesboro, TN.

17. John Williams, *Leaves of a Trooper's Diary*, 56.

18. Robert Minty, Letter to Backus—November 11, 1906; Abraham Buford, *Official Records*, Series 1, Volume 20, Part 1, 970; Eugene Bronson, January 22, 1863, letter.

19. Benjamin Burke, *A Terry's Ranger Write Home: Letters of Pvt. Benjamin F. Burke*, Jessie Burke Head, ed., compiled 1965, January 16, 1863 letter, Missouri History Museum, St. Louis; Joseph Wheeler, *Official Records*, Series 1, Volume 20, Part 1, 959; Drucilla Lyttle Watkins, "Memories of Drucilla Lyttle Watkins," Stones River National Park, Technical Information Center, Murfreesboro; John N. Smith, Letters—January 10, 1863, "The Confederate Letters of John Newton Smith," Stones River National Park, Technical Information Center, Murfreesboro.

20. J. D. Webb, *Official Records*, Series 1, Volume 20, Part 1, 964; Michael M. Bailey, "From Pensacola to Bentonville: The War History of the Prattville Dragoons, 3rd Alabama Regimental File," SG024911, Folder 8, ADHA; N. W. Sample, "Autobiographical Sketch of N. W. Sample," 15th Pennsylvania Regimental Files, Stones River National Park, Technical Information Center, Murfreesboro, 9.

21. William Lamers, *The Edge of Glory: A Biography of General William S. Rosecrans, U.S.A.* (New York: Harcourt, Brace & World, Inc., 1961), 235.

22. Alexander Stevenson, *Battle of Stones River near Murfreesboro, Tennessee* (Boston: J. R. Osgood & Co., 1884), 121; David Stanley, *An American General*, 154; Thomas Crittenden, "The Union Left at Stone's River," In *Battles and Leaders of the Civil War*, Volume III (New York: Century Company, 1888), 634; Donn Piatt, *General George H. Thomas, A Critical Biography* (Cincinnati: Robert Clarke & Co., 1893), 212.

23. William Lamers, *The Edge of Glory*, 235.

24. John Wharton, *Official Records*, Series 1, Volume 20, Part 1, 968; Edward Longacre, "Fightin' Joe," *America's Civil War*, Vol. 23 Issue 2 (May 2010), 50–57; Joseph Vale, *Minty and the Cavalry*, 116.

25. Theodore M. Banta, *Sayre Family Lineage of Thomas Sayre* (New York: De Vinne Press, 1901), 502; Jack D. Welsh, *Medical Histories of Confederate Generals* (Kent, OH: Kent State University Press, 1995), 5; Newspaper clipping of French, L. Virginia (Lucy Virginia), 1825–1881, Diaries, Tennessee State Library and Archives, ID# 36077-07 Tennessee State Library and Archives; Stirling D. Popejoy, "The Second Tennessee Cavalry in the American Civil War," Master's Thesis, 2014, U.S. Army Command and General Staff College, Fort Leavenworth, KS, 49; Mamie Yeary, *Reminiscences of the Boys in Gray, 1861–1865* (Dallas: Smith and Lamar Publishers, Dallas, 1912), 739.

26. Stirling D. Popejoy, "The Second Tennessee Cavalry in the American Civil War," 47.

27. Baxter Smith, "8th Tennessee Cavalry Regiment, Confederate, History of Regiment and Biographical information," Box 107, Folder 10, undated, USAHEC, 20.

28. Gilbert C. Kniffin, *The Third Day at Stone's River* (District of Columbia: Military Order of the Loyal Legion, 1907), 9; W. L. Curry, *Four Years in the Saddle: History of First Regiment Ohio Volunteer Cavalry* (Columbus: Champlin Printing Co., 1898), 85–86.

29. John Euclid Magee, Diary entry, December 31, 1862, James Euclid Magee Papers (1861–1863), David M. Rubenstein Rare Book & Manuscript Library, Duke University.

30. Lucy Virginia French, Diary—December 31, 1862, French, L. Virginia (Lucy Virginia), 1825–1881, Tennessee State Library and Archives, Nashville, Tennessee.

31. T. F. Dornblaser, *Sabre Strokes of the Pennsylvania Dragoons in the War of 1861–1865* (Philadelphia: Lutheran Publication Society, 1884), 103. [Grands rounds referred to officers inspecting the conditions of sentinels.]

32. Thomas Connelly, *Autumn of Glory: The Army of Tennessee 1862–1865* (Baton Rouge: Louisiana State University Press, 1971), 57.

33. Joseph Wheeler, "The Battle of Murfreesboro," Joseph Wheeler Papers, Chicago Historical Society, Chicago.

Chapter 12

1. Braxton Bragg, *Official Records*, Series 1, Volume 20, Part 1, 667.

2. N. W. Sample, "Autobiographical Sketch of N. W. Sample," 15th Pennsylvania Regimental Files, Stones River, 10–11; Wilmon Blackmar, "The Charge on Infantry at Stone River," In *History of the Fifteenth Pennsylvania Volunteer Cavalry*, Charles Kirk, ed. (Philadelphia, PA: Society of the Fifteenth Pennsylvania Cavalry, 1906), 114; John Crittenden, Letter to Wife, January 11, 1863, Crittenden, John letters (1862–1865), Record Group 765, Auburn University, Auburn, Alabama.

3. Joseph Burke, *Official Records*, Series 1, Volume 20, Part 1, 654; John Witherspoon Dubose, "3rd Alabama Cavalry," unpublished manuscript, SG024911, Alabama Department of History and Archives, Montgomery; Baxter Smith, "8th Tennessee Cavalry Regiment, Confederate, History of Regiment and Biographical information," Box 107, Folder 10, undated, USAHEC.

4. Lewis Zahm, *Official Records*, Series 1, Volume 20, Part 1, 634; John Witherspoon Dubose, "3rd Alabama Cavalry," unpublished manuscript, SG024911, Alabama Department of History and Archives, Montgomery; Baxter Smith, "8th Tennessee Cavalry Regiment, Confederate, History of Regiment and Biographical information," Box 107, Folder 10, undated, USAHEC.

5. Lewis Zahm, *Official Records*, Series 1, Volume 20, Part 1, 634.

6. Joseph Burke, *Official Records*, Series 1, Volume 20, Part 1, 655; Baxter Smith, "8th Tennessee Cavalry Regiment, Confederate, History of Regiment and Biographical information," Box 107, Folder 10, undated, USAHEC.

7. James King, Letter January 3, 1863, Federal Collection Box F 25, Folder 8, Tennessee State Library and Archives.

8. Gerould Otis Gibson, Diary—January 1, 1863, Pennsylvania Regimental Files, Stones River National Park, Technical Information Center, Murfreesboro, TN; Henry Albert Potter, Letter—January 8, 1863, Correspondence—MS 91-480: Henry Albert Potter Collection; Accession Box 461 Folder 3, Archives of Michigan, Lansing, Michigan.

9. Lewis Zahm, *Official Records*, Series 1, Volume 20, Part 1, 637–638; James Weir Diary, William Palmer Papers, Colorado Springs Pioneers Museum; "A Lancaster Boy in the Anderson Cavalry," *Lancaster Daily Express*, January 16, 1863.

10. Zahm, *Ibid*.

11. Isaac Skillman, Diary—January 1, 1863, MMS

1083, Bowling Green State University, Bowling Green Ohio; Lancaster Thomas, Letter—January 4, 1863, Civil War Collection, USAHEC, Carlisle, Pennsylvania.

12. J. Ferrell Colton and Antoinette Smith, editors, *Column South with the Fifteenth Pennsylvania Cavalry* (Flagstaff: J. P. Colton & Co., 1960), 45.

13. J. Ferrell Colton and Antoinette Smith, editors, *Column South with the Fifteenth Pennsylvania Cavalry*, 44.

14. Mark Hoffman, *My Brave Mechanics: The First Michigan Engineers and Their Civil War* (Detroit: Wayne State University Press, 2007), 115–122.

15. Mark Hoffman, *My Brave Mechanics: The First Michigan Engineers and Their Civil War*, 122–125; Charles R. Sligh, *The History of the Services of the First Regiment Michigan Engineers and Mechanics: During the Civil War 1861–1865* (Grand Rapids: n.p., 1921), 14; William Innes, *Official Records*, Series 1, Volume 20, Part 1, 651.

16. William D. Bickham, *Rosecrans' Campaign with the Fourteenth Army Corps, of the Army of the Cumberland* (Cincinnati: Moore, Wilstach, Keys & Co., 1863), 300–301; Mark Hoffman, *My Brave Mechanics*, 126–128; William Innes, *Official Records*, Series 1, Volume 20, Part 1, 651; John Fitch, *Annals of the Army of the Cumberland* (Philadelphia: J. B. Lippincott, 1863), 411–412.

17. William D. Bickham, *Ibid.*; Mark Hoffman, *My Brave Mechanics: The First Michigan Engineers and Their Civil War*, 122–128.

18. Baxter Smith, "8th Tennessee Cavalry," p. 20; John Wharton, *Official Records*, Series 1, Volume 20, Part 1, 968–969; J. K. P. Blackburn, *Reminiscences of the Terry Rangers* (n. p.: University of Texas, 1919), 38.

19. William Innes, *Official Records*, Series 1, Volume 20, Part 1, 651; Charles R. Sligh, *The History of the Services of the First Regiment Michigan Engineers and Mechanics*, 16.

20. Joseph Burke, *Official Records*, Series 1, Volume 20, Part 1, 655.

21. John Wharton, *Official Records*, Series 1, Volume 20, Part 1, 968; Joseph Burke, *Official Records*, Series 1, Volume 20, Part 1, 656.

22. David Stanley, *Official Records*, Series 1, Volume 20, Part 1, 618; Robert Burns, Letter Book, January 14, 1863, M642, Minnesota Historical Society, St. Paul; Henry Albert Potter, Diary—January 1, 1863, MS 89-535 Henry Albert Potter Collection; Accession Box 459 Folder 14, Archives of Michigan, Lansing, Michigan.

23. J. Ferrell Colton and Antoinette Smith, editors, *Column South*, 46.

24. Alexis Cope, *The Fifteenth Ohio Volunteers and Its Campaigns, 1861–1865* (Columbus, OH: Published by Author, 1916), 239; R. B. Stewart, "The Battle of Stone River: As Seen by One Who Was There," *Blue and Gray*, Volume 1, 1895 (January), 10–11.

25. Braxton Bragg, *Official Records*, Series 1, Volume 52, Part 2, 402; Wilson Vance, *Stone's River: The Turning-Point of the Civil War* (New York: The Neale Publishing Co., 1914), 10; R. D. Jackson, Letter to wife—January (n.d.) 1863, Alabama Department of History and Archives; Edward Longacre, "Fightin' Joe," *America's Civil War*, Vol. 23 Issue 2 (May 2010), 50–57.

26. Braxton Bragg, *Official Records*, Series 1, Volume 20, Part 1, 667.

27. Larry Daniel, *Days of Glory*, 219–222; John C. Breckinridge, "Murfreesboro," *Southern Historical Society Papers*, Vol. 5, Number 5 (May 1878), 211–213; H. G. Bradt, *History of the Services of the Third Battery Wisconsin Light Artillery in the Civil War of the United States, 1861–1865* (Berlin, WI: Courant Press, 1902), 17; George Brent, "Journal of George Brent," January 2, 1863, Braxton Bragg Papers, MS 2000, Series II, Box 4, Folder 22, Western Reserve Historical Society, Cleveland Ohio; John M. Hollis, Diary, January 1 and 2, 1863, John M. Hollis Papers, MS.3222, Box 1, Folder 1, University of Tennessee Libraries, Special Collections, Knoxville.

28. Lewis Wolfley, Letter, January 23, 1863, Wolfey Family Papers, Mss. CW, Filson History Society, Louisville.

29. John C. Breckinridge, *Official Records*, Series 1, Volume 20, Part 1, 785; Braxton Bragg, *Official Records*, Series 1, Volume 20, Part 1, 668.

30. Ed Porter Thompson, *History of the Orphan Brigade* (Louisville: Lewis N. Thompson, 1898), 178; John C. Breckinridge, *Official Records*, Series 1, Volume 20, Part 1, 785.

31. John Wharton, *Official Records*, Series 1, Volume 20, Part 1, 969.

32. William Preston, *Official Records*, Series 1, Volume 20, Part 1, 813; H. B. Clay, "On the Right at Murfreesboro," 588–589; Edwin Bearss, "The Union Artillery and Breckinridge's Attack," Research Project 2, 1959, Stones River National Park, Technical Information Center, Murfreesboro, TN, 64; John Wharton, *Official Records*, Series 1, Volume 20, Part 1, 969.

33. J. S. Johnston, *Kentucky: Confederate History*, Volume IX (Atlanta: Confederate Publishing, 1899), 160–162.

34. H. B. Clay, "On the Right at Murfreesboro," 588–589.

35. M. B. Butler, *My Story of the Civil War and Underground Railroad* (Huntington, IN: United Brethren Publishing Establishment, 1914), 273–276.

36. William C. Davis, *Breckinridge: Stateman, Soldier, Symbol* (Baton Rouge: Louisiana State University Press, 1974), 340–344.

37. William C. Davis, *Ibid.*; George Brent, March 15, 1863 letter, Appendix to the Breckinridge Report, Braxton Bragg Papers, Western Reserve Historical Society, Cleveland, Ohio.

38. George Brent, *Official Records*, Series 1, Volume 20, Part 1, 790; John C. Breckinridge, *Official Records*, Series 1, Volume 20, Part 1, 791; John Wharton, *Official Records*, Series 1, Volume 20, Part 1, 969; Baxter Smith, "8th Tennessee Cavalry Regiment, Confederate, History of Regiment and Biographical information," Box 107, Folder 10, undated, USAHEC; R. F. Bunting, Undated (1863–1865) biography of John A. Wharton, Wharton, John Austin Papers, 1862–1866, Accession Number, 25-0567, Galveston and Texas History Center, Rosenberg Library, Galveston, TX.; George Brent, Orders to John Pegram, January 2, 1863, Appendix to the Breckinridge Report, Braxton Bragg Papers, Western Reserve Historical Society, Cleveland, Ohio; William C. Davis, *Breckinridge: Statesman, Soldier, Symbol* (Baton Rouge: Louisiana State University Press, 1974), 343.

39. Gideon Pillow, *Official Records*, Series 1, Volume 20, Part 1, 810; William C. Davis, *Breckinridge: Statesman, Soldier, Symbol* (Baton Rouge: Louisiana State University Press, 1974), 343–344.

40. H. B. Clay, "On the Right at Murfreesboro," *Confederate Veteran*, Volume 21, 588; Baxter Smith, "8th Tennessee Cavalry," p.21.

41. Steven L. Wright, *Kentucky Soldiers and Their Regiments in the Civil War, 1863*, Volume III (Utica, KY: McDowell Publications, 2009), 32, 71, 81–82; Nathaniel

Cheairs Hughes, Jr., and Thomas Clayton Ware, *Theodore O'Hara: Poet-Soldier of the Old South* (Knoxville: University of Tennessee Press, 1998), 127–128.

42. William E. Crane, "William E. Crane's Daily Journal of Life in the Field during the War of the Rebellion," January 3, 1862, entry, Mss. 980, Cincinnati Historical Society, Cincinnati Museum Center; Lewis Zahm, *Official Records*, Series 1, Volume 20, Part 1, 638.

43. Abraham Buford, *Official Records*, Series 1, Volume 20, Part 1, 971; Joseph Wheeler, *Official Records*, Series 1, Volume 20, Part 1, 959; John Berrien Lindsley, *The Military Annals of Tennessee. Confederate* (Nashville: J. M. Lindsley & Co., Publishers, 1886), 715–716; R. D. Jackson, Letter to wife—January (n.d.) 1863, Robert D. Jackson Family Papers, [1857–1914], Alabama Department of History and Archives; Daniel McCook, *Official Records*, Series 1, Volume 20, Part 1, 445.

44. Isaac Skillman, Diary—January 3, 1863, MMS 1083, Bowling Green State University, Bowling Green Ohio; *Dayton Daily Empire*, "Murfreesboro Fight," January 5, 1863, a. c. 1.

45. James J. Johnston diary, January 3, 1863, entry, Mss A J72b/1, Filson Historical Society; Baxter Smith, "8th Tennessee Cavalry," p. 21.

46. William E. Crane, "William E. Crane's Daily Journal," January 4, 1863; Tommie Clack, Microfilm 824, Confederate Collection, Reel 6 (Box 15, Folder 4), Tennessee State Library and Archives; George W. Dillion, "War Diaries of George W. Dillon, January 5, 1863, Microfilm 1656, Tennessee State Library and Archives.

47. Vincent Dunn, Letter, January 19, 1863, Dunn Family Papers, 1854–1977, Correspondence, Mss./A/D923, Filson Historical Society, Louisville, Kentucky; Robert Burns, Letter book, January 16, 1863, M642, Minnesota Historical Society, St. Paul; William E. Crane, *Ibid*.

48. "The Story of a Cavalry Soldier," *Lancaster Daily Evening Express*, January 28, 1863; Ganum Vineyard, "Letter from Sgt. Ganum Vineyard at the Battle of Murfreesboro to His Wife in Grainger County, Tennessee," *Tennessee Ancestors*, Volume 16, Number 2 (August 2000), 123–124; Othniel Gooding, Letter, January 12 and 18, 1863, Othniel Gooding Letters (c.00275), Michigan State University Archives & Historical Collections, Michigan State University, East Lansing; Milton Weaver, Letter, January 14, 1863, Milton Weaver Collection, MS.2128, Folder 4, Item 1, University of Tennessee Libraries, Special Collections, Knoxville.

49. Braxton Bragg, *Official Records*, Series 1, Volume 20, Part 1, 669; Edward G. Longacre, *A Soldier to the Last: Maj. Gen. Joseph Wheeler in Blue and Gray* (Washington: Potomac Books Inc., 2007), 83; Peter Cozzens, *No Better Place to Die: The Battle of Stones River* (Urbana and Chicago: University of Illinois Press, 1991), 200; St. John Liddell, *Liddell's Record*, Nathaniel Hughes, Jr., ed. (Baton Rouge: Louisiana State University Press, 1997), 115; Stanley Horn, *The Army of Tennessee* (Wilmington, NC: Broadfoot Publishing Co., 1987), 209; Andrew Haughton, *Training, Tactics, and Leadership in the Confederate Army of Tennessee* (Portland, OR: Frank Cass Publishers, 2000), 110.

50. John Connelly, *Autumn of Glory*, 67; William Hardee, Letter to Breckinridge, January 12, 1863, Breckinridge Papers, New-York Historical Society.

51. Joseph Wheeler, "The Battle of Murfreesboro," Joseph Wheeler Papers, Chicago Historical Society, Chicago; L. H. Stout, *Reminiscences of General Braxton Bragg* (Hattiesburg, MS: The Book Farm, 1942), 21–22.

52. Lucy Virginia French, Diary—January 4, 1863, French, L. Virginia (Lucy Virginia), 1825–1881, Tennessee State Library and Archives, Nashville, Tennessee.

53. David S. Stanley, "Report of the Battle Stone River," West, Stanley, Wright Family Papers, Boxes 1 and 5, US-AHEC; Robert Minty, *Official Records*, Series 1, Volume 20, Part 1, 623; William E. Crane, "William E. Crane's Daily Journal," January 5, 1863; Edward Crippen, "The Diary of Edward C. Crippen, Private 27th Illinois Volunteers, War of the Rebellion, August 7, 1861 to September 19, 1863," Ed. Robert J. Kerner, *Illinois State Historical Society Transactions*, Volume 10 (1909): 220–282, 257.

54. William E. Crane, "William E. Crane's Daily Journal," January 5, 1863; Edward Hill, Letters—1st Ohio Cavalry, March 1863, USAHEC, Civil War Collection, Box 55, Folder 18, Carlisle, PA.

55. Howell Carter, *A Cavalryman's Reminiscences of the Civil War* (Port Hudson, LA; Old South Book, 1979), 54.

56. Edward Amsden, Letter—January 5, 1863, Collection of Edward W. Amsden, D company, 3rd Regiment, Ohio, cavalry, Gilder Lehrman Collection#: GLC02156-02156.07, The Gilder Lehrman Institute of American History, New York City; James Wiswell, Letter to father, January 8, 1863, James Wiswell Papers (1861–1867), David M. Rubenstein Rare Book & Manuscript Library, Duke University; William Rosecrans, Letters to Wife, January 20, 1863, February 9, 1863, University of California Los Angeles, Special Collections, Manuscript 663, Box 59, Folder 70 and 73.

57. Joseph Johnston, *Official Records*, Series 1, Volume 20, Part 2, 487.

58. William Hardee, *Official Records*, Series 1, Volume 20, Part 2, 147–149; Ralston Skinner, Report, William S. Rosecrans Papers: 1810–1920, Collection 663, Box 76, Folder 98A, University of California, Los Angeles, Department of Special Collections, Los Angeles; Joseph H. Parks, *General Leonidas Polk, CSA: The Fighting Bishop* (Baton Rouge: Louisiana State University Press, 1990), 293–295; Charles George, Letter to Brother, January 24, 1863, George Family Papers, Record Group 85, Auburn University; Nathaniel Cheairs Hughes, Jr., *General William J. Hardee: Old Reliable* (Baton Rouge: Louisiana State University, 1965), 147–149.

Conclusion

1. Basil Duke, *Morgan's Cavalry* (New York: The Neale Publishing Co., 1909), 343; John W. DuBose, *General Joseph Wheeler and the Army of Tennessee* (New York: The Neale Publishing Co., 1912), 135; Cecil Fletcher Holland, *Morgan and His Raiders: A Biography of the Confederate General* (New York: The MacMillan Company, 1942) 187.

2. David Stanley, *Official Records*, Series 1, Volume 20, Part 1, 619.

3. James Alex Baggett, *Homegrown Yankees: Tennessee's Union Cavalry in the Civil War* (Baton Rouge: Louisiana State University, 2009), 60; Richard Hall, *Patriots in Disguise: Women Warriors in the Civil War* (New York: Paragon House, 1994), 27.

4. William Rosecrans, *Official Records*, Series 1, Volume 20, Part 1, 214. [There are math errors in this official report.]

5. Third Ohio Cavalry Regimental Papers, Semi Weekly Reports, December 22, 1862, January 19, 1863, Record Group 94, Box 3512, Third Ohio Cavalry, National Archives, Washington, D.C.; Fourth Ohio Cavalry Papers,

Semi Weekly Reports, December 25, 1862, January 12, 1863, Record Group 94, Box 3518, Fourth Ohio Cavalry, National Archives, Washington, D.C.

6. Reginald Stuart, "The Role of the Cavalry in the Western Theatre of the American Civil War from the Battle of Shiloh to the Tullahoma Campaign," Master's Thesis 1968, University of British Columbia, Vancouver, British Columbia, 132.

7. Frank Mix, Letter from Frank Mix, January 9, 1863, Elisha Mix Papers, 1818–1898, Bentley Historical Library, University of Michigan, Ann Arbor.

8. Mark Hoffman, *My Brave Mechanics: The First Michigan Engineers and Their Civil War* (Detroit: Wayne State University Press, 2007), 132; James W. Sligh papers, 1842–1865 (Box 1), Bentley Historical Library, University of Michigan, Ann Arbor.

9. Nancy Pape-Findley, *The Invincibles: The Story of Fourth Ohio Veteran Volunteer Cavalry* (Tecumseh, Michigan; Blood Road Publishing: 2002), 112, 299, 360; United States Census, 1860; C. S. Williams, *Williams' Cincinnati Directory* (Cincinnati: C. S. Williams Publisher, 1860), 254; Lucien Wulsin, *The Fourth Regiment Ohio Veteran Volunteer* Cavalry (Cincinnati: Fourth Ohio Volunteer Cavalry Association, 1912), 157; Lucien Wulsin, *Roster of Surviving Members of the 4th Regiment Ohio Volunteer Cavalry* (Cincinnati: Charles Thompson, Printer, 1891), 8.

10. William E. Crane, "William E. Crane's Daily Journal of Life in the Field during the War of the Rebellion," January 24–25, 1863, entry, Mss. 980, Cincinnati Historical Society, Cincinnati Museum Center.

11. Alexander McCook, *Official Records*, Series 1, Volume 20, Part 1, 258; William Rosecrans, *Official Records*, Series 1, Volume 20, Part 1, 198.

12. William Palmer, *Letters, 1853–1868, Genl. Wm. J. Palmer* (Philadelphia: Ketterlinus, 1906), 73–74.

13. David Stanley, *Official Records*, Series 1, Volume 20, Part 1, 619–620.

14. David Stanley, *An American General—The Memoirs of David Sloan Stanley*, Samuel W. Fordyce IV, ed. Santa Barbara, CA: The Narrative Press, 2004), 150–155; William Rosecrans, *Official Records*, Series 1, Volume 20, Part 2, 6; Stephen Z. Starr, *The Union Cavalry in the Civil War: The War in the West*, Volume III (Baton Rouge: Louisiana State University, 2007), 114; James Parkhurst, "Recollections of Stone's River," In Michigan MOLLUS Papers (Detroit: Winn, Hammond, Printers and Binders, 1890), 13.

15. Braxton Bragg, *Official Records*, Series 1, Volume 20, Part 1, 674; William Wiles, *Official Records*, Series 1, Volume 20, Part 1, 233.

16. Joseph Wheeler, *Official Records*, Series 1, Volume 20, Part 1, 960; John Wharton, *Official Records*, Series 1, Volume 20, Part 1, 968; Abraham Buford, *Official Records*, Series 1, Volume 20, Part 1, 971.

17. Joseph Wheeler, *Official Records*, Series 1, Volume 20, Part 1, 958.

18. *American Civil War: The Definitive Encyclopedia and Document Collection,* edited by Spencer C. Tucker (Santa Barbara: ABC–Clio LLC, 2013), 251; Bruce Allardice and Lawrence Lee Hewitt, *Kentuckians in Gray: Confederate Generals and Field Officers of the Bluegrass State* (Lexington: University of Kentucky Press, 2008), 51–52.

19. Christopher S. Dwyer, "Raiding Strategy: As Applied by the Western Confederate Cavalry in the American Civil War." *The Journal of Military History*, 63 (April 1999): 263–281, 272.

20. Henry Albert Potter, March 8, 1863, Letter, MS 91–480 Henry Albert Potter Collection, Accession Box 461 Folder 2, Archives of Michigan, Historical Society of Michigan, Lansing; E. S. Godfrey, "Revolver versus Saber—The Report of the Cavalry Board," *Journal of the United States Cavalry Association*, Volume 17, Number 61 (July 1906): 42–47.

21. Jonathan Wither, *Official Records*, Series 1, Volume 23, Part 2, 620; Daniel S. Donelson, *Official Records*, Series 1, Volume 23, Part 2, 711.

Bibliography

Primary Sources

PUBLISHED LETTERS, DIARIES, JOURNALS AND OTHER MANUSCRIPTS

Batchelor, Benjamin Franklin and George Batchelor. *Batchelor-Turner Letters, 1861–1864: Written by Two of Terry's Texas Rangers*, H. J. H. Rugeley, editor. Austin: The Streck Company, 1961.

Beatty, John. *The Citizen Soldier: The Memoirs of a Civil War Volunteer*. Lincoln and London: Bison Books University of Nebraska Press, 1998.

Clark, William Allen. "'Please Send Stamps: The Civil War Letters of William Allen Clark," Part IV, ed. Margaret Black Tatum, *Indiana Magazine of History*, Volume 91, Issue 4 (1995), pp. 407–437.

Cutrer, Thomas W. *Our Trust Is in the God of Battles: The Civil War Letters of Robert Franklin Bunting, Chaplain, Terry's Texas Rangers*. Knoxville: University of Tennessee Press, 2006.

Davis, Jefferson. *Papers of Jefferson Davis*, Volume 8, Linda Lasswell Crist, Mary Seaton Dix, and Kenneth H. Williams, editors. Baton Rouge and London: Louisiana State University Press, 1995.

Dodd, Ephraim. *Diary of Ephraim Shelby Dodd*. Austin: Press of E. L. Steck, 1914.

Fisher, Horace Cecil. *The Personal Experiences of Colonel Horace Newton Fisher in the Civil War; a Staff Officer's Story*. Boston: Thomas Todd Company, 1960.

Fobes, George. "An Account of the Mutiny in the Anderson Cavalry, at Nashville, Tenn., December 1862," In *Leaves of a Trooper's Dairy*, John Williams. Philadelphia: Published by Author, 1869.

Fremantle, Arthur. *Three Months in the Southern States, April–June, 1863*. New York: John Bradburn Co., 1864.

Grant, U.S. *Papers of Ulysses S. Grant: September 1–December 8, 1862*, John Y. Simon, ed. Carbondale: Southern Illinois University Press, 1977.

Green, John W. *Johnny Green of the Orphan Brigade: The Journal of a Confederate Soldier*. Lexington: University of Kentucky Press, 1956.

Liddell, St. John. *Liddell's Record*, Nathaniel Hughes, Jr., ed. Baton Rouge, Louisiana State University Press, 1997.

Longacre, Glenn V. and John E. Haas, ed., *To Battle for God and the Right: the Civil War: Letterbooks of Emerson Opdycke*. Urbana and Chicago: University of Illinois Press, 2003.

Miller, George Knox. *An Uncompromising Secessionist: The Civil War of George Knox Miller, Eighth (Wade's) Confederate Cavalry*, edited by Richard M. McMurry. Tuscaloosa: University of Alabama Press, 2007.

Morton, John Watson. *The Artillery of Nathan Bedford Forrest's Cavalry*. Nashville, Tennessee and Dallas, Texas: Publishing House of the M. E. Church, 1909.

Palmer, William. *Letters, 1853–1868, Genl. Wm. J. Palmer*. Philadelphia: Ketterlinus, 1906.

Shelly, Joseph Frederick. "The Shelly Papers," Fanny Anderson, ed. *Indiana Magazine of History*, 44, no. 2 (June 1948): 181–198.

Womack, J. J. *A Civil War Diary of Captain J. J. Womack, Company E 16th Tennessee Volunteers*. McMinnville, TN: Womack, 1961.

UNPUBLISHED LETTERS, DIARIES, JOURNALS AND OTHER MANUSCRIPTS

Alabama Department of Archives and History, Montgomery

John W. Dubose, 8th Confederate Cavalry
John W. Dubose, 3rd Confederate Cavalry
8th Confederate Cavalry Regimental File
51st Alabama Partisan Rangers
1st Alabama Cavalry Regimental File
1st Confederate Cavalry Regimental File
R. R. Gaines Papers
James Hagan Papers
William Hardee Papers, Hardee Family Papers, [1862–1962]
Robert D. Jackson Family Papers, [1857–1914]
Mrs. L. Kirkpatrick's Scrapbook
Nimrod William Ezekial Long Papers, [1860–1865]
George Knox Miller Papers
Henry Clay Reynolds Papers, [1838–1920]
James R. Riggs Civil War letters
3rd Alabama Cavalry Regimental File
Joseph Wheeler Family Papers, [1809–1943]

American Civil War Museum, Richmond, Va.

Sgt. Tucker St. Joseph Randolph, Letters, Co. F, 21st Virginia Infantry and staff of Gen. John Pegram, May 1861–May 1864

Auburn University Libraries Special Collections & Archives Department

John Crittenden, letters (1862–1865)
George Family Papers, letters (1861–1865)

Bowling Green State University, William T. Jerome Library

Askew Family Correspondence
George Kryder, Diary
Daniel Prickitt, Diary
Isaac Skillman, Diary

Chicago Historical Society
Joseph Wheeler Papers

Cincinnati Historical Society, Cincinnati Museum Center
William E. Crane, "William E. Crane's Daily Journal of Life in the Field During the War of the Rebellion"

Colorado Springs Pioneers Museum
William Palmer Papers
James Weir Diary

Duke University, David M. Rubenstein Rare Book & Manuscript Library
Marvin Benjamin Butler Papers (1861–1864)
William Culbertson Papers (1861–1863)
John Euclid Magee, Diary
Benjamin F. Nourse Papers
Elisha A. Peterson Papers (1862–1865)
James H Wiswell Papers (1861–1867)

Emory University, Manuscript, Archives, and Rare Book Library
W. B. Corbitt, Civil War-era documents (1860–1865)

Filson Historical Society, Louisville, Kentucky
John Daeuble Papers (1839–1864), Mss. A D123
Eleanor Diehl Papers (1899–1918), Mss. C/D
Vincent Dunn, Dunn Family Papers, 1854–1977, Mss. A/D923
J. Stoddard Johnston Papers, Mss A72-16
John Lillyett, Correspondence in Don Carlos Buell Papers, 1818–1898, Letters Received, Mss A B928
Thomas B Thompson, Diary, Mss A T477.
Lewis Wolfley, Mss. Murfreesboro (Tenn.), Battle of, 1862–1863 C. Wolfley Family Papers

Galveston and Texas History Center, Rosenberg Library
John Austin Wharton Papers, 1862–1866, Accession Number, 25-0567

Georgia Department of Archives and History
Julius Lafayette Dowda, Diary, Reference: AC 70-069, MF 159; Drawer 283, Box 24

Gettysburg College, Musselman Library
George C. Wynkoop Papers, MS—076

The Gilder Lehrman Institute of American History, New York City
Collection of Edward W. Amsden, D Company, 3rd Regiment, Ohio cavalry

Harvard University, Dearborn Collection, Houghton Library
John A. Wharton Letter
Wheeler correspondence

Indiana Historical Society
Daniel Wait Howe Papers (1824–1920), Correspondence and Diary

Kalamazoo College, Kalamazoo
Eugene Bronson Collection

Kentucky Historical Society
D. Howard Smith Papers, 1821–1889, 85M03

Louisiana State University Libraries Special Collections, Louisiana and Lower Mississippi Valley Collections
James Hagan and Family Papers Mss. 1485 [1833–1901]

Masters, Jack Personal Collection
John Weatherred, "The Wartime Diary of John Weatherred," private collection of Jack Masters, Gallatin, TN.

Michigan Historical Society, Lansing, Michigan
Henry Albert Potter Collection. MS 91-480, Accession Box 461 Folder 2

Michigan State University Archives & Historical Collections, Michigan State University
Othniel Gooding Letters (c.00275)
John McLain Diary and Papers (c.00111)

Minnesota Historical Society, St. Paul, Minnesota
Robert Burns Letters (Mss. M642)

Missouri Historical Society, St. Louis
Benjamin Burke, *A Terry's Ranger Write Home: Letters of Pvt. Benjamin F. Burke*

National Archives, Washington, D.C.
Correspondence, First Cavalry Division, Record Group 393
Fourth Ohio Cavalry Papers, Record Group 94, Box 3518
Fifth Tennessee Cavalry Papers, Record Group 94, Box 4667
Letters and Orders by the Chief of Cavalry, Record Group 393, Part 2, Number 2469
Letters and Orders, First Cavalry Division, Record Group 393, Part 2, Number 2468
Letters Sent, First Cavalry Division, Record Group 393
Organization Charts, Record Group 393, Part 2, Number 2477
Second Tennessee Regimental Papers, Record Group 94, Box 4661
David Stanley, Personnel Records ACP 000183, National Archives Microfiche
David Stanley, Union General Papers. Record Group 94, Entry 159, Box 28.
Third Kentucky Cavalry Papers, Record Group 94, Box 1366
Third Ohio Cavalry Regimental Papers, Record Group 94, Box 3512

New-York Historical Society
Braxton Bragg Scrapbook
John C. Breckinridge Papers/ Braxton Bragg, Battle of Stones River Papers

Ohio Historical Society, Columbus
John W. Large Papers, 1862–1863, [VFM 455]

Historical Society of Pennsylvania, Philadelphia
Charles Malone Betts Papers (#1889)

Perryville Battlefield State Historic Site
Corporal Barton Ulmer Letter Letters

Stones River National Park, Technical Information Center, Murfreesboro, Tennessee
Philemon Baldwin Papers

A. S. Bloomfield, Letter—January 16, 1863, Battery A, 1st Ohio (Artillery)
Henry G. Cooley, Diary
Inslee Deaderick Papers
George Garrett, Letters
Gerould, Otis Gibson, Diary
F. M Ison, Letters
Josiah Lewis, Letter
N. W. Sample Papers
Confederate Civil War Letters of John N. Smith
Drucilla Lyttle Watkins Papers

Tennessee State Library and Archives, Nashville, Tennessee

Lyman Ayer Letters, Civil War Collection (Box F 25, Folder 6)
Tommie Clack, Microfilm 824, Confederate Collection (Box 15, Folder 4)
Carroll Henderson Clark, "Memoir," Confederate Collection (Box 12, Folder 9)
George W. Dillion, "War Diaries of George W. Dillon," (Microfilm 1656)
Alfred Tyler Fielder, "Diaries of Alfred Tyler Fielder," (Microfilm 1003)
Lucy Virginia French, "Lucy Virginia French Diaries," (Microfilm 1816)
George B. Guild, "Memoirs," Confederate Collection (Box C27, Folder 8)
William Henry Harder, Diary 1861–1865 (Microfilm 574)
James Knight, Letters (Federal Collection Box F 25, Folder 8)
James Lacy, Letters (Confederate Collection, Box C28, Folder 17)
John M. Porter, "Memoir," (Confederate Collection, Box 14, Folder 11)
John M. Routt, Papers (Confederate Collection, Box 11, Folder 15)
William Thompson Letters, December 11, 1862, [warr 002]

U.S. Army Heritage and Education Center, Carlisle, Pennsylvania (Usahec)

Paul Hersh, Papers, Civil War Misc. Collection
Edward Hill, Letters, Civil War Collection
Eli Long, Diary and Papers 1855–1892, Civil War Collection
John C. McLain, Diary, Civil War Collection
Robert Minty Papers, Civil War Collection, Box 1 and 2
Frances W. Reed Papers, Civil War Times Illustrated Collection
Baxter Smith, "8th Tennessee Cavalry Regiment, Confederate, History of Regiment and Biographical information"
Lancaster Thomas, Letters, Civil War Collection
Stanley West, Wright Family Papers, Box 1 and 5

University of California, Los Angeles, Department of Special Collections

William S. Rosecrans Papers: 1810–1920, Collection 663
Ralston Skinner Report

University of Georgia, Hargett Rare Book & Manuscript Library, Athens, Georgia

Erastus Newton Bates Papers (MS 6)
William Joseph and Nancy Wallis Short Family Papers (MS 3863)

University of Michigan, Bentley Historical Library

Elisha Mix Papers (1818–1898)
James W. Sligh Papers (1842–1865)

University of North Carolina, Chapel Hill, The Wilson Library

Isaac Barton Ulmer Papers, Southern Historical Collection

University of Notre Dame Archives (Unda), Notre Dame

Conyngham, David Power, Papers (Con)

University of Tennessee, Knoxville

John M. Hollis Papers, Diary
William A. Huddard, Papers
Ezra T. Stringer, Correspondence
Milton Weaver Collection

University of Texas at Austin, Briscoe Center for American History

Crimmins (Martin Lalor) Papers, David S. Stanley, "David Stanley Diary, United States 2nd Dragoons of a March from Fort Smith, Arkansas, to San Diego, California, made in 1853," Accession No.: 1936; 1950.

University of Virginia

Theodore O'Hara Papers, MS 11914

Francis Weigley Papers, Private Collection

Francis Weigley Letters

Western Michigan University, Kalamazoo, Michigan

Cyrus Thomas, Diary

Western Reserve Historical Society

Bound Letter Copy Books, 1861–1864, Braxton Bragg Papers, Ms 2000
George Brent, Journal, Braxton Bragg Papers, Ms 2000
Headquarters and Personnel Records Braxton Bragg Papers, Ms 2000

REGIMENTAL HISTORIES

Andes, John and Will McTeer. *Loyal Mountain Troops: The Second and Third Tennessee Volunteer Cavalry*. Maryville, Tennessee: Blount County Genealogical and Historical Society, 1992.
Bailey, Chester. *The Mansfield Men in the Seventh Pennsylvania Cavalry, Eighth Regiment*. Mansfield, Pennsylvania: Published by Author, 1986.
Bailey, Michael M. *From Pensacola to Bentonville: The War History of the Prattville Dragoons*. 3rd Alabama Regimental File, SG024911, Alabama Department of Archives and History.
Bennett, Charles W. *Historical Sketches of the Ninth Michigan Infantry*. Coldwater, MI: Daily Courier Print, 1913.
Bennett L. G. and William. M. Haigh, *History of the Thirty-Sixth Regiment Illinois Volunteers, During the War of the Rebellion*. Aurora, IL: Knickerbocker & Hodder, Printers And Binders, 1876.
Blackburn, J. K. P. *Reminiscences of the Terry Rangers*. n.p.: University of Texas, 1919.
Bradt, H. H. G. *History of the Services of the Third Battery*

Wisconsin Light Artillery in the Civil War of the United States, 1861–1865. Berlin, WI: Courant Press, 1902.
Burlingame, E. P. "Company L, First Ohio Volunteer Cavalry," In *History of Washington County Ohio with Illustrations and Biographical Sketches*. Cleveland: W.W. Williams Publishers, 1881.
Bush, Bryan S. *Terry's Texas Rangers: History of the Eighth Texas Cavalry*. Paducah, KY: Turner Publishing Co., 2002.
Butler, M. B. *My Story of the Civil War and Underground Railroad*. Huntington, Indiana: United Brethren Publishing Establishment, 1914.
Carter, Howell. *A Cavalryman's Reminiscences of the Civil War*. Port Hudson, LA: Old South Books, 1979.
Carter, Howell. *A Cavalryman's Reminiscences of the Civil War*. New Orleans: American Printing Co., n.d.
Carter, W. R. *History of the First Regiment of Tennessee Volunteer Cavalry*. Knoxville: Gaut-Ogden Co., Printers and Binders, 1902.
Cavender, Michael Bower. *The First Georgia Cavalry in the Civil War: A History and Roster*. Jefferson, NC: McFarland, 2016.
Colton, J. Ferrell and Antoinette Smith, editors. *Column South with the Fifteenth Pennsylvania Cavalry*. Flagstaff: J. P. Colton & Co., 1960.
Cope, Alexis. *The Fifteenth Ohio Volunteers and Its Campaigns, 1861–1865*. Columbus, Ohio: Published by Author, 1916.
Crofts, Thomas. *History of the Service of the Third Ohio Veteran Volunteer Cavalry*. Toledo: Stoneman Press, 1910.
Curry, W. L. *Four Years in the Saddle: History of the First Regiment Ohio Volunteer Cavalry*. Columbus, OH: Champlin Printing Co., 1898.
Davis, William C. *The Orphan Brigade: Kentucky Confederates Who Couldn't Go Home*. Garden City, NY: Doubleday & Co., 1980.
Dornblaser, T. F. *Sabre Strokes of the Pennsylvania Dragoons in the War of 1861–1865.Interspersed with Personal Reminiscences*. Philadelphia: Lutheran Publication Society, 1884.
Giles, L. B. *Terry's Texas Rangers*. n.p.: L. B. Giles, 1911.
Gremillion, Nelson. *Company G, 1st Regiment Louisiana Cavalry CSA: A Narrative*. Lafayette, LA: W.N. Gremillion, Sr., in cooperation with Center for Louisiana Studies, University of Southwestern Louisiana, 1986.
Guild, George. *A Brief Narrative of the Fourth Tennessee Cavalry Regiment*. Nashville: n.p., 1913.
Hight, John J. *History of the Fifty-Eighth Regiment Indiana Volunteer Infantry*. Princeton: Press of the Clarion, 1895.
Hoffman, Mark. *My Brave Mechanics: The First Michigan Engineers and their Civil War*. Detroit: Wayne State University Press, 2007.
Jeffries, C. C. *Terry's Rangers*. New York: Vantage Press, 1961.
Kirk, Charles. *History of the Fifteenth Pennsylvania Volunteer Cavalry*. Philadelphia, PA: Society of the Fifteenth Pennsylvania Cavalry, 1906.
A Military Record of Battery D, First Ohio Veteran Volunteers, Light Artillery. Oil City, Pennsylvania: The Derrick Publishing Co., 1908.
Miller, Rex. *Wheeler's Favorites: A Regimental History of the 51st Alabama Cavalry Regiment*. Depew, NY: Patrex Press, 1991.
Mims, Wilbur F. *War History of the Prattville Dragoons*. Prattville, AL: n.p., n.d.
Pape-Findley, Nancy. *The Invincibles: The Story of Fourth Ohio Veteran Volunteer Cavalry*. Tecumseh, MI: Blood Road Publishing: 2002.
Payne, Edwin W. *History of the Thirty-Fourth Regiment of Illinois Volunteer Infantry*. Clinton, IO: Allen Printing Co., 1902.
Pickerill, W. N. *History of the Third Indiana Cavalry*. Indianapolis: Aetna Printing Co., 1906.
Poole, John Randolph. *Cracker Cavaliers: The 2nd Georgia Cavalry under Wheeler and Forrest*. Macon, GA: Mercer University Press, 2000.
Popejoy, Stirling D. "The Second Tennessee Cavalry in the American Civil War," Master's Thesis, 2014, U.S. Army Command and General Staff College, Fort Leavenworth.
Sipes, William. *History and Roster of the 7th Pennsylvania Veteran Volunteers*. Pottsville: Miners' Journal Print, 1905.
Sligh, Charles R. *The History of the Services of the First Regiment Michigan Engineers and Mechanics*. Grand Rapids: n.p., 1921.
Tarrant, Eastham. *The Wild Riders of the First Kentucky Cavalry*. Louisville: Press of R. H. Caruthers, 1894.
Thompson, Ed Porter. *History of the Orphan Brigade*. Louisville: Louis N. Thompson, 1898.
Vale, Joseph. *Minty and the Cavalry: A History of Cavalry Campaigns in the Western Armies*. Harrisburg, Pennsylvania: Edwin K. Myers, Printer and Binder, 1886.
Walker, C. I. *Rolls and Historical Sketch of the 10th Regiment So. Ca. Volunteers*. Charleston, SC: Walker, Evans and Cogswell Printers, 1881.
Weatherbee, F. W. *The 5th (1st Middle) Tennessee Cavalry Regiment, USA*. Carrollton, MS: Pioneer Publishing Co., 1992.
Williams, L. B. *A Revised History of the 33rd Alabama Volunteer Infantry Regiment: In Cleburne's Elite Division, Army of Tennessee, 1862–1865*. Auburn, AL: Auburn University Printing Service, 1998.
Wulsin, Lucien. *The Fourth Regiment Ohio Veteran Volunteer Cavalry*. Cincinnati: Fourth Ohio Volunteer Cavalry Association, 1912.

OFFICIAL DOCUMENTS

Journal of the Congress of the Confederate States of America, 1861–1865 Vol. III. Washington: Government Printing Office, 1904.
United States Census, 1860
United States Record and Pension Office. "Compiled Service Records of Volunteer Union Soldiers Who Served in Organizations from the State of Tennessee." Washington, D.C.: National Archives, 1962.
United States War Department, *Cavalry Tactics*, Volumes 1–3. Philadelphia: J. B. Lippincott, & Co. 1862.
The War of the Rebellion. A Compilation of the Official Records of the Union and Confederate Armies. Washington, D.C.: U.S. Government Printing Office, 1880–1901.

JOURNAL ARTICLES

Breckinridge, John C., "Murfreesboro." *Southern Historical Society Papers*, Vol. 5, Number 5 (May 1878): 211–213.
Brooksher, William and David Snider. "The War Child Rides: Joe Wheeler at Stones River." *Civil War Times Illustrated*, Vol. 14 (1976): 4–10.
Carraway, William E. "The Mutiny of the 15th Pennsylvania Volunteer Cavalry." *The Denver Westerners Monthly Roundup*, Volume XVII, No. 11 (November 1961): 5–17.

Clay, H. B. "On the Right at Murfreesboro." *Confederate Veteran*, Volume 21:588.
Crippen, Edward. "The Diary of Edward C. Crippen, Private 27th Illinois Volunteers, War of the Rebellion, August 7, 1861 to September 19, 1863," Ed. Robert J. Kerner. *Illinois State Historical Society Transactions*, Volume 10 (1909): 220–282.
Dwyer, Christopher S. "Raiding Strategy: As Applied by the Western Confederate Cavalry in the American Civil War." *The Journal of Military History*, Vol. 63 (April 1999): 263–281.
Dyer, John P. "The Civil War Career of General Joseph Wheeler." *The Georgia Historical Quarterly*, Vol. 19, No. 1 (Mar. 1935): 17–46.
Emanuel, S. "Promoted on the Field for Gallantry." *Confederate Veteran*, Volume 13 (1905): 17.
Godfrey, E. S. "Revolver versus Saber—The Report of the Cavalry Board." *Journal of the United States Cavalry Association*, Vol. 17, Number 61 (July 1906): 42–47.
Groce, William Wharton. "Major General John A. Wharton." *The Southwestern Historical Quarterly*, Vol. 19, No. 3 (Jan. 1916): 271–278.
Harris, Moses. "Some Thoughts on Equipment." *Journal of the United States Cavalry Association*, Vol. 4 (1891): 166–178.
Hickman, F. G. "Events in the Battle of Murfreesboro." *Confederate Veteran*, Vol. 3 (1895): 162.
Holman, J. A. "Letters from Veterans." In *Confederate Veteran*, Volume 2 (1894): 227.
James, Alfred P. "General James Scott Negley." *Western Pennsylvania Historical Magazine*, Volume 14, Number 2 (April 1931): 69–91.
Johnson, E. Polk. "The First Kentucky Cavalry." *Confederate Veteran*, Volume 21 (1913): 479.
Johnston, J. Stoddard. "Sketch of Theodore O'Hara." *The Register of the Kentucky State Historical Society*, Volume 11, Number 33 (September 1913): 67–72.
Johnston, J. Stoddard. "Sketches of Operations of General John C. Breckinridge." *Southern Historical Society Papers*, Vol. 7 (1879): 385–392.
Jones, William B. "The Late Maj. Gen. William Wirt Allen." *Confederate Veteran*, Volume 2, Number 11 (November 1894): 324.
Kniffin, G. C. "The Third Day at Stone's River," In *War Papers*, Paper Number 69. Military Order of the Loyal Legion of the United States, Commandery of the District of Columbia, 1907, 22 pages.
Longacre, Edward. "Fightin' Joe." *America's Civil War*, Vol. 23 Issue 2 (May 2010): 50–57.
"The Lookout Rangers Colonel Henry Marshall Ashby and the 2nd Tennessee Cavalry." *The Silver Gray*, Volume 17, Number 11 (November 2012): 2–4.
Otey, W. N. Mercer. "Organizing a Signal Corps." *Confederate Veteran*, Vol. 7 (1899): 549–551.
Pickett, W. D. "Reminiscences of Murfreesboro." *Confederate Veteran*, Vol. 16 (1908): 449–454.
Quisenberry, A. C. "The Confederate Campaign in Kentucky: The Battle of Perryville." *The Register of the Kentucky Historical Society*, Volume 17 (January 1919): 30–38.
Ramsdell, Charles W. "General Robert E. Lee's Horse Supply, 1862–1865." *The American Historical Review*, 35 (July 1930): 758–777.
Schiller, Laurence D. "Of Sabers and Carbines: The Emergence of the Federal Dragoon." *The Papers of the Blue & Gay Education Society*, Monograph Number 11, August 1, 2001.

Seay, Samuel. "A Private at Stone River." *Southern Bivouac* Vol. 4 (1887): 156–160.
"Six Brothers Confederate Survivors," *Confederate Veteran*, Vol. 10 (1902): 114.
Starr, Stephen. "Cold Steel: The Saber and the Union Cavalry." *Civil War History*, Volume 18, Number 2, 1965: 142–159.
Starr, Stephen Z. "The Third Ohio Volunteer Cavalry: A View from the Inside." *Ohio History*, Volume 85 (Autumn 1976) Number 4: 306–318.
Stewart, R. B. "The Battle of Stone River: As Seen by One Who Was There." *Blue and Gray*, Volume 1, 1895 (January): 10–14.
Tullidge, Edward, editor. "Governor Murray and Family." *Tullidge Quarterly Magazine*, Volume 1, Number 3 (1881): 496–501.
Vineyard, Ganum. "Letter from Sgt. Ganum Vineyard at the Battle of Murfreesboro to his Wife in Grainger County, Tennessee." *Tennessee Ancestors*, Volume 16, Number 2 (August 2000): 123–124.
Wendel, Vickie. "Ordinary Heroes: The Second Minnesota Battery of Light Artillery." *Minnesota History Quarterly*, Volume 59, Number 4 (Winter 2004–2005): 141–153.
Williams, T. Harry. "Voters in Blue: The Citizen Soldiers of the Civil War." *The Mississippi Valley Historical Review*, Vol. 31, No. 2 (Sept., 1944): 187–204.

NEWSPAPERS

Columbia Daily Tribune (Columbia, MO)
Daily Dispatch (Richmond, VA)
Daily State Sentinel (Selma, AL)
The Daily Wabash Express (Terra-Haute, IN)
Dayton (Ohio) Daily Empire
Franklin (Tennessee) Sentinel
Harper's Weekly Potter Journal (Coudersport, PA)
Highland Weekly News (Hillsboro, OH)
Lancaster Daily Evening Express (Pennsylvania)
Lancaster (Ohio) Gazette
The Nashville American
National Tribune (Washington, D.C.)
New York Daily Tribune
New York Times
Newark (Ohio) Advocate
Northern Indianian (Warsaw)
Perrysburg Journal (Ohio)
Rome Tri-Weekly Courier (Georgia)
The Vevay Reveille (Vevay, IN)

Other Sources

Allardice, Bruce S. *Confederate Colonels: A Biographical Register*. Columbia: University of Missouri Press, 2008.
Allardice, Bruce and Lawrence Lee Hewitt. *Kentuckians in Gray: Confederate Generals and Field Officers of the Bluegrass State*. Lexington: University of Kentucky Press, 2008.
Allardice, Bruce S. *More Generals in Gray*. Baton Rouge: Louisiana State University Press, 1995.
Aster Aaron. *Civil War Along Tennessee's Cumberland Plateau*. Charleston: History Press, 2015.
Baggett, James Alex. *Homegrown Yankees: Tennessee's Union Cavalry in the Civil War*. Baton Rouge: Louisiana State University, 2009.
Banta, Theodore M. *Sayre Family Lineage of Thomas Sayre*. New York: De Vinne Press, 1901.

Bates, Samuel P. *History of the Pennsylvania Volunteers, 1861-65*. Harrisburg: B. Singerly, State Printer, 1870.

Battle, Frank. "Colonel Baxter Smith's Orders," In *Gray Riders: Stories from the Confederate Cavalry*, Lee Jacobs, compiler. Shippensburg, PA: Burd Street Press, 1999.

Bearss, Edwin C. "The Battle of Hartsville and Morgan's Second Kentucky Raid." Research Project #4—Stones River National Park, Technical Information Center, Murfreesboro, TN, 1960.

Bearss, Edwin C. "Cavalry Operations—Battle of Stones River." Stones River National Park, Technical Information Center, 1959.

Bearss, Edwin C. "Cavalry Operations in the Stones River Campaign," In *The Battle of Stones River*, Volume 4, Timothy Johnson, editor. Nashville: Tennessee Historical Society, 2012.

Bearss, Edwin C. "Rebels Concentrate at Stones River." Research Project Number 5, Stones River National Park, Technical Information Center, Murfreesboro, TN, 1960.

Bearss, Edwin C. "The Union Artillery and Breckinridge's Attack." Research Project 2, Stones River National Park, Technical Information Center, Murfreesboro, TN, 1959.

Beatty, John. *The Citizen Soldier: The Memoirs of a Civil War Volunteer*. Lincoln and London: Bison Books University of Nebraska Press, 1998.

Belcher, Dennis W. *General David S. Stanley, USA*. Jefferson, NC: McFarland, 2014.

Bergeron, Arthur W., Jr. *Guide to Louisiana Confederate Military Units, 1861-1865*. Baton Rouge: Louisiana State University Press, 1989.

Berry, Thomas Franklin. *Four Years with Morgan and Forrest*. Oklahoma City: Harlow-Ratliff Company, 1914.

Bickham, William D. *Rosecrans' Campaign with the Fourteenth Army Corps, of the Army of the Cumberland*. Cincinnati: Moore Wilstach, Keys & Co., 1863.

Billings, John D. *Hardtack and Coffee, or, The Unwritten Story of Army Life*. Boston: George M. Smith and Company, 1887.

Biographical and Historical Souvenir for the Counties of Clark, Crawford, Harrison, Floyd, Jefferson, Jennings, Scott and Washington, Indiana. Chicago: John M. Gresham & Co., 1889.

Blackmar, Wilmon. "The Charge on Infantry at Stone River," In *History of the Fifteenth Pennsylvania Volunteer Cavalry*, Charles Kirk, ed. Philadelphia, PA: Society of the Fifteenth Pennsylvania Cavalry, 1906.

Boniface, Jonathan J. *The Cavalry Horse and His Pack*. Kansas City: Hudson-Kimberly Publishing Co., 1908.

Bradley, Michael R. *The Raiding Winter*. Gretna, Louisiana: Pelican Publishing Co., 2013.

Bradley, Michael R. *They Rode with Forrest*. Gretna, Louisiana: Pelican Publishing Co., 2012.

Brewer, Willis. *Alabama, Her History, Resources, War Record, and Public Men*. Montgomery: Barrett & Brown, Steam Printers and Book Binders, 1872.

Brown, Dee Alexander. *Morgan's Raiders*. New York: Smithmark Publishers, 1959.

Buell, Don Carlos. "East Tennessee and the Campaign of Perryville," In *Battles and Leaders of the Civil War*, Volume III. New York: The Century Company, 1888.

Cameron, Robert S. *Staff Ride Handbook for the Battle of Perryville, 8 October, 1862*. Fort Leavenworth, KS: Combat Studies Institute Press, n.d.

Cannon, Newton. *The Reminiscences of Newton Cannon: First Sergeant, CSA*, Campbell Brown, editor. Franklin, TN: Carter House Association, 1963.

Carmichael, Peter. *Lee's Young Artillerist: William R.J. Pegram*. Charlottesville: University of Virginia Press, 1995.

The Catalogue and History of Sigma Chi. Chicago: Published by the Fraternity, 1890.

Cist, Henry M. *The Army of the Cumberland, Campaigns of the Civil War*, Volume VII. New York: Charles Scribner's Sons, 1909.

Cone, Stephen D. *Biographical and Historical Sketches and a Narrative of Hamilton and Its Residents*. Hamilton, Ohio: Republican Publishing Co., 1896.

Connelly, Thomas Lawrence. *Army of the Heartland: The Army of Tennessee, 1861-1862*. Baton Rouge: Louisiana State University Press, 1967.

Connelly, Thomas L. *Autumn of Glory: The Army of Tennessee 1862-1865*. Baton Rouge: Louisiana State University Press, 1971.

Cozzens, Peter. *No Better Place to Die: The Battle of Stones River*. Urbana, Chicago: University of Illinois Press, 1991.

Crane, William E. "Bugle Blasts," In *Sketches of War History 1861-1865* (MOLLUS, Ohio, Volume 1). Cincinnati, OH: Robert Clarke, 1888.

Crittenden, Thomas. "The Union Left at Stone's River," In *Battles and Leaders of the Civil War*, Volume III. New York: Century Company, 1888.

Crute, Joseph H. *Units of the Confederate States Army*. Midlothian, Virginia: Derwent Books, 1987.

Cullum, George. *Biographical Register of the Officers and Graduates of the U.S. Military Academy, 1841-1867*, Vol. II. New York: D. Van Nostrand, 1868.

Cullum, George W. *Biographical Register of Officers and Graduates of the U.S. Military Academy*, Volume II. New York: D. Van Nostrand, 1879.

Curry, L. M. *Legal Justification of the South in Secession*. Atlanta: Confederate Publishing Co., 1899.

Dalessandro, Robert J. "Major General William S. Rosecrans and the Transformation of the Staff of the Army of the Cumberland: A Case Study." Strategy Research Project, U.S. Army War College, Carlisle Barracks, PA, 2002.

Daniel, Larry J. *The Battle of Stones River*. Baton Rouge: Louisiana State University Press, 2012.

Daniel, Larry J. *Days of Glory: The Army of the Cumberland, 1861-1865*. Baton Rouge: Louisiana State University Press, 2006.

Davis, J. Lucius. *The Trooper's Manual*. Richmond: A. Morris Publisher, 1861.

Davis, William C. *Breckinridge: Statesman, Soldier, Symbol*. Baton Rouge: Louisiana State University Press, 1974.

Dawes, R. R. "Lieutenant Timothy L. Condit," In *Marietta College in the War of Succession: 1861-1865*. Cincinnati: Peter Thomson, 1878.

De Land, T. A. and A. Davis Smith, *Northern Alabama Historical and Biographical Illustrated*. Birmingham: Donohue and Henneberry Printers, 1888.

Dodson, W. C. *Campaigns of Wheeler and His Cavalry, 1862-1865*. Atlanta: Hudgins Publishing Co., 1899.

Dornblaser, T. F. *My Life Story for Young and Old*. USA: Privately printed, 1930.

DuBose, John W. *General Joseph Wheeler and the Army of Tennessee*. New York: The Neale Publishing Co., 1912.

Duke, Basil W. *History of Morgan's Cavalry*. Cincinnati: Miami Printing and Publishing Co., 1867.

Duke, Basil W. *Morgan's Cavalry*. New York: The Neale Publishing Co., 1909.

Duke, Basil. "Morgan's Cavalry During the Bragg Invasion," In *Battles and Leaders of the Civil War*, Volume III. New York: The Century Company, 1888.

Duncan, L. Wallace and Charles F. Scott, editors. *History of Allen and Woodson Counties, Kansas: Embellished with Portraits of Well-Known People of These Counties, with Biographies of Our Representative Citizens, Cuts of Public Buildings and a Map of Each County.* Iola, KS: Iola Registers, Printers and Binders, 1901.

Dyer, Frederick H. *A Compendium of the War of the Rebellion.* Des Moines: The Dyer Publishing Co., 1908.

Dyer, John P. *From Shiloh to San Juan: The Life of "Fightin' Joe Wheeler."* Baton Rouge: Louisiana State University, 1989.

Eby, Henry H. *Observations of an Illinois Boy in Battle, Camp and Prisons—1861 to 1865.* Mendota, IL: Published by the Author, 1910.

Edwards, Lawyn C. "Confederate Cavalry at Chickamauga: What Went Wrong." Master's Thesis, U.S. Army Command and General Staff College, Fort Leavenworth, Kansas, 1990.

Ellis, J. Tandy. *Report of the Adjutant General of the State of Kentucky: Confederate Kentucky Volunteers.* Hartford, Kentucky: McDowell Publications, 1979.

Estes, Claud. *List of Officers, Regiments and Battalions in the Confederate States Army.* Macon, Georgia: J. W. Burke Co., 1912.

Evans, Clement, editor. *Confederate Military History*, Volume 1 and 3. Atlanta: Confederate Publishing Co., 1899.

Evans, David. *Sherman's Horsemen.* Bloomington: Indiana University Press, 1996.

Field, Ron. *The Confederate Army 1861-1865: Florida, Alabama & Georgia.* New York, Oxford: Osprey Publishing, 2005.

Fitch, John. *Annals of the Army of the Cumberland.* Philadelphia: J. B. Lippincott and Co., 1864.

Freeman, Henry V. "Some Battle Recollections of Stone's River," In *Military Essays and Recollections*, Volume III. Chicago: The Dial Press, 1899.

Friend, W. R. "Rout of Rosecrans," In *New Annals of the Civil War*, edited by Peter Cozzens and Robert Girardi. Mechanicsburg, PA: Stackpole Books, 2004.

Fry, H. C. "The Death of Martin L. Hill," In *History of the Fifteenth Pennsylvania Volunteer Cavalry*. Philadelphia: n.p., 1906.

Ganoe, William A. *The History of the United States Army.* New York: D. Appleton and Co., Publishers, 1924.

Garrard, Kenner and Lewis Edward Nolan. *Nolan's System for Training Cavalry Horses.* New York: D. Van Nostrand, 1862.

Goebel, David P. "Organizational Turbulence and Army Performance: A Comparison of the Confederate Army of Northern Virginia and the Army of Tennessee." Master's Thesis, U.S. Army Command and General Staff College Fort Leavenworth, KS, 1993.

Graber, H. W. *The Life Record of H. W. Graber: A Terry Texas Ranger, 1861-1865.* n.p.: H.W. Garber Publisher, 1916.

Grant, Ulysses Simpson. *Personal Memoirs of U.S. Grant.* New York: Charles L. Webster & Co., 1894.

Griffith, Paddy. *Battle Tactics of the Civil War.* New Haven, CT: Yale University Press, 2001.

Griggs, Walter, Jr. *General John Pegram, CSA.* Lynchburg, VA: H. E. Howard, Inc., 1993.

Griggs, Walter, Jr. *Hidden History of Richmond.* Charleston, SC: Arcadia Publishing Co., 2012.

Groce, W. Todd. *Mountain Rebels: East Tennessee Confederates and the Civil War, 1860-1870.* Knoxville, University of Tennessee Press, 1999.

Hafendorfer, Kenneth. *They Died by Twos and Tens: The Confederate Cavalry in the Kentucky Campaign of 1862.* Louisville, KY: KH Press, 1995.

Hall, Richard. *Patriots in Disguise: Women Warriors in the Civil War.* New York: Paragon House, 1994.

Hardie, William H. *Brothers in Arms: The Hardie Family in the Civil War.* Mobile, AL: Thornhill Foundation, 1994, 1998.

Haughton, Andrew. *Training, Tactics, and Leadership in the Confederate Army of Tennessee.* Portland, OR: Frank Cass Publishers, 2000.

Hazzard, George. *Hazzard's History of Henry County, Indiana, 1822-1906*, Volume 1. New Castle, IN: George Hazzard Publisher, 1906.

Hewitt, Lawrence Lee and Arthur Bergeron. *Confederate Generals in the Western Theater*, Volume 3. Knoxville: University of Tennessee Press, 2011.

Holland, Cecil Fletcher. *Morgan and His Raiders: A Biography of the Confederate General.* New York: The MacMillan Company, 1942.

Horn, Stanley. *The Army of Tennessee.* Norman: University of Oklahoma Press, 1952.

Hughes, Nathaniel Cheairs, Jr. *General William J. Hardee: Old Reliable.* Baton Rouge: Louisiana State University, 1965.

Hughes, Nathaniel Cheairs, Jr., and Thomas Clayton Ware. *Theodore O'Hara: Poet-Soldier of the Old South.* Knoxville: University of Tennessee Press, 1998.

Johnson, Richard. "Losing a Division at Stones River," In *Battles and Leaders of the Civil War*, Volume 5, Peter Cozzens, editor. Urbana and Chicago: University of Illinois Press, 2002.

Johnson, Richard. *A Soldier's Reminiscences in Peace and War.* Philadelphia: J. P. Lippincott and Company, 1886.

Johnston, J. S. *Kentucky: Confederate History*, Volume IX. Atlanta: Confederate Publishing Co., 1899.

Jones, Charles E. *Georgia in the Civil War 1861-1865.* Augusta: n.p., 1909.

Jones, Terry L. *Campbell Brown's Civil War: With Ewell and the Army of Northern Virginia.* Baton Rouge: Louisiana State University Press, 2001.

Jones, Terry L. *Historical Dictionary of the Civil War*, Volume 1. Lanham, MD: Scarecrow Press Inc., 2011.

Jordan, Thomas and J. P. Pryor. *The Campaigns of Lieut.-Gen. Nathan B. Forrest of Forrest's Cavalry.* New Orleans, Memphis, New York: Blelock & Co., 1868.

Kendall, Henry M. *The Battle of Stones River.* District of Columbia: Military Order of the Loyal Legion United States, 1903.

Kennett, John. "History of the First Cavalry Division from November 1, 1862, to January 1, 1863," In *G.A.R. War Papers*. Cincinnati, OH: Fred C. Jones Post, 1891.

King, Michael R. "Brigadier General St. John R. Liddell's Division at Chickamauga: The Study of a Division's Performance in Battle." Master's Thesis, U.S. Army Command and General Staff College, Ft. Leavenworth, KS.

Knight, Lucian Lamar. *A Standard History of Georgia and Georgians*, Volume IV. Chicago, New York: The Lewis Publishing Co., 1917.

Kniffin, Gilbert. "The Battle of Stone's River," In *Battles and Leaders of the Civil War* Volume 3. New York: The Century Company, 1888.

Krick, Robert. *Lee's Colonels: A Biographical Register of the Field Officers of the Army of Northern Virginia.* Dayton, OH: Morningside Bookshop, 1992.

Lamers, William. *The Edge of Glory: A Biography of General William S. Rosecrans, U.S.A.* New York: Harcourt, Brace & World, Inc., 1961.

Lane, Mills. *"Dear Mother: Don't grieve about me. If I get killed, I'll only be dead": Letters from Georgia Soldiers in the Civil War.* Savannah, GA: Beehive Press, 1977.

Lewis, Berkley. *Notes on Cavalry Weapons of the Civil War, 1861–1865.* Washington, D.C.: American Ordnance Association, 1961.

Lewis, Lloyd. *Sherman: Fighting Prophet.* Lincoln: University of Nebraska Press, 1960.

Lindsley, John Berrien, editor. *The Military Annals of Tennessee. Confederate.* Nashville: J. M. Lindsley & Co., Publishers, 1886.

Londa, John. *The Role of Union Cavalry during the Chickamauga Campaign.* Master's Thesis, U.S. Army Command and General Staff College, Leavenworth, KS, 1980.

Longacre, Edward. *Mounted Raids of the Civil War.* Lincoln, Nebraska and London: University of Nebraska Press, 1975.

Longacre, Edward G. *A Soldier to the Last: Maj. Gen. Joseph Wheeler in Blue and Gray.* Washington: Potomac Books Inc., 2007.

McClurg, Alexander C. "An American Soldier, Minor Millikin," In *Military Essays and Recollections: Papers Read Before the Commandery of the State of Illinois.* Chicago: A. C. McClurg and Company, 1894.

McWhiney, Grady. *Braxton Bragg and the Confederate Defeat, Volume I.* New York and London: Columbia University Press, 1969.

McWhiney, Grady and Perry Jamieson. *Attack and Die: Civil War Military Tactics and the Southern Heritage.* Tuscaloosa: University of Alabama Press, 1982.

Medlock, Chelsea A. "Delayed Obsolescence: The Horse in European and American Warfare from the Crimean War to the Second World War." Master's Thesis, Oklahoma State University, 2009.

Miller, George Knox. *An Uncompromising Secessionist: The Civil War of George Knox Miller, Eighth (Wade's) Confederate Cavalry,* edited by Richard M. McMurry. Tuscaloosa: University of Alabama Press, 2007.

Morton, John Watson. *The Artillery of Nathan Bedford Forrest's Cavalry.* Nashville, Tennessee and Dallas, Texas: Publishing House of the M. E. Church, 1909.

Myers, Barton. *Rebels against the Confederacy.* New York: Cambridge University Press, 2014.

National Cyclopedia of American Biography, Volume II and VI. New York: James T. White Co., 1896.

Oates, Stephen B. *Confederate Cavalry West of the River.* Austin: University of Texas Press, 1961.

Official Register of the Officers and Cadets of the U.S. Military Academy. West Point, NY: U.S. Military Academy, June 1852.

Osborn, Thomas. "Osborn, Thomas H.," In *The History of the Cincinnati Society of Army and Navy Officers.* Cincinnati: Peter G. Thomson, Publisher, 1880.

Otis, Ephraim. "The Murfreesboro Campaign," In *Campaigns in Kentucky and Tennessee including the Battle of Chickamauga, 1862–1864, Papers of the Military Historical Society of Massachusetts* Vol. VII. Boston: Military Historical Society of Massachusetts, 1908.

Otto, John Henry. *Memoirs of a Durch Mudsill,* David Gould and James B. Kennedy, editors. Kent and London: Kent State University Press, 2004.

Owens, Ira S. *Greene County Soldiers in the Late War. Being a History of the Seventy-Fourth O. V. I.* Dayton, OH: Christian Publishing, 1884.

Page, Walter Hines and Arthur Wilson Page, editors. *The World's Work: A History of Our Time,* Volume 15. New York: Doubleday, Page, and Co., 1908.

Parkhurst, James. "Recollections of Stone's River," In Michigan MOLLUS Papers. Detroit: Winn, Hammond, Printers and Binders, 1890.

Parks, Joseph Howard. *General Edmund Kirby Smith, C.S.A.* Baton Rouge: Louisiana State University Press, 1992.

Parks, Joseph H. *General Leonidas Polk, CSA: The Fighting Bishop.* Baton Rouge: Louisiana State University Press, 1990.

Piatt, Donn. *General George H. Thomas, A Critical Biography.* Cincinnati: Robert Clarke & Co., 1893.

Pirtle, Alfred. "Stone River Sketches," In *Sketches of War History,* edited by Theodore Allen, Edward McKee and Gordon Taylor. Cincinnati: Monfort & Co., 1908.

Polk, William. *Leonidas Polk—Bishop and General,* Volume 2. New York: Longmans, Green and Co., 1915.

Powell, David. *The Chickamauga Campaign: A Mad Irregular Battle.* El Dorado Hills, CA: Savas Beatie, 2014.

Powell, David. *Failure in the Saddle.* New York and California: Savas Beatie, 2010.

Powell, William Henry, editor. *Officers of the Army and Navy (volunteer) Who Served in the Civil War.* Philadelphia: L. R. Hamersly, 1893.

Reid, Whitelaw. *Ohio in the War: Her Statesmen, Her Generals, and Soldiers,* Volume I. New York: Moore, Wilstach & Baldwin: 1868.

Ridley, Bromfield L. *Battle Sketches of the Army of Tennessee.* Mexico, Missouri: Mexico Printing & Publishing Co., 1906.

Rodenbough, T. F. *From Everglade to Canon with the Second Dragoons.* New York: D. Van Nostrand, 1875.

Rowland, Dunbar. *The Official and Statistical Register of the State of Mississippi.* Nashville: Brandon Printing Co., 1908.

Schaefer, James Arthur. "The Tactical and Strategic Evolution of Cavalry during the American Civil War." Ph.D. Dissertation, The University of Toledo, 1982.

Sheridan, Philip. *Personal Memoirs of Philip H. Sheridan. General United States Army.* Volume 1. New York: D. Appleton and Company, 1902.

Sifakis, Stewart. *Compendium of the Confederate Armies; Compendium of the Confederate States Army for South Carolina and Georgia* Volume 7. New York: Facts on File, 1995.

Smith, D. Howard. *Life, Army Record, and Public Services of D. Howard Smith.* Louisville: Bradley and Gilbert Company, 1890.

Smith, Lanny. *The Stone's River Campaign: 26 December 1862–5 January 1863, Army of Tennessee.* n.p.: Lanny Smith, 2010.

Smith, Myron J., Jr. *Civil War Biographies from the Western Waters: Confederate and Union Naval Officials, Steamboat Pilots and Others.* Jefferson, NC: McFarland, 2015.

Society of the Army of the Cumberland, *Twenty-seventh Reunion.* Cincinnati, OH: The Robert Clark Company, 1898.

Speed, Thomas "Cavalry Operations in the West under Rosecrans and Sherman," In *Battles and Leaders of the Civil War,* Volume IV. New York: Century Company, 1888.

Speed, Thomas. *The Union Cause in Kentucky: 1860–1865.* New York: G. P. Putnam's Sons, 1907.

Speed, Thomas. *Union Regiments of Kentucky Volume I.*

Louisville: The Courier Journal Job Printing Co., 1897.

[A] Staff Officer, *Synopsis of the Military Career of Gen. Joseph Wheeler*. New York: n.p., 1865.

Stanley, David S. *An American General—The Memoirs of David Sloan Stanley*. Samuel W. Fordyce IV, ed. Santa Barbara, CA: The Narrative Press, 2004.

Stanley, David S. *Personal Memoirs of Major-General D. S. Stanley, USA*. Cambridge, Massachusetts: Harvard University Press, 1917.

Starr, Stephen Z. "Cold Steel: The Sabre and Union Cavalry," In *Battles Lost and Won: Essays from Civil War History*, John T. Hubbell, ed. Westport, CN: Greenwood Press, 1975.

Starr, Stephen Z. *The Union Cavalry in the Civil War, Volume 3: The War in the West, 1861–1865*. Baton Rouge: Louisiana State University Press, 1985.

Stevenson, Alexander. *Battle of Stones River near Murfreesboro, Tennessee*. Boston: J. R. Osgood and Company, 1884.

Stout, L. H. *Reminiscences of General Braxton Bragg*. Hattiesburg, MS: The Book Farm, 1942.

Stuart, Reginald. "The Role of the Cavalry in the Western Theatre of the American Civil War from the Battle of Shiloh to the Tullahoma Campaign," Master's Thesis, University of British Columbia, Vancouver, 1968.

Styles, Sean. *Stones River National Battlefield: Historical Resource Study*. Atlanta: National Parks Service, 2004.

Swiggett, Howard. *The Rebel Raider: The Life of John Hunt Morgan*. Garden City, NY: Garden City Publishing Co., 1937.

Tennesseans in the Civil War, Vol. 1. Nashville: Civil War Centennial Commission of Tennessee, 1964.

Thruston, Gates P. "Personal Recollections of the Battle in the Rear at Stone's River, Tennessee, with Two Maps," In *Sketches of War History 1861–1865, Papers Prepared for the Commandery of the State of Ohio, Military Order of the Loyal Legion of the United States*, Volume IV, Theodore F. Allen, Edward S. McKee, and J. Gordon Taylor, eds. Cincinnati: Monfort & Co., 1908.

Tucker, Spencer, editor. *American Civil War: The Definitive Encyclopedia and Document Collection*. Santa Barbara: ABC–Clio LLC, 2013.

Urquhart, David. "Bragg's Advance and Retreat," In *Battles and Leaders of the Civil War*, Volume III. New York: The Century Company, 1888.

Vance, Wilson J. *Stone's River: The Turning-Point of the Civil War*. New York: The Neale Publishing Co., 1914.

Vincent, Thomas M. "David Sloane Stanley," In *The Thirty-fourth Annual Reunion of the Association Graduates of the United States Military Academy at West Point, New York*. Saginaw, Michigan: Seeman & Peters, Printers and Binders, 1903.

Walsh, George. *Those Damn Horse Soldiers*. New York: Thom Doherty Associates, 2006.

Warner, Ezra J. *Generals in Gray: Lives of the Confederate Commanders*. Baton Rouge: Louisiana State University Press, 1959.

Welsh, Jack D. *Medical Histories of Confederate Generals*. Kent, Ohio: Kent State University Press, 1995.

Wheeler, Joseph. "Bragg's Invasion of Kentucky," In *Battles and Leaders of the Civil War*, Volume III. New York: The Century Company, 1888.

Williams, C. S. *Williams' Cincinnati Directory*. Cincinnati: C. S. Williams, 1860.

Wright, Stephen. *Kentucky Soldiers and Their Regiments in the Civil War*, Volume III. Utica, Kentucky: McDowell Publications, 2009.

Wulsin, Lucien. *Roster of Surviving Members of the 4th Regiment Ohio Volunteer Cavalry*. Cincinnati: Charles Thompson, Printer, 1891.

Wyeth, John Allan. *The Life General Nathan Bedford Forrest*. New York and London: Harper Brothers, 1899.

Wyeth, John Allan. *With Sabre and Scalpel: The Autobiography of a Soldier and Surgeon*. New York and London: Harper Brothers, 1914.

Yaryan, John Lee. "Stone River," In *War Papers Read before the Indiana Commandery MOLLUS*. Indianapolis: MOLLUS, 1898.

Yeary, Mamie. *Reminiscences of the Boys in Gray*. Smith and Lamar: Dallas, 1912.

Young, Bennett. *Confederate Wizards of the Saddle*. Boston: Chapple Publishing, 1914.

Index

Page numbers in ***bold italics*** indicate pages with illustrations.

Adams, Brig. Gen. Daniel 197, 203, 205
Adrian, Lieut. Col. T.W. 14, 50
Affleck, Dunbar 195
Airey, Sgt. Maj. Washington 142
Alabama Mounted Rifles *see* Alabama Units, 3rd Cavalry
Alabama Units:
 1st Cavalry 13, 50, 53, 105–106, 219, 249–250; battle on December 31 216; flag of truce incident 70–72; Wheeler's Raid 145, 148
 1st Cavalry Battalion 106
 3rd Cavalry 13, 50, 106, 121, 148
 4th Cavalry 50; 11th Cavalry 96
 14th Cavalry Battalion 94–95, 118; battle with 1st Michigan Engineers 227; skirmish at Franklin 127, 136
 16th Infantry 124, 126
 19th Infantry 16, 111
 33rd Infantry 124
 34th Infantry 25, 222
 51st (Partisan) Cavalry 29, 39, 50, 94, 107, 120–121, 133, 249; battle on December 31 217; Stewarts Creek bridge battle 129–130; Wheeler's Raid 145
 Howard's Cavalry Battalion 96
 Lumsden's Battery 199
 Semple's Battery 199
Allen, Col. William Wirt 13, 105–106, 243, 250; battle on December 31 216, 219, 249; Wheeler's Raid 147
Allston, Brig. Gen. Benjamin 14
Ambrose, Pvt. H.L. 165–166, 191, 193
ammunition trains *see* wagon trains
Amsden, Edward 240
Anderson, Capt. Paul F. 155, 231
Anderson, Brig. Gen. Robert 86, 91
Anderson Cavalry *see* Pennsylvania Units, 15th Cavalry
Antietam, Battle of 86, 91, 217
Arkansas Units:
 2nd Cavalry 111

2nd Light Artillery 110
Calvert's Battery 50
Calvert's Battery (Hanley's Section) 14
Clark County Artillery 110
Wiggins' Battery 59, 105, 110; December 26 actions 120; Wheeler's Raid 145
Army of Kentucky (CSA) 10–11, 14–16, 18–19, 25, 27, 33, 52, 55, 206
Army of Kentucky (U.S.) 23
Army of Middle Tennessee 29, 36, 47
Army of Mississippi 9–11, 13, 16, 18, 25–26, 29, 33, 46, 55; arrives in Middle Tennessee 35
Army of the Cumberland 1–2, 9, 32, 34, 37, 42, 48–49, 54–55, 57–58, 70–71, 115, 138–139, 149, 152, 173, 186, 191, 199, 228, 240, 243, 245, 251; battle begins 154–158; cavalry division 54, 66, 77–93; Rosecrans assumes command 35
Army of the Mississippi 41, 78
Army of the Ohio 11, 15, 17, 22–23, 29, 55, 77, 87, 91; cavalry 23–25
Army of the Potomac 66, 83
Asbury Church 144, 173, 180, 182, 211, 218
Ashby, Col. Henry M. 11, 14–17, 19, 49, 101, 104, 155; December 31 actions 181–183
Ashby, Col. Turner ***104***
Askew, Mathew 163
Austin, Maj. John E. 200
Ayer, Lyman 168

Baird, Maj. A.H. 50
Baldwin, Col. Philemon 144, 154, 157, 162–165
Barnes, Lt. Col. Milton 59
Barnett, Col. James 83
Baskerville, Lt. Col. Charles 108–109
Baskerville's Battalion *see* Confederate Units, 8th Cavalry

Battle, Capt. Lee W. 129
Battle Creek, skirmish at 96, 248
Bayles, Col. Jesse 25
Beatty, Brig. Gen. John 54
Beatty, Col. Samuel 230
Beauregard, Gen. Pierre 10, 102
Bell, Maj. Solon 109
Bell's Battalion (8th Confederate Cavalry)
Bennett, Charles 212
Bennett, Col. James D. 14, 61, 97
Betts, Sgt. Charles M. 93, 142
Bickham, William D. 87, 187, 227
Big Rockcastle Creek 18
Blackburn, James 115, 158, 166, 228
Blackland, skirmish at 96, 105, 109
Blackmar, Wilmon 222
blacksmith 47, 53, 114
Bledsoe, Maj. Willis Scott 50, 98, 103, 155
Blood's Hill *see* Cox's Hill
Bloomfield, Pvt. Alpheus S. 162
Bole Jack Pass, skirmish at 117
Bole Jack Road 132, 139, 142
Boonville, skirmish at 105, 109
Boyle, Lt. Col. John 25
Bragg, Gen. Braxton 3–4, ***10***, 35, 37–38, 46–53, 55, 57–59, 64–65, 68–74, 96, 98, 100–102, 104–106, 109–111, 113–115, 118–120, 122–124, 127–128, 130–138, 140–141, 143–145, 149–154, 156 159, 171, 173, 195, 211, 213, 219, 221–222, 229, 242–245, 250–252; Breckinridge's attack on January 2, 230–231, 233–236; Kentucky campaign 9–11, 13, 15–21, 23–31, 33; Pegram's cavalry on December 31, 196–197, 199–209; withdrawal after the battle, 236–241
Branner, Lt. Col. Benjamin M. 103–104
Brazelton, Jr., Lt. Col. William 103
Breckinridge, Maj. Gen. John C. 11, 13, 28–29, 35, 47, 59, 69, 114, 131, 134, 150–151, 156, 244–245, 250; December 31 actions 196–

285

197, 199–209, 211; January 2 attack 230–236, 240
Brewer, Col. Richard H. 108–109
Brewer's Battalion *see* Confederate Units, 8th Cavalry
Bridgeland, Col. John A. 79
Bronson, Eugene 213, 216
Buck, Capt. Martin 77–78
Buckley, Col. Harvey M. 59
Buckner, Col. John 202, 205
Buckner Guards 14
Buell, Maj. Gen. Don Carlos 9–11, 14–15, 17–*19*, 20–25, 28–31, 33, 41–42, 55, 58, 78, 80, 84, 86–87, 91, 93
Buford, Brig. Gen. Abraham 19, 50–51, 56, 94, 99–*100*, 101, 112, 115, 152, 156, 196, 230, 244–245, 249–250, 252; December 31 actions 185–186, 211–217; January 1 actions 222–225; January 3 actions 237
Buford, Brig. Gen. John 99
Buford, Maj. Gen. Napoleon 99
"bull pups" (mountain howitzers) 61, 207–208
Burdsall, Lt. Col. Henry W. 82
Burford, Lt. E.S. 250
Burke, Pvt. Benjamin 53, 127, 144, 168, 217
Burke, Col. Joseph 148, 223–224, 228
Burlingame, Sgt. E.P. 161
Burns, Lt. Robert *73*, 120, 122, 222, 228, 238
Butcher, Sgt. Henry C. 216
Butler, Col. J. Russell 50, 100, 215, 250
Butler, M.B. 190, 233–234

Caldwell, Maj. John W. 14
Calvert's Battery *see* Arkansas Units
Campbell, Lt. Col. Archibald 25
Campbell, Capt. William 215, 250
carbines 33, 66–67, 73, 77, 85–86, 88–90, 106, 112, 141, 161, 183, 213, 252
Carlin, Col. William 115, 117, 154
Carlisle Barracks 16, 43, 86, 91, 110
Carter, Col. James E. 49, 103, 216
Carter, Lt. Julius 129
Carter, Brig. Gen. Samuel 69–70
Carter's Raid 69–70
casualties, cavalry 40, 62–63, 246, 249
cavalry tactics 88–91, 166, 217; *see also* raiding strategy
Cavalry Tactics 32
"Cedars" 199
Chalmers, Brig. Gen. James R. 108–109
Charlton, Lt. Col. Richard 125–126
Cheatham, Maj. Gen. Benjamin 59–60, 69, 131, 134, 150, 238
Chenault, Col. D.W. 49, 61, 63

Chenoweth, Maj. James 215, 250
Chilton, William P. 107
Christian, Capt. S.P. 168, 189
Church, Capt. Josiah 212
Claiborne, Col. Thomas 96
Claiborne's Cavalry *see* Confederate Units, 1st Cavalry
Clanton, Col. James H. 105
Clare, Maj. William 203–204
Clark, Carroll Henderson 23
Clark, Governor Henry 94
Clark, William Allen 62
Clay, Capt. H.B. 204, 207, 233–234, 236
Cleburne, Brig. Gen. Patrick 67, 114, 124, 131, 134, 152–154, 159, 162
Clements, Capt. Robert 201
Cluke, Col. R.S. 49, 61, 63
Collins, Maj. Joseph 125–126
Collins House 208
Colony, William H. 179
Colt revolving rifles 48, 66, 68, 73, 88–89, 213; *see also* carbines
Colton, Ball 225
Condit, Lt. Timothy 182–183, 249
Confederate Department Number Two 35
Confederate Units:
 1st Cavalry 94–96, 126, 155, 167, 227
 3rd Cavalry 16, 50, 94, 96, 124, 155, 158, 183, 250
 6th Cavalry 13, 95–96
 8th Cavalry 10, 14–15, 50, 53, 60, 94, 105, 108–109, 111, 121, 130–131, 134–135, 145, 149
 12th Cavalry 96
 16th Cavalry 96
Cook, Lt. Col. William R. 85
Cooke, Philip St. George 32
Cooley, Henry 212
Cope, Alexis 163
Cope, Corp. Morris 168
Corinth, Battle of 10–11, 27–28, 41–42, 54, 221
Corinth, Siege of 10, 16, 23, 42–43, 79, 81–82, 87, 102
couriers 46, 50, 131, 181, 195
Cox, Maj. J.J. 199
Cox, Col. John T. 96, 155, 161, 167–169, 180–181, 186, 227
Cox's Hill, skirmish at 236–237, 245
Crab Orchard, Kentucky 17, 19
Crane, Capt. William 75, 118, 127, 139, *141*, 157, 185, 237–239, 248
Crawford, Col. Martin Jenkins 97
Crews, Col. Charles C. 97
Crittenden, John 25, 222
Crittenden, Maj. Gen. Thomas L. 44–46, 48, 58, 72, 77, 113–114, *119*–124, 127–128, 130–132, 135, 137–139, 150, 153–154, 165, 176, 196, 199, 211, 218–219, 223
Crocheron Light Dragoons *see* Alabama Units, 3rd Cavalry
Crofts, Sgt. Thomas 82, 156

Cruft, Brig. Gen. Charles 121
Cumberland Gap 10–11, 19, 26–27, 30, 84, 103
Cupp, Capt. Valentine 159, 161, 182
Curry, Capt. W.L. 88, 173, 220

Danville, Kentucky 15–16, 99, 110
Davis, President Jefferson 16, 26–27, 35, 51, 64; concerns of local citizens 68
Davis, Brig. Gen. Jefferson C. 114–115, 123, 153–154, 164, 168, 179
Davis, Maj. John R. 14, 98
Davis, Maj. N.H. 91–93
Deaderick, David Anderson 208
Department of East Tennessee 27, 35, 104, 252
Department of the Cumberland 21, 30–31
Dibrell, Col. George 39, 47
Dickinson, Lt. Col. William H. 54, 71, 78, 80, 224, 228, 247
Diehl, C. Lewis 142
Dillion, George W. 237
dismounted cavalry 15, 18, 29, 33, 59, 61, 63, 65, 67, 73, 90, 118, 121, 126, 142, 149, 158, 162, 211–213, 215, 227, 233, 237, 252
Dodge, Col. J.B. 153, 167
Dollinger, Sgt. Maj. John 186
Dornblaser, T.F. 180, 220
Douglass, Maj. DeWitt C. 39, 50, 105, 108, 145
DuBose, John Witherspoon 13, 107, 148, 223
Ducat, Lt. Col. Arthur 44–45, 48
Duke, Col. Basil 10, 17, 49, 61–62, 240, 245
Dunlop, Lt. Col. James E. 97, 155
Dunn, Vincent 169, 238
Dure's Battery *see* Georgia Units

East Tennessee Units *see* Tennessee Units
Eckman, Joseph 142
Ector, Brig. Gen. Mathew D. 154, 162
Edgarton, Capt. Warren P. 125–126, 161
Edgefield Attack *see* Nashville Attack
Ellis, Lt. William 250
Elmore, Capt. V.M. 250
Estes, Lt. Col. William N. 96, 155
European interests in the war 57–58

Fambro, Pvt. James 168
Farrish, Pvt. James 192
Fielder, Alfred Tyler 69
Fitt, Lt. William M. 129
flags of truce 70–72, 210, 227
Floyd Bush Rangers *see* Alabama Units, 3rd Cavalry
Fobes, George 92–93
Folk, Lieut. Col. G.N. 50

Fordyce, Lt. Sam 182
Forrest, Nathan Bedford 1, 11, 13, 17–18, 28–29, 31, 33–34, 44, 46–53, 56, 64, 68–70, 72, 75, 78–80, 86–88, 97–99, 102, 104, 107–108, 111–112, 206, 243, 245, 249, 252; battle at Nashville **38**–44
Fort Donelson 13, 83, 102
Foster, Maj. John 25
Franklin: December 9 skirmish 66–68; December 26 skirmish 113, 118–119; December 27 skirmish 127
Freeman, Capt. Samuel 39–40, 68
Fremantle, Sir Arthur 111
French, Lucy Virginia 220, 239
Friend, W.R. 162, 185–186, 189
Fry, James 24
Fyffe, Col. James B. 190–191, 234

Gailbreath, Capt. R.J.C. 250
Gallatin, Tennessee: skirmish 14, 80
Gano, Col. R.M. 49, 61, 63
Gareschè, Lt. Col. Julius 134, 138, 151, 187, 210
Garner, George 25
Garnett, Brig. Gen. Robert 101
Garrett, Sgt. George 93
Gay, Capt./acting Brig. Gen. Ebenezer 17–18, 22–25, 54, 77
George, Charles 240
Georgia Units:
  1st Cavalry 14, 50, 52, 65, 104–105, 196, 200–201, 203, 205–206, 209, 233, 245, 251
  2nd Battalion Sharpshooters 99
  2nd Cavalry 13–14, 50, 74, 94, 96–97, 155, 158, 168, 183, 195
  3rd Cavalry 79, 94, 97, 181–182
  5th Infantry 240
  16th Battalion Partisan Rangers 50
  21st Infantry 105
  Dure's Battery 28
  Smith's Cavalry Battalion 14
Gibson, Sgt. Gerould 179, 224
Gibson, Col. William 166 167, 179, 229
Gilbert, Capt./Maj. Gen. Charles 23
Gilbert, Lt. James 228
Godfrey, Col. E.S. 252
Goodspeed, Capt. Wilbur 163
Gorgas, Col. Josiah 29
Granger, Maj. Gen. Gordon 69
Grant, Capt. Marcus 227
Grant, Maj. Gen. Ulysses S. 11, 30, 41–42, 64–65, 68, 70–71, 78, 240
Grenfell, Col. George 203–205
Grigsby, Col. J. Warren 14, 100, 215
Grose, Col. William 230

Hagan, Col. James 13, **106**–107, 111
Hall, Lt. William 133

Halleck, Henry General-in-Chief **20**–21, 30–31, 37, 42, 48, 55, 57–58, 65, 74–75
Hanley, 2nd Lieut. S.G. 14
Hanley's Section *see* Arkansas Units
Hanson, Col./Brig. Gen. Roger W. 39, 197, 199–200, 203–204, 206–**207**; actions at Hartsville 59–63
Hardee, Lt. Gen. William 13, 15, 35, 48–49, 51, 69, 72, 99, 113–114, 117–118, 123–**124**, 125, 130–134, 144–145, 150–156, 158, 161–162, 164–166, 184, 194–195, 203, 234, 241
Harder, Capt. William Henry 164, 184, 195
Hardy, Capt. L.T. 155, 182
Hardy's Escort Company 181–183
Harker, Col. Charles 45, 128, 137, 184, 197, 199
Harlan, Col. John M. 61, 63
Harper, Lt. Col. Armistead 105; actions on December 31 200, 202, 205–206
Harris, Governor Isham Green 28, 103, 239
Harrison, Col. Thomas 14, 58, 99, 117, 123, 155, 158–159, 168–169, 181–182, 228, 249
Hart, Col. John R. 14
Hartsville, Battle of 60–66, 79
Hartsville, Tennessee 44–47, 59
Hascall, Brig. Gen. Milo Smith 59, 128–129, 199, 201
Hawkins, W.H. 71
Hazen, Col. William B. 15–16, 18–19, 128–130, 132, **199**
Heath, Lt. R.J. 162
Hickman, Dr. F.G. 181
Hill, Pvt. Martin 92
Hill, Maj. Samuel 62–63
Holman, Maj. Daniel W. 50, 58–59, 73–74, 105, 108, **145**
Holman, J.A. 193
Holt, Pvt. L.B. 216
Hood, Lt. Col. Arthur 13
Hoover's Ford 200–205, 209
Hord, Mildred Amelia 192
Hord, Thomas 192
Hord House 192
horses 1, 17–18, 26, 32–33, 41, 43, 45, 53, 55–57, 60, 62, 68, 70, 74, 84, 86, 88, 98–99, 118, 129, 131, 133, 145, 153, 157–157, 161, 164, 166–167, 179, 181, 184, 186, 190, 213, 216–217, 219–220, 223–224, 227, 236, 246; care of 89; equipment 32, 90, 112; horse holders 90; method of replacement 89–90, 98, 112
Howard, Col. James R. 16–17, 49, 96
Hower's house 234
Hunt, Col. Thomas 61

Illinois Units:
  16th Infantry 38

19th Infantry 60
24th Infantry 147
34th Infantry 162
36th Cavalry *see* 36th Infantry
36th Infantry 25, 115, 123
43rd Infantry 58
59th Infantry 164
74th Infantry 164, 168
75th Infantry 164, 168
100th Infantry 129
104th Infantry 60–62
Chicago Board of Trade Artillery 70
Indiana Units:
  2nd Cavalry 17–18, 25, 54, 77, 79, 128, 138, 246; at Hartsville 60–63
  3rd Cavalry 25, 59, 77, 83, 125, 132, 134–135, 156, 159, 169, 172, 181, 186, 189–190, 221, 244, 246, 249
  4th Cavalry 25
  5th Artillery 125
  6th Infantry 164
  7th Artillery 65–66, 190–191, 194
  9th Infantry 18
  13th Battery 63
  19th Infantry 32
  22nd Infantry 164, 223, 227
  29th Infantry 125–126
  30th Infantry 167
  31st Infantry 121
  35th Infantry 65
  39th Infantry 162, 167
  44th Infantry 190, 223
  58th Infantry 208
  72nd Infantry 62
  Swallow's Battery *see* 7th Artillery
Innes, Col. William P. **226**–228
Insane Asylum Hill *see* Cox's Hill
Ireland, Capt. Thom A. 13
Island Number 10, Siege of 42, 54, 87
Ison, Maj. Francis M. 97
Iuka, Battle of 10–11, 27, 41–43, 87, 221

Jackson, Brig. Gen. James S. 82
Jackson, Brig. Gen. John K. 131, 203, 205
Jackson, Col. William "Red" 111
Jaggers, Corp. Wilson 192
James, Lt. Col. Thomas 25
Jeffries, C.C. 193
Jennings, Maj. William H. 80, 210–211
Johnson, Brig. Gen. Bushrod 154, 163, 184
Johnson, Penelope 95
Johnson, Brig. Gen. Richard W. 114, 119, 127, 144, 150, 152–**155**, 156, 159, 161, 163–164, 177, 179, 181, 210
Johnston, Gen. Albert Sidney 96, 111
Johnston, Gen. Joseph 51, 64, 68, 117, 240

Index

Johnston, Col. J. Stoddard 111, 200, 203, 233
Jones, Maj. Gen. Sam 27–29, 33

Kansas Units:
 8th Infantry 66
Kennett, Col. John 17, 19, 22–25, 37, 44–**49**, 54, 77–78, 82, 86, 112, 119, 156, 172, 190–193, 195, 210, 230, 244, 246–249
Kentucky Units (CSA):
 1st Cavalry 13–14
 2nd Cavalry 14, 22, 61
 2nd Cavalry Battalion 49, 105, 145
 2nd Infantry 59, 63
 3rd Cavalry 19, 22, 49–50, 100, 211, 215, 250
 5th Cavalry 19, 50, 100, 211, 215
 6th Cavalry 14, 19, 50, 100–101, 211, 215
 7th Cavalry 14, 49
 8th Cavalry 14, 49, 61
 9th Cavalry 14, 22, 39, 61
 9th Infantry 59, 63
 11th Cavalry 14, 49, 61
 Arnett's Kentucky Howitzer Battery 49
 (W.C.P.) Breckinridge's Cavalry Battalion 49
 Cobb's Battery 59, 199
 Kentucky Mounted Rangers see Confederate Units, 1st Cavalry
Kentucky Units (U.S.):
 1st Cavalry 15, 17, 22, 25, 77
 1st Infantry 121
 2nd Cavalry 25, 147, 202
 3rd Cavalry 25, 38, 54, 67, 77–79, 92, 120, 128, 138, 142, 149, 156, 165–166, 169, 172, 181, 186, 188–194, 210, 221, 230, 238–239, 244, 246, 249–250
 4th Cavalry 25
 5th Cavalry 25, 73, 77
 5th Infantry 59
 6th Cavalry 24–25
 7th Cavalry 24
 8th Infantry 65
 9th Cavalry 25
 11th Cavalry 24, 60, 62–63
 Fry's Kentucky Scouts 25
 Twyman's Scouts 25, 38
Kimbrough's Mill, skirmish at 59
King, Maj. Henry C. 96
King, James 176, 224
King's Battalion see Confederate Units, 1st Cavalry
Kirk, Brig. Gen. Edward N. 53, 150, 154, 162–164, 167, 181
Kirkpatrick, Capt. M.L. 129
Klein, Lt. Col. Robert 83–**84**, 125–126, 132–135, 156, 169, 189–190, 193–194, 249
Kniffin, Capt. G.C. 46, 176, 194, 219
Knight, James 151
knives 90

Knob Gap, fighting at 115
Knox, Capt. George G. 71

Lacy, Lt. A.J. 41
Lancaster, Kentucky 17
La Vergne, skirmishes at 4, 47, 53, 60, 65, 107, 117, 119–123, 128, 148–149; January 1 skirmish 223–229
Lawton, Col. Winburn J. 96–97
Lay's Cavalry see Confederate Units, 1st Cavalry
Ledyard, Lt. Edward S. 250
Lexington Rifles 14
Liddell, St. John R. 154, 162, 184, 238
Livingston, Lt. Cortland 208
Long, Capt. Eli **189**, 246, 248
Louisiana Units:
 1st Cavalry 14, 17, 50, 52, 102–103, 196, 206–207, 233, 240
 4th Battalion (sharpshooters) 200
 Holmes' Louisiana Battery 50
 Washington Artillery 199
Louisville and Nashville Railroad 14, 37, 64
Lubbock, Lt. Col. Thomas S. 99

Magee, James E. 220
Malone, Lt. Col. James Chappell, Jr. 95, 118–119, 136, 155, 227
Maney, Brig. Gen. George 120
Maple, Lt. Thomas 25, 228
Martin, F.M. 125
Martin, Pvt. Frank 246
Mathews, Capt. Peter 185
Mathews' Rangers see Alabama Units, 3rd Cavalry
Matthews, Col. Stanley 65–66
Maynard, Representative Horace 70
McCann, Maj. Richard "Dick" 105, 107–108, 145, 250
McClellan, Maj. Gen. George 41–42, 101
McClellan, Col. George R. 104
McCook, Maj. Gen. Alexander 29, 44, 48, 58, 74, 112–115, 117–120, 122–**123**, 124–128, 130, 132–135, 138–139, 141, 144, 149–156, 158–159, 161–166, 179–181, 189, 199, 208, 210, 212, 218, 239, 248
McCook, Col. Edward 15, 17, 19, 23–25, 45, 54–**55**, 56, 60, 67, 77–79, 83, 97
McCown, Maj. Gen. John Porter 27, 131, 134, 152–156, 159, 162–163
McCown's Escort Company 155
McFadden's Ford 199
McGregor's house 211
McKenzie, Lieut. Col. G.W. 50
McLain, John C. 213
McNair, Brig. Gen. Evander 154, 162–**163**, 171
Memphis Mounted Rebels see Confederate Units, 1st Cavalry

Merrill carbines 85–86, 213
Mexican War 14, 52, 99, 105–107, 109
Michigan Units:
 1st Artillery 212, 237–238
 1st Engineers and Mechanics 224, 226–229, 247, 250
 2nd Cavalry 24–25, 70, 80
 3rd Artillery 54
 3rd Cavalry 80
 4th Cavalry 23, 54, 58, 67–68, 70–73, 77–80, 120, 122, 133, 135, 149, 156, 186, 210–211, 213, 215–216, 218, 224, 228–229, 238–239, 246–247, 249; at Stewarts Creek bridge 128–130
 7th Cavalry 66
 7th Infantry 54
 9th Infantry 97, 185, 211–212
 10th Infantry 58
 11th Infantry 151, 176, 224
 14th Infantry 39–40
 Loomis' Artillery see Michigan Units, 1st Artillery
Middle Tennessee Units see Tennessee Units
Miller, Col. Abram 61, 63
Miller, George Knox 10–11, 35, 53, 60, 109, 121–122, 130–131, 134–135, 137, 145, 148–149
Miller, Col. John 237
Millikin, Col. Minor 22–24, 54, 78, 81, 156, 165, 182–**183**, 184–186, 194, 246
Minnesota Units:
 2nd Battery 115, 168
 5th Infantry 43
Minty, Col. Robert H.G. 2, 54, 56, 58, 77, 79–80, 83, 88, 128, 131, 138, 142, 149–151, 156, 169, 195, 219–220, 228–229, 239, 243–244, 246–247, 249; begins the advance 113, 119–123; December 31 afternoon actions 210–217; flag of truce incident **71**–72; moves to Stewarts Creek 149–151; Rural Hill skirmish 72–73
Mississippi Units:
 1st Cavalry 111
 1st Infantry 109
 10th Infantry 109
 45th Infantry 124–125
 Darden's Battery 124–126
Mitchell, Capt. Joseph A.S. 77, 79, 138
Mitchell, Lt. Thomas 246
Mix, Capt. Frank 73, 128–**130**, 215–216, 247
Mobile Humphries Dragoons see Alabama Units, 3rd Cavalry
Montgomery Mounted Rifles see Alabama Units, 1st Cavalry
Moore, Col. Absalom B. 60–62, 64
Moore, Maj. David 161, 165, 182, 246
Morgan, Brig. Gen. James 59
Morgan, Brig. Gen. John Hunt 1,

10-11, 14-17, 21-24, 29, 31, 33-34, 37-41, 44-*52*, 56-57, 59-68, 78-80, 82, 87-88, 108, 112, 207, 243, 245, 248-249, 252; "Christmas Raid" 69-70, 72, 75, 240; marriage 69
Morgan, Col. John Tyler *107*-108, 148
Morrison, Col. James J. 50, 104-105
Morton, Governor Oliver P. 21
Morton's Pioneer Brigade 201, 206, 209
Mount Vernon, Kentucky 18
mountain howitzers see "bull pups"
Munfordville, skirmish at 13, 49, 82
Murphy's Independent Company see Alabama Units, 3rd Cavalry
Murray, Lieut. Col. Douglas A. 25, 54, 78, *82*, 139, 156, 164
Murray, Col. Eli H. 25, 54, 78-79, 138, 142, 156, 165, 191-*192*, 193, 249
Murray, Col. John P. 98, 155, 227
mutiny of 15th Pennsylvania Cavalry 77, 91-93, 247

Nashville (Edgefield) Attack 37-41
Nashville and Chattanooga Railroad 30, 113
Negley, Brig. Gen. James 24, 28-29, 37-*40*, 41, 46-47, 70, 73, 75, 108, 114, 119, 123, 127-128
Nelson, Maj. Gen. William "Bull" 23
Newell, Lt. Nathaniel M. 54, 78, 81-83, 120-121, 156, 210, 224
Nicholas, Maj. Thomas P. 202
Nix, Lt. Col. Francis M. 50
Nixon, Lieut. Col. James O. 50, 103, *201*
North Carolina Units:
 5th Cavalry Battalion 50
 7th Cavalry Battalion 50
 Thomas' Cavalry Regiment 50

O'Hara, Theodore 202, 204
O'Higgins, Father 151
Ohio Units:
 1st Artillery 54, 78, 81-82, 120, 125-126, 161-163, 168, 210, 224
 1st Cavalry 15, 22, 24-25, 54, 77-78, 81-82, 88, 127, 139, 156, 159, 161, 165-166, 182-186, 190, 194, 220, 236, 246
 1st Infantry 59, 163
 3rd Cavalry 21, 25, 54, 77-78, 80-82, 118, 127-128, 139, 144, 156, 159, 161, 164-167, 182, 184-187, 189-190, 192, 224-225, 237, 240, 247
 4th Cavalry 21-22, 25, 46-47, 54, 75, 77-78, 81-82, 118, 127, 139, 141, 144, 156-157, 159, 166, 168, 182, 184-185, 224, 236-237, 239, 246-248

7th Cavalry 70
10th Infantry 148, 151, 175, 223, 228
15th Infantry 163, 168, 229
18th Infantry 102
49th Infantry 166
51st Infantry 63
69th Infantry 39
93rd Infantry 59
97th Infantry 59
106th Infantry 60, 62, 64
108th Infantry 60, 62-64
"Old Wristbreaker" see sabers
Oliver, Bettie 107
Osborn, Sgt. Thomas 168-169
Otis, Capt. Elmer 45, 54, 78, 83, 114, 156, *187*, 189, 193-194, 249
Otis, Ephraim 152
Otto, Capt. John Henry 147
Owsley, Maj. John 25

Palmer, Maj. Gen. John 119, 121, 128, 137, 150, 192, 211, 230
Palmer, Col. Joseph B. 39, 197, 206-207
Palmer, Capt./Col. William J. 86, 91-92, 248
Paramore, Maj. James W. 186-187, 189-190, 192-193
Paris, skirmish at 96
Parkhurst, Lt. Col. John 185, 212
Partisan Ranger Act 94
Pea Ridge, Battle of 79
Pease, Capt. Henry 179
Pegram, Brig. Gen. John 4, 19, 25, 49-52, 56, *65*, 73, 94, 101, 103-104, 112, 115, 120, 131, 134, 145, 156, 181, 219, 242-245, 249-252; December 31 actions 196-209; January 2 actions 230-236
Pell, Lieut. Col. James 13
Pennsylvania Units:
 7th Cavalry 25, 39, 54, 67-68, 77-80, 120, 128, 133, 138, 149, 156, 165, 169, 172, 179-180, 186, 191, 195, 210-211, 213, 215-216, 218, 221, 224, 239, 244, 246, 249
 9th Cavalry 24-25, 70
 15th Cavalry 25, 48, 50, 54-55, 58, 66-67, 77-78, 83, 86, 91-93, 117, 126, 136, 138, 151, 156, 177, 186, 195, 210-213, 215-217, 222, 224-226, 228-229, 245-249; fight with South Carolina Infantry 139-143; mutiny see mutiny of 15th Pennsylvania Cavalry
 78th Infantry 39-40
 79th Infantry 147
Percy Walker Rangers see Alabama Units, 3rd Cavalry
Perryville Campaign 9-21
Pickett, Col. William D. 72, 123, 195
Piepho, Capt. Carlo 64
Pillow, Brig. Gen. Gideon 234-*235*, 236
Pinson, Col. R.A. 111

Pioneer Brigade see Morton's Pioneer Brigade
Pirtle, Lt. Alfred 175
Pitman's Crossroads 18
Poinsett Tactics 32
Polk, Lt. Gen. Leonidas 13, 18-19, 27, 35, 48-50, 69-70, 114, 120, 131-*133*, 134, 145, 151-153, 165, 207, 219
Polk, Lucius E. 154
Porter, John M. 39
Post, Col. P. Sidney 74, 115, 154, 162-164
Prattville Dragoons see Alabama Units, 3rd Cavalry
Prentice, Maj. Clarence J. 250
Preston, Brig. Gen. William 197, 205, 233
Preston, William C. 95
Price, Col. Samuel 201, 208
Price, Maj. Gen. Sterling 11
Prim's Blacksmith Shop 114
Pritchard, Capt. Benjamin 130
Pugh, Maj. John L. 25, 54, 78, 82, 141, 156, 168, 182, 184, 248

"raiding strategy" 112, 242, 247, 251
Rains, Brig. Gen. James 154, 162
Randolph, Secretary of War George 27-29
Randolph, Sgt. Tucker St. Joseph 101
Ransom, Lt. Albert 126
Ransom, Col. Owen P. 81
"Rape of Athens" 102
Ray, Col. Daniel M. 83-85
Ready, Col. Charles, Jr. 69
Ready, Martha 69
Regulations and Instructions for the Field Service of the United States Cavalry in Time of War 32
Reiff, J.C. 216
Rendelbrook, Lt. Joseph 228
revolvers 33, 66, 90, 98, 106, 112, 141, 168, 183, 185, 217-218, 262
Reynolds, Sgt. Henry Clay 29
Rich Mountain, Battle of 41, 52, 101, 250
Richmond, Battle of 23, 27, 105
Robbins' Rangers see Alabama Units, 3rd Cavalry
Robie, Lt. Col. Oliver P. 248
Roddey, Col. Phillip D. 50
Rosecrans, Maj. Gen. William 2, 11, *31*, 33, 37, 41-48, 51-52, 54-55, 57, 60, 63, 69, 71, 73, 78, 80, 83, 87-88, 91, 101, 117, 122-124, 128, 131-135, 138, 143-145, 147-154, 156, 159, 161-162, 165, 171, 173, 175, 180-181, 186-187, 191, 195, 197, 199, 203, 205, 210-213, 218-219, 221-224, 229-231, 236-240, 242, 244-252; assumes command 21, 29-31; begins the advance 74-75, 113-114; communication issues with

the cavalry 44–48; issues with Washington 57–58
Rosengarten, Maj. Adolph G. 83, 92, 117, 126, 142–*143*, 177, 226, 246, 249
Rothrock, Lt. N.D. 250
Round Forest 199, 202–203
Routt, John 164
Rucker, Maj. E.W. 50
Ruffin Rangers *see* Alabama Units, 3rd Cavalry
Rural Hill skirmish 72–73

saber 4, 29, 32–33, 43, 67, 80, 88, 90, 112, 141, 182–184, 216–217, 244, 252; 1860 Light Cavalry Saber 32
"Sabre Brigade" 80
Sacramento, skirmish at 79
Sample, Nathaniel W. 212, 217, 222
Savers, Billy 228
Scott, Col. John 11, 14–18, 29, 50, 101–*103*; arrest 17
Scott, Col. Joseph 60
Scott, Lt. William 182, 246
Seidel, Maj. Charles: capture of Union cavalry 21–22
Shacklett, Maj. Aaron 169
Sharp, Lt. W.H. 250
Sheridan, Brig. Gen. Phil 74, 87, 114, 117, 123, 154, 165, 179, 199, 211
Shiloh, Battle of 10, 13–14, 16, 23, 44, 79, 82–83, 86–87, 95–99, 102, 105–106, 108–109, 111
Short, William "Joe" 195
shotguns 33, 73, 89–90, 108, 112, 166
Sill, Brig. Gen. Joshua 48, 53, 154, 229
Simonson, Capt. Peter 125; *see also* Indiana Units, 5th Artillery
Sinclair, Maj. William Henry 54
Sipes, Lt. Col. William B. 80
Skillman, Sgt. Isaac 159, 161, 165, 225, 237
Slater, Capt. Frederick 62
Smith, Brig. Gen. A.J. 9, 23
Smith, Maj./Col. Baxter 13, *67*–68, 70, 97–98, 111, 118–119, 127–128, 134, 136, 155, 161, 180–181, 187, 194, 219, 221, 223–224, 227, 235, 237
Smith, Col. Dabney Howard 100
Smith, Maj. Gen. E. Kirby 10–11, 14–21, 23, 25–*27*, 29, 33, 35, 48–52, 55, 65, 68, 96, 101–102, 104, 111, 112, 114, 117, 206, 250
Smith, Pvt. John N. 148
Smith, Col. Robert 38
Smith, Brig. Gen. William Sooy 18
Solomon Fork, skirmish at 43
South Carolina Units:
 10th Infantry 142–143, 152
 19th Infantry 142–143
South Tunnel *see* Louisville and Nashville Railroad
Sparta, Tennessee 14, 50, 102

Spence, Capt. D.H.S. 206–207
Spencer, Lt./Lt. Col. William 92–93
Stanley, Brig. Gen. David S. 2–4, 9, 31–32, 34, 41–*42*, 48, 54–56, 65–66, 69, 72–75, 78–83, 86–89, 93–94, 97, 112–114, 117–119, 123, 125–127, 132–133, 135, 139, 142–144, 149–152, 156–158, 169, 171, 186–187, 191, 195, 202, 218–220, 229, 236, 239, 242–244, 246–249, 252; assessment of cavalry 55–56, 88; beginning advance to Murfreesboro 77, 132–133, 138; cavalry tactics 88–89; conversion to Catholicism 42–43; December 31 attack 210–217; Franklin skirmish 66–68; frontier duty 43; Whipple's expedition 43
Stanton, Secretary of War Edwin 42, 48
Starkweather, Col. John 147–*148*, 149
Stevenson, Maj. Gen. Carter 19, 68
Stewart, Lt. Col. Robert 17, 25, 54, 60, 62, 73
Stewarts Creek bridge: capture by 4th Michigan 128–131
Stokes, Col. William B. 39–40, 83, *85*–86
Stoner, Maj. Robert G. 61
Stuart, Maj. Gen. J.E.B. 33, 43, 111
supply trains *see* wagon trains
Swallow, Capt. George 65–66, 190–191, 194; *see also* Indiana Units, 7th Artillery
swords *see* sabers

Tafel, Lt. Col. Gustavus 64
Tarver, William 219
Teeter, Capt. Henry B. 185
Tennessee Units (CSA):
 1st Cavalry 14, 49–50, 67, 103–104, 145, 196, 216, 237
 2nd Cavalry 14, 52, 103–104, 155, 181, 183, 196, 219
 3rd (Starnes') Cavalry 14, 39
 4th Cavalry (Murray's) 97–98, 155, 227, 250
 4th Cavalry (Smith's) 13, 50, 67, 94, 97–98, 127–128, 134, 136, 155, 166, 180, 223, 227
 4th Cavalry (Starnes') 40, 97–98
 4th Cavalry Battalion 103
 4th Infantry 99
 5th Cavalry 50
 5th Cavalry Battalion 104
 7th Infantry 108
 8th Cavalry 40–41, 97
 9th Cavalry 14, 41, 50, 61
 11th Cavalry 58, 108
 12th Cavalry 14, 50
 12th Infantry 50, 69
 14th Cavalry Battalion 103
 16th Cavalry Battalion 50
 16th Infantry 23, 64
 18th Infantry 207, 237

20th Infantry 115
21st Infantry 96, 108
22nd Infantry 71
23rd Infantry 164, 184, 195
44th Infantry 164
Anderson's Company 50, 155
Bacot's Cavalry Battalion 39
Bledsoe's Cavalry Battalion 50, 98
Brazelton's Battalion 103
Davis' Cavalry Battalion 14
Douglass' Battalion 39, 50, 105, 108, 145
Freeman's Battery 39–40, 68
Holman's Cavalry Battalion 50, 58–59, 73–74, 105, 108, 145
Huwald's Battery 233
Marshall's Battery 49
McCann's Cavalry Battalion 105, 107–108
Murray's Cavalry Regiment 94
Roberts' Battery 39
Russell's Partisan Rangers 39
White's Battery 50, 94, 99–100, 115, 126, 155, 161, 166, 171, 181–182, 184–185, 193–194, 221, 243
Tennessee Units (U.S.):
 1st Cavalry 48, 67, 239
 2nd Cavalry 48, 67, 83–*85*, 117, 133, 139, 142–144, 156–157, 159–160, 166, 169, 182, 185, 223–225, 227–229, 239, 245–247
 3rd Cavalry 236
 3rd Infantry 84
 4th Cavalry 92
 5th Cavalry 25, 39–40, 48, 58, 67, 77, 83, 85–86, 126, 142, 151, 156, 210–211, 213, 218, 239, 246
Terry, Col. Benjamin F. 95, 99
Terry's Texas Rangers *see* Texas Units, 8th Cavalry
Texas Units:
 8th Cavalry 14, 50, 53, 55, 68, 74, 94–95, 115, 123, 127, 141, 144, 155, 158, 162, 166–168, 181–183, 185–186, 189, 193, 195, 217, 228, 235, 249–250, 252
Thomas, Maj. Gen. George 30–31, 45, 72, 81, 118–119, *127*
Thomas, Lancaster 213, 215, 225
Thomas, Col. W.H. 50
Thompson, Maj. De Witt 155
Thompson, John Edgar 86
Thompson, Maj. Robert 97
Thompson, William 64
Thruston, Capt. Gates 9, 161, *179*–182, 184–186, 194–195
Tod, Governor David 30
Trabue, Col. Robert 206
Trecy, Father Jeremiah F. 44
Trooper's Manual 33
Turchin, Col. John 102
Twyman, Capt. Henry G. 38
Twyman's Scouts *see* Kentucky Units, U.S.

Ulmer, Barton 106, 124
United States Military Academy 13, 16, 26, 43, 101, 250

United States Units:
1st Dragoons 16, 110
2nd Cavalry 82
2nd Dragoons 23
4th Cavalry 25, 45, 54, 77–78, 83, 113–114, 143, 156, 172, 186–187, 189–191, 193–194, 221, 228, 238–240, 243–244, 246–249
4th Light Artillery 77
9th Cavalry 252
Mounted Rifles 16, 105–106
Urquhart, Col. David 204

Van Cleve, Maj. Gen. Horatio 72, 137, 150, 152, 199–**202**, 205–206, 208–209, 230, 233, 244
Van Dorn, Maj. Gen. Earl 11, 28, 64–65, 70
Vanosdol, Capt. Argus 59
Vineyard, Sgt. Ganum 238
Virginia Units:
20th Infantry 101

Wade, Col. William B. 14–15, **108**–109, 111, 137
Wagner, Col. George 128
wagon trains 18–19, 29, 50, 59, 64–65, 67, 86, 114, 131–132, 148–151, 161, 173, **175**, **176**, **177**
Wailes, Lt. William E. 250
Walker, Lt. Col. John G. 99
Walker, Col. Moses 127, 133, 149, 168, 212
Wallace, Col. William H. 166
Ward, Maj. Frank B. 83, 92, 142–**143**, 177, 246, 249
Watson, Assistant Secretary of War P.H. 66
Wayne's Hill 137, 151, 199–200, 206–207, 230
weapons see carbines; knives; revolvers; shotguns
Weatherred, John 41
Webb, Lt. Col. James D. 121, 129–130, 217–**218**, 219, 249
Webster, W.M. 120
Weigley, Francis 213
Weikel, Orlando 225
Weir, James 92–93

West Point see United States Military Academy
Whaley, Maj. C.A. 14
Wharton, Brig. Gen. John 11, 13–17, 19, 21, 35, 47, 49–**51**, 56, 66–68, 70, 72–75, 94–95, 97–100, 111–112, 120, 122, 131–132, 134–135, 138–139, 141, 144–145, 152–154, 209, 212–213, 215–224, 226–229, 242–244, 249–252; actions at Nolensville 114–115, 117–118; actions at Triune 124–127; December 31 early attack 155–163, 165–169, 171; December 31 late morning attack 173, 175–176, 178–179, 181–185; December 31 Union counterattack 186–196; January 2 actions 230–236; repulse by 1st Michigan Engineers 226–228
Wharton, William 95
Wheeler, Brig. Gen. Joseph 1–4, 28–29, 31, 33–35, 46–**47**, 48–53, 56, 59–60, 65–66, 68–69, 73, 75, 87, 88, 94–95, 99, 103–112, 115, 117, 119, 134–135, 137, 150–151, 156–159, 171, 173, 177, 186, 195–196, 204, 209, 230, 242–245; cavalry raid see Wheeler's raid; cavalry tactics 90; December 31 afternoon cavalry battle 210–221; "Fightin' Joe" 110; January 1 actions 222–229; January 3 actions 236–239; Perryville Campaign 9, 11, 13–19; "Point" 110; resists Crittenden's advance 120–122, 124, 127–131
Wheeler's Raid 145–149
Whipple, Lt. A.W. 43
Whitaker, Col. Walter 121
White, Capt. Benjamin H. 99
White, Lt. Carrol 142
Widow Burris's house 173, 180, 182, 184, 211, 213, 215, 217
Wiggins, Capt. Jannedens H. see Arkansas Units, Wiggin's Battery
Wilcox Rangers see Alabama Units, 3rd Cavalry

Wild Cat Mountain 18
Wilder, Col. John 90
Wilderness Road 19–20
Williams, John 177, 179, 215, 217
Willich, Brig. Gen. August 72, 132–134, 150, 154–155, 157–**158**, 162–164, 166–167
Wilson, Maj. James 205
Wilson's Creek Campaign 41, 87
Wirth, Dr. Randolph 220
Wisconsin Units:
3rd Battery 208, 230
5th Battery 115, 164, 168
21st Infantry 147
Wolfley, Maj. Lewis 92, 138, 169, 230
Wolford, Col. Frank 15–17, 25
Wood, Brig. Gen. S.A.M. 114, 117, 124–127, 162
Wood, Brig. Gen. Thomas 59, 122, 128–129, 137, 150
Woodruff, Col. William 115, 154
Woodson's Gap, skirmish at 104
Wright, Maj. Gen. Horatio 21, 23, 66, **69**–70
Wynkoop, Col. George 39, 80
Wynkoop, Maj. John E. 25, 54, 79–80, 138, 156, 165, 195, 249
Wynkoop, Lt. Nicholas 80

Yaryan, John Lee 32
Young, Bennett 63

Zahm, Col. Lewis 17, 24–25, 45, 54, 56, 77–78, 80–**81**, 82–83, 113, 123, 126–128, 131, 133, 135, 138–139, 141–142, 144, 215, 243–247, 249; December 26–27 actions at Franklin 118–119, 127; December 31 afternoon actions 211–212; December 31 early morning actions 156–159, 161, 165–169, 171–172; December 31 late morning actions 178, 180–182, 184–186, 189, 191; January 1 action 220–229; January 3 actions 236–240

www.ingramcontent.com/pod-product-compliance
Lightning Source LLC
Chambersburg PA
CBHW081542300426
44116CB00015B/2721